NATURAL RESOURCES MANAGEMENT AND LIVELIHOOD SECURITY

About the Editors

K.V. Sundaram is Founder & Chairman of Bhoovigyan Vikas Foundation, dealing with earth-care policies, tuned to the Third World Countries. He was former Chief Technical Adviser FAO/UN and had worked with the Indian Planning Commission and UN Organisations on various prestigious regional and local-level planning projects in India and other Asian and African countries. He was conferred D. Litt degree for his published work from the University of Mysore (1977) and a Senior Nuffield Fellowship from UK (1978-79) for his post-doctoral work in the Centre of South Asian Studies, University of Cambridge (UK). His publications include 15 books and more than 160 research papers. His technical expertise covers urban and regional planning, rural area development, multilevel planning, eco-development and human resources development.

M. Moni is a senior technocrat of National Informatics Centre (Government of India), currently working as its Deputy Director General. With more than 24 years of professional experience, he has held several prestigious assignments including sharing important responsibilities as Principal Systems Analyst to the Former Finance Minister of India during 1985-88. He pioneered to establish the District Information System of National Informatics Centre (DISNIC) in the 520 districts of India during 1987-96. He is currently leading the Group for formulating ICT Plans for increasing productivity in Agriculture and Allied sectors and Water Resources Development. His research interests span over a wide area of agricultural economics and informatics, micro-level planning, regional and sustainable development, infrastructure systems and networking (ICT), decision support system and fusion of technologies for increased agricultural productivity. He is the author of more than 20 technical reports and a number of research papers. He is also the Secretary General of the Bhoovigyan Vikas Foundation.

Mrityunjay Mohan Jha is a *Fellow* with the Bhoovigyan Vikas Foundation, New Delhi, and is dealing with issues pertaining to food security, land use and participatory planning. He was awarded with the Senior Research Fellowship of the University Grants Commission during 1993-98. He has authored a book *on Food Security: Dynamics and Dimensions*, besides some research papers on population, food security, land use dynamics and primary education.

NATURAL RESOURCES MANAGEMENT AND LIVELIHOOD SECURITY

Survival Strategies and Sustainable Policies

Edited by
K.V. Sundaram
M. Moni
Mrityunjay M. Jha

Published for
BHOOVIGYAN VIKAS FOUNDATION
by
CONCEPT PUBLISHING COMPANY, NEW DELHI-110059

Disclaimers

The responsibility for facts and Views expressed in various sections of this book are entirely those of the contributors, and do not reflect those of Bhoovigyan Vikas Foundation or the publishers.

ISBN 81-8069-096-2

First Published 2004

Published and Printed by
Ashok Kumar Mittal
Concept Publishing Company
A/15-16, Commercial Block, Mohan Garden
New Delhi-110059 (INDIA)

Phones : 25351460, 25351794
Fax : 091-11-25357103
Email : publishing@conceptpub.com.

SOMPAL
MEMBER
PLANNING COMMISSION
XII FINANCE COMMISSION
GOVERNMENT OF INDIA

सत्यमेव जयते

YOJANA BHAWAN
PARLIAMENT STREET
NEW DELHI - 110 001
PHONE : 2 3 0 9 6 5 6 9
FAX : 2 3 0 9 6 5 6 8
e-mail: sompal@yojana.nic.in

Foreword

The present book is an outcome of the 2nd International Conference of the Bhoovigyan Vikas Foundation, held during 18-20 December, 2002 at New Delhi (India). This conference closely followed the deliberations of the World Summit on Sustainable Development (WSSD) held in August 2002 at Johannesburg, South Africa. This Summit aimed to move from commitments to action in five specific areas viz. Water, Energy, Health, Agriculture and Biodiversity. The 3-day conference organised by the Bhoovigyan Vikas Foundation, besides keeping the aim of Caring for the Earth as an arching policy to help improve the condition of the world's people, focussed on two principal issues relating to Sustainable Agriculture (including sustainable livestock development) and Water Resources Development along with the fusion of technologies needed to transform our economy shaped largely by market forces into one shaped by the principles of ecology.

This volume consists of 20 research papers contributed by eminent scientists, who are experts in their own lines of specialisation. They were specially invited to write these papers. Caring for the earth as the underlying emphasis, the papers in this Volume deal with the conservation, management and development of natural resources, pertaining to agriculture, livestock and water resources development. The issues involved here have been seen by the experts in the context of social, economic and technical measures, aimed at sustainability at local, regional and national levels. The contributions advocate survival strategies and sustainable policies that are needed to save the mankind and our planet in the new millennium.

Thus the book provides a comprehensive analysis of India's natural and human resources development and management problems in the context of sustainability. The book will be a valuable addition to the growing literature on sustainable development issues by the Foundation and will be useful to researchers, academics and development planners all over the world.

(SOMPAL)

Acknowledgements

We are greatly indebted to Shri Sompal, Member, Planning Commission, Government of India, our Chief Mentor and the Chairman of the Conference Advisory Committee. He also kindly looked into the contributions in this volume and wrote the Foreword to this publication.

We gratefully acknowledge the assistance provided by Dr. N.A. Siddiqui, our Fellow Member, in the initial stages of editing of this book.

We would like to express our warm appreciation to our secretariat staff Mr. T.S. Sankaran and Mr. B. Ganesan for their untiring help in preparing the first manuscript.

We gratefully acknowledge the generous financial assistance provided by NABARD, Department of Science and Technology (NRDMS Division) and National Horticulture Board, which helped us in bringing out this publication.

Finally our sincere thanks are due to the publisher, the Concept Publishing Company for their excellent cooperation in nicely bringing out this publication in a short time.

Editors

Contents

PART II
SUSTAINABLE LIVESTOCK DEVELOPMENT

PART III
SUSTAINABLE AGRICULTURE

PART IV
POLICIES FOR THE NEW MILLENNIUM

PART V
FOUNDATION DAY LECTURE

Introduction

This book on "Natural Resources Management and Livelihood Security—Survival Strategies and Sustainable Policies", consists of 20 selected theme papers contributed by experts to the 2nd International Conference on "Sustainable Agriculture, Water Resources Development and Earth Care Policies", organised by the Bhoovigyan Vikas Foundation during 18-20 December, 2002 at New Delhi. The text has four parts:

Part I with six chapters, deals with natural resources, their conservation, development and management in relation to livestock development, sustainable agriculture and the development of water resources;

Part II has two papers relating to the strategic approach to livestock development;

Part III has six papers related to sustainable agriculture, covering a wide spectrum of issues relating to farming systems, rural livelihoods, renewable energy sources, climate change, urban and peri-urban agriculture and agricultural information and communication network;

Part IV consists of five papers, all of which address issues relating to policies for the new millennium.

The last chapter is the *Foundation Day lecture,* which deals with "knowledge revolution" in the new millennium.

The contributions made in this volume, address the vital issues that would shape policies and enable decision-making affecting the course of development and condition of our environment in the new millennium.

In the subsequent paragraphs, we have provided a brief resume of each paper, hitting at some high spots.

PART I

N.G. Hegde, in his paper on "*Management of Natural Resources for Sustainable Livelihood: BAIF's Approach*", has discussed the approach to attain sustainable livelihoods, through effective management of natural resources. He considers quality of life, perennial employment opportunities and women empowerment, as critical aspects of sustainable livelihoods, and maintains that all development programmes should also take care of conservation of natural resources and protection of the environment. The livelihood security to the resource poor and landless, has been identified as one of the biggest challenges, confronting development agencies. Presently, all the important natural resources, like land, water, forest and livestock, which are critical resources for providing gainful self-employment, are not properly managed. Integrated livestock and dairy development, development of community pastures, tree-based farming and water resources development can play very important role in achieving sustainable livelihoods. Lack of infrastructure, inadequate financial resources and poor managerial capabilities, come in the way of tackling poverty and ensuring livelihood opportunities. Motivation and training of weaker sections of the society, awareness generation about natural resources, introduction of multidisciplinary programmes and appropriate technologies, and establishment of people's organisation have been suggested as key to success for ensuring sustainable livelihood to the rural poor.

D.K. Paul's paper on "*Natural Resource Management—for Food Security and Sustaining Agriculture*", has its major thrust on management of various natural resources, viz. soil, water, weather, biodiversity etc., in order to address the issues of food insecurity, persisting poverty and sustainability of agriculture. The paper argues that despite high growth achieved in food grain production in the last thirty years, poverty and food insecurity still plague a large number of Indian population. The yields of rice and wheat have stagnated in the last few years. There is perceptible concern about the ongoing process of degradation of resources, which are related to agricultural production and livelihood support system. This paper suggests strategies for natural resources management in the new millennium, and also emphasizes the participatory approach to natural resources management. As a new paradigm, this approach addresses the natural resources degradation problem as perceived by farmers and provides economically viable, and environmentally friendly measures for ensuring sustainable production. Finally, for sustaining productivity and to ensure food security, some recommendations have been suggested.

Mohan Dharia, in his paper on "*Management of water, development of wastelands and other natural resources for a self-reliant India*", explains that sustainable Development depends on very judicious use of lands, forests, water, cattle wealth and fish of the country. The ever-shining solar energy should be tapped fully to achieve unlimited energy, nutrition for plants and animal and human life. Instead of large dam projects, preference should be given to micro watershed development schemes focused on all-round development. Example of one such successful effort can be witnessed in Gawadawadi village of Pune district (Maharashtra) which now has encouraged another 300 villages to follow its approach. The village has now no scarcity of water supply for drinking and other purposes. 500-600 acres of land is now sown with crops. Milk collection has gone up from 200 litres to 7000 litres per day. Every house now has latrine and gobargas plant. Cent-per-cent literacy has been achieved and people have started going back from Mumbai to settle in their original village. All this could be possible through people and their united efforts.

D.K. Chadha in his paper titled "*Ground Water Potential, Development and Regulation—A Critical Review*", discusses the varied dimensions of groundwater resources. The fast development of groundwater resources since the last two decades has increased the irrigation potential from 23 mha to 50 mha, meeting the almost entire demand of rural drinking water and more than 52 per cent of urban and industrial requirements, but has converted many of the surplus ground water areas/watersheds to critical areas, where withdrawal has exceeded the annual replenishment. Contrary to decline in water levels, an area of 3.11m sq. km is waterlogged and another 5.04 m sq. km is prone to water logging mostly along the canal command areas of major and medium irrigation projects. Such problems need to be addressed immediately through regulatory measures and artificial recharge. It is also observed that in many areas, anomalies exist between the stage of ground water development and actual field observations, requiring collection of more input data for better estimation of ground water resources. It is estimated that 214 BCM of water can be stored in underground reservoirs, utilizing a part of the 865 BCM of surplus monsoon runoff. Master plan prepared for artificial recharge has established that 36.2 BCM of under ground storage is possible through simple structures. The concept of surface storages and distribution of water through a network of canal system is now replaced with sub-surface storages in the aquifer system, which being multi-layered and laterally extensive can take care of transferring the water. In the 21st century, the main concerns in ground water development will be: (i) the protection of ground water against depletion and pollution, the central and state ground water regulatory authorities will have to be strengthened and the implementing agencies educated on ground water systems; (ii) management of trans-boundary aquifers across national and international boundaries; (iii) formulation of an exclusive **National Ground Water Policy** defining the custodianship of natural and recharged ground water; (iv) monitoring and management of waterlogged and Inland Salinity areas; and (v) accelerating the research and development activities in updating the treatment technologies to tackle the problems of fluoride, arsenic, nitrate and selenium.

S.S. Meenakshisundaram, in his paper *"Drinking Water Supply in India: A Strategic Policy Analysis"*, deals with the drinking water availability in different climatic regions of India. Fresh water is like many other resources a scarce commodity. On the one hand, there is the increase in demand in the section of agriculture and industry. On the other, population explosion change in life stage and change of technology also further accentuate the progress. The supply or availability of fresh water per capita has come down from 5000 cubic metres per annum to 2000 cm and shall further reduce. Rural water supply in India is the largest in the world. Drinking water should be pure, i.e. free from excessive mineral content or brackishness. There are many issues relevant to assured water supply of sufficient quality of drinking or fresh water. For sustainable assured water supply, strategy for the future is required to answer the three key challenges in the rural sector: (i) full coverage of all habitations with potable drinking water, (ii) water quality problems and (iii) sustainability. A comprehensive survey of habitations and drinking water sources should be undertaken. G.I.S. and remote sensing may be used for this purpose. Community participation in *Swajaldhara* projects should be encouraged. Watershed Development programmes should be undertaken to promote sustaining water resources in the rural areas. Rainwater harvesting is to be launched. Finally, reliable data of rainfall, hydrological conditions, location for potential recharge, rate of permeability etc. should be periodically obtained. It shall help in the propagation and implementation of programmes.

A.M. Michael, in his paper on "*Blue Revolution*", calls for ushering in *Blue Revolution*, by adopting efficient water conservation and management, small holder irrigation and waste water reuse. Globally, the availability of fresh water is due to the ever-increasing rise of population, improved standard of living and to meet the requirement for environmental management. The available water resources are to be optimally harnessed and beneficially utilized with appropriate priorities of use. The competing demands of water are mainly for irrigation, industry, domestic water supply and environmental management. This paper presents broad estimates of the demand for water in the various sectors and the opportunities for more efficient utilization of water. Sustainable development and management of water resources will require a holistic approach and simultaneous attention to all aspects of water use and management. Some of the issues causing much concern and threatening sustainability relate to water quality management across the sectors, including ecology and environment, inadequate development and management of the catchment areas of irrigation systems, inefficient water distribution and control at the farm level, water logging, salt problems in agriculture and absence of on-farm drainage. Conjunctive use of surface and ground water, utilization of canal flows during non-demand periods in agriculture, controlling rapid silting up of reservoirs and river beds and increasing flood damage, water quality management of lakes, rivers and tanks, recycling and proper treatment of industrial and domestic effluents and lack of adequate attention to preventive and regular maintenance of the water infrastructure are the major problems to be addressed. Here, India's water budget and the various factors influencing the availability of water in different regions of India are discussed in detail. Opportunities for conjunctive use of surface and ground water and the resulting advantages in increasing agricultural productivity are presented. A major opportunity in increasing crop yields and water use efficiency in a particular environment is to select plant species adapted to the available amount and distribution of water. Participatory management of irrigation systems, in which the beneficiary farmers have a major role, is an essential requirement to increase the efficiency of the irrigation sector. The productivity of most of the crops in India is much below those in developed countries, in spite of the fact that the required technology to substantially increase crop productivity is available. To achieve quick and spectacular increase in agricultural production, it is necessary to establish models of integrated village agricultural technology transfer programmes at district/block/panchayat levels. Case studies on the spectacular success achieved by the Indian Agricultural Research Institute in establishing such models in difficult and far-flung areas have been described.

PART II

S.N. Mishra, in his paper on "*Sustainable Livestock Development in India: A Strategic Approach*", has made an attempt to distinguish between different livestock farming systems and has concluded that the mixed farming system, in which livestock and agriculture are integrated or interdependent, is environmentally most benign. Based on the experience of mixed farming system in India, a system that constitutes the predominant mode in practice, he has delineated its characteristics, the linkages between livestock and agriculture, between the livestock population and livestock production system, and the impact of the latter on environment, both on its input as well as output side. He has given a brief quantitative account of India's livestock economy in order to prepare the ground for examining the conditions of its sustainable development. A system based upon renewable sources of material inputs and energy is by definition sustainable. India's mixed farming system is open for sustainable development in future, provided appropriate state policies are adopted. In the past, policies have been formulated and implemented from top down. Success, however, depends upon reversing the direction of policy formulation and implementation. It has also been pointed out that information base and socio-economic research relating to livestock in India, so crucial for formulation of right policies and their implementation, are woefully inadequate.

P.N. Bhat advocates the need for a *Livestock Revolution*, as one of the effective means to alleviate poverty from rural India. Livestock Revolution, like Green Revolution, summarizes a complex series of interrelated processes and outcomes in production, consumption, and economic growth. The changes in dietary habits of people and change in purchasing power shall further augment the demand for animal-based food products. The increase in healthy, well-bred and well-nourished animals will provide economic resources of a high order for both agriculture and industry. Future shall be promising, if due care is given to make Livestock Revolution a success. In the world, especially developing countries, among them India is the natural pathbreaker. The strategy for successful sustainable development needs special steps to eradicate the weaknesses of livestock husbandry in India. First, partnership of the farmer with the professional should be developed. Second, the Indian consumer is to be addressed, as domestic market. Third, is the livestock farming itself. Science and Technology have the key to resolve these problems.

PART III

S.L. Mehta and A. Bandyopadhyay's paper titled "*Sustainable Agriculture: Farming Systems & Natural Resources*", examines the various aspects of the sustainability of the farming systems in India, in view of the environmental concerns and near-stagnant productivity in the major food grain production. The spectacular growth in agricultural production since 1960s has been mainly due to the new technologies, high receptivity of the farmers and the policies adopted by the government. Now, we have a huge buffer stock to face even a severe drought situation. This paper draws attention to the falling growth rates and declining per capita availability of food grain and examines this trend in all the five agro-ecosystems, viz. irrigated, coastal, arid, rainfed and hill and mountains. Sustainable technologies for these agro-ecosystems have been discussed, including 'zero tillage for rice-wheat production systems', crop residue management for rice and wheat, organic matter recycling and soil enrichment, integrated pest management, moisture conservation etc. Indigenous Technical Knowledge (ITK) and Precision Farming have been identified as the key elements for sustainability in all agro-ecosystems. The National Agricultural Technology Project (NATP) has given the right importance to ITK by including it as a 'Mission Mode' project for the 'collection, documentation and validation', of the technologies. The management of natural resources and integrated pest management hold the key to the preservation of soil fertility and our leadership in the international market. Renewed emphasis on organic farming, protection of environment, restoring and maintaining the health of soil are critical to sustainability and increase in agricultural production for meeting the demands of the ever increasing population.

S.S. Acharya in his paper on "*Sustainable Agriculture and Rural Livelihoods*", has brought out the salient issues relating to sustainable agriculture and rural livelihoods; analyses agricultural development initiatives in India; and suggests some areas of action to resolve the conflicts, which confront the policy makers in developing countries including India. In the context of trade off involved in achieving the overall goal of inter-generational equity, the paper raises several questions related to intra-generational inequality and asks who should set the priorities. The paper argues that political economy will not allow the neglect of present demands of the poor in pursuance of better future for others. For the hungry, malnourished and poor/food insecure, the needs of present generation and children are far more important than the needs of the future generations. Reviewing the situation of poverty, food insecurity and malnutrition at global level, the paper argues that large populated countries like China and India, pursuing the goal of near self-sufficiency in staple foods is a welcome development for the macro food security of medium size and low-income countries of the developing world. The paper has reviewed the Indian agricultural development strategy since independence and brought out how it has helped in improving macro and household food security. An analysis of poverty levels and rural livelihoods in India has also been presented in the paper. The implications of liberalized trade in agricultural commodities on rural livelihoods in India have been brought out. Based on the lessons derived from the development processes, a strategic approach to sustainable agricultural and rural livelihoods is presented.

It has been brought out that poor families derive their livelihoods from agriculture and natural resource base. Hence, the Preservation and Conservation of natural resources is equally important for them. However, these sections of society are concerned more for the improvement in the livelihoods of their present generation and removal of hunger and malnutrition of their children, which is their second generation. The strategic and priority goal of sustainable agriculture and rural livelihoods should, therefore, be removal of hunger and rapid reduction in poverty and malnutrition. In achieving this goal, the well-to-do and richer sections would need to make a definite sacrifice by changing their lifestyles, which would conserve natural resources of water, bio-diversity and land. Policy framework, institutional changes and technological development would have to be consistent with the priorities for achieving a win-win situation. State, market, civil society, science and technology and local institutions, all have important and critical roles in achieving the goals of sustainable agriculture and better rural livelihoods. A prerequisite for sustainable agricultural development and better rural livelihoods in India is a vibrant agriculture. A package of agricultural sector reforms suggested in this paper would help in making Indian agriculture more efficient and improve rural livelihoods on sustained basis.

A.N. Mathur, in his paper on *"Sustainable Agriculture Systems: Reduced Reliance on Non-Renewable Energy Sources and Substitution of Renewable Energy Sources"*, examines the status of various energy resources in India, environmental aspects of fossil fuels, need for renewable sources of energy and new technologies for sustainable power supply to agriculture. He admits that the present energy scenario is heavily biased towards the conventional energy sources, such as petroleum products, coal, atomic energy etc., which are finite in nature, besides causing environmental pollution. He has also attempted the SWOT analysis of renewable energy sources and technologies and has delineated the role played by them in supplementing the conventional energy sources in agriculture. Discussing the renewable energy sources, he has recognised that small hydro projects can play a critical role in improving the overall energy scenario in the country, particularly in remote and inaccessible areas. Apart from hydro power, the importance of solar energy, bio gas, wind power, wood and other biomass have also been discussed. The extensive use of renewable energy sources to complement the existing energy sources is an option to sustainable energy flow in the rural areas. He is of the view that the control of environmental pollution, which is likely to reach a new height in the times to come, can be achieved by the new technologies.

J.S. Samra, in his paper on *"Impacts, Adaptation and Mitigation of Climate Change in Indian Agriculture"*, has looked into the possible impact of climate change on Indian Agriculture, and further on food security scenario. According to his findings, in the next 20 years, India has to increase its food grains production by 1.5 times of the highest achievements made so far in order to meet the requirements of our growing population. Arable land resources will shrink due to increased demands for non-agricultural land use. Climatic changes are also going to impact on food security system. Anticipatory research is being strengthened to analyse impacts of global warming on overall food security system. Increased concentrations of carbon dioxide are expected to raise productivity, whereas high temperature will produce negative impacts. Spatial and temporal shifts in land use pattern and bio-diversity in response to snow melts, redistribution of rainfall and water have been modelled. Rise in sea level may submerge some islands and coastal areas, which will necessitate human migration, resettlement and resolution of social issues. Management of rice cultivation and resource conserving technologies for minimizing greenhouse gases production have been evolved. Sequestration of carbon in soil and agro-forestry systems has been argued for trading in emission gases. Watershed management practices to combat shifts in the patterns of erosion of resources, floods and droughts have been described. Technologies for ground water recharging to absorb contingencies of reduced rainfall in some regions and increased precipitation elsewhere are described. The need of a futuristic, pro-active and anticipatory multi-disciplinary research for minimizing inputs and adverse impacts of climatic changes has been emphasized. Agriculture is a lesser source of greenhouse gases, but a greater sink for managing impacts of global warming and climatic changes.

Madhusree Mazumdar, in her paper on "*Role of Urban and Peri-Urban Agriculture in Sustainable Development of a Metropolitan City: A Case of Delhi*", has brought out the significance of agriculture, in the ever-expanding urban areas. It includes horticulture, pisciculture, livestock rearing, dairying, floriculture and food processing and vending, including the production of exotic varieties of food, flowers and vegetables that is in demand in cities. It has been observed that the larger the population, the more varied is the food requirements and more expansive is urban agriculture. What attracts such activities to a city, is its ready market: of consumers as well as labour. Apart from the socio-economic benefits, urban agriculture contributes to environmental improvement within cities, like solid, liquid and gaseous waste assimilation, conservation of water, prevention of pollution and improvement in the quality of life. This paper has also brought out the important role, which the peri-urban agriculture can play in improving food availability and livelihood opportunities. This paper examines the concept and characteristics of urban agriculture and discerns its potential role in sustainable urban development. It also tries to find out if the national plans and policies that promote environmental management in India, support urban agriculture, creating a niche for it in city planning.

M. Moni's paper on *"Agricultural Informatics and Communication Network (AGRISNET): An ICT Strategy to Usher in Digital Opportunities for Sustainable Agricultural Development in India"*, brings to focus the emerging areas in information and communication technology and its role in sustainable agricultural development in India. The growing demand for food grains, vegetables, fruits, milk etc. present greater and newer challenges to agriculture. This paper stresses that 'informatics led agriculture development' can take India forward towards precision agriculture and enhancement of quality of life of the farming communities. Here, he has examined the impact of ICT diffusion on economic growth and sustainable development. ICT diffusion derives economic force from the complementary development of a knowledge-intensive society. AGRISNET will take advantage of convergence of technologies and service sectors for promotion of e-governance in the agricultural and cooperation sector, by incorporating applications like unified messaging, collaborative data sharing, network security etc. Thus, ICT network envisages to facilitate an integrated approach of internet technology and sustainable agricultural, rural and backward areas development with its farm and non-farm linkages.

PART IV

R.S. Deshpande, L. Venkatachalam and A. Narayanamoorthy in their paper on "*Policies for Access, Equity and Equality: Physical Resources and Human Resources*", seek to address the issues relating to access, equity and equality in physical and human resources, especially in the Indian context. The 'vicious circle of poverty' that prevails in many of the developing countries warrants the appropriate intervention in the form of enhancing the access to basic resources such as land and water to the individuals. Such policy interventions would eventually address the equity and equality issues so that the benefits could reach the needy. But the implementation process may distort even this logical sequence and hence added emphasis is needed for internalizing the equity and equality aspects. In the first part of this paper, a focused review of the trends in the Human Development Index and its components is incorporated. An integrated approach in providing education, healthcare, water supply and sanitation in an efficient and equitable manner to different groups seems to be the immediate need. Historical aspects of land policy in India that include three aspects, namely distribution of land, targeted land development programme and soil and water conservation programmes, are discussed to highlight the issues related to access to land resources. The weaker sections of the society seem to have been marginalised in terms of land holdings. Analysis of water resources and its distribution across farm sizes suggests that the growth rate of all the major sources of irrigation is inversely related to the farm size in majority of the states. After recognising that the access, equity and equality in resource- sharing is an institutional phenomenon, the paper suggests region-specific policy imperatives to handle the problems of equity and related aspects.

K.V. Raman's paper on "*Social and Economic Equity, Poverty Reduction and Employment Generation*", advocates harmonization of various policies relating to eradication of poverty, socio-economic equality and employment generation. Agricultural growth, as an important factor in reducing poverty has been recognised. Here, the provision for multiple livelihood opportunities has been suggested, as a strategy for the integrated development. This would include value addition of products, produced with the locally available resources. Diversification of agriculture and its integration with aquaculture and livestock, is am important suggestion. Focusing on agriculture, this paper also dwells upon the productivity improvement, detailing out the required interventions, in terms of natural resources management.

Gopal Krishan, in his paper, *"A Development Perspective for Punjab"*, emphasizes managing carrying capacity, in order to achieve sustainability. For years, Punjab effectively demonstrated its salience as the nation's leading state in agricultural and rural development. Today, it is yearning to be led for a recovery of its impaired economic and ecological base. With a view to capturing this scenario and offering a development strategy for Punjab, this paper attempts to spell out a vision for the state. It reviews the development perspectives and priorities under its successive Five Year Plans, analyses the performance of various sectors of economy and society on the 'SWOT' parameters, and highlights the ecological stress the state is currently experiencing. In that context, some seminal questions are raised: In which manner should Punjab manage its carrying capacity so that a-regular rise in relative prosperity in ensured ? How should it respond to the emerging challenge of globalisation, which is having an adverse effect on its agriculture and small-scale industry, in particular? In what way should it promote a culture of electing 'optimal locations' for any development investment, wherein economics leads politics rather than the other way round? For that some hard choices and decisions need to be made. These include: diversification of economy from agriculture to non-agriculture; that of agriculture towards non-farm activities; and, further that of cropping pattern from the stubborn wheat-rice rotation to an ecologically viable regime. This, however, is not enough, upgradation of the quality of habitat, both rural and urban, is essential. On the demographic front, the recent obnoxious tendency towards female foeticide is to be curbed. Rejuvenation of the economic dynamism, quality upgradation of the service provision, and management reforms in operating the system emerge as three vital ingredients of reinventing Punjab. Decentralised good governance, administrative area reform, and micro-level planning are identified as the three major instrumentalities for the purpose. The envisaged outcome is a 'progressive civil society', on a sustained basis.

K.V. Sundaram, in his paper on *"Policies for our Plundered Planet—Some Pathways to the Future"*, outlines the contours of some priority policies, related to the problems emerging from Earth-Man interface and their various consequences, which call for urgent action along several fronts. The paper underlines the fact that humanity's stake in earth protection is enormous in the new millennium, as the sane earth care policies, necessary in this behalf, have been neglected too often in the past. The basic dilemma here is related to the two-way relationship between development and environment. Covering a wide spectrum of issues, viz. environmental degradation, food security, water security, sustainable energy, rural development, population and carrying capacity, this paper expresses the twin concerns, viz. (i) environment without development would be life without opportunities; and (ii) development without adequate environmental protection would inflict serious environmental damage and destroy earth's delicate natural balance and hasten its very end. He has advocated for stringent environmental laws and economic instruments for promoting sustainable development. A new paradigm has also been suggested involving local communities and community-based organisations, for achieving sustainable earth care.

Shantanu Mathur's paper on *"Towards an Innovative Institutional Architecture to Promote the Development and Diffusion of Sustainable Pro-Poor Technologies"*, examines the institutional mechanism, responsible for transfer of technologies to farming communities. During 1980s and uptill mid-90s, there was little explicit pro-poor emphasis, with focus on scale-neutral technologies, at the same time crops and commodities produced and consumed by the society was emphasized. The paper discusses the IFAD's experiences in the past, and how they addressed the challenges, which came from different quarters. Evaluation of R&D programmes using participatory approaches showed higher benefits to the rural poor through increasing their adoption of the technologies developed with their involvement—leading to enhanced on-farm production and incomes. He gives emphasis on the community participation and recognizes that local farmer organizations are often better equipped than their upstream research partners, owing to their access to location-specific, agro-ecological and socio-economic information, and can make use of the upcoming technologies. Referring to the emergence of high-end biotechnology, space and information and communication technologies (ICTs), he sees opportunities for new forms of partnerships and IFAD's niche in ICTs would lie in promoting knowledge management aspects, including knowledge management and empowerment of its target groups through *Farmer Field Fora* (FFFs) and Telecentres.

Foundation Day Lecture

While delivering the 2nd Bhoovigyan Vikas Foundation Day Lecture, Dr. K. Venkatasubramanian, Member, Planning Commission, Government of India, stressed the need for a "*Knowledge Revolution*" in India, as the key to overall development in the country. Describing the knowledge concepts and its various related elements, he expressed the view that our country is on the brink of a period of profound societal change, and the government should invest in the areas of research in science and technology, to make India a Super Power in the new millennium with a Super Knowledge Society. This would need a movement towards four goals, viz. innovation goal, economic goal, environmental goal and social goal. In order to focus on the development of knowledge society in India, the government should give top priority to ensure infrastructure development for knowledge dissemination. He congratulated the Foundation in spreading the message of earth care and sustainability through the Earth Day Celebrations and Earth Care Awareness Campaigns with Earth Trustee Vision.

Part I

Natural Resources Development and Management

1

Management of Natural Resources for Sustainable Livelihood

BAIF's Approach*

NARAYAN G. HEGDE

Background

With the increasing population, demand for basic needs has been steeply rising during the past five decades in most of the developing countries. The growing populations need food, clothing, shelter, fuel and fodder for their livestock. In India, over 60-70 per cent of the people are living in rural areas who neither have adequate land holdings nor alternate service opportunities to produce or procure these commodities. In the absence of adequate employment opportunities, the rural people are unable to generate enough wages to sustain their livelihood. As a result, 40 per cent families, who earn less than Rs. 11,000 per annum are classified as poor. Apart from lower income, rural people also suffer from shortage of clean drinking water, poor health care and illiteracy, which adversely affect the quality of life. Presently, about 25 per cent of the villages do not have assured source of drinking water for about 4-5 months during the year and about 70-75 per cent of the water does not meet the standard prescribed by WHO. Poor quality drinking water is adversely affecting the health and diarrhoea is an important cause of infant mortality.

Traditionaler Indian communities being male dominated, women have been suppressed till recently. While the average literacy rate in rural areas is around 50-65 per cent, it is as low as

* Bharatiya Agro Industries Foundation's (BAIFs).

20-25 per cent among women in backward areas. Education of girls was felt to be unnecessary in the past and this has seriously affected their quality of life. Illiteracy has also suppressed their development due to lack of communication with the outside world. They are slow in adopting new practices, which are essential with the changing times. Apart from lack of communication, social taboo has also hindered their progress. Several vested interests, both local and outsiders have exploited this situation. The rich landlords did not want any infrastructure development, which would benefit the poor, because of the fear that they would not get cheap labour to work on their farms. The local moneylenders did not want alternate financial institutions to provide cheaper credit needed by the poor. The traditional healers canvassed against modern medicine under the garb of religion and divine power. Thus, the poor continued to live in the clutches of the powerful, accepting it as their destiny. They avoided confrontation and preferred to live a voiceless and suppressed life. Tolerating the worst and hoping for better days has been their way of life. It is a vicious cycle, and development programmes to address their livelihood improvement and food security can help them to come out of this cycle.

Problems of Livelihood

In India, although the contribution of agriculture to the Gross National Product (GNP) is around 35 per cent, in the absence of employment opportunities in industrial and service sectors, over 85 per cent of the rural income is generated from agriculture, who spend about 75-80 per cent of their earnings on food. Agriculture is the major source of livelihood but most of the illiterate farmers have not been successful in cultivating their land economically. They have been treating agriculture as a family tradition, following age old practices, and adopted new changes only after observing the success of their neighbours. Over 12-15 per cent of the rural families are landless and among the land holders, 69 per cent are marginal farmers with less than 1 ha holding (17% of the total land) and about 21 per cent are small farmers with 1-2 ha holdings (34% of the land). Thus about 90 per cent families own less than 51 per cent lands, with a per capita holding of 0.19 ha. Out of the 147 million ha agricultural lands, about 60 million ha are located in arid zones, which are mostly owned by the poor families. As the chances of crop failure on these lands is very high, the farmers generally do not invest in external inputs like improved seeds, fertilisers and plant protection measures and end up with poor crop yields, even during normal years.

Apart from private holdings, pastures and common lands owned by the government and community are also being used in many ways, particularly for fuel and fodder collection. The Government has reserved about 10 per cent of the total land in each village for livestock grazing. The ownership of this land is with the Village Panchayat (Local Government) and all the members of the community have free access. The Panchayat has no control over the use while the community does not consider it to be their responsibility to manage the pasture. This has resulted in over-exploitation and denudation of the pastures. The same situation prevailed on village woodlots and community forests. Thus, in spite of land scarcity, over 50 per cent of the total land are either idle or under-utilised. Such wastelands, unable to retain the rainwater are promoting soil erosion, flooding of rivers and silting of tank beds. They are also hosting a wide range of pests and diseases. Management of these wastelands to improve the productivity can revive the supply of fodder and fuel, facilitate the percolation of rainwater and improve agricultural production.

Water is a critical input for human consumption as well as for crop production but grossly neglected by the community. Major sources of water supply are rainfall, lakes, rivers, snowy mountains and underground storage. Except wells and small tanks, the other sources of water are collectively owned by the community. However, the powerful lobbies and vested interests have been taking advantage of these water resources for their own benefits, while the poor have no means of utilising their share. This has been accelerating the economic imbalance between the small and large landholders.

Rainfall is the main source of water for agricultural production in India. However, in the absence of adequate soil and water conservation practices, it is estimated that over 65 per cent rainwater runs off, flooding the rivers. About 28 per cent of the total cropping area in the country are under irrigation, where farmers have a tendency to use excessive water. In the absence of adequate training and demonstration, they believe that excess water can enhance their crop yields. Moreover, as the water charges are fixed on the basis of the area covered under irrigation instead of on the quantity of water supplied, farmers do not want to restrict the use of water. As a result of poor soil and water conservation measures, the average yield of food crops in India is only 1.9 tonnes/ha as compared to 4.0 tonnes/ha in China. Due to excessive use of water for irrigation, over 9.00 million ha fertile lands have turned into sodic and saline wastelands, thereby posing a serious threat not only to food security and employment generation but also to community health, biodiversity and the environment.

Forests have been providing many direct and indirect benefits to rural communities. As against the recommended 33 per cent of the total geographical area to be placed under forest cover, only 22 per cent land is under the Forest Department in India. Out of this area, over 50 per cent land is devoid of vegetation due to over-exploitation and biotic pressure. As a result, the existence of over 80 million tribals, who were dependent on forest products for livelihood has been threatened. Ill-effects of deforestation are evident in the form of shortage of fodder, fuel, timber, non-wood forest products and medicinal herbs. The indirect losses in the form of soil erosion, deepening of ground water table and reduction in green cover are far more serious. Deforestation has been directly suppressing agricultural production, which is yet to be realised by a major section of the rural society. Like community wastelands, the forests are under the ownership of the Government but these precious resources cannot be protected unless the local communities come forward to conserve it.

Livestock is an important source of supplementary income. Mixed farming has been serving as an insurance against natural calamities, while supporting food security and nutrient recycling. India has over 500 million livestock, which include cattle, buffaloes, sheep and goats. Among them, cattle and buffaloes are popular for milk production. As milk is an important part of the Indian diet and bullock power is essential for farming and rural transportation, rural families maintain 2-3 animals, but over 70 per cent of them are uneconomical due to low genetic base and poor management. The average milk yield of cows in India is 987 kg/lactation as compared to 4,233 kg in Europe. This is because out of the 100 million cattle, over 90 per cent are indigenous which yield less than 250 kg milk per lactation, while about 10 per cent of the crossbred yield about 2,000-3,000 kg milk per lactation. The poor and landless prefer to maintain sheep or goats and let them loose for grazing on community pastures. Such animals are a liability.

Poor productivity of the land and livestock and inefficient use of forests are the causes of seasonal employment in villages. Small farmers have work only for 100-120 days for growing one crop in a year, which is not adequate to sustain their livelihood. Hence, they have to struggle to earn additional wages by working in irrigated areas or migrate to urban areas. The migration pattern varies with the region, opportunities and socio-economic status of the families. The poorest families, particularly the landless and marginal holders owning poor quality land tend to migrate with the entire family. Many tribal families migrate to cities as construction workers and return at the onset of the rains. Such migrations severely affect the quality of life, due to poor health, lack of education and social pressures leading to erosion of moral values.

After independence, poverty alleviation was the major agenda of the Government of India. Thus various community development programmes were initiated to build the capabilities of the poor. These programmes provided skill oriented training to build the capabilities and supplied critical agricultural inputs either free or at subsided cost. However, most of these programmes did not succeed due to lack of people's participation. They were suspicious about the relevance of the programme and also lost confidence in the programme due to frequent failures. Subsequently, they lost confidence in themselves and also lost initiatives to work hard. This situation can be termed as mental poverty or psychological poverty. Thus, it is necessary to fight mental poverty through motivation, awareness and capacity building before initiating any livelihood activities.

BAIF's Approach

BAIF Development Research Foundation (formerly registered as the Bharatiya Agro Industries Foundation) is a voluntary organisation, established in 1967, as a Public Charitable Trust. Considering the challenges in rural areas, BAIF has set its mission to create opportunities of gainful self-employment for the rural families, especially disadvantaged sections, ensuring sustainable livelihood, enriched environment, improved quality of life and good human values. This is being achieved through development research, effective use of local resources, extension of appropriate technologies and upgradation of skills and capabilities with community participation. BAIF is a non-political, secular and professionally managed organisation, presently operating in 12,000 villages in India.

Family as a Unit for Development: BAIF considers poor rural family as a basic unit for development. This provides an opportunity to identify the target families who require different types of support to come out of poverty. Generally most of the community development programmes consider village as an unit of development where the well to do and influential sections of the society dominate over the poor and exploit the benefit to the maximum extent. Thus such development projects may often create a wider gap between the rich and poor with in the community.

Focus on Quality of Life: The overall goal of BAIF is to ensure better quality of life, through promotion of various development activities related to livelihood, health, literacy and moral development. Starvation being the most serious form of poverty, livelihood programme was considered as a priority but it was soon realised that good health and education are basic needs even for taking up livelihood activities. With generation of income, good moral values are also essential for happiness. Excess money, without strong moral education has been distracting the youth towards unproductive and unethical activities. Hence, BAIF is emphasising on blending livelihood programme with education, health care and moral development activities. The essential components of moral development are—willingness to take part in community development, non-violence, de-addiction from alcohol, drugs, narcotics and gambling, respect for women and concern for environmental protection. These components are generally acceptable to the community, irrespective of their religious and ethnic backgrounds, which have brought about a significant change in the attitude of the target communities.

Assured Livelihood: While promoting various development programmes, the primary goal is to help the target family to come out of poverty, within a shortest period. The dairy development programme has a gestation period of 3-4 years, till the newly born calf comes into milk production. In land based development programmes the gestation period may vary from 2 to 6 years, depending on the type of farming systems practiced by the farmers. In case of arable crop production, the gestation period is short due to short rotation crops while the fruit and tree crops take 5-6 years to generate income. While promoting these income generation activities, there are two critical factors which affect the success of the programmes. Firstly, the programme should be well planned to generate substantial income to enable the participating families to come out of poverty. Generally small farmers having poor quality land and livestock may not be able to earn substantial income with only one intervention. Hence multi-disciplinary programmes have the advantage. Similarly, small interventions such as kitchen garden, vermi-composting, homestead horticulture in isolation will not help the poor. These interventions can be helpful as a part of an integrated programme.

The other important aspect is to provide support during the gestation period. Many of the poor who do not have any resources even to procure their daily ration, are likely to neglect their development work, if no support is available in the form of assistance or wages to ensure their food security. Hence different short term income generation activities need to be designed till the income starts generating from the major interventions.

Women Empowerment: Involvement of women in all the development programmes right from the stage of project planning is essential. Although women represent 50 per cent of the population, they also have the major responsibility of grooming children and procuring the basic needs required for food, fuel and fodder securities. Active participation of women in development programmes will help to identify their problems and reduce their drudgery.

Environmental Protection: In all the development programmes conservation of the natural resources and protection of the environment are essentially built in, as these are critical for sustainable development. This is particularly important, while dealing with the poor as their primary objective is to earn their livelihood and the development organisations have the obligation to carefully design the programme to ensure environmental protection with income generation activities.

Blending Development with Research and Training: For effective implementation of various development programmes, the development programmes are supported by applied research and training activities. It is realised that any development programme without research back up is outdated and any research programme without development and extension outlets is academic. Training of the field functionaries and farmers is essential for effective transferring of technologies from laboratories to the field.

People's Organisations: To sustain the benefits of various projects particularly after the completion of the project, BAIF has developed a strategy to promote grassroots level People's Organisations, right at the initiation of the projects. Several types of local People's Organisations such Self Help Groups (SHGs), Village Level Planning Committees, Users' Groups of various goods and services, networks and federations of SHGs and village level Organisations, processing and marketing cooperatives are some of the organisations promoted in the field. These organisations are helpful in motivating the members of the community, particularly the backward and shy members to sustain their interest and take active involvement in various development initiatives. These organisations are also effective in procuring necessary agricultural inputs, disseminating technology, organising post-harvest handling, processing and marketing the produce. Subsequently they work closely with the Panchayati Raj Institutions to participate in various states sponsored development activities as well as to ensure the welfare of their community.

'Jana Utthan': Our New Approach

Over the long field experience, BAIF has realised that the development organisations approach the rural communities with specific activities, which benefit only a few sections of the community, while the others are left out, due to lack of resources or skills. In this process, it is often the poor who are left out of these development programmes. Therefore to overcome this situation, the new approach—known as 'Jana Utthan Approach' has been developed. Under this approach, the Extension Workers interact with the local community with an open mind and to bring them together to identify the local problems. The community is then encouraged to interact closely and identify the members into

3-4 economic categories based on their income and the access to various resources. Then the local groups identify the resources and the opportunities for the individual families belonging to different categories with an objective of bringing all the sections above poverty. In this process, while the marginally poor get smaller support through 1 or 2 development intervention, to come out of poverty, the poorest families having limited resources are given opportunity to participate in multiple activities. Thus the poor have scope to earn their income from several sources and the chances of failure are low. This approach helps to maintain transparency of the programme and promotes harmony among the members of different economic categories.

The Jana Utthan Approach also poses a challenge to the development agencies to find suitable solutions to the problems of the landless and resource poor families. This calls for the search of suitable off-farm production and service activities to be undertaken by the poor, particularly the landless. Some of the important off-farm activities are pottery, smithy, carpentry, textile and services such as automobile hire and repairs, electrical wiring and repairs, masonry, production of pre-casted materials, civil construction, consumer stores, etc. While the off-farm activities have serious limitation due to poor infrastructure for input supply and marketing, the success of most of the on-farm activities are dependent on the productivity and management of the natural resources.

Presently, all the important natural resources like land, water, forest vegetation and livestock, which are critical inputs for providing gainful self-employment and generation of GNP are underutilised. These resources, which are the basic assets for providing sustainable livelihood are proving to be liabilities. Therefore, the strategy for sustainable development is to improve the productivity of the natural resources and develop the capabilities of the local communities to make optimum use of these resources for their livelihood. Efficient management of the natural resources can generate secondary resources, which in turn can provide additional employment opportunities. With this background, BAIF has developed a multi-disciplinary programme for sustainable management of natural resources, which include livestock development, watershed development, agroforestry and promotion of post-production and non-farm activities. These activities have good potential to provide employment opportunities even to the landless, small landholders and women, while conserving environment and biodiversity.

Programme Impact

Dairy Development: BAIF initiated livestock development programme through the upgradation of local cattle and buffaloes for milk production as most of the rural families including the landless maintain livestock most of the rural families benefited from this programme. Indeed, the poor are more dependent on the livestock than the rich as they do not have adequate land and water resources to engage in agricultural development activities.

Realising the drawback of the local cattle with respect to productive and reproductive inefficiencies, BAIF has taken up the crossbreeding of such low productive, non-descript cattle. The programme also covers the buffaloe improvement by breeding non-descript with improved breeds. Under this programme a cluster of 10-15 villages will be headed by a trained technician who will provide breeding services to cows and buffaloes at the doorsteps of the farmers, using frozen semen of superior sires. Motivation, awareness about the benefits, delivery of various services, regular follow up, technical guidance, timely health care, supply of critical inputs have been helpful to the farmers to take full advantage of this programme.

Crossbred calves born at the doorsteps of the rural families come to milk production at the age of 28-32 months and yield about 2,500-2,700 kg milk per lactation (300 days). This programme encourages the farmers to stall feed their valuable animals and reduce the herd size by selling un-productive animals. A crossbred cow is able to contribute a net income of Rs. 5,000 per year apart from other benefits such as supply of milk for home consumption, particularly for children, dung for biogas and manure and efficient use of various agricultural by-products as feed. The programme provides an excellent opportunity for the empowerment of women and improve the eco-system by reversing the unhealthy trends of stray grazing, inbreeding and spread of diseases. A family with three crossbred cows is able to remain out of poverty and lead a sustainable livelihood.

Presently, BAIF's programme is spread over 12,000 villages

through 740 cattle development centres in eight states. At least 2 lakh female crossbred cattle and buffaloe calves are born every year and value of the milk produced from this programme is over Rs. 800 crores per annum. Presently, at least 5 lakh families have taken advantage of this programme to come out of poverty. This programme has the potential to expand throughout the country, as milk is a staple food for the growing population of the country.

Development of Community Pastures: In drought prone regions of Rajasthan, where rainfall is erratic, farmers are more dependent on livestock than on agriculture for their survival. In such areas, the community pastures have been heavily degraded due to uncontrolled grazing. With the degradation of community lands, the other problems such as soil erosion, deforestation and depletion of ground water have been accelerated further affecting the natural resources. Therefore, BAIF decided to take up community pasture development on a pilot basis in Bhilwara district of Rajasthan. Initially, the work was undertaken at village Kavlas by identifying 10 ha of pasture land out of 200 ha belonging to a temple trust. The villagers were reluctant, as there was a fear of land that the land brought under such development will not be available for their use. Fortunately, as BAIF was already operating a cattle development centre in the village, the villagers had full faith in the organisation and were willing to take part in this experiment.

The project was initiated with the formation of a pasture committee, taking one representative from each of the 10 communities. The major activities proposed were to dig trench-cum-mould for establishing live hedges, contour bunding, gully plugging, sowing of seeds of forage of legumes and grass species to enrich the quality of forage. Over the next 3 years, the villagers participated in protection, collection of seeds, harvesting grass and trimming of the trees grown in the pasture. The villagers were extremely happy to realise that with the investment of Rs. 10,000 per ha they were able to generate output worth Rs. 6,000-7,000 every year in the form of fodder and fuelwood. Looking to the success, additional areas were brought under community pasture development not only in Kavlas but also in 15 different villages in Rajasthan. Apart from the production of forage, there were several other benefits such as recharging the ground water, reduction in soil erosion resulting in improved agricultural production in the neighbouring areas, rehabilitation of wild animals like blue bulls in the pasture which were damaging agricultural crops. There was good harmony established among various sections of the society and there was a direct benefit on the productivity of livestock in these villages. Looking to this success, the Government of India has now provided additional support to expand this programme in about 200 villages.

Water Resource Development: Development of water resources and wastelands are other important activities, having good potential for supporting the livelihood. However, with watershed development alone particularly the small farmers owning poor quality land, cannot take advantage as they do not have the capacity to invest in land development and critical agricultural inputs. Hence they do not take active part in such programmes. Therefore the strategy adopted is to combine watershed management with development of low productive agricultural lands and wastelands owned by the weaker sections of the society. As there is a close link between poor quality land and poverty, BAIF has been taking up the development of private lands on priority to ensure adequate income generation for the poor, before expecting them to participate in community land development. Such a step has helped to motivate the community to conserve the community pastures and forests in the future.

In all the watershed development programmes, involvement of the community right from the stage of planning has been a critical factor, for the success. Mobilising the community through entry point activities and establishing effective communication through SHGs and village level planning committees, participation of the community in resource identification and development have been the important elements of the programme. With watershed development, introduction of the improved agricultural practices such as use of certified seeds, promotion of timely tillage operations, integrated pest management, supply of micro-credit to procure inputs, setting up of grain bank to meet the emergency needs of the poor etc. have played a very significant role in building the confidence of the community and sustain their interest.

Active involvement of the local community in watershed development has also helped in tapping their traditional wisdom and come out with several innovations. In South Karnataka, where the soil is sandy and the annual rainfall is only 750 mm, traditional approach of contour bunding was not feasible and construction of percolation tanks could benefit only a few farmers, having their land on lower portion of the grid. Hence the farmers come up with the idea of digging 1-2 farm ponds per hectare to retain rainwater in their own fields. Thus in a cluster of 4-5 villages near Mainahalli in Hassan district, 350 farm ponds were dug and interconnected to capture the surplus water coming out from the ponds located on higher elevations. The size of the pond varied from 6 × 6 × 3m to 10 × 10 × 3m and cost about Rs. 3,000-4,000 only in the form of labour. Such ponds could retain water up to December-January and this water could be used for watering fruit and vegetable crops, during the Kharif and Rabi seasons. Other major benefits were prevention of soil erosion, which resulted in improved soil productivity, recharging of the open wells and borewells, and revival of the old rivulets. The yield of coconut plantation in the surrounding had also increased significantly. With effective recharging of ground water, farmers gained their confidence and brought their barren lands under fruit and plantation crops. It was estimated that over four years the ground water table had increased by 3.79 m and 175 ha were brought under irrigation. Two ephemeral streams have started flowing throughout the year. The problem of drinking water has been completely solved. Apart from increased agricultural production, the community has gained confidence in their capabilities, which has helped them to take active part in other development programmes promoted by the Panchayati Raj Institutions and other community development programmes.

Introduction of cattle development in the watershed has also played a very significant role in improving the economic viability of the programme. It has been observed that most prominent and immediate benefit of watershed development is conservation of soil and water, resulting in increased grass production on field bunds, borders and on all the available cultivated and non-cultivated lands. The advantage of this grass output can be harnessed only when the farmers own valuable livestock, which can respond suitably through higher milk production. Such Multidisciplinary activities have helped in taking best advantage of the watershed development programmes.

Tree Based Farming: While promoting land development

programmes along with watershed development, tree based farming has several advantages. Tree are hardy, capable of withstanding harsh weather conditions and to provide income for a long period. However, crop selection is dependent on the soil productivity and moisture supply. Most of the small farmers prefer fruit crops, as they can earn regular income, although there is high demand for labour.

Promotion of tree based farming on private wastelands for food security and income generation is a major programme of BAIF. This programme to promote agri-horti-forestry for food and fodder security and marginal lands also covers women empowerment, community health, drinking water supply, hygiene and sanitation and capacity building. The poor families participating in this programme establish drought tolerant fruit crops such as mango, cashew, tamarind, custard apple, ber, etc. on their marginal or wastelands covering 0.4 to 1.0 ha. The interspace is used for cultivating arable crops, which they have been growing earlier and the field bunds and borders are used to establish hardy shrubs and trees useful for fodder, fuel, timber and herbal medicines.

This programme for rehabilitation of poor tribal families on their own degraded lands, popularly known as "Wadi" (Orchard Development) has helped over 25,000 families to conserve and improve the productivity of the natural resources while improving their agricultural production. The green coverage of the land through fruit trees enabled them to earn regular income without destroying the vegetation. Efficient field bunding promoted soil and water conservation and active presence of the farmers in the field helped them to enhance their crop yields by 50-100 per cent as compared to their normal yields. There were opportunities for them to meet their basic needs such as fodder, fuel, timber and medicinal herbs without depending on the community lands and forests. This not only saved their time but also enhanced their dignity and status in the society.

Organisations at various levels have been created to motivate the community, mobilise resources, initiate marketing and other community development activities. Such people's organisations play a very vital role in sustaining the programmes beyond the project period.

Key to Success

As the natural resources which are critical inputs for providing sustainable livelihood to the rural poor are in a degraded condition, it is difficult for the small and marginal farmers to generate gainful employment in rural areas and to come out of poverty. Lack of infrastructure, inadequate financial resources and poor managerial capabilities have further shaken their confidence to fight poverty. Therefore, the following components play a critical role in successful implementation of rural development programmes in the country.

- Motivation and training of the weaker sections of the society.
- Introduction of multidisciplinary programmes.
- Introduction of appropriate technologies.
- Direct linkage with the consumers and market.
- Establishment of people's organisations to sustain the development.

These critical factors will empower the poor to earn their livelihood from various activities and establish a good network with other members of the community to fight poverty with unity.

2

Natural Resource Management for Food Security and Sustaining Agriculture

D.K. PAUL

Agricultural developments in India through increased use of high yielding varieties, irrigation and fertilizer resulted in spectacular fourfold increase in production of food grains from a mere 50.8 million tonnes in 1950-51 to 202.53 million tonnes in 1998-99. But it slowed down in last few years as food grain production has stabilised around 200 million tonnes. Concerns have been raised about stagnation of yield levels of rice and wheat with 0.1 to 1 per cent increase recently compelling serious considerations to address major issues regarding sustainability of agriculture development and food security of the the nation with ever increasing population. There is perceptible concern from ongoing process of degradation of resource which are related to agricultural production from the land encompassing all the resources. Land degradation in India, like in all the developing country, is a serious facet of agriculture as soil erosion, nutrient depletion, soil and water quality degeneration are affecting quality of life. Livelihood support system, with adequate distribution of the developmental funding for income distribution in the rural India is a great task as and poverty interact in a destructive cycle as increased natural resource degradation is often rooted in food insecurity, poverty and urban crowding and reduced health and hygiene.

In view of this, the management of various natural resources, namely weather, soil, water, bio-diversity including multi-purpose tree species assume paramount importance for the maintenance of food security in India. Detailed discussion about the implication of food security and management of those resources are given sectionwise.

What is Food Security?

Food security is regarded as one of the major index of development of a country and is said to exist when the people, at all times, have physical and economic access to sufficient, safe and nutritious food to meet their dietary needs and food preferences for an active and healthy life. As per the Rome Declaration on World Food Security and Plan of Action by the World Food Summit, food security could be assessed at several levels—individual, household, national, regional and global. Here, food security fundamentally is about production of food and its access by the population to meet the present and anticipated future need, over the cycle of normal and adverse years.

Food security has three important criteria

- *Availability*: sufficient supplies of appropriate quality of food consistently available to all at all times,
- *Access*: all have adequate resources to produce or buy appropriate foods for a nutritious diet;
- *Utilization*: proper biological use of food through adequate diet, water, sanitation and health care.

It is estimated that a large population in India (about 200 million) exist on less than a dollar per day, are not having food security due to various reasons. Poverty is the main obstacle to food security as low income denies access to resources needed to produce food (land, supplies, credit) or prevent the people from buying it. The deprived people are especially vulnerable when food prices increases due to low production or other factors affecting food security like weather condition, conflict, joblessness, low returns to farmers, unsustainable resource-use, debt service, overvalued exchange rates between countries, and distorted international markets. During World Food Conference (held in 1974) the global community pledged to end world hunger thus food insecurity within 10 years but even after 25 years, it was the most overriding concern for Summit at Sustainable Development at the Earth Summit at Johannesberg, South Africa (2002).

Even before 1974, the world's nations recognized the right to food. The Universal Declaration of Human Rights states that "every human being has the right to a standard of living adequate for the health and well-being of himself (herself) and family, including food." The governments at the World Conference (1974), took a unique policy decision on 'right to food' which proclaims that "every man, woman and child has the inalienable right to be free from hunger and malnutrition" and endorsed the goal of eradicating food insecurity "within a decade".

So what went wrong? On careful analysis we can say that there are many reasons like population explosion (in the food insecure countries) combined with unsustainable agriculture with high degree of land degradation due to enhanced pressure on land and water coupled with unscientific cultivation practices especially misuse of water and neglect of its management aspects.

Management of Weather Resources

India is blessed with a good amount of rainfall receiving 400 million-hectare metres. However, the regional distribution of rainfall varies from less than 100 mm in the extreme arid parts of western Rajasthan to the highest rainfall region (> 10,000 mm) in the Cherrapunji and adjoining Khasi hill regions of Assam. About 80 per cent of the annual rainfall as a whole and in some areas 90 per cent of it is received in the monsoon period (June-October) alone with high co-efficient of variability.

This pattern of alternation calls for adopting suitable seasonal cropping along with contingency plans. There are two patterns in rainfall distribution; the first is a spatial pattern, in which the rainfall over eastern India and the rest of India is in opposition. The second pattern is that the rainfall over Peninsular India fluctuates in opposition to north-western India. Also rainfall behaves in a coherent manner over wide tracks of the country, which has been utilised in developing long-range prediction techniques by IMD, for the seasonal rainfall for the country.

Besides rainfall, thermal regime acquires importance as it controls physical and chemical reactions vital for plant growth and productivity. Fortunately, most of the country's cultivable area is under tropical climate where temperature is not a limiting factor.

Relative humidity influences plant water use and the incidence of pests and diseases. High atmospheric humidity conditions during the active monsoon period show with the morning RH values around 80 to 85 per cent more so in coastal and north-eastern region of the country and decrease in the interior inland regions.

Mean hours of highest sunshine are lowest in the north-eastern region (5.8 hours), and are highest in western Rajasthan (9.1 hours). During summer periods (March to May) sunshine hours reach to more than 10 hrs per day in Rajasthan, Madhya Pradesh and Gujarat regions. With the onset of monsoon, the hours of bright sunshine decrease sharply and remain around 3 to 7 hours per day over many parts of the country.

The mean wind speeds are lowest during the winter months (3-6 km/h) and the wind regime builds up with the initiation of summer season and is at peak during the pre-monsoon periods of April to June (6-10 km/h).

Based on the soil characteristics, rainfall pattern and ET demand, the length of growing season (LPG) varies from 90 days in NW India to about 300 days in NE region. In the semi-arid region, the LPG varies between 120-150 days while in the dry sub-humid climates it is 150-180 days

Weather/climate as a natural resource defines the choice of crops and cropping patterns in a given region (Table 2.1). In the arid regions where rainfall is above 300 mm, the length of humid period is about 1 to 4 weeks. Short duration drought resistant pulses such as mungbean, mothbean, cowpea, and cereals of 10 to 12 weeks duration such as pearl millet and minor millets are suitable. In semi-arid regions, where the length of the humid period is around 6 weeks, rainy season crops are grown in soils that have a capacity of holding less than 150 mm of water. Additional post-rainy season crops can be grown on conserved soil moisture, in soils that can hold more than 200 mm. In soils with 150-200 mm capacity, inter-cropping is possible. In sub-humid areas, where humid period is more than 12 weeks duration and the rainfall is twice that of PET, paddy based cropping system is suitable as other crops cannot tolerate water stagnation.

Table 2.1: Choice of Cropping Patterns for Different Growing Periods

Length of Growing Period	*Cropping System that can be Adopted*
< 75 days	Perennial vegetation Monocropping of short duration pulses
75-140 days	Monocropping
140-180 days	Inter-cropping
> 180 days	Double cropping.

Management of Land Resources

A large varieties of soils spreading all over the subcontinent are derived from a wide range of geological rocks and parent materials interacting with soil forming factors like climate, vegetation, topography, for varying time period. The 329 m ha land surface of, India is covered with 105.5 m ha red soils, 73.5 m ha black soils, 58.4 m ha alluvial soils, 11.7 m ha laterite soils and 30 m ha hill and terai soils.

The Alluvial soils of Indo-Gangetic Plains is supporting agriculture for more than 330 million people of the subcontinent and a good part of which are irrigated. Red soils which occur in peninsular region have been developed from granite and granite-gneiss and support many plantation and horticultural crops besides, the common agricultural crops. They respond well to management inputs such as tillage and irrigation. The black soils occur mostly in central, western India and part of southern India. The laterites occurring in high rainfall zones of the country are poor soils because of low base saturation and nutrient retention capacity. Most of the desert soils in western part of the country are sandy soils with low water and nutrient holding capacity. The hills and Terai soils of India are located mostly in northern and north-eastern part of the country and are characterized by cooler temperature and high rainfall which help in high carbon status and have very high potential for horticulture and agri-horti system, but faces serious water erosion problem.

Soil being a finite resource, its capacity to produce is limited by intrinsic characteristics, agro-ecological setting and the land and water management practices. The nature and distribution of different kinds of soils have been surveyed by state and central soil survey organizations under the overall coordination of

National Bureau of Soil Survey and Land Use Planning of thc ICAR and soil maps at 1:250,000 scale have been prepared. Detailed maps at 1:50,000 scale for district level planning and at 1:10,000 scale for watershed level planning have also been developed on demand for selected areas.

Both due to intrinsic features and human interventions, the soil resources of the country are being constantly exposed to different forces of degradation. The reported statistics of land degradation in India varies widely. The potential human induced land degradation is reported to be as high as 187.7 mha. At least 32.7 per cent of geographical area of country suffers from different forms of land degradation and water erosion accounts for 65 per cent of land degradation (Table 2.2).

Table 2.2: Land Degradation Status in India

Type of Degradation	*Area (million ha)*
Water erosion	57.16
Wind erosion	10.46
Salt affected and water logging	9.52
Shifting cultivation	2.38
Ravines	2.68
Degraded forests	24.90
Others (Mines & querry, land slides & acid sulphate)	0.34
Total	107.43

Source: Ministry of Agriculture, Govt. of India, 1994.

Management of Water Resources

Though renewable water resources of the country is about 4 per cent of global availability, still 70 per cent of runoff goes waste to the sea without utilisation. In the past five decades commendable work on water resource utilisation has been achieved for irrigation, power generation, drinking water, industrial uses and civic supplies. Even then we have to take renewed efforts in developing our vast water resources prudently in the next millennium to cater to demands of different sectors. The per capita availability of water over the country has dropped down from 5300 m^3 in 1955 to 2200 m^3 recently, compared to 7420 m^3 world and 3240 m^3 Asian average. It may touch 1500 m^3 by 2025 making country water stressed as already many parts of the country are water stressed as scarcity limit of less than 1000 m^3 is existing in many places, forcing us to take priority remedial measures.

Agriculture is the largest consumer of water but demand for domestic and industrial sectors would also increase by 3-4 times and for power by 7-8 times forcing the farming community to adopt better water management practices as scarcity of good quality water would be the major challenge in next millennium. The actual water use efficiency in the command areas, including tube well command are very low with a tremendous scope for improvement.

In India, an estimated 80 per cent of the population use ground water for their domestic needs (UNICEF 1998). The ground water availability, vary from most potential aquifers of Indo-Gangetic-Brahmaputra alluvium to the comparatively low yielding hard rock formations of peninsular India. Overexploitation of ground water is evident for irrigation in quite a few states due to 'ground and water rights' to the land owners. Ground water needs to be managed as common property resources for which the quality of ground water at many places needs to be monitored for presence of fluoride, arsenic, iron etc. All these call for scientific management of ground water for equilibrium withdrawals. As domestic and municipal effluents are estimated to constitute 75 per cent of India's waste water by volume (MOEF 1992), affecting 241 towns in 14 States of India, it is indicated that on an average, 90 per cent of the water supply is polluted and only 1.6 per cent of polluted wastewater gets treated (Central Pollution Control Board, Report).

Management of Crops and Plant Resources

Land utilization pattern of 305 m ha reported area depicts 68.8 m ha area under forest, 93.8 m ha not being cultivated and 142.22 m ha is the net sown area, of which only 37.6 per cent is under irrigation. The cropping intensity is 131.2 per cent with 44.4 m ha area sown more than once in a year (1999).

In effect cropping systems, are decided by a complex agro-climatic, socio-economic and trade related factors, viz. climate, soil, irrigation, marketing, socio-economics, food habit, availability of labour and technological innovations.

More than 250 important cropping systems are being followed

throughout the country. Sequential multiple cropping, using short duration crop cultivars and intensive input management is practiced, to enhance land use efficiency especially in irrigated eco-system for increasing productivity. In areas with assured irrigation only few cropping systems have been perfected for high productivity. However, a large diversity of cropping systems exists under rainfed and dry land areas with an overriding practice of inter-cropping to cover risks of single crop failures.

Review of Developmental Programme on Natural Resource Management

The problem of natural resource rehabilitation management in the country is a complex and multi-dimensional one and requires a scientific and non-conventional approach. Over the years, the Planning Commission, the National Commission on Agriculture and various concerned ministries and the state governments, have dealt with this difficult problem in a traditional manner with limited success.

Review of Watershed Development Programmes

ICAR's took up Operational Research Projects on Watershed Management with the funding from the Central Government in collaboration with the State Government with a view to develop location specific soil and water management methodologies and consequent adoption of production technologies on a large scale. A review of 47 Operational Research Projects of Watershed Management was published few years back by the ICAR. Most of the projects had been undertaken by the Central Soil and Water Conservation Research and Training Institute, Dehradun, through a dozen or more Research Centres undertaken all over the country (mostly in the Arid and Semi-Arid Zones), notably Dehradun, Chandigarh, Agra, Kota, Bellay, Ootacamund, Datia, Koraput and Vasad (Gujarat). Other (ICAR) institutes also took up some projects, e.g. Grassland and Fodder Research Institute, Jhansi project at Tejapura.

State Programmes of Soil and Water Conservation on Watershed Basis: On the basis of that finding presently all states now prepare watershed projects, though comprehensive multi-disciplinary holistic approach may be wanting in some areas. From the first plan period up to 1993-94, an area of 33.3 m ha was treated under the earlier schemes in the State Sector with an expenditure of Rs. 27,036.6 crores. Since Eighth Plan Central Ministries (Agrculture, Rural Development, Envirornment and Forest) are taking up watershed development projects in large areas with the funding from them. Some of the important and significant ongoing Watershed Development Projects are documented here below:

The Scheme on Soil Conservation for Enhancing Productivity of Degraded Lands in the Catchments of River Valley Projects (RVP): The scheme covers 31 catchments in 18 States. Mostly Inter-State River Valley Projects are selected.

Scheme on Soil Conservation for Enhancing Productivity of Degraded Lands in the Catchments of Flood Prone Rivers: The purpose was to reduce flood hazard by controlling runoff and sediments generated in the catchments.

Watershed Development Project for Shifting Cultivation Areas: This scheme first operated on family basis for the North East Region, but has now been restarted on watershed basis. IX Plan outlay of Rs. 75 crores with a target of 1.5 lakh ha has been proposed.

National Watershed Development Project for Rainfed Areas (NWDPRA): First started in the VIII Plan, this scheme is the most talked about venture in Agriculture today and aims for integrated development of the rainfed areas. During VIIIth Plan period an area of 4.3 million hactares is claimed to have been treated at an estimated cost of Rs. 1,274 crores; and Rs. 1,050 crores is proposed to be spent under this centrally sponsored scheme during Ninth Five Year Plan.

Internationally Aided Watershed Development Projects: These projects are primarily funded by the World Bank, DANIDA, Swiss Development Corporation, EEC, KFW, FAO/UNDP and Government of Netherlands. They are mostly NGO oriented.

Drought Prone Areas Programme (DPAP): Frequent drought compelling the Central Government to provide relief gave rise to an area development programme for the drought prone blocks of the country in 1973-74, later on taken up on watershed basis. The DPAP is under implementation in 947 blocks of 155 districts spread over 13 States. Work is taken up units of 500 ha watersheds. Since 1995-96, about 6,875 Watersheds Development Projects have been sanctioned.

Desert Development Programme (DDP): The Desert Development Programme aims at economic development, especially of the weaker sections of society, for checking desertification, and increase in productivity. The scheme was started in 1977-78 and currently operates in 227 blocks of 36 districts in 7 States, over an area of 45.7 m ha since 1995-96, under the watershed approach.

Outlay of the Government Programme: The amounts that are presently available from schemes which have an important component of natural resource management, i.e. afforestation, soil and water conservation etc. is more than Rs. 6,000 crores per year, which advocates management of the natural resources through State oriented management interventions in India. Apart from the investment collectively made by various governments and agencies, farmers are also using their own resources for soil and moisture conservation works on their own lands, the total availability of funds adds up to more than Rs. 7,000 crores a year.

Strategies of Natural Resource Management in this Millennium

In the ensuing millennium favourable land and water, which were available till now, will not be available in plenty in future as degradation of natural resources at higher level of production is eminent reducing the agricultural production base. Decreased per capita availability of land, water, vegetation, as no area expansion is possible forcing the cultivator to go for intensive cultivation with application of science and technology, especially in the hither to neglected area of management of natural resources.

The problem of natural resource rehabilitation and management in the country is a complex and multi-dimensional one and requires a scientific and non-conventional approach. Over the years, the Planning Commission, the National Commission on Agriculture and various concerned ministries and the state governments, have dealt with this difficult problem in a traditional manner with limited success.

The Indian agriculture is often considered a 'gamble on the monsoon rains' as the monsoon activity controls a major quantum (about 80%) of the annual rainfall. Rainfall decides the adequate availability of irrigation water in the reservoirs in the irrigated areas, both for rainy season and dry period. With a large area still being cultivated under rainfed conditions, the impact of weather conditions during the cropping season play a dominant role in deciding the cultivated net area and the productivity of many important. This calls for better management of the natural resources judiciously for sustainable agriculture.

Thus greater understanding of the local features, potentials and problems of the soils, water, plant and biodiversity should form the starting point for agriculture development planning and optimum utilisation of arable and non-arable areas in the country.

The degraded lands offer great avenues for horizontal expansion in future with intensive soil and water conservation measures of these fragile land resources. It is necessary to rejuvenate degraded forest by way of development of silvi-pastoral—multi-purpose plus trees system, there is a dire necessity to develop agro forestry system which is compatible with the general agriculture. This requires the development of area-specific agro forestry models on watershed approach. Agro-forestry will have the distinction of being the most dependable farming system in the non-forest areas of arid, semi-arid (dryland) besides the humid tropical regions to meet the challenges of deficits of fodder, firewood, timber, pulp wood and system sustainability.

Paradigm Shift for Participatory Natural Resource Management

The thinking and an analysis of other national and indigenous case studies of people's participation in WM (Sharma, 1997) as well as new knowledge based on many failed experience in the last ten years or so (Sanders, 1990; Dent, 1997), has given rise to a new paradigm for people's participation in natural resource management.

This new paradigm addresses the natural resources degradation problem as perceived by farmers and gives economically viable, environmentally sustainable production oriented, conservation alternatives that are built upon their indigenous knowledge for their overall development. Out of the prevalent two schools of thoughts on people's involvement, the one is that involvement through people will result into declining role of professionals and technicians is gradually being discounted.

The thinking that empowerment of people will result into more empowerment of the professionals for development agents/social workers as they gain more love and trust of the people is gaining ground. This will happen when the professionals and development agents become true facilitators and this can come by with the large scale involvement of the largely unbiased youth in the developmental process.

Renewed Involvement of the People: It is necessary to have coordination of the central and state governments, dealing with development of land and water and to accept the micro-watershed approach for integrated and holistic development. For management of Natural Resource in a time bound manner, there should be commonality of approach to the programmes to be implemented by the various ministries or states with close monitoring and review of the progress of the plan at district level with active involvement of people's group/organisations as well, as research organisations (ICAR), with peoples participation at every stage. The planning process should take into account the available manpower both of skilled and unskilled in the targeted developmental area. A conscious effort should be made to integrate and accommodate the available male and female in a village in the developmental programme with prior consultation and division of labour and responsibility.

Sometime back, the Ministry of Human Resource Development, Department of Youth and Sports has announced a scheme of involving the youth in the national re-construction activities by creation of a national volunteer force. Youth of age group from 18 to 25 are proposed to be given 2 years training programme and after the training, their services are to be utilised for implementation of the developmental programme in the villages/blocks. This should be implemented urgently, with a bit of planning and coordination among various levels of workers, it will be possible to involve the youth in large scale in all the developmental scheme/project which have a direct relevance to the natural resource management.

Scientific Temparament Building: Research systems in India could play the vital role in finding appropriate methodology and location specific technology for the management of the natural resources so as to add to their productivity. It is very clear that rampant use of chemicals and fertilizers and pesticides has been doing great harm to our lands and their fertility and has become one of the major reasons for their degradation. Natural manures, bio-fertilizers and bio-pesticides, along with balanced use of inorganic fertilizers have to be encouraged in a planned way all over the country to preserve the soil texture and fertility for sustainable development.

Integration of Gender Concerns: A majority of the farmers in the rainfed watersheds are women. They spent long hours on agricultural as well as other natural resources management activities, in addition keeping the home hearth fires burning, in most of the Asian countries. Hence, urgent action is needed to correct the imbalance caused by lack of awareness to integrate the gender concerns. Also special efforts at confidence building of women farmers are needed as they have been the most neglected. To do this, the gender concerns and remedy for alleviating inequalities (also for disadvantaged classes/castes) need to be designed and main-streamed into watershed development programmes.

Assured and Quick Benefit Generation: It is by now very clear that unless the NRM activities result in quick (preferably within a crop season or a year) net direct benefits to the participating farmers, their participation should not be expected. Without this, there will not be any on-farm level conservation and better utilisation of natural resources. On common property resources also, if they are to be managed better by the people, they must produce quick benefits to them. Hence, if a activity does not result into quick and assured benefits, it should not be treated as a WM activity as the people in any case will not implement it.

Desired Action for Sustaining Productivity to Ensure Food Security

To realise a vision of eco-friendly production and productivity goals with high efficiency of inputs, while ensuring sustainable use of natural resources following strategies are advocated in the present-millennium:

- Convergence of policy and effective coordination among various Ministries of Government of India for sustainable management of rainfed areas (78 million ha) for meeting future production goals.

- Management of degraded lands or waste land estimated to be 107.43 million ha to produce fuel and fodder with intensive soil and water conservation measures on watershed approach for their protection and maintenance.
- Applied areas of science and technology like biotechnology, integrated nutrient and pest management, post-harvest technology, information technology should be used for enhancing input use efficiency for sustainable of management of natural resources.
- Inventorisation, characterisation and monitoring of various natural resources using remote sensing and GIS tools. Utilisation of sustainable land use plans for each agro-ecological sub-region in the country by the State Agricultural/Extension Department.
- Creation of sufficient live storage capacity by completion/formulation of big and small dams and other water bodies while discussing ecological fallouts and social considerations with the people so that a part of monsoon flow going waste could be used for enhancing ground water recharging and *in situ* water utilisation.
- Raising the efficiency of water use for agriculture by rationalising the price structure by prudent sectoral management of water resources jointly with stake holders and realizations of the economic value from the consumers.
- Improve on-farm irrigation water management to enhance water-use efficiency by about 10 per cent from the current level. Refinement of technology for economical utilisation of poor and marginal quality waters for agriculture. Development of cost effective drainage technology including bio-drainage for saline and water-logged situations to reduce cost of reclamation by about 25 per cent.
- Development of location specific model watersheds in various agro ecological zones of the rainfed areas so as to be used as demonstration models to farmers to enhance the average productivity from 0.8 t/ha to 2.0 t/ha with adoption of cost effective conservation technology.
- Increasing the fertilizer use efficiency by 8-10 per cent from the current level and integrated use of organics and

bio-fertilizers to meet about one-third of the plant nutrient needs through integrated plant nutrient management.

- Increasing overall cropping intensity by 20-30 per cent over the current level with emphasis on energy efficiency and alternate agriculture with preference for low water requiring crops.
- Management of soil and water resources for development of agro-eco-zone specific farming systems with emphasis with diversified agriculture and precision farming
- Popularisation of agro forestry system, to enhance the tree cover in agricultural lands for supply of fodder, fuel, industrial wood and small timber requirements on a sustainable and cost effective basis through the ongoing watershed development projects.
- Monitoring and dissemination of climate change and mitigation of its adverse effects on agricultural production systems by adopting preventive measure with weather based expert systems for enhanced production and improvement in agromet advisory services.

REFERENCES

Agricultural Research Data Book (2000), IASRI, ICAR, New Delhi.

Annonymous (2002). *Agricultural Statistics at a Glance*. Directorate of Economics and Statistics, Department of Agriculture & Cooperation, Ministry of Agriculture, Govt. of India, NewDelhi, pp. 10276.

Irrigation Commission, Ministry of Irrigation & Power, Govt. of India (1972). *Report of the Irrigation Commission*, Vol. I. India, Ministry of Information & Broadcasting, Govt. of India, 2002; A Reference Mannual.

Ministry of Water Resources, (1999). *National Water Policy*.

Moench, Marcus. (2000). *Ground water and food security in India. Proceeding International Conference on* "Sustainable Development of Water Resources: Socio-economic, Institutional and Environmental Aspects", (Agricultural and Environmental Aspects), November 27-30, 2000, Institute for Resource Management and Economic Development, New Delhi. pp. 58-73.

Paul, D.K., (1988). Methodologies for Research on Water Management in rainfed areas with emphasis on rainfed rice. *Proc. IRRI-WTC Workshop on:* Methodologies of research on water management in rice production, Coimbatore, India, Dec. 5-6, 1988.

Paul, D.K. and Chauhan, V.S., (1990). Determination of natural ground water recharge in rainfed high rainfall area. *Proc. XIth Intl. Cong. Use of plastics in Agril.* New Delhi: 35-43.

Paul, D.K. and Tiwari, K.N., (1993). Results and lessons from Research in rain water storage systems for increasing riceland productivity: Opportunities and unresolved issue. S.I. Bhiyan, ed. *On Farm reservoir system for rainfed ricelands.* IRRI. Philippines. pp. 127-40.

Paul, D.K. (1995). Integrated Management Information System for sustainable agricultural development. *Intensive Agril.* 34(788): pp. 8-11.

Paul, D.K. (1995). Rainfed Farming System Development in India in retrospective and perspective. Ed. John Farrington, *ICAR-ODA workshop on research for rainfed areas.* CRIDA Hyderabad. pp. 34-45.

Paul, D.K. (1980). *Reclamation of water-logged soils—a new engineering technique.* Abs. 3rd Afro-Asian Reg. ICID Conf. on "Mgt. of Wat. Irrig. Sys. etc." at New Delhi.

Paul, D.K. (2000). *Management strategy for development of wetlands in Assam.* Proc. Sem. by SLUB, Assam, Gauhati, pp. 56-63.

Paul, D.K. & Sharma, B.R. (2001). Developmental Issues for Sustainable Management of Watershed in Twenty First Century in India. *Proc. National Workshop on Watershed Management Strategies*: A New Outlook for 21st Century. IRMED, New Delhi.

Samra, J.S. & Paul, D.K. (2001). A critique on Watershed Development in North Eastern Region of India. *Proc. Nat. Sem. Wat. & Land Manage.* Incl. CAD for Soc.-Econ. Uplift. of NE Reg, Guwahati, Vol. 2, pp. 23-26.

3

Management of Water, Development of Wastelands and Other Natural Resources for a Self-reliant India

MOHAN DHARIA

Sustainable development has become a matter of serious concern for the world. Though the International Conference held at Stockholm in 1972 to some extent attracted the attention of the world towards nature, in Rio de Janeiro International Conference held in 1992, this serious issue was recognised by the whole world. In this Conference a conscious decision was taken to protect nature and its regenerating capacity for sustainable development. Though some action was initiated on the agenda accepted by Rio de Janeiro Conference, the progress was too inadequate. In August 2002 an International Conference was held at Johannesburg to review the Conference since 1992 and to take further decisions to implement the accepted agenda. In this Conference representatives of nearly 183 countries met at Johannesburg from 26 August to 4th September 2002. Heads of all important countries with an exception of USA and India, participated and forcefully made their representation. In spite of differences over approaches and actions, by and large the Summit agreed in principle to work on the following programmes:

Water and Sanitation—To halve proportion of people without access to proper sanitation by 2015, a goal Washington had resisted.

Energy—To take actions to improve access to affordable energy. The Summit however failed to agree on specific targets to increase share of world energy produced from renewable 'green' sources such as solar or wind power.

Fish—A target to restore depleted fish stocks by 2015 at the latest, recognising oceans are essential to the ecosystem and a critical source of food, especially in poor countries.

Chemicals—By 2020 chemicals will be made and used in ways to minimise severe harmful impact on humans and the environment.

Health—The World Trade Organisation accord on patents should not prevent poor countries providing medicines for all, a key issue as they often cannot afford aids and other costly drugs.

Aid—Substantial increase in aid for poor countries to meet agreed development goals. It urged rich countries to give 0.7 per cent of the national income, a target first set in 1970. Only five countries have reached that level.

Trade—The meeting's plan bolsters trade and environment without saying that World Trade Organisation rules override global environmental treaties. This was seen as a victory for environmental groups, who feared deals such as Kyoto Protocol could be undermined. Wealthy countries reaffirmed their will to lower trade-distorting subsidies.

Biological Diversity—To cut significantly by 2010 the rate at which rare animals and plants are becoming extinct.

Governance—Good governance, nationally and internationally, is essential for sustainable development. All appreciated that aid be tied to less corruption and more democracy.

It could be observed from the summary of the decisions of the Summit that the Summit has not bothered to abolish poverty, unemployment, provison for potable drinking water, control the population explosion and similar such basic issues as a time bound programme. From the deliberations, I genuinely believe that the rich countries are only interested in better marketing opportunities for the goods produced by them. The very fact that barring a few rich countries the decisions taken at the Rio De Janeiro Summit held in 1992 have remained unimplemented, is adequate to reflect on the attitude of the rich countries. On this background, India and other poor countries are left with no other choice but to develop their own lands, water and other natural resources, by involving millions of masses and march towards self-reliance. Whenever I think of India, 1 believe that our massive lands, water, forests, medicinal and other species, cattle-wealth, sea-shore of 7,000 km, internal sweet water reservoirs, ever shining sun, mines, minerals and millions of hands are our real strength. Most of these resources have either remained underdeveloped or undeveloped. If we could systematically develop these resources, food and water security or other essentials could never be a problem for India. Advanced science and technology, in particular, the information technology has to be extensively used for this purpose.

Land

India has total geographical area of 329 mha, out of which nearly 175 mha including forest lands are waste or degraded. To me, they are not waste but wasted lands. With scientific micro watershed approach, it is possible to conserve every drop of water wherever and whenever it rains, to prevent soil erosion and make most of these lands productive through forests, horticulture, silvi pasture, agriculture, etc. It is indeed a man made tragedy that, 50 per cent of our lands should be in poor condition and 50 per cent people should remain poor or below poverty line. As suggested by the High Level Policy Committee constituted by Central Government under my chairmanship, it is possible to make all our lands productive, generate employment opportunities to millions of people, raise food grain production from 210 m tonnes to 450 m tonnes, bring 30 per cent of our area under forests or green cover and achieve the objective of self-reliance along with sustainable development with social justice, I am glad that after great efforts and persuasion, the Central Government has accepted the recommendations of my Committee and has created a separate Land Resource Department to execute them. My proposal to constitute Loknayak Jayaprakash Narayan National Mission for Development of Wastelands and other natural resources, is under consideration of Government Hon'ble Prime Minister and concerned colleagues have assured me to constitute the Mission in the Birth Centenary year of late Loknayak Jayaprakash Narayan, for implementing a time bound programme within 15 years.

Forests

Out of 6 lakh villages in the country, nearly 2 lakh villages are on the periphery or in the forests. While 1 was a member of the undivided Wastelands Development Board, my suggestion to introduce Joint Forestry Management was accepted by the then Government. Ever since 1st June,1991 till today people's committees have been established in about 60,000 villages. Though unbelievable, in spite of illegal tree felling more than 14 m ha of lands have come under additional green cover in the country. In a National Conference convened by the Minister for Environment and Forests, Shri T. R. Balu, on 23rd July, 2002 it has been resolved to constitute J.F.M. Committees in all the 2 lakh villages within next 5 years and to have green cover on all the forest lands in India. Out of 75 m ha forest lands, nearly 40 m ha are without forest cover.

Production and Productivity

Average production of food grains and other crops in India compared to other countries is too low. While average production of food grains in India is 1950 kg per ha, in China it is 4000 kg and nearly 5000 kg in Canada, Australia and Japan. Similarly our forest wealth per ha is also poor, which is of order of 10 cubic metres as against 80-90 cubic metres in some other countries. There is a vast scope to improve upon the productivity per ha, including waste or degraded lands in India. It would thus be clear that the fears expressed by the international experts that food and water security shall be the most acute problem for India in 21st Century, have no basis, provided we firmly decide to make all our lands effectively productive.

Water

When one observes occurrence of famine and scarcity of water in several parts of the country, it is genuinely felt that India will have to face acute scarcity of water in next few years. I am not inclined to believe in this assessment. India is one of the most fortunate countries in the world, which gets nearly 400 m ha metres of water every year. So far India has spent Rs. 130,000 crores over big or medium dams. Besides huge amount has also been spent over minor or medium projects. In spite of all these investments it has not been possible for us to harvest even 10 per cent of the water, made available to us by great nature. I am not opposed to big dams, if they are unavoidable to generate energy or to carry water to areas where it is not possible to conserve a drop of water. We should however emphasize on scientific micro watershed development programme all over the country. Perennial irrigation facilities may reach 40 or 45 per cent of the total lands. They cannot cover the whole of the country. Therefore micro watershed programmes could be the proper solution. Along with conserving every drop of water, judicious use of every drop of water is equally important. India cannot afford the luxury to make water available without any charges. They may be lower for agriculture or domestic purpose. However, every citizen must be under an obligation to pay for the consumed water. We have been reading regarding controversy over the use of Kaveri waters. Time is more than ripe to treat all the water as a national resource and all states and citizens should have equitable right over the same. This is equally important to maintain the integrity of our country.

When I think of future, I may like to emphasize on the proposal of Dr. Rao and the Garland Canal project prepared by M's. Dastur and Co., to link all the rivers in the country which deserves serious consideration by the country. With proper management of water, it is possible to take due care of states such as the Punjab, Haryana, Uttar Pradesh, Bihar and to carry the remaining water to all parts of the country as suggested in their reports. Similarly, all waters received by the western parts of Sahyadris passing through Maharashtra, Goa, Karnataka, Kerala and Tamil Nadu, now directly flow to Arabian seas. They should also be directed to eastern parts after taking due care of the concerned states.

With the above mentioned approaches, I am sure that there cannot be a problem of food and water security in 21st century as forecast by eminent experts. On the contrary, India would be in a position to feed dying countries or provide water to the thirsty countries.

Cattle-wealth and Fish

India is perhaps a rare country having one cattle per two persons. The number of cows and she buffaloes in India, is about 200 million. Of course, we have to control and gradually bring down this strength. With better fodder, feed and health care even if we could increase their milk yield even by one litre, the country could produce additional 200 m litres of milk everyday. India is already number one country in the world in producing milk. Similar is the case with goats, sheep, chickens, etc. Seashore of 7,000 km and internal sweet water reservoirs, have a potential to produce fish on a massive scale. With this approach, India could capture all world market by exporting fish, meat, poultry, milk, milk products, etc.

Spicies, Herbal Medicines, Species and Perfumes

Barring some individuals or firms, India has never emphasized on scientifically cultivating several spices, herbal medicines, perfumery and other species. They could be grown in between the trees, on bunds of farms and even through systematic plantations. While the world is tired of the side effects of the antibiotics and allopathic drugs, it is leaning towards natural medicines. In this regard, India could be a pioneer country in meeting the ever increasing needs and earning foreign exchange. The lead provided by China is an eye opener for India.

Ever Shining Sun and Energy

India has a rare privilege to enjoy the shining sun for more than ten months. Whenever a controversy appears on 'Enron' and the corrupt deals the sun is virtually laughing at our inability to use his great source of energy. Along with unlimited energy, the sun has tremendous potential to provide food and colour trees, fruits, flowers and vegetables. Besides with increasing tree cover and agro produce we could use biomass to produce energy on large scale. Similarly, micro hydro energy plants could be installed in many parts of the country. This would be the most appropriate approach to generate ample energy for the country in a decentralised way.

To develop all the above mentioned and other natural resources, modern science, technology and in particular the information technology will have to be extensively used, preferably in regional languages. To connect like drinking water, school or an approach road for every village, a computerised knowledge centre should be treated as a part of the basic need.

Our farmers are always penalised as they do not secure reasonable remunerative price to their produce. Many times to produce more becomes a crime. Cooperative institutions could play a vital role in securing a remunerative prices to the farmers and also making available their produce to the consumers. In the name of free market economy, instead of undermining the co-operative movement it would be advisable to create a network from production to marketing, as being demonstrated by Amul or Dhara. In a massive populous country like India cooperatives could be the most effective instrument for socio-economic transformation and social justice.

I have covered vital areas related with our lands, water and other natural resources. I have however not mentioned our mines and minerals, I believe that being exhaustible, such resources should be sparingly used. On the basis of various experiments carried through my organisation 'Vanarai' and various other voluntary organisations, I may like to state with all force at my command that it is possible to make all such resources productive with minimum investments and produce food grains, pulses, edible oils, fruits, vegetables, timber, energy, milk, mutton, etc. in abundance, generate employment opportunities to millions of our masses, bring 1/3rd area under green cover and to attain the objective of self-reliance, along with sustainable development.

Inspired by Vanarai, people have initiated their activities in more than 300 villages. Village Gawadewadi, in Pune District, where drinking water had to be supplied through tankers, conserved every drop of water falling in the vicinity, prevented soil erosion and there is no scarcity of drinking water. On the contrary, the village produced crops on almost 500-600 acres of land as seasonal crops. Vanarai has introduced new technologies and as a result, the milk collection per day has gone up from 200 litres to 7,000 litres and the members earn about Rs. 60,000 to 70,000 per day. The production of tomatoes gone up from 5000 kg to 25,000-30,000 kg per acre. This is a rare village, where every house has a latrine and a gobar gas plant. Nobody is now illiterate. People strictly observe family planning. All are above the BPL and above all nearly 135 families, living in filthy slums of Mumbai have returned back to the village. They are earning more incomes and leading a better life. The village is always clean and green with 6,00,000 trees all around. There are computers in schools and it is regarded as one ideal self-reliant village in the state. Marriages and the social events are performed collectively in a simple manner. It has a modern gymnasium and a decent library. Though Vanarai has provided the lead, the people and their united leadership have brought this change.

I may like to add that, though difficult, we have to create conducive environment in the country to attain these objectives. In this regard I would like to insist on:

1. Eradicating illiteracy and ignorance within the next three to five years basically by involving our teachers, professors, college students and social workers, whose strength is of the order of 20 million.
2. Bringing down the growth rate of birth and controlling the explosion of population as effectively demonstrated by the Kerala state. We should aim at stabilising our population by 2015 and should not cross 115 crore. We should resolve to prove wrong the great demographers, who have projected that population of India will stabilise by the year 2050, when it would be of order of 160 crore.
3. Introducing discipline and work culture in all walks of our life. Present perverse attitude that disciplines and democracy cannot go together must be reversed.
4. Controlling the craze for ugly urbanisation and mega cities. No city above a population of one million should be allowed to grow further. Self-reliant green villages with modern facilities of education, health, drinking water, roads, communications and local employment can prevent the influx of the people going to cities. Besides, if needed New Growth Centres may be created to save the cities. It has however to be realised that healthy rural development with ideal villages having modern facilities including local employment generation programmes could alone save the cities.
5. Accepting new lifestyle as against the luxury oriented living has become imperative. It may not be possible to consider "High Thinking and Simple Living." However, for sustainable development to adopt "High Thinking and Moderate Living", has become unavoidable!

4

Groundwater Potential, Development and Regulation

A Critical Review

D.K. CHADHA

Introduction

The availability and development of groundwater resources have played a significant role in increasing the agricultural production and sustainable development by meeting the water demands of various sectors in India. Groundwater is contributing more than 85 per cent of the drinking water requirements of rural areas, about 58 per cent of irrigation requirements and more than 50 per cent of the urban and industrial water supplies. It shall continue to play a key role in meeting the water needs of irrigated agriculture and related fields in a big way in the next millennium as well. Given the greater convenience and reliability of groundwater and continuous technology development in water, well drilling and pumping devices, it is expected that there is going to be much greater emphasis on groundwater development and utilization. The output/hectare of groundwater-irrigated land is greater than output per hectare of surface water irrigated land, *certeris paribus*. Several studies support this hypothesis, and Dhawan (1989) compared the land productivity per net hectare of net cropped area for canal irrigated and groundwater irrigated areas in Punjab and Tamil Nadu and concluded that productivity in groundwater irrigated area was high throughout by almost 1.5-2 times. Similar evidences have been documented in a number of early studies in Pakistan (Meinzen-Dick, 1996), Gujarat and Eastern U.P. in India

(Shah, 1993). It is reported that the contribution of groundwater in India's GDP is 9 per cent although public investment have been very low. It is also realised that uncontrolled development, in future, will de-saturate the less sustainable hard rock aquifers in South India, the recharging of depleting aquifers, proper management of water logged areas and regulating the development of groundwater resources will become a compulsion.

Water Resources—A Critical Review

The accurate assessment of the water resources, both surface and ground water, is an essential prerequisite for proper planning to their utilisation for different purposes. The assessment of surface water resources is done by Central Water Commission and of the groundwater by state organization with close association of Central Groundwater Board.

The assessment of surface water resources has been attempted from time to time, the first being done during 1901-03 by Irrigation Commission and assessed as 1,443.2 BCM excluding the potential in Assam. Subsequently, the assessment was made by Dr. A.N. Khosla (1945-46) as 1,673 BCM; CWC&PC (1954-66) 1,881 BCM and lately CWC (1993) estimated it to be 1,869 BCM incorporating the additional data of river discharges (Table 4.1). It is observed that in spite of collection of additional hydrological data there is not much difference between the figures calculated during 1901 and now. The National Commission on Integrated Water Resources Development Plan (1999) has commented on the reliability of water resources data and advised for reassessment.

Out of the total availability of 1,869 BCM of water (this figure has been accepted and incorporated in the National Water Policy), it is possible to have surface water storages in different river basins to the extent of 690 BCM. The total surface water storages till the end of 8th Plan has been 214 BCM of the completed projects, and another 35 BCM will be added on completion of on-going projects by 2025. It is further estimated that another 132 BCM is possible till 2050, making the total storage capacity as 381 BCM. The ultimate storage of 690 BCM, thus, needs to be reassessed for future planning. The surface water storages of different water basins of the projects completed, under execution and those under consideration are given in Table 4.2.

Table 4.1: Estimated Utilizable Flow in Different River Basins

Live Storage Capacity of Projects (MCM)			*Gross Storage*		
S. No.	*River Basin*	*Catchment Area, km²*	*Water Resources, km³/per year*		*Utilizable Surface Water*
			As per CWC 1993	*As per NCIWRDP 1999*	
(1)	(2)	(3)	(4)	(5)	(6)
1.	Indus	3,21,289	73.31	73.31	46
2.	Ganga Brahmaputra-Barak (Meghana)				
	a. Ganga sub-basin	8,62,769	525.02	525.02	250
	b. Brahmaputra and Barak sub-basins	1,97,316	537.24	629.05	24
		41,157	48.36	48.36	24
3.	Subernarekha	29,196	12.37	12.37	6.81
4.	Brahmani-Baitarni	51,822	28.48	28.48	18.3
5.	Mahanadi	1,41,589	66.88	66.88	49.99
6.	Godawari	3,12,812	110.54	110.54	76.3
7	Krishna	2,58,948	78.12	69.81	58
8.	Pennar	55,213	6.32	6.32	6.86
9.	Cauvery	87,900	21.36	21.36	19
10.	Tapi	65,145	14.88	14.88	14.5
11.	Narmada	98,796	45.64	45.64	34.5
12.	Mahi	34,842	11.02	11.02	3.1
13.	Sabarmati	21,674	3.81	3.81	1.93
14.	West flowing rivers of Kuchchh, Saurashtra and Luni	3,34,390	15.1	15.1	14.98
15.	West flowing rivers South of Tapi	1,13,057	200.94	200.94	36.21
16.	East flowing rivers between Mahanadi and Krishna	49,570	17.08	17.08	13.11
17.	East flowing rivers between Godavari and Krishna	12,289	1.81	1.81	13.11
18.	East flowing rivers between Krishna and Pennar	24,649	3.63	3.63	13.11
19.	East flowing rivers between Pennar and Cauvery	64,751	9.98	9.98	16.73
20.	East flowing rivers south of Cauvery	35,026	6.48	6.48	16.73

(Contd.)

Table 4.1 (*contd.*)

(1)	(2)	(3)	(4)	(5)	(6)
21.	Area of North Ladakh not draining into Indus	28,478	0	0	NA
22.	River draining into Bangladesh	10,031	8.57	8.57	NA
23.	River draining into Myanmar	26,271	22.43	22.43	NA
24.	Drainage areas of Andaman, Nicobar and Lakshadweep Islands	8,280	0	0	NA
	Total	32,87,260	18,69.37	1,952.87	690.32

Table 4.2: Basin-wise Surface Water Storage

		Live Storage Capacity of Projects (MCM)				*Gross Storage*
S. No.	*River Basin*	*Completed*	*Under Constuc-tion* (2025)	*Under Conside-ration* (2050)	*Total*	*Completed Projects*
(1)	*(2)*	*(3)*	*(4)*	*(5)*	*(6)*	*(7)*
1.	Indus	13,831.90	2,453.55	272.95	16,558.4	18,263
2.	Ganga-Brahama-putra-Barak (Meghana)	36,842.91	17,119.76	29,558.16	83,520.83	44,742
	(a) Ganga sub-basin	1,094.46	2,398.90	63,347.84	66,841.2	1,381
	(b) Brahmaputra and Barak sub-basins	19,505.3	10,651.93	8,283.61	38,440.84	26,274
3.	Godawari	34,476.7	7,775.96	127.53	42,380.19	43,614
4.	Krishna	7,431.6	386.27	342.69	8,160.56	8,214
5.	Cauvery	380.31	2,133.69	0	2,514.03	403
6.	Pennar	663.81	1,650.19	1,592.73	3,906.73	781
7.	Subarnarekha Burhabalang and others	4,760.23	239.6	8,721.19	13,721.02	5,580
8.	Brahmani-Baitarni	8,492.36	5,390.91	10,958.91	24,842.18	11,435
9.	Mahanadi	4,754.61	355.28	22.5	5,132.39	5,536
10.	Mahi	1,349.76	121.99	92.02	1,563.77	1,559
11.	Sabarmati	6,601.16	16,723.04	465.73	27,789.93	7,983
12.	Narmada	8,531.81	1,005.47	1,988.56	11,525.84	10,953
13.	Tapi	7,103.00	2,655.21	838.75	10,596.96	7,714

(Contd.)

Table 4.2 (*contd.*)

(1)	(2)	(3)	(4)	(5)	(6)	(7)
14.	West flowing rivers between Tapi to Tadri	10,243.49	2,310.79	1,702.57	14,256.85	11,378
15.	West flowing rivers between Tadri to Kanyakumari	1,628.94	1,448.18	862.18	3,939.3	1,839
16.	East flowing rivers between Mahanadi and Pennar	1,416.71	24.25	0	1,440.96	1,507
17.	East flowing rivers between Pennar to Kanyakumari	4,308.44	577.55	3,145.96	8,031.96	4,707
18.	West flowing rivers of Kutch, Saurashtra and Luni	0	0	0	0	0
19.	Area of inland drainage of Rajasthan	312.00	0	0	312.00	329
20.	Minors rivers draining into Myanmar and Bangladesh					
	Total	1,73,729.50	75,422.5	1,32,323.9	3,81,475.9	2,14,192

Groundwater Potential

The study of groundwater resources in India started during 1929 but the first systematic assessment was made only during 1993, using methodology recommended by Groundwater Estimation Committee constituted by the Government of India in 1984 (refered to as GEC-84 methodology). Prior to this, the National Commission on Agriculture (1976) estimated the groundwater resources as 350 BCM, of which 260 BCM was considered as available for irrigation. The Groundwater Over-Exploitation Committee (1979), constituted by ARDC (now NABARD) estimated the groundwater potential as 467.9 BCM. Based on the available field data of different inputs for calculation of total recharge potential, it is estimated that the annual replenishable groundwater resources (called dynamic resource) as 432 BCM (Table 4.3). The status of groundwater development during

1998, as indicated in Table 4.4, was 37 per cent which has now increased to about 40 per cent. However, the total potential available *vis-a-vis* stage of development does not match with the long term behaviour of water levels and this analogous situation is observed in many blocks particularly in hard rock areas. The groundwater potential is being worked out by using updated methodology (GEC-97) which would possibly give better information on the assessment and development status.

In addition to the replenishable dynamic resource, the country is blessed with enormous groundwater resources below the lowest level of groundwater fluctuation termed as in-storage groundwater resource. The first approximation indicates in-storage fresh groundwater resource as 10,812 BCM up to the depth of 450 metres in alluvial aquifer and 150 metres in hard rock aquifers. The exploratory drillings have now given adequate information on the geometry of aquifer system particularly of Indo-Gangetic Basin, it is therefore required that the groundwater resources are calculated separately for different aquifers. The present calculation of dynamic and in-storage resources for alluvial aquifers should be alternatively done for unconfined aquifer for better understanding of the groundwater potential and planning for utilization.

Groundwater Development

The development of minor irrigation has created an irrigation potential of about 58.93 mha at the end of 8th Plan (groundwater contributing 45.73 mha and surface water 13.2) whereas potential from major and medium projects is only 32.96 mha. During 9th Plan, an additional potential of 4.49 mha has been created through groundwater and 1.45 mha through surface minor irrigation whereas the potential created through the major and medium structures is not indicated so far.

The development of groundwater resources in the last two decades had been very rapid increasing the number of groundwater structures from 12 million during 1983 to 17.3 million during 1997 increasing the irrigation potential from 6.5 mha during 1951 to 45.73 mha till 1997, i.e at the end of 8th Plan (Table 4.5). In addition to the substantial increase in irrigation potential, the development of groundwater is meeting the drinking water requirements of 85 per cent of the rural population and catering for more than 50 per cent of the urban and industrial water requirements.

Table 4.3: Groundwater Resources in India

S.No.	State	Total Replenishable Groundwater Resources (MhaM/Yr)	Available Groundwater Resource for Irrigation in Net Terms (MhaM/Yr)	Net Draft (MhaM/Yr)	Level of Ground Water Development
1.	Andhra Pradesh	—	2.9973	0.78304	26.10
2.	Arunachal Pradesh	0.14385	0.12227	—	—
3.	Assam	2.24786	1.91068	0.14249	7.46
4.	Bihar	2.69796	2.29327	0.82527	35.99
5.	Chhattisgarh	1.60705	1.36599	0.07647	5.60
6.	Goa	0.02182	0.01855	0.00154	8.30
7.	Gujarat	2.0367	1.73199	0.85327	49.27
8.	Haryana	1.11794	0.95025	0.71846	75.61
9.	Himachal Pradesh	0.02926	0.02487	0.00413	16.63
10.	Jammu & Kashmir	0.44257	0.37620	0.00413	1.07
11.	Jharkhand	0.66045	0.56138	0.12146	21.64
12.	Karnataka	1.61750	1.37564	0.45481	33.06
13.	Kerala	0.79003	0.65869	0.12509	18.99
14.	Madhya Pradesh	3.48186	2.95958	0.73846	24.95
15.	Maharashtra	3.78677	2.54704	0.8837	34.70
16.	Manipur	0.31540	0.26810	Neg.	Neg.
17.	Meghalaya	0.05397	0.04587	0.00182	Neg.
18.	Mizoram				
19.	Nagaland	0.07240	0.06150	Neg.	Neg.
20.	Orissa	2.01287	1.71094	0.26037	15.22
21.	Punjab	1.81923	1.63730	1.61020	98.34
22.	Rajasthan	1.26021	1.06044	0.77245	72.84
23.	Sikkim				
24.	Tamil Nadu	2.64069	2.24458	1.40398	62.55
25.	Tripura	0.06634	0.05639	0.01885	33.43
26.	Uttar Pradesh	8.25459	7.01640	2.97619	42.42
27.	Uttaranchal	0.28411	0.24149	0.06843	28.34
28.	West Bengal	2.30914	1.96277	0.63175	32.19
	Total States	43.30063	36.20191	13.47627	37.23
	Union Territories				
1.	Andaman & Nicobar	0.00297	0.00252	0.00245	—
2.	Chandigarh	0.00422	0.00359	0.00046	12.81
3.	Dadra & N. Haveli	0.00071	0.00060	0.00048	80.00
4.	Daman & Diu	0.00037	0.00031	0.00029	94.84
5.	NCT Delhi	0.02916	0.00977	0.01180	120.78
6.	Lakshadweep	0.03042	0.00195	0.00076	39.12
7.	Pondicherry	0.01746	0.01484	0.01152	77.63
	Grand Total	43.38593	36.25938	13.50404	37.24

Table 4.4: Static Fresh Water Resource State-wise

S. No.	*States*	*Static Fresh Groundwater Resources*		
		Alluvium/ Unconsolidated Rocks (BCM)	*Hard Rocks (BCM)*	*Total (BCM)*
1.	Andhra Pradesh	76	26	102
2.	Assam	920	0	920
3.	Bihar	2,557	11	2,568
4.	Gujarat	92	12	104
5.	Haryana	420	1	421
6.	Himachal Pradesh	13	0	13
7.	Jammu & Kashmir	35	0	35
8.	Karnataka	0	17	17
9.	Kerala	5	6	11
10.	Madhya Pradesh	14	27	41
11.	Maharashtra	16	22	38
12.	Orissa	162	13	175
13.	Punjab	910	0	910
14.	Rajasthan	115	13	128
15.	Tamil Nadu	98	0	98
16.	Tripura	101	0	101
17.	Uttar Pradesh	3,470	30	3,500
18.	West Bengal	1,625	1	1,626
19.	Delhi	3	0	3
20.	Chandigarh	1	0	1
	Total	10,633	179	10,812

Table 4.5: Growth of Groundwater Structures and Irrigation Potential

Year	*Dug wells*	*Private Tube wells*	*Public Tube Wells*	*Total*	*Cumulative Irrigation Potential Created Groundwater (mha)*
	←	*('000)*		→	
March, 1951	3,860	3	2.4	3,865.4	6.5
March, 1980	7,786	2,132	33.3	9,951.3	22.0
March, 1985	8,742	3,359	46.2	12,147.2	27.82
March, 1990	9,407	4,754	63.6	14,224.6	35.62
March, 1992	10,120	5,379	67.6	15,566.6	38.89
March, 1997	10,501	6,743	90.0	17,334.0	45.73

The development of the groundwater resources will further increase as the surface water storages remained almost static since last 5 years and the possibility of additional storages in the near future being uncertain, the stress on different aquifers is imperative.

The ultimate irrigation potential from groundwater is estimated to be 64 mha and has been approved for its development but this needs revision as the return irrigation flow to groundwater from applied irrigation has not been considered besides other factors. The irrigation potential created and utilized during each plan period is given in Table 4.6.

Table 4.6: Development of Irrigation Potential (Cumulative) Through Plan Periods

(In mha)

Plan	*Major/Medium Irrigation*		*Minor Irrigation*		*Total Irrigation*		*Gross Irrigated Area as per Land Utl. Statistics*
	Pot	*Utl.*	*Pot.*	*Utl.*	*Pot.*	*Utl.*	
Pre-plan	9.70	9.70	12.90	12.90	22.60	22.60	22.50
First (1951-56)	12.20	10.98	14.06	14.06	26.26	25.04	25.64
Second (1956-61)	14.33	13.05	14.75 (8.25)	14.75 (8.25)	29.08	27.80	27.98
Third (1961-66)	16.57	15.17	17.00	17.00	35.57	32.17	30.90
Annual (1966-69)	18.10	16.75	19.00 (12.50)	19.00 (12.50)	37.10	35.75	35.48
Fourth (1969-74)	20.70	18.69	23.50 (16.44)	23.50 (16.44)	44.20	42.19	40.28
Fifth (1974-78)	24.72	21.16	27.30 (19.80)	27.30 (19.80)	52.02	48.46	46.08
Annual (1978-80)	26.61	22.64	30.00 (22.00)	30.00 (22.00)	56.61	52.64	49.21
Sixth (1980-85)	27.70	23.57	37.52 (27.82)	35.25 926.24)	65.22	58.82	54.53
Seventh (1985-90)	29.92	25.47	46.61 (35.62)	43.12 (35.15)	76.53	68.59	61.85
Annual (1990-92)	30.74	26.32	50.35 (38.89)	46.54 (36.35)	81.09	72.86	65.68
Eighth (1992-97)	32.96	28.49	56.60 (44.35)	52.32 (41.50)	89.56	80.76	70.64

Note : Figures in brackets indicate the potential created and utilized by groundwater development.
Pot. - Potential; Utl. - Utilization

It is to be seen that the potential to be created in each plan period always fall short of the stipulated targets and this is also true in case of its utilization as well. In the 9th Plan, irrigation potential through minor irrigation was planned to be 12 mha (groundwater 10 mha, surface water 2 mha), but the actual achievement has been much less. The irrigation potential created through groundwater was only 4.49 mha and from surface water 1.45 mha. The gap between potential created and utilized at the end of 1995-96 was 9.43 mha out of which the gap in case of groundwater was 3.59 mha and of surface water (Minor irrigation) 1.38 mha. For the 10th Plan, the irrigation potential to be created through groundwater is stipulated to be 5 mha and surface water (minor irrigation) 2.0 mha. The gap between groundwater potential created and utilized till 9th Plan and proposed for 10th Plan is already meeting 70 per cent of the stipulated targets, therefore steps must be taken for maximum utilization of the irrigation potential created. In the case of groundwater the gap between the irrigation potential created and utilized is indicated as 3.59 mha but this need to be reconciled as the potential created is almost fully utilized immediately.

The continuous and sustained development of groundwater resources have already resulted in decline of water levels in many parts of the country, the number of over exploited and dark blocks have increased from 253 during 1984-85 to 445 during 1997-98 and there is further increase in their numbers but the data is not available.

Table 4.7: Status of Over-exploited and Dark Blocks in Different States of India

State	*Number of Dark Block*		
	1984-85	*1992-93*	*1997-98*
Andhra Pradesh	0	30	26
Bihar	14	1	11
Gujarat	6	26	28
Haryana	31	51	41
Karnataka	3	18	16
Madhya Pradesh	0	3	3
Punjab	64	70	83
Rajasthan	21	56	94
Tamil Nadu	61	97	103
U.P.	53	31	40
Total	253	383	445

The categorization of different blocks as over-exploited, dark, grey and white has been contested by the World Bank in their report and opined that the categorization should not be used to calculate the level of groundwater development or to guide development finances and abstraction regulation. The full development of groundwater resources assumes the total recoverable recharge in individual development units should be captured. It is irrespective of depletion of base flow, saline water intrusion and declines in groundwater level reaching unacceptable levels long before total recharge is captured The comments are very valid as the areas which still shows development of 60 per cent or so records continuous decline of water levels making it a over-exploited block and it sounds unreasonable.

The present categorization should be done away in case of alluvial aquifers in the Ganga-Brahmaputra Basin as the aquifer system is very deep, interconnected and multi-layered. The present lowering of the water levels in certain areas categorized under over-exploited and dark blocks is also expected to get stabilized because of high permeability values of the different aquifer zones.

Projected Water Demands

National Commission for Integrated Water Resources Development has estimated that the total water requirements for various uses will substantially increase, and by the year 2050, it is expected to vary between 973 to 1,180 BCM (Table 4.8).

Table 4.8: Estimated Sectoral Water Requirement (BCM)

S.No.	*Uses*	*Year 2010*		*Year 2025*		*Year 2050*	
		Low	*High*	*Low*	*High*	*Low*	*High*
1.	Irrigation	543	557	561	611	628	807
2.	Domestic	42	43	55	62	90	111
3.	Industries	37	37	67	67	81	81
4.	Energy	18	19	31	33	63	70
5.	Inland Navigation in addition to ecological need	7	7	10	10	15	15
6.	Flood Control						
7.	Environment (1) Afforestation						
8.	Environment (2) Ecology	5	5	10	10	20	20
9.	Evaporation	42	42	50	50	76	76
	Total	694	710	796	784	973	1180

The irrigation water requirements will increase from present availability/utilization of 454 BCM to a minimum of 973 BCM and maximum of 1,180 BCM. The present agricultural production of about 210 m tonnes utilizes irrigation potential of 93 mha only. The present production is in excess to the real demand for a population of 1.02 billion whereas the projected water demand of 973 BCM for a production of 420 m tonnes to 494 m tonnes for the projected population of 1.6 billion does not sound reasonable as the production per hectare will increase from 2.5 tonne per hectare to at least 3.5 tonne per hectare, therefore it is felt that the projected water demand will be much less than stipulated minimum demand of 973 BCM.

The total water requirements for irrigation sector need to be properly assessed and then demand for future should be projected. At present the water utilization in the agriculture sector in India is 93 per cent of the total availability as compared to 69 per cent world-wide.

In addition to the development of identified shallow aquifer systems, efforts should be made to identify new deep aquifers in the alluvial aquifers of Ganga-Brahmaputra belt, limestone and sandstone aquifers of hard rock areas and develop the brackish/saline aquifers to maintain the saline/fresh interface. As the demand for water may substantially increase in certain critical areas requiring further development of groundwater resources, it is recommended that the aquifers not considered in the dynamic groundwater resources should be considered for development, which is explained below:

Development of Deeper Aquifers in Ganga-Indus Basin: The large alluvial tract in the Indo-Ganga-Brahmaputra basins extending over a distance of 2,000 km from Punjab in the west to Assam in the east, constitutes one of the largest and most potential groundwater reservoirs in the world. The aquifer systems are extensive, thick, hydraulically interconnected and moderate to high yielding. To the north of this tract all along the Himalayan foothills, occur the linear belt of Bhabar piedmont and Terai belt down slope with characteristics of auto-flowing conditions along the spring line.

The Ganga basin covering an area of 2,50,000 sq. km is the repository of very vast multi-aquifer system extending up to a depth of 2,000 m and remains almost untapped resource of fresh water estimated to be 7,000 BCM. The development of these aquifers particularly the shallow aquifer up to 100 m are very essential so that, these aquifers which are fully saturated are developed and recharged by artificial recharge using water from monsoon runoff. An exploratory well of 600 m near Meerut city is giving a discharge of 0.5 mlpd and water temperature is 52°C and another well in Patna city has yielded 2 million litre per day. It is, therefore, essential that deep aquifers are also developed whenever and wherever scarcity of water is felt for assured irrigation or for domestic water supply.

Development of Saline/Brackish Aquifers: In many parts of the country particularly the intensively irrigated areas, the groundwater is brackish at shallow and deep depth whereas in the coastal areas, the shallow aquifers are brackish to saline in character. The large scale development of fresh water resources has resulted in the ingress of brackish water, which now occupies almost 0.20m km area. It is estimated that brackish and saline water resources are about 1,164 BCM. It is very essential that these resources are utilized to check their further expansion and their depletion can be made good by recharging the aquifer with the monsoon runoff or any surplus water available, which may be treated waste water/sewerage or industrial effluents from the urban areas.

Palaeo-Channels of Rivers: The Palaeo-channels of the migrating rivers constitute potential fresh water areas particularly in arid and semi-arid areas where the groundwater is brackish. The palaeo channels are identified by river borne sediments and are saturated with fresh water. The hydro-geological and geophysical survey of the palaeo-channels in the Saraswati basin have indicated the presence of fresh water pockets within the saline aquifers. Similarly detailed studies should be taken up in other river basins for identification of palaeo channels and if proved successful can then be planned for development to meet the water requirements for drinking purpose and their use for irrigation should be prohibited by law.

Recycling/Reuse of Water: Water used for domestic and industrial purposes is mostly non-consumptive and about 80 to 85 per cent water is usually available for further utilization. Recycling and reuse are the two actions in modern technology for waste water management. Reclaimed water after treatment can be used for irrigation, cooling and other useful purposes. Recycling and reuse of waste water would help in minimizing the requirement of fresh water and reducing the quality of water for final treatment before letting it off into the river/stream.

Constraints in Groundwater Development

The development of groundwater resources is not uniform as it depends mostly on the availability of surface water and irrigation requirements. For this reason some parts of the country are now over-exploited because of high irrigation demand but in certain areas development of groundwater has been very low, particularly in eastern states where surface water is adequately available. The poor development of groundwater in irrigation commands has resulted in serious problems of water logging and soil salinity. The following are some of the main factors responsible for poor development of groundwater particularly in eastern India.

Fragmented Land Holdings: At present the availability of institutional financial assistance is for construction and energization of wells and tube wells in areas where their construction is found to be technically feasible and economically viable. The assistance to individual farmers for these works is available only if the land holding is big enough to guarantee the return from the investments. Because of small size and fragmented nature of land holdings in the eastern states, the small or marginal farmers are not able to generate the amount required by them to contribute either from their own saving or through loans from banks. This poses a big constraint in flow of institutional finance to the farmers and the recovery of the loans by banking sector.

Lack of Public Funding

Public funds, in groundwater sector, are used generally for the investigation of groundwater resources and for providing subsidy for construction and energisation of groundwater abstraction structures. However, since majority of the land holdings in the country are non-bankable and cannot sustain of their own. Moreover lack of efforts in funding the construction of wells and tube wells from public resources is proving to be a constraint in the development of ground water.

Lack of Consultancy in Hydrogeology: The technical and scientific support required in location of sites, construction and design of groundwater structures and pumping devices and operation and maintenance, etc. is not been available to the farmers on site with the result the construction of wells and tube wells are not yielding optimum discharge and the rate of success is also poor. This aspect needs to be addressed and there should be a national level institute to provide consultancy in all aspects of ground water.

Non-Availability of Assured Power Supply: The availability of assured electric power supply for pumps is prerequisite for better water management and utilization of man power. At present the power supply is irregular in most of the states and in case available is not of the right voltage. This has invariably caused failures of pumps and burning of control panels. Thefts of electricity from the main feeders have also been a cause of reduction in voltage which in turn affect the running of electric pumps. The non-availability of assured power supply of required voltage has also proved to be a bottleneck in the accelerated development of ground water.

Subsidized Water Rates in Canal Commands: In canal commands of major and medium irrigation projects, water rates are highly subsidized. On the other hand, all states do not provide subsidy for development of groundwater, as a result farmers opt for utilizing canal water instead of constructing tube wells from their own resources. In order to optimally use the surface water resources in the canal command and develop the groundwater, to check water logging and meet the additional demand of water, the water rates both for utilization of surface and groundwater should be rationalized.

Waterlogging and Inland Salinity

The adverse affect of Canal irrigation in the fertile areas of Punjab, Haryana, U.P. and Rajasthan is the waterlogging which is increasing each year in spite of continuous expenditure under CADA programme to improve surface drainage. It is estimated that large areas, particularly in the command areas of major and medium irrigation projects suffer from waterlogging largely because of seepage from carrier channels, application of excessive water at farm level, poor and inadequate extraction of groundwater by farmers because of poor quality of ground water, sub-surface flow of groundwater towards areas prone to waterlogging because of the natural gradient, blockage of natural drainage by way of construction of roads, railways, canals, etc.

The assessment of area under waterlogging is required to be monitored regularly which is not being done and for want of information on the critical waterlogged areas under the threat of becoming waterlogged, the country is losing highly productive land. The National Commission on Agriculture assessed an area of 6.0 mha as waterlogged out of which surface water stagnation is in 3.4 mha and groundwater 2.6 mha. The Ministry of Water Resource in 1991 reported 2.46 mha as water logged in the command area of major and medium irrigation schemes. After the correct information on waterlogging was not available, so CGWB made an assessment during 1998-99 and observed that in November 1998 about 31.12 mha is water logged and another 50.41 mha area was prone to waterlogging. However during May 1999, the waterlogging was observed only in 1.87 mha and 10.02 mha as prone to waterlogging (Table 4.9). The problem of waterlogging should be viewed as a serious national concern, requiring immediate action to dewater-log the affected areas.

Waterlogging can be controlled by adopting suitable measures to reduce the recharge and increase the discharge from the shallow unconfined aquifer in the problem areas. The water-logging can only be effectively checked by constructing shallow tube wells for conjunctive use with surface water. The various other measures by which this can be achieved are (i) control of surface drainage into the area, (ii) provision of an efficient surface drainage system, (iii) lining of canals and watercourses, (iv) planning and adoption of rational agricultural practices, (v) adopting judicious water management practices and improving subsurface drainage.

Ministry of Water Resources (1986) had setup a working group to outline the adverse effects of waterlogging and salinity which is observed to be a big constraint in achieving optimum agriculture production. The report of the committee estimated that with an area of 5.8 mha is under waterlogging and soil salinity/alkalinity in the canal command of major/medium irrigation projects. This problem is responsible for a loss of 17 million tons of food grain and now the area under waterlogging has increased to about 30 mha, the loss is almost 80 million tons of food grain.

Table 4.9: State-wise Waterlogged and Areas Prone to Waterlogging

S. No.	State	November 1998		May 1999	
		Water Logged Area (0-2m)	Areas Prone to Water Logging (2-3m)	Water Logged Area (0-2m)	Area Prone to Water Logging (2-3)
		Sq.Km.	Sq.Km.	Sq.Km.	Sq.Km.
1.	Andhra Pradesh	58,300	61,690	3,401	9,886
2.	Arunachal Pradesh	0	0	6,060	0
3.	Assam	6,475	9,350	1,030	10,725
4.	Bihar	28,925	48,000	150	7,495
5.	Goa	278	392		
6.	Gujarat	4,330	5,550	600	2,900
7.	Haryana	5,478	5,455	794	3,335
8.	Himachal Predesh	110	190	121	148
9.	Jammu & Kashmir	504	566	346	295
10.	Karnataka	15,152	49,683	624	22,493
11.	Kerala	3,500	2,800	730	1,355
12.	Madhya Pradesh	25,666	16,993	25	2,186
13.	Maharashtra	44,250	91,090	439	4,306
14.	Manipur	Not Available			
15.	Meghalaya	950	950	100	325
16.	Mizoram	Not Available			
17.	Nagaland	0	0	0	0
18.	Orissa	47,492	28,317	1,180	4,583
19.	Punjab	4,875	4,500	2,350	5,000
20.	Rajasthan	2,779	1,680	880	1,611
21.	Sikkim	0	0		
22.	Tamil Nadu	30,918	52,640	4,850	5,115
23.	Tripura	0	0	0	50
24.	Uttar Pradesh	20,566	59,680	908	17,626
25.	West Bengal	10,298	64,128	0	630
	Total	3,10,846	5,03,654	18,589	1,00,064
Union Territories					
1.	Andaman & Nicobar				
2.	Chandigarh				
3.	Dadra & N. Haveli	200	480	0	0
4.	Daman & Diu				
5.	NCT Delhi				
6.	Lakshadweep				
7.	Pondicherry	202	0	100	120
	Grand Total	3,11,248	5,04,134	18,689	1,00,184

Artificial Recharge

The increased demand for water for various uses require some urgent steps to supplement the water resources which is either possible through transfer of water from surplus areas through construction of reservoirs and transfer of water through canals or conserve and recharge the groundwater by utilizing the monsoon run off. The scarcity of water is perpetual in about 947 blocks but in many other areas the scarcity is created by increasing the demand by cultivating water intensive crops in otherwise low rainfall and water deficit areas.

In order to meet the demand of water scarcity areas, it was earlier conceived that by interlinking of different rivers the water could be transferred. It is understood that when such a proposal was conceived not much information was available on the disposition of aquifer system under different geological formations, the capacity of the different aquifer systems to yield water and their recharge potential. A few link proposals are being worked out and the possibility of such links will be known when the detailed project reports of some links are made public. It is known that by the middle of the third millennium, surface water resources which is likely to be about 240 BCM by 2025 will be fully committed. The dynamic groundwater resources will also be fully utilized in the hard rock areas and in certain areas the in storage groundwater potential will be under exploitation. Considering geology, topography and rainfall pattern, the best option is to conserve and recharge the aquifers through artificial recharge.

The field experimentation and construction of a few artificial recharge demonstrative projects show that it would be possible to recharge the groundwater through construction of structures such as check dams, sub-surface dykes, gabion, percolation tanks and injection wells. It is evident that artificial recharge is going to be one of the important planning necessities for the country in the times to come. The groundwater reservoirs (aquifer) offer technically feasible alternative to store additional quantity of water available in the country. The storage of water underground minimizes evaporation losses; checks and even reverse declining trends of groundwater levels; check the ingress of saline water to the water—fresh water. Sub-surface storage has some other comparative advantages compare to surface water storage and the comparative advantages are given in Table 4.10

Table 4.10: Characteristics of Groundwater Storage, Small Dam Storage and Large Dam Reservoirs

	Groundwater Storage	*Small Dam and Surface Reservoirs*	*Large Dam Reservoirs*
Advantages	Little evaporation Widely distributed Operational efficiency Available on demand Water quality	Ease of operation Response to rainfall Multiple use Groundwater recharge	Large, reliable yield Carryover capacity Low cost per m^3 water stored Multi-purpose (power % flood control) Groundwater recharge
Limitations	Slow recharge rate Groundwater contamination Cost of extraction Recoverable fraction	High evaporation losses Relatively high unit cost Absence of over-year storage	Complexity of operation siting High initial investment cost Time needed to plan and construct
Key issues	Declining water levels Rising water levels Management of access and use Groundwater salinization Groundwater pollution	Sedimentation Adequate design Dam safety Environmental impacts	Social impacts Environmental impacts Sedimentation Dam safety

Source: IWMI Research Report No. 39: Water Scarcity and the Role of Storage in Development.

It is estimated that out of 4,000 BCM of average annual participation in the country, about 1,140 BCM is annually lost as surface runoff and out of this balance, 865 BCM of surplus monsoon runoff is available for additional recharge to ground water. It is estimated that it is possible to store in aquifers 214 BCM of water, out of which 160 BCM is retrievable (CGWB, 1996). As a first step towards utilization of surplus monsoon runoff in different states, the master plan prepared established that an additional potential of 36.2 BCM can be created through construction of simple structures.

In addition to the recharge utilizing the monsoon runoff, it is possible to recharge the aquifers on a large scale to mitigate any water shortages by utilization of water from water logged areas, recharging the aquifers in flood plains and utilizing the storm water and treated sewerage water.

Utilizing Water from Waterlogged Areas. It is estimated that about 01.12 mha area is water logged (0-2m depth) and another 50.41 mha is prone to waterlogging. This potential can be gainfully utilized to recharge the over-exploited shallow and deep aquifers of Punjab, Haryana, U.P., Rajasthan and other areas with waterlogging problem provided the hydro-geological conditions permit. The estimated groundwater resources does not include the groundwater potential of waterlogged and inland salinity areas. The large water potential (roughly about 800 BCM) available in the waterlogged areas can be utilized for recharging the depleting aquifers and through conjunctive use with the surface water. It is, therefore, necessary to conduct field experiments and model demonstrative projects to work out the feasible plans to overcome the problem and utilize this resource.

Another serious problem is the inland salinity, which covers an area of about 20 mha and it is increasing over the years for want of its utilization.

The solution to these two twin problems should be a national priority and there should also be a national debate on these issues. There should also be legal provision to compensate poor farmers with land holding of less than 5 ha who have lost their livelihood because of these problems.

Recharge of Aquifers in Flood Plains: The aquifers in the flood plains of the different rivers can be over-exploited and then recharged by using water of the monsoon runoff. In the flood plains large recharge structures like spreading basins, induced recharge structures can be made in the river flood plains or nearby where underground aquifers are at shallow depth and the project proposals meet the other technical requirements. An experimental study for recharging the aquifer by induced recharge method was carried out at village Tatiana in Ghaggar river basin during 1976-78 by CGWB. It was observed that if the well is pumped at the rate of 1,728 m^3/day, about 97 per cent of the well recharge will be contributed by the river after 94 days of continuous pumping in the form of induced recharge. The Yamuna flood plain of Delhi is also the ideal site for induced recharge as the fresh water aquifers are at shallow depth and enough water is available during flood period.

In addition to the induce recharge the large scale artificial recharge can be done by using the latest Aquifer Storage and

Recovery (ASR) technique which is defined as "the storage of water in a suitable aquifer through a well during times when the water is available and recovery of water from the same well during times when it is needed." Large volume of water can be stored underground thereby reducing the need to construct expensive surface reservoirs. In ASR technique the storm water and the treated sewerage water to the desired quality can be used for recharge.

National Water Policy

The reference to water as a whole is given in the Constitution under:

- *Entry 17—List II:* In the Constitution, "Water, that is to say, water supplies, irrigation and canals, drainage and embankments, water storage and water power."
- *Entry 56—List II:* "Regulation and development of inter-state rivers valleys to the extent to which such regulation and development under the control of the Union is declared by the parliament by law to be expedient in the public interest."

The reference to water is only with regard to surface water and there is no mention to groundwater directly or indirectly. In this regard, National Commission observed: "It seems the word 'water' may have been taken to include groundwater although there is no specific reference to the later, the constitution makers seem to have been thinking mainly of river waters."

The reference of the custodianship of groundwater is given in the Indian Easement Act, 1882 which defines this as:

> "The right of every owner of land to collect and dispose within his own limits of all water under the land which does not pass in a defined channel. All groundwater existing and found beneath private property is fully under the control of the owner of the land, who is free to extract and use it as he or she deems fit. This has led to a *de facto* right at the field level where affluent farmers with higher pumping capacity and deeper tube wells have disproportionate claims over the resources than others."

In the National Water Policy of 1987, there was no reference to the ownership of groundwater and many other issues pertaining to ground water. The revised National Water Policy of 1987 released during April, 2002 does not show any significant changes with regard to groundwater although the development of groundwater increased the irrigation potential from 27 mha to 45 mha besides meeting bulk requirements of drinking water in rural sector and of the industry and urban areas. The comparative statement of the National Water Policy of 1987 and 2002 is given in Table 4.11.

Table 4.11: A Comparative Statement of the National Water Policy of 1987 and 2002

NWP 1987	*NWP 2002*
1. There should be a periodical reassessment of the ground water potential on a scientific basis, taking into consideration the quality of the water available and economic viability.	1. There should be a periodical reassessment of the ground water potential on a scientific basis, taking into consideration the quality of the water available and economic viability *of its extraction.*
2. Exploitation of ground water resources should be so regulated as not to exceed the recharging possibilities, as also to ensure social equity. Ground water recharge projects should be developed and implemented for augmenting the available supplies.	2. Exploitation of ground water resources should be so regulated as not to exceed the recharging possibilities, as also to ensure social equity. *The detrimental environmental consequences of over-exploitation of ground water need to be effectively prevented by the Central and State Governments.* Ground water recharge projects should be developed and implemented for *improving both the quality and availability of ground water resource.*
3. Integrated and coordinated development of surface water and ground water resources and their conjunctive use, should be envisaged right from the project planning stage and should form an essential part of the project.	3. Integrated and coordinated development of surface water and ground water resources and their conjunctive use, should be envisaged right from the project planning stage and should form an integral part of the project implementation.
4. Over exploitation of ground water should be avoided especially near the coast to prevent ingress of seawater into sweet water aquifers.	4. Over exploitation of ground water should be avoided especially near the coast to prevent ingress of seawater into sweet water aquifers.

It is also well recognized that the large scale development of groundwater resource is likely to continue through this century fully exploiting the dynamic resource and also some percentage of the in storage in hard rock areas, coastal aquifers, sandstone and limestone aquifers of arid and semi-arid areas. The development and management of artificially recharged aquifers, custodianship of groundwater having been recognized as a common pool property, the problem of water logging and inland salinity and legal issues connected with it, etc. have raised many questions, therefore, all these issues need to be debated and addressed to in any new policies to be framed in future. There is also a need to frame separate policies for development of groundwater for the five different major aquifer systems as each of the system has different aquifer geometry, sustainability and potential to get recharged. There is thus, a need to have a separate National Groundwater Policy so that the aquifers are managed and utilized properly. The policy also need to be worked out for transboundary aquifers between the states as future development of groundwater in such areas will lead to conflicts.

Transboundary Aquifers

The distribution of surface water resources of the rivers cutting across international boundaries is governed by treaties between the countries and within the country by agreement between the states but in case of groundwater it was neither found necessary nor there was a need for it as the groundwater was being selectively exploited. The increasing water demands, scarcity during drought periods and changing water scenario will compel water managers to work for mapping of aquifers which extend across the international boundaries particularly where the aquifers receive the majority of its recharge transboundary and the majority of its discharge occur in the neibouring country. Under such a situation, the development of groundwater or pollution to groundwater in one country will become areas of conflict. This situation may also arise within the country between different states as the over-exploitation of common aquifers and non-implementation of regulatory measures to check industrial pollution. This has been observed in case of Pondicherry and Tamil Nadu, the former has Ground Water Regulatory Act and implementing it whereas Tamil Nadu is not adhering to the guidelines for treating the industrial effluents.

India has the international borders with Pakistan, Bangladesh, Nepal, Bhutan and Burma (Myanmar), the aquifers in case of

Burma and Bhutan may not be the cause of immediate concern but the aquifers in case of other countries are very extensive and problems will definitely arise in future. In case of border with Pakistan, the aquifers of Indus basin transgress across the borders. This requires detailed mapping of the aquifers up to the basement formation. Similarly the border with Nepal has extensive aquifer system and still to be fully exploited but the increase in demand particularly for irrigation will lead to conflict issues. It is therefore essential that a beginning is made to prepare database of the hydro geological data available and sub-surface geological cross-sections are plotted and aquifers delineated particularly of Rajasthan and Gujarat. A committee of technical professionals should be constituted to undertake the work.

Water Quality and Pollution

Man has lived in urbanized areas for centuries in environment naturally protected from pollution. Population concentrations, increased urbanization, industrialization and modern agriculture practices have created a slowly increasing pollution of the environment, both of the air and water including ground water.

The sources of groundwater pollution may be either geo-generic, i.e. the substancesminerals that occurs naturally like Fe, Mn, F, toxic elements (As and Se) and radio nuclides (radium, uranium and radon) or anthropogenic resulting from human activities *i.e.* bacteria, viruses, nitrate, synthetic organic chemicals (pesticides), hydrocarbons and heavy metals. They are introduced into ground water from a variety of sources like urban (municipal), industrial and agricultural land uses, domestic and environmental.

In the context of developing water crisis scenario, many problematic areas have been identified in almost all the states of the country. The problems are associated with ground water pollution due to contamination with heavy metals, Nitrate, Fluoride, Arsenic, Selenium, etc. At some places pesticides, phenolic compounds, cyanide and pathogenic organisms have been detected. Fluoride, Nitrate are predominant pollutants present in groundwater of all the states, Arsenic in the eastern end of the Ganga basin and Selenium in Hoshiarpur district of Punjab.

Nitrate

Nitrate contamination of groundwater occurs mostly in urbanized areas all over the world. The substances set free by human activities and transported conservatively under ground including unplanned disposal of domestic sewage and industrial wastes, livestock operations, use of nitrate based fertilizers, are sources of concern to the society presented by increasing contaminant concentrations.

The consumption of well water containing higher concentrations of nitrate more than 100 mg/l is linked with methemoglobinemia in infants. The highest concentration of 3,000 mg/l is observed in district Bikaner, Rajasthan.

Fluoride

Fluoride poses a serious health hazard affecting a large segment of rural population estimated to be 25 million spread over more than 200 districts in 17 states. High fluoride in groundwater has been reported in Rajasthan, Andhra Pradesh, Karnataka, Tamil Nadu, Madhya Pradesh, Maharashtra, Gujarat, Punjab, Haryana, Uttar Pradesh, Bihar, Orissa, Kerala, West Bengal and Delhi. Among these states, Rajasthan and Andhra Pradesh are the most seriously affected areas (Table 4.12).

Table 4.12: Rural Population Consuming Fluoride-Contamination Water (1999) in the 17 Endemic States

State	*Total*	*Rural*	*Rural affected*	*Percentage of Rural*
Andhra Pradesh	74.62	52.31	13.50	18.1%
Bihar	98.12	83.67	Na	Na
Delhi	13.42	1.23	0.16**	1-1.4%
Gujarat	47.56	29.45	4.78	10.1%
Haryana	19.83	14.57	2.17	10.9%
Jammu & Kashmir	9.17	7.22	Na	Na
Karnataka	51.65	34.42	6.90	13.4%
Kerala	32.08	22.43	Na	Na
Madhya Pradesh	78.81	58.36	1.68	2.1%
Maharashtra	90.45	52.84	0.14	0.2%
Orissa	35.53	29.80	3.26	9.2%
Punjab	23.28	16.05	2.07	8.9%
Rajasthan	52.94	39.82	10.90	20.6%
Tamil Nadu	61.43	39.19	7.64	12.4%
Uttar Pradesh	167.66	130.83	11.77	7.0%
West Bengal	78.32	56.21	1.65	2.1%
Assam	25.88	22.62	Na	Na
All India*	961.29	691.02	66.62	6.9%

* Total population of 17 endemic States.

** Estimates for Delhi include average of both rural and urban populations "Na" indicated not assessed.

Arsenic

Contamination of groundwater used for drinking purposes, with arsenic (As) has emerged as serious health threat in recent years in India too. Eight districts comprising 68 blocks in West Bengal have arsenic levels in groundwater above the BIS and WHO maximum permissible limit of 50 μg/l. The affected districts are Malda, Murshidabad, Nadia, North 24 Paraganas, South 24 Parganas, Hugli, Howrah and Burdhwan and about 6 million people living in there districts are in the risk zone (Table 4.13). Besides the West Bengal. Rajnandgaon of Madhya Pradesh, some isolated patches in Madras city and in one or two places in the flood plain of river Yamuna have recently been found to be affected with arsenic.

Arsenic toxicity produces myriad problems in the human body, chromine exposure to as also results in arsenosis, Hyperpigmentation, depilmentation, keratosis and peripheral vascular disorder are the most commonly reported symptoms. Skin cancer, cario vascular and neurological diseases have also been found lose linked to arsenic ingestion.

Table 4.13: District-wise Spread of Arsenic in Groundwater—May 1998

District	*Blocks*		*Affected Areas*			*Population at Risk (in million)*
	Total	*Affected*	*Hab.*	*NMA*	*MA*	
Malda	15	5	379	–	–	0.54
Murshidabad	26	15	367	–	–	1.17
Nadia	17	13	455	7	1	0.92
Burdhwan	31	2	7	–	–	0.02
Hugli	18	1	15	1	–	0.03
Howrah	14	3	6	–	1	0.19
N 24 Parganas	22	19	671	2	7	1.57
S 24 Parganas	29	10	1,243	–	–	0.91
Total	172	68	3133	15	9	5.31

Hab.—Habitations; NMA—Non-Municipal Area; MA—Municipal Area.

Selenium

The occurrence of Selenium (Se) in excess to the acceptable limit of 0.05 ppm has been reported in India only in the Nawansahar and Hoshiarpur districts of Punjab. The most affected villages are Mahendpur, Barwa, Rakkar, Jainpur (Nawansahar district); Simble and Nazarpur in Hoshiarpur district where Selenium toxicity has been noticed in soil, plants as well as in drinking water, thus posing a serious threat to crops and human life. In human being there is loss of hair, malformation of nails, oozing of blood from the finger tips. In animals, characteristic symptoms of developing up cracks in the hoofs and horns. Selenium toxicity symptoms can be seen in wheat, sugar cane and some plants which exhibited papery snow/*white* chlorosis of leaves with pinkish coloration on the surface of leaves (Table 4.14).

The selenium in ground water ranges from 0.025 mg/l to 0.69 mg/l. The water samples collected from different villages showing concentration of selenium is given below:

Table 4.14: Concentration of Selenium in Groundwater Collected from Selenium Affected Areas in Punjab

S. No.	*Location Villages*	*Sources*	*Depth*	*Temp. °C*	*Selenium/ (ppm)*
1.	Simbal Majra	Hand Pump	20 metres	24°C	0.102
2.	Rokkra	Hand Pump	15 metres	24°C	0.100
3.	Barwa	Tube well	25 metres	24°C	0.277
4.	Mehandpur	Hand Pump	15 metres	22°C	0.094
5.	Mehandpur	Dug-cum-bore well (Cavity)	24 metres	22°C	0.118
6.	Mahendpur	-do-	33 metres	22°C	0.479
7.	Simbli	Hand Pump	15 metres	24°C	0.150
8.	Mahendpur	Hand Pump	22 metres	24°C	0.227
9.	Jainpur	Hand Pump	15 metres	22°C	0.164
10.	Jainpur	Bore well	25 metres	22°C	0.297
11.	Simbli	Hand Pump	15 metres	22°C	0.131
12.	Nizzarpur	Dug-cum-Bore well	35 metres	24°C	0.220
13.	Nizzarpur	Hand Pump	15 metres	24°C	0.119

Note: In drinking water the acceptable limit is 0.05 mg/l and of the irrigation water 0.02 mg/l.

Legal, Moral and Ethical Issues

Legal Issues

Groundwater Regulation: The documented reference to the ownership of groundwater in pre-British period is not available and the only early documented reference is available in section 7 of the Indian Easement Act, 1882 which refers to the right of every owner of land to collect and dispose within his own limits of all water under the land which does not pass in a defined channel.

This property-based rights were thought of when there was hardly any development of groundwater but under the prevailing conditions, the Act needs thorough revision as groundwater is a shared common good property. Many independent stakeholders and government organizations are exploiting this resource in excess to the renewable recharge resulting in continuous decline of water levels and many problems associated with it and this may lead to the "tragedy of the commons".

In order to check, control and regulate the groundwater from its overexploitation by the individuals and government organizations, Government of India circulated a Model Bill in the year 1970, which was later on revised in 1992 and 1996. The salient features of Model Bill (1970) are:

- The state governments to acquire powers to restrict the construction of groundwater structures.
- Groundwater Authority to be constituted by each state under Legislation.
- Permission to construct tube well for all industrial and agriculture purposes except domestic use.
- Groundwater Authority vested with the power to cancel any permits, registrations or licences issued by them.
- Support to enforce the various provisions of the legislation. Orders issued by the Authority would fall outside the perview of the Civil Court.

The following provisions were included in the revised version of Model Bill (1992):

- Extension of the bill to cover all uses including drinking and domestic use, exemption of small and marginal farmers from obtaining prior permission for construction of groundwater structures for their exclusive use
- Small and marginal farmers are not required to obtain permit to extract and use groundwater in the notified areas.

Later on during 1996, the provisions in the Model Bill were further modified to allow the construction of the well to be fitted with a hand operated manual pump or with manual devices.

Although the model Bill was circulated as early as 1970 but no action was taken by the State Governments to control the heavy withdrawal of groundwater and regulate its development. The continuous declining of the water levels particularly in the

National Capital Territory of Delhi was reported in the National newspaper, *'Indian Express'*. Based on the news item, public interest litigation was filed in the Supreme Court who directed the Government of India to constitute the Central Authority under the Environment Act of 1986. The operating paragraph of Supreme Court judgment is "The Central Government in the Ministry of Environment and Forest shall constitute the Central Groundwater Board as an Authority under Section 3(3) of the Act. The Authority so constituted shall exercise all the powers under the Act necessary for the purpose of regulation and control of groundwater management and development. The Central Government shall confer on the Authority the power to give directions under Section 5 of the Act and also powers to take such measures or pass any orders in respect of all the matters referred to in Sub-section (3) of the Act." As directed by Hon'ble Supreme Court, the Ministry of Environment and Forest issued the Gazette Notification on 14th January 1997 constituting the Authority for a period of one year with the objective to regulate indiscriminate boring and withdrawal of groundwater in the country and to issue necessary regulatory directions with a view to preserve and protect the ground water. The authority will have the following powers to function under the Environmental Act, 1986.

> Exercise of powers under section 5 of the Environment (Protection) Act, 1986 for issuing directions and taking such measures in respect of all the matters referred to in sub-section (2) of Section 3 of the said Act.
>
> To resort to the penal provision contained in Sections 15 to 21 of the said Act.

Subsequent to the notification of 14th January, 1997, Ministry of Environment and Forest issued revised notifications on 13th January, 1998 and 6th November, 2000 modifying the structure of the authority by adding more members and making it a permanent Authority. The Authority has framed the rules for regulating the groundwater development but the rules are still to be notified.

The problem of depletion of aquifer storages and lowering of water levels having become acute in many parts of the country, some of the State Governments took action towards regulating the development of groundwater resources but there is a need that all states should regulate the withdrawal even in the areas where the development is limited but likely to take up in the near future.

The existing framework of the functioning of the Authority is given in Fig. 4.1 and the alternative management framework given in the World Bank Report (1998) is given in Fig. 4.2.

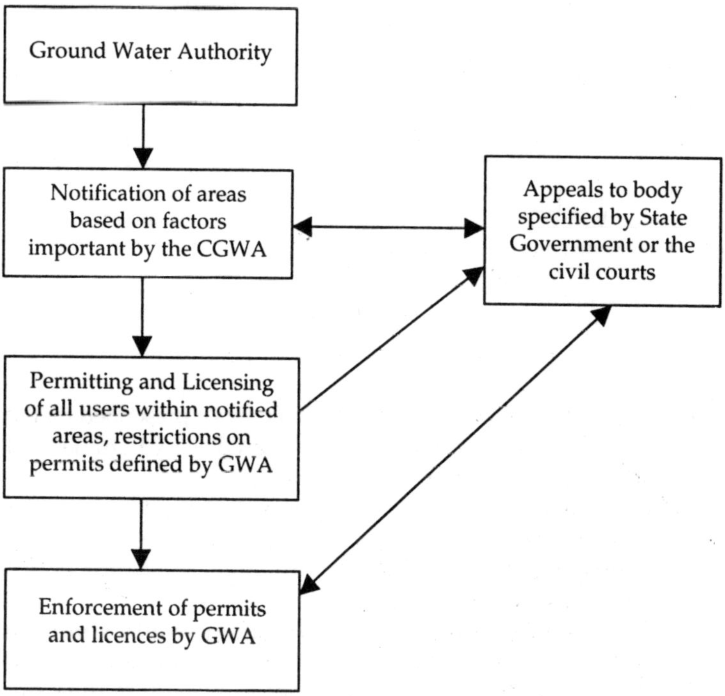

Fig. 4.1: Management Process Proposed in the Implicit Legislation.

The fast development of the groundwater resources have changed the scenario which existed at the time when the groundwater ownership rights and provision in the constitutions were defined. In view of this, the property based groundwater rights are unsuited to the present conditions when the water resources are scarce, fierce competition for its availability and not easy co-operation on water issues. Moreover, the artificial recharge being done by NGO and individual has also put a question mark on the ownership rights when groundwater aquifers are a common pool property.

The National Commission on integrated water resources management suggested the following legal and institutional mechanisms for regulation the groundwater in dark and over exploited areas:

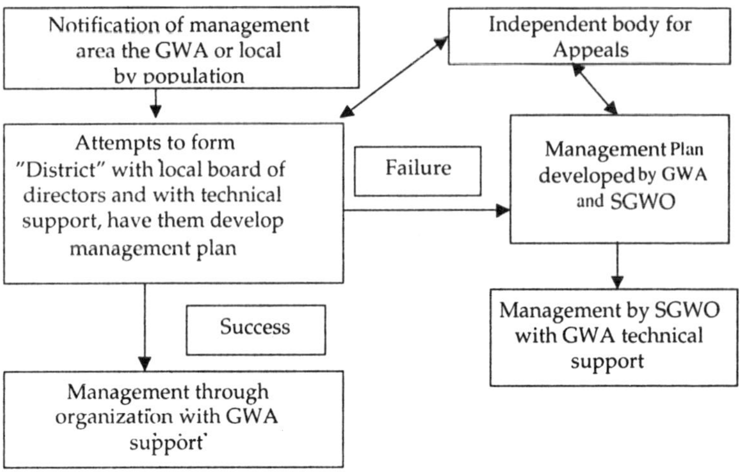

Fig. 4.2: Alternative Management Framework.

- The overall guidelines of regulation may be prescribed by the Groundwater Authority concerned, based on local studies and surveys, until a law on groundwater is enacted.
- Panchayats should get the approval of the Gram Sabha (village community), as a whole on groundwater management; where villages are large, the Sabha could be formed for smaller areas.
- The use of groundwater for irrigation would similarly require approval of the Gram Sabha. This would ensure that the village community determines whether the groundwater should be used and if so in what quantity, based on the technical information and the advice received from the state groundwater officials.
- The sale of groundwater needs to be prohibited for the simple reason that it converts a scarce natural good into 'commodity' and dealing in commodities must meet the requirements of public interest, which it does not do in 'dark' and 'over exploited' areas.
- The village community may be inspired and enabled to undertake groundwater recharging operations and conserve the utilization of water in the village area.
- The central and state groundwater officials may be required to extend full cooperation, rendering technical service and advice to village communities.

The relation between the Central Authority constituted under Environmental Act and State Authorities under Legislation is that the Central Authority will have the overriding power of the actions taken by the State Authority. It is still to be seen how the implementation of the guidelines of Central Authority which is only a regulatory authority will get its directions implemented in the States having their own Authority. The casual approach towards regulating the development and pollution of groundwater resources is fast turning surplus areas to water deficit areas and ending up importing the water from other areas. It is also a matter of concern that the states groundwater authorities being constituted under legislation act are headed by political leaders instead of scientists which may defeat the very purpose of regulating the depletion and pollution.

Moral and Ethical Issues

The control of water is the control of life and livelihood. As the water is connected to human dignity and basic needs for sustaining life, Universal declaration on human rights (1948) found a close link of water to broader social and ethical concerns. Over the last two decades, several important International Conferences have called for an ethical commitment to provide for humanity's basic water needs such as Maer del plata in 1977, the Rio earth summit in 1992; the Unsponsored comprehensive assessment of world's freshwater resources in 1997 and others. Linkages between water policy and ethics are increasingly found throughout the world.

The importance of water has also been refereed to in almost all the religious books of Hinduism, Islam, Christianity, Buddhism. In the Rig-Veda, a water prayer is offered " The waters in the sky, the waters of rivers and water in the well whose source is the ocean, may all these scared waters protect me." In Islamic tradition, the Shariah literally means the " source of water".

World water statistics are becoming familiar. According to Water Supply and Sanitation Council, roughly 1.4 billion people (25% of the world) still have no access to water supply and 2.9 billion people (50 – 60% of the world) have no access to sanitation services.

In the developing world, 90 per cent of such diseases are related to water. The UN agencies collective declaration on occasion of 1999 World Water Day stated that the amount of donors money necessary to bring low cost safe water and sanitation in eight to ten years was equivalent to the money spent in pet food in North America and Europe.

The UNESCO working group on fresh water uses has been looking at the ethics of managing various water uses; water and food security; water and health and sanitation; water and natural disasters; decision making and water management; water and ecology; the special role of women in water; water history and broader social ethics; challenges of technology and standards of professionalism; special issues related to the recent intense use of ground water in arid countries; water and conflict and elements of a new ethic of water.

Most responses to water require finding a balance among uses, among traditional and technological solutions and will differ among regions. A new sense of water ethics at the personal and social level is needed. Most of the earth has been built and rebuilt and today the fundamental need of water managers is for an ethic of ecological design and not just preservation.

There are profound ethical implications in the management of all aspects of the traditional water uses such as flood control and management; drought contingency planning and management; irrigation; hydroelectric power and agriculture; water supply and sanitation; navigation; ecological maintenance and health; public health and disease control and others. Ethical considerations concerning water tend to revolve around the distribution of benefits and costs of the services; who gets how much of the water and who pays; the distribution of risks; who is vulnerable and to what degree. Today, this includes service for nature and ecology as well as people. Ethical considerations also depend on whether the uses are seen as an end in themselves or a means to some other ends such as economic development.

Conclusion

In this millennium, the development of groundwater will continue at the present rate of development and it is likely to fully utilize the dynamic potential other than of the eastern states, which have very extensive groundwater reservoirs. This calls for shift from development to management and it is imperative. The perpetual scarcity areas and those having water intensive cropping pattern must go for large scale recharge projects and for water recycling. This is also very essential to prepare the code of practice for different recharge structures, water quality to be recharged and also to conduct regular training programme at the Panchayat level so that the recharge planning is successfully implemented.

In the drought prone and arid areas the cultivation of water intensive crops should be discouraged and the water available in the aquifers should be exclusively used for drinking purpose as the aquifers are not getting recharged to the extent they are being exploited. The quality of groundwater particularly the problem of arsenic and fluoride need to be intensively monitored and the information on update treatment technologies for their removal are disseminated through publications, creating a web site for the purpose and through mass awareness programmes.

The availability of fresh water aquifers getting reduced because of the pollution by the industrial effluents, therefore, the groundwater pollution need to be tackled strictly and the offenders punished and the polluters pay concept is seriously implemented.

It is now realized that the ground water is at the crossroads, past development efforts have been successful but the future development of the resource will face many challenges to maintain the sustainability, therefore, the change in mindset and the following points need consideration:

- A separate National Ground Water Policy covering all aspects from ownership rights to management issues may be framed.
- The ultimate irrigation potential which at present is taken as 64 mha should be reassessed considering return flow from the groundwater irrigated lands and 10 per cent which at present has been kept as a contingency.
- The potential of groundwater in hard rock areas to be reassessed, working out separately for each of the three major hard rock aquifers.
- Strengthening of groundwater institutions, along with capacity building, training and education in specific areas like artificial recharge, groundwater modelling, watershed management, quality monitoring and aquifer remediation on a continuous basis.
- The solution to the problem of water logging and inland salinity to be taken up on priority. Legal provision to be incorporated to compensate the affected farmers.
- New techniques of artificial recharge such as ASR (Aquifer storage recovery) and induced recharge practices should be experimented and used for creating large recharge potential together with management of recharged aquifer code for practice of all the recharge techniques should be prepared and widely circulated for practice.

REFERENCES

Central Ground Water Board, (1991). "Special Issue on Ground Water Statistics." *Bhu Jal News* 6(1): 1-162.

Central Ground Water Board, (1995). *Groundwater Resources of India.* Faridabad: Ministry of Water Resources, Government of India.

Central Ground Water Board, (1998). Activities and Achievements of Central Ground Water Board on Rain Water Harvesting and Artificial Recharge, Government of India.

Central Ground Water Board, (2002). Action Plan for Artificial Recharge to Ground Water in India, Ministry of Water Resources, Government of India.

Central Ground Water Board, (1994). *Manual on Artificial Recharge of Ground Water* pp. 1-215.

Central Ground Water Board, (2000). 'Rain Water Harvesting and Artificial Recharge –Technological Developments' National, '*Seminar on Rain Water Harvesting*'.

Chadha, D.K., (1999) 'A proposed New Diagram for Geochemical Classification of Natural Waters and Interpretation of Chemical Data'. *Hydrogeology Journal* – Volume-7, pp. 431-439.

Chadha, D.K., (1999) Challenges in Ground Water Management in India – *Proceedings of* National Workshop on 'Challenges in the Management of Water Resources and Environment in Next Millennium: Need for Inter-Institute Collaboration', New Delhi – pp. 219-228.

Chadha, D.K., (1998) Imbalance in groundwater development and its consequences. Ninth National Symposium on Hydrology, Amritsar, India. Pp. 1-11.

Chadha, D.K., (2000)' Technologies Developments in Artificial Recharge of Ground Water-Case Studies in India, *Seminar* on 'Management of Aquifer Recharge for Sustainability'.

Dhawan, B.D., (1989a). Preventing Groundwater Over-Exploitation. Workshop on Efficiency and Equity in Ground Water use and Management. Anand, Gujarat: Institute of Rural Management.

Dhawan, B.D., (1989b). *Studies in Irrigation and Water Management*. New Delhi: Commonwealth Publishers.

Dillon, P., Pavelic, P., Sibernaler, X., Gerges, N., and Clerk, R. (1997) Aquifer storage and recovery to storm water runoff. *AWWA J. Water* 24 (4) 7-11.

Laamas, M.R., Priscoli, J.D. (2000). Report of the Unesco Working group on the Ethics of Freshwater use. Foundation Marcelino Botin.

M. Ramon Llamas, Jerome Delli Priscoli, *Water and Ethics,* Special Issue, Foundation Marcelino Botin.

Martin Russel, Dillon Peter (2001), Aquifer Storage Recovery, CSIRO, Australia

Meinzen-Dick, R., (1996). *Groundwater Markets in Pakistan: Participation and Productivity*. Washington, DC: International Food Policy Research Institute.

Ministry of Water Resources, (1992). "Waterlogging, Soil Salinity, and Alkalinity Report of the Working Group on Problem Identification in Irrigated Areas." New Delhi.

Ministry of Water Resources, (1996). "World Bank – India Water Resources Management Sector Work, Report of the Sub-Group on Ground Water." New Delhi.

Ministry of Water Resources, (1997), "Ground Water Resources Estimation Methodology, Report of the Ground Water Resources Estimation Committee."

Ministry of Water Resources, (1999). "Integrated Water Resources Development: A Plan for Action, Report of the National Commission for Integrated Water Resources Development Plan."

Ministry of Water Resources, (1992). Model Bill to Regulate and Control the Development of Ground Water.

Ministry of Water Resources, (2002). National Water Policy.

Puri, S., *et al.* (2001). Internationally Shared (Transboundary) Aquifer Resources Management, Paris, Unesco.

Shah, T., (1993). *Groundwater Markets and Irrigation Development: Political Economy and Practical Policy*. Bombay: Oxford University Press.

World Bank, (1998). India-Water Resources Management Sector Review: Groundwater Regulation and Management Report, South Asia Rural Development Unit.

World Bank, (1998). Water Resources Management Sector Review: Rural Water Supply and Sanitation Report. Washington, DC: South Asia Rural Development Unit.

World Bank, (1998b). "Groundwater Regulation and Management Report," under the India Water Resources. Management Sector Review Programme. Washington, DC: World Bank, South Asia Rural Development Unit.

5

Drinking Water Supply in India

A Strategic Policy Analysis

S.S. MEENAKSHISUNDARAM, *I.A.S.*

Fresh water, which was once viewed as an infinitely renewable natural resource, is no longer available in plenty. Most of the countries that were having sufficient fresh water supplies are currently facing problems on account of increasing demand due to population pressure, over-exploitation of resources and rapid growth in agriculture and industry, besides urbanization. In India, per capita water availability was over 5,000 cubic metres per annum in 1950. Now, it stands at about 2,000 cubic metres, and it is estimated that by 2025, per capita availability would be around 1,500 cubic metres.

The demand for fresh water from different sectors has been growing against an almost fixed availability, resulting in a scarcity situation in different parts of India. Water distress is visible in desert and drought prone areas. Apart from the increasing mismatch in the supply-demand scenario, gross mismanagement of water resources, coupled with neglect of traditional water resources environment have further aggravated the situation. The result is seen in the form of falling water levels, water scarcity, degradation of quality and prevalence of water borne and water related diseases in several parts of India. We need, therefore, to protect, allocate and manage our available water most judiciously to ensure water security, food security, livelihood security, health security and ecological security for the people.

Rural water supply in India is the largest of its kind in the world. Significant progress has been achieved in the drinking water sector due to sustained efforts by the Governments, both at the Centre and in the States. An impressive achievement has been the reported coverage of about 90 per cent habitations with adequate drinking water, i.e. 40 litres per capita per day (lpcd). Annually, the Government of India is providing to the State Governments, more than Rs.2,200 crore as central share and equal matching share is coming from the State Governments.

This significant coverage of drinking water in rural and urban areas, however, is not without any environmental costs. Heavy dependence on ground water for drinking water supply as well as irrigation coupled with inadequate recharging efforts, ineffective conjunctive use of water sources and the neglect of traditional practices and systems including rainwater harvesting have resulted in the depletion of ground water levels. In several districts of India, the ground water levels have fallen by more than 4 metres during 1981-2000, i.e. 20 cms per year. This had led to the emergence of water quality problems in several areas of the country. In addition, several habitations which were fully covered with the required water supply, a few years ago, have now slipped into the category of 'Not Covered' or 'Partially Covered' villages. The country is now facing three major challenges in the water sector: (a) slippage of covered habitations; (b) water quality problems, and (c) sustainability of sources and systems. We propose to examine in this paper, these issues in some detail. A substantial portion of this paper will summarize the magnitude of each of these problems as well as the efforts put in by the Central and State Governments to deal with them. The rest of the paper will be to suggest possible directions for a future strategy.

Coverage of Habitations

A national water supply and sanitation programme was first introduced by the Government of India in the year 1954. The Central Government then provided assistance to the States to establish special investigation divisions, to identify the problem villages. Taking into account the magnitude of the problem and to accelerate the pace of coverage of the problem villages, the Government of India introduced the Accelerated Rural Water Supply Programme (ARWSP) in 1972-73 to assist the States and the Union Territories with 100 per cent grants-in-aid to implement water supply schemes in such villages. This programme continued till 1973-74. With the introduction of the Minimum Needs Programme (MNP) during the Fifth Five Year Plan (from 1974-75), ARWSP was withdrawn. It was, however, reintroduced in 1977-78 when it was felt that the supply of safe drinking water to the identified problem villages was not adequately focused under the MNP.

In 1986, providing drinking water was identified as one of the key areas where a mission approach was needed to achieve the goal of providing potable drinking water to all the citizens of the country. A technology mission on drinking water management, called the National Drinking Water Mission was, therefore, set up in 1986 and this was subsequently renamed as Rajiv Gandhi National Drinking Water Mission (RGNDWM) in 1991. The National Agenda for Governance announced by the Government of India in 1999 again focused its attention towards attaining the goal of providing safe drinking water to all rural habitations within a period of 5 years, i.e. by April 2004. The key strategies identified by the Government to achieve this goal are: (a) ensure coverage of all rural habitations, especially by reaching the unreached with access to safe drinking water; (b) ensure sustainability of the systems and sources; and (c) tackle the water quality problems in all the affected habitations.

Water is defined as safe, if it is free from biological contamination (gini worm, cholera, typhoid etc.) and chemical contamination (excessfluoride, brackishness, iron, arsenic, nitrate etc.). A habitation is declared 'Fully Covered' if the following goals are achieved while providing drinking water to that habitation: (a) 40 ltrs per capita per day (lpcd) of safe drinking water for human beings; (b) 30 ltrs per capita per day (lpcd) additional for cattle in the desert areas; and (c) one hand-pump or stand post for every 250 persons residing in the habitation. The water source should exist within or nearby the habitation, i.e. within 1.6 kms in the Plains and within 100 metres elevation in the Hilly areas. These norms were recently relaxed to provide for 55 lpcd with the sources within 0.5 kms in the Plains and 50 metres elevation in the hills, to those States who have achieved the coverage of all 'Not Covered' (NC) and 'Partially Covered' (PC) rural habitations as per the existing norms of 40 lpcd.

The ARWSP is the key vehicle that provides the funds for water supply schemes in the States. The criteria for allocation of ARWSP funds to the States as of now is indicated below:

	Weightage for	*Percentage (%)*
1.	Rural Population	40
2.	States under Desert Development Programme (DDP), Drought Prone Area Programme (DPAP), Hill Area Development Programme (HADP) & special category Hill States in terms of rural areas	35
3.	NC/PC villages (at 2:1 ratio between NC and PC)	15
4.	Quality affected villages (40:40:15:5)*	10
	TOTAL	100

* Keeping in view the differential impact of chemicals such as Fluoride, Arsenic, Brackishness and Iron on human health, higher weightage have been given to Fluoride (40%) and arsenic (40%) affected habitations which have serious health problems when compared to Brackishness (15%) and Iron (5%) while arriving at quality parameters.

Allocation of funds to the States, based on the above criteria, would be subject to the matching provision/expenditure by the States from their own resources. About 5 per cent of Annual Plan allocation is earmarked to States covered by Desert Development Programme (DDP). The share of the States is determined in proportion to the NC and PC habitations of DDP areas without insisting on States' matching contribution. States are authorized to utilize up to 15 per cent of ARWSP funds for operation and maintenance of the Rural Water Supply Schemes. Further 5 per cent of ARWSP funds are earmarked to meet natural calamities and emergent situations. Funds remaining unutilized in February under this head will be pooled back to normal ARWSP funds and allotted to better performing States.

The status of coverage of rural habitations with drinking water facilities as reported by the States/UTs and compiled by the Government of India as on 25th November, 2002 is as under:

Type of coverage	*No. of habitations*	*Per cent*
Total	1,422,664	
Fully Covered (FC)	1,284,203	90.27
Partially Covered (PC)	123,359	8.67
Not Covered (NC)	15,102	1.06

The exact status with regard to slippage of some FC habitations into PC and NC category and the PC habitations becoming NC habitations might not have been reflected in the above table. At any given point of time the ground situation is bound to be different owing to increase in population and the number of habitations; systems having outlived their life span or becoming defunct possibly due to poor maintenance; sources going dry due to depletion in ground water levels and sources having become quality affected.

The following table summarizes the outlay and expenditure (in crores) incurred during the Ninth Five Year Plan in the drinking water supply sector:

Year	*Outlay*	*Expenditure*	*State Share*	*Total*
1997-1998	1,302.00	1,299.91	1,676.99	2,976.90
1998-1999	1,612.00	1,600.64	1,897.07	3,497.71
1999-2000	1,715.00	1,714.41	2,471.77	4,186.18
2000-2001	1,960.00	1,896.55	2,366.32	4,262.87
2001-2002	1,975.00	1,943.05	2,029.53	3,972.58
Total	8,564.00	8,454.56	10,441.68	18,896.24

The Central outlay for the Rural Water Supply Sector for the year 2002-03 is Rs.2,235 crore.

Quality Problems

Despite the improved coverage and access to water supply, the disease burden from infectious diseases suggests that the impact in improving access has not been as great as may have been hoped. In India, nearly 400,000 children die due to diarrhoeal diseases attributable to feacally contaminated water and poor health and hygiene practices. Apart from this, 66 million people in 19 States are at risk due to high fluoride in drinking water and another 13 million are at risk due to high arsenic concentration in drinking water in West Bengal. Excess arsenic has also been reported from Bihar and Madhya Pradesh. Other water quality problems include iron, salinity and nitrates. Some water quality problems are of geological origin and others are due to man-made causes. Unlike iron and salinity, the presence of arsenic, fluoride and bacteriological pollution does not result in change in colour or taste of water to warn the user. As a result, a large number of people are unknowingly drinking contaminated water, and are at health risk.

As already mentioned, almost 85 per cent of the drinking water supply in rural India is dependent on ground water sources. In the absence of adequate and reliable water quality data, it is difficult to have an accurate assessment of the situation. On the basis of the information furnished by the State Governments, the Government of India have identified 217,211 rural habitations with quality problems as on 1st April, 1999. The following table summarizes the nature of the quality problem and the habitations affected with them.

Nature of Quality Problem	*No. of Affected Habitations*
Excess Fluoride	36,988
Excess Arsenic	3,553
Excess Salinity	32,597
Excess Iron	138,670
Excess Nitrate	4,003
Other reasons	1,400
TOTAL	217,211

Since the quality problems are dynamic in nature, to assess the actual scenario at any point of time, the State Governments carry out a 5-10 per cent stratified sampling survey, taking the community development block as the unit. On identification of the quality affected Blocks, 100 per cent survey of the sources in those Blocks are carried out. The exact magnitude of the problem is assessed only after the results of these surveys are available. However, it can be estimated that around 15 per cent of the drinking water sources in India are generally affected by water quality problems.

To address the identified quality problems, exclusive Sub-Missions were constituted under the RGNDWM for initiating preventive and remedial measures. From 1998 onwards, the States were empowered to implement Sub-Mission programmes themselves to improve water quality by availing 15 per cent allocation under ARWSP. Combating water quality problems included provision of safe water sources or treatment units and establishment of district water testing laboratories.

However, the water quality testing infrastructure in most States is still weak. Donor partners, who took initiative include DANIDA, GTZ, UNICEF and WHO. UNICEF support include R&D initiatives for the development of domestic defluoridation unit and user friendly and reliable field test kits for testing limited water quality parameters, desk studies, supply of water quality testing equipment and training of water analysts. The R&D initiative for the chemical parameters was taken by the National Chemical Laboratory (NCL), Pune. The refinement of bacteriological test kit was carried out by the Defence Food Research Laboratory (DFRL), Mysore, in cooperation with eight leading Indian educational/research institutions.

As adequate and reliable water quality data is not available, it is difficult to identify hot spots and optimally target limited resources. It is also not possible to carry out risk assessment and, therefore, interventions in most cases are post-epidemic rather than preventive. Secondly, the district level water testing infrastructure is weak in most States. In many districts, labs are yet to be established. Many district labs do not have qualified and experienced staff, and adequate transport facilities and fund allocation. Many labs face financial crunch. It will take quite some time before the district labs will conform to acceptable norms. Due to these shortcomings, they are unable to respond to the needs immediately and effectively. Thirdly, over 10 million public and private water sources (dug wells, shallow handpumps, etc.) including nearly 3 million deep-well public handpumps are spread over 1.4 million habitations. The dispersed nature of water sources poses immense logistic problems in transporting water samples to the district laboratories and conveying results to the community as frequently as necessary. Regular sanitary inspections are necessary to prevent bacteriological pollution, but these are rarely conducted.

Keeping in view the above issues and constraints, the "National Workshop on Water Quality Monitoring and Surveillance" during August 1997, recommended adoption of community based water quality monitoring and involvement of the Health Department in water quality surveillance on a continuing basis. As a follow-up, RGNDWM has been advocating

"Catchment Area Approach" involving locally available infrastructure and institutions for water quality testing at the habitation level with support from the district labs.

However, to implement the community based "Catchment Area Approach" on a large scale, availability of user friendly and reliable water quality field test kits is a prerequisite. Fortunately, as a result of efforts by NCL and DFRL user friendly and reliable water test kits are now available for testing the presence or absence of health threatening pollutants (arsenic, fluoride, nitrate and bacteriological) in drinking water supply.

Although these test kits have undergone laboratory and field checks, it is necessary to closely scrutinize their efficacy on two counts, namely, user-friendliness and reliability. Only then their potential for large scale use can be determined. Secondly, standardization of these kits may be necessary to facilitate local manufacture, training community representatives as well as decentralized marketing of these kits in district/block level shops. There is also a need for an institutional arrangement for assuring quality, receiving feedback from the users and periodical design refinement of these kits.

Time has come to make a paradigm shift in the water quality monitoring strategy to move from district laboratory based approach to the catchment area approach, involving communities, local infrastructure and district laboratories. Empowering the communities in testing water quality of their own sources is the only way for users to know if their water sources are safe and also to initiate remedial action without any delay.

Sustainability

Sustainability in rural drinking water supply has two aspects. First is the sustainability of sources and the second is sustainability of systems. The rapid increase in ground water extraction, both for the purposes of drinking water and irrigation, has caused substantial ground water depletion, as already indicated. This has affected the drinking water supply sources adversely. During summer months, the ground water depletion shows up significantly, resulting in acute scarcity of drinking water in several areas. It has also been noticed that ground water depletion has aggravated water quality problems like excess fluoride, arsenic and brackishness. This has resulted, in diseases like fluorosis and arsenical dermatitis. The need to sustain the existing water sources for drinking water supply is thus acute.

In order to tackle the problem of sustainability of sources, Sub-Missions have been established under RGNDWM. The Sub-Mission on sustainability includes projects for water conservation as well as rainwater harvesting. 5 per cent of ARWSP funds have been earmarked exclusively for the Sub-Mission on sustainability. In addition, the Ministry of Urban Development has also initiated steps to make rainwater harvesting structures mandatory in urban constructions. The Ministry of Water Resources has undertaken specific programmes to promote water harvesting measures in the States. Under Programmes like the Members of Parliament Local Area Development Scheme and the Members of Legislative Assembly Local Area Development Scheme, water harvesting schemes are to be given high priority. The State Governments have also been requested to get the ground water regulations enacted in their States to prevent haphazard location of tubewells, especially for purposes of irrigation.

The sustainability of systems is equally important. There are more than 3.5 million handpumps and over 1.5 lakh piped water supply schemes in the country already. While the investment costs so far are of the order of Rs. 35,000 crore, the estimated cost for operation and maintenance (O&M) of these systems would be around Rs. 5,000 crore per year. Though the States are permitted to utilize 15 per cent of the funds available under ARWSP for O&M of the existing systems, the gap between the total requirement of funds for O&M and the resources available is quite huge. In addition, since the people consider these assets created for water supply as government property, they do not come forward to maintain the systems. The State Government Departments, particularly the Public Health Engineering Department, is looked upon as the agency with the responsibility to maintain the water supply systems, and the role of the people has been restricted to making a mere complaint to the concerned local officer of the department. Under these circumstances, the only possible solution to make the systems sustainable appears to be to decentralize their O&M by transferring these systems to the local communities and the panchayats, who should be empowered to collect water charges from the users.

Keeping this in view, the Government of India has recently introduced the Sector Reforms Projects under ARWSP. Under these projects, which have been taken up on a pilot basis in 67 districts in 26 States, attempt has been made to institutionalize a community based demand-driven rural water supply programme, gradually replacing the existing supply-driven, centrally monitored and implemented rural water supply schemes. 20 per cent of the annual outlay under ARWSP has been earmarked for taking up projects by the State Governments to institutionalize community-based rural water supply schemes by strictly following three basic principles, namely (a) adoption of demand-responsive approach based on empowerment of villagers in the choice of scheme design, control of finances and management, so as to ensure their full participation in decision making with regard to rural water supply projects; (b) partial capital cost sharing by the community/panchayats either in cash or in kind or in both, in addition to taking full responsibility of O&M by the users and (c) shifting the role of government departments from direct service delivery to that of planning, policy formulation, monitoring and evaluation, besides partial financial support. The project area covers the entire district and the communities/panchayats are expected to share not less than 10 per cent of the capital costs.

The Sector Reforms Projects are expected to be process projects. Their main objective is not just physical implementation of a water supply scheme, but institutionalization of a new concept, which envisages enhancement of people's awareness and participation. In these projects, the communities are expected to identify their needs, discuss the various possible technology options to meet those needs, their merits, demerits and cost implications and then decide on a suitable scheme. The objective is to equip the rural population with competencies to plan, fund, control, implement, operate and maintain the rural water supply scheme of their choice themselves.

This being a rather difficult and challenging process, there have been several teething problems in the beginning and the projects have gained momentum only very recently. In most of these projects, the awareness generation and capacity building phase is just over and the installation of hardware has just commenced. The Sector Reforms Projects are implemented usually through the Zilla Panchayats and where these panchayats are not strong enough to undertake Sector Reforms Projects, they can be implemented through a District Water and Sanitation Mission (DWSM) constituted at the district level as a registered society, functioning under the overall supervision, control and guidance of the Zilla Panchayat. The funds for implementation of these projects are being released directly to the District Implementation Agencies.

On the basis of the experience gained, it has been decided to extend the Sector Reforms Projects to cover the whole country under a new programme called *Swajaldhara*, wherein water supply schemes following Sector Reforms principles can be taken up even in a smaller geographical area, namely, a village, Gram Panchayat (GP) or a Block Panchayat (BP). Unlike the Sector Reforms Projects, they need not have to cover the entire district at the initial stage, but can be extended subsequently. The *Swajaldhara* projects will be sanctioned by the Department of Drinking Water Supply, if the proposals are found to have (a) the commitment of the concerned District Implementing Agency and the State Government for compliance of reform principles; (b) 10 per cent of the estimated capital cost of the Schemes (5 per cent in case of Scheduled Castes and Scheduled Tribes Gram Panchayats/villages where 50 per cent of the population is Scheduled Caste or/and Scheduled Tribe as per 2001 census) is paid by the community, in cash, as their contribution to the Implementing Agency. The cost of the project, excluding community contribution, will be fully met by Government of India.

State Government/State Water and Sanitation Mission (SWSM) will engage the agencies undertaking rural drinking water supply programmes who will be designated as the District Implementing Agencies (DIAs) for these projects. For the implementation of the projects, the sanctioned funds will be released in two equal installments to the DIA which will be responsible to release the same to concerned Block Panchayats/Gram Panchayats/Village Water and Sanitation Committees (VWSC)/Beneficiary Groups (BGs), and also for proper management of funds. DIA would also be responsible for (a) the formulation, implementation and management of the project; (b) receipt and management of Central funds for the project; (c) selection of agencies for project implementation by BP/GP/VWSC/BG; and (d) sanctioning of the schemes and entering into bipartite/tripartite agreement between BG/GP/VWSC/BP. Providing water supply facilities in schools and NC, PC and water scarcity habitations and revival of traditional water sources to ensure drinking water sustainability will get priority under *Swajaldhara*.

- BP/GP/VWSC/BG will be responsible for—execution of the sanctioned schemes;
- place the progress of scheme implementation in each Gram Sabha meeting;
- ensure community participation in scheme activities;
- arrange community contribution towards capital cost, in cash;
- open and manage bank accounts for management of project funds;
- procure construction materials/goods and select contractors for construction activities;
- supervise construction activities;
- commission and takeover completed water supply works; and
- collect funds, and manage O&M of water supply works.

After the completion of the scheme, the same shall be commissioned and taken over for operation and maintenance by the GP/VWSC/BG in a Gram Sabha meeting. In case of implementation of schemes by any government agency, no centraly, departmental, administrative or overhead charges will be admissible. Under *Swajaldhara*, one time operation and maintenance grant would be released to BG/GP/VWSC/BP within 6 months of takeover of the schemes by them. This start up grant is not in lieu of community contribution for O&M but to maintain as O&M revolving fund and will be sanctioned on case-to-case basis. The O&M grant will be considered for release only after assessing the actual costs of operation and maintenance of the scheme.

HRD and IEC

Human Resource Development (HRD) and Information, Education and Communication (IEC) activities are the key support requirements for any successful community-based development programme. In 1994, the Government of India launched a National Human Resource Development Programme (NHRDP) specifically in the water supply sector. Under this programme, two types of orientation courses are designed—one for the grassroots level workers at the village level and the other for the sector professionals. Workshops are also organized for stakeholders at the District and State levels to improve coordination in their activities. The HRD programme aims at training functionaries of the Panchayati Raj Institutions (PRIs) with the objective of enabling them to take up O&M activities. It also aims at capacity building of local communities by giving requisite training to mechanics, health motivators, masons, etc. especially women to operate and maintain handpumps and the components of other water supply systems.

The information, education and communication (IEC) strategy introduced alongside the NHRDP is now under implementation in 55 pilot districts. The emphasis of IEC programmes has been the frontloading of software with the objective of generating mass awareness regarding the need for safe drinking water and also on health related issues. The programme also focuses on the need for the community to participate in decision making and empowering them to effectively participate in the water supply programmes. The service of the State publicity/public relations department have also been utilized to provide adequate publicity to the rural water supply programmes through the mass media to disseminate information about the programme as well as emphasizing the use of safe water to overcome water borne diseases, etc. Treating water as a socio-economic good and the need to conserve the same are also highlighted through appropriate methods like folk songs, dramas, documentary films, plays and other local means suited to the area.

A national level Management Information Systems (MIS) programme for effective planning, monitoring and implementation of various activities under Rural Water Supply and Sanitation Sector also has been designed by the RGNDWM. The system provides for : (i) maintenance of micro-level status of water supply to ensure planning and monitoring; (ii) assistance for computer facilities up to division level in phases to ensure latest technology for processing and storing data and its communication from one office to another; (iii) assistance for conducting training programmes; and (iv) development of customized software for enabling States/UTs to fully utilize computer systems for planning, monitoring and implementation of various activities in the sector. The Mission also provides financial assistance to the States/UTs to take up computerization of the rural water supply sector in a phased manner.

Strategy for the Future

As mentioned earlier, the three-key challenges in the rural water supply sector in the country today relate to full coverage of all habitations with potable drinking water, water quality problems and sustainability. In view of the reported slippages of several FC habitations into the category of PC and NC habitations, the ideal starting point should be to take up a fresh survey of all rural habitations to assess the coverage status as on a particular date, say 1st January, 2003. If in a particular village, potable drinking water is available for the public even through a private drinking water source, that can be taken as a PC/FC village, depending upon the quantity of water available. Each State should have the list of NC and PC habitations as on 1st January, 2002, which will constitute the benchmark for further development in the rural water supply sector. A two-pronged attack will be mounted—first to sustain the sources in the FC habitations and the second to identify sources for the NC and PC habitations in a scientific manner. The NC and PC villages should be taken up on priority basis for execution of schemes preferably under the *Swajaldhara*, as that would ensure their sustainability.

Remote sensing and GIS have emerged as powerful tools in the management of natural resources. India has been launching its own remote sensing satellites with increasing capabilities. Good amount of ground facilities and infrastructure have also been established to generate quality information. The remote sensing techniques can be used to identify the location of drinking water wells in the NC and PC habitations, which can be updated periodically. A survey/census of all drinking water sources requiring rejuvenation must also be undertaken so that a plan of action can be drawn up for augmentation under the *Swajaldhara* mode with people's participation/community contribution. Sinking of new borewells should be avoided to the maximum extent possible, as that would deplete the ground water levels further. Only in exceptional cases, new borewells can be sunk, subject however to the condition that a water harvesting structure should be simultaneously established in the catchment area of that borewell. The expertise available with National Remote Sensing Agency (NRSA), Hyderabad, should be made use of to identify points where the new borewells can be sunk and the supporting water harvesting structures can be constructed.

There is a need to reduce the allocation under the supply-driven top-down ARWSP and correspondingly increase the allocations under *Swajaldhara* in a phased manner. ARWSP will be gradually restricted to dealing with research (including action research) on quality and sustainability issues, in addition to meeting natural calamities and emergent situations. As a matter of policy, the communities/panchayats should own, operate and maintain the water supply schemes meant for them. The State and Central Governments should facilitate the smooth transfer of assets, wherever necessary, by bringing in suitable policy changes.

The concept of community participation in India is still in a transient stage. It has to gradually move into community ownership. The communities have to be motivated to convert themselves into responsible civil society organizations to manage water resources sustainably. There should be a clear distinction between the primary stakeholders and supportive stakeholders in the process of decision making. Local community as the primary stakeholder should take key decisions. They should be supported by other structures such as the State and local governments, the NGOs and other technical institutions who have the knowledge base. The role of support structures and institutions should be to provide technical and financial support to the primary stakeholders. The existing water managers should gradually upgrade their technical outlook to get a professional perspective. Their role should be to provide the technological options to the people and assist them in making their choice, keeping the sustainability and cost effectiveness of systems in view.

There is an urgent need for a water legislation and a clear water policy at the State and Central levels. Water has to be realized as an economic good, in addition to being a basic right for the citizens. It has to be priced appropriately for all uses. While full cost recovery has to be insisted upon for economic use, a reasonable pricing may have to be necessary for other uses, if need be, by adopting principles of cross subsidization. The IEC programmes should concentrate on water conservation and educate the people on water being a precious and scarce resource. Private rights in ground water should not come in the way of treatment of ground water as a common pool resource.

In the case of surface water, there should be no ownership or proprietary rights on the part of any individual or institution, who may at best have only usufructory rights. Even the State does not own the water, but merely has the power to legislate and regulate. State regulation over the use of water, whether ground water or surface water, is very necessary, but it should not undermine the rights and responsibilities of the civil society. The regulations of ground water extraction and the maintenance of ground water quality should, therefore, provide for involvement of the community in the various control systems to be effected.

At present, there is no comprehensive water legislation reflecting the diverse aspects of water, namely, water as a scarce and precious resource; water as a basic right; conservation of water; social justice and equity in its distribution; use and control. There is also a need to bring in a regulation, which should have provisions to control the present tendencies to disturb the catchment areas and sand quarrying in river beds. All local bodies should be made responsible for maintenance of all water bodies within their jurisdiction, as envisaged under the Constitution (Seventy-Third) Amendment Act. The reform principles now adopted under *Swajaldhara* have to be universalized and all schemes taken up for water supply, even with external assistance should, as a rule, have community participation, both in designing and in O&M of the water supply schemes in future.

The quality of both surface and ground water sources have to be monitored periodically. A methodology for water quality monitoring by the panchayats/communities at local levels has to be evolved and adopted quickly. Technological solutions have to be found for effectively dealing with quality problems through local research institutions. Adopting locally acceptable solutions by the communities will have to be consciously encouraged.

Recharge of ground water through Watershed development programmes have to be promoted for sustaining drinking water sources in the rural areas. A massive national level awareness campaign will have to be launched on rainwater harvesting as a simple and effective means of utilizing rainwater directly for domestic purposes. The awareness campaign should be followed up with simple messages on rainwater harvesting along with information on actual rainwater harvesting structures that can be put up by individuals as well as communities. The standardization of such structures by agencies, like the Bureau of Indian Standards, can be taken up thereafter so that government and non-government agencies can promote the production of such structures on a commercially viable scale. Rainwater harvesting can also be permitted as a means of flood mitigation and should be encouraged in the storm water management systems of local bodies. Individual house owners should be encouraged to allow flow of surface water to residential premises for ground water recharge.

Legislation and enforcement through building plan regulations and development control rules in both urban and rural areas will be necessary for ensuring wider and full coverage of rainwater harvesting by all sections of the society. Traditional rainwater harvesting methods and traditional wisdom for improving water quality available in different parts of the country should be actively reintroduced with appropriate modifications relevant to the present day conditions. The government as well as non-government agencies must not only document such wisdom, but also take an active part in reviving them for location-specific applications. The involvement of schools, youth and women's groups will also be necessary to make rainwater harvesting campaign a mass movement.

Finally, data from government and non-government agencies on rainfall, hydrogeological conditions, locations for potential recharge, rate of permeability of different soils and all other information relevant to rural water supply as well as rainwater harvesting should be made available periodically through government publications/website. This would help the agencies, institutions and communities making full use of the information, not only for research but also for propagation and implementation of programmes. There should be transparency and willingness to exchange data between government, national and international agencies and the voluntary organisations. Making available fresh water to the ever-increasing population to meet their needs is a dynamic problem, which cannot be left to the government alone. It has to be the joint responsibility of the governments, civil society organizations and also the community.

6

Blue Revolution

A Step towards Water Conservation and Management, small holder irrigation, drainage and waste water reuse, to achieve sustainable public health engineering and food security, and ushering in Second Green Revolution in India

A.M. MICHAEL

Water is a precious natural resource, a basic human need and a prime national asset. The extent to which water is plentiful or scarce, clean or polluted, beneficial or destructive, greatly influence the extent and quality of human life. Rapid development of human civilisation and advances in science and technology are changing the condition of life on earth, emanating basic transformations of the environment. Ever increasing population growth and the resulting rise in the demand for water require careful planning and management of the limited water resources. In India, the annual population growth is about 2 per cent per year. It is necessary that the food production is increased by about 2.5 per cent annually in order to provide a better food intake than at present. The available water resources are to be optimally harnessed and beneficially utilized with appropriate priorities of use.

The competing demands for water are for irrigation, industry, domestic water supply, hydro-power generation and environmental management. Provisions for water transport, recreation and fresh water fisheries are also to be considered. World-wide water use has increased over ten-fold during the 20th century. There has been a sharp rise in water use in the second half of the 20th century. The demand rate in each of the sectors will further increase in the 21st century to meet the need of better living standards. Water is unevenly distributed over the world and is usually scarce in many of the regions where the mass of the people live. There are large seasonal variations. For example, large parts of India and Bangladesh suffer from floods during the monsoon period, which is followed by a period of water shortage. Water scarcity is not a general phenomenon but is a regionally, locally and seasonally specific problem. The UN Water Conference held at Mar del Plata(Argentina) in 1977 drew attention to the basic lacuna in water management in several countries. The 1992 the International Conference on Water and Environment in Dublin, Ireland, laid major emphasis on the need for intensive and serious consideration at different levels on the limited availability of water and the possibilities of exploiting and managing the earth's fresh water resources. The Dublin Statement (1992) on Water and Sustainable Development and Agenda 21 of the UN Conference (1992) in Rio de Janeiro stressed on the need for intensive efforts to appropriately develop and efficiently manage the world's scarce fresh water resource, based on a participatory approach involving users, planners and policy makers at all levels. It was emphasised that water has an economic value in all its competing uses and should be recognised as an economic good. It was pointed out that women play a major role in the provision, management and safeguarding of water and their effective involvement in efficient water management is important. To take advantage of the information and technology developed and made available globally, the Global Water Partnership was established in 1996. It has been stressed that in order to manage water efficiently for continued human development, the competing uses for water must be reconciled.

Diverse Uses of Water

The diverse uses of water can be broadly classified as (i) offstream use and (ii) instream use. Offstream use involves the consumption of water as is the case in its use for irrigation, domestic and industrial water supply and thermal and nuclear power generation. Offstream use of water in India in 1999 was 92 per cent for irrigation, 5 per cent for domestic use and 3 per cent for industry. Instream use does not involve the consumption of water.

It includes the use for hydro-electric power generation, fisheries, navigation and recreation.

Irrigation: Irrigation is the artificial application of water to soil for crop production to supplement the water available from rainfall, soil moisture in the crop root zone and the contribution to soil moisture from ground water. In may areas of the world the amount and timing of the rainfall are not adequate to meet the moisture requirement of crops and irrigation is essential to raise crops necessary to meet the food and fiber requirements of the growing population. With the population growth rate of about 2 per cent, there is need to increase the irrigated area and obtain optimum productivity levels of crops to the maximum possible extent.

Water requirement for domestic use: Water for drinking is a basic human need. In addition, community water supply has to meet the needs for cooking, washing, bathing and sanitation. The water use for community water supply in India in the year 1989 was 25 cu.km. It was estimated to reach 34 cu.km by the year 2000. The estimate for the year 2025 is 52 cu.km, based on projections in population rise.

Water requirement for industries: The requirement of water in the industrial sector is usually high especially in mining, chemicals, fertilizers, petrochemicals, paper and pulp, and textiles. The National Commission on Integrated Water Resources Development Plan (NCIWRD) in 1999 has estimated the water requirement for industrial development as 37cu.km, 67 cu.km and 103 cu.km for the years 2010, 2025 and 2050, respectively, based on the demand rates of water prevailing in 1998-99. However, the NCIWRDP (1999) projected an alternative figure of 81 cu.km for the year 2050, assuming that by then the industries would adopt major water saving technology in industrial production and it would be possible to utilize 80 per cent of the industrial effluent after proper treatment. On this consideration there would be a reduction in the water requirement of 67 cu.km estimated for the year 2025. It is estimated that 70 per cent of the industrial water requirement would be met from surface water sources and the remaining 30 per cent from ground water.

Water requirement for power development: Water use in power generation includes both offstream and instream uses. Offstream uses are for thermal and nuclear power generation while the instream use is for hydro-power generation. Coal, petroleum oil and gas are used for thermal power plants. Coal-based thermal power plants and hydro-power have been the mainstay of electricity generation in India. Oil, natural gas and nuclear power account for a smaller portion of the total power supply. The installed capacity of thermal, hydro-electric and nuclear power stations are around 73 per cent, 24 per cent and 3 per cent, respectively. Hydro-electricity is still an underutilized resource potential. The consumptive use of water by thermal power plants in India in the year 1989 was about 4 cu.km. It was to increase to 6 cu.km by the year 2000. For nuclear power plants, with projected installed capacity of 10,000 MW by the year 2000, the estimated consumptive use of water was 0.3 cu. km. It is estimated that India has harnessed only about 15 per cent of its hydro-power potential. Hydro-electrical source of power generation is low in cost, renewable, clean and pollution free. The consumptive use component of water for hydro-power generation is only by way of evaporation from the reservoirs. Thus, there is great scope for hydro-power development in India.

Inland water transport: In comparison to road and rail transport, inland water transport is low in cost. The consumptive use of water in this sector is insignificant.

Fisheries: There is considerable scope for substantially increasing fisheries production on scientific lines in inland water bodies, water conveyance systems and storage reservoirs.

Water requirement for protection of environment and ecology: Increasing water shortage and water pollution are major ecological concerns. In India, the dense forests which was estimated at 40 per cent of land area in the early part of the 20th century has reduced to less than 14 per cent by the year 2000. Many of the rivers now carry polluted water during non-monsoon periods. Protection, enhancement and restoration of water quality and prevention of water pollution are essential for providing safe drinking water and maintaining human health. It is also important for sustaining land quality, and agricultural and industrial production.

Water requirement for environmental protection comprise of (i) the requirement for forestry and tree planting, and (ii) the requirement for the abatement of water pollution and maintaining safe quality for drinking and other uses in the streams/rivers/ponds/reservoirs. The water requirement for afforestation is mostly met from rainfall and soil moisture and water conservation programmes in the catchment areas. The major contributor of water pollution is urban sewage. Industrial waste, though small in volume contributes significantly to the pollution load. There are many instances of high pollution from irrigated lands using heavy doses of fertilizers and insecticides. Estimation of the quantity of water required for managing ecological standards for all water bodies, including lakes and rivers on sustainable basis is difficult at present suitable methods will have to be evolved and operationalised for an effective ecological protection system. The (NCIWRDP 1999) has made a token provision of 5 cu.km, 10 cu.km, and 20 cu.km of water for ecological management in India for the years 2010, 2025 and 2050, respectively.

Sustainable Development and Management of Water Resources

Sustainable development and management of water resources will require a holistic approach and simultaneous attention to all aspects of water use and management. Some of the issues causing much concern and threaten sustainability relate to water quality management across the sectors, including ecology and environment, waterlogging, salt problems in agriculture and absence of on-farm drainage. Conjunctive use of surface and groundwater, utilisation of canal flows during non-demand periods in agriculture, rapid silting up of reservoirs and river beds and increases flood damages due to uncontrolled development of catchment areas and watersheds, water quality management of lakes and tanks, recycling and proper treatment of industrial effluents and lack of adequate attention to preventive and regular maintenance of water infrastructure are the major problems to be addressed.

A major challenge today is to introduce economies in agricultural, municipal and industrial water use. The efficiency level of water use in irrigation in the developing countries is only 25-40 per cent. Water losses in the cities of developing countries are usually about 50 per cent and above. These high losses could be greatly reduced by the application of appropriate technology in the respective fields. Major areas of wastage of water in canal irrigation are under utilisation of night supplies, canal flow going waste in non-demand seasons due to lack of crop diversification and absence of storage tanks/reservoirs within the command area (system storage), improper canal water releases, excessive seepage losses in water conveyance systems, field-to-field irrigation in rice crops and unscientific irrigation methods. Conveyance losses are often high in urban water supply systems as well. Leaking pipelines, resulting from corrosion and incrustation in pipes and faulty pipe joints coupled with intermittent water supply result in serious water pollution problems.

Contamination of water with harmful and pathogenic substances is a major problem of the industrialised countries. In developing countries also it is on the increase. The factors influencing contamination are untreated or inadequately treated industrial effluents, and contamination by mining. Dumping municipal waste on lands at higher reaches of streams and rivers and its flow into waterways is a serious problem. In India it is reported that only a few of the cities are having satisfactory wastewater treatment plants. Poor quality drinking water, in combination with inadequate sanitary conditions at the domestic and industrial levels, are the major causes of the high incidence of diseases, especially among children in the developing countries.

India's Water Budget

India is a vast country with extremes of climate. Rainfall varies from 100mm in western Rajasthan to over 11000mm at Cherapunji in Meghalaya in the north-east. Variability of annual and seasonal rainfall at the same place is high, resulting in droughts and floods. One-third area of India is drought-prone, while over one-eighth is flood-prone. India's topography comprises of towering mountain ranges rolling hills lofty plateaus and extensive plains traversed by major rivers. The presence of the great mountain mass formed by the Himalayas and its spurs in the north and of the Indian Ocean on the south are the two major physical features influencing the climate of India. The Himalayas provide an impenetrable barrier to the influence of cold winds from Central Asia and gives the subcontinent the elements of tropical type of climate. The Indian Ocean is the source of cool moisture-laden winds reaching India and giving it the elements of the oceanic type of climate. India has great diversity and a variety of climate, and extremes of weather conditions. The climate ranges from continental to oceanic, from extremes of heat and cold and from aridity and negligible rainfall to excessive humidity and heavy rainfall. The climatic factors profoundly influence the availability and utilisation of water resources.

Precipitation: The basic source of water is precipitation in the form of rainfall or snowfall. Runoff from precipitation drains through streams and rivers or collects in surface depressions forming tanks or ponds. Water of streams and rivers is stored in reservoirs or is diverted directly through canal systems for irrigation. Runoff water stored in tanks or ponds is also regulated for irrigation through suitable control and conveyance systems. A part of the rainfall is stored as soil moisture and groundwater.

Rainfall in India varies from place to place and from year to year. The annual average rainfall of the country is about 1200mm which when considered over the geographical area of over 328 million ha amounts to 390 million ha-metres. The contribution of snowfall is estimated to range from 80-100 mm. Thus the total precipitation amounts to 400 million ha-metres. Rainfall in India is dependent in different degrees on the south-west and north-east monsoons, on shallow cyclonic depressions and disturbances and on violent local storms which form in regions where cool humid winds from the sea meet hot dry winds from the land (which occasionally reach cyclonic dimensions). Most of the rainfall in India takes place under the influence of south-west monsoon between June to September. The south-west monsoon starting from the equatorial belt comes over the Indian sub-continent in two distinct wind currents known as the Bay of Bengal branch and the Arabian sea branch. The influence of the north-east monsoon is mainly in the south-eastern and the southern parts of the country spread over the eastern regions of Tamil Nadu, Andhra Pradesh and most parts of Kerala during the months of October and November.

When rain falls, a portion of it soon evaporates from the ground or the vegetation that may intercept it, another portion infiltrates into the soil and the rest flows away over the land surface as runoff. It is estimated that out of the average annual precipitation of 400 million ha-metres, about 70 million ha-metres is lost to the atmosphere. Of the remaining 330 million ha-metres, about 115 million ha-metres flows as surface runoff and the rest 215 million ha-metres infiltrates into the ground, a part of which joins the streams as subsurface flow. The Irrigation Commission of India (1972) and the National Commission on Agriculture (1976) placed the total annual surface water flows in India at 180 million ha-metres. It includes about 20 million ha-metres brought in by streams and rivers from catchments lying outside the country. About 45 million ha-metres of water that pertain to regenerated flow from ground water as assessed from river flow during non-rainy months. The remaining 115 million ha-metres constitute direct contribution by precipitation, of which about 10 million ha-metres is received as snowfall. The latest estimate of the Central Water Commission on surface water flows in India is 185 million ha-metres.

While the above figure of 185 million ha-metres represents the average annual surface water runoff available, the amount of water that can actually be put to beneficial use is much less. India has monsoon climate. Over 90 per cent of the annual runoff in peninsular rivers and over 80 per cent of the annual runoff in Himalayan rivers occur during the four monsoon months of June to September. There is need to store maximum possible water in surface reservoirs during this period. The Central Water Commission has estimated that within the limitations of topography, legal constraints and the technology of water development available at present, the utilizable water from surface structures is about 69 million ha-metres only (about 30% of the total).

Soil moisture and ground water recharge: Of the annual rainfall and snowfall of 400 million ha-metres, about 215 million ha-metres infiltrates into the soil. A major part of it, amounting to about 165 million ha-metres, is retained as soil moisture to support the growth of vegetation. After the soil has absorbed water to its field capacity the water starts percolating down to water table and adds to the ground water reservoir. The contribution of rainfall to ground water in any area depends upon the intensity of rainfall, the depth of soil and its permeability and the nature of vegetative cover. It has been estimated that on an average about 12.5 per cent of the precipitation infiltrates to the ground water table. This amounts to about 29 million ha-metres. Various soil and water conservation measures further increase the amount of ground water recharge in an area during the rainy season when the rivers are in high stages of flow their water surface in many areas are higher than the surrounding land. Some river flow therefore seeps to the adjoining land area and adds to ground water. Such an addition in an average year is estimated to be about 5 million ha-metres. Another source of substantial contribution to ground water is from canal irrigation systems in irrigation command areas through seepage from the water conveyance systems and percolation below the crop root zone in irrigated fields. Deep percolation losses are large in wetland rice areas. In other areas also the losses are high inadequately levelled fields and under faulty surface irrigation methods. Ground water contribution from these sources could be as high as rainfall contribution. Such a situation calls for intensive efforts to step up ground water utilization in canal command areas.

Groundwater: Groundwater occurs in the zone of saturation below the land surface. Ground water is in a dynamic state and moves slowly. Part of the ground water is in the form of subsurface flow, a major part of which joins the surface water bodies like streams, rivers and tanks. However, a sizable part of ground water is retained in the porous strata, commonly known as aquifer as groundwater storage, which is available for extraction. The quantity of water, which can be extracted economically every year is considered as the groundwater potential of an area. It implies that water extracted in any year should be returned to the aquifers in the form of recharge from the succeeding precipitation, so that over a cycle of 2, 3, or 5 years the groundwater table does not go down progressively. The groundwater has two components, namely, static and dynamic. The static fresh water, comprise of the quantity of water that lies in the aquifer zones below the level of water table fluctuation. Generally, the static water resource is not regularly replenished on an annual basis. The dynamic resource is replenished annually. As per the National Water Policy, in general, the development of groundwater resource is to be limited to the dynamic component of groundwater. When there is over-exploitation of groundwater, the water table goes down. Such over-exploitations have occurred at many places in India. This has induced saline waters of the sea into the coastal areas at several places or has resulted in lowering of water table below the economic level of pumping.

Based on the occurrence of water in geological formations, nature and extent of groundwater bodies and flow characteristics, the Central Ground Water Board has generalised the geo-hydrological formations of India as (i) unconsolidated formations, (ii) semi-consolidated formations, and (iii) consolidated formations. The alluvial formations of the Indo-Gangetic plains and the coastal alluvial belts are the important unconsolidated formations of India. Semi-consolidated formations are composed chiefly of shale, sandstone and limestone of the north-western region and the terrestrial deposits of the Deccan region. A large portion of the country, extending to about 120 million ha comprise of consolidated hard rock formation. The water yields of such formations is low. The yield of ground water in semi-consolidated formations is moderate. There are large areas of unconsolidated alluvial formations which include valleys like Kashmir, the Indus basin, Ganga-Brahmaputra-Meghana basin, and coastal regions (especially of the east coast) which yield substantial quantities of ground water. There is a narrow band of artesian ground water reservoir just below the Himalayas adjoining the sub-mountain tracts. A broad assessment of ground water resources of India has been attempted by the Central Ground Water Board. It is estimated that the annual utilizable ground water resource of India constitute about 423 cu.km and the current level of utilisation is about 25 per cent of the total utilizable resource.

In areas having shallow water aquifers, it is economical to utilise ground water, as compared to surface water through storage reservoirs and canal systems. Ground water accounts for about 50 per cent of the water utilised in irrigation, 80 per cent water for domestic use in rural areas and 50 per cent water for urban and industrial uses.

The management of ground water resources of India requires detailed studies to regulate and maintain a hydrological balance so that ground water is exploited on a sustainable basis. For accurate assessment of ground water resources, detailed and reliable information relating to hydro-geological formations and the water balance of the various river basins of the entire country are necessary. The utilizable ground water potential of India is limited and is to be utilised judicially.

Presently, the ground water available at a place is considered as the property of the landowner. In many of the developed countries the ownership of the land does not permit the land owner to utilise the ground water indiscriminately. In view of the importance of ground water, the Government of India, Ministry of Agriculture, as far back as 1970 drafted a model bill called Ground Water Control and Regulation Bill and circulated it to all the states for possible adoption by the State Governments. However, only a few states have enacted laws providing for the rational use of ground water in some of the regions of the respective states.

Conjunctive Use of Surface and Ground Water

The basic source of water for both surface water and ground water is the same, namely, precipitation. Conjunctive use is the management of all water resources of an area, including surface and ground water, in a harmonious manner such that the total water use in the area over a period of time is optimised. Normally, under such a use, the combined availability of water is more than that is available from the separate components of the two sources in that region. Conjunctive use mitigates the problems of high water table and salinity resulting from canal irrigation and facilitates the use of high salinity ground water by dilution with canal water cannot otherwise be used directly for irrigation.

Several of the existing canal irrigation systems in India suffer from inadequate supplies. The available supply in most of the canal systems in northern India, for instance, is often only a fourth to a third of the amount needed for intensive agriculture. The total quantity of irrigation water is neither adequate nor is supplied satisfactorily in time. This calls for making combined or conjunctive use of surface and ground waters wherever possible.

The conjunctive use of surface and ground waters can take the form of full utilization of surface water supplies, supplemented by ground water or the direct use of ground water during periods of low canal supplies or canal closures. It can also take the form of irrigating a part of the canal command area exclusively with ground water.

Conjunctive use of surface and ground water may be planned to augment canal supplies, to combat waterlogging and facilitate irrigation with poor quality ground water. An outstanding example of conjunctive use which has shown spectacular results in rice cultivation is the raising of paddy nurseries, utilizing ground water so that the seedlings are ready for transplanting at the time of the onset of the monsoon, which often coincides with the release of canal supplies as well. It provides for early start of the transplanted crop, the growth period of which is covered mostly during the monsoon season. The early harvesting resulting from the above practice will allow time for seedbed preparation of the succeeding rabi crop. The conjunctive use of surface and ground water will substantially increase the irrigation potential of an area and will lead to efficient use of the land and water resources. Conjunctive use technology in water resources utilization is situation specific. Appropriate technologies for conjunctive use should be developed to effectively implement the programme. Such programmes often call for active involvement of the beneficiary farmers in the programme.

India: Physiography, Soil Resources, Land Holdings, Cropping Systems

Physiography: The origin, distribution and utilization of water resources of any country are profoundly influenced by its physiography, climate and soils. The diversity of land forms in India is matched by the diversity of its climate, its people and its cultures. Towering mountain ranges, rolling hills, lofty plateaus and extensive plains, have all played major roles in shaping the physical features of the country and the cultural, economic and political history of its people. Physiographically, India can be divided into the following seven regions: (i) the northern mountains, (ii) the great plains, (iii) the central highlands, (iv) the peninsular plateau, (v) the east coast belt, (vi) the west coast belt, and (vii) the islands. Each region has its own specific adaptability to water management requirements.

Soil Resources: Soil, water and air are basic to the sustenance of life on earth. Man has been relying on the soil for his sustenance for food, cloths and shelter. The pressure on land has increased to an extent that the relationship between the living beings and the soil has become critical. Deforestation, accelerated soil erosion, deterioration of soil physical environment, increasing waterlogging and salinity in canal irrigated areas, declining water table due to over-exploitation of ground water, poor management of rain water, lower efficiency in water use and fertilizer and agro-chemicals, and rapid industrialization coupled with pollution and environmental degradation have aggravated the deterioration of our precious soil resources.

The cultivable area of India is estimated to be 186 million ha. The cultivated area at the end of 1993-94 was about 142 million ha. Because of pressure on land due to increasing population it may not be possible to increase the area under cultivation. The cultivated area is expected to stabilise at 140 to 145 million ha. ea. Nearly all cultivable area which can be brought under rainfed farming is already cropped. Further increase in cropped area is possible only by bringing more area under irrigation and by increasing irrigation intensities. About 80 per cent of the cultivated area in India is under food grains. The productivity of irrigated land on an average in 2000 A.D. has been about 2.5 tonnes/ha and 0.7 tonnes/ha for rainfed land. This is low compared to world standards. With advances in technology and breakthrough in scientific farming practices it is possible to increase the productivity levels of irrigated and unirrigated lands to over 3.5 to 5 tonnes/ha and over 1 to 2 tonnes/ha, respectively within a short time span. To achieve a production of 450 million tonnes of food grains by the year 2050, it is necessary to bring at least 150 ha under irrigation, out of which 120 million ha should be under food crops. The gross area under rainfed agriculture in 2050 should increase by about 40 million ha, of which about 30 million ha would be covered by food crops. To increase the productivity of rainfed agriculture, effective watershed management to increase productivity is necessary. Introduction of supplementary irrigation inasmuch area as possible, adopting water harvesting procedures, will be of great benefit.

Land Holdings, Land Utilization and Cropping SystemsL: The land holdings of India are predominantly of small size. Marginal size holdings (<1 ha) with an average size of 0.4 ha constitute 59 per cent and small holdings of 1 to 2 ha size constitute 19 per cent of the total land holdings. Semi-medium holdings of 2 to 4 ha account for 13.2 per cent and the rest are medium (7.2%) and large (1.6%). Increasing fragmentation of land holdings adversely affects crop production. In the recent past, the evolution of the cultivated area has presented two distinct phases. From 1950 to 1970 the cultivated area rose by 1.8 per cent a year, while the cropping intensity increased from 1.11 per cent to 1.18 per cent. From 1970 to 1990 the cultivated area rose by 2 per cent per year while the cropping intensity increased to 130 per cent.

The major cereals grown are rice, wheat, maize, barley, sorghum, ragi and pearl millet. Food grains cultivation formed 70 per cent of the total cropped area, consisting of 57 per cent under cereals and 13 per cent under pulses. Among the cereals rice and wheat formed 23 per cent and 13 per cent, respectively of the total cropped area. The percentage of cropped area under rice remained almost constant at 23 per cent from the year 1950-51 to 1992-93. For wheat also it remained constant at 13 per cent for the period 1980-81 to 1992-93, while for earlier period it varied from 8 per cent to 11 per cent from 1950-51 to 1970-71. There is a declining trend in the area under sorghum, pearl millet, barley and coarse cereals. Declining trend has been observed in case of gram also which has come down to 3 per cent in 1992-93 from 6 per cent in 1950-51. The area under sugarcane increased from 1.3 per cent in 1950-51 to 2.2 per cent in 1992-93. There has been an appreciable increase in the area under fruits and vegetables (from 1.7% in 1950-51 to 3.7 per cent in 1992-93). The proportion of total oilseeds increased from 8 per cent in 1950-51 to 14 per cent in 1992-93. The area under cotton has remained constant at about 4 per cent. The average cereal yield increased from 522 kg/ha in 1950-51 to 11457kg/ha in 1992, i.e. an average annual growth rate of 2.5 per cent.

The net rainfed cropped area of India is 91.8 million ha. Forests occupy 22.4 per cent of the total geographical area. However, many forests are under varying degrees of degradation in spite of stringent laws for their maintenance. The remaining area are grouped into area under non-agricultural uses (7.2%), barren and uncultivable land (6.2%), pasture and grazing land (3.7%), groves and tree crops (1.2%), cultivable waste land (4.7%), current fallows (4.7%) and other fallows (3.2%).

Surface Water Sources

Precipitation in the form of rainfall occurs only for a few days in a year. Hence, there is a need to conserve it in the soil profile, aquifers, ponds, lakes, reservoirs and rivers for use during the dry periods. The management of surface and ground water resources requires a thorough understanding of the hydrology of the surface and ground water systems, agro-eco systems, soil-water-plant-environment interactions, existing and expected demands of water, availability of energy for pumping and social dynamics. For sustained agricultural production it is necessary to manage and utilize the water resources optimally so that (i) both surface and ground water supplies are maintained at the desired level, and (ii) the quality of land and water resources does not deteriorate with time.

Water for irrigation is obtained from natural streams or rivers, from surface reservoirs and from underground reservoirs. Flood water from rivers is collected in surface reservoirs by constructing dams at suitable sites and by diverting water by constructing weirs/barrages at appropriate locations. Runoff water from small areas can be collected by constructing ponds or tanks. Ground water is utilized by constructing wells and installing pumps or other water lifts. Water from surface reservoirs or diversion points is conveyed through canals. Canals run from higher to lower elevations and water flows in them by the force of gravity.

Based on whether the source of water is above or below the field surface, irrigation is classified into two types: (i) flow irrigation where the water reaches the field from the source by gravity flow, and lift irrigation requiring the water to be raised or lifted from its source to the field surface.

River Systems of India: India is blessed with a large number of big and small rivers, the sweet waters of which can be put to many uses such as drinking, other domestic needs, agricultural and industrial uses, navigation, recreation, power generation and other uses. In the national strategy for water resources utilization, drinking water requirement is given priority over all other needs.

The river systems of India can be classified into four groups, namely (i) Himalayan rivers, (ii) Deccan rivers, (iii) coastal rivers, and (iv) rivers of the inland drainage basins. The Himalayan rivers derive their flow from rainfall runoff and by melting of snows and glaciers. Therefore, they have nearly continuous flow throughout the year. During the monsoon months, Himalayas receive heavy rainfall and rivers swell, causing frequent floods. The Deccan rivers are rainfed. Hence, they have major fluctuations in the volume of flow. Many of them are non-perennial. The coastal rivers, especially on the west coast, are short in length and have limited catchment areas. Most of them are non-perennial. The streams of inland drainage basins of western Rajasthan are few and far apart. They drain into salt lakes like Sambhar, or disappear in sands with no outlet to the sea.

Water resource regions can be planned on the basis of river basins which are the natural physiographical units. A river basin has a defined watershed boundary. It has relationship with ground water resources in most of the cases. The development of a balanced plan for water resources utilization requires detailed knowledge of the quantity, quality and distribution of water resources over space and time. Information on the changing pattern of land use in the entire watershed and its influence on the river flows are required.

The Ganga-Brahmaputra-Meghana basin is the largest in India, receiving water from an area which comprises about one-quarter of the total area of India. The second largest basin is that of Godavary which covers about 10 per cent of the total area of India.

The average annual surface water flows in India has been estimated as 1869 billion cu.m, of which only 690 billion cu.m can be utilized, if appropriate storages can be created. The reason for this major difference between availability and possible utilization is due to the monsoon climate as well as topographical and geological limitations. Due to the monsoon climate almost the entire surface flow is limited to about 4 months of the year and the spatial and temporal distribution of rainfall is so uneven that annual averages have little significance for practical purposes. About one-third of the country is under threat of drought, not necessarily due deficient rainfall but many times due to its uneven occurrence.

At the end of 1996-97 the gross irrigation potential created was 90.8 million ha, against 22.6 million ha in 2000, the expansion of irrigation system along with the increased use of fertilizers, high yielding crop varieties and scientific agronomic practices have substantially increased the production of major crops, especially wheat and rice, between 1950-51 and 1996-97. India has been able to successfully combat severe droughts like the one in 1987-88, the worst of the country.

Cropping Systems and Water Management

The primary objective in the development of an irrigation system is to increase agricultural production on a sustained basis. Plants vary in their requirements for water and adaptability to environment. Irrigation systems are planned to meet the water requirement of crops under a specified cropping system. Alternatively, cropping patterns can be modified to suit the availability on water in a project and its distribution in space and time. Water requirements of crops can be met from rainfall contribution, soil moisture storage in the crop root zone, capillary rise from shallow ground water, and by irrigation from canals and ground water pumping or canal or river water through lift irrigation systems. All these components of the water source of an area should be taken into account while planning cropping systems in an irrigated area.

Cropping pattern of an area is determined by many factors, including the type of soil, climate, rainfall characteristics, farmer's requirement of food grains for self-consumption and market supply and net rate of financial gain resulting from various alternative crops that can be grown in the area. Assured water supply will induce the farmer to change over to more profitable crops which could not be grown before the introduction of irrigation, provided the soils are suitable and the expected rates of net return from such crops are high. The climate of a place influences almost all the parameters of a crop production enterprise, including processing and the marketing of the produce. Long term planning needs a clear vision for land and water resource management, keeping in view the constraints regarding their availability, productivity, technology available and environmental impacts.

A major opportunity of increasing crop yields and water use efficiency in a particular environment is to select plant species adapted to the available amount and distribution of water. The plant characteristics influencing water requirements include the length of growing season, extensiveness of the root system, leaf area, and distribution and size of stomata. The selection of the crop and its species are vital. Research efforts in plant breeding have contributed greatly in increasing the efficiency of the applied water to a given area. Today the farmer can select specific varieties of a particular crop to suit the amount of water and its availability at different stages of the growth of the crop. There are early sown and late sown varieties in almost all major crops. There are short duration, medium duration and long duration varieties in most of the cereal crops. A short duration rice variety, for instance, is selected when the succeeding crop requires early sowing, as is the case in many of the pulse and oilseed crops. The resulting crop production in one of the crops is often not significant and may be compensated by the combined productivity of the two crops. There are crop varieties can tolerate soil moisture stress to a great extent. Resistance to pests and diseases is another beneficial characteristic of a good crop variety. With the aid of suitable prediction on soil moisture availability from rainfall, ground water and surface water sources, it is possible to arrive at suitable cropping patterns to make the maximum use of the available water in an area. However, there is need to restrict the area under high water demanding crops like rice and sugar cane, when the available water supply is low.

Irrigation Systems

Surface water stored in reservoirs or diverted directly from streams and rivers is distributed for irrigation through the canal irrigation network. A canal takes of from the head-works of either a water storage dam (Fig. 6.1) or barrage (Fig. 6.2) or a diversion dam.

Fig. 6.1: A view of the Nagarjuna Sagar Dam, Andhra Pradesh. Courtesy: PIB, Govt. of India.

Fig. 6.2: A view of Durgapur Barrage on River Damodar in West Bengal. Courtesy: PIB, Govt. of India.

Kolhapur Type Weirs. A comparatively new technology, originally developed in the Kolhapur region of Maharashtra, with applicability in other regions, specially in the plateau region of India (comprising over one-third of the land area of the country), is the Kohlapur Type Weir, popularly known as KT weirs (Fig. 6.3). They are used to intercept and store the receding monsoon flows in streams and rivers. They comprise of masonry piers and removable R.C.C. boards. The weirs are kept open during the main monsoon period. They are inserted one by one into the slots in the weirs during the receding phase of the monsoon to store the river flow. The water stored in the river course is pumped from suitable sites for irrigation and water supply. The system has been widely adopted in the region. Large areas of lands on either side of the river are provided with supplementary irrigation during the dry season.

Fig. 6.3: A view of a Kolhapur Type weir near Pune, Maharashtra. At the top is a view of the weir taken from upstream. At the bottom is a close view of the top of the weir. Note the piers with slots for inserting R.C.C boards (not seen in the picture) to control the river flow and store water for irrigation by installing river pumping systems. The boards are removed during the period of heavy rain, but are put in place well before the recession of the south-west monsoon.

Tank Irrigation in India: Surface reservoirs storing rainfall runoff from catchment areas of contributing watershed and collecting seepage from surrounding underground water bearing formations are called tanks or ponds (Fig. 6.4). They are of varying types and are used for irrigation, water supply and ground water recharge. Tank irrigation is popular in Tamil Nadu, Karnataka, Andhra Pradesh, Maharashtra, Madhya Pradesh, Chattisgarh and West Bengal. The Telengana region of Andhra Pradesh has been termed as "the land of rice and tanks" where tank irrigation has been developed extensively since the ancient times. Unfortunately, tank irrigation has not received the right attention in the large scale irrigation development during the Five Year Plans which

Fig. 6.4.: An irrigation and headwater flood control tank at Sukhomanjari near Chandigarh.

commenced in 2000, the extent of irrigation by tanks has remained nearly the same, except in Maharashtra. Tanks formed the source of water for irrigating about 50 per cent of the cropped area during the pre-independence period. Today it accounts for only about 10 per cent of the cropped area. There are ample opportunities for substantially increasing the area under tank irrigation and improving the performance of the existing tank systems. These include improvement in the silt-free runoff volume stored in the tanks, use of lift irrigation from tanks, and efficient management of the flow irrigation potential through farmer participation and adoption of appropriate technology in the construction of the water distribution systems and scientific farming practices. A nearly unutilised potential is the construction of system storage reservoirs in canal command areas to store excess flows during the periods in the crop season when the demand for water is low.

Classification of Irrigation Projects: Post-independence development of irrigation projects India have been on the basis of classification of works into major, medium and minor projects. All irrigation schemes with a culturable command area of 10,000 ha or more are classified as major irrigation projects. They are essentially surface water projects involving large scale storage and diversion works. Medium irrigation projects are those having command areas ranging from 2000 to 10,000 ha. They are also usually surface water projects, excepting a few large lift irrigation schemes. Minor irrigation schemes have culturable command areas up to 2000 ha. Minor irrigation schemes are of two types: (i) Surface water minor irrigation schemes, and (ii) Ground water minor irrigation schemes.

Canal water distribution network: In a canal irrigation system water flows through the complete canal system before it reaches the farmer's field to be irrigated. The canal network consists of the main canal, branch canals, distributaries, water courses and field channels which are termed according to their capacity and orientation with respect to the head-works. It is the head regulator with its hydro-mechanical devices at the head end of a canal system which controls and regulates the water from the reservoir or diversion point. Major distributaries distribute water to different reaches of the canal command area. Often there are minor distributaries taking of from the major distributaries to distribute the water to a group of canal outlets. In India the canals and branches up to minor distributaries and the outlets are generally constructed, operated and maintained by the government. It has been observed that there exists large gaps between the development of irrigation potential and its utilization, mainly in the first few decades after the commissioning of major and medium irrigation projects. The major reasons for this deficiency is the inadequate attention given to command area development, including effective agricultural extension programmes emphasising on efficient irrigation water management.

Canal Outlets: Outlets are provided in irrigation canal systems at suitable points. The water course originates from the canal outlet. The size of an outlet depends upon the area to be irrigated. The common types of canal outlets used in India are the adjustable proportionate module outlet (APM) and pipe outlets. The APM type outlets can be fixed to obtain the desired discharge from an outlet, depending on the culturable command area of the outlet. The discharge of the outlet varies with the level of water in the distributary channel. The outlet capacity commonly fixed is at the full supply level of the channel, supply water to it. There is no regulation of the supply at the outlet level.

Night irrigation in canal systems: Most of the canal irrigation systems in south and southeast Asia continue to flow throughout the day and night. Inefficient water application, breaches in channels and wasted water flowing into drains are common during the night. A good part of the canal discharges in the night are inefficiently used or wasted, except in areas where land consolidation and rectangulation of field boundaries have taken place and warabandi system of canal water delivery to fields are functioning effectively. In most areas where these practices have not been effective, a good part of the night supply flows into the drainage systems and is lost, unless they are stored in tanks and reservoirs in the command area and used for irrigation later or are reused for irrigation in the lower reaches.

Darkness, cold, fear, departure from normal working hours and desire for sleep deter irrigation staff and farmers from activities at and control of water at the farm level. It requires smaller irrigation streams for irrigation at night. Night irrigation usually needs additional efforts and a greater degree of regulation graded fields. However, paddy, tree crops and other widely spaced crops are easy to irrigate at night as well.

The warabandi system of scheduling water delivery to different land holdings is based on the area of the field belonging to the farmer. The available flow in a week is distributed to the farmers in proportion to the size of the land holding. There is no distinction between the flow in the day and the night. Farmers of north India (mainly Punjab, Haryana and Western Uttar Pradesh) and the Indus basin of Pakistan have accepted the system without any complaints. Important features of the area favouring the adoption of the warabandi system are nearly level fields, consolidated rectangular land holdings and scarcity in the availability of canal water for irrigation. However, in most other regions of India and in many of the developing countries, especially under undulating topography, introduction of warabandi in the same manner has not been successful. Many adaptations of the warabandi system have been attempted with varying degrees of success. The need to ensure equitable distribution of water amongst the farmers of the command area of a canal outlet has been recognised by all. An essential requirement in ensuring this objective is effective participation and involvement of the farmers of the outlet command area.

Possible measures of moderating the canal flows in the night are reducing irrigation at night through regulating sluice releases or diversion of flows, providing intermediate storage systems in the command area, diversion of flows to adjust for travel time in the canal system, redistribution of day time water, passing over to drains and escapes and adoption of water application methods which require less human intervention (examples, sprinkler and drip methods of irrigation), choice of crops and distributing flows in distinct zones of the command area. The ease or difficulty of irrigation during the night will depend on field conditions, the rate of flow in the water conveyance system and the type of crop. The smaller and more sloping the field is the more difficult night irrigation becomes. Some large flat lands can be left to flood the whole night. Adaptability to night irrigation also depends on the type of soil. Night irrigation is easier in soils which are not sticky. It is often difficult in black cotton soils. Hence, warabandi, as followed in north India is difficult to be adapted in black soils. The feasibility of efficient night irrigation also depends on the size of the irrigation stream to be handled. Optimum flow rate in the night should be lower than the day supply. The type of crop and its stage of growth profoundly influence the ease and efficiency of night irrigation. The easiest crops are paddy and tree crops; paddy can be flooded. Overflows may not raise serious problems.

Similarly, trees are tolerant to standing water for some hours. Widely spaced crops and those in earlier stages of growth are easier to irrigate at night than those which are high, dense, or in their later stages of growth.

When night irrigation is not possible, the excess flows can be released to drains and escapes than allowed to flood the outlet command area which will result in waterlogging and salt problems. Uncontrolled large flows may result in stream channel erosion especially at the tail end reaches of a canal system. Drainage of excess flows at non-erosive velocities may sometimes be beneficial at the lower reaches of the command area. Whether the water is wasted or not will depend on the possibilities of its utilization in the lower reaches. In regions where there is a cascade or chain of tanks, wastage through night flows in the upper tank may fill the tank lower down. Such benefits are common in south India. Reducing irrigation at night has many potential advantages, including saving water, convenience to all concerned, and limiting the damage (flooding, waterlogging, soil erosion) which uncontrolled night flows can cause.

The following are some of the ways in which night irrigation supplies can be reduced or improved:

(i) *Regulating sluices releases or diversion of flows in streams.* The size of an irrigation system determines whether night irrigation can be reduced by regulating sluice releases or diversion to downstream river course. On small reservoirs with command area less than 200 ha, the sluices are usually closed at night. Where canals are long and large, sluice or diversions to reduce night supplies becomes infeasible.

(ii) *Intermediate night storage reservoirs/system storage tanks:* Night storage in intermediate reservoirs or diverting part of the night flows to tanks are often beneficial to the region. This can reduce night irrigation, save water and introduce flexibility in canal system management. It can also be used to reduce the design capacity of canals. However, design of intermediate storages within the canal network needs careful considerations in relation to silting of canals as influenced by the storage reservoir.

Storage of water can be at the field level as well, if the field conditions and the crop will permit. It is most feasible with paddy. It is a common practice in Sri Lanka to hold as much water as possible in the upper paddy basins and release it to the lower fields on the following days.

(iii) *Zoning for night flows:* Where a farm or an outlet receives water throughout the day and night, the day flows can be used to irrigate the more difficult soils and crops, and the night flows for those which are easier.

(iv) *On-farm engineering measures:* Night irrigation can be substantially improved by providing appropriate structures in the water distribution network and adopting water application methods having low requirement for close observation, adjustment and physical manipulations. Water in paddy fields is easily monitored in level fields. Border strip irrigation requires greater attention but is easier when the fields are well planned and properly graded. In general, greater attention is required to maintain field channels and field shaping where irrigation is by night than by day.

(v) *Choice of crops:* Night irrigation can be improved by choosing crops tolerant to flooding and easy to irrigate.

Waste Water Management and Pollution Control

Pollution of streams, rivers and reservoirs due to toxic effluents resulting from over use of fertilizers and agricultural chemicals, agricultural wastes, contaminated effluents from sewerage systems and toxic effluents from industries are causing serious problems to mankind. Rivers, lakes and wetlands are important natural sources of water. Maintaining water quality in them is vital for all life. Most of the major rivers in the developing countries suffer from pollution in one stretch or the other. The river Ganga is probably one of the most polluted rivers in India today. The first major river cleaning programme in India was started with the launching of the Ganga Action Plan in 1985. The objective is to clean the main river and its major tributary the Yamuna in a phased manner, as the river system is grossly polluted due to indiscriminate discharge of sewage and industrial effluents from 25 major towns spread over the states of Uttar Pradesh, Bihar and West Bengal. The Phase I of the Ganga Action Plan has been implemented and the Phase II programme is being implemented to cover the remaining works. The Government of India has initiated similar pollution control measures to clean other important rivers under the National River Conservation Plan in a phased manner. The rivers include Godavary, Sabarmati, Brahmani, Tapti, Kavery, Krishna, Mahanadi, Subarnarekha, and Narmada and its tributaries.

Sewage Irrigation

Using treated waste water is usually a favourable proposal .The plant nutrients present in treated wastewater are useful in irrigation. There are several examples of using sewage water for irrigation. They can be successfully adopted wherever feasible. However, sewage water is unsafe for irrigating leafy and root type vegetable crops where the edible part is eaten raw. Wastewater could be used for secondary domestic/muncipal purposes such as flushing of toilets and watering of lawns. Only countries with a high level of technology for the operation and monitoring of advanced techniques of wastewater treatment can consider reusing wastewater for domestic purposes. The quality of industrial and municipal wastewater require to be constantly monitored, because such waters may have long term adverse effects, both on the crops and on the health of the people.

Environmental Impact of Irrigation Projects

Any direct human influence on environment has a positive objective, namely, to raise the living standards of a given group of people. However, certain activities could cause undesirable side effects, leading to unexpected changes in the environment, unless the projects are carefully planned and executed. Improperly planned projects may give rise to irreversible processes, causing deterioration of the desirable balance of nature.

All water resources development projects have social and environmental implications. The environmental impacts of irrigation projects vary with the physiography of the region, climate, soil, the characteristics of river flow and the size of the project. Irrigation projects invariably change the river flow characteristics and ecosystem of the downstream river course and works of the project, downstream from the head-works, in the original river course, along the routes of the canal system and in the extensive irrigation command areas.

Global attention to environmental problems was drawn by the United Nations Conference on Environment at Stockholm, Sweden in 1972. Following the establishment of the United Nations Environment Programme (UNEP), international organizations like UNDP, UNICEF. FAO and WHO have engaged themselves in programmes of environmental improvement and the relationship between development and environment. The need for adopting suitable steps to reduce the adverse environmental impacts of development projects have been stressed in many international conferences. They have drawn attention to the various aspects of the problem and suggested policies and action plans for adoption by different countries.

Energy Requirement in Irrigation

Careful planning of energy sources and their efficient utilization are vital in meeting the water needs of agriculture and other uses. Agricultural production in many situations is limited by the non-availability of power to lift water for irrigation from ground water and surface water sources. Energy requirement in irrigation pumping may be broadly grouped into the following two categories: (i) Pumping from wells, and (ii) River and canal pumping. Irrigation wells are classified into open wells, shallow tube wells and deep tube wells. Water is lifted from open wells by manually operated and animal operated water lifts and pumps driven by diesel engines and electric motors. Water lifting from shallow tube wells and deep tube wells are almost exclusively by pumps operated by diesel engines and electric motors. The power requirement in river and canal pumping is also met by diesel engine or electric motor driven pump sets. The consequent higher demand for power in the irrigation sector has to form an integral part of planning irrigation systems.

Human and animal power will continue to be the main sources of energy in small scale irrigation pumping and domestic water supply in many of the developing countries. From a purely economic standpoint, the cost of water lifting per unit quantity of water lifted is substantially higher in case of human and animal power than with mechanically powered pumps. In spite of economic disadvantages, animal and human power will continue to be in use for small scale water lifting in many of the developing countries. However, their use will be on the decline. Whenever electric power is available, it is the most convenient and efficient source of energy in irrigation pumping. The reliability and efficiency of electrically operated pumping sets are high, provided they are properly selected, installed and maintained. To achieve the goal of efficient utilization of land and water resources, it is essential that the concerned agencies including power generation and distribution, irrigation and agriculture work in close coordination.

Lift Irrigation Systems

In lift irrigation projects, water is lifted directly from rivers or streams or from suitable points at different segments of a canal system. River lift irrigation schemes are feasible in regions where the stream flow is adequate during the peak period of irrigation demand by the crops and where electricity or diesel oil is available at reasonable cost. Canal lift irrigation schemes are beneficial in many areas where sizable land area adjoining a canal, but lying at higher elevations cannot be irrigated through gravity flow from the canal. Often such areas can be brought under irrigation by installing low and medium head, high discharge pumping sets. The water can be pumped to one or more distribution chambers located at suitable points in the command area from where it is distributed through appropriate water distribution systems.

There has been a spurt in the growth of river lift irrigation schemes in India since 1970. The total number of lift irrigation schemes in India was estimated to be about 500,000 in 1987. Lift irrigation schemes are being implemented mostly by cooperative societies, state owned lift irrigation corporations and minor irrigation departments of state governments. The schemes in the cooperative sector usually avail credit facilities of the National Bank for Agriculture and Rural Development (NABARD), land development banks, and commercial banks, availing refinance facilities of the NABARD.

The state of Maharashtra has made significant progress in the development of financially viable lift irrigation projects in the cooperative sector, availing institutional financing, mainly through the NABARD. The other states where lift irrigation systems have been developed as significant source of irrigation are Andhra Pradesh, Karnataka, Madhya Pradesh, Bihar, Orissa, West Bengal and Tamil Nadu. Most state governments have set up separate statutory corporations to undertake minor irrigation works, including river lift irrigation systems. Direct lifting of water from rivers, steams and canals is extensively practiced in rural water supply schemes where it may be the only source of potable water. However, lift irrigation is still an under-utilised potential in water resource development. There is considerable scope to increase the quantity of surface water that could be lifted and the area covered by such schemes in the irrigation sector.

Major Opportunities in Increasing Irrigation Efficiency in Command Areas

A properly designed water distribution system will make irrigation easy and efficient. Several types of structures are used to convey, divert and control irrigation water. Good farm irrigation structures are an essential part of an irrigation layout. Properly designed structures will prevent seepage in the water conveyance system, avoid leakage from outlets and diversion structures and provide for the control of water released to the lower reaches of the canal network and to the farm land. They will also facilitate effective on-farm water management and result in labour saving in irrigation application. In many areas a substantial amount of water conveyed through open channel systems is lost through seepage, evaporation through the usually wide unlined channels, transpiration from the weeds on the banks of the conveyance channels, breaches in the canal banks, leakage through gates and turnouts and operational losses. Operational losses include return flow to drains due to faulty canal regulation, inadequate arrangement for irrigation in the night and unused flows during periods when there is no demand for the crops or diversion to downstream river course. On small reservoirs with command area less than 200 ha, the sluices are usually closed at night. Where canals are long and large, sluice or diversions to reduce night supplies becomes infeasible.

While some loss in the canal system is unavoidable, a good part of it could be avoided by the proper design and management of the system. Operational waste in most canal systems could be reduced considerably by providing equalizing reservoirs.

The major component of water loss in irrigation conveyance systems is in seepage (Fig. 6.5). Seepage control measures, comprising essentially of lining of the permeable reaches of the water conveyance system provide the greatest opportunity in saving water supplies developed at a high cost (Fig. 6.6). The water thus saved can be used for irrigating additional areas or for more

Fig. 6.5: A small diversion canal in a highly permeable soil near Leh, District Ladakh, Jammu and Kashmir. It is estimated that about 70% of the water diverted to the canal is lost by seepage in a length of about 5 km of the canal.

Fig. 6.6: Lining of a water course in the West Yamuna Canal Circle near Rohtak, Haryana in 1973. The lining consists of bricks on the sides and stone slabs at the bottom, both laid in cement mortar. Note the rectangular cross-section of the lined water course.

intensive irrigation in the existing areas. Little can be done to save the evaporation loss in the conveyance system, which in any case is small. Losses due to transpiration through vegetation in canal banks and canal beds are reduced by keeping the banks and beds clear of weeds and lining with masonry material. In addition to the major objective of saving irrigation water seepage control measures contribute greatly to solving the problems of waterlogging and salt problems in land areas adjoining the canal system. Water which seeps through main canals and laterals collect in low lying areas. The problem of waterlogging in an irrigated area could often be attributed to the faulty design of the water distribution system and poor water management. There are also other benefits resulting from minimizing the water loss in the conveyance system. Unlined channels are to be designed with wide beds and flat slopes, in order to make them stable. In a lined channel, much higher velocities are allowed. A deeper and narrower section is possible, resulting in saving in land, cost and earthwork. Lining results in a general reduction in the size of the channel and hence the cost of canal structures. Lined channels are easier and less costly to maintain and have safer banks. In case of an on-farm system, the bed level of the water courses and field channels are raised which usually result in an increase in the command area of the canal systems. Canal systems which take of directly from diversion works on rivers usually have silty water and do not present serious weed problems. The canal systems originating from reservoirs are often infested with weeds, which greatly reduce their capacity and make canal operations difficult. Lining of canals have the added advantage of eliminating the problem. Lining assumes special importance in areas, which on introduction of irrigation, would be liable to waterlogging and salinity.

Farm irrigation distribution systems for surface irrigation methods can be classified into two groups—surface channels and underground pipelines. Facilities for the conveyance and control of irrigation water are different for each type. Field channels may be either unlined earth channels or lined channels. The extent of seepage in canals is influenced mainly by the permeability of the soils through which it travels.

Earthen channel are lined with impervious materials to

prevent seepage and the growth of weeds. Lining is important in on-farm irrigation systems, irrespective of whether they are fed by canals or ground water. In permeable soils like sands and sandy loams, the losses in earth channels may often be as high as 20 per cent to 40 per cent of the water delivered at the outlet. Any masonry material locally available and laid in cement mortar, after proper consolidation of the channel bed is ideally suited to line on-farm water conveyance systems. Choice of the material, whether bricks or stones, will essentially be based on their relative costs.

On-Farm Structures for Water Conveyance, Control and Distribution: Appropriate structures in the on-farm water distribution system are an integral component of an effective and efficient irrigation system. On-farm structures are often a neglected area in irrigation system planning and development, even in projects where there is a provision for lining of water courses and field channels. Such situations will result in erosion of channel beds, obstructions in movement of farm machinery, access to fields and lack of control and regulation of water supplied to the fields. On-farm structures are grouped into four groups: (i) structures for control of erosion in channel beds, (ii) structures for water surface control in water courses and field channels, (iii) structures at channel crossings, and (iv) structures for water diversion and regulation. On-farm erosion control structures are drop structures, chute spillways, and drop inlet structures. Low cost designs are available in case of all of them. Proper care in planning will result in substantial savings in the cost of projects because of the large number of structures required in an area. Structures for control of water surface level in open channels include check gates (built-in, precast and portable). Diversion structures are necessary to carry water to different farms or to different parts of the same farm (Fig. 6.7). Two-way or three-way diversions made of check gates with seal strips provide leak-proof check gates. Structures at channel crossings include flumes, culverts and inverted siphons. Various alternative types are available in on-farm structures to suit location specific requirements. Proper selection of the type of structures, their design, and materials and methods of their construction provide ample scope to achieve efficiency and economy in farm irrigation systems.

Fig. 6.7: A 2-way division box in a field channel made of prefabricated concrete channel sections. The division box is made of brick masonry. Low-cost valves of the type shown in the figure provide leak-proof outlets in field channels.

On-farm water conveyance and distribution systems in canal irrigation command areas. Water conveyance and distribution systems in canal irrigation project areas comprise of open channels and ancillary structures designed to ensure efficient supply of water to the farmer's fields in areas under the command of an irrigation outlet. Till the later part of the 19th century, irrigation project development was essentially to provide water at the canal outlet. The farmers were given the responsibility to manage water below the outlet. This led to numerous problems. Water distribution efficiency in the command area was poor. The problems of unequal distribution of water to the beneficiary farmers of the outlet of an irrigation system, such as waterlogging and soil salinity, resulted in serious problems. Pioneering efforts in developing efficient and low cost structures in farm irrigation systems were made at the regional centres of the Central Soil and Water Conservation Research Institute, Dehra Dun and at the College of Agriculture, Jobner, Rajasthan in early 1960s. The first major effort in large scale introduction of lining of water courses was by the states of Haryana and Punjab in early 1970s, availing refinancing by the Agricultural Refinance Corporation (now NABARD). The effort has been a great success. However, a major lacuna was the near absence of ancillary structures in the water distribution system.

The first national level effort to focus attention on the problems of canal irrigation command areas has been the establishment of Command Area Development Programme in the mid-1970s by the Government of India and its adoption by most of the state governments. Simultaneously, many of the research institutes of state irrigation departments, command area development authorities, agricultural universities and research institutions, and water and land management institutions of the states concentrated their efforts in developing technology and man power in command area development. The Water Technology Centre of IARI, New Delhi has contributed substantially to the development of technology for on-farm water conveyance and distribution and to solve other problems of irrigation command areas. A policy decision was taken to reach canal water supplies to serve outlets with command an area not exceeding 8 ha. Wherever possible, the water courses were to be laid along the ridge line of the outlet command area so that water could be diverted to both the sides of the channel. In case of sloping land, the channels are laid across the slope on the higher reach of the field and water flows to the downfield area. The downfield area is levelled to non-erosive grades. Proper survey and planning of the fields of the outlet command area is essential to ensure efficient water management. There are many cases where the location of the canal outlet is not on the basis of the topography of the outlet command area. Such outlets are to be relocated. In all cases where water courses are not laid to serve all the farmers of the command area, there is an immediate need to realign the existing channels and provide branch water courses to ensure equitable water allocation to every farmer of the outlet command area. Unlined water conveyance systems in permeable soils are to be lined with appropriate lining materials. Provision of appropriate structures for water conveyance and distribution are essential.

Underground Pipeline Water Conveyance and Control: An underground pipeline water distribution system consists of buried pipes for conveying water to different points on the farm and allied structures required for the efficient functioning of the system. The system offers many advantages over open channels in water conveyance and distribution. The pipes are laid underground. Hence, cultivation can be done above the pipeline; no culverts or other structures are required. Open channels often take 2 per cent to 4 per cent of the land area out of cultivation, which is saved by adopting the underground system. The pipelines do not interfere with the farming operations. Efficient use can be made of modern farm machinery because fields are not cut into short runs by channels. When properly installed, the pipelines have long life and low maintenance cost. They are essentially leak-proof. Their placement below the ground level prevents damage to pipes and eliminates water loss by seepage and evaporation. Water supply to the field plots is controlled precisely with leak-proof riser valves used in the distribution system. As underground pipelines operate under pressure, they can be laid uphill or downhill, thus permitting delivery of irrigation water to areas not accessible by open channels. With an underground pipeline system, the irrigation wells need not be located at a high point on the farm, but may be at a location that provides the best water supply. The water can be pumped directly to the head end of the distribution system or a low height overhead tank. The pipelines are not clogged by vegetation and wind blown material. Underground pipelines are ideally suited to undulating topography and to reach water to fragmented and isolated locations on the farm. They are preferred in areas where land is costly.

Underground pipeline irrigation water distribution systems have a high initial cost, as compared to lined open channels. They may, however, be more economical under many field situations, including the fields being located in benches at different elevations. Generally, underground pipelines are not suitable in canal irrigation systems because of insufficient head and silt-laden water. Therefore, open channel systems are commonly used.

Underground pipeline water distribution systems are usually constructed of concrete or PVC pipes. The choice of the material of the pipe depends on the conditions under which the pipe is to operate and the relative costs. Concrete pipes are not suitable in salt affected soils, specially soils high in sulphates. In such situations either special sulphate resistant cement is used in manufacturing the pipes or other types of pipes like PVC or vitrified clay pipes are used.

The water distribution systems of deep tube wells which are owned by the government or cooperative or group farming societies, usually comprise of open channels or buried pipes with outlets at suitable points in the tube well command area. Buried pipeline water distribution systems, though comparatively more expensive, have major advantages over the conventional water distribution systems comprising of a network of field channels. Underground pipeline systems for deep tube wells may be laid in loop network or in branching network systems. Loop network systems are preferred in nearly level areas and branching networks on comparatively undulating land. Closed loop systems are designed to have only one valve in a loop operating at a time. Usually two loops are provided to distribute water on either side of the deep tube well. Outlets with valves are provided along the underground pipeline to supply water to each field plot. It is a good practice to locate the outlet on the boundary between two or more land holdings.

Buried pipeline water distribution systems are ideally suited to rotational water supply to the beneficiary farmers of the command area. The system ensures reliable supply of water to the beneficiary farmers at fixed time intervals, like once a week in each of the command areas of the loop segment. The success of the system will, however, depend upon the availability of electrical power supply without interruptions.

Land Drainage and Reclamation

Waterlogging and salt accumulation are major constraints to agricultural production in most countries of the world. In Monsoon Asia, particularly in Southeast Asia, a major potential for increasing agricultural production lies in the reclamation and management of swampy and marshy areas (Fig. 6.8). Low lying areas are usually flat lands which are often prone to waterlogging due to accumulation of rainfall runoff and seepage water from higher reaches. In regions where canal irrigation has been introduced, seepage from the water distribution network and deep percolation of excess water applied to the land cause the rise of the water table, which in many situations result in the accumulation of salts in the crop root zone. Salt problems are more acute in the Central Asian countries, West Asia and North Africa.

With the rapid increase in canal irrigation in South Asia, especially India and Pakistan, drainage problems were major constraints in sustained agricultural production.

Fig. 6.8: A view of the waterlogged marshy land in the low lying area of Punjab Agricultural University main farm at Ludhiana in 1966, prior to undertaking drainage and reclamation work.

Estimates shows the waterlogged area in India range from 6.5 to 12 million ha. Nearly half of this area face problems of excess salt accumulation in the crop root zone. Early years of the post-independence period witnessed substantial effort by the Punjab Government to combat waterlogging and salt problems by constructing a series of large outlet drains benefiting major areas of the state. There was also substantial increase in the use of ground water through shallow and deep tube wells. These efforts resulted in controlling the problem to a great extent. However, there are still large areas requiring drainage and reclamation at the farm level.

Serious problems of waterlogging and salt accumulation were observed in the Chambal canal command areas in Rajasthan and Madhya Pradesh. Concentrated efforts in the Kota region of the Chambal canal command area met with substantial success in diagnosing the problem and providing surface and subsurface drainage and undertaking reclamation measures. In the Indira Gandhi Canal Project area in Western Rajasthan, however, much greater attention is required to adequately combat the drainage problem facing arid zone irrigation. Many of the major and medium irrigation projects of the alluvial Gangetic plains of north and east India and in the Brahmaputra valley in the north-west face serious problems due to waterlogging and accumulation of salts. In Peninsular India as well as the deltaic regions of the east coast, there are extensive areas affected by waterlogging and salt problems. In addition, there are localised low-lying areas suffering from waterlogging and salt accumulation, especially in the semi-arid regions. These lands usually have high agricultural production potential and may be reclaimed by undertaking drainage and reclamation measures. Unfortunately, in India and most other developing countries drainage was given low priority in the development projects. High embankments of rail lines and highways often lead to obstruction to natural drainage, resulting in waterlogging and salt accumulation in vast areas lying between them at places where adequate drainage provisions have not been made. Similar is the situation when the canals are constructed with raised embankments, without provision for smooth drainage of water accumulated in compartments of land areas formed by canals, accumulation of rainfall runoff in low lying areas for want of suitable outlets and over-irrigation. High water tables and salt problems often develop as a result of canal irrigation on fields well drained before introducing canal irrigation. They may not have drainage facilities to take care of the additional ground water resulting from over-irrigation, seepage, and faulty canal regulation and water releases. In such cases the ground water level may rise from a considerable depth to the crop root zone or the land surface in a relatively short time.

Canal regulation and water release patterns profoundly influence the amount of water received in an area. Indiscriminate water releases in canal systems, including wastage of much of the water released in the night, where rotational irrigation supply system is not practiced, will lead to accumulation of excess water in the area. Improperly designed and constructed water control structures, canal outlets without control gates, leaking canal gates and other structural deficiencies in the water distribution system as well as improper water application methods add to the problem of waterlogging and salt build-up in the crop root zone. Water management at the headworks and at the farm level provide major opportunities in increasing the efficiency of canal irrigation system and consequent reduction of the problem of waterlogging and salt build-up.

Successful drainage of waterlogged lands depends on a correct diagnosis of the problem. A programme of drainage of waterlogged lands should comprise the identification of the source of waterlogging and the extent of drainage required in the problem area. A suitable drainage system is then designed and constructed to obtain a proper environment for plant growth on a permanent basis (Fig. 6.9). Equally important are the planning and development of the reclaimed area (Fig. 6.10). Appropriate maintenance of drainage systems assumes major importance.

Fig. 6.9: A part of the main outlet drain soon after its construction during June–September 1966. The entire stretch of the outlet drain was on the land belonging to the farmers of the adjoining village who had willingly cooperated in the drainage project in view of the benefits from the project.

Fig. 6.10: Layout of the drained area of the Punjab Agricultural University Farm, Ludhiana, laid out for raising the rabi crop during 1986-87. The construction of outlet drain, followed by an interceptor drain lowered the water table by about 60 to 90 cm.

Drains blocked by excessive weed growth and silting are serious problems adversely affecting drainage systems in the developing world (Fig. 11). Areas in which the maintenance is improper revert back to problem areas within a short time span (Fig. 6.12). Participation and involvement of the beneficiary farmers are essential for the proper maintenance of drainage systems.

Fig. 6.11: A surface drain in the Chambal canal command area, Rajasthan blocked by excessive weed growth.

Source: Rajasthan Agricultural Drainasge Res. Project Progress Report, 1995 ed.

Fig. 6.12: A view of surface water standing in farm land in the Left Main Canal command area of Chambal Canal system, Rajasthan.

Source: Rajasthan Agricultural Drainage Res. Project Progress Report, 1995 ed.

Farmers' Participation in Irrigation System Management

The traditional system of irrigation the world over had a built-in system of distribution of water among the beneficiaries, thereby linking utilization with the creation of irrigation systems. In India, the management of tanks and small-scale river diversion schemes had provision to involve the beneficiary farmers in the maintenance of the system and distribution of water as well as in modalities of resolving conflicts. There was an unwritten convention among the farmers of tank command areas to use water on a weekly rotation. One farmer among the beneficiaries acted as the coordinator and leader for water distribution within the unit. Similarly, the supply of water to a field on a particular day was decided by the farmers on mutually agreed terms.

Against the above background, major canal irrigation projects of India developed in the 20th century, in most cases, did not have any role for the beneficiary farmer in canal system development and management. The responsibility of the irrigation department was deemed to end at the point where water was released at the outlet. The planners and executors of irrigation projects have tended to focus largely on engineering aspects of the project with little attention to socio-economic dimensions, and modern methods of water management. There has been a general lack of constructive and functional relationship between irrigation officials and the farmers. Thus, the farmer who had the most important stake in the proper management of irrigation water as the ultimate beneficiary, had little role to play in the management of irrigation under the prevailing system. This realization lead the Government of India to lay emphasis on the need for the participation of farmers in the management of irrigation water. In 1987, the Ministry of Water Resources, Government of India, issued guidelines to state governments to reduce its sphere of responsibility and involve farmers organizations to takeover maintenance, management of water allocation, and collection of water charges with a view to develop participatory mode of management in irrigation systems.

Participatory irrigation management refers to the involvement of irrigation users in part or all aspects of irrigation management and at all levels. This implies initial planning and design, construction, supervision, financing, framing of rules of operation, maintenance, monitoring and evaluation of the system.

Even though the irrigation systems are meant for the farmers, the countries around the globe have promoted the development of irrigation projects primarily through their governments. Only in 1950s to 1970s, several countries started providing incentives to their farmers to takeover the management of operation and maintenance of irrigation systems, leaving the government organizations to concentrate on the main system. There has been major effort in South-east Asian countries and the Far East, particularly Indonesia, The Philippines, Thailand, Taiwan, Malaysia and Korea to involve farmers at various levels of planning, operation and management of irrigation systems. Farm level irrigation management has been given to a large extent to farmer organizations. These systems have produced substantial benefits in these countries. This is in spite of the situation that there are problems due to lack of funds for construction, operation and maintenance of on-farm water management systems. Difficulties in optimizing water use and a lack of incentives and training for those charged with operation and maintenance of the schemes still remain as constraints. The main lessons learned from South-east Asia countries are that farmers should begin to participate in irrigation schemes at the planning stage itself and that adequate funds should be set apart for irrigation system maintenance.

In many states of India, efforts have been made on people participation in irrigation management. The first Water User's Association (WUA) in India was established in India in 1980s, and 4403 WUAs had been formed by March 1997, managing an irrigated area of about 397,100 ha under major and medium irrigation schemes. For minor irrigation schemes (mostly tube wells) about 10,400 WUAs had been formed, managing an irrigated area of about 50,000 ha. The Government of Andhra Pradesh promulgated the Andhra Pradesh Irrigation and Command Area Development Act, 1984 authorised the creation of command area development authorities and pipe (canal outlet) committees. The pipe committees, charged with the responsibilities of internal distribution of water below the canal outlet and maintenance of the water courses and field channels, were the first steps in the direction of participatory irrigation management. However, there were problems due to the lack of coordination between the irrigation and command area development authorities, and poor reliability of water supply at the outlet. In 1995 the Government of Andhra Pradesh issued an order to promote WUAs for the management of irrigation systems at the canal minor level covering areas of 400 to 750 ha. The WUAs are to function as autonomous bodies on democratic lines and are responsible for the maintenance and operation of irrigation network within the area of their operation. To begin with, WUAs were required to cover about 268,000 ha command area of Sriramsagar and 55,000 ha of Srisailam Right Bank Canal Projects.

In Gujarat in 1997 there were 33 WUAs at the minor level of various canal irrigation projects. The Mohini Cooperative Distributary Society, which was formed in 1979 in the command area of Bhestan Minor of Ukkai Kakrapar Irrigation Project made spectacular success due to strong government backing, effective local leadership, and income generating cropping system. However, due to local problems its functioning is reported to have declined. The Government of Gujarat has taken a policy decision to distribute water on volumetric basis to WUAs at the level of the minors of Sardar Sarovar Irrigation Project. It has also issued instructions to its irrigation department to provide compensation to farmers if the department is unable to supply water to the farmers as per agreement. The governments of Orissa, Rajasthan, Madhya Pradesh, Maharashtra, Karnataka, Tamil Nadu, Uttar Pradesh and West Bengal are among the other states which initiated steps to promote people's participation in irrigation system management, specially at the level of canal minors.

Involvement of farmers on different aspects and levels of irrigation system management varies from one state to the other. All the states envisage the retention of ownership of the main canal system from headworks to the branch canals of major and medium projects. In different states of India, WUAs are envisaged at outlet, minor and distributary levels.

The WUAs have different responsibilities in respect of maintenance, operation, and collection of water charges. The rules for water allocation and distribution also differ from one state to the other. The performance of the programme of participatary irrigation management in India is yet to be evaluated.

Ushering in Second Green Revolution in India Through Soil and Water Management Based Agricultural Technology Transfer Programme

The status information on land water resources of India, the various uses of water and the panorama of opportunities in increasing the efficiency of irrigation projects and providing environmental and ecological safeguards are presented in the preceding sections. There is immense scope to achieve revolutionary progress in agricultural production, adopting efficient land and water management based agricultural technology transfer. Appropriate technology is available and improved procedures are continuously being upgraded through research and development in different research and development institutions in the country. Global information is also available through computer-based information system and other information dissemination sources. However, adoption of scientific technology in soil and water management and scientific farming practices is far below the desired level in most regions of the country. Only a fraction of the production potential of crops has been achieved. The productivity of most crops is below international levels. The major limiting factor in obtaining substantially higher crop productivity is the lack of adequate and intensive efforts in the transfer of scientific agricultural practices at the farm level.

To achieve quick and spectacular results it is necessary to establish models of appropriate transfer of technology at district, block and panchayat levels spread over the entire country as the first step in the programme. The 'whole village agricultural transfer of technology' programme implemented by the Indian Agricultural Research Institute, New Delhi, which had concentrated its efforts during the period 1984-1990 provides an in-sight on the immense potential of effective transfer of technology in land and water management based agricultural technology transfer and achievement of spectacular increase in agricultural production (Figs. 6.13 to 6.20). The programme was spread over the districts of Gurgaon (Haryana), Fatehpur, Banda, Rae Bareli, Sultanpur and Lakhimpur Khiri (Uttar Pradesh), Raighar (Madhya Pradesh), and Munger (Bihar). The programme was to establish models of transfer of technology, adopting the

Fig. 6.13: Farmers pooling their bullocks and ploughs in a community farming block of 3000 ha flood-prone area adjoining the Yamuna in Khora Kanak village, Fatehpur District, U.P.

Fig. 6.14: Demonstration of seed-cum-fertilizer drilling machine in farmer's field for rabi 1985-86 sowing.

Fig. 6.15: Organised visit of farmers of nearby areas to fields covered under the IARI's Transfer of Technology Programme, 1987.

Fig. 6.16: A view of a bumper crop of Pusa-189 paddy variety in farmer's land, Bhoye village, Jamo Block, Sultanpur.

Fig. 6.17: High yielding wheat in IARI's Laboratory-to-Land Programme in Pachua Bara village, Sultanpur district, U.P., 1985-86.

Fig. 6.18: High yielding pegeon pea variety Pusa-84 in famer's land in Baliapur village, Haswa Block, Fatehpur district, U.P., 1987.

Fig. 6.19: High yielding tomato (Pusa ruby) in the Technology Transfer area in Bhoye village, Jamo Block, Sultanpur district, U.P., 1986.

Fig. 6.20: Rich growth of high yielding mustard in a compact 3000 ha community farming block of the unirrigated flood plain of Khora Kanak, Fatehpur district, U.P., December,1988.

"Whole Village Development" concept. At least 70 per cent of the farmers in Programme Village were members of the project. The involvement of the concerned State Departments formed an integral part of the programme. The emphasis in the programme was (i) to asses the capability of the land, (ii) to conduct rapid soil survey to evaluate the basic soil properties and the nutrient and micro-nutrient status of the soils of the programme areas and the requirement of fertilizers and micro-nutrients, (iii) study the climatic factors influencing pest and disease problems of the crops in the cropping plan for the area, (iv) make arrangements for appropriate farm power and machinery required for crop production and crop product processing, (v) ensure the availability of quality seeds of crop varieties suiting the climate of the area and the cropping system envisaged, (vi) organise group efforts for timely raising of paddy nurseries, involving at least one farmer having an irrigation well, (vii) ensure timely preparation of seed beds and proper placement of seeds (and fertilizes whenever required), (viii) provide the correct and timely plant protection measures, as and when required, (ix) provide suitable scheduling of irrigation applications, (x) arrange timely harvesting, threshing and crop processing operations and storage of the crop produce, using appropriate machinery and organizing group efforts, wherever required, and (xi) ensure farmer-friendly marketing arrangements, avoiding middlemen to the extent possible.

An important observation made during implementation of the programme was that the quality of seeds get progressively deteriorated and the seeds are to be replaced with good quality ones produced by approved seed farms, once every 3 to 4 years. The quantity of seeds available from organised seed agencies like the National Seeds Corporations and state level seed agencies could meet only about 5 to 7 per cent of the annual requirement of seeds in an area. Timely availability of seeds and other crop production inputs are essential requirements to ensure a successful crop production programme. A feasible procedure effectively implemented in the IARI's Transfer of Technology Programme was the introduction of "Farmer-to-Farmer Seed Production and Seed-Grain Exchange Programme."

Under the above concept seed farmers were selected from the villages concerned and quality seeds were grown by them under the guidance and close supervision of the scientists and meeting the seed quality requirements and seed production procedures as prescribed by the Seed Act. One seed farmer was required to produce and exchange for grains in sufficient quantity the seed requirement of 20 farmers of the village in return of grain produced by them. An exchange rate formula accepted by the farmers was to supply 1.5 kg good quality grains for 1 kg seeds produced by the seed farmer. All those farmers who receive quality seeds in a year under the programme would be included as seed farmers in the next year and the process of quality seed multiplication will increase many fold. It was predicted that progressively an entire district could be covered to meet its full requirement in about 5 years, with the committed and concerted efforts of the scientists and the programme farmers whose number continuously increase over the years.

The Technology Transfer Programme of IARI achieved spectacular success, commencing the very first year. The performance of paddy and wheat crops in selected areas in Sultanpur and Rae Bareli districts of Uttar Pradesh under the programme. Similar results were obtained in other areas as well. The unprecedented success of the programme attracted the attention of all concerned, the farmers of the area and the surrounding areas, the policy makers, the officials of the concerned government departments, and the media. Leading news agencies deputed their representatives to cover the story. *The Hindustan Times* in its October 25, 1987 edition covered the news in the tribal villages of Chandan Chouki, Lakhimpur Khiri district of Uttar Pradesh under the title "Green Revolution in Terai". It quoted that the per ha yield of paddy rose from the normal about nine quintals to 51 quintals in the area covered in the programme. The same agency in its October 28, 1987 issue covered the information relating to Sultanpur district under the heading "An oasis in a desert of drought."

The success of mustard production programme in the flood prone areas of Fatehpur district of U.P. is equally revealing. Almost the entire flood prone area on either side of river Yamuna had been lying almost barren with the farmers following the age-old farming practice of mixed cropping in some of the years. The yields were depressingly low. Realising the immense potential of the area with its suitability for mustard and gram production, the scientists of IARI motivated the farmers to form themselves in viable groups and resort to growing mustard in large blocks. Mustard crop could be raised utilising the soil moisture stored in the crop root zone in the preceding monsoon. The basic requirement was timely and proper sowing of seeds of good quality. The results surprised all, including the farmers and agriculture department officials. *The*

Hindustan Times covered the success story of mustard production in the flood-prone Gangetic plains in its editions of January 1, 2 and 3,1990 under the headings "Mustard Miracle in the Flood Prone Areas", "IARI Men Behind the Golden Harvest", and "Oil Self Sufficiency Through Mustard". Record yields ranging from 2 to 3 tonnes per ha could be harvested in 1989 and 1990 in large blocks extending to thousands of hectares in one stretch. The technology spread to the neighbouring districts, including Mirzapur in the subsequent years.

A notable feature of the above cited case study has been that the beneficiary farmers were highly responsive to receiving the benefits of the programme almost uniformly in all the areas covered, irrespective of widely varying socio-economic conditions spread over the four states. Once convinced of the commitment and competence of the programme implementers, the cooperation of the farming community is always forthcoming.

REFERENCES

Bhattacharya, A.K. and Michael, A.M. (2002/2003). *Land Drainage—Principles, Methods and Applications.* Pub. Konark Publishers Pvt. Ltd., Shakarpur, Delhi (in Press).

Biswas, A.K. and El-Habr, H.N.(1993). *Environment and Water Resources Management: The Need for a Holistic Approach.* Water Resources Development, Vol. 3, No. 2. pp. 117-25.

Biswas, A.K. and Qu Geping, eds. (1987). *Environmental Impact Assessment for Developing Countries.* Pub. for the United Nations University by Tycooly International, London.

Biswas, A.K., Mohammad Jellali and Slout, G. eds. (1993). *Water for Sustainable Development in the 21st Century.* Pub. Oxford University Press, Oxford, U.K.

Central Ground Water Board (1982). *Ground Water Resources and Development Potential in India.* Min. of Irrigation, Govt. of India, New Delhi.

Central Ground Water Board (1995). *Ground Water Resources of India.* Min. of Water Resources, Govt. of India, Faridabad, Haryana.

Central Water Commission (2000). *Water and Related Statistics.* Information System Directorate, Performance Overview and Management Information Organistation. Min. of Water Resources, Govt. of India.

Chambers, R. (1998). *Managing Canal Irrigation.* Pub. Oxford and IBH Pub. Co. Pvt. Ltd., New Delhi.

Chithale, N.A. (2000). *A Blue Revolution*. Pub. Bharatiya Vidya Bhawan, Pune.

Food and Agriculture Organization of the United Nations (1978). *World Irrigation and Land Use Statistics.* FAO Production Yearbook, Vol. 32. *FAO Statistics Series,* No. 22, FAO, Rome.

Food and Agriculture Organization of the United Nations (2000). *FAO Database, 2000.* On-line internet, 18th July, 2000. Available from http. apps. fao.org. page collections.

Food and Agricultural Organization of the United Nations (2001). *AQUASTAT Database, 2001.* Available from http://www.fao.org./waicent/faoinfo/agricult/agl/aglw/aqastat/profile.htm

Indian National Academy of Engineering (1990). *Water Management Prospective: Problems and Policy Issues*. Pub. INAE, New Delhi.

Indian Water Resources Society (1997). *River Basin Management : Issues and Options.* Theme Paper, IWRS, New Delhi.

Maria Saleth, R. (1996). *Water Institutions of India : Economics, Land and Policy.* Pub. Commonwealth Publishers, New Delhi (for Institute of Economic Growth, Delhi).

Michael, A.M. (1986). *Conjunctive Use of Surface and Ground Water for Irrigation in Bangladesh* (Report W.M. 6286). Submitted to Bangladesh Agricultural Research Council, Winrock Intetrnational Institute for International Development, Dacca.

Michael, A.M. (1987). "Environmental Impact Assessment of a Major Water Development Project in India: A Case Study of the Mahi Right Bank Canal System, Gujarat" in Biswas, A.K. and Qu Geping, eds. *Environmental Impact Assesment for Developing Countries*. Pub. for the United Nations University by Tycooly International, London. pp. 126-59.

Michael, A.M. and Khepar, S.D. (1989). *Water Well and Pump Engineering*. Pub.Tata McGraw Hill Pub. Co. Ltd., New Delhi.

Michael, A.M. and Ojha, T.P. (1999). *Principles of Agricultural Engineering*, Vol.II. Pub. Jain Brothers Pub. House, Karol Bagh, New Delhi.

Michael, A.M. (2000/2003). *Irrigation Theory and Practice,* 2nd ed. Pub. Vikas Pub. House, New Delhi/Chennai. (in Press).

Michael, A.M., Walia, S. and Parmar, V.S. (1993). *Emerging Water Quality Hazards and Their Management in Populated Alluvial Zones of India*. Proc. Stockholm Water Symposium, 10-14 August, 1992. Stockholm, Sweden. pp. 253-65.

Ministry of Water Resources, Govt. of India (1987). *National Water Policy*.

Minstry of Water Resources, Govt. of India (1999). Report of the National Commission for Integrated Water Resources Development Plan. New Delhi.

Ministry of Water Resources, Govt. of India (1999). *Water Resources Development Plan of India: Policy and Issues.* New Delhi.

Ministry of Water Resources, Govt. of India (1997). Report of the Working Group on Participatory Irrigation Management for the IX Five Year Plan. Command Area Development Wing, New Delhi.

National Land Use and Conservation Board, Ministry of Agriculture, Govt. of India, New Delhi (1991). *National Consultation on Perspective Plan for Conservation*, Management and Development of Land Resources of the Country. Discussion Paper, Oct. 21-24, 1991, New Delhi.

Punjab Agricultural University, Ludhiana (!967). *Evolving Design Criteria for Surface and Subsurface Drainage for Affected Areas in Punjab.* PAU, College of Agricultural Engineering, Drainage Research Scheme Annual Report 1966-67.

Rajasthan Agricultural Drainage Research Project (1995). *Analysis of Subsurface Drainage Design Criteria.* Chambal Command Area Development Authority, Kota, Rajasthan and Canadian International Development Agency. Report. 1995 ed.

Singh, S.R. (1998). *People Managed Irrigation Systems in Partnership Mode—Status and Methods for Performance Evaluation.* International Workshop on People's Participation in Irrigation Systems Management, Div. of Natural Resources Management, ICAR, New Delhi, April 22-24, 1998.

Water Technology Centre, Indian Agricultural Research Institute, New Delhi (1983). *Resource Analysis and Plan for Efficient Water Management: A Case Study of Mahi Right Bank Canal Command Area, Gujarat.*

Wolf, P. (1999). On the Sustainability of Water Use. *Natural Resources and Development*, Vol. 49/50. Institute for Scientific Cooperation, Tibingen, Germany.

World Bank (1998). *India: Water Resources Management*, Sectoral Review: Report on the Irrigation Sector. Report No.18416. IN, Rural Development Unit, South Asia Region, World Bank, New Delhi.

Part II

Sustainable Livestock Development

7

Sustainable Livestock Development in India

A Strategic Approach

S.N. MISHRA

Introduction

In the present paper our main concern is to articulate a long-term strategy for sustainable livestock development in India. Sustainability problem of development in general has arisen from environmental concerns, about development's impact on the local (national) and global environment, and about the manner and mode of utilisation of natural resources, renewable and non-renewable. Livestock anywhere are a renewable natural resource. A given livestock population is sustainable in the sense that it can be replaced (renewed) by breeding. But livestock *production*, viewed as *flow* of livestock products from the population need not be, sustainable, since production requires additional natural resources like land, feed and water, which may not be available in required quantity and quality. It is, therefore, necessary to explore and set the conditions for sustainable livestock production.

However, these conditions can't be the same for all types of livestock production systems and resource endowments. In the world today there are many livestock production systems. These are classified into three broad groups: (1) *pasturage* (grazing) systems, (2) *mixed farming* systems in which livestock production is integrated with agriculture, and (3) industrial systems in which livestock production is organised along industrial business lines. The characteristic differences among these broad groups are touched upon in the following section. In terms of their relative contribution to world output of milk and meat, the mixed farming system appears to be the most prevalent system. According to one estimate, it accounts for 90 per cent of world's milk output. Of the balance of meat output, pasturage provides only 9 per cent; and industrial system 37 per cent, which is largely concentrated in the developed world (Cees de Haan *et al.* 1997).

In India also mixed farming system predominates, and there again large ruminants have predominant position. A general framework of the mixed farming system as practiced in India, depicting the linkages between agriculture, ruminant livestock population and production system and environment, is presented in section 3. Section 4 is devoted to a brief description of the state of livestock economy against the general background. Both these sections are preparatory to articulation of the strategy for sustainable development of the system. The discussion in section 5 pertains to the latter. Public policy implication of the strategy are discussed in section 6. The summary and conclusion of the study are presented in the last section.

Livestock Production Systems

As mentioned earlier livestock farming, rather production systems, currently in practice around the world, fall into three broad groups: *pasturage, mixed farming,* and *industrial production systems.* The systems are distinguished, one from the other, according to the mode of sourcing feed for the livestock. In the pasturage system, as the name suggests, animals directly feed themselves by grazing and browsing on pastures or open rangelands. In the temperate regions of North and South America, pasturage is practiced in the form of ranching in which vast tracts of pasture lands are privately owned or held on lease. The forage availability on such pastures is maintained by periodic seeding and fertilizer applications. In contrast to this in the arid, semi-arid and mountainous regions of Asia and Africa, pasturage is traditionally practiced by pastoral communities on open, public rangelands. Since forage availability on the rangelands varies with climatic conditions and seasons of the year, these communities usually follow a transhumance cycle, moving herds from one to the other rangeland. In Western Himalayas0, for example, pastoral communities like Gujar and Gaddies move their herds from high to low altitudes in summer.

Irrespective, of its form, pasturage is an extensive system of livestock production, requiring considerable area of land per head of livestock.

The mixed farming system, in which animal husbandry is integrated with crop production, is an intensive system of production. Animal feed—dry fodder (crop residues) and green fodder—is produced and fed to animals at the level of the farming unit. Concentrates as by-products of grain processing such as husk, bran, broken foodgrain residues (*chunni, khuddi*) were earlier also produced at the farm households using traditional labour intensive technology. Oilcake too was produced not beyond the village level using bullock-drawn rotary press. This traditional system was almost wholly self-reliant. With industrial development, grain processing has increasingly moved away to power driven milling industry. As a result, concentrate by-products now flow back to farms either directly from the mills or in the form of compounded feed through marketing channels. This development has reduced the self-reliance of the mixed farming system at the farm level, but not at the macro, national level.

Unlike pasturage and mixed farming system, industrial livestock production system is free from land constraint for sourcing feed. All of its feed requirements is met from external supplies through the market. Typical examples are feed-lot system in the advanced industrial countries and dairy production enterprises in the urban and pre-urban areas of the developing countries. In the first case meat animals (cattle or pigs) are subjected to close door intensive feeding for fattening before being sent out for slaughter. In the second case too animals in-milk (cow or buffalo) are kept on high rations, while dry animals and calfs as far as possible, are removed from the production enterprise. The industrial system at the enterprise level or even at the national economy level may appear to be free from land constraint, but as animal feed at the primary stage comes from land, this system as well makes a demand on land within or outside of the country concerned. If a Dutch swine is fattened on cassava feed imported from Thailand, Thailand must allocate land for cassava production to that extent.

The livestock production systems also differ in their economic motivations. The industrial livestock production system is driven by profit motive, and is subject to market forces of supply and demand for inputs and outputs. If, for some reason market price of feed rises much faster than that of milk, an urban dairy enterprise may decide to reduce its milk output by reducing its scale of operation or by reducing the feed ration of the animals in its herd. Thus, the industrial system is an open-ended system, at the input as well as output end of the production process.

The motive of production under pasturage and mixed farming vary across countries and regions depending upon the general level of the economic development and relative resource endowment in particular as between land and labour. Ranchers in North and South America are driven by profit motive, and produce for the market. For the pastoral communities in Asia and Africa, pasturage, on the hand, is simply a source of livelihood. Similar differences exist in the developed and developing world in respect of mixed farming. In the European Community 'dairy farmers', who produce forage crop for feeding their dairy herd. On the farm, are *profit maximisers*. Quite, in contrast mixed farmers in the densely populated South Asian region, where foodgrains production is the primary goal, *maximise milk output* from the few dairy animals they are able to maintain on their farms in addition to plough bullocks. They look to livestock as a secondary source of income, and employment of family labour.

Just as livestock production system differ in their economic motives, so they do in respect of their interactions with the environment. Interaction is mostly situation (site) specific with the natural resource base land, water, plant, microflora, biodiversity and air. There is, however, one common global atmospheric impact from all types of ruminant production system, namely emission of methane (CH_4) which contributes to global warming, hence climate change. As regards situation specific interaction of different livestock production system it is not our purpose to discuss it in any detail. A good account can be found in Cees de Haan *et al.* (1997) referred earlier.

For illustrative purpose, let us consider interaction with land. Pasturage in the aird and semi-arid regions can be in balance with the area of the rangeland, if stocking rate is consistent with forage renerative capacity of the top soils, in other words 'carrying capacity' of the rangeland. Overstocking leads to overgrazing which expose the soil to erosion and reduces forage affects the health of the herd and its productivity.

In the mixed farming system, wherein animals are fed agricultural by-products, livestock production make little claim on land, secondly, dung used as manure replaces chemical fertilizers, maintains natural fertility of the soil, and protects soil-born micro-organisms. The industrial system, on the other hand, based as it is on intensive concentrate feeding, makes a large claim on land resource base, domestic or foreign, for feedgrains and tuber production. The system produces mountains of animal excreta. The latter, whether disposed in slurry pits or spread on fields, has a damaging effect on the local land base. Clearly, from environmental angle, mixed farming systems appears to be most beneficial.

Mixed Farming System: A General Framework

In the present section we provide a general framework of livestock production under mixed farming system. It is based upon the experience of mixed farming as practiced in India. It relates to bovine stock, cattle and buffaloes, with which agriculture is integrated. Small ruminant (sheep and goat) production takes place on the side lines of this system. The framework, as can be seen from the accompanying chart, demonstrates the relationships or linkages that exist between livestock production and livestock population, agriculture and environment. It is meant to guide us in articulating the strategy for sustainable development in the subsequent sections. It may be noted that the term livestock hereafter is used synonymously with cattle or buffaloes.

Livestock production, like any other, can be viewed as a process of transformation of certain inputs into outputs. However, there is a basic difference between livestock and other production processes. An animal involved in the production process is not a mere machine which can be made and remade at will. On the contrary, it is a living being subject to life-processes, and produced by a breeding population of which it is a member. Consider a cow producing milk. Suppose 6 months before she had given birth to her first calf—a she-calf, so to say. This daughter after a period of growth to maturity, say 3 years since birth, will give birth to her first calf 2½ years from now, and will enter into milk production process. Her growth to maturity is another process of production, rather a sequence of annual production processes, the output of which are additions to her body weight and age. From an economic angle this is what is known as investment or capital formation. While this daughter will be producing milk, her mother after completing her lactation period, may have gone through a dry period, and be ready to give birth to another calf and start milk production again. And, during the same period under consideration, her grandmother should have given birth to her second, third or fourth calf and entered another period of milk production.

The overlapping time sequences of births, maturity to productive age and lactation periods over three generations of cows described above reveals several characteristics of a cattle production system. *First*, an animal involved in the production process is genetically related to other animals. *Second*, the animals together constitute a population. *Third*, they are products of reproduction of that population. *Fourth*, the animals in the population differ among themselves by age, sex and function. And, *finally*, during any year there are three production processes simultaneously going on: (1) cows producing milk, (2) cows in their dry period undergoing physiological and hormonal changes before producing their crop of calfs, and (3) young calfs born in the current year as well as from the preceding years growing in age and body-weight. These production processes, when animals are considered in groups, together constitute a macro system of production in which the whole cattle population is involved. This holds good in the case of buffaloes also.

Consider now the movement of the system over time. It is easy to see that the movement is, *ceteris paribus*, determined by the reproduction process of the population, cattle or buffaloes. Reproduction is a biological process in which several factors play a role. Critical factors are: (1) the initial size of the breedable stock, i.e. the number of cows in their reproductive period, (2) breeding efficiency of the stock, i.e. the ratio of cows giving birth to a calf during the year to the total number of breedable cows, (3) age and sex specific mortality rates, and (4) maturity age of males and females, i.e. the age at which they enter their reproductive life. For a given set of values of these parameters and the initial size of the breedable stock, reproduction will make a change in the size of the livestock population in question, and also in its age, sex and functional composition. The direction of change, i.e. whether the population would be growing remain stationary, or declining, will depend upon the configuration of the parameter values. Concomitant to change in the population there will be change in the volume of production.

The exposition above is a bio-physical representation of a livestock production system. But humans rear livestock for economic purposes. Therefore, the system needs to be looked at from an economic view-point. From this view-point growth in the body mass of a calf is not considered an output of the system, through it is an output from bio-physical perspective. The calf, through its metabolic processes, converts the feed (input) fed to it into bodymass (output) only milk is the only output of the above system, when looked at from an economic angle.

The size and composition of the livestock population resulting from natural reproduction processes is also open to human intervention to suit economic purposes. In the developed world dairy farmers, who do not need plough bullocks since crop production is mechanised, dispose of their males for beef production purposes. Their slaughter drastically reduces male to female ratio in the cattle population. At the same time, it results into desired output of beef, in addition to output of milk from the system. In a developing country like India, since buffalo males are not normally used as plough-bullocks, buffalo male calfs after weaning were traditionally left to die their natural death, of course from starvation and uncare. Now, when commercial spirit has gripped the land, it is likely that farmers will take care of the calfs up to a certain age before disposing them of for slaughter. Either way the male to female ratio in the buffalo population is reduced to suit economic purposes.

It is clear from the above discussion that in practice every livestock production system has certain socially desired output goals. Let us illustrate this with reference to mixed farming system of India. In India, cattle traditionally have been (are) reared primarily to provide animal draught power (animal energy as shown in the chart) for purposes of agricultural operations. Milk output from the cattle system is a second priority. In fact, one might say milk is produced anyway since certain number of cows have to be maintained for replacing the required stock of working bullocks. Quite in contrast, milk output is the first priority goal of the buffalo system. Since buffalo bullocks are very rarely used in agricultural operations in India, animal draught power is hardly a goal of the buffalo production system, although for the sake of symmetry, animal energy has been shown in the chart as a system goal for bovines (cattle and buffaloes). As regards meat output, it is not a system goal either of cattle or buffaloes. Cow is sacred to Hindus. Accordingly, beef does not enter a Hindu kitchen. And, under constitutional provisions in most Indian states there is either prohibition or restriction on slaughter of 'cow and its progeny'. Buffalo is neither sacred, nor is there restriction on slaughter of buffaloes. Yet Hindus in general are averse to eating buffalo meat. However, and despite religious taboo and preferences of the Hindus, some beef and buffalo meat is produced in the country, which supplies to the needs of non-Hindus, Muslims and Christians in particular. Even though meat production is a residual activity, we have shown in the chart meat as an output goal of the system.

It is necessary to note that in addition to socially desired output goals of the system, the system produces outputs of joint products and by-products. The joint products are: (1) dung and urine excreted by the animals, and (2) methane, a greenhouse gas, formed in the digestive tracts of the animals in the process of feed fermentation (enteric fermentation) and released by them largely through eructation. The joint products have important environmental implications, as we will see later. The outputs of by-products come from slaughtered and dead animals. There are many by-products such as hides, hoof, horn, hair, bone, offals and casings. The outputs of these go as raw materials to various crafts and industries in which leather industry is the most prominent.

Let us now consider inputs to the production system. From an economic perspective animals engaged in production are *capital goods, bio-capital* so to say. However, when an animal is slaughtered for meat, it is deemed as a consumption goods. A *capital goods* is the one which has a productive or working life stretching over more than one period of production. Accordingly, it appears, or is used in more than one round or period of production. Cows and bullocks are examples of capital goods. A growing calf, female or male, until it has reached maturity is an 'unfinished capital goods' also known as 'investment goods' in the process of capital formation. Animals apart, production system requires some other capital goods such as animal shed or shelter, feeding stall, milking bucket, tethering material etc.

Among *current inputs*, i.e. inputs consumed within the same period of production, feed fed to animals is of course the most important input. The next most important input is human labour involved in the upkeep and care of animals, in feed preparation and feeding, in grazing if there are grazing grounds, in milking etc. Then, there are sundry items like medicine, salt, veterinary service which call for some money expenditure.

So far we have focused on the livestock (bovines) production system. It is time now to look at its linkages with agriculture. Feed input to the system comes from agriculture, at the micro farm level, as well as at the macro level. Much of it consists of agricultural by-products—dry fodder and concentrates. To provide for green fodder, some land is allocated to production of fodder crops. At the farm level people also collect green fodder from standing crops of foodgrains and oilseeds during weeding and thinning operations. Livestock system provides animal energy to agriculture. Animal energy is a flow from the stock of working animals. It is embodied in the work performed by the latter for various agricultural operations. Thus, there is an *interdependence* between livestock and agriculture through energy exchange between the two. Energy (and nutrients) in the form of feed flows to livestock from agriculture and a part of that is returned to agriculture in the form of animal energy. Another part of that energy and nutrients is returned to agriculture in the form of dung (urine) used as manure.

The *interdependence* just noted is at first weakened and then, finally, eliminated by agricultural mechanisation. Animal energy which was internally generated in the mixed farming system is now replaced by externally supplied fossil fuel. The self-reliance characteristics of the system is thereby lost. In a situation of mechanised agriculture, mixed livestock farming simply means that the farmer produces forage crops and feed grains for feeding the livestock on the farm. It is in this sense that livestock production is integrated with agriculture. This is the form of mixed farming currently practiced in the developed world. In India, despite growing mechanisation of agriculture, mixed farming of the original type outlined in the preceding paragraph still remains the predominant mode, as we will see in the following section.

The environmental impact of this mode of mixed farming is depicted in the accompanying chart. The livestock production system under this mode of mixed farming has environmental impact both on its input as well as output side. On the input side the impact is largely on the natural resource base, land in particular. To the extent agricultural by-products—dry fodder and concentrates—are utilised as animal feed, the system saves land, in other words, does not make a claim on additional land for feed production. From another perspective the livestock work as a recycling machine for agricultural 'waste' (crop residues and concentrates), which are inedible for human consumption. Recycling of any waste materials, organic or inorganic, is an environmentally beneficial strategy.

On the output side, environmental impacts are due to animal energy used in agriculture, management and utilisation of dung output, and methane production from enteric fermentation of feed. The stock of working animals from which energy is derived is a renewable source of energy. Secondly, animal energy use saves fossil-fuel, a non-renewable source of energy. And, finally it prevents emission of greenhouse gases, CO_2 in particular, from burning of fossil-fuel, if the animal energy were to be replaced by fossil-fuel.

As mentioned in the preceding section dung used as manure replaces chemical fertilizers. As against the latter, it is a renewable organic source of soil fertilization. To the extent it replaces chemical fertilizers, it prevents greenhouse gases emission that would otherwise occur in their manufacture, and saves non-renewable mineral resources required for manufacture. In India part of the dung output is used as domestic fuel in the form of dry dung-cake, specially by farm households for cooking purposes. In this form dung is a renewable bio-energy source. It saves fossil fuel (coal) or alternative bio-fuel like firewood. There is no net emission of CO_2 from its burning as the carbon emitted is sequestered by the surrounding plant biomass, in other words, utilised to form carbohydrates through photosynthesis.

We, thus, see that most environmental impacts of the mixed farming system are of beneficial nature. Methane output from enteric fermentation of feed is the only one that has negative environmental impact. Its emission contributes to global warming and climate change. We shall think about its containment in the section on the

Chart Showing Linkages between Livestock Population (Bovines), Production System and Environment

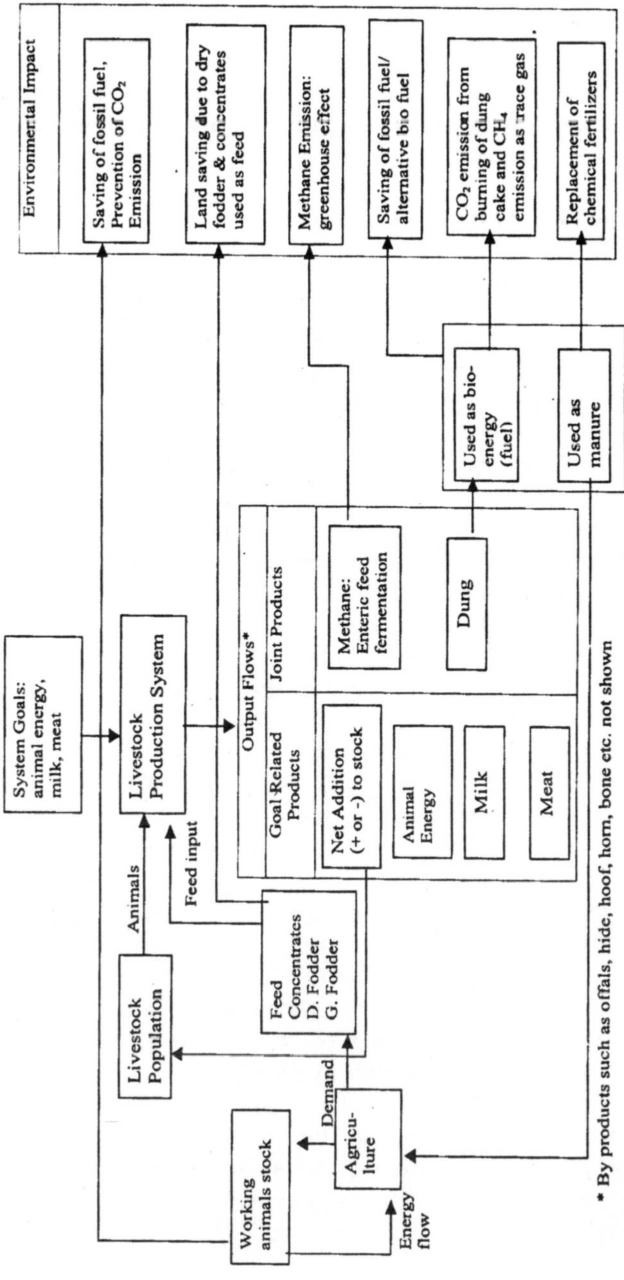

* By products such as offals, hide, hoof, horn, bone etc. not shown

D: Dry
G: Green

strategy of sustainable development. In the meanwhile, against the backdrop of mixed farming framework presented in this section we give a brief empirical account of the current state of livestock economy of India. This will provide us a sort of given initial conditions which to a certain extent determine the nature of the strategy for sustainable development of the economy.

State of the Livestock Economy

Livestock Population

India has world's largest livestock population. In 1992, the year for which livestock census data are available, there were 471 million heads of livestock in the country. In this the largest number was that of bovines, cattle (205 million), and buffaloes (84 million), followed by goat (115 million) and sheep (51 million) (GOI, Ministry of Agriculture, Livestock Census, 1992, Vol. I). The rest comprised of small numbers of equines—horses, mules and ponies—donkey, camel, yak and mithun. India's cattle accounted for about 16 per cent and buffaloes for more than 50 per cent of the world's respective populations (FAO, 1993). Ten years later in 2002, the numbers of bovines and ovines must have increased, but only marginally, except in the case of goats. The observed annual compound growth rates during 1982-92 were as follows: cattle—about 1.0 per cent, buffaloes—1.9 per cent, and goat—about 2.0 per cent (Birthal & Parthasarthi Rao, 2002). Other species like sheep, horses and ponies, camel, donkey, yak have either remained stagnant or declined in number, posing a threat to survival in the case of the latter.

As noted in the preceding section, bovines are the backbone of mixed farming system in India. Difference in the growth rates of cattle and buffaloes indicates their relative importance and changing composition of the bovine stock. Notable compositional changes are the following: (1) increase in the share of buffaloes and consequent reduction in the share of cattle, (2) in cattle as well as buffaloes increase in the share of breedable females and decrease in the share of working adult males, and (3) among the young stock, the share of females rising and that of males falling. The sex and age specific composition of cattle and buffaloes has slowly but surely been moving in favour of increasing milk production and against production of animal energy. Growing agricultural mechanisation has played an important role in this. Indeed, as a result of this the number of cattle bullocks—the livestock census category designated as 'males over 3 years used for work only', whose share in the total working bovines is preponderant, declined from 71 million in 1972 to about 53 million in 1992. During the same period, the number of agricultural tractors increased from 142 thousand in 1972 to 1.22 million in 1992. Since net cultivated area in the country remained stagnant between 140 to 143 million hectare, the density of tractors rapidly increased. A set of two public policies followed since mid-1960s promoted agricultural mechanisation: (1) soft credit and subsidy for purchase of tractors and low priced supply of diesel oil and (2) a cattle breeding policy which exclusively focused on cross-breeding of indigenous cows with exotic breeds aimed at maximising milk production, completely ignoring the fact that indigenous cattle for over thousands of years had been reared and evolved producing and reproducing bullocks required for agriculture.

Livestock Biodiversity

For a large size country like India with her varied topography and climate ranging from snow covered Himalaya in the north to sub-tropical conditions in the southern Peninsula, a high degree of livestock biodiversity is naturally expected. Biodiversity is indicated by the number of species and sub-species present, and the number of different breeds within species. The latter also indicates genetic variability with species.

As enumerated in livestock censuses, there are 10 species of livestock in India. These are: cattle, buffaloes, sheep, goat, horses and ponies, donkey, camel, yak, mithun and pigs. Yak and mithun are sub-species of cattle. On the basis of current knowledge, cattle, excluding yak and mithun have as many as 26 well defined indigenous breeds. Buffaloes have no less than 15 breeds; some of these are considered as best milk-breeds in the world. Goats have 20 breeds, and sheep as many as 40 breeds, though as we mentioned earlier sheep population is now stagnant around 50 million heads (GOI, Ministry of Agriculture, Dept. of Animal Husbandry and Dairying, 1996).

The number of breeds within a species indicates genetic variability. The numbers regarding breeds given above are not based upon up-to-date and complete scientific knowledge. Only now the National Bureau of Animal Genetic Resource (NBAGR) has initiated a programmer of genetic mapping. As a matter of a fact, till recently conservation of livestock biodiversity was not a concern of public policy. A programme of cross-breeding of indigenous cattle, goat and sheep, including females of well defined breeds, with selected exotic gene pools has gone on for decades, unmindful that it will reduce the genetic variability of the indigenous stocks. Thankfully, in case of goat and sheep trials at experimental level itself proved infructuous. Cross-breeds neither yielded expected productivity gains (milk, meat, wool per animal) nor could withstand environmental stress, and, therefore, yielded to high mortality rates (GOI, Min. of Agriculture, Dept. of Animal Husbandry & Dairying, 1996). The most ambitious programme, that of cattle crossbreeding too has yielded modest result. In 1992, after 30 years since programme was started, there were only 15 million crossbreeds (with about 6 million milch cows) in a total cattle population of 205 million. Pretty early in 1970s, after a detailed and careful evaluation of an Intensive Cattle Development Project (ICDP, Pune), I had demonstrated that success of crossbreeding was doubtful since benefit-cost ratios of the project from the private angle of the farmers were less than one, both at the market as well social prices. Main reason was the loss of bullocks required for agriculture following the process of transformation of the indigenous cattle stock of the project into a crossbred one (Mishra, S.N. 1978). At the national level, apart from draught power requirement, general preference of the population for buffalo milk with higher fat content also operated as a constraint on the success of cattle cross-breeding programme. Nevertheless, even with modest success cattle cross breeding has adversely affected genetic variability of the indigenous cattle population.

Production Performance

Average yield of output per animal in India, whether it is milk, meat, wool or any other product, is admittedly very low compared to average yields attained in the temperate and developed regions of the world. During the hay days of crossbreeding programme in 1960s and 1970s it was quite common to advance such yield differences as a stock argument in favour of crossbreeding. But the comparison was (is) unscientific. A valid comparison required some common denominator between the entities compared. Think of a Holstein-Freizian cow in Holland and a Haryana cow in India. Except that they both belong to the same species, cattle, there is no common denominator between them. They differ in their evolutionary history, in genetic make-up and genetically determined milk production traits, in their natural environment, in their economic environment, feed intake, bodymass and so on. Given these inherent differences, the Indian cattle stock, including crossbreds, can never reach the milk yield levels attainted in the developed, temperate regions of the world. If the idea is, as it ought to be, to raise the milk yield of the domestic animals, one should better look for the potential in yield differences that exist across the country within each group of animals, i.e. indigenous cows, crossbred cows, and buffaloes.

Available estimates of milk yield of these groups in different parts of the country are presented in Table 7.1. The figures show the range between the minimum and maximum yield. The difference between these for a given group and a given region indicates the potential for raising the yield. Yield is affected by climate and topography. Long ago W. Burns (1944) noted an inverse relationship between yield and intensity of rainfall. Yet the difference between minimum and maximum yield within a region and also between regions can't be exclusively due to this effect. With this caveat, the figures in Table 7.1 reveal the following.

Consider first the difference within regions. Compared to minimum the maximum achieved milk yield is higher in every region, between 25 to 33 per cent in the case of indigenous cows (leaving aside North-East region), between 20 to 100 per cent in case of crossbreds, and between 50 to 60 per cent in case of buffalos. Across regions the difference is much higher. Compared to minimum the maximum achieved yield is higher by as much as 400 per cent in the case of indigenous cows, 200 per cent in case of crossbreds, and 300 per cent in case of buffaloes. Thus, there is ample potential for increasing milk yield in the country as a whole and in every region.

Table 7.1: Average Milk Yield Per Cow in Milk (kg/day), 1993-94

S. No.	Region/States	Non-Descript Indigenous Cows	Crossbred Cows	Buffaloes
1.	North-West (Haryana, Punjab, Gujarat, Rajasthan)	2.77 – 3.93	6.44 – 7.86	3.71 – 5.63
2.	Central Plateau Region (M.P., Maharashtra, Andhra Pradesh, Karnataka)	1.20 – 1.51	5.47 – 6.95	2.34 – 3.25
3.	Gangetic Plain (Uttar Pradesh, Bihar, West Bengal)	1.66 – 1.95	4.77 – 5.56	3.5 – 4.33
4.	North-East (Assam, Manipur, Meghalaya, Mizoram, Nagaland)	0.69 – 1.37	4.05* – 8.42**	2.14 – 3.25

* Relates to Warm Assam Plain; ** Relates to Cooler Highlands

Source: GOI, Ministry of Agriculture, Dept. of Animal Husbandry and Dairying, 1999, Table 9-11.

There is little reliable information on yield rates of meat, wool, dung and by-products from slaughted and dead animals. From sundry information it is reported that average live weight of cattle at slaughter is 200-250 kg and that of buffaloes 200 kg. And the corresponding boneless meat per carcass is reported to be 50 and 60 kg respectively. The average carcass weight of sheep and goat is put at 12 and 10 kg respectively (GOI, Ministry of Agriculture, Dept. of Animal Husbandry & Dairying, 1996). Data for a few states on dung evacuation rates obtained from Department of Animal Husbandry & Dairying shows that the mean rate is a little over 6.0 kg per bovine per day. Animal category-wise information is not at all available.

Despite messy statistic on yields of various products concerned authorities some how make estimates of output and gross domestic product of the livestock sector. By the dint of sheer livestock numbers India produced 58 million tonnes of milk, a little over 3.4 million tonnes of meat, and 39 million kg of wool in 1993-94 (Min. of Agriculture, Dept. of Animal Husbandry & Dairying 1999). In relation to human population these output numbers are pretty small. The per capita availability of milk, the most important source of animal protein for Indians, was no more than 182 gm (1992-93) per person per day as against recommended nutritional norm of about 250 gms by the Indian Council of Medical Research.

In Table 7.2 are presented value of output and gross domestic product (GDP), of the livestock sector and its share in agriculture and national GDP at 1980-81 prices. In 1993-94 livestock sector produced value of output to the tune of about Rs. 20 thousand crore, and GDP of the order of Rs. 14 thousand crore. It is also clear from the table that livestock sub-sector's share in agricultural sector's value of output in real terms increased from about 19 per cent in 1980-81 to 23 per cent in 1993-94. Its share in agricultural GDP increased from 13 per cent to 20 per cent during the same period. And, its share in the national GDP marginally increased, while that of agricultural sector as whole declined from about 38 to 30 per cent. In brief, while livestock's share in national GDP remained stable between 5 to 6 per cent, its share in agricultural GDP substantially increased from 13 to 20 per cent through the period of 1980s and first half of 1990s. The change in general has, thus, been in favour of the livestock sector. Why that is so? The simple answer is that with rise in per capita incomes beyond a certain food from livestock sources gains in relative importance over foodgrains. That gets translated into change of the production structure in favour of the livestock sector. This seems to have been happening in

Table 7.2: Value of Output and Gross Domestic Product of the Livestock Sector

(In Rs. crores, at 1980-81 prices)

S. No	*Particulars*	*1980-81*	*1993-94*
A.	*Value of output*		
1.	Agriculture and allied Activities	56875 (100.00)	86318 (100.00)
2.	Livestock	10597 (18.63)	19627 (22.74)
B.	*Gross Domestic Product*		
1.	National	122427 (100.00)	236064 (100.00)
2.	Agriculture and allied Activities	46649 (38.10)	70231 (29.75)
3.	Livestock	5913 (4.83)	13912 (5.89)
4.	Livestock share in Agriculture & allied Activities	(12.67)	(19.81)

Source: CSO, National Accounts Statistics, 1993 and 1996.
Note: Figures in brackets are percentages.

India during the 1980s and 1990s. Be that as it may, it is important to note that the value of output from the sector does not include the value of animal energy livestock sector supplies to agriculture. In 1992 there were a total of 70 million working animals in India, out of which 63 million were cattle bullocks and rest buffalo bullocks contributing animal energy.

Livestock economy is important from another angle too, that of employment opportunity it provides to the people. Unlike agriculture, animal husbandry is a more regular activity through the seasons of the year. For the last three decades it has remained a key element of the governments' anti-poverty programme. Rural poor, landless, marginal and small farmers are provided credit and subsidy support to acquire productive animals so as to improve their employment and income position. A rough idea of how much employment the sector provides can be had from the following discussion.

The National Sample Survey Organisation (NSSO) periodically conducts surveys on employment and unemployment in the country. The results of the latest survey, NSS 55th Round (July 1999-June 2000) have recently been released (NSSO, 2001). From the Report we can get number of persons employed in agriculture and allied activities, livestock being one such activity. Suppose that labour absorbed per unit of output in livestock is the same as in agriculture. Then, the proportion of persons employed in livestock will be equal to its share in the value of output (refer to Table 7.2) of the agriculture. According to the NSS Report No. 458, just mentioned total work force consisted of 337 million persons in 1999-2000, out of which 202 million were usually employed in agriculture. Assuming that livestock's share in the value of output of agriculture remained at the level of 1993-94, i.e. 23 per cent, the number of persons employed in livestock activities works out to over 46 million. Note that while the energy output of the working animals is not included in the value of output of the livestock sector, the labour of upkeep of those animals is included in this 46 million. This number indicates the order of magnitude, rather than an exact estimate. Furthermore, it should not be interpreted as if so many persons were engaged wholly in livestock activities round the year. It simply means livestock activities absorbed the labour equal to the work of so many persons for most part of the year. In addition to the direct employment of this order, millions of people are employed in industries using livestock raw materials, the residual products of the livestock production system, and in dairy industry.

Feed Availability, Requirement and Consumption

The feed available in India, as noted in section 3, consists of agricultural by-products—dry fodder and concentrates—and cultivated green fodder. The availability of both the components depends upon the volume of agricultural output, which in turn depends upon yields of crops and cropped area. The quantity of cultivated green fodder too depends upon the yield and area allocated for fodder crop production. A notable point is that there is an actual and potential trade-off between availability of feed as by-product of agricultural crops and feed from fodder crops production. With negligible scope for increasing land area under cultivation as is presently the case in India, a shift of area under fodder crops, *ceteris paribus*, will add to fodder output but there will be a corresponding fall in the by-product feed from other crops.

There are a few other aspects of feed availability that need to be noted. With increasing agro-processing industries, manufacture of animal feed has been growing in India. But manufactured feed is not an additional source of feed availability. It is no more than compounding of available feeds with additives like minerals, vitamins and chemicals like urea. Secondly, tradable feeds like feed-grains and oil-cakes and manufactured composites affect domestic availability through export and import. India has for long been an exporter of oil-cake and meal, largely to European Community (EC) countries. To the extent of such exports, net domestic availability of concentrates is reduced. Finally, availability is also affected by non-feed uses of agricultural by-products. There are reports that a good portion of soybean oil-cake output in India finds its way to human consumption. Similarly, in agriculturally advanced regions of the country such as Punjab rice straw is burned after harvest, not to mention its increasing use as a packaging material in the country.

The nutritional requirement of an animal is made up of two parts: requirement for *maintenance* and *production*. The part that enables the animal to carry on the 'essential life processes while at rest' is called *maintenance requirement*. It depends upon several factors, for instance, body weight, body surface of the animal, and environmental conditions. *Production requirement* is generally considered additive to maintenance requirement. It varies with the level or the rate of production (growth of young animal, milk-yield, work intensity). But there is an element of interdependence between the two. A high-yielding milk-breed cow, say a crossbred, apart from yield related production ration requires larger maintenance ration compared to a low-yielding indigenous cow of the same body weight. This is because in the high-yielder tissue metabolism is faster and tissue wear-and-tear more (ICAR, Scientific Panel, 1985). Furthermore, if due to better nutrition there is general body-weight gain in the livestock population over time, its maintenance requirement proportionately goes up.

The nutritional *requirement* of a livestock population in any year may be more, equal to or less than the *availability* of feed. On the other hand, actual *consumption* in any year cannot exceed availability net of carry over to the following year. In short, considered *ex-post* consumption must equal availability. This condition also provides a check on the validity of consumption and availability estimates. If, *post facto*, the two are not equal to each other then the estimate of either of the two or both are incorrect. Estimate of consumption is required not just to check the validity of availability estimate. It has acquired another importance it never had before. All the direct and indirect environmental effects of a livestock production system, as we will see in the following sub-section, are related to feed consumption rather than feed availability or requirement.

A number of official committees and individual researchers have made attempts since early 1950s to estimate feed availability and requirement of livestock population, in most cases the bovine population. The motivation generally was how to increase milk production or meet minimum nutritional requirement of milk of the human population. Quite often the estimate of feed availability and requirement are for a year in future, involving projections of the relevant variables and parameters. In this context it is notable that the National Commission on Agriculture (NCA) made a heroic effort of projecting India's livestock population and its composition in precise detail, its feed requirement and availability from various sources in A.D. 2000, i.e. a quarter century away from the base year (Ministry of Agriculture, NCA, Report, Part VII, 1976). Incidentally, projections are hardly conformed by the reality. And, longer the period of projection, more distant from reality it turns out to be, and, therefore, more futile.

Be that as it may, no two studies are comparable since they relate to different years, notwithstanding the differences in their estimation procedure and the values of relevant variables and parameters used in preparing the estimates. Major studies up to the end of 1980s are briefly reviewed in Mishra and Sharma (1990). Notable additions in 1990s are those by Pandey (1995) and the World Bank (1999). Since the World Bank study is the first one by an international agency, it deserves some comments. Contrary to the usual run of Indian studies it has prepared what it calls India's 'feed balance estimates' for 1995, in which the term feed 'demand' and 'supply' are used, instead of feed requirement and availability, giving the impression that the estimates have something to do with market processes. A closer examination suggests that their 'supply' is nothing but availability assumed to be equal to production. And, the 'demand' is some sort of requirement of the projected livestock population (large and small ruminants and pigs) including poultry at the assumed rates of requirement of concentrates and roughages per animal per day. The basis of these rates have not been explained. However, an interesting result of the study is that in 1995 India was *surplus in concentrates* and there was *large deficit in roughages* (World Bank, 1999, Statistical Annex Table 3.2C). Almost all Indian studies, on the contrary, have concluded that there was deficit in both, and more so in concentrates.

There are two Indian studies, which stand out of the long line of studies since early 1950s, which need some discussion. These are by Amble *et al.* (1965) and by Jain and Shivtar Singh (1990). In both of these *consumptions* of different types of feed per day per animal of the different categories of bovines, rather than the *nutritional norms* were, *inter alia*, used for estimating *requirement* of the bovine stock (projected) in the concerned year. The primary source for arriving at the all India feed consumption rates in both these studies are sample surveys, including repeat surveys conducted by the Indian Agricultural Statistics Research Institute (IASRI) since the second half of 1950s to early 1980s, mainly to find out milk-yields and feed consumption per animal per day for different categories of bovines. The surveys were conducted in the typical livestock tracts of the country. Both sets of estimates of all India consumption rates of bovines involve wide assumptions. However, in comparison to Amble's rates, in every item Jain and Shivtar Singh's rates are higher, as expected. Note that agricultural production had been growing roughly at a tend rate of 3.0 per cent a year over the period 1966-85. Accordingly, by-product feed output had been growing at the same rate. Since bovine stock had been growing at about 1.0 per cent a year, per animal feed availability had been growing (Mishra and Sharma, 1990). Finally, it may be noted that it is neither feed availability nor requirement but actual feed consumption, i.e. the feed input to the livestock production system, as indicated in the chart, that has environmental impact to which we turn now in the following sub-section. For interested readers feed consumption rates of the bovines from Jain and Shivtar Singh (1990) are given in the Annexure to this chapter.

Environmental Impact

The environmental impacts or effects of the mixed livestock farming system as practiced in India were identified in the preceding section (see the chart). Here we present some estimates of those effects with reference to cattle and buffalo population as of 1992. These estimates are taken from a major study we recently did with financial support from the National Dairy Development Board (NDDB), (S.N. Mishra & A.K. Dikshit, 2001). The effects fall into two broad groups: global and local (national). Emission of green house gases or their emission prevented has global warming effect. Local effects are in the nature of resource saving.

According to our estimate, in 1992 total methane (CH_4) emission from the livestock production system was of the order of 9.767 million metric tonnes (MT). Most of it is from enteric fermentation of feed fed to animals, as emission from 'manure management' (0.202 MT) and from burning of dung cake (0.21 MT) as negligible. At the same time, 6.0 MT of CO_2 emission was prevented due to animal energy used in agriculture in place of fossil fuel (diesel). This much of emission would occur if over 70 million working animals were to be replaced by tractors. At the replacement rate of 12 bullocks to a tractor, replacement of the stock would require 6.0 million tractors and about 20 million tonnes of diesel oil to run them annually, burning of which would cause CO_2 emission. Thus, use of animal energy yields double environmental benefit; saves fossil fuel and prevents CO_2 emission. Furthermore, it contributes to India's self-reliance as the country imports 70 per cent of its petroleum requirement.

Local impacts are all environmentally beneficial. Our estimates show that if agricultural by-products—dry fodder and concentrates—used as animal feed were to be replace by cultivated green fodder, as much as 46 million hectares of land would be required to produce it. Currently India devotes about 5 per cent of the total cropped area, i.e. not more than 8 million hectare for green fodder production. Dry dung cake is a renewable bioenergy source. If it was to be replaced by another bioenergy source, fuel wood, production of latter would require 2.0 million hectare of land to be kept continuously under fuel wood plantation. Besides considerable land saving due to the system, dung used as manure in terms of nutrients saves 2.5 million tonnes of ammonium sulphate, about 0.5 million tonnes of superphosphate and 0.8 million tonnes of muriate of potash. And, being an organic fertilizer it sustains natural fertility of the soil. We also attempted, under certain assumptions, to estimate the value of these benefits. We found that the total value of the benefits (about Rs. 1,20,000 crore) was larger than the value of output of the livestock sector (Rs. 79,000 crore) in 1997-98 (for details refer to Mishra & Dikshit, 2001). One obvious conclusion is that any sustainable development strategy of the livestock economy should be able to retain, rather enhance its environmental benefits.

Sustainable Development Strategy

General Observations

A production system is *sustainable* in the sense that output flow from the system can be maintained indefinitely in future, if the materials and energy inputs to the system are derived from renewable resources. If input level remains constant, the output flow will remain constant, and, thus, the system will remain stationary, just replacing itself as time passes. But human effort always is to increase the flow of output either by increasing the level of inputs or by changing the technology of production, i.e. the proportions in which inputs are combined. This is what is known as development. However, irrespective of technology, there is an upper limit to the flow of materials and energy inputs from the renewable resources, if the latter are not depleted, damaged or endangered in the process of pushing up the flow of inputs. Therefore, development can be sustainable only if the renewable resources, from which the production system receives its materials and energy inputs, are maintained in future, in quantity and quality.

A livestock production system is sustainable since the animals engaged in the production process receive nutrients and energy from feed, and feed is a renewable resource. However, feed production depends upon land, which is an all time limitational resource. This is true whether feed is obtained from grazing on rangeland, or *produced using land* as by-products of agriculture. Therefore, or a given level of output flow sustainable development of the system depends upon the development or growth of feed availability from limited land resource. For a given growth rate of feed availability, growth in output flow can take place either by increasing the size of livestock population, or increasing yield rates of animals or both. If, the initial or actually realised yield rates are lower than the potential rates, the latter course of development is more efficient.

The sustainability conditions discussed above relate to renewable and limitational resource base of the livestock production system. There are two more conditions system's sustainable development ought to satisfy. Firstly, it should not reduce livestock biodiversity and genetic variability. These are now considered as *genetic wealth* of the country concerned, inherited from the past. The present generation, therefore, has no right to tamper with it, and should leave it as such for future generations. Secondly, harmful environmental effects of the production system like emission of greenhouse gases should not increase, rather be reduced in the course of development.

Mixed Farming System: A Sustainable Development Strategy

In the light of above observations and the state of livestock economy of India described in the preceding section we turn to articulation of a development strategy for the livestock economy. We take it for granted that in India mixed farming mode will continue to be in practice in future. We also assume that, following the past trend, the bovine population which is at the core of the mixed farming system, will not be growing at a rate higher than 1.0 per cent a year. Indeed, it may come to stabilise at a certain level, since growth rates of cattle and level since growth rates of cattle and buffaloes have been decelerating (Birthal & Parthasarthy Rao, 2002). A development strategy, in general, consists of three sets of elements: (1) goals, (2) means to achieve the goals, and (3) policies to put the means into action. The strategy of development in our specific context is discussed below.

Development Goals

At present livestock production system is geared to production of milk, meat and animal energy. The social preference ordering among these products was discussed in section 3. This preference ordering is not likely to change in the near future. In the long run, however, if agricultural mechanisation is not contained, the demand for animal energy will decline. This will have two consequential effects—one environmental, and the other economic. The environmental effect would be increasing use of non-renewable fossil-fuel sources of energy in agriculture, and corresponding rise in emission of greenhouse gases, CO_2 in particular. This one is clearly a negative effect from the angle of sustainability. The second effect would be declining rate of replacement of working animals' stock, particularly of cattle bullocks, the predominant part of the stock. This will pose the increasing problem of disposal of male cattle calfs, more so if the reproduction rate of the cattle population were to increase as it ought to increase, since the breeding efficiency of the population (ratio of cows in-milk to total number of breedable cows) is presently quite low, less than 50 per cent. The traditional mode of male calf disposal, as in the case of buffaloes, of letting it die of starvation, besides being cruel, is economically inefficient, since a certain cost has been incurred from its embryo stage to birth and on to suckling age. Even if the replacement rate of cattle bullock stocks is restrained from falling as a matter of sustainable development strategy, improvement in the breeding efficiency of the cattle population will continue to pose this problem. Since the scope for culling by slaughter is extremely limited, male calfs (including of buffaloes) should be reared up to a certain age, before being exported for meat to other countries. This will enlarge the opportunity to produce milk for domestic demand and bovine meat animals for world demand.

Thus, the goals of sustainable livestock development in India ought to be:

(1) To increase flow of outputs of *milk* and *meat animals*;
(2) To continue using animal energy in agriculture;
(3) To conserve livestock biodiversity and genetic variability within species; and
(4) To minimise greenhouse gases emission from the production system.

It may be noted that there is no conflict among these goals, conservation of biodiversity and genetic variability is an ethical goal. So it stands on its own. And, goal numbers (1), (2) and (4) are simultaneously achievable without affecting each other adversely.

Means to Achieve the Goals

The essential means to achieve the goals is a well fed, healthy animal, irrespective of its age, sex and function. That every member of the livestock population acquires such a status, the enabling means are availability of feed and fodder sufficient to meet the nutritional requirement of the population and health care facilities. Availability of dry fodder and concentrates has been growing *paripasu* with growth in agricultural production. Green fodder availability has also been growing with increase in area under irrigation, even though the share of fodder area to cropped are has remained constant. In fact, because agriculture's growth rate has been substantially higher compared to the growth rate of livestock population, per animal availability has been increasing (Mishra and Sharma, 1990). During 1990s agricultural growth had slackened, but it was still higher than the growth rate of the livestock population. The prospect for increasing per animal feed availability in future appear promising also because of current policy emphasis on agricultural diversification which favours livestock production. The real problem is how to enhance nutritive value of available feed, specially of dry roughages at the field level. We shall return to this in the following sub-section.

As regards health care facilities, these fall into two groups: (1) facilities for surveillance, prevention and control of epidemic diseases like rinder pest, foot and mouth disease, and (2) veterinary facilities, including artificial insemination centres which cater to livestock with individual farmers. There is already a vast infrastructure in the country of the second type of facilities under public sector. Quality of services, however, is reported to be poor. With increasing market orientation in all sorts of services, it is likely that veterinary facilities will increase under private initiative. The first type of facilities by their very nature belong to public sector. Provision of these facilities is found to be very inadequate (Dept. of A.H. & D., Steering Group, 1996).

As nutrition and health of the livestock population improves with time, its reproductive and productive characteristics are bound to improve. Better nutritive feeding alone will lead to increase in the breeding efficiency of cattle and buffaloes, will reduce the age at first calving, prolong the productive age, and will reduce age and sex-specific mortality rates. It will increase the milk yield per milch animal, as also yield per animal in-milk. We have already seen considerable, large gap between the potential and realised milk yield per animal in-milk in all types of the bovine population.

Besides nutrition and health related means, purposive intervention in the breeding processes is another means to improve the productive traits of animals. Crossbreeding of indigenous cows with exotic breeds started in early 1960s and pursued till date in India is a classic example of such intervention with single purpose of increasing milk production in the country, completely ignoring the other goal of the cattle system, namely animal energy (stock of bullocks) required for agriculture. As we have seen earlier, judged in terms the number of crossbred cattle and breedable cows generated so far, this long concerted public effort has been a failure. Originally crossbreeding was supposed to cover only so called 'non-descript' indigenous cows. But latter it was extended to cover even well defined indigenous cattle breeds like Haryana, Gir, Rathi, Tharparker and Sahiwal. Along the same line, the 'non-descript' buffaloes across the country began to be crossed with well-known breeds like Murrah for the same purpose. Admittedly, behind all this effort at crossbreeding, there was no consciousness regarding conservation of genetic variability within the cattle and buffalo population in the country. Possibly, even today it is not there.

Man has been doing selective breeding, choosing best bulls to sire the females in his stock from the time livestock were domesticated. This route to improve productive traits does not interfere with the genetic variability of a population composed of several breeds, provided selection is within breeds. The point is that selective breeding is the suitable means for increasing productive traits as well as for serving the third goal of sustainable livestock development, namely conservation of livestock biodiversity and genetic variability.

Policy Options

The means to achieve goals of sustainable livestock development require a package of state policies to set them in action. It must be recognised, however, that the role of the state is limited since livestock production is in private hands. Wherever private agents are involved, policies can be only *promotional*, and can be implemented through a set of incentives and disincentives. There are, however, areas of social interest in which private behaviour needs to be regulated or direct state action is necessary, as for instance health related areas. Let us now consider policy options that exist in respect of feeding, breeding and animal health.

Feeding of animals is in private hands. Better digestibility of feed, specially of roughages, is known to contribute to better nutrition and productivity on once hand and reduce methane emission from enteric fermentation of feed. Considerable research on feed digestibility has been done in the country. But adoption of techniques and methane for improving digestibility at the farmers' level is poor (Khub Singh and C.S. Prasad, 2002). Perhaps involvement of farmers in generation and adoption of technology may yield better result. As mentioned earlier production of concentrate by-products has been moving to milling industries. This has led to fast growth of compound feed manufacturing. Here it is necessary for the state to set quality standards and monitor its implementation.

As regards *breeding policy*, we have already commented upon indiscriminate crossbreeding followed so far. The focus should now shift to selective breeding, keeping in view the agro-climatic conditions in which well known breeds have evolved. As regards the unknown category bracketed as 'non-descript', the urgent task is to do their genetic mapping in different livestock tracts of the country. Conservation of threatened species like donkey, camel, horses and ponies and yak should also from part of the breeding policy. Here again the success of breeding and conservation policy will depend upon cooperation and involvement of concerned people such as farmers, their association, breeders' village level associations.

In the course of half a century of development planning, a vast network of health related infrastructure has already been built in the country. All that is needed is to improve the quality of the services provided to livestock holders. It has been suggested charging a fee for the service provided may help in toning up the system. However, infrastructure for surveillance and disease control and so also quarantine facilities at ports are quite inadequate. These need to be strengthened. A health inspection system would become necessary before quarantine stage when export of bovine male calf for meat production in other countries becomes a feasible proposition.

Research and development (R&D) in animal sciences and technologies relating to feeding, breeding and health is a necessary complement of any livestock development strategy. Under the aegis of the Indian Council of Agricultural Research (ICAR) a pretty large establishment in terms of the number of scientists, labs and research stations is already there. A review of technologies generated in various areas shows impressive performance. But their extension rather adoption at field level appears to be woofully inadequate. How to achieve this end should be the major question before policy makers. For the animal scientists and technologists it is now necessary to integrate environmental aspects of livestock and livestock production system into their work.

Finally, mechanisation of agriculture based on fossil-fuel needs to be contained in the interest of sustainable development of the mixed farming system. State governments have been providing subsidy and soft loan to farmers, mostly large farmers for purchase of tractors. Then there are instances of free power supply to farmers under political considerations. All these incentives must be removed. From environmental angle alternative to animal energy are other renewable sources of energy such as solar and wind-based energy.

Information Base and Socio-Economic Research

In a recent invited lecture I have reviewed the status of livestock statistics in India (Mishra, 1999). You look at any aspect, be it livestock numbers, feed fed to animals, output quantities, estimates of output values or of value added, available statistics suffer from lack of quality, reliability and timeliness. Then, there are aspects on which statistics are simply not available. It is not without reason that in section 3 we have quoted decade old data on livestock numbers or feed consumption rates (Annexure). A good and updated information base is as much necessary for policy making as for economic and social research relating to livestock. And, for the success or failure of policies at the ground level, research of the latter type is equally necessary.

But economic and social research relating to livestock has not received the attention it deserves (Mishra, 1995). Indeed, it has been the last priority among academic professionals or government research institutions. There are in the country umpteen number of Agricultural Economics Research Centres maintained by the Ministry of Agriculture, Government of India. But livestock is assiduously kept out of their research purview. It should come as no surprise that there is not even one centre in this large country devoted to economic and social research on livestock, or for that matter, on environmental aspects of the livestock production systems. In this direction we have recently made a modest effort, for the first time in the country to set up a Livestock Research and Conservation Centre committed to such research and building up of an information base concerning all of the livestock species. One palpable reason for poor research interest in this area has been lack of promotion and financial support from public agencies, including those that are directly concerned with agricultural or livestock development in the country.

Annexure

AVERAGE FEED CONSUMPTION PER DAY PER ANIMAL

Classification of Animals	*Category*	*Concentrates (gms)*								*Roughages (Kg)*		*Nutrient (Kg)*	
		Oil cakes	*Bran*	*Husk*	*Cereals*	*Pulses*	*Cotton seed*	*Others*	*Total*[b] *(Kg.)*	*Green*[a]	*Dry*	*DCP*	*TDN*
In Milk	Cow	96	22	16	14	38	19	68	0.273	5.09	5.01	0.235	3.49
	Buffalo	398	81	28	39	89	181	131	0.947	8.77	6.41	0.373	5.24
Dry	Cow	40	12	3	1	7	1	17	0.081	3.96	4.38	0.131	2.69
	Buffalo	89	58	9	9	28	5	35	0.233	6.84	5.22	0.158	4.49
Adult Males	Cattle	58	11	5	55	125	6	17	0.277	5.90	5.48	0.251	3.56
	Buffalo	36	19	65	–	41	12	–	0.174	6.51	5.44	0.178	3.11
Young Stock Cattle	Male	17	3	2	9	23	1	5	0.060	1.95	1.97	0.089	2.00
	Female	13	2	1	1	6	–	6	0.028	1.61	2.36	0.059	1.98
Buffalo	Male	1	–	–	–	12	7	3	0.023	1.80	1.53	0.056	1.52
	Female	1	–	–	5	38	5	–	0.049	2.19	2.55	0.082	2.13

Notes: (*a*) Excludes the quantity Consumed through grazing.
(*b*) Includes Salt, Gur, Methi, Oil, Cattle feed etc.

Source: J.P. Jain and Shivtar Singh, 1990.

Concluding Observations

In this paper, we have made an attempt to distinguish between different livestock farming systems and then have claimed that the mixed farming system, in which livestock and agriculture are integrated or interdependent, is environmentally most benign. Based on the experience of mixed farming system in India, a system that constitutes the predominant mode in practice, we have delineated its characteristics, the linkages between livestock and agriculture, between the livestock population and livestock production system, and the impact of the latter on environment, both on its input as well as output side. We have then given a brief quantitive account of India's livestock economy in order to prepare the ground for examining the conditions of its sustainable development. A system based upon renewable sources of material inputs and energy is by definition sustainable. So, we have concluded that India's mixed farming system is open for sustainable development in future, provided appropriate state policies are adopted. In the past policies have been formulated and implemented from top down. Success, however, depends upon reversing the direction of policy formulation and implementation. Finally, we have pointed out that information base and socio-economic research relating to livestock in India, so crucial for formulation of right policies and their implementation, is woofully inadequate. Surely, in this attempt we may not have been able to cover all aspects of sustainable livestock development. But, hopefully, it may contribute to a better understanding of the problems of sustainable livestock development in India.

REFERENCES

Amble, V.N. *et al.* 1965(a) 'Feed Requirement of Bovines and Possibilities of Meeting Them', *Indian Journal of Agricultural Economics*, Vol. 20, No. 1, January-March.

Burns, W. (1944), *Technological Possibilities of Agricultural Development in India*, Superintendent of Government Printing, Punjab, Lahore.

Birthal, P. and Parthasarthy Rao, P. (eds), (2002). *Technology Options for Sustainable Livestock Production in India*: Proceedings of the Workshop on Documentation, Adoption, and Impact of Livestock Technologies in India, 18-19 Jan. 2001, ICRISAT-Patancheru, India.

Cees de Haan, *et al.*, (1997), *Livestock and the Environment: Finding A Balance*, Report of Study coordinated by the FAO of the United Nations, the United States Agency for International Development and the World Bank, FAO, Rome.

FAO, (1993), *Production Year Book*, FAO, Rome.

Government of India, *15th Indian Livestock Census, 1992*, Directorate of Economics and Statistics, Department of Agriculture & Cooperation, Ministry of Agriculture, New Delhi.

Government of India, Ministry of Agriculture, Deptt. of Animal Husbandry, (1976). *Report of the National Commission on Agriculture*, Part-VII, New Delhi.

Government of India, Ministry of Agriculture, Deptt. of Animal Husbandry and Dairying, (1996). *Report of the Steering Group on National Livestock Policy*, New Delhi.

Government of India, Department of Animal Husbandry and Dairying, Ministry of Agriculture, *Basic Animal Husbandry Statistics*, AHS series-7, (1999), New Delhi.

Indian Council of Agricultural Research, Scientific Panel on Animal Nutrition and Physiology, (1985), Nutritional Requirement of Livestock and Poultry, ICAR, New Delhi.

Jain, J.P and Singh Shivtar, (1990) 'Qualitative and Quantitative Insufficiency of Livestock Feeds by 2001 AD, and Possibilities of Bridging the Gap'. *Indian Journal of Animal Sciences*, 60 (10), 1224-1229, ICAR, New Delhi.

Mishra, S.N., (1978), *Livestock Planning in India*, Institute of Economic Growth, Vikas Publishing House, Delhi.

Mishra, S.N, (1995), 'India's Livestock Economy: A Perspective on Research' *Indian Journal of Agricultural Economics*, Vol. 50, No. 3.

Mishra, S.N., (1999), 'Dr. V.G. Panse Memorial Lecture: The Status of Livestock Statistics in India,' *Journal of the Indian Society of Agricultural Statistics*, Vol. 52 (3): 273-89.

Mishra, S.N. and Sharma, R.K., (1990). *Livestock Development in India: An Appraisal*, Institute of Economic Growth (IEG), Vikas Publishing House, Delhi.

Mishra, S.N. and Dikshit, A.K., (2001). *Environmental Contributions of Livestock in India*, Society for Economic & Social Research (SESR), Delhi (forthcoming).

National Sample Survey Organisation (NSSO), (2001), *Employment and Unemployment Situation in India*, 1999-2000, Report No. 458, NSSO, New Delhi.

Pandey, U.K., (1995), 'The Livestock Economy of India: A profile,' *Indian Journal of Agriculture Economics*, Vol. 50, No. 3.

Singh, Khub and Prasad C.S., 'Potential of Nutritonal Technologies in Improving Livestock Productivity' in Birthal and Parthasarthy Rao (ed.), *op. cit*.

World Bank, (1999), '*Indian Livestock Sector Review: Enhancing Growth and Development*', Rural Development Sector Unit, South Asian Region, Delhi.

8

Livestock Revolution as a Sustainable Alternative for Poverty Alleviation

A Strategic Approach

P.N. BHAT

Livestock production is an important source of income for the rural poor in developing countries. It enables poor and landless farmers to earn income using common-property resources, crop by-products that would otherwise become waste; use land that has no other sustainable agricultural use. Livestock products are an important source of nutrients. The addition of milk and meat to the diet provides protein, calcium, vitamins, and other nutrients that are lacking in their usual diets. Besides providing food, the driving force behind increased livestock production, they have other valuable uses. Livestock remain the most important if not the sole form of non-human power available to poor farmers. The poor, in particular, use fertilizer from livestock operations. Livestock also store value and provide insurance for people who have no other financial market available to them. Skins, wool, fat and other resources are used as inputs in other industries. The rapid growth in livestock production is critical to designing policies that promote the incorporation of the rural poor into economically and environmentally sustainable growth patterns.

Although traditionally livestock, dairying and fisheries sectors have been treated as integral parts of agriculture as allied sectors, these sectors have some unique characteristics of their own. They have problems as well as opportunities, which need consideration individually without being allied with crop agriculture and/or industry. It is felt that the approach for achieving higher growth rate in this sector has clearly to be spelled out and the proportional investments made on infrastructure and reform in policy framework, a growth rate of 6 to 8 per cent in the livestock sector must be obtained in order that an overall growth rate of 4 per cent is realized for agricultural sector as a whole in India during 10th Plan period.

Currently three categories of production systems within a continuum of development both within a country and between the countries exist. The first category is:

> *Subsistence-based Production*—The poorest of the world's poor people comprise hundreds of millions of families existing on less than $1 per day. Approximately 50 per cent of these families own livestock and in some parts of the world will remain reliant for at least some more human generations on adapted genetic resources that can cope with low-input, high-stress production systems to provide food, fibre and hides for home use and local sales; serve as a source of traction and fuel; meet cultural and religious needs and provide a reliable and readily convertible means of managing family resources. Low literacy rates and very real risks of hunger are common problems. Consequently, programme and policies' have to be adjusted to their needs.
>
> *Market-based Production*—Opportunities for small to medium scale commercial animal production reflect global patterns of urbanization, economic development and globalization. These changes provide opportunities for farmers to move from subsistence production for primarily home use to market-oriented production with attendant demands for greater consistency of production, more reliable and predictable product quality, better producer organization, equitable price negotiations, reliable product delivery, access to credit, greater economic risk, and increasing competition for resources, markets, credit and political favours from outside the traditional agricultural sector. This system relies on increasing external inputs.
>
> *High-Input Production*—High-input production increasingly is becoming a global phenomenon. In the

mature, developed economies food costs are a relatively small percentage of disposable income, food security has been essentially achieved, and per capita consumption of animal products is stable or declining. In these economies issues of food quality, food safety and respect for animal welfare and the environment are of increasing importance. Farmers in developing nations must also address these issues if they aspire to market products in the most developed nations. High input livestock production is also becoming common in peri-urban areas of developing countries as urban populations expand and economic development leads to larger, more lucrative and more consistent markets for animal products. These systems often attract investments from outside traditional agricultural communities which do not contribute to facilitate rural development.

Policy makers must address the desired mix of systems including the need of each system to be as a part of comprehensive national development strategy. Moving away from the subsistence production is generally a development goal although the desired mix of households in other systems is much less clear, but will have a profound effect on the proportion of a nation's households involved in agriculture, and will likely differ among countries, depending on other, non-agricultural development goals.

It is within these three categories that scientists have to interphase the technologies for alleviation of poverty, generation of wealth and employment. This conference must therefore address these issues in a holistic manner.

The proportionate contribution of livestock sector (4-8. 6-5%) to total Gross Domestic Product Growth (GDP) has remained constant; its contribution to agricultural GDP has gone up to 22.6 per cent by 1998-99. This however does not include animal power, which is valued at between Rs. 4,000 and Rs. 9,500 crore in terms of fuel equivalent. The contribution of milk alone (Rs. 82, 624 crore) was higher than paddy (Rs. 68,230 crore), wheat (Rs. 40,323 crore) and sugarcane (Rs. 23,314 crore). Against this, the investments of the Government of India including share of States in Animal Husbandry and Dairying Sector is extremely low and varied between 0.4 per cent and 1.0 per cent. The investments in AH&D as a percentage to total investment of Government of India in 9th Plan was 0.4 per cent only. This calls for revision and massive investments during 10th Plan.

Animal Husbandry sector provides large self-employment to millions of households in rural areas. Employment in Animal Husbandry sector was 9.8 million in Principal status (out of which 7.90 million were in rural areas) and 8.6 million in subsidiary status, this does not include persons employed in sale, re-processing and transport of animal products at secondary market level. Apart from these, large manpower is involved in livestock related activities, viz. manufacture of animal food products and beverages, manufacture of woolens, tanning and dressing of leather, farming of animals, production, processing and preserving meat and meat products, manufacture of dairy products, retail and wholesale trade of livestock products, etc.

The rural women have a special place in this sector. They play a significant role in animal husbandry. Women constitute 71 per cent of the labour force in livestock farming. In dairying, 75 million women are engaged as against 15 million men, while in case of small ruminants, the sharing of work with men is almost equal. Decisions in livestock production lie with men while those of feeding and milk production, breeding of animal and fodder cultivation lie with women. Although, women are involved in most livestock operations, their knowledge level is low. Therefore, in order to further increase income from livestock farming, knowledge level of women has to be increased. Special programmes need be taken up to move this employment growth to 9 per cent during 10th Plan.

Population growth, urbanization and income growth in developing countries are fuelling a massive global increase in demand for food of animal origin. Twenty-three per cent of the world's population living in developed countries presently consume three to four times the meat and fish and five to six times the milk per capita as those in developing countries. A change has taken place, massive annual increases in the aggregate consumption of animal products are occurring in developing countries. From the early 1970s to the mid-1990s, consumption of meat in developing countries grew by 70 million metric tonnes, whereas consumption in developed countries grew by only 26 million metric tons. In value and caloric terms, meat consumption in developing countries increased by more than three times the increases in developed countries. Milk consumption in the developing world increased by more than twice as much as milk consumption in the developed world in terms of quantity, money value and calories. In India food consumption basket is also diversified in favour of non-food grain items like milk, meat, egg and fish. The consumption of food of animal origin is however small, income increases would make people consume more of these items resulting in improved overall nutrition, export potential is immense which should be realised.

The demand for foods of animal origin comes from changes in the diets of billions of people and could provide income growth opportunities for many rural poor. It has been designated as *Livestock Revolution.* Like the well-known Green Revolution, the label is a simple and convenient expression that summarizes a complex series of interrelated processes and outcomes in production, consumption, and economic growth. As in the case of cereals, the stakes for the poor are enormous. And unlike the Green Revolution, the transformation has been brought in by new biology, which has changed the technologies, are knowledge intensive. The two revolutions differ in one fundamental respect: the Green Revolution was supply-driven, whereas the Livestock Revolution is driven by demand. The demand driven 'Livestock Revolution' will stretch the capacity of existing production and distribution systems and exacerbate environmental and public health problems. Governments and industry must prepare themselves for this continuing transformation with long-term policies and investments that will satisfy consumer demand, improve nutrition, direct income growth opportunities to those who need them most, and alleviate environmental and public health stress.

Our target group consists of 67 per cent farmers (small, marginal, landless labour and women) who have limited access to land and are resource poor. We need to help them to convert whatever assets (Labour and Livestock) they have, to generate wealth and employment. So that they participate in growth process directly and come out of poverty net.

What are the options available to them? Become a part of this Revolution and convert our surpluses to dollars and use them as input in fuelling growth in livestock sector and eradicate poverty. Alternatively do nothing as usual. If they chose option one—they have to use (i) Technology and Science for effective transition; and (ii) generate enough surplus goods for export to fuel the livestock revolution in the country. If export is not possible in near future to developed countries because of tariff and non-tariff barriers. Export to developing countries in Asia and Africa. The domestic demand itself will lead to household, nutritional security in the near future that itself is no small achievement.

The basic platform therefore will be financially viable livestock units underwritten by service provider and supported by financial institutions such that he can convert slowly from subsistence farming (1, 2 animals) to financially viable livestock units of 5, 10 cows/buffaloes through an appropriate technology underwriting by the service provider and credit by financial institutions.

The rapid increase in this demand presents crucially important policy dilemmas that must be resolved for the well being of both rural and urban people in our country. These dilemmas involve complex environmental and public health issues in the context of weak regulatory environment. Taken together, the many opportunities and dangers of the Livestock Revolution suggest that it would be foolish for us to adopt a *laissez faire* policy for livestock development. Many specific recommendations for concrete action have been discussed hereunder.

Technological progress in the production, processing, and distribution of livestock products will be central to the positive outcome of the Livestock Revolution. Rapid advances in feed improvement and genetic and reproductive technologies offer scope for overcoming many of the technical problems posed by increased livestock production. Institutional and regulatory development will also be critical to securing desirable environmental and public health outcomes. In sum, the demand-driven Livestock Revolution is one of the largest structural shifts to ever affect food markets in developing countries and how it is handled, is crucial for future growth prospects in developing livestock for food security and the livelihoods of the rural poor, and for environmental sustainability.

Strategy

Livestock, as they are raised presently at subsistence farming level, is financially unviable but by increasing the unit size and using current technologies it has an opportunity of generating wealth and employment. Livestock enterprises with crossbred cattle and high yielding buffaloes have shown to be a remunerative business. Studies have shown that dairy enterprise as against crops in rural areas gave larger profit margins in marginal, small and medium holdings. Studies have also shown that dairying and crop production together for small farmers having irrigated land was more profitable than crop farming alone. Profitability of dairy farming for different herd sizes has also been demonstrated. Various animals' models (sheep, goat, pig and poultry) in different agro-climatic regions under specialized and mixed farming situations, depending upon people's preferences and under different systems (extensive, semi-intensive and intensive). Economic viability of these models has been demonstrated. On the macro level, the livestock sector in India looks bright and is steadily marching to prepare itself for the challenges in the next millennium. In India the land-man ratio is low and distribution of land is skewed; diversification of a crop based rural economy into an animal husbandry, mixed farming system must be encouraged for rapid economic development and generating equitable income and employment in the country.

The key issue for future development of livestock is whether India can address her major weaknesses while remaining true to the basic principle that have been the foundation of this success. In the answers to the question lie the international competitive advantages that to our farmers and our industry will get in 21st century. The task before us is not to become the bigger but the best. The building blocks of our success are well known, if not well understood. First is the partnership of farmer with the professional. The second block is the Indian consumers who constitute the largest domestic market. Third is our system of livestock farming which contribute to crop farming, do not compete with human beings in terms of food and gives India a tremendous competitive advantage in terms of energy efficiency. Fourth block is quality of products. Science and Technology is extremely important so far as the first and the last blocks are concerned. This is not realized.

Productivity is the key to growth. We have no option but to raise the productivity of our livestock through breeding, feeding and management, the goal is no longer the farmers share of the consumers rupees. It is significant and sustained increase in farmer's income and employment. Quality is the bedrock of success for any enterprise and there is no substitute for consistent, superior quality. Our system has not yet built in quality at every stage from the udder to the consumer. Until India achieves world-standard quality, it will not only find access to markets abroad limited or difficult and will continue to be vulnerable to challenges at home. The wisdom and energy of the farmers combined with the knowledge and skills of the professionals would create the conditions of confidence and strength that has brought out success stories and instances of miracles.

Through meeting the needs of our domestic consumers demand, we expand and achieve superior economics in production, transport, processing and marketing. The answers of 90's may no longer work today, much less tomorrow. We must restructure our total solutions uniquely appropriate to our own environment and accord highest priority to generation and dissemination of appropriate technologies. Our infrastructure, though strong and widespread, is aging and too often poorly used. The cost of traditional livestock based enterprises is increasing. Our research and design must provide new answers to new questions. Our support to client must help raising significantly their efficiency and economy. The future of livestock sector rests not only on the farmer, but on the scientist, the technologist and the professional. We must equip a new generation to compete head on with the best human resources of the advanced nations. In this backdrop, it becomes difficult to remain divorced from the personnel and organizational structure, which is to formulate policies and execute programme for the development of the animal husbandry sector.

Animal husbandry and dairying should receive a high priority in the efforts for generating wealth and employment, increasing animal protein availability in the food basket and for generating exportable surpluses. A sustainable and financially viable livestock and poultry farming, which will generate wealth and self- employment through entrepreneurs hip, is need of the day. The overall focus will be on the four broad pillars, viz. (i) removing policy distortions that is hindering the natural growth of livestock production; (ii) building participatory institutions of collective action for small scale farmers that allow them to get vertically integrated with livestock processors and input suppliers; (iii) creating the environment in which farmers will increase investment in ways to improve productivity in the livestock sector; and (iv) promoting effective regulatory institutions to deal with the threat of environmental and health crises stemming from livestock.

Use of technological and marketing interventions in production, processing, and distribution of livestock products will be central theme of any future programme for livestock development. Technology support is imperative not only for enhancement of productivity but also for reduction of per unit cost. Generation and dissemination of appropriate technologies in the field of animal production as also health care to enhance production and productivity levels will be given greater attention.

External markets are an extremely important source of demand and these should be tapped much more aggressively. In order to encourage exports, all licensing control for processing of livestock products/bye products should be repealed and all restrictions on the export of livestock and its products need to be removed. The immediate focus should on export of Indian dairy products, buffalo meat and poultry products to Asian and African countries. The minimum requirements for sustainable export are creation of disease free zone, organic farming and potable water; these should be made available in selected areas having large marketable surplus.

Sustainable rapid growth and development in this sector can only be ensured if the livestock owners, service providers, veterinarians and planners become knowledge based and acquire the ability to absorb, assimilate and adopt the spectacular development in the veterinary sciences and related technologies. A massive programme encompassing village schools, veterinary colleges and universities should be taken up in collaboration with Indian Council of Agricultural Research (ICAR) to improve the skills and competence of all the stakeholders.

Resides the Ministry of Agriculture, schemes relating to animal husbandry and dairying are also being implemented by other ministries, viz. Ministry of Rural Development, Ministry of Non-Conventional Energy Resources, Ministry of Environment (Animal Welfare Department) etc. Many schemes operated by these ministries have similar and overlapping objectives targeting the same population. Generic components like extension, training, and infrastructure get repeated in most of such schemes and are not complementary. Thus, there is a need for consolidation and convergence of all such activities, schemes and funds. Department of Animal Husbandry and Dairying being the nodal department should address all the issues in totality.

Most of the livestock services like A-I, vaccination, deworming etc. are time sensitive which government institutions at times are not able to deliver due to financial as well as bureaucratic constraints. This necessitates the need for providing efficient and effective decentralized services in tune with demands emanating from users. Such services should be delivered at farmers door and linked with cost recovery for economic viability. However limited government involvement should be continued for people below poverty line who are vulnerable, illiterate and unable to integrate with the mainstream.

The Department of Animal Husbandry and Dairying should play a role of regulatory authority rather than disbursement of central kitty, which is the current focus. It should have legal authority for certification and enforcement of quality/standards of veterinary biological, feeds, pharmaceutical products and livestock and livestock products.

A national livestock breeding strategy needs to be evolved to meet the requirements of milk, meat, egg and other livestock products and transport. Major thrust will be on genetic up gradation of indigenous/native cattle and buffaloes using proven semen and high quality pedigreed bulls and by expanding artificial insemination network to provide services at the farmer's level.

Since animal disease eradication and quarantine is critical to exports, animal health system will be strengthened and disease free zones created. After the successful eradication of rinderpest disease, the major thrust will now be to adopt a National Immunization Programme against most prevalent animal diseases e.g. Hemorrhagic Septicaemia and Black Quarter in large ruminants, PPR and Poxes in small ruminants, Swine fever in pigs (Ranikhet in poultry).

Conservation of threatened breeds of livestock and improvement of breeds used for draught and pack animal should be the major goal of the Tenth Plan. It should be a national priority to maintain diversity of breeds and preserve those showing decline in number or facing extinction.

The importance of feed and fodder in livestock production hardly needs to be emphasized. Attention is needed for cultivation of fodder crops and fodder trees to improve animal nutrition. The area under permanent pasture and grazing land has been estimated at 11.06 million ha. However, actual availability appears to be much less. An integrated approach for regeneration of the grazing lands needs to be evolved. Due to improper management of common property resources and lack of coordination between different agencies involved, the productivity as well as carrying capacity of the present public and forestland are decreasing. This problem needs to be attended on priority basis for sustainable and economic livestock production.

Livestock extension is presently a part of agriculture extension. Livestock extension, is primarily based on providing services and goods, needs to be treated differently from crop related extension activities that are based on transfer of knowledge. Animal husbandry extension worker is basically a service provider. Panchayats, Cooperatives and NGO's should play a leading role in generating dedicated band of service providers at the farmers doorstep in their respective areas.

Public sector lending in livestock sector is abysmally low and such inadequate credit support leads to poor capital formation. As the organized financial sector is unwilling to finance livestock programme that are not in their interest especially after the initiation of financial sector reform, the livestock farmers are mainly dependent on the financial intermediaries and they end up bearing a higher interest rate than that would be available otherwise. NABARD should ensure that at least 20 per cent of the total agriculture sector lending is reserved for Animal Husbandry and Dairying Sector for both short term and long term capital requirement. Financing should be done against model projects that have demonstrated their economic viability. A conducive climate is to be created through favourable price and trade regime to promote farmer's own investment as well as private sector investment.

The country needs a computer based 'National Animal Health and Production Information System' with active involvement of institutions, government departments, private industries. cooperative, and NGO's.

Priority attention should also be given to improve the processing, marketing and transport facilities, with emphasis on modernization of abattoirs, carcass utilization and value addition thereon. Incentives for livestock production activities should be brought at par with incentives for crop production. Development of marketing network and remunerative price support to the producers will be a great incentive for higher animal productivity both in quantity and quality. Creation of a permanent institution, which will estimate the cost of production of various livestock products and suggest remunerative price is needed so that farmers are not exploited.

Issue of animal management and welfare during natural calamities and disaster will require attention and suitable programme need to be developed since such asset loss can drive the poor into destitution. Animal welfare is also related directly with the productivity of the animal. The well being of animal is hampered during management under intensive production system, in the animal market, during handling and transportation in animal market, rearing of newly born male calves in urban areas etc. There is a great deal of wastage and losses, as well as animal suffering due to ill designed agri-implements, carts and implements attached to animal. Veterinary universities/colleges and other institutions like veterinary hospital, dispensary, NGO's working on livestock care system need to be strengthened so that they can ensure and promote animal care and well-being.

In India poultry neither enjoys the status of agriculture nor does it enjoy the status of industry. This uncertainty does not auger well for consistent development of the sector. Poultry establishments having less than 10,000 birds should be treated as agricultural activity for the benefit of the poultry farmer and extend the same benefit/incentives/concessions to this sector, as applicable to agriculture; for units having capacity greater than 10,000 birds it should be treated as industry with all the benefits as extended to industry.

Quality and safety of livestock products depend upon quality and safety assurance system for which legislation is an obligatory mechanism for setting up standards, which should correspond to Codex standard. These do not exist nor is there any method for reviewing and rationalizing the quality and safety guidelines. Enforcement of the legislation would also be one of the important areas of action. For these, infrastructure facilities for testing food quality and safety need to be harmonized with DIE and SPS system. It is needed to establish a permanent Directorate/ Regulatory agency in DAHD supported by an Expert Committee for review of WTO/SPS related issues, regulatory requirement *vis-a-vis* Indian Legislation, control of import if necessary, counter measures against unjustified/arbitrary WTO/SPS measures adopted by other nations, helping export of livestock products and matters related to trade of livestock and its product on a regular basis.

Livestock farming is a major player in dry lands and hill regions. But the focus of investment and developmental strategy is on crop agriculture. The focus in these regions should have been on livestock production as more than 70 per cent of family income is derived from livestock. This will help to alleviate poverty and increase the family income of those who are poorest of poor.

Ever since draught power was allocated to Ministry of Non-Conventional Energy Sources (MNES), very little developmental work has been done. For the development and efficient utilization of draught animal power in the country, the Ministry of Agriculture should work as a nodal ministry. A National Centre for Animal Energy Development can be established under the Department of Animal Husbandry and Dairying as a Central Sector Scheme to coordinate all the activities related to the efficient utilization of DAP in collaboration with other Ministries/Departments. A new programme focused exclusively on improvement and conservation of draught breeds of livestock may be initiated during Tenth Plan.

Remove the present restriction on establishing new milk processing capacity under MMPO. Rules and regulation regarding registration of milk plants as practiced globally should be framed. MMPO should concentrate on quality and food safety only. To enable the dairy and poultry cooperatives to compete with private companies, it is necessary that cooperatives are free of shackles of archaic laws and bureaucratic interference. Time has come to bring about structural changes in the unorganized sector; programme should be designed and implemented to restructure this sector.

Government should recognize that culling and utilization of surplus animals is an established norm for animal production and improvement. Animal preservation acts of the states need to be reviewed so that constraints, if any, affecting proper utilization of livestock could be removed. Registration of the all slaughterhouses in the city/town is must for clean meat production and protection of the environment. Establishing Rural Based Abattoirs (RBA) in animal tracts would drastically reduce the need for transportation of live animals to urban areas for slaughter.

The Livestock Census Scheme suffers from timeliness and quantitative as well as qualitative problems. Livestock census should be based on cent-per-cent coverage of all households in the country on a specific date through the State Animal Husbandry Directorate and the Department of Animal Husbandry & Dairying at the Central level.

The government should endeavour to create a favourable economic environment for increasing capital formation and private investment by removing distortions in the incentive regime for livestock production and bringing about external and domestic market reforms and backed by rationalization of tax structure. Resource Mobilization has to come through, institutional financing, capital market and private investments, which are to be tapped as a major drive to put the infrastructure in place.

The export surplus should be used to develop the infrastructure. Presently, country is exporting leather and leather goods worth Rs. 17,000 crores year. None of this is ploughed back into improvements of livestock so that quality skins and hides are produced nor in creating environmental friendly carcass utilization centres for dead and fallen animals. Similarly, country exports carpets worth Rs. 1,500 crores a year and none of this goes back to growth of indigenous sheep industry. A cess on leather, leather goods and carpets should be imposed and this would be ploughed back to improve the related industries at the level of farmers. The delivery and input cost of all the services provided by State Veterinary Department should be recovered on commercial basis except for those farmers who are identified as being below the poverty line.

The venture capital fund should be created in the Department of Animal Husbandry and Dairying (in collaboration with NABARD) for establishment of infrastructure by private entrepreneurs like veterinary hospitals, vaccine production units, feed plants, fodder seed production facilities, processing plants for western and indigenous dairy, meat and egg products, semen production units including bull mother farms and network for delivery of semen to the farmers. These activities should also get credit under the head of Priority Sector Lending from commercial and co-operative banks. The concept of working capital loan is not in operation in the livestock sector. Like in small-scale sector, this sector requires a provision of working capital loan to enable the entrepreneurs to use it judiciously. Such provision will help the entrepreneur to avoid rushing to the bank for further financial help and make a long wait by which time the activity might suffer irreparable loss. Introduction of Dairy and Poultry Farmers Credit Card (like Kisan Credit Card) would solve the problem of working capital under this programme the farmer will get credit against the future production and he will be free to purchase the inputs at a competitive price from his selected shop. Government should come out with a margin money scheme on the lines of KVIC's Margin Money Scheme where entrepreneurs are required to contribute only a sum equal to 5 or 10 per cent of the cost of the project from their own sources. Alternatively, a soft loan scheme with confessional rate of interest to meet the margin money should be formulated with the help of NABARD.

The perception of bankers is that the financing of animal husbandry activities is a risky proposition and many loans are likely to become bad. It is this factor, which forces the financial institutions to go in for collateral security either in the form of mortgage of land or third party guarantee. Such units will be security oriented rather than commercially designed. In case of commercial units, where technology plays an important role and the size of land holding need not be large, the collateral becomes insufficient in the bankers perception. Removal of collateral security wherever warranted will prove to be of great help to qualified and skilled entrepreneurs to establish financially viable units.

The share of animal husbandry and dairying sector was only

5.7 per cent of total ground level credit offered through NABARD for agriculture and allied activities during 1999-2000. Only term loan to the tune of Rs. 2366 crore was given to Animal Husbandry and Dairying; no production credit or short-term credit was given. NABARD should ensure that at least 20 per cent of the total ground level credit becomes available to animal husbandry sector. Financing should be done against model projects that have demonstrated their economic viability. A reasonable unit size depending upon the capacity of an individual is to be determined and necessary schematic lending has to be provided to establish the same.

Besides the funding by Department of Animal Husbandry and Dairying, a minimum portion of the budget (10% of the budget or Rs. 3000 crore per annum) of Ministry of Rural Development should be earmarked for animal husbandry and dairying activities as a legitimate share of rural development.

SAARC Poverty Commission Report in 1990 which has became the part of Dakha Declaration had made two significant points, it warns that open economy and the free markets were alright only so long it could carry along poor. South Asia, which is home to nearly half of the world's poor could not leave them to fend for themselves and hope their problems to disappear. The developmental process in the countries of this region could proceed ahead only if it stood on two legs. The second important point that the Poverty Commission made was that you don't have to make the poor dependent on the governments hand outs, if they have survived conditions of abject poverty, they must have their own capacity for survival and renovation. All you need to do is to make it work. What they need are some strategic inputs such as micro-credit, some basic training, access to technology underwriting, easy access to market in ways *designated to incorporate them into the development process*. They have the capacity to realize their productive potential if only they could be provided certain basic inputs and some economic space to operate in. In practical terms, that takes into accounts decentralization, grassroots organizations and relatively meagre financial inputs. This is essentially the basic bedrock of this present report. The demand driven livestock revolution can easily be brought in and activated in a manner that the small and marginal farmers and landless labour who own livestock can move from the present non-viable occupation to a financially viably entrepreneurship through the provision of some organizational help, micro-credit training and access to technology underwriting through a service provider, he could participate directly in the growth process.

Part III

Sustainable Agriculture

9

Sustainable Agriculture

Farming Systems and Natural Resources

S.L. MEHTA & A. BANDYOPADHYAY

Introduction

The spectacular agriculture growth since 1960s has been mainly due to development of new technology by our scientists, high receptivity of the farmers and good policies by the Government of India. In a span of five decades food grain production which was barely 51 million tonnes in 1950-51crossed 200 million tonnes mark in 2000. India during this period became the second largest producer of wheat, rice and sorghum, the third largest producer of sugar cane and the fourth largest producer of cotton. In fruits and vegetable production we share the first position with China. Likewise in the animal husbandry and dairy sector also the progress has been very impressive with milk production increasing form 17 million tonnes in 1950-51 to over 75 million tonnes now (Table 9.1).

The country today is not only self-sufficient in meeting the food needs of the vastly increased population but also has built a buffer stock of over 50 million tonnes of food grains to tide over any shortages which may arise because of bad weather conditions. The new technologies developed by the Scientists in the State Agricultural Universities and the ICAR Institutes helped to achieve this favourable position.

Table 9.1: India's share in the world production and area for major crops, 1995-97

Crops	*India's share (%)*		*India's rank*	
	Production	*Area*	*Production*	*Area*
Wheat	11.4	11.2	2	2
Rice	21.4	28.5	2	1
Pulses	26.0	36.6	1	1
Groundnut	28.6	35.2	1	1
Sugar cane	22.6	20.0	2	2
Tea	28.3	18.5	1	2
Jute	52.5	51.5	1	1
Cotton (lint)	14.0	20.7	3	1

Falling Growth Rates and Declining Per Capita Availability of Food Grains

Falling Growth Rates and Declining Per Capita Availability of Food Grains

During 70s' food grains production had annual growth of 2 per cent (Table 9.2). It increased to 4.7 per cent during 80s. But during 1990s, the annual growth rate declined to 2.0 per cent. Rice production increased by 2.78 per cent annually during 80s. During 90s, however, the growth rate of rice production sharply declined to 0.76 per cent per annum. Pulses production is stagnant at around 13 to 14 million tonnes over the last 40 years, resulting in sharp decline of daily per capita availability of pulses from 51 gms in 1951 to 35 gms in 1997. As a result of deceleration in growth rate

Table 9.2: Food grains production: decadal figures

Year	*Food grains Production (Million tonnes)*	*Decadal Increase*
1950	50	–
1960	82	32
1970	108	26
1980	129	21
1990	176	47
2000	196	20

of food production, daily per capita availability of food grains has declined from 510 gms in 1991 to 484 gms in 1998.

Total Factor Productivity (TFP)

Total Factor Productivity is an important measure to evaluate the performance of any production system and sustainability of growth processes. Performance of TFP was more impressive in 1980s than 1990s. TFP of crop sector in Indo-Gangetic Plains (IGP) witnessed 2 per cent growth per annum in 1980s and which became negative in 1990s (Praduman Kumar, personnel communication).

The sustainability issues of crop sector in IGP are emerging and the decline of TFP raises a need for holistic approach for increasing productivity keeping sustainability of the Agro-eco-system in view.

Despite ushering in green revolution, the impact of technologies has not been uniform across the regions mainly due to biophysical and socio-economic factors. The indiscriminate exploitation of natural resources in these intensively cultivated areas has raised concerns about the long-term sustainability of the agricultural production system and environment. In the recent past, several indicators highlight that natural resources of the region, especially, land, water and bio-diversity are under severe pressure to meet the growing food demand due to increasing population and income. At the same time, the productivity of this system has now started showing signs of decline at a few places and stagnation at many places in the region. There are also concerns of declining soil health and other related environmental problems associated with sustainability.

Sustainability in agriculture is a complex concept, which has been defined in a number of ways. However, the World Commission on Economic Development (1987) has tried to capture the basic philosophy of the concept by defining, "Agriculture is considered sustainable if it ensures that today's development is not at the cost of tomorrow's prospects." The major components of such sustainability are (i) economic profitability, (ii) environmental health, and social and economic equity. The British Columbia Rural Table on the Environment and Economy (CEPAL, 1994) has identified following the key acts for achieving sustainability:

(i) Limit the impact on the overall carrying system within its capacity.

(ii) Present and project the environment including causation of biodiversity and other resources.

(iii) Minimum depletion of non-renewable resources.

(iv) Diversity and increased resource use efficiency so that benefits are increased without affecting the environment assets.

(v) Equitable distribution of the benefits and costs of resources used and environment protection.

(vi) Productive, participatory and long term system of decision-making and governance.

(vii) Use information and education to inculcate the philosophy.

In the Indian context the carrying capacity of the system is of the highest concern. The food grain production has to be increased from about 210 million tonnes now to about 300 million tonnes by the year 2020 (Bhalla *et al.*, 1999). The enormity of the task at hand can be viewed with the following analysis of population supporting capacity of land (Eswaran *et al.*, 2002) in three land management input levels (FAO, 1976). The estimates (Table 9.3) are based on considerations of inherent land quality, current climate and estimated population levels.

Table 9.3: Carrying Capacity at three Land Management Level

Input Level	*Carrying capacity (No. of persons in thousands)*	*Population ratio*	
		At 2025 level to the carrying capacity	*At 2000 level to the carrying capacity*
Low	309,938	3.55	4.4
Medium	541,665	2.03	2.6
High	878,222	1.25	1.6

Although, the Indian Council of Agricultural Research (ICAR) has divided the country into 20 agro-eco regions and 60 agro-eco-sub-regions, under NATP five major agro-eco-systems have been supported for addressing sustainability issues and research programmes have been focused on the Production System

Research (PSR) by integrating all the system components for improving the productivity and profitability of the system. The five agro-eco systems are: Irrigated, Coastal, Arid, Rainfed and Hill & Mountains.

Agro-Ecosystems

Irrigated Agro-Ecosystem

The Irrigated Agro-eco-system which was the backbone of the green revolution with 38 per cent of arable land provides for 55 per cent of total agricultural production. The irrigated agro-eco-system has played and continues to play a critical role in fulfilling country's demand for foodgrains, pulses, oilseeds, fruits, vegetables, milk and milk products. Rice-wheat, cotton-wheat and sugarcane based cropping systems are the important production systems in this region. Plateuing of yields, decrease in total factor productivity, heavy losses (20-25%) in yield due to pests and diseases, erosion of genetic diversity, inadequate production of quality seeds, excessive ground water depletion, rise in ground water in areas with poor quality aquifers, emergence of micro-nutrient deficiencies in excessive cultivated area are the major concerns in increasing the production and productivity of the systems.

Rainfed Agro-Ecosystem

This covers 90 million ha area, which is nearly 60 per cent of the net-cropped area whose productivity potential has yet to be realized. Productivity and stability in this region is low as it contributes only 45 per cent of the country's production because of vagaries of monsoon. The main crops in the region include pearl millet, cotton, sorghum and pulses, which not only yield low but also have wide technology transfer gaps. The poor resource farmers in the region have low risk-taking ability and, therefore, the agriculture continues to be much less remunerative.

Arid Agro-Ecosystem

This region with 62 million ha, covering 19 per cent of the total geographical areas of the country is highly vulnerable. The major production constraints consist of low precipitation, high potential evapotranspiration-transpiration and land degradation due to biotic pressure. Droughts marked by long, dry spells are common. Region also is characterized by 70 per cent of the ground waters in the salinity range. However, the strength of the region is the live-stock population which is backbone of livelihood security along with and agri-silvi-hort-pastoral system including multi-purpose trees. In this agro-ecosystem sustainability depends, on agro-forestry, agri-silvi, agri-horticulture system and the livestock and fish production.

Coastal Agro-Ecosystem

The country has over 8000 km long coastline and this provides opportunities for development of fisheries, along with plantation crops and cropping systems which could be sustained with saline/brackish water. It supports the livelihood security of several million poor and contributes to the national economy in large measure. Its strength is diverse vegetation ranging from rich tropical rain forests to coastal mangroves. Therefore, in this region for sustainability fisheries and live-stock production system and agri-horticulture production system assume importance.

Hill and Mountain Agro-Ecosystem

Hill & mountain agro-ecosystem with climatic variations, sloping land, small holdings and absence of irrigation, comprises of fragile and complex farming systems, encompassing agriculture, animal husbandry, horticulture, fisheries and agro and social forestry. The sustainability issues are unique and call for concerted approach from water harvesting, soil conservation, IPM, INM to post harvest technology and value addition.

The improvements in productivity, stability and sustainability of each production system, therefore, have tremendous impact on a range of national objectives including:

- National food security;
- Household food security, poverty alleviation and equity;
- Conservation of the environment and/or biodiversity;

- Sustainability in the use of natural resources;
- Product or rural income diversification;
- Welfare of tribal people, women or other disadvantaged groups; and
- Exploiting latent commercial or export potentials.

Scientists in the NARS have addressed many of the important issues and some of the high lights are presented here for different agro-eco-system.

Some Sustainable Technologies for Different Agro-Ecosystem

Irrigated Agro-Ecosystem

Zero Tillage for Rice-Wheat Production System: Importance of minimum tillage was realized about three decades back but it could not pickup due to non-availability of suitable seeding machine. The development of zero till drill at Pantnagar, and its fine-tuning has paved the way for agricultural transformation all around particularly in the rice-wheat system. Out of four different tillage practices tried in wheat, i.e. Zero Tillage, Strip Till Drill, Roto Drill and Bed Planter, Zero Tillage exhibited its superiority and out yielded all other practices. Zero tillage has now been adopted over large area. The farmers who are adopting the zero tillage technology have indicated the following advantages:

- Saving in cost of seedbed preparation to the tune of approximately Rs. 2,500-4,000/ha.
- Saving in fuel to the tune of 37.3 to 70 litres of diesel per hectare depending upon soil condition.
- Advancement in sowing time over conventional system by 2-4 weeks depending upon the type of soil.
- Saving in water to the tune of about 30 per cent.
- Reduction in incidence of *Phalaris minor* the tune of about 40-50 per cent.
- Increase in yield by 5-15 per cent over the conventional system.

Last years about 0.1 million-hectare area of wheat was sown with zero-tillage in areas of rice-wheat cropping system. Farmers in Haryana have adopted zero tillage on large scale. There were 2,055 drills in the state and over 3000 have been fabricated this year. Village Teek in Kaithal district, Pirthla in Fatehabad district, Bhani Khund in Karnal district and Govindgarh in Karnal district in Haryana have been saturated with zero-tillage last year. Zero-tillage technology was demonstrated in more than 500 villages in different states. Most centres specially in the Eastern sector have demanded more number of drills to further improve the adoption of zero tillage. This year in view of its advantages, it is expected to cover about 30 million ha.

Bed planting system for increasing the yield and input use efficiencies under different cropping systems: Research in the past have revealed that raised bed and furrow system has numerous advantages like better irrigation management, better plant establishment, ability to use inter-bed cultivation for weed control, lowering seeding rate, less crop lodging and opportunity to use same beds to plant a succeeding crop with minimum tillage as compared to flat bed system.

Sowing of wheat on beds is now possible with development of a bed planter which enables two wheat rows 20 cm apart on 37.5 cm wide bed and 30 cm wide furrow between two beds. An adjustment in these distances is also feasible with this planter.

The wheat yield under bed planting was either similar or higher to conventional method of sowing in both on-station and on-farm trials. The yield of wheat could be maintained by using PBW 343 variety, 75 kg seed/ha, 180 kg N/ha applied ½ at sowing and remaining half dose as drilling on beds at first irrigation, irrigating the crop at 50 mm CPE value and controlling weeds with sulfosulfuron weedicide. This new technology leads to saving of irrigation water up to 30 per cent.

In *kharif* also yield of soybean and maize were higher in bed planting than flat sowing. Planting of two-rows/bed of soybean and one row/bed of maize was found better. Application of 150 kg N/ha in two splits, ½ at sowing and ½ at flowering produced higher yield of soybean.

Bed planting system could therefore help in giving comparatively better yield by efficient use of input resources, i.e. water, fertilizer, seed and weedicide. The use of permanent beds would also help in reducing tillage cost and greenhouse gas emissions from burning diesel and stubble retention system would also reduce loss of soil organic matter. The bed planting system has great potential due to water saving where water table is going down. Following success in wheat farmers have started growing rice on raised beds. This leads to saving of 30 per cent water and paddy fetches them Rs.10 per quintal extra because grains are bold and lustrous.

Crop Residue Management for Rice and Wheat: In Punjab 91 per cent of the rice crops is harvested by machine and about 10.7 million tonnes straw is burnt annually. In Haryana only 45 per cent of rice is machine harvested and major portion of it (37%), which is estimated to be 2.5 mt/annum, is completely burnt. In Terai region of Uttar Pradesh, 55 per cent rice is machine harvested and whole of it or partly is burnt. Under wheat, the machine harvested area is 82 per cent in Punjab, 30 per cent in Haryana, 55 per cent in Terai region and 31 per cent in eastern Uttar Pradesh. A substantial amount of wheat straw is also burnt in these areas (3.1 mt in Punjab, 1.3 mt in Haryana and 4.2 mt in eastern Uttar Pradesh). This huge amount of residue burning causes great loss of soil organic matter, plant nutrients and also causes environmental pollution.

Studies revealed that in rice-wheat system, rice residue burning which causes environmental pollution and deterioration of soil quality could effectively be managed by incorporating it into the soil. Rice residue can be effectively incorporated in coarse to medium textured soil with four to five operations of disc harrow. Rice residue may effectively be incorporated in soil without any deleterious effects on wheat yield irrespective of date of sowing and decomposition period.

Organic Matter Recycling and Soil Enrichment for Rice-Wheat System: Sustainable production of rice-wheat system demand maintenance of quality of natural resources. It is, therefore, necessary to enhance the contribution of organics to meet about one-third of plant nutrients need through integrated plant nutrient management. Recycling of wastes in agriculture brings in the much-needed organic and mineral matter to the soils. Since most recyclable wastes are organic, they directly add organic matter and the plant nutrients contained in it. While the nutrient input improves soil fertility, the organic input has a profound and vital role to play in improving soil physical properties such as its tilth, water holding capacity and providing a more favourable environment for root growth.

Experiments on organic matter recycling have demonstrated that 25 per cent recommended N dose for rice can be substituted through Farm Yard Manure (FYM) or moong straw (Table 9.4). Similarly, during the year 2001-2002, 75 per cent N from urea + 25 per cent N from mung straw produced maximum grain yield of rice (5.83 t/ha) followed by 75 per cent N from urea + 25 per cent N from farmyard manure (4.97 t/ha).

Table 9.4: Influence of chemical fertilizers and organics on yield of wheat and rice

Treatment	*Grain Yield t/ha*	
	Wheat	*Rice*
Control (no fertilizer)	2.76	1.73
100% N (120 kg./ha) as chemical fertilizer	4.9	2.9
75% N as chemical fertilizer + 25% N as carpet waste	5.1	3.22
25% N as chemical fertilizer + 25% N as digested sludge + 25% N as press mud + 25% N as carpet waste	5.4	3.57
1/3 N as digested sludge + 1/3 N as press mud + 1/3 N as carpet waste	5.9	3.6

Resources management of rice-wheat cropping system through inclusion of legumes, Indian mustard and potato: The rice-wheat is the most dominant cropping system in northern plains and has brought in focus new problems like, (i) disturbed soil resource and formation of sub-surface hard pan due to widely adopted practice of puddling in rice cultivation; (ii) building up of *Phalaris minor* population under continued rice-wheat cultivation; (iii) declining factor of the productivity specially to fertilizer use; (iv) receding water table in certain areas; and (v) development of multiple nutrient deficiencies are matter of concern. Therefore, to tackle these problems the following most efficient cropping system have been identified which proved to be better than existing rice-wheat cropping system.

Diversification of the system through introduction of crops of diverse nature is a good preposition to break the monotony of the system and help to sustain productivity over a period of time. Diversification will not only help in reducing ill effects of continuous rice-wheat cropping but also result in (i) much needed increase in productivity of oilseeds and pulses, which had been pushed back to low productivity marginal lands, (ii) improvement in intake of protein component in the diets of vegetarian population and fodder quality of animals, (iii) increase in economic returns of farmers, and (iv) exploitation of legumes for their atmospheric N-fixing capacity to reduce fertilizer requirements and addition of organic matter in the soil to reduce the fertilizer requirements and improving productivity system. Inclusion of short duration legumes, potato, Indian mustard, etc. intermittently in RWCS holds great promise in sustaining high production levels of the system as well as long-term soil health.

Rainfed Agro-Ecosystem

Rainwater Harvesting and Recycling for Rainfed Rice: Managing rainwater is crucial for stabilizing rice production in the states of Chattisgarh, Madhya Pradesh, Orissa and Jharkhand. These states receive relatively high rainfall (>1200 mm) and yet kharif rice suffers from dry spells mainly due to poor water management. A construction of On Farm Reservoirs (OFRs) of 1000-2000 cu-m capacity dug on individual holdings to collect excess runoff water along the slope and recycling for crop use during dry periods or for raising the rabi crop could help in increasing production. Experiments at different locations revealed that 40-60 per cent of the surplus runoff could be collected and recycled for rice crop. A 1000 cu-m OFR saves about 1 ha rice area from drought. The additional rice yields due to the use of harvested water ranged from 55-200 per cent at Baghbara (Chhattisgarh) and 11-29 per cent at Dindori (M.P.) on different farmers fields. Greater availability of conserved moisture enabled to take up rabi crops successfully at all the locations. The cropping intensity increased by 139 per cent at Baghbara and 149 per cent at Dindori.

Integrated Plant Nutrient Management in Rice: Fertilizer use in the eastern region is quite low which is one of the major constraints limiting rice productivity. Chemical fertilizers at recommended dose are rarely applied by the farmers due to their poor resource base. The integrated nutrient management package for rainfed rice was compared with the farmers practice and chemical fertilizers alone in Orissa, Jharkhand and Chattisgarh. In uplands, application of 75 per cent recommended fertilizer dose (RDF), five tonnes of farm yard manure (FYM) and incorporation of intercropped greengram as manure-cum-mulch produced higher grain yield of rice (25.29 q/ha and 36.40 q/ha respectively at Phulbani and Darisai) as compared to farmers practice (12.9 and 14.2 q/ha). In medium lands, transplanted rice produced significantly higher grain yield with integrated use of 100 per cent RDF, five tonnes FYM and *in situ* green manure as compared to farmers practice and 100 per cent RDF. This indicates the possibility of enhancement of productivity with lesser input using INM.

Paddy Based Farming System in Tribal Areas: In the tribal areas of Jharkhand and Chattisgarh, the yields of paddy are quite low due to low input use. Since the holdings are small, the tribals are unable to eke out livelihood from cropping alone. Therefore, a paddy based farming system model including rice cum-fish-cum duck and rice-cum-fish-cum-pig was tested in tribal areas of Jharkhand and Chhattisgarh. The paddy-cum-fish culture (in the ponds) was integrated where in the fish and duck manure was used for the rice crop. Initial results from the project and the mid-term impact assessment by NCAP indicated up to 100 per cent increase in income to the tribals is possible by adopting farming systems approach over cultivation of paddy crop alone or duck rearing. The paddy crop benefited from the duck manure. The local races of ducks survived better than the introduced Khaki Campbell ducks.

Integrated Pest Management in Oilseed Crops: Pests and diseases cause serious yield losses in oilseed crops. A number of IPM modules were evolved by the research institutes based on on-station research but they been have rarely tested on farmers fields. The recommended IPM modules specific to each location and cropping system were tried in five states involving crops/cropping systems like mustard, groundnut, sunflower + groundnut, mungbean-safflower and safflower + chickpea systems. At all the centres, bio-intensive and chemo-intensive modules were evaluated and the advantages of eco friendly pest management were demonstrated to the farmers. In case of mustard, seed treatment with *Trichoderma viride* @ 2 g/kg seeds and soil application @ 1 kg/acre (mixed with 25 kg FYM and spread on 1 acre land) was effective for controlling *Alternaria* leaf blight and white rust diseases. For castor, a bio-intensive module consisting of crop rotation, summer ploughing, use of resistant variety, removal of alternate hosts, seed treatment, hand picking of larval masses and use of neem seed kernal emulsion (NSKE 5%) was found effective for control of semilooper in alfisols of Telangana, Andhra Pradesh. The recommended location specific IPM modules could be validated under farmers conditions for mustard at Gurgaon and Hissar, for groundnut at Anantapur, sunflower+ groundnut at Raichur, Mungbean – safflower at Parbhani, Sunflower + Chickpea at Solapur and castor at Hyderabad and Palem.

New Biofertilizer Formulation for Pulses: Biofertilizers like *Rhizobium* and PSB are important components of the IPNS for pulse cultivation. A new *Rhizobium* formulation based on liquid inoculant was standardized for major pulse and oilseed crops. This is based on use of cell protectants to prolong the shelf life. This formulation proved superior in terms of quality, shelf life (up to one year) and field efficacy as compared to the commercial carrier based inoculants. On farm trials at 140 locations in 7 states during kharif 2001 revealed a mean pod yield increase with liquid inoculants by about 2-15 per cent over the carrier based inoculant with maximum advantage in soybean (20%) and least in pigeonpea 2 per cent.

Benefits of Integrating Component Technologies for Pulses: Moisture conservation, nutrient management and pest control are important components of the improved technology for pulse cultivation besides the use of HYV. However, these components of the production technology have rarely been integrated on farmer's fields and the agronomic and economic advantages assessed. On-farm trials on pigeonpea conducted in several states. Have shown that HYV recommended intercropping, INM, moisture conservation and IPM packages gave higher returns over farmers practice with a BC ratio of 2.2 to 3.1 for different crops.

Rainwater Management in Cotton Based Production System: Soil moisture availability during the crop growth period is a major determining factor in rainfed cotton production. Cotton is cultivated on different top sequences (upper, middle and lower plains) in the Deccan plateau, which requires suitable land configurations for conservation of moisture during deficit periods and removal of excess water on the lower plains. Cotton as a sole crop and intercropped/sequence cropped with pulses and oilseeds was tried on flat bed + RDF, ridges and furrows + RDF, raised and sunken beds + RDF and farmers practice. The results showed that all moisture conservation measures increased seed cotton yield over flat bed sowing. On upper plains, ridges and furrows over flat bed sowing improved the yield by about 3 q, owing to increased *in situ* conservation of moisture while raised and sunken beds increased the seed cotton yield by about 5 q over flat sowing on the lower plains, mainly due to the removal of excess water.

Introduction of Legumes in Finger-millet Based Cropping System: Finger-millet crop is generally grown in tribal and remote areas with low yields and economic returns to the farmers. Traditionally in tribal belts miner millets are still grown which have not seen the impact of new technology scientists have demonstrated benefits of soil moisture conservation and inter cropping with legumes on producing introducing legumes like pigeonpea, cowpea and blackgram as inter/sequence crops in the fingermillet based cropping system led to higher gross monitoring returns.

Moisture Conservation in Pearl-millet Based Cropping System: Soil and moisture management are the two key requirements for stabilizing the pearlmillet productivity in semi-arid tropics. On-farm trials (involving 10 farmers from each location) in three states, i.e. Maharashtra, Karnataka and Tamil Nadu revealed that, paired row planting at 30/60 cm and opening of furrows in wider rows at 35 DAS along with the best INM package (50% RDF + FYM + biofertiliser) registered highest gross (Rs. 11,715/ha) and net returns (Rs. 4,914/ha) and B:C ratio (1:1.73). This opens up the possibility of increasing yield in pearl-millet based cropping system.

Intercropping in sugar cane based production system: Sugar cane being a long duration widely spaced and one time income-generating crop lends ample scope for crop diversification. Inclusion of short duration high value crops in sugar cane based production system as intercrop holds great promise in increasing the land utilization efficiency, reducing the production cost, economizing the use of market purchased costly inputs and making the system sustainable. This in turn raises the socio-economic status of small and marginal resource constrained farmers.

Integrated Pest Management in Plantation Crops: The major pests of palms including coconut, areca nut and oil palm in India are the rhinoceros beetle *(Oryctes rhinoceros)*, the red palm weevil *(Rhynchophorus ferrugineus* F.) the leaf eating caterpillar *(Opisina arenosella* wlk) and the white grub *(Leucopholis coneophora* Burm) and these seriously affect yield from plantation crops. IPM technologies have been developed for control of rhinoceros, beetle, red palm, weevil and leaf eating caterpillar are quite effective.

Coastal Agro-Ecosystem

Western ghats running along the west coast are fragile but endowed with potentially rich natural resources conducive to develop a sustainable agricultural growth. Excessive surface runoff and soil erosion due to high rainfall with higher intensity and erosivity, drying of mountain streams, frequently occurring moisture stress/drought and inadequate water management are the major factors attributing to low productivity in the region. Proper soil and water conservation measures including micro scale water resource development are the foundation for sustainable production system. Low cost vegetative barriers and mechanical engineering measures like bunding and terracing have been effective in control of soil runoff losses.

Arid Agro-Ecosystem

Sustainability of the agro-ecosystem depends largely on the agri-silvi-horti production system. Researches over the last 2 decades have identified cropping patterns, which could bring higher economic benefits to the farming commuters. Rotation of pearl millet with cluster bean leads to not only savings of fertilizer N but also provides additional income. Since the region is characterised by low rainfall, watershed management could prove to be a beneficial for sustainability. Use of polythene much could further improve soil moisture conservation in watershed areas. The regions economy also is development on medicinal and aromatic plants.

Simple technologies of bracketing crop residues, their enrichment with molasses and mineral supplement have further potential to increase live stock products of the region.

The region's major aquifer consists of brackish water. The fishery scientists have demonstrated fish culture in brackish water. The success has led many farmers in Rajasthan, Gujarat and Haryana to undertake fisheries. This has opened an alternative source of income and employment in the arid region.

Hill and Mountain Agro-Ecosystem

Agri-Horti Production System: Studies have demonstrated substantial increase in productivity by the use of IPNS consisting of NPK fertilizers with FYM in the rice relevant cropping system. Green manuring also has shown significant increase in soybean yield.

At Almora, a yield increase of 24.3 per cent and 15.4 per cent was observed in french bean when treated with runoff from oak and pine ecosystems, respectively. In the succeeding tomato crop, the yield increase was 28.6 per cent and 21.9 per cent when treated with pine and oak runoff, respectively.

Tomato yield was maximum (255.7 ha^{-1}) with french bean residue incorporation, while french bean and cauliflower yields were highest (62.1 and 124.5 q ha^{-1} respectively) with tomato + sunhemp + french bean residue incorporation.

The region also derives major economic returns from horticultural crops. The technologies have been developed which permit control of the major insect-pests and diseases of the crops which has led to prosperity in the region as a result of increase in productivity. Growing of off-season vegetables following improved IPNS of IPM package of practices farmers have been able to obtain high yields and returns. Improved soil conservation and water management has led to increase in cropping intensity and higher income to the farming community.

Use of *geojute* has been found to have high potential in reducing the soil erosion of the sloping hillsides and increase their sustainability by making revegetation feasible.

Indigenous Technical Knowledge

The growing emphasis on sustainable agriculture since the late eighties has evoked deep interest in indigenous technical knowledge (ITK) that has the element of the use of natural products and indigenous wisdom to solve the problems pertaining to agriculture and allied activities. Indian farmers, over the centuries, have learnt to grow food and to survive in difficult environments, where the rich traditions of ITK have been interwoven with the agricultural practices followed by them.

India's rich civilisation is 5000 years old. India's ancient scriptures consisting of four Vedas, 108 Upanishads, two epics, the Bhagwad Gita, Brahmasutras, 18 Puranas, the Manu Smriti, the Kautilya Shastra and the Smritis, as well as the teachings of innumerable sayings, proverbs and sages contain profound literature providing ideas, concepts and practices for agriculture designed to address the process of building harmonious relationship among the man, animal and the nature.

Indigenous Traditional Knowledge (ITK) refers to the unique, traditional, local knowledge existing within and developed around the specific conditions of women and men indigenous to particular geographic area (Gremier, Louise 1998). ITK are seldom documented, and so are often lost, if not passed on from generation to generation or protected and practised by the local people. It is imperative to document and protect our valuable ITK for the posterity. In the context of agricultural sustainability, ITK is also required to be properly documented for the benefit of researchers, planners and development officials. Validation of the ITK is a logical step to qualify and quantify the effectiveness of the practices. Suitable modifications of the local practices, through research and development will help to develop appropriate and acceptable technologies that are more suited to our farming situations.

The NATP has given the right importance to ITK by including it as a Mission Mode project on 'Collection, Documentation and validation of indigenous Technical Knowledge'. The objectives of the project are the following:

- Identify, collect, classify and document ITK and its variants in different agro-climatic regions in respect of production systems, farming systems and situations.
- Catalogue and characterize the information for developing a database.
- Ascertain the propensity of the extent and level of use of

various ITK by the farmers in the management of various farming systems.

- Validation of ITK through a quick screening method and through formal experimentation, wherever needed.
- Evolve a mechanism to protect property rights and facilitate the process of sharing the benefit by the farming community.

In the project already documentation of 1473 ITKs under 18 categories has been done.

ITK Class	*Number collected*
Rainwater management	41
Soil and water erosion management	10
Tillage and interculture	10
Crops and cropping systems	117
Pest and disease management	237
Soil fertility management	53
Farm implements	131
Post harvest technology	34
Grain and seed storage	67
Horticulture	112
Veterinary Sciences and animal husbandry	595
Fishery	2
Methods of weather forecasting	22
Food product development	19
Ethno botany and agro biodiversity	3
Agro-animal based yarns, natural dyes and weaves	6
Low cost housing material	1
TOTAL	1473

The collection represent only a fraction of the traditional wisdom. But it is encouraging to find how much knowledge already exists among the farmers on key sustainability issues like rain water management, management of soil and water erosion, soil fertility management and pest and disease management. It is first necessary now to understand this knowledge scientifically. There is always a science behind these traditional technologies (Arunachalam, 2001). These technologies could be undertaken for verification in association with the farmer and integrating those which stand test with modern production technologies. A basic concept of sustainability is its location specificity and the advantages of these ITK are that they are location specific. A harmony between the livestock and crop husbandry has been the mainstay of Indian agriculture. That is reflected in the largest number of ITK collected on veterinary science and animal husbandry. This synergy is gaining back importance in the context of organic matter recycling in INM. If the livestock sector in India is to be improved and sustained, the value of indigenous technical knowledge has to be recognised and blended with scientific information (Ramkumar, 1998).

An analysis of limited ITKs documented on crops and cropping systems highlight two important points: (i) examples of crop diversification abound, and (ii) the awareness of the use of specific cropping systems to enhance the sustainability and efficiency of the system.

It is refreshing to note that ITKs on management of pests and diseases are almost in complete agreement with most of the non-synthetic pesticide components of various IPM packages. It is time that a thorough review by scientists of the ITKs is undertaken to establish the scientific basis and then integrate them in IPM packages in participation with the farmers.

An often-noted trend of modern agriculture is the decreasing coping mechanism on the basis of indigenous knowledge of the communities (Elliot, 1994). But application of indigenous knowledge in agricultural extension has been rare (Sharland, 1991). Indigenous technology can provide the basis of design concepts that could easily be adopted and diffused. What is required is a methodology that will facilitate the use of indigenous technology as a basis for appropriate technology development (Massaquoi, 1993). The ultimate solution for rural development is not the dumping of more scientists upon rural people to make exogenously generated technologies more adaptable and in line with people's problems, but to empower and legitimise indigenous capacities for identifying problems and developing solutions for these problems (Den Biggelaar, C., 1991). The empowerment of the indigenous knowledge/technology system may well be a very important step in dealing with indigenous problems.

Women are a very important group of owners of ITK in all traditional systems. Women in countries like India and Nepal possess deep-rooted knowledge about their immediate environment due to their economic dependence on their surroundings. Even if there are contradictions in the goals of international development work, it is possible to combine them in the agricultural, livestock and natural resource management sector, when women's knowledge is used in the right manner (Petersen, 1999).

The ITK is not a static process but a dynamic one, which develops slowly, requires small investment and is usually carried out in small-scale units. In the context of development, indigenous technology may have either a positive or negative effect on the development process depending on the way it is used (Song and Wang, 1991). Hence documentation and assimilation of ITK is a continuous process where identifying, nurturing and sustaining nascent ITKs is a very important component of sustainable social systems.

Global environmental concerns have diverted attention for productivity concerns, thereby resorting to some of the softer options, which emphasize indigenous technology, low cost measures and participatory institutional development. Such policy changes have resulted in the removal of substantial investment in land, which farmers cannot afford to do (Shah, 1998). In the ultimate analysis sustainability is enriched and further sustained by the ecological and intellectual knowledge held by the cultures and their economies dependent upon the specific geographic region in which they reside (Zasada, J.C., 2000).

Natural Resource Management (NRM)

Efficient use of natural resources of land, water, energy, forests and biological resources is important for the survival of humanity and for sustainability of future agriculture. Due to increase in population the per capita land availability has declined to 0.14 ha and is expected to decline to 0.10 ha per capita by the year 2025 AD. Additionally good agricultural land is declining due to increased population pressure, urbanization, and industrialization. This necessitates use of science-based, eco-friendly technology for efficient use of natural resources.

Integrated Nutrients Management

Intensive agriculture has led to decline in soil fertility mainly because of mans greed. By harvesting 200 mt of food grains every year we are removing about 25 mt of plant nutrients whereas the annual input from external sources in the form of fertilizers and manures is hardly 17.5 mt. By the year 2025 AD for producing 300 mt of food grains, India will need about 45 mt of nutrients (Kanwar & Katyal, 1997). Already micronutriens and secondary nutrient deficiencies have reached alarming situation. These if not corrected would lead to serious effects on human health as well. In future micronutrient (Zn, Fe, Mn, Cu, Bo) requirements, therefore, are going to be much higher.

Imbalanced fertilizer use and overuse of nitrogen alone, high losses, removal and depletion of plant nutrients is leading to decline in productivity. Integrated Nutrient Management System using organic and inorganic resources and monitoring of nutrient status of soil and input-output relationship hold key to sustainability. Researchers have clearly demonstrated beneficial effects of FYM, *green manuring* as well as bio-fertilizers not only on yield but most importantly on soil health. Even the simple technique of using leaf colour charts in rice savings in nitrogen application could be made. Fertilizer application based on soil test values coupled with balanced use of fertilizer will lead not only in optimization of fertilizer use but would lead to maintaining productive capacity of soil.

Intensive agriculture and also crop rotation like wheat rice monocropping year after year involving high yielding varieties have brought in micro and secondary nutrient deficiencies and seriously affecting yield and productivity (Table 9.5). Farm Yard Manure (FYM) supplement could correct to a large extent these deficiencies. The integrated plant nutrient system is, therefore, essential and a necessity for sustainability of agriculture. Crop rotations involving restoration and exhaustive crops such as legumes and cereals also is a necessity for increasing fertilizer use efficiency and sustainability.

Table 9.5: Micronutrient deficiencies in soils of some states

State	*No. of samples*	*Per cent samples deficient*			
		Zn	*Cu*	*Fe*	*Mn*
Andhra Pradesh	8,158	49	<1	3	1
Bihar	19,214	54	3	6	2
Haryana	21,848	61	2	20	4
Punjab	16,483	48	1	14	2
Tamil Nadu	20,087	58	6	17	6
Uttar Pradesh	26,126	46	1	7	1

Source: Singh (1998).

A few issues on INM: An ideal INM system should be able to define the cropping system for a particular soil environment with nutrition and water use efficiency of the component crops and the varieties used in the component crops. Recent developments in molecular biology, root biology, rhizosphere interactions, and modelling present new opportunities for the understanding and improvement of crop nutrient efficiency (Lynch, 1998). Breeding for nutrient use efficiency of crops to suit defined cropping systems is possible and necessary. It must be emphasized here that this breeding will be meaningful only when the cropping system is kept in mind. Wiesler *et al.* (2001) have emphasised the role of nitrogen efficient cultivars in sustainable agriculture. However, it is now important to develop cultivars which have higher efficiency for P, K and especially micronutrients like Fe, Zn; and/or Mn. Finding of various scientists indicate that crop genotypes differ in nutrient uptake and this variation could be made use of in developing cultivars with higher designer nutrient uptake. Tools of molecular biology and recombinant DNA technology permit transfer of genes across species barrier. Already groups led by Dr. Ingo Potrypens have engineered rice variety with higher iron content. Biochemical and physiological understanding of nutrient uptake help in genetic engineering for higher uptake of plant nutrients and blocking toxic constituents and help in alliviating toxicity problems.

The role of soil moisture in the INM has many dimensions. Moisture availability determines nutrient uptake, it determines the activities of soil biota, chemical changes in soil and nutrient loss through water. Loss of nutrient through water has been studied to some extent. But moisture *vis-à-vis* nutrient use efficiently has not received adequate attention. Interesting results have come up when such relationships have been studied. In a ten-year trial, various combinations of chemical fertilizers, FYM and biofertilizer influenced the water efficiency of wheat and winter maize. Maximum water expense efficiency of 98.2 and 100.3 kg/ha-cm for wheat and winter maize respectively, could be achieved with 100 per cent chemical fertilizers combined with FYM and blue-green algae (Mishra, 2000).

The effect of various nutrients on the soil biota is a component little studied in term of INM. So is the case with effect of nutrients on general crop health, not only nutritional but also that affected by insects and diseases. The productive capacity of a cropping system will depend on optimum crop health. Since soil is a dynamic living system it is important to have detailed study of effects of chemical use on microorganism both beneficial and harmful. In the long-term strategy it is important to build up useful microorganism because they not only fix plant nutrients or mobilize them, they also produce constituents that promote plant growth and maintain a dynamic balance with harmful microbes. Dynamics of various practices on soil biology need to be studied far more in depth than at present.

Further, INM requires social interventions to arrive at technologies that simultaneously improve soil fertility in sustainable way, and make sense to farmers given their social and economic milieu (Deugd, Roling and Smaling, 1998).

Precision Farming

Precision farming has been getting attention by many concerned with the production of food, feed and fibre and sustainability and efficiency of agricultural systems. Swaminathan (2002) while discussing the new gains to be made towards sustainability and food security advised, that at the production level, precision farming practices will have to be developed and popularized.

A precision farming is a management strategy that uses information technologies to bring data from multiple sources to bear on decisions associated with crop production (Committee on Assessing Crop Yield: Site Specific Farming, Information System, and Research Opportunities, National Research Council, 1997). It has three components: capture of data, interpretation and analysis of that data, and implementation of a management response at an appropriate role and time. The key difference between conventional agricultural management and precision agriculture is the application of modern information technology in micro-level decision making based on multi-source data of high spatial and temporal resolution. Even though farmers know from experience that yields are higher in some parts of the field than in others, conventional management focuses on input application at a given rate to the whole field. Precision agriculture on the other hand permits to apply input at smaller scales based on new tools of leaf and soil nutrient analysis to account for the variability in the field. Variability management is the key approach in precision farming, using field maps and real time sensing for temporal and spatial variation in soils, plant growth and yield and other parameters related to cultivation (Sasao and Shibusawa, 2000).

Precision agriculture entails a paradigm shift for the agricultural research system, extension system, the farming system, and infrastructure and public policy. For this, total system orientation will be required for agricultural research with close partnership of agricultural scientists, economists and information specialists. The research focus will have to shift from the controlled experimental plots to on farm dynamic experimentation. The system being dependent on generation of vast amount of real time data on crop variability, soil analysis, cropping intensity, disease intensity and so on, a whole line of fast and precise system of sampling and analysis has to be developed. The data so generated should be amenable to user-friendly decision support system. Understanding of the complex interactions among multiple factors affecting crop growth and farm decision-making wasted help in developing system for maximising productivity with increased efficiency of various inputs. The farmers will become partners in research for precision farming.

Precision agricultural technologies are data intensive and geographically dispersed. Hence, a highly dispersed extension system, private or public will be required. Adequately trained professional will be required to form the bridge between the farmer and science and technology. Existing extension specialists will need continuing education and remote-site learning in precision agricultural technologies because they will have to interpret information and help the farmer take decision at the farm level. Farmers owned information tools will have to be organised. But at the micro level a new breed of information and input service providers will possibly be the backbone of precision agriculture technology dissemination. These service providers will be entrepreneurs. It is likely that a combination of services and products will result in which services are needed to be customized for each farmer's operation.

High-speed data connectivity and accessibility will be the most important infrastructural support in rural areas to encourage precision farming.

As precision agriculture is information based major policy

decision on data ownership and privacy rights will have to be in place. Data collected for use at the sub field and field levels have additional value for research, testing, evaluation, and marketing when assembled into regional databases. Mechanisms are needed to create and use this value, including data collection and transfer standards; institutions for collecting, managing or networking data and policies to facilitate data sharing and access while protecting proprietary interests and confidentiality. As precision agriculture involves a fundamental paradigm shift the agricultural education system has also to be reoriented to information based agriculture with direct partnership with the farmer.

Precision agriculture even in the developed countries is still at the innovation stage. Unbiased, systematic, rigorous evaluations of the economic and environmental benefits and cost of precision agriculture will be required. Complexity and costs are the barriers to adoption by interested farmers even in the U.S. However, the economics of precision farming look to be attractive (Harris and Stafford, 1997).

A survey in Denmark, UK and USA conducted with farmers who have adopted precision farming (Pedersen *et al.*, 2001) show that the farmers are in general optimistic. But precision agriculture, which is actually a suite of technologies and practices, has been partially adopted by these farmers. Most of them are optimistic about the variable rate of application of fertilizers. In some cases farmers have been satisfied with solutions to site-specific application of pesticides saving up to 13 per cent spray (Secher *et al.*, 2000).

Indian farming situation appears to be in an advantageous position with respect to precision farming. Precision farming deals with information at small scales. The Indian farmers already deal in small scales and as such they have more detailed information on their farms. But the organisational set up to make data acquisition; processing and decision support system available to each farmer has to be developed. In the beginning the high input-high value cropping systems should be targeted. The gains will then diffuse to other systems. On the other hand for the fragile agro-eco systems like the arid agro-ecosystem and the hill-mountain system, precision agriculture can provide extensive database and a means of controlling micro-agro environments to prevent deterioration. It is envisaged that a precision farming system will involve a complex network of farmers, government agencies, large information and input providers, private industries and local highly skilled service-entrepreneurs. Human capital will be highly important in the system.

It is certain that precision agriculture will improve profitability through targeted and efficient application of inputs, which in turn besides reducing cost will reduce the polluting effects of inputs that do not reach the target several studies confirm this. For example, reduction of N_2O emission due to site-specific reduction in fertilizer application has been well documented (Munch *et al.*, 2001. However, there is a possibility that precision agriculture may have less positive impact on environment than expected, for two reasons. First, reduction in fertilizer and pesticide applications may not give a proportionate reduction in their concentration in environment because natural degradation rates may be positively proportional to concentration. Second, increase in crop response to inputs like fertilizers and pesticides may induce the farmer to use more of the inputs. Similarly, better information about soil may induce farmers to increase the yield potential through more inputs.

Precision agriculture has the potential of making organic farming and low input agriculture feasible provided they became profitable to both the farm service sector and the farmer. At one time it was hypothesized that precision farming wasted entail heavy expenditure but it is not so. The government has already developed support policies in this direction mainly to increase the work and nutrient use efficiency reducing environmental pollution and propelling sustainable agriculture. Of course, technology gap still exits and that need to be bridged.

Integrated Water Management

Water is getting scarce and scarce and this has led states like Karnataka and Tamil Nadu fight for irrigation water. In fact, over exploitation of water with little attention to water recharge has brought water scarcity in sharp focus in more than one ways. Decrease in per capita water availability due to increased population, diversion for urban areas and increased domestic use is already compounding water availability for agriculture. Under this scenario, it is important to adopt technologies for conservation of water, its conjunctive use, improving water use efficiency through use of sprinkler and drip irrigation, diversification of agriculture involving shift from high water requiring crops to crops with low water requirement, development of watersheds and use in critical period of shortage and recycling of run off water. Rejuvenation of tank system and improved water management in command areas will help mitigate some of the problems.

Integrated Pest Management (IPM)

Bhopal gas tragedy and awareness among people about environment protection and effect of pesticide residues on human health have given impetus to our efforts in promoting Integrated Pest Management (IPM) strategies. IPM is now a well-recognised technology for achieving our goals of increasing production in harmony with the imperatives of sustainable agriculture. Researches over last two decades have demonstrated that with IPM use pesticides could be completely eliminated in various crops whose production is threatened by serious pests. It also leads to ensuring the safety of the ecological foundations of agriculture such as land, water, forests, environment, biodiversity etc. Intensive agriculture, a necessity of mid-sixties and seventies to meet our needs of burgeoning population, increased genetic uniformity and crop intensity, mono-cropping, higher chemical inputs including fertilisers, pesticides, herbicides, irrigation water, and inappropriate and unsustainable cropping systems. All these favoured insect pests and diseases. Despite increased use of pesticides crops continue to suffer heavy yield losses. The increased pesticide use has also brought in increased resistance among pests necessitating higher levels of pesticide use or more potent broad-spectrum systemic pesticides, which pose serious health hazards. The number of deaths of farmers because of crop losses despite pesticide use highlights the problems of quality of pesticide and inherent danger in development of insect resistance.

The alternative, therefore, for sustainability of the production systems lay in adoption of IPM technology as an integral component of farming system. It is ironical that despite scientists, over the years, having demonstrated the efficacy of IPM, it is still practised in a very small and insignificant area if we consider the total cropped area in the country. However, this does not detract us from the fact that the area under IPM has been increasing each year.

The basic strategy of IPM is to contain pest build up early and check through an integrated approach involving resistant varieties, crop rotation, use of predators and natural enemies of pests, planting repellent crop, use of biopesticides, emphasis on good crop management etc. Complete packages of practices for major crops like, cotton, pigeon pea, groundnut and chickpea, vegetables, like tomato and cabbage, fruits like, apple and mango, which traditionally account for maximum pesticide use, have been worked out. Under NATP the IPM technology has been demonstrated over 690 ha involving 464 farmers families in 31 villages of 8 states in different agro ecosystems covering crops mentioned earlier. This effort still is too small and there is need to have national level development plan for IPM over a large area. This would require partnership among the private sector including pesticide industries, the government agencies, NGOs and farmers.

The basic reasons for the unsatisfactory adoption of IPM are the following:

(i) Lack of a system approach.
(ii) Not making the main stakeholders, the farmer, the farm-level input provider and the consumer, partners in IPM development and planning.
(iii) Inadequate policy framework encouraging IPM.
(iv) Lack of effective interface among institutions.
(v) Inadequate extension efforts.

The pest system is first a part of the cropping system as a whole and then a part of the agro-eco system. The pest system involves, insect-pest, diseases, weeds, beneficial organisms above and in the soil and the cropping system. But practically no IPM system tries to address all these components together. That is why still today we talk of IPM for individual pests or diseases of specified crops. Strangely, weed is always dealt with completely separately though it is a component of the pest system not only because of its direct effects on productivity but also because there is an intricate relationship among diseases, insect pests, soil microbes and weeds.

India has now a fairly widespread IPM generation and dissemination system through ICAR institutes, SAUs and the 26

Central IPM centres under the Directorate of Plant Protection, Quarantine and Storage. But still we find reports, like " ...a series of short duration training courses on IPM in rice....", "...IPM package of practices for 11 rabi crops were finalised" and so on. It is not unusual to find reports on IPM for individual pests and diseases.

Not adopting a system approach for IPM in research and technology development hinders the spread of IPM. The emphasis is still on remedial actions, though natural products are replacing the synthetic chemicals. It is worth mentioning here that very little work has been done on development of resistance to the botanicals etc.

Results of IPM are not spectacular and immediate like the application of synthetic pesticides. It is often very difficult to make the average farmer understand the benefits of IPM in the long run. IPM practices are information intensive and do include understanding the local biotic system, the effects of IPM on productivity of the cropping system and the long-term sustainability of the system. A consumer movement will be helpful in spreading the benefit of IPM.

In India some policy support is emerging like phasing out subsidy on pesticides and diverting resultant savings for promotion of IPM, liberalised registration of Bio-pesticides and botanicals, facilitation of production and use of biocontrol agents etc. However, a well planned delivery and quality management system for knowledge and information, and physical inputs are not available to the stakeholders. Here, a policy framework needs to be developed.

IPM is beneficial despite the fragmentary approach to IPM. It has led to reduction of in use of pesticides by 25 per cent, from 61,357 tonnes during 1994-95 to 46,195 tonnes during 1999-2000 in India (Pawar and Mishra, personal communication). A real integrated approach to and adoption of IPM philosophy will be a boon to sustainable agriculture. Efficacy of IPM packages have been demonstrated on farmers' fields in almost all the states of the country under the Production System Research mode of the NATP in the different agro-ecosystems and these practices have shown cost benefit ratio of 1:3-5 in crops like rice, pigeon pea, mustard and cotton.

Epilogue

The sustainability of the farming system has drawn attention of scientists, administrators, government officials, farmers and consumers alike in view of the environmental concerns and declining or near-stagnant productivity in major food grain production bowls in the country. Fortunately, we have a vast untapped reservoir in the rainfed agro-ecosystem and the north eastern region in which application of science and technology could bring major gains in food grain production. Developments in science and technology, specially in molecular biology now are revolutionary and scientists have power to engineer and transfer genes across species barrier. This has opened vast opportunities to use recombinant DNA technology for addressing many issues of sustainability of different farming systems. India is rich in biodiversity and this national wealth could be fruitfully utilised not only for conomic gains but also for agricultural transformation. Given the technology development, achieving the target of 300 million tonnes of foodgrains is not a difficult task. But it is not an easy target either. In view of the phytosanitary regulations quality of produce assumes importance. Management of natural resources and IPM hold the key to our leadership in the international market. Resumed emphasis on organic farming, protection of environment, restoring and maintaining the health of soil are critical to sustainability and increase in agricultural production for meeting the demands of the ever increasing population.

REFERENCES

Arunachalam, V. (2001). The science behind tradition. *Current Science*, 80:1272-1275.

Bhalla, G.S., Peter Hazell and John Kerr. (1999). *Prospect for India's cereal system and demand to 2020.* International Food Policy Research Institute, Washington D.C., Discussion Paper 29, pp. 24.

CEPAL. (1994). *Panorama Social de America Latina.* Commision Economica America Latina, Chile.

Das, P., Das, S.K., Arya, H.P. S., Subba Reddy, G and Mishra, A. (2002) *Inventory of Indigenous Technical Knowledge in Agriculture*, Document 1, Pub. DIPA, ICAR, New Delhi, pp. 411.

Den Biggelar, C. (1991). *Farming systems development: synthesising indigenous and scientific knowledge systems*. Agriculture and Human Values, 8:25-36.

Deugd, M., Roling, N. and Smaling, E.M.A. (1998). *A new praxeology for integrated nutrient management, facilitating innovation with and by farmers. Special issue: nutrient balances as indicators of productivity and sustainability in sub-Saharan African agriculture*. Agriculture, Ecosystems and Environment, 71: 269-283.

Ellott, A. (1994). *An introduction to sustainable development: the developing world.* Pub. Routledge, London, U.K., pp. 121.

Eswaran, H., Reich, P. and Beinforth, F. (2002). *Land resources of South Asia—stresses, quality and population supporting capacity*. Procd. International Conference on Managing Natural Resources for Sustainable Agricultural Production in the 21st Century (Invited papers), 2000, pp. 97-109.

FAO. (1976). A framework for land evaluation. *FAO Soils Bulletin* No. 32, Rome, Italy: FAO, pp. 72.

Harris, D. and Stafford, J.V. (1997). *Risk Management in precision farming*. Precision Agriculture '97, Vol. II: Technology, IT and management, Papers presented at the First European Conference on Precision Agriculture, Warwick University, U.K., 7–10 September, 1997, pp. 851-59.

Lynch, J. (1998). The role of nutrient-efficient crops in modern agriculture. *Journal of Crop Production*, 1:241-64.

Kanwar, J.S., Katyal, J. C. (Eds.). (1997). *Plant nutrient needs, supply, efficiency and policy issues 2000-2025*. National Academy of Agricultural Science, New Delhi.

Massaquoi, J.G.M. (1993). *Indigenous technology for off-farm rural activities*. Indigenous Knowledge and Development Monitor, 1:2-3.

Mishra, V.K. (2000). Water expense and nutrient use efficiency of wheat and winter maize as influenced by integrated nutrient management. *Agropedology*, 10:1-5.

Munch, J.C., Berkenkamp, A. and Sehy, U. (2001). The effect of site-specific fertilization on N_2O emissions and N-leaching measurements and simulation. In Hort, W.S. *et al.* (ed.), *Plant Nutrition: food security and sustainability of agro-ecosystems through basic and applied research*—Fourteenth International Plant Nutrition Colloquiums, Hannover, Germany, pp. 102-903.

Pedersen, S.N., Ferguson, R.B. and Lark, R.M. (2001). A multinational survey of precision farming early adopters. *Farm Management*, 11:147-62.

Petersen, P.H. (1998). Agriculture, forestry and knowledge in communication technology. In Andersen, K.E. and Dolberg, F. (Ed.), Procd. of *"Women in agriculture and modern communication technology"*, Tune Landboskole, Denmark, 30 March- 3 April, 1998; 1999:94-101.

Ram Kumar, S. (1998). Realising the reality: the first step in sustainable agricultural development. *Newsletter of the Agricultural Research and Extension Network*, 37:22-24.

Sasas, A. and Shibusawa, S. (2000). Prospects and strategies for precision farming in Japan. *Japan Agricultural Research Quarterly*, 34: 233-38. Committee on Assessing Crop yield—Site-specific farming, Information Systems and Research Opportunities, National Research Council (U.S.) 1997. *Precision agriculture in the 21st Century: geospatial and information technologies in crop management*. Pub. National Academy Press (U.S.), pp. 149.

Secher, B.J.M., Bjerre, K.D. and Seiero, M. (2000). *Site-specific control of pest and diseases—a challenge and an opportunity*. The BCPC Conference: Pests and diseases, Vol. 2: Procd. International Conference, Brighton, U.K., 13–16 November, 200, pp. 607-14.

Shah, A. (1998). Watershed development programmes in India: Emerging issues for environment-development perspectives. *Economic and Political Weekly*, 33:26.

Sharland, R. (1991). ITK and extension: how can extension to low-resource, subsistence farmers better relate to indigenous knowledge? *Bulletin of the University of Reading agricultural extension and Rural Development Department*, 31:3-11.

Singh, M.V. (1998). Micronutrient Management. In Singh, G.B. and Sharma, B.R. (ed.), *50 years of Natural Resource Management Research*, Indian Council of Agricultural Research, New Delhi, India, pp. 177-98.

Song, H.K. and Wang, I.K. (1991). Indigenous and new technologies—basic implications for technology development. Seoul National University *Journal of Agricultural Sciences*, 16:247-255.

Swaminathan, M.S. (2002). Food security and sustainable development. In Acharya, S.S., Surjit Singh and Vidya Sagar (ed.), *Sustainable Agriculture, Poverty and Food Security: agenda for Asian economies* Vol. I, pp. 11-32.

Wiesler, F., Behrens, T. and Horst, W. J. (2001). The role of nitrogen-efficient cultivars in sustainable agriculture. In Galloway, J.N., Cowling, E.B., Erisman, J.W. and Wisniewski, J. (ed.), *Procd. of the Second International Nitrogen Conference* on Science and Policy, Potomac, MD, U.S.A., 14-18 October 2001. pp. 61-69.

World Commission on Economic Development. (1987). *Our common future*. Oxford University Press.

Zasada, J.C. (2000). Intellectual and ecological traditional knowledge: can it be sustained through natural products development? Case studies from Thailand, Tibet, Ghana, and Guatemala. In Flaster, T., Davidson, Hunt I. And Duchense, L.C. (Ed.), General Technical Report of the North Central Research Station, USDA Forest Service, No. NC-217, 49-65.

10

Sustainable Agriculture and Rural Livelihoods

S.S. ACHARYA

Introduction

The global consciousness on ecology, environment and poverty was brought to the centre stage of development during the first UN Conference on human environment held in 1972 at Stockholm. However, a conceptual break through on sustainable development was achieved through the Brundtland Commission Report 1987. Subsequently, in June 1992, a blue print for sustainable development was adopted as Agenda 21 during the UN Conference on Environment and Development held at Rio de Janeiro. Ten years later, World Summit on Sustainable Development (WSSD) was held at Johannesburg in August 2002 with the objective of moving from commitment to action in this important area. The debates and concerns being expressed following WSSD need to be understood clearly as these have far reaching implications for improving the livelihoods and food security of the marginalized sections in developing countries. The objective of this paper is to bring out some of these issues relating to sustainable agricultural and rural livelihoods; to analyse agricultural sector development initiative in India; and to suggest some areas of action to resolve the conflicts which confront the policy makers in developing countries including India.

The paper has been divided into ten sections. Basic concepts of sustainable development, sustainable agriculture, rural livelihoods and entitlement to livelihoods are briefly presented in the second section. Some salient aspects of the debate and issues concerning sustainable agricultural development and rural livelihoods have been brought out in the third section. The fourth section covers the status of poverty, food insecurity and inequalities at the global level. Status of agricultural development, food security, rural livelihoods and inequalities in India are discussed in the fifth section. The sixth section covers globalization, implications of WTO agreement and India's prospects in international agricultural trade. A brief comment on economic reforms in India and their implications on rural livelihoods are also given in the sixth section. In the seventh section, some lessons and experiences of development and improvement of rural livelihoods are presented. The strategic approach towards movement to sustainable agriculture and rural livelihoods is discussed in the eighth section. Some suggestions for agricultural reforms in India are presented in the ninth section. Concluding observations are given in the last section.

The Concepts

Since the Earth Summit 1992, use of the expression sustainable development has received increasing attention and became inevitable in development discourse. Sustainable development has been defined in several ways. The World Commission on Environment and Development (WCED) has defined sustainable development as the development that meets the needs of present generation without compromising the ability of future generations to meet their own needs.

Applying this basic intent of sustainability to the agricultural sector, the notion of sustainable agricultural development emerges clearly. Food and Agriculture Organisation (FAO) has defined sustainable agriculture as "the management and conservation of resource base and the orientation of technological and institutional changes in such a manner that ensures attainment and continued satisfaction of human needs for present and future generations. It follows that sustainable agricultural development is that path of agricultural development which is environmentally non-degrading, technologically appropriate, economically viable and socially acceptable" (FAO, 1991).

Livelihood is defined as adequate stock and flows of food and cash with an individual or a family to meet basic needs. Given this, the livelihood security can be understood to encompass secured ownership of, or access to, resources and income earning activities, including reserves and assets to offset risks, ease shocks and meet contingencies. Accordingly, sustainable livelihood refers to maintenance or enhancement of access to food and income earning activities on a long-term basis (Chambers, 1988). Sustainable livelihood is thus a multi-faceted concept as against sustainable food security, which is an uni-dimensional concept (Maxwell and Frankenberger, 1992).

The use of the concept of livelihoods, rather than job or work, is appropriate in the case of farmers and rural poor, because most of these families work in agriculture only seasonally and often part-time. Individuals and households in rural areas create a living from various sources, viz., farming, rural non-farm work and seasonal migration to elsewhere. A working definition of livelihood adopted by Lipton *et al.* (1996) was 200 days of working year, considered sufficient to produce enough income to keep a worker, plus independents, out of poverty (Lipton, 1996).

There are four ways of acquiring or gaining livelihoods by the rural families. First is production-based entitlements. A large proportion of the small and marginal farmers gain livelihoods and food through production on the small pieces of land. Availability or access to inputs and techniques of production are quite critical for the livelihoods of this section of rural people. Second is the labour-based entitlements. Assetless rural families derive livelihoods by selling their labour. For their livelihoods, demand for labour, wage rates and prices of food and other essentials are critical factors. Third, is exchange or market based entitlements. Those rural families who produce surplus food and non-food agricultural products or non-farm goods earn their livelihoods by selling these surpluses in the market. The marketing system for these products and relative prices of what they sell and what they buy affect their livelihoods. The fourth set of entitlements is transfer-based entitlements. The families without any income earning asset or able-bodied person to work depend for their livelihoods on transfers from government or other social organizations. Government's social security programmes are relevant for this group of rural households in fulfilling their livelihood requirements. Entitlement of livelihoods is gained by anyone or a combination of these four modes. The rural families adopt different coping and adaptive strategies for gaining entitlements to livelihoods. The rural livelihood systems in developing countries thus encompass a broad range of factors and depend on several other systems.

Food security is an important and most critical subset of livelihoods. Food security has been defined as physical and economic access to sufficient food, of all people at all times, to meet their dietary needs for a healthy and productive life. In this sense, there are three essential components of food security, viz. food availability, food access and food consumption/absorption.

Issues and Concerns

Sustainable agricultural development and rural livelihoods basically imply attainment of the objective of inter-generational equity. As there is a trade off involved in achieving this over riding goal of sustainability, the important issue of setting the priorities arises. As there is considerable intra-generational inequity, several questions need to be answered. Who sets the priorities? Who defines the needs of present generation? Needs of which section of present generation to be accorded priority over others and future generations? Who defines the discount rates for comparing cost and benefits of the future generations *vs.* present generation? Obviously, the problem gets compounded due to existence of very large inter-personal, inter-regional and inter-country inequalities in livelihoods of even the present generation. If entitling of adequate food and safe drinking water to 30 per cent of the population, who live below the poverty line, is considered not sustainable by the remaining population, should these be deprived of food and water in the interest of future generations (of whom?). There is also the important issue of projections of the needs of future generations, their lifestyles and future technologies. Can this projection be done with reasonable degree of precision?

A related issue that needs attention is the basis of imputation of social costs and benefits for comparison with individual costs and benefits. There is considerable divergence between nominal costs/benefits *vs.* environmental costs and benefits. Internalization of environmental accounting has not become a practice in several societies.

There is also a source of conflict between developing and developed societies in protecting the global environment. The damage to the environment in low-income countries is very low compared to the developed societies. It has been quoted that in 1996, per capita corbon dioxide emission in low-income countries was 1.1 metric tons as against 12.3 metric tons in high-income countries. Given this, setting of similar standards of reducing emissions is being contested on the world fora. Even if it is recognized that environmental degradation is public bad, the shadow price for valuation of degradation cannot be uniform across countries. It is being argued that the shadow prices ought to be a sovereign decision of a country and should not be dictated by those who do more damage to the environment. Debroy (2002) argues that if 38 per cent of population of Bhutan does not have access to potable water and 47 per cent of Napalese children (under 5) are under-weight, should these countries worry about air-pollution or spend on primary education and health care? The decisions relating to marginal social costs and benefits and discount rates for future stream of social costs and benefits are a function of country's stage of development and internal to the country. These cannot be made a cross-border issue. Political economy will not allow the neglect of present demands of the poor in pursuance of better future for others (Vyas and Reddy, 1996).

In this context, Chambers (1988) argues that sustainable development can be achieved by securing livelihoods for the critical group of very poor, not through unproductive conservation but through development with a positive impact on livelihoods, which, in turn, later becomes sustainable. Short-term improvements in living create conditions for later livelihood-intensive and sustainable human use of environment.

However, Reddy (1996) argues that these solutions hold good for resource poor regions where majority lives below poverty line. When these cross this line, they tend to over-exploit natural system. Of course, in the developed regions, there are certain activities which are beyond sustainable line. He argues that sustainability follows a cyclical pattern. In the case of sustainable agriculture, cyclical pattern takes place due to (lopsided) policies of the state, which are biased towards well-endowed regions in the beginning and later shifting towards fragile resource regions. However, the course of the cycle can be altered if appropriate interventions are made either by the state or civil society. People's awareness through education, institutions and technology can alter the curve.

The incidence of poverty is very high among tribal societies. Out of all the societies, tribals live closest to the nature and environment. Their access to markets is limited. Development initiatives of these societies and regions have received considerable attention and debated upon. In this connection, late Pandit Jawaharlal Nehru once said, "nothing should be denied to them". Dalai Lama said "no matter how attractive a traditional rural society may seem, its people should not be denied the opportunity to enjoy the benefits of modern development". As regards the issue of poverty reduction *vs.* environmental preservation, Smt. Indira Gandhi, addressing the World Forum had said, "poverty is the worst polluter of environment". In this context, a development course which alleviates poverty is not the cause but cure of environment problems.

Given the debate and trade off in sustainable development and rural livelihoods, following needs to be recognized:

(i) For hungry, malnourished and poor/food insecure, needs of present generation and children are more important than the needs of future generations. Their rates of discounting future benefits and costs are very high.

(ii) While economic development policies and actions could not ignore environmental damage, environmental policies and management should not ignore economic welfare losses of poor, malnourished and food insecure in the short run.

(iii) In predominantly agricultural and rural countries, livelihoods of farmers and rural families is difficult to improve without causing some damage to the natural resources and environment.

(iv) Sustainability of agriculture is the question of degree and not neither/or.

(v) Complete prevention of natural resources and environmental damage is neither feasible nor socially/ economically desirable. Therefore, attempt should be to abate it or reduce it. Some important issues in reducing or abating the environmental damage are (a) costs of reducing the damage; (b) effect of reduction of damage on economic welfare of the poor; and (c) effectiveness of fiscal or economic instruments for reducing the damage.

7World Scene of Poverty and Food Insecurity

Poverty continues to be a major problem in many parts of the world. If poverty line is defined as one dollar per day, nearly 1.2 billion people live below this poverty line. Poverty is more pronounced in rural areas. Seventy-five per cent of the total poor live and work in rural areas. Nearly 90 per cent of total poor live in Asia and Sub-Saharan Africa (SSA). Asia accounts for about two-thirds of the total world poor, with South Asia accounting for 43 per cent (IFPRI, 2001).

A significant proportion of the rural poor live in less favoured areas that are challenged by difficult agro-climatic conditions such as poor soil, low and unstable rainfall, steep slopes, short growing season and inadequate infrastructure and support services.

Most of the poor people are also food insecure. During the last three decades, there has been considerable improvement in food security situation. The number of food insecure declined by 17 per cent from 940 million to 780 million. The percentage of food insecure declined from 37 per cent to 18 per cent. The major decline in food insecure population occurred in China and South-east Asian countries. In South Asia, there was a slight increase in food insecure population. However, in Sub-Saharan Africa, the number of food insecure doubled during this period (IFPRI, 2002).

Another dimension of inadequate livelihoods is the malnutrition. Despite considerable improvement in the status of malnutrition during the last two to three decades, the situation continues to be alarming. The average calorie and protein intake has gone up by 27 per cent and the incidence of malnutrition has declined from 57 per cent to 31 per cent. The number of malnourished children also declined by 31 million during this period, but 170 million under—5 children continue to be malnourished. Most of these live in Sub-Saharan Africa and South Asia. In fact, the number of malnourished children has gone up in SSA during the last couple of decades.

A more disquieting feature has been the continued and growing inequalities in the world. The richest one per cent of the population accounts for an income which is equivalent to the sum total of the income of 57 per cent of the poorest population. The ratio of per capita income of developed world to the per capita income of Sub-Saharan Africa which was around eight a couple of decades ago has gone up to 18 in recent years.

In the developing countries, the food availability continues to be from the domestic sources. However, their dependence on food imports has shown an increasing trend. Combined food imports of developing countries, as proportion of their total food availability has gone up from 10 per cent two decades ago to 15 per cent in recent years. However, the inter-year variability in availability of food has declined from 33 per cent to 20 per cent in recent years. For the developing world as a whole, the burden of food imports bill, defined as value of food imports as percentage of their total exports, declined from 20 per cent to only six per cent during this period. However, for 49 least developed countries, the food import bill continues to stay at around 20 per cent. Many of these countries face huge debt burden and are constrained to import needed food for their population. In this context, large populated countries like China and India pursuing the goal of near self-sufficiency in staple foods, is a welcome development for the macro food security of medium and small low-income countries of the developing world.

Indian Agriculture, Food Security and Status of Livelihoods

Main Features of Agricultural Development Strategy

Ever since independence, the concern for food security has been the major focus of agricultural development policy in India. The necessity for this arose from the situation of food supplies falling short of the demand by a substantial margin, inadequacy of the then existing system to induce farmers to increase food production at a rapid rate and pervasive poverty and low purchasing power of the masses.

In the fifties and upto the middle of sixties, as the main concern of the food policy was to ensure that the gap between demand and supply of food did not result in excessive rise in consumer prices, India imported considerable quantities of cereals. During the middle of sixties, India was importing about 16 per cent of the net availability of food grains. This period was a turning point in the approach to food security in India. Apart from the increased dependence on imports for meeting the food needs, it were two severe consecutive drought years in mid-sixties, which led to the launch of a new strategy of agricultural development for increasing the output of food grains. The strategy was based on the recognition that for building a sound agricultural economy, simultaneous attention is necessary on three foundations, viz.: (a) provision of an improved technology package for the farmers; (b) creation of an efficient system of delivery of inputs and services including credit; and (a) assurance of quick market clearance and a remunerative price environment for the farmers. As a part of this strategy, apart from investment in agricultural research, extension education, input supply system including credit, expansion in irrigation and infrastructure, the Food Corporation of India (FCI) was established as the sole agency of the state for the purchase, storage, transport and distribution of food grains. Simultaneously, the Agricultural Prices Commission was set up to advise the government on matters relating to agricultural and food price policy in the context of the need to raise production of agricultural commodities particularly of food grains and give relief to the consumers.

A large number of policy instruments were used to achieve the stated objectives. The policy and instruments were reviewed from time to time. The main instruments of food management policy in India currently in vogue include the following:

(i) Fixation of minimum support prices for all major cereals and pulses. The support prices are announced before the sowing season for 25 farm products including paddy, maize, sorghum, pearl millet, ragi, wheat, barley, pigeon pea, green gram, black gram and chick pea;

(ii) Arrangements for purchase of the produce offered by the farmers at guaranteed prices. The designated nodal agency for undertaking price support operations is Food Corporation of India (FCI) for cereals and National Agricultural Cooperative Marketing Federation (NAFED) for pulses;

(iii) Building up of a buffer stock of cereals through price support operations and imports;

(iv) Distribution of cereals at prices lower than the economic cost under public distribution system and through anti-poverty, employment generation and nutrition programmes;

(v) Control and/or restrictions on the activities of private trade through a series of legal and other instruments like levy on rice millers, limits on stocks with traders and millers and mandatory quality standards;

(vi) Regulation of imports and exports through canalization, quantitative ceilings or tariffs;

(vii) Creation of physical and institutional infrastructure for improved performance of the marketing system which include primary market yards, roads and communication facilities;

(viii) Provision of food and input subsidies to reconcile the conflicting objectives of food grain producers and consumers.

It may be mentioned here that one of the main objectives of the policy has been to assure a remunerative and relatively stable price environment for the farmers for inducing them to adopt new technology and modern inputs and thereby augment the availability of food grains. Further, the policy also sought to make available food grains to masses at reasonable prices.

Status of Macro Food Security

The new strategy adopted in India since the mid-sixties paid rich dividends. The change in the status of food security can be measured from several angles:

(i) The most significant change has been the increase in domestic output of cereals. The production of cereals went up from 72.0 million tonnes during the triennium ending (TE) 1964-65 to 189.8 million tonnes during TE 2000-01 (Table 10.1).

Table 10.1: Production of Foodgrains in India

	TE 1951-52	*TE 1964-65*	*TE 2000-01*
Rice	21.8	36.5	87.3
Wheat	6.3	10.9	71.8
Coarse Cereals	16.1	24.6	30.7
Total Cereals	44.2	72.0	189.8
Pulses	8.3	11.3	13.1
Total Foodgrains	52.5	83.3	202.9

TE—Triennium ending

Source: Government of India (2002).

(ii) Owing to the increases recorded in the output of cereals, not only the dependence on imports for meeting the domestic needs was eliminated but also the country has even emerged as marginal exporter of cereals.

(iii) Apart from the increase in the level of cereal output, the instability in the availability of cereals from domestic sources went down considerably. Between TE 1964-65 and TE 2000-01, in the incremental production of 117.8 million tonnes of cereals, the contribution of wheat and rice has been as much as 111.7 million tonnes. With rice and wheat contributing the bulk of additional output, the share of coarse cereals, a component subject to wide inter-year fluctuations, in the total output of cereals, decreased from 34 per cent during TE 1964-65 to 16 per cent during TE 2000-01.

(iv) Further, a geographically dispersed growth of cereals helped in increasing physical access to food in different parts of the country. During the last one and half decades, the contribution of rice, the production of which is more dispersed, to the incremental production of cereals was considerably higher than that of other cereals. Between TE 1984-85 and TE 2000-01, out of the incremental production of 59.5 million tonnes of cereals, rice contributed as much as 32.1 million tonnes (54 per cent), whereas its contribution was only 32 per cent in the incremental production of cereals between TE 1964-65 and TE 1984-85.

(v) Another important development contributing to the food security has been the increase in economic access to cereals. With the retail prices of rice and wheat increasing at a rate lower than the increase in average per capita income of the country, the proportion of average per capita income required to buy a quintal of wheat declined from 12.9 per cent in 1972-73 to 4.4 per cent in 1999-2000 in rural areas and from 13.7 per cent to 5.4 per cent in urban areas. Similarly, average per capita income required to buy a quintal of rice declined from 17.2 per cent to 6.5 per cent in rural areas and from 19.5 per cent to 7.3 per cent in urban areas (Table 10.2).

Table 10.2: Per cent of Per Capita Income to buy a Quintal of Rice/Wheat in India

Year	Rice		Wheat		One-day wage Equivalent
	Rural	Urban	Rural	Urban	
1972-73	17.2	19.5	12.9	13.7	One kg
1999-2000	6.5	7.3	4.4	5.4	4 to 6 kg

Source: Acharya (2002).

(vi) With the increase in physical and economic access to staple cereals, important shifts in production and consumption patterns occurred. Farmers in several areas diverted their resources from low-yielding cereals to other crops which *inter-alia* helped in improving the availability of other food items like edible oils, vegetables, fruits, milk, eggs and meat/fish (Table 10.3). The pattern of consumption expenditure also shifted in favour of other nutritive foods like vegetables, fruits, milk and milk products etc. This happened even in rural areas. There was also improvement in calorie intake in low-income households and shift in the sources of calorie.

Table 10.3: Per Capita Availability of Food Items in India

Item	1980-81	1999-2000
Edible Oils (kg)	5.0	10.6
Pulses (kg)	11.3	13.5
Sugar (kg)	7.3	15.6
Milk (kg)	46.7	76.0
Eggs (No.)	16.7	30.7
Fish (kg)	3.4	5.5
Meat (kg)	NA	44.7
Fruits (kg.)	13.3	34.3
Vegetables (kg)	NA	85.8

Source: Acharya (2002).

(vii) These positive developments, by and large, reduced the food insecurity in the country to a very great extent. However, hunger at household and at individual level could not be eliminated. Surveys conducted by NSSO have reported that nearly 8 per cent of rural population do not get two square meals a day (Asthana, 2001). According to NSSO (1997), during 1993-94, 6.4 million people were reported to be starkly hungry (without two square meals a day). The number of partially hungry people in the country was quite large at 44.8 million. This is reflected in quite high levels of infant and maternal mortality rates, and high proportion of under-5 malnourished children.

Use of Land and Water Resources

Yield-raising technologies, viz. high-yielding varieties, better and improved seeds, fertilizers, diseases and pest-control methods were instrumental in improving the productivities of land and water. Nevertheless, augmentation of land and water resources also contributed to the improvement in food and nutritional security:

(i) Cultivated area (net sown areas plus current fallow) in the country was extended from 129.5 million hectares during 1950-51 to 156.1 million hectares during 1998-99. With 26.6 million hectares of additional land brought under cultivation, cultivated area as a proportion of total geographical area went up from 39.4 per cent to 47.5 per cent during this period. The area under forests also increased considerably. However, a disquieting feature of land use has been a decline in pastures and grazing lands from 26.5 million hectares to 14.7 million hectares during the last 50 years (Table 10.4).

Table 10.4: Land Use Changes in India

Classes	*1950-51*		*1998-99*	
	Million Ha	*%*	*Million Ha*	*%*
Net sown area + current fallow	129.5	39.4	156.1	47.5
Not available for cultivation	47.5	14.4	42.4	12.9
Forests	40.5	12.3	69.0	21.0
Pastures	26.5	8.1	14.7	4.5
Old fallows	17.4	5.3	9.9	3.0
Culturable Waste	22.9	7.0	14.0	4.3
Not reported	44.4	13.5	22.6	6.8
Total GA	328.7	100.0	328.7	100.0

Source: Compiled from Government of India (2002).

(ii) Apart from the expansion in cultivated area, expansion in irrigation facilities has been another important source of increasing agricultural production in India. The net irrigated area in the country went up from 20.8 million hectares during 1950-51 to 57.0 million hectares during 1998-99. In 1950-51, 17.6 per cent of net sown area (118.8 m.ha) had irrigation facilities whereas in 1998-99, as much as 40 per cent of net sown area (142.6 ha) had this facility (Table 10.5). The expansion in gross irrigated area was even higher than that in net irrigated area. The gross irrigated area in the country increased from 22.6 million hectares during 1950-51 to 75.6 million hectares during 1998-99.

Table 10.5: Irrigation Expansion in India

Particulars	*1950-51*	*1998-99*	*Change*
NAS (m.ha)	118.8	142.6	+23.8
NAS as % of GA	36.1	43.4	+ 7.3
NIA (m.ha)	20.8	57.0	+36.2
NIA as % of NAS	17.6	40.0	+22.4
GCA (m.ha)	131.9	192.6	+60.7
GIA (m.ha)	22.6	75.6	+53.0
GIA as % of GCA	17.1	39.2	+22.1

Source: Compiled from Government of India (2002).

(iii) Out of the incremental gross irrigated area of 53 million hectares, 27.2 million hectares was added between 1950 and 1980 and 25.8 million hectares was added between 1980 and 1998. The pattern of allocation of incremental areas to various crops or crop group was considerably different during the two periods (Table 10.6). Between 1950 to 1980, as much as 50.4 per cent of incremental irrigated area went to wheat whereas during the later period, wheat accounted for only 25.5 per cent of the incremental irrigated area. During the later period 27.5 per cent of incremental irrigated area went to rice and 13.7 per cent to oilseeds. By and large, allocation of incremental irrigated area was consistent with the objective of assuring macro food security and encouragement to low-water requiring crops like oilseeds (Table 10.6).

Table 10.6: Allocation of Incremental Irrigated Area in India

(% of Total Incremental)

Crops	*1950 to 1980*	*1980 to 1998*
Wheat	50.4	25.5
Rice	24.2	27.5
Coarse cereals	3.2	(–) 1.2
All cereals	77.8	51.8
Pulses	0.8	3.2
Oilseeds	8.3	13.7
Cotton	6.1	4.3
Sugar cane	3.7	6.0
Others	3.3	21.0
Total	100.0	100.0
(Change in GIA) m.ha	27.2	25.8

(iv) In spite of considerable increase in irrigation facilities, 60 per cent of gross cropped area continues to remain without irrigation. Unirrigated or rainfed area is 47.7 per cent in rice, 88 per cent in coarse grains, 87.9 per cent in pulses, 76.8 per cent in oilseeds and 65.1 per cent in cotton. It is only in the case of wheat that the unirrigated area is only 14.2 per cent (Table 10.7)

Table 10.7: Per cent Irrigated and Rainfed Areas (1998-99) under Important Crops in India

Major Crops	*Irrigated*		*Unirrigated*		*Total*
	52-53	98-99	52-53	98-99	
Rice	31.7	52.3	68.3	47.7	100
Wheat	34.0	85.8	66.0	14.2	100
Coarse grains	7.9	12.0	92.1	88.0	100
All cereals	20.5	49.6	79.5	50.4	100
Pulses	9.4	12.1	90.6	87.9	100
Oilseeds	0.8	23.2	99.2	76.8	100
Cotton	8.2	34.9	91.8	65.1	100

Source: Compiled from Government of India (2002).

Status of Poverty and Livelihoods

The number of poor in India, which hovered around 321 million during 1973-74, 1983 and 1993-94, declined to 260 million during

1999-2000. The poverty ratio, defined as number of poor as a percentage of total population, however, declined continuously from 54.9 per cent during 1973-74 to 44.5 per cent during 1983, 36.0 per cent during 1993-94 and further to 26.1 per cent during 1999-2000 (Table 10.8).

Table 10.8: Number of Poor and Poverty Ratio in India

Period		Rural	Urban	Total
1973-74				
	Million	261	60	321
	Ratio	56.4	49.0	54.9
1983				
	Million	252	71	323
	Ratio	45.7	40.8	44.5
1993-94				
	Million	244	76	320
	Ratio	37.3	32.4	36.0
1999-2000				
	Million	193	67	260
	Ratio	27.1	23.6	26.1

Source: Planning Commission, Government of India, quoted by Mohanti (2002)

Spatial distribution of poor in India (Table 10.9) shows that 48.3 per cent of poor live in three states, viz., Bihar, Uttar Pradesh and Madhya Pradesh. Maharashtra, Orissa and West Bengal account for 23.4 per cent of India's poor. These six states together account for 71.7 per cent of India's poor.

Table 10.9: Spatial Distribution of Poor in India (1993-94)

States	Cumulative %
Bihar, UP, MP (3)	48.3
Maharashtra, Orissa, WB (3)	71.7
AP, Karnataka, TN (3)	85.3
Assam, Rajasthan (2)	92.1
All India	100.0
Rural India	74.0
Urban India	26.0

The studies show that the incidence of poverty is higher among scheduled caste and scheduled tribe families. Similarly, the incidence is higher among illiterates than among literates. Further, poverty ratio is higher among families in low-rainfall and irrigated areas than others. Across rural occupational categories, the incidence of poverty is the highest among agricultural labourers (up to 90%), followed by other labour households (up to 78%), self-employed in non-agricultural activities (up to 62%) and self-employed in farming (up to 56%).

There are 106.6 million operational holdings in India, of which 59.4 per cent (63.4 million) operate less than one hectare of land and 18.8 per cent (20.1 million) operate between one and two hectares of land. Thus, 78.2 per cent (83.5 million) holdings are less than two hectares in size (Table 10.10). The families dependent on these holdings are not able to earn enough livelihoods for their members. They produce mostly for home consumption. For the livelihood and food security of these families, availability of inputs and their prices are more important. These families account for 36.9 per cent of gross cropped area, 47.7 per cent of paddy area, 43.1 per cent of wheat area, 43.4 per cent of net irrigated area, 41.6 per cent of gross irrigated areas, 53.9 per cent of electric pumps, 41.7 per cent of total fertilizer use, 50.4 per cent of power tillers and 58.7 per cent of power operated sprayers/dusters (Table 10.11). In this context, it is important to keep in view the food security and livelihoods of small and marginal farmers while raising the user charges for electricity and canal water and increasing fertilizer prices. These measures will increase the cost of food produced by these families mostly for self-consumption.

Table 10.10: Size Distribution of Farmers in India

Size	*1960-61*		*1990-91*		+
	Number (Million)	%	*Number (Million)*	%	
Marginal	19.90	40.7	63.39	59.4	43.49
Small	10.88	22.3	20.10	18.8	9.22
Semi-Medium	9.22	18.9	13.92	13.1	4.70
Medium	6.57	13.4	7.58	7.1	1.01
Large	2.31	4.7	1.65	1.6	– 0.66
Total	48.88	100.0	106.64	100.0	57.76

Source: Government of India (2002).

Table 10.11: Share of Small (+M) Farmers in Important Inputs in India

Item	*Unit*	*Total*	*Small Farmers*	%
Net Sown Area	Lakh ha	1,354	471	34.8
Gross Cropped Area	"	1,702	629	36.9
Paddy Area	"	454	217	47.7
Wheat Area	"	234	101	43.1
Net Irrigated Area	"	485	204	43.4
Gross Irrigated Area	"	633	263	41.6
Electric Pumps	No. in lakh	93	50	53.9
Diesel Pumps	"	69	41	58.9
Fertilizer Use (nutrients)	Lakh tonnes	103	43	41.7
Fertilized Area	Lakh ha	1,005	397	39.4
Institutional Borrowers	No. in lakhs	174	125	71.8
Power Tillers	"	11	5	50.4
Power Operated spayers/ dusters	"	16	9	58.7
Other Power Operated M.	"	52	23	44.6

Source: Compiled from Government of India (2000).

Consumption Pattern

With the increase in physical and economic access of two important staple cereals viz., rice and wheat, there have been considerable changes in the consumption pattern at the household level. Per capita consumption of wheat increased but that of rice and coarse cereals decreased. The decrease was much more pronounced in coarse cereals. The average annual per capita consumption of coarse cereals declined from 56.7 kg in 1977 to 17.7 kg in 1999. Another important change in the consumption basked has been the decrease in average consumption of cereals as a group and of sugar/gur and increase in the consumption of nutritive foods like pulses, milk and milk products, edible oils, vegetables, fruits and meat, eggs & fish group (Table 10.12).

The shift in consumption pattern in favour of more nutritive foods occurred owing mainly to smaller percentage of income of a household now required to meet its staple food needs. The proportion of total expenditure on rice plus wheat declined from 29.8 per cent in 1972-73 to 20.5 per cent in 1999-2000 and on coarse cereals declined from 10.8 per cent to 1.7 per cent during this period. As a consequence, food accounted for only 59.4 per cent of total expenditure during 1999-2000 as against 72.8 per cent during 1972-73 (Table 10.13). Thus, an average Indian family now has a relatively larger proportion of income to spend on non-food items like education, health and durables.

Table 10.12: Change in Food Consumption (Kg. per person per year)

Items	*1977*	*1999*	*Change*
Rice	86.5	81.0	–
Wheat	49.4	53.9	+
Coarse grains	56.7	17.7	–
Total cereals	192.6	152.6	–
Pulses	8.7	10.1	+
Milk + Products	24.6	50.5	+
Edible oils	2.7	6.0	+
Vegetables	24.7	66.0	+
Fruits	2.6	17.0	+
Meat, eggs, fish	2.7	5.0	+
Sugar, gur	13.5	10.1	–

Source: NSSO, quoted by Ramesh (2002).

Table 10.13: Consumption Pattern: Per cent Share in Total Expenditure in India (Rural)

Items	*1972-73*	*1999-2000*
Rice + Wheat	29.8	20.5
Coarse grains	10.8	1.7
Other foods	32.2	37.2
Total food	72.8	59.4
Non-food	27.2	40.6
Total	100.0	100.0

Source: NSSO Reports.

Inequalities

Sustainable agricultural and rural livelihoods also depend on inequalities that exist in the present generation. Beyond a point, the inequalities get reflected in practices, which conflict with sustainability of natural resources. A few aspects of trends in inequalities need to be noted.

(i) During the last two decades, the state level averages of per capita income have diverged more. The ratio of state level highest per capita income to the lowest per capita income went up from 4.4 during the early eighties to 5.4 during 1999-2000.

(ii) The coefficient of variation of state level rural per capita income increased from 20 per cent during early 1980s to 28 per cent during 1999-2000.

(iii) The inequality between rural and urban areas also went up considerably during this period. The ratio of gross domestic product per worker in urban areas to that in rural areas went up from 2.43 in 1950-51 to 3.84 in 1980-81 and further to 5.56 in later half of nineties (Table 10.14).

Table 10.14: Rural Urban Inequality in India: Ratio of GDP Per Worker (1980-81 Prices)

Year	*Ag.*	*Non-Ag.*	*Ratio Non-Ag. to Ag.*
1950-51	2,138	5,189	2.43
1960-61	2,274	6,120	2.69
1970-71	2,854	9,945	3.48
1980-81	2,668	10,238	3.84
1990-91	3,323	15,448	4.65
1996-97	3,648	20,272	5.56

Globalization

Globalization basically means flow of goods/services, capital and finance, technology, information, labour and culture from one country to the other across the world. But all of these have not flowed equally owing to the restrictive policies pursued by almost all the countries. For these flows not getting tilted in favour/against some countries, there is a need for some rules/norms agreed upon by all the countries. The setting up of World Trade Organization (WTO) in 1995 was a step in this direction. For, the benefits of globalization to percolate to rural areas and marginalized sections of developing countries, or to put it differently, for the losses of globalization not to be born by those who are already poor, the developing countries need to reformulate their domestic marketing policies. In fact, domestic market liberalization should have preceded the opening up of international trade policy regime. However, in the case of agricultural sector, it did not happen in several developing countries including India, which has far-reaching implications for sustainable agriculture and rural livelihoods.

After the establishment of WTO, the international trade in agricultural commodities has increased but the benefits of increased trade have not flowed adequately to the developing countries. There are several reasons for this situation. As per commitments under Agreement on Agriculture (AoA) under WTO, many developed countries have not reduced their support to the agricultural sector. Some developed countries have changed the forms of subsidizing farmers to make them WTO compatible. Further, even if developed countries had reduced their support at committed levels, these would have been still at much higher levels compared to the support being given in the developing world. On the other hand, developing countries have an aggregate support, which is negative, and the indirect support in the form of input subsidies existing in these countries is being reduced due to domestic economic compulsions.

As far as freeing of agricultural trade is concerned, it is now becoming increasingly clear that it may not be a reality in the foreseeable future. International trade in agricultural commodities continues to be residual in nature. Further, every country—developed or developing—continues to provide some degree of protection to its farmers. Political economy compulsions dictate protection to farming. In developing countries, where a large proportion of population derives its livelihoods from the agricultural activities, protection to farmers in the form of subsidies has a justification from the point of view of livelihood security of rural population.

Large populated countries like India need to analyse globalization in relation to agricultural commodities keeping the food security and rural livelihoods security as the prime concern. For example, rice consumed in India is around four times the total international trade in rice. While looking at India's share in world trade, one should not ignore India's share in world consumers of rice. Further, if initial trade volumes are low, figures of growth in trade volumes may be, sometimes misleading. One other important aspect, which needs to be kept in view while analysing the degree of globalization, is that the international prices of agricultural commodities continue to be more volatile than the prices in the domestic market. Complete free trade, thus may mean importing volatility in agricultural prices. The livelihoods of small farmers and poor consumers are likely to suffer if this happens.

The international market in agricultural commodities continues to remain distorted. Further, small country assumption does not hold for countries like India and China. The studies have shown that if India enters the international market as exporter, its FoB price is lower than the international prices. If it enters as a buyer, its CIF price is much higher than the international prices (Chand and Jha, 2001). As regards India's prospects of international trade, it needs to be recognized that India is a competitive producer of many agricultural commodities if farm gate cost of production is taken as the criteria. The main problem arises when domestic price is compared with international prices. India's transaction costs, arising mainly due to inefficiency of the marketing system, are unduly high. Nevertheless, India has comparative advantage in rice, raw cotton, fresh and processed fruits and vegetables, marine products, flowers, spices and meat products. Another advantage to India in the international trade arena is its large domestic market, which works as a buffer to exporters in the event of setbacks in the international market. However, our sanitary conditions come in the way of taking full advantage of export opportunities available after 1995.

The most important aspect of international trade for India is the redistributive effect it results in. Whenever, a commodity is imported, the consumers gain whereas the producers of this community lose. On the contrary, if a commodity is exported, the producers gain and consumers of this commodity lose. The studies conducted in India to estimate the gains, losses and net social welfare from freeing of trade in major agricultural commodities show that net social welfare from imports of edible oils is close to zero but there is considerable redistribute effect (Chand and Jha, 2001). The loss is mainly to oilseed growers who are mostly resource poor farmers in dry land areas or farmers without irrigation facilities. Free imports of edible oils at low duties thus adversely affect the livelihoods of poor farmers. In the context of these implications of globalization of agriculture, it is being pointed out that India should pay attention to (a) raising tariffs on imports of edible oils and pulses; (b) removal of domestic market restrictions on agricultural commodities; (c) investing in rural infrastructure; and (d) encouragement to agro-processing and value addition in agriculture.

Some Lessons and Experiences

In an attempt to identify the strategic approach towards sustainable agriculture and rural livelihoods, it is relevant to take stock of the lessons and experiences in this regard.

(i) Dangers to the environment in the developing world arise owing to the following:
   (a) A very large proportion of poor individuals, households and communities depend for their livelihoods on land, water and bio-diversity which are vulnerable to damage;
   (b) Environment policies and institutional framework for overseeing the environment are weak;
   (c) Raise in environmental standards either raises the costs or adversely affects the livelihoods of the poor, which creates a climate of popular resistance; and
   (d) Border, caste or communal conflicts are a common features leading to far reaching implications for environmental damage/protection.

(ii) If the pace and pattern of development remains as at present and no special initiatives are taken, the number of food insecure in the world would decline to 675 million up to 2015, which shall be considerable higher than the target of 400 million set by the World Food Summit.

(iii) In developing countries with a large population dependent on agriculture, if priority in development agenda is accorded to agricultural growth, rural infrastructure and employment in non-farm sector, the poverty and food insecurity can be reduced at a rapid rate,

(iv) If the character of the agricultural growth is broad-based *i.e.*, small, marginal and dry-land farmers also participate in the growth process and farmers are able to retain higher incomes, the backward and forwarded linkages generated by this kind of growth process help in reducing rural poverty at a rapid rate.

(v) The experience shows that rural livelihoods can be

improved in a sustainable way if the following conditions hold true:

(a) Availability of appropriate technology to rural households;
(b) Availability of inputs, services and credit to farmers and rural families;
(c) Availability of market support to farmers and rural households;
(d) Adequate local institutions and social capital;
(e) Security of tenure or rights to resources;
(f) Absence of poor non-friendly macro policies; and
(g) Good governance.

(vi) For sustainable natural resource use practices and simultaneous improvements in rural livelihoods, there is a need for institutional mechanisms for resolution of contradictions in development and environment. For example, construction of rural roads for linking marginalized communities to social services (health and education) and to the market also increases extraction of natural resources from remote areas. If grazing lands or pastures are closed to avoid over-grazing, the livelihoods of poor livestock owners are adversely affected. Some environmental protection measures increase the workload of rural women, which is already very heavy. The other examples of contradictions are found in policies that discourage the use of chemicals in agriculture. As these policies adversely affect the interests of the entire chemical industry, it is bound to lobby against such policies.

(vii) Science and technology offers tremendous opportunities in simultaneous achievements of the goals of sustainable agriculture and improving the rural livelihoods. A blend of indigenous knowledge and new technology is a desirable option in this regard. The information technology has opened considerable opportunities for the rural poor both in terms of direct employment and in improving their linkages with the market. Demand for high value food marketing services is growing at a very rapid rate. Technological change in marketing provides considerable potential of creating rural non-farm employment. Rural institutional framework also needs to undergo a drastic change for increasing the scale of marketing.

(viii) Agricultural and rural marketing system improvement is another area for moving towards a sustainable agri-system. At present 90 per cent of the food marketing system is in the unorganized sector, where physical losses are considerably high. Contrary to general belief, 80 per cent of the trade in agricultural commodities is handled by the private sector, with cooperatives and public sector handling ten per cent each (Acharya, 1998). The private sector is mainly constrained by a plethora of market regulations and non-availability of credit for marketing from financial institutions. With the increase in demand for marketing services, there is a need to encourage private sector for making investment in agricultural marketing system and thereby reducing the marketing costs and gross marketing margins.

Strategic Approach to Sustainable Agriculture and Rural Livelihoods

The strategic approach to sustainable agriculture and rural livelihoods should recognize the following:

(i) The developing countries cannot and should not ignore the fact that the priority goal of development strategy ought to be in the order of removal of hunger, providing safe drinking water to all, lifting all above the poverty line, removing malnutrition among children and reducing inter-personal inequalities in levels of living.

(ii) Environmental accounting needs to be made an essential part of policy formulation, planning and development decision-making. There is not enough knowledge of environmental costs at all the stages of decision making and policy formulation. According to some estimates, between 1980 and 1999, if the cost of environmental damage is taken into account, India's economic growth rate comes to minus (–) 5.73 per cent per annum as against plus (+) 5.66 per cent estimated otherwise. The estimates of soil degradation during the eighties and nineties range from 11 to 26 per cent of gross domestic product. The cost of water logging and salinity (11 per cent of area) has been estimated at Rs. 120 billion to Rs. 270 billion.

(iii) There is considerable wastewater, which, if recycled can help in easing the demand for water in urban areas. It has been estimated that the wastewater in urban areas of India is around 200 billion litres, out of which only 10 per cent is treated as present. Finding alternative sources for meeting fuel wood demand in rural areas is another area, which needs attention both for sustainable land use practices and improving rural livelihoods. The existing fuel wood demand is estimated to be six times the sustainable supply of fuel wood.

(iv) As there is an element of trade off between environmental protection and welfare loss of the present generation, valuation of individual and social costs and benefits is quite critical in development decisions. While looking at the environmental costs in terms of degradation of forest lands, the benefits in terms of new plantations should also be simultaneously estimated. It has been found that paddy fields emit methane gas, which is environment polluting, but this may not be true in all the rice growing areas of the world. It is being argued that methane gas emission from paddy fields is either very low or negligible in Asia. Similarly, excessive use of fertilizers is only a limited phenomenon. In several areas of India, the fertilizer use is still at sub-optimum levels. If new technology and high yielding practices help resource poor farmers in improving their livelihoods and thereby reduces the incidence of hunger and malnutrition, there is a basis of the argument that in the event of a trade off, removal of hunger and malnutrition should get precedence over environmental degradation.

(v) There is an on-going debate between protagonists of agricultural development and environmentalists. While those who give precedence to removal of hunger and malnutrition suggest that irrigation facilities should be expanded further, environmentalists argue that water use in agriculture should be brought down. However, the best course to reconcile the conflicting objectives is to adopt a strategy which increases water use efficiency, measured as maximum biomass per drop of water. This would require technological changes in terms of low-water using varieties of crops and adoption of such nutrient management and agronomic practices, which reduce water use. Apart from technological changes, conducive policy environment would equally be important. Sometimes, it is argued that the main problem with current agricultural development paradigm is that it is a shift away from the traditional system of water and natural resource management. In this context, it should not be forgotten that current socio-economic environment is distinctly different from an environment in which traditional system was evolved and had worked. These days the conflicts in the use of natural resources like water have increased manifold. The conflicts arise because the limited amount of water that has been harnessed needs to be shared between individuals, between sectors, between states, between countries and even between man and other living beings (animals and birds).

(vi) India receives about 4,000 billion cubic metres (BCM) of water annually in the form of precipitation/rainfall. Nearly 75 per cent of this is received within 100 hours. Harnessing water through either surface or sub-surface water storage structure is, therefore, inevitable. However, so far, only 1900 BCM of water is utilized for irrigation, which account for around 90 per cent of total water utilized in the country. Nearly one-third of total water is received in Ganga, Brahmaputra and Meghna basins. Rest of the country's area receives two-third of total precipitation in India. Given such an uneven distribution of rainfall, floods in some regions and droughts in several other regions are bound to occur. There is, therefore, a basis for launching a long-term programme of linking different river basins of the country to tackle the problems of floods and droughts.

(vii) There are some welcome initiatives both by the government and the non-governmental organizations in the last decade. The country has launched a programme of providing safe drinking water to all the villages by 2004. A massive programme of constructing rural roads has been launched by the Centre and states to provide connectivity to all the 1,000+ villages by 2003 and 500+ villages by 2007. The Bio-diversity Bill has been passed by the Parliament in 2000. The National Agricultural Research System has evolved several drought resistent varieties and has perfected water and soil conserving agronomic practices. Non-governmental organizations have convincingly demonstrated that the involvement of communities is critical in successfully adopting environmental-friendly natural resource development activities. Role of civil society and community groups in the areas of watershed based development programmes, water conservation, tree plantations, forest management, water use and canal water management has been brought to the fore by way of several successful community based projects spread throughout the country.

Considering these developments, the approach to sustainable agriculture and rural livelihoods should emphasize the following:

(a) A win-win situation is when both the goals of poverty, food security and malnutrition reduction and environmental preservation are achieved simultaneously. However, in the situation of a trade off, first priority needs to be accorded to elimination of hunger and reduction of poverty and malnutrition.
(b) In achieving these goals, technology, institutions, social capital, market and the state, all have distinct and important roles.
(c) Improvement in the efficiency of available water, land and bio-resources is going to be a key area for achieving the twin goals of a win-win situation. Technological innovations, institutional changes, built-up of social capital, market performance and the state policies will be quite critical in this regard.
(d) Improving the access of the poor and food insecure to resources including land, water and enhancement of their skills is another area for moving to a regime of sustainable agricultural and rural livelihoods.
(e) Development of rural infrastructure and improvement in

the existing marketing system is another area, which needs the attention of government. Complementary investment by the state and deregulation of domestic markets will encourage investment in rural areas, which will open up several opportunities for employment in rural non-farm sector.

(f) One other area in which the state has a critical role is good governance, decentralized planning and legal reforms for creating a poor-friendly and natural resource-friendly environment.

(g) Cost effective pollution abatement policies are also important for moving to a paradigm of sustainable agricultural and rural livelihoods. Where individual benefits and social costs are high, the pollution abatement policies should be strictly and effectively implemented. Economic incentives and disincentives work where average income levels are relatively high. In such cases, the principle of "polluter must pay" should be applied.

(h) The importance of social capital is increasing day be day. The role of civil society in sustainable development and simultaneous elimination of hunger and reduction of poverty and malnutrition is quite significant. The emerging trend in this regard is quite encouraging.

Suggestions for Agricultural Reforms in India

The objectives of reforms should be, apart from moving to a sustainable pattern of natural resource use, aimed at further improvement in food and nutrition security at the macro as well as household level; reduction in levels of poverty; development of backward and less developed areas; reduction in inter-personal and inter-regional disparities in development; and overall accelerated growth of the agricultural sector and in turn of the whole economy. The achievement of all these objectives simultaneously is a tall order and calls for considerable balancing of conflicting interests. Keeping the imperatives of sustainable agriculture and improved rural livelihoods, directions for agricultural reforms ought to be as follows (Acharya and Chaudhri, 2001).

(i) Before linking the domestic markets with the world market, it would be important to first improve the functioning of the domestic market and to undertake strengthening of farm, non-farm linkages so that farmers are able to realise better prices without adversely affecting the interests of economically weaker sections who are least able to bear the burden of reforms.

(ii) The policies and policy instruments, which come in the way of the efficient functioning of domestic market for agricultural commodities, should be phased out. Some of these are:

   (a) Levy on rice millers;
   (b) Statutory rationing of foodgrains in Calcutta;
   (c) Monopsony procurement of raw cotton in Maharashtra;
   (d) Levy on sugar mills and distribution of sugar under PDS;
   (e) System of state advised prices of sugarcane prevalent in some states;
   (f) Imposition of stocking limits on traders and processors;
   (g) Imposition of inter-state movement restrictions; and
   (h) Monopoly of Agricultural Produce Market Committees in setting up markets.

(iii) The food management system, including buffer stocking built up over the years, needs to be retained as an important instrument of food security policy. However, the management system should be decentralized to improve efficiency and the distribution of subsidized food grains should be progressively targeted to only economically weaker sections of the society.

(iv) The subsidies enjoyed by the non-poor in the non-farm sector and urban areas need to be phased out first to release more resources for the agricultural sector and social development. However, the food and input subsidies need to be retained for sometime more as essential components of policy of development with equity. But these need to be progressively targeted to only the poor and small farmers.

(v) The policy of minimum support prices for important agricultural commodities needs to be continued but its effective implementation should be ensured in all the areas of the country. This apart, for those commodities, which are not covered under the minimum price support policy a selective market support scheme needs to be put in place for stabilizing the prices received by the farmers producing these commodities.

(vi) For the benefits of growth to reach the rural areas and the poor, the marketing infrastructure needs strengthening in far-flung rural areas. Rural roads, storage and processing facilities need to be developed for both accelerating the growth and hastening the process of trickle-down effect to reduce poverty at a rapid rate (Fan *et al.*, 1999).

(vii) India has created a network of agricultural marketing institutions, which include state agricultural marketing boards, agricultural produce market committees and commodity corporations/boards. There is a need to review and redefine their role and functioning in the liberalized trade and economic environment.

(viii) Keeping in view the small size of agricultural holdings and the very small-marketed surplus with them, there is a need to create an environment for the development of a network of farmers corporations which would improve the efficiency both in production and marketing of farm products. This arrangement will also help in reaching the gains of scale and technology to small and marginal farmers. This has become necessary because the experience with the cooperatives in India has been a mixed one. Even the successful cooperatives are now aspiring to shift to the corporate model of management for competing with multinationals. Developing a hybrid between the two as an innovative organizational structure needs exploration.

(ix) Land is an important input in agriculture but the market for land is highly distorted. Soon after independence, the government intervened in the land market and land reforms, which were comprised of a series of measures, were introduced. These measures helped in protecting the cultivating rights of the tillers of land, which improved incentives for farming as an occupation. Land ceiling laws were enacted to reduce inequalities in land ownership. These apart, several legal restrictions on the transfer or sale of land, leasing of land and land rents were imposed. The situation has now considerably changed. The average farm size is getting progressively smaller and over the years the proportion of marginal and small farms has substantially increased upto 80 per cent of the total. Most of these farmers are unable to provide even the barest minimum income required for the sustenance of an average family. Owing to the increasing pressure of population on land, there is considerable flouting of the provisions of land laws, and this affects the poor more. In a regime of concealed tenancy, for example, it is the poor who suffer the most. Though the issue of withdrawal of ceilings on land requires debate, there is certainly a case for liberalization of the land market within the ceiling limits. While the complete opening up of the land market may require more research in terms of its implications for efficiency and equity, the opening up of the lease market needs to be priority area in the liberalized economic environment. Legalization of the land-lease market would not only help in improving efficiency within agriculture but also help the poor farm families in augmenting their income either by leasing in land or shifting to more remunerative occupations by leasing out their tiny holdings.

(x) Consequences of trade liberalization are going to differ across commodities, regions and different sections of the society. To some extent, the adverse impact of liberalization on weaker sections and poorer regions can be mitigated through timely action on tariffs and through the public distribution system of food. Total freeing of imports and exports would make poorer sections and regions worse off and richer producers and regions better off. To counter the adverse impact of trade liberalization on the poor, there is a need to maintain a distinction between free trade and liberalized trade. The WTO member countries are under an obligation to liberalize trade and to dismantle physical restrictions on trade, replacing them by appropriate tariffs. This may not require totally free trade. Thus, tariffs should be used as a safeguard, where necessary.

(xi) In the matter of exports, India should follow a consistent policy of exporting basmati rice, non-basmati rice, wheat and raw cotton to establish itself as a reliable supplier in the world market. However, there is no need for subsidizing exports except when management of excessive public stocks calls for this route.

(xii) India should also encourage exports of processed and high-value commodities such as fruits, vegetable products and spices, in which the country has a comparative advantage.

(xiii) The equity implications of imports are quite serious. The tariff on imports of edible oils should be maintained at sufficient levels to balance the losses to the producers and gains to the consumers. These apart, there is also a need to raise the bound tariff rates of soybean oil and rapeseed/ mustard oil, which were pegged at 45 per cent and 75 per cent respectively during initial negotiations in WTO. In the case of pulses, the tariff walls should be at low levels. For sugar, the international prices should be carefully monitored and the option of using even the countervailing duties to restrict the excessive imports in some years should be kept open.

(xiv) Apart from the unilateral actions, India should try strategically to play an active role in the on-going negotiations in the framework of World Trade Organization (WTO). The critical areas affecting India and several other developing countries include seeking adequate market access for agricultural commodities by asking (a) that the commitments made by developed countries for reducing high level of domestic support to agriculture be fulfilled; (b) that the high level of tariffs and tariff rate quotas be reduced; and (c) that distortions such as discriminatory sanitary and phytosanitary standards and other technical barriers be removed.

(xv) Crop pattern changes in favour of rice and wheat and horticultural crops have improved income, which in turn has favourable impact on household food and nutrition security even for the marginal farm households. These changes in cropping pattern, therefore, need to be sustained.

(xvi) In the liberalized economic environment there has been an increase in mechanization and fertilizer use but there is a reduction in the use of farm labour per unit of land. This has resulted in improvement in crop production efficiency. Further, rural literacy has emerged as an important source in adoption of technology and use of modern inputs. Literacy and school education is going to play a far more important role in output growth than it did in the past. Increase in investment in agricultural research and extension, improvement in rural literacy, rural electrification and irrigation, which are found to be the most important instruments for growth in productivity, should, therefore, continue to receive priority.

Conclusions

Poor families derive their livelihoods from agriculture and natural resource base. Preservation and conservation of natural resources is equally important for them. However, these sections of society are concerned more for the improvement in the livelihoods of their present generation and removal of hunger and malnutrition of their children, which is their second generation. The strategic and priority goal of sustainable agriculture and rural livelihoods should, therefore, be removal of hunger and rapid reduction in poverty and malnutrition. In achieving this goal, the well-to-do and richer sections would need to make a definite sacrifice by changing their lifestyles, which conserve natural resources of water, bio-diversity and land. Policy framework, institutional changes and technological development would have to be consistent with the priorities for achieving a win-win situation. State, market, civil society, science and technology and local institutions, all have important and critical roles in achieving the goals of sustainable agriculture and better rural livelihoods. A pre-requisite for sustainable agricultural development and better rural livelihoods in India is a vibrant agriculture. A package of agricultural sector reforms suggested in this paper would help in making Indian agriculture more efficient and improve rural livelihoods on sustained basis.

REFERENCES

Acharya, S.S. (1998), "Agricultural Marketing in India: Some Facts and Emerging Issues", *Indian Journal of Agricultural Economics*, Vol. 53, No. 8, July-September.

Acharya, S.S. (2002), "Towards Sustainable Food Security at State Level—A Case of Rajasthan with Special Reference to Role of Food Assistance Programmes", paper presented and published in the Proceedings of State Level Consultation on Food and Nutrition Security in Rajasthan, organized by the World Food Programme, Government of Rajasthan and M.S. Swaminathan Research Foundation at Jaipur, June 25-26.

Acharya, S.S. and Chaudhri, D.P. (2001), *Indian Agricultural Policy at the Crossroads*, Rawat Publications, New Delhi.

Asthana, M.D. (2001), "Introduction to the Book Towards Hunger Free India: Agenda and Imperatives", by M.D. Asthana and P. Medrano (Editors), Manohar, New Delhi, January.

Chand, R. And Jha, D. (2001), "Trade Liberalisation, Agricultural Prices and Social Welfare", in Acharya and Chaudhri (2001).

Chambers, R. (1988), "Sustainable Rural Livelihoods: A Key Strategy for People, Environment and Development", in C. Conroy and M. Litvinoff (Eds), *The Greening of Aid*, Earthscan, London.

Debroy, B. (2002), "Sustainable Development and Protection", *Financial Express*, Sept. 24.

Diaz-Bonilla, E. and Robinson, S. (Ed) (2001), "Shaping Globalization for Poverty Alleviation and Food Security", *Focus* (8), 2020 *Vision*, IFPRI, Washington D.C.

Fan S., Peter Hazell and S. Thorat (1999), "Linkages between Government Spending, Growth and Poverty in Rural India", IFPRI, *Research Report* 110, Washington D.C.

FAO (1991), "Sustainable Agriculture and Rural Development in Asia and Pacific", Regional Document No. 2, FAO/Netherlands Conference on Agriculture and Environment, April 15-19.

Government of India (2000), All India Report on "Input Survey 1991-92", Ministry of Agriculture, New Delhi.

Government of India (2002), Agricultural Statistics at a Glance, Directorate of Economics and Statistics, Ministry of Agriculture, New Delhi.

International Food Policy Research Institute (IFPRI) (2001), "Agricultural Research and Poverty Reduction", Food, Agriculture and Environment Discussion Paper 34, September.

IFPRI (2002), "Reaching Sustainable Food Security for All by 2020", Washington D.C. May.

Lipton, M. (1996), "Rural Reforms and Rural Livelihoods: The Context of International Experience", in Lipton, M. *et al.* (Ed), *Land, Labour and Livelihoods in Rural South Africa*, Vol. 1, Western Cape, Indicator Press, Durban (South Africa).

Lipton M., Klerk, M. and Lipton Merle (Ed) (1996), *Land, Labour and Livelihoods in Rural South Africa*, Vol. 1: Western Cape, Indicator Press, Durban (South Africa).

Maxwell, S. and Frankenberger, T.R. (1992), *Household Food Security: Concepts, Indicators and Measurement*, UNICEF New York and IFAD, Rome.

Mohanti, T.K. (2002), "Poverty in India", *Economic Times*, April 1.

National Sample Survey Organization (NSSO) (1997), "Reported Inadequacy of Food Intake in India: 1993-94", 50th Quinquennial Survey of Consumer Expenditure, NSS, 50th Round, Department of Statistics, Government of India, Report No. 415, September.

Ramesh Chand (2002), *Government Intervention in Foodgrain Markets in the New Context*, National Centre for Agricultural Economics and Policy Research, New Delhi.

Reddy, V. Ratna (1996), "Environment and Sustainable Agricultural Development: Conflicts and Contradictions", in Rathore, M.S. (Ed), *Environment and Development*, Rawat Publications, Jaipur and New Delhi.

Vyas, V.S. and Ratna Reddy, V. (1996), "Environmental Policies and Policy Implementation in India: An Assessment", in M.S. Rathore (Ed), *Environment and Development*, Rawat Publications, Jaipur and New Delhi.

11

Sustainable Agricultural System

Reduced Reliance on Non-Renewable Energy Sources and Substitution of Renewable Energy Sources

A.N. MATHUR

Man and Energy

Energy is the key input for technological, industrial, social and economical development of a nation. The present energy scenario is heavily biased towards the conventional energy sources such as petroleum products, coal, atomic energy etc., which are finite in nature, besides causing environmental pollution. Of the available energy, the present energy utilisation pattern is heavily biased for meeting the energy requirement in urban and metropolitan cities.

The man's thrust to use more energy after the invention of fire about 150 thousand years ago, invention of wheel, use of petroleum products for power generation and invention of steam and coal has brought him to use the energy all available energy sources for his comfort irrespective of the environmental consideration. The extensive use of energy operated devices in domestic, industrial, transport and agriculture sectors in urban and rural areas have resulted in overall economical development of the society. The standard of living enjoyed by the people in US, Japan, Germany, many countries of Europe and other industrially developed nations resulted in consumption of larger part of available world's conventional fuel. The per capita consumption of energy in USA is about 8000 kW in comparison to India's 400 kWh shows that USA having 7 per cent of world's population consumes 32 per cent of total world's energy, while India with

20 per cent population hardly get little over 1 per cent of energy share. Of the total energy consumed in India 68 per cent in urban areas is from commercial energy sources while in rural areas 68 per cent energy in household sectors is from biomass, whereas, in urban areas the household sector consumed 13-15 per cent while industrial sector 42-51 per cent. The flow of energy in the form of fertilizer, insecticides, hi-yielding seeds, irrigation system etc. have made a significant impact on the Indian agriculture. India was net food grain import country at the time of independence in 1947, for feeding 360 million people, whereas, today after feeding 1000 million people we are exporting food grain. The electricity available for farming operations and in the rural and urban areas is being generated using the fossil and static energy resources such as petroleum oil, coal, and atomic energy and to a limited extent by hydro power. These all sources have a great influence on our economy and environmental aspects. This has resulted in a serious consideration for the use and availability of various energy sources. To the individual farmer, restricted supply of electric power and frequent shortage of diesel oil pose the most disturbing and immediate energy problem. Therefore, the use of conventional power will not only result in significant environmental degradation but also shifting away our progress in agriculture far from the sustainable growth.

Energy Resources and Their Status

The energy generation sources and capacity in India have some limitations. Staring from 1347 MW of installed power capacity in 1947 and limited food production, today we are generating above 95,000 MW, whereas we need around 1,20,000 MW power to meet our requirement in all sectors, including intensive agriculture. The peak hour shortage is estimated to be 20 per cent. The agriculture sector is worst affected from the shortage of power. Despite of promise and our serious efforts we are unable to provide electricity even for 8 hours during standing crop irrigation period in rural areas. The progress during the last five yearly plans in the power sector have not been very encouraging, as we could not increase our production capacity more impressively. This sector was even opened to private and MNCs, but the picture has not changed significantly. Of the 90,000 MW proposal submitted by the private sectors during VIII Plan only 50 per cent were of serious in nature, however, for various reasons they did not take off. Surprisingly none of the proposals contained the scheme for creating or revamping the transmission and distribution network. The Ninth Plan also failed to meet the projections and we have to scale down our target to less than 50 per cent. Therefore, taping this important power source alone to electrify the uncovered rural areas and continuous flow of power in agriculture will have a serious adverse effect on our overall development, as it will result in increased gap between demand and supply. The power sector is using the carbon rich fuels for generation of electricity producing high volume of CO_2, which will cause the environmental pollution.

Globally, about 40 per cent of world's energy needs are being met from petroleum products as of today. The anticipated growth in demand was expected to be 7 per cent. There has been a significant and impressive growth in the sector, which has surpassed and failed all the estimates, forecasts and projections made in this regard. It is estimated that the world oil consumption will increase from 68 million barrel per day to 94 million barrel per day in next decade. The importance of the hydrocarbon sector in the Indian economy is well known and needs no emphasis. The supply of the crude oil, and, therefore, of petroleum products affects all sectors of our economy. India is net oil import country and its oil import bill increased after the oil price shocks of the 1970s and the early 1980s. In the 1960s, oil imports accounted for less than nine per cent of the foreign exchange earnings through the agriculture commodity exports; it increased to 30 per cent in 1973-74 (following the first oil crisis) and to over 75 per cent in 1980-81 (after the second oil crisis). Currently due to international prices fluctuation and increase in indigenous production it has resulted in the oil import bill being 32 per cent of the net foreign exchange earnings, which stands over Rs. 75,000 crores. India is hard pressed for this important modern resource and is making all possible efforts to explore the off and on shore crude and gas production. With the indigenous production of 25 MMT and import of 80 MMT up to 2000-01 and 350 MT by 2025 AD (according to the Hydro Carbon Vision 2025) the consumption is likely to increase to 150 MMT by next eight years, which will be difficult to meet with indigenous reserves, which are only 0.6 per cent of world reserve. This will increase the import bill to an all time high during next decade.

It is a good source of energy for the agriculture but requires to overcome the acute problems of rising import expenses and environmental problems in several aspects including the technological. One of them is the present conversion technology of harnessing motive power or electricity from petroleum oils work at an efficiency of 30-35 per cent. This results in wasting of 70-65 per cent heat to the environment. The exhaust gases discharged into the atmosphere increase the CO_2 concentration in the environment causing global warming. Similarly, the transportation of the fuels from the oil sources and refineries, through road, rail or pipelines is a major problem today. We will have to think to make available this important source to our automobile industry to increase the living standard and mobility of the rural people. Therefore use of the petroleum oil requires a serious consideration.

Coal currently contributes over 50 per cent of the share of total commercial energy in India with over 65 per cent of the electricity generated is from coal based power stations. In spite of the energy-environment conflict on use of coal, transportation cost, high amount of ash content and poor washability characteristics, it will continue to meet the future energy demands in all the sectors as indicated in the Table 11.1 of sector-wise coal demand.

Table 11.1: Sector-wise coal demand (Projected)

Sector	*VIII Plan End (1996-97)*		*IX Plan End (2001-02)*		*X Plan End (2006-07)*	
	in mt	*%*	*in mt*	*%*	*in mt*	*%*
Steel (including private cookeries)	40	13.4	55	12.9	59.1	10.9
Power (Utilities)	188.5	62	279	65.4	379	70.2
Cement	17.1	5.7	25	5.9	30	5.6
Fertiliser	4.4	1.4	4.7	1.1	4.7	0.9
Others	52.4	17.5	62.7	14.7	67.2	12.4
Total	299.4	100	426.4	100	540	100

The Indian coal reserves are estimated to be 187 billion tonnes of which non cooking coal is 85 per cent. There exist no sufficient washery for the quality of coal available in India and 60 per cent of it is utilized as such in power sector. Except importing some good quality coal, the internal demand is met from the potential areas located in the eastern sector of the country. The mining of the coal is itself an environmentally hazardous operation.

Besides, the coal based power stations discharge the solid effluent and cause air pollution, which are the main concern of the environmentalist even today. With projected increase in coal demand to 580 MMT by next decade the situation will be worst causing serious environmental problems in future.

The atomic energy would have been an important fuel of future power plants but for the constraint on the uranium reserves and safety in use have slowed down the progress. We have the installed capacity of over 5000 MW of power from this source whereas it is expected that the installed capacity may increase to about 10,000 MW by 2002-03. This is a very prominent energy source and may remain so for a long time to come, but for the serious hazards. As such despite of the indigenous and perfect technology available we are going ahead very cautiously.

Environment Aspects of Fossil Fuels

Of the different fuels used, the coal, which accounts for about 60 per cent use in calorific terms, followed by liquid petroleum about 30 per cent and the rest natural gas; the CO_2 emissions result largely from coal burning. Coal contributed about 87 per cent of the emissions in 1950 and 71 per cent in 1991 at the same time, the petroleum fraction increased from 11 to 22 per cent (Table 11.2).

Table 11.2: Relative emissions from coal, petroleum and natural gas in TgC/year

Year	*Coal*	*Petroleum*	*Natural gas*	*Cement and Gas Flaring*
1950-51	16.0 (87%)	2.0 (11%)	9.9 (–)	0.4 (2%)
1960-61	26.8 (81%)	5.3 (16%)	0.0 (–)	1.1 (3%)
1970-71	37.7 (71%)	13.1 (24%)	0.3 (1%)	2.2 (4%)
1980-81	69.7 (73%)	22.4 (23%)	0.7 (1%)	2.7 (3%)
1990-91	130.1 (71%)	39.6 (22%)	5.2 (2%)	9.4 (5%)

CO_2 and Climate Change Reach New High

The Worldwatch Institute released its Vital Signs 1998: The Environmental Trends Shaping Our Future. It reports that climate change carbon emissions reached a record high worldwide in 1997, totalling 6.3 billion tonnes, up 1.5 per cent from 6.2 billion tonnes in 1996. Atmospheric concentrations of CO_2 climbed to 364 parts per million, the highest so far. With record high world temperature in 1997, the 14 warmest years since record keeping began in 1866 have all occurred since 1979. Evidences of the warming can be found in melting icecaps, shrinking glaciers in Alps, and the break-up of the sea ice around Antarctica. This has occurred despite non-CO_2 emitting wind power has grown by 26 per cent a year, growth in the sale of solar cells averaging 15 per cent annually from 1990 through 1996, jumped phenomenal 43 per cent in 1997.

The depletion of the Ozone layer located at a height of 30 km from the earth surface is another serious problem we are facing due to excessive use of the fossil fuels and other chemicals. It is reported that there are evidences of a hole of the size of the country like Australia and it is attracting the concern of the entire world. Even 1 per cent depletion in the Ozone layer, it will be sufficient to cause cancer like diseases in 10,000 people leading to fatal damage to life on the earth.

The Nature of the Energy and Environment Problems

Both energy and environmental problems are multidimensional, multidisciplinary, and dynamic, and require positive and timely responses. Often, there are no unique solutions, but a matrix/mix/multiple solution. Both require an integrated approach, integrating technology and management, education and training, and social and economical aspects and S & T and management aspects. In particular, energy problems require an integrated approach to energy and materials, conventional and non-conventional energy sources and non-renewable and renewable energy sources in agriculture and other development sectors. In a similar fashion, environmental problems require an integrated approach to chemical solutions biological solutions, abatement and prevention, waste reduction and recycling, environment and development, environment and safety, and environment and health.

Therefore, serious efforts are required to save as much of our installed electrical power of about 100,000 MW through use of renewable energy sources. This will result in saving of power, which could be used for other pressing sectors including the agriculture and checking the growth of the CO_2 concentration level. The two significant statements of World Energy Conference, Montreal, 1989 with respect to a case for energy conservation to meet the world's growing energy demand due to increase in population and more energy intensive lifestyles and a nexus between Agriculture, Energy and Environment requires the much dependence on renewable energy resources. This makes a strong case for the use of renewable energy in the highest priority sector of agriculture.

Renewable Energy Sources in Agriculture

Table provides the details of SWOT analysis of renewable energy sources and technologies and delineates the role they can play in supplementing the conventional energy sources in agriculture. This also highlights the barriers to its commercialisation and use, which need to be overcome for they become viable solution.

SWOT Analysis of Renewable Energy Sources for Agriculture

Strengths

- Unlimited/Perennial potential.
- Environmentally benign.
- Favoured option for sustainable development and equitable distribution of benefits.
- Naturally recycled resource base.
- The system and devices are modular in size decentralised energy option.
- Most appropriate for agriculture sector, as the operations can be done, when they are available.
- Only solution for rural electrification.
- Can be matched with the scale of use.

Weaknesses

- Impose greater demand on labour.
- More capital intensive.

- Lower capacity utilisation, because of low density.

Opportunities

- Energy availability is seasonal and intermittent.
- Usually of low density, requiring large areas of space.
- Environment driven awareness.
- Policy initiatives at global and national levels.
- Short gestation schemes; quicker project implementation.
- Easy to install stand alone systems.
- Generates rural employment.
- Fuel transportation costs eliminated.
- Social benefits.
- Can be matched with the scale of use.

Threats

- Closely linked with environmental concerns.
- R & D efforts inadequate.
- If social and environment costs are ignored, RET cannot compete with conventional energy.
- Incentive/subsidy driven momentum is short timed and under criticism.

The renewable energy can be used to replace various activities in rural areas and in crop production. Among various energy intensive activities in agriculture the maximum energy is used in land operations and irrigation. The RET can substitute the conventional energy source to a great extent as indicated in Table 11.3.

Table 11.3: The options and RET for various operations

Options	*Operations in rural areas based on RET*
Solar Energy	Water pumping for irrigation, post harvest operations, domestic cooking, power generation through solar p-v and thermal mode.
Biogas	Fuel for domestic use, motive power and slurry as manure-use solar p-v, thermal technologies use bio-energy sources.
Biomass	Domestic cooking, power generation through gasification and biomethanation route.
Fuel cells	Power generation.

Solar Energy and its Importance

Solar Energy is a natural gift and is of prime importance in the field of energy. In fact, all other natural resources of energy are also obtained indirectly from the solar energy. Therefore, Sun is recognised as father of all sources of energy. The sun radiates energy continuously through conversion of hydrogen into helium, and thereby the solar energy is available on the earth's surface everywhere free of cost. It has been calculated that a single day's solar energy falling on the earth's surface is sufficient to meet the energy needs of the globe for 15 years.

Solar energy is not a new source of energy; human being has used it since its creation. In 212 BC, Archimedes used solar energy to burn the sails of enemy ships. In Chile, a big solar still was made to give 25 m^3 fresh water per day in 1872. Similarly in many other countries like France, Egypt and Canada, solar energy was used for different applications. It has been a favoured option for post harvest technology of crop.

It is hoped that up to mid of 21st century, perhaps our civilisation may be powered directly and totally by the solar energy. In India the agricultural production is emerging as an important consumer of commercial energy. Solar energy has wide prospectus for utilisation in agriculture, as the sun's energy is available when the agriculture operations are donc.

Potential of Solar Power

It has greatest potential among all other energy sources, as it will be available, when all other energy sources may deplete in future.

The amount of solar power entering into earth's atmosphere is 17^{17} watt whereas available on earth's surface it is 10^{16} watt. The world energy requirement at present is 10^{13} watt. Therefore, if we harness even one per cent of solar power, it will be 10 times more than our requirement. The energy available to us on clear sunny day is 1 kW per sq. metre, on an average and may vary at place to place and season to season from 550 to 1000 watt per sq. m surface. This can be harnessed to raise temperature of the matter to 50°C, 60°C, 100°C and more and even up to 5000°C or to generate electricity through the thermal route. The agriculture operations require energy at 60-70°C or up to 100°C, which can be met from this source. As such for sustainable development of agriculture in India, the solar energy will remain a favoured option due to its perennial availability.

Power from Solar Photovoltaic Source

The solar photovoltaic is one of the clean option for power production from sun's energy, which causes no pollution. The decentralised power from the source has been in application ever since its invention in early fifties of the current century. The source has been accepted commercially also. It has a very bright future to be the single power source during early next century. The cost of the setting up of the power station is around Rs. 20-25 crore a MW, which is very high in comparison to other conventional sources. Looking to the global research efforts it is bound to come down to a level comparable to all other sources. The time is not far when each farm, each house and each industry will be generating the required power at their roof using this technique. Even with this high cost of installation, the activities are gaining momentum worldwide. The world's largest and most technically advanced rooftop photovoltaic plant has been installed on the hail rooftops of the New Munich Trade Fair Centre. With a peak output of 1 MW, it will feed around 1 million kW hours of solar power into the grid of the New Munich Trade Fair Centre and thereby contributing to meeting the centre's own power requirement. In addition all those involved hope that this unique project will send out a strong signal. The plant can be built in a record time; in this case it took just seven weeks. It has a total of 7812 solar modules covering 7916 sq. m mounted on the roof of the six northern halls of the New Munich Trade Fair Centre Site. The project has cost 14 million DM (Rs. 28 crores approximately) with no pollution at all.

Solar photovoltaics are specially suitable for rural and isolated areas. Photovoltaic systems have emerged as strong and useful power sources not only for applications such as water pumping, domestic lighting and other agricultural operations, but also as power plants for meeting the electrical energy needs of remotely villages which are not covered under the rural electrification programme. Our country has developed indigenous production capabilities as well as a strong research base in this field. So far 9.20 lakh SPV systems with an aggregate capacity of 82 MWp have been deployed. More than 6.0 lakh solar lighting systems have been in use. Besides this, 26 grid interactive SPV power projects with an aggregate capacity of 1.9 MWp have been installed.

Solar Water Pumping

Small capacity (360 W) surface mounted photovoltaic inverter pumping systems for canal irrigation are available in India. These pumps are capable of yielding 20-30 cu m of water on a clear sunny day, from a depth of 3-5 metres. For small land holdings, horticulture and cash crops where the canal irrigation system with small lift is used the 360 W pumps are reasonably effective and economical.

Further, a variety of higher capacity and deep well water pumping units operated on solar energy, both DC and AC options are available. Submersible pumps suitable for photovoltaic operation and installed in 4 inch diameter bore is also available. A simple PV water pumping system consists of a PV array, a motor/pump set, a manual/automatic tracking type metallic structure, delivery pipe network and wires. When a DC motor/pump set is used, power conditioning is not required. For an AC motor, an inverter is needed. The design of a system and choice of components are determined as a function of water demand and the characteristics of the solar and water resources. In general, the well depth and solar resources determine array size and power conditioning requirements.

For static heads up to about 10 metres, a single stage centrifugal pump directly coupled to a DC motor can be used. Such a motor-pump combination can be designed so that its optimum efficiency curve coincides closely with that of the photovoltaic array under varying levels of solar radiance.

100 KWp grid interactive SPV power project at Village Harriya, Distt. Basti, UP for voltage support application in rural grid.

A 25 KWp SPV power project at Vidhyuth Bhawanam, in Thiruvananthapuram, Kerala.

For higher head pumping, positive displacement pumps can be used but they don't have characteristics that can be well matched directly to a PV array. It is, therefore, necessary to introduce a small battery or maximum power point tracer to overcome the impedance mismatch to some extent. High head pumping may also be achieved using a submerged multi-stage centrifugal motor/pump set.

The selection of the motor for the PV water pumping system is dependent on the size, requirement, need for the motor to be submerged or not and availability of driving electronics. There are three basic types of motors such as; Permanent magnet DC motors (with or without brushes), Wound-field DC motors and AC motors. As the PV arrays produce DC power, the use of DC motors is, therefore, preferred for photovoltaic water pumping system. However, AC motors in conjunction with DC-AC high efficiency inverts can be used for high power and high head applications.

Solar Lantern

A typical solar lantern consists of a small photovoltaic module, a light source, a high frequency inverter/ballast, a battery, charge controller and appropriate unit. During the day hours, the module facing south is placed in the sun and it converts the solar radiation into electricity and charges the battery, which is connected to the lantern through a cable. In the evening, the lantern with the charged battery is disconnected from the module and is available for indoor or outdoor use.

The solar lantern is a very simple unit that can be used for lighting. It has no operating and maintenance cost except the change of battery after about four to five years of use. Many state governments have subsidised the cost of solar lanterns and these are available at a unit price of Rs. 1500 to Rs. 2500 in different states, though its cost is about Rs. 4000.

Street Lighting System

The solar PV based street lighting system has following three models, namely:

(a) Single module, three hour operation, and fluorescent lamp with timer control,
(b) Two module, six hour operation, fluorescent lamp with timer control, and
(c) Two module, all night operation, with compact fluorescent lamp (CFL) and day/night sensor.

The other components and principle of operation is same as that of solar lantern in all models.

Domestic Lighting System

The following three types of domestic lighting systems are available in our country:

(a) Fixed domestic lighting units (one 10 W module, 7 watt 2 CFL with sealed battery and controls).
(b) Portable lighting units—lanterns (10 W module, 5-7 watt CFL and sealed battery).
(c) Service connections from photovoltaic power plants.

There is no installation cost or cost of setting up power lines, it makes the solar lantern and street light very cheap in far-flung areas having non-access to electricity.

Community PV Lighting Systems and PV Power Plants

The solar power plants working on the solar p-v technology have been set up in many villages. The systems available are of two types, a 300 Wp PV installation for the community centres in villages, largely comprising lights and village based PV power plants of 2 to 25 kW capacity or even higher capacity plants.

A typical village based PV power plant consists of an array, a battery bank housed in a small shed, a power conditioning unit, meters, controls and distribution system. The connected load may be for lighting, TV, radio, flour mill and drinking water supply pumps.

The solar photovoltaic based systems for small power applications such as telecommunication, railway signalling microwave repeater stations, cathodic protection of oil pipelines, powering of telemetric equipment, off-shore oil platforms and unmanned television transmitters etc. are also commercially available.

Box Type Solar Cookers

Box type solar cookers are capable of cooking different types of food including rice, vegetables, *dals*, chicken, fish, and for steaming, roasting, boiling etc. It works as an airtight box with double glass covers. A reflector is placed over it for boosting the solar radiation and thus its temperature increases. Because of its simplicity and ease of handling, the box type solar cooker has found wider acceptance especially in urban areas. More than 0.3 million such cookers have been sold in the country. The technology has been fully commercialised and many variety of cookers are available in the market with ISI mark in the price range of Rs. 1200 to 2500. The Ministry of Non-Conventional Energy Sources, Government of India and Bureau of Indian Standards have brought out Indian Standards for box type solar cookers beside it has set up one national testing centre and six regional test centres for testing of solar cookers in different region of the country. The similar designs have found applications in agriculture sector for baking animal feed which is a common practice in rural areas.

Solar Air and Water Heating System

It is a flat plate collector with built-in channels or riser tubes attached to the absorber sheet. With a black paint coated on the absorber plate, the air and water can be heated up to a temperature of 60 to 90°C, while in selectively coated system the temperature can be raised to 85 to 100°C. Presently, the solar heating systems are used for domestic water and space heating, commercial and industrial applications. A temperature of 60°C is sufficient for domestic use and as such black paint coated absorbers are normally used in such domestic solar water heating systems. Solar water heating systems are mainly useful for agro-processing units, milk dairy plants besides several other applications. The water heaters are commercially available in the range of 100 litres per day to over 200,000 litres per day capacity at 85 to 90°C with or without the selective coated absorber systems. With the launch of evacuated tube collectors, it is expected that the solar energy will be successfully used for high temperature steam generation for use in agriculture. So far, water heaters with a total of 600,000 sq. m of collector area have been installed against the estimated potential of 140-million sq. m.

A concentrating type solar cooker for community use developed by Maharashtra Gandhi Samarak Nidhi, Pune.

Solar still for potable water

A solar still can produce about 4 to 6 litres of distilled water for every square meter of basin area in a day of 8-9 sunshine hours. The yield of a solar still depends on solar isolation, ambient temperature, quality of the glazing, temperature of the water inside the basin, shallow water layer in the basin, air velocity etc.

Presently, fibreglass body basin type solar still is available commercially in the market for industrial and other applications. The cost of such solar still is about Rs. 2500 per square metre area, which works out to be Rs. 800 per litres per day capacity. Further, presently, concrete based solar still could be installed at the rate of Rs. 450 to 500 per liter per day capacity. The land requirement for installation of a 100-lpd solar distillation system would be about 30 to 40 m^2. The solar distilled water can be used for drinking purposes where the safe drinking water is not available. It helps converting brackish water into potable water.

200 lpd capacity domestic solar water heating system installed under IREDA's intermediary scheme in Karnataka.

Solar Crop Drying and Driers

Indian economy, unlike the developed countries, predominantly depends upon the agriculture. Its 70 per cent population living in rural areas is engaged in production of food grain, fruits, vegetables and milk. India has emerged as grain export nation with nearly 210 million tonne of grain production every year. It has huge stock of food grain to meet any scarcity and emergency. The country is number one in milk production with 86 million tonne milk production per day. We are ranked second in fruit and vegetables production. This shows a tremendous possibility of processing of farm produces and their value addition for commercialisation. Of the total grains produced, it is estimated that about 30 per cent are retained by farmers for their use and the remaining 70 per cent is marketed. An estimated 10 per cent of food grains and 30 per cent fruits and vegetables are lost every year before they reach the consumer. These losses are mainly from spoilage, contamination, and attack by insects and deterioration in storage and drying. The safety of the stored grains largely depends on post harvest management, control of moisture in the product, aeration and change in temperature. Of these, the moisture content of the grain is the most important factor. The high initial moisture content leads to high respiration of grains in storage, with the result that a hot and humid atmosphere is developed which is conducive to the growth and multiplication of insects and other micro-organisms.

The economical standard of the farmer can be improved, if the produce is stored or value added to fetch good price in the lean season. To regulate the flow of food grains into the market and to meet the requirements of lean period, huge stocks of food grains have to be stored in the public and private sectors. The drying of crop is one of the important post harvest operation for safe storage of the grain.

The term crop drying refers to removal of moisture to a level necessary for its safe storage. This will prevent the grain from the molds, enzymic action, and insects. Most of the crops are harvested at moisture content of 14-25 per cent as such they require drying. The adequacy of drying often determines the additional measures to minimize the losses from the farmer's field to the dining table. For example, if the groundnut pods could be maintained at five per cent or lower moisture content practically no deterioration is expected for more than a year and no additional treatment will be called for. Thus drying is a very important post harvest operation to increase self life of the produce.

Traditional drying technology

The traditionally drying of grain in our country is achieved by leaving the harvested produce in the open fields or cemented floor or even on road for several days. The drying time depends on the weather, if the weather stays favourable, the adequate drying takes place, however, if the weather turns bad, significant produce losses often result. Thus practically there is no control over the drying. Practically, often the rains during kharif and rabi harvesting seasons have been causing concern in recent years. The Indian agriculture is faced with the prospects of heavy spoilage of their produce due to the rains despite of bumper harvest on several occasions. The procuring agencies face the challenge of handling wet produce. The additional field losses during drying and storage due to insect-pests, birds and animals are also well documented.

The natural climate in India is suitable for safe storage of well dried grain provided properly designed and well-engineered storage structures are used. The benefit from early harvest of crops can be fully obtained only if there are proper drying and storage facilities. If paddy harvested at moisture levels of 21-24 per cent is dried to 14 per cent wet basis moisture content, the head rice recovery during milling increases by 5-10 per cent. Paddy and soybean, when harvested at 20-25 per cent wet basis moisture content need to be dried to 10-12 per cent wet basis for safe storage.

Other methods of drying

Apart from the traditional drying methods, there are several other energy based methods in use in developed and energy rich countries, agro-industries and by progressive farmers. These methods required high quality energy such as Electricity, Natural or Liquefied Petroleum Gas, or other Petroleum products. These processes will increase the cost of drying operation.

The use of Solar Energy for the drying of the grain is an age old practice used in agriculture. The dryers have been developed to meet the specific requirement of various produces.

Table 11.4 gives the drying requirement of selected grains and other farm produces.

Classification of solar dryers

On the basis of exposure of products: *Direct and Indirect Dryers*
On the basis of flow of air: *Natural Circulation and Forced Circulation Type Dryers*
On the basis of storage of produce to be dried: *Tray, Bin and Cabinet Type*
On the basis of supplementary heating system: *Agricultural waste, biogas, and other conventional fuel heated*
On the basis of produce to be dried: *Grain, fruits and vegetable dryers*

Dryers Developed in India

The conventional energy based dryers working on furnace oil fired

LSU were in use in the country particularly in paddy processing units in early 1950s. As the prices of petroleum products increased the use of such dryers became prohibitive. It was in late 1970s that there was a shift from conventional fuel based dryer to non-conventional fuel based dryers. The efforts were made and succeeded to the development of efficient rice husk fired furnaces for steam and hot air generation for the drying of paddy. The efforts of the research scientists also include the use of alternative energy sources such as solar and biomass, alone or integrated, for drying purposes. During past few years numbers of dryers have been designed, developed, perfected and commercialised for practically all agricultural materials. The drying technique developed, perfected and drying characteristics studied under laboratory and as well as field conditions.

Table 11.4: Drying requirements of agricultural and farm produces

S. No.	*Product*	*Temp. Reuired °C*	*Initial Moisture Content % (wb)*	*Final Moisture Content % (wb)*	*Type of solar drying*
1.	Apple	66	60-70	11-20	Direct
2.	Beans (green)	65	10-20	5	Direct
3.	Sulitfied cabbage	74	80	<5	Direct
4.	Sultified carrots	70	70-80	4-5	Direct
5.	Cauliflower	60	80	3	Indirect
6.	Chillies	60	70-80	10	Direct
7.	Corn (sweet)	65	80-85	10-15	Direct
8.	Date	35-50	65	4	Indirect
9.	Fish	50	65-75	15	Direct
10.	Garlic	43-48	70-80	6-7	Direct
11.	Grapes	60	80-85	13-15	Direct
12.	Ginger	60	83-85	10-16	Direct
13.	Groundnut (shelled)	45	40-60	9	Direct
14.	Sorghum	45	20-25	10	Direct
15.	Onion	71	80-86	3-5	Indirect
16.	Paddy	60	20-25	10	Direct
17.	Rice (milled)	60	15	9	Direct
18.	Soybeans	45	20-30	7-8	Direct
19.	Sweet Potato	65	70-80	5	Direct
20.	Tomatoes	65	85-90	< 3	Direct

India is among few world leaders in the area of development of solar dryers for drying of various farm produces. The development includes both natural and forced convection type solar dryers. Natural circulation type dryers are generally suitable for drying of fruits and vegetables, as these dryers cannot work against high static pressure. The forced circulation type dryers are more suitable for commercial or large quantity drying.

The Tamil Nadu Agricultural University has developed a Conventional fuel based Osmotic dryer for dehydration of fruits and vegetables. A lab model plant of 5 kg fruit holding capacity was designed, developed and evaluated for its performance with banana and grapes. The maximum water loss of 42.5 per cent in banana and 24.6 per cent in grape was observed after 5 h of osmosis at flow rate of 12 lpm and under static conditions the water loss was 38.5 per cent and 22.7 per cent, respectively.

The Indian Institute of Technology, Kharagpur has developed a re-circulatory hot air dryer for chilies and grapes. The green chilies cut into two halves along length gave best retention of colour and lesser drying time. Studies showed that green chilies took 4 h to dry at 70°C temperature and 90.6 per cent re-circulation with a tray loading of 4 kg/m^2 and air velocity 2 m/s. The energy required to remove 1 kg of water was 2.55 kWh.

IIT Kharagpur also developed a dryer for the drying of garlic. The Garlic cloves were dried with hot air and combined microwave-hot air drying methods. The combined microwave-hot air drying experiments were carried out with 100 g sample sizes at temperature of 40, 50, 60 and 70°C and at air velocities of 1 and 2 m/s, using continuous microwave power of 40 W. The combined microwave hot air drying results in a reduction in the drying time to an extent of 80-90 per cent in comparison to conventional hot air drying and a superior quality final product.

The TNAU Coimbatore also worked on Fluidized bed drying system for mushroom. There are various methods of drying of mushroom, viz. sun drying, thin layer drying, solar cabinet drying and fluidized bed drying. Fluidized bed drying of mushrooms at 50°C with an air flow rate of 35 m^3/min dried the mushroom with in 2 h to a final moisture content of about 9 per cent db. The loss of nutrients and browning was less in fluidized bed drying compared to other methods of drying. The GB Pant University of Agriculture and Technology, Pantnagar, also used Osmo-air drying method for mushrooms successfully. The drying behaviour of button mushrooms slices (3-4 mm thick) pre-treated with salt solution at three levels of temperature (25°C, 40°C and 50°C) and three different weights of mushrooms to salt solution ratio (1:4,1:6 and 1:8) were used and it was reported that approximately 50 per cent moisture was reduced in about 16.5 h osmotic drying at 85°C and at 100 m/min of air velocity.

Sun Drying

Selection of sun drying surfaces

At CIAE Bhopal, GBPUA&T Pantnagar and PKV Akola studies have been undertaken on selection of surfaces for faster and quality sun drying. Tarpaulin, hessian, canvas cloth, black and white polyethylene and concrete surfaces have been evaluated and compared with mud floor used in rural areas. Tarpaulin (olive green), black polyethylene and concrete surface have been found reducing drying time by 10-20 per cent. It was observed that the drying was slow on horizontal elevated 0.5m, 1.0m wire mesh surface than blackish concrete surface, whereas, the sand bed gave faster drying but created sand separation problem. Tarpaulin and GI sheet were found significantly meritorious than mud floor.

Solar Dryers: Natural Convection Type

Solar cabinet dryer

A single glass shielded 2 x 1 m size solar cabinet dryer was designed and evaluated for chilly drying compared with sun drying on selective surfaces with mud floor as control at CIAE, Bhopal. In November at 3 kg/m^2 materials load the cabinet dryer reduced drying time to ½ to 1/3 rd of sun drying on tarpaulin. Even at 12 kg/m^2 material load cabinet dryer performed well. Techno-economic study revealed that cabinet dryers are desirable for drying at material load of 6 kg/m^2 or more. However its performance was affected in areas having strong northern wind.

Further improvements were made by designing and installing an aspirator of 0.25 m diameter and 1.2 m height to make the dryer work independent of the wind direction, to create 1 m^3/min of air flow at average wind velocity of 4 kmph.

The cabinet dryers are suitable for drying of perishable and semi-perishable products including plantation crop.

Rack type natural circulation solar dryer

The PAU, Ludhiana has developed single rack, multi-rack and mini multi-rack cabinet type dryers. A single rack cabinet dryer is a wooden hot box having a transparent glass at the top. The produce to be dried is placed on a perforated tray. For natural convective flow of air, holes are provided at the bottom of the dryer. In the cabinet dryer the hot air comes in contact with the product only once, whereas the air still has capacity to remove more moisture if it could be passed through additional layers of the product. Based on this principle a multi-rack dryer has been developed. The product to be dried has been stacked at several levels one after the other.

The dryer was tested with cauliflower, onions, spinach, potato chips, etc. It took about 2-2.5 days to dry each of these vegetables (2 kg each). With this unit, it was possible to remove 2.88 kg moisture per day/m^2 glazing area higher than the moisture removal rate of cabinet dryer (1.5 kg/day/m^2).

A multi-tray type natural convection solar cabinet dryer was developed at the CTAE, Udaipur. The dryer is fabricated from materials such as wood, plywood, wire mesh, MS sheet, angle iron, glass, etc. The cabinet is made in such a way that the front surface is inclined at an angle of 25° to the horizontal, which is approximately equal to latitude of Udaipur. A 25 mm side slit is provided at bottom of cabinet for fresh air entry. At the top, two draught pipes each of diameter 200 mm and length 1000 mm are provided to carry away warm moist air by natural convection. Twelve perforated trays each of size 1000 x 455 mm are provided to place material to be dried. The inside of side and rear panel of the cabinet is pasted with a reflecting material, Mylar. The trays are painted with black colour for maximum absorption of solar radiation. The semi processed food products, fruits or vegetable such as potato chips, ginger, turmeric, chilies, onion, garlic, leafy vegetables, etc. can be successfully dried in a batch of 60-75 kg. Only 2-3 man hr/day are needed to perform the operation in comparison to 6-8 days/batch in open sun drying.

A 25 kg batch capacity natural convection solar dryer with flat plate solar collector and drying chamber having provision of direct as well as indirect heating was also developed at CTAE,

Udaipur for simultaneously drying of peanuts and leafy vegetables. It removed moisture by 21 per cent in 8 hrs. A comparative study was also undertaken to evaluate the quality of selected leafy vegetables (fenugreek, coriander, bathua and spinach) dried in solar dryer and open sun. The initial moisture content of the fresh vegetables varied in the range of 86-94 per cent wb, which was reduced to 7.7 to 15.0 per cent during drying. Results revealed that the drying time varied from 3-4 h in solar dryer (60-65° C temperature) and 8-12 h under open sun, indicating 50-75 per cent reduction in the drying time as compared to sun drying. Retention of ascorbic acid was found higher in solar dried vegetables. Beside these, the total scores of 8 (on the scale of 10) obtained for the colour, flavour and overall appearance of all the leafy vegetables dried by this method and they were also found better than that of open sun dried.

The Central Arid Zone Research Institute, Jodhpur (CAZRI) has also worked on cabinet dryer with heat storage in pebbles for continuous drying of chilies and other produces even after sunset. In order to capture maximum energy throughout the year CAZRI Jodhpur developed an inclined direct type solar dryer, thus it reduced the size of the dryer. The solar dryer has a provision of adjustable stand and stacking of material, which reduced the drying time of chilics by about 40 per cent compared to simple cabinet dryer.

At CAZRI a large size (batch capacity 100 kg vegetable) solar drier, which can be commercially used for drying of fruits and vegetables, was constructed.

A step type natural convection solar dryer for drying of fruits and algae was developed at TNAU, Coimbatore. The solar dried product fetched 13.75 per cent more return compared to open sun dried product by adjusting air inlet and outlet openings.

Forced convection solar dryers

Three forced hot air circulation type solar dryers of capacity 0.25t, 1t and 10t per day were developed for paddy drying at PAU, Ludhiana. The air channel is made of GI sheet and painted with black board paint at the top. The layer of grain is supported on the wire net. The hot air from the solar air heater is passed through the paddy lot. The wet paddy was dried at a constant air flow rate of 4.3 kg/h/kg of dried paddy during the month of October-November. The performance of the solar crop dryer was assessed by comparing it with paddy dried in an electrically operated dryer and drying of un-threshed paddy suspended on ropes in the open sun. It took 6-7 h to dry paddy to safe moisture content in solar as well as electrically operated dryer compared to 4-5 days in open field drying.

Solar batch-in-bin dryer

The Jabalpur centre of the Post-harvest Technology Scheme (ICAR) developed a low cost dryer, which gave 9°C temperature rise at an air flow of about 38 m^3/min in bright sunny weather at an ambient air temperature of 22.5° C. The dryer consists of 1 t circular aeration bin for grain storage, 0.5 hp blowers and an unshielded absorber solar collector created on south facing wall enclosing the motor. This dryer was adopted for groundnut drying (from 40 per cent to 10 per cent wb) at the CIAE, Bhopal with suitable modifications making use of the standard size of sheet metal available, making it light for portability and reducing cost. It has batch capacity of 1.36 m^3. In December, it gave an air temperature rise of 6°C (4 to 6°C range). In cloudy weather it ranged from 2 to 4°C with average of 3.5°C. Experimental results suggest additional supplemental heating for groundnut drying.

Roof built-in solar dryer

The existing roof of grain storage room made of 20 gauge corrugated GI sheet is covered with 6 mm thick transparent glass maintaining 50 mm clearance between the roof surface and the glass. The air duct (200 x 200 mm) receives hot air from the solar collectors through a blower and carries to the drying chamber.

At CIAE Bhopal a roof built-in one tonne capacity grain dryer was developed and installed under the roof built-in-solar collector (i.e. shed). The grain was envisaged to be held between the two concentric perforated cylinders through which air diffuses. Preliminary testing of the system indicted that 38.1 cum/min hot air (50°C temperature) can be generated. On an average 25-30°C above ambient temperature was obtained.

A low cost dryer with mobility mounted on cart using engine

waste heat in addition to solar energy for the batch drying was fabricated and tested at Jabalpur. It is designed to fit in to "Balwan" cart with ADV tyres, consisted of 1.77 × 1.09 × 1.00 m aeration bin with 225 mm deep plenum, using the two-third waste heat of engine. In November, in partial overcast weather, using 1.9 hp (petrol) engine 8.8°C temperature rise was obtained, 5.8°C from solar energy and 3.0°C from engine waste heat.

Biogas aided solar roof dryer

A biogas aided solar roof dryer was designed and tested by TNAU Coimbatore. The dryer consisted of solar flat plate collector at the roof, ducting, a blower, a rectangular drying bin and a biogas burner for air heating, so that the dryer can also be used under inclement weather conditions. Testing of dryer was done with 1 t paddy, its moisture reduced from 23 per cent to 12 per cent wb in 16 h in open sun drying, 9 h in solar roof dryer and 8 h in biogas aided solar drying system.

At many places dryers with additional heat from the burning of agriculture wastes have been designed and tested. It consisted of a simple furnace made of bricks in clay mortar having horizontal grate and a chimney, indirect MS heat exchanger, electric blower and an aeration bin. The blown air passes through the heat exchanger and than into the plenum of the aeration bin. Agricultural wastes such as cotton stalks, sorghum stubbles, pigeon pea stalks, rice husk etc. are used as fuel. A batch of 1.5 q of sorghum grains required 2.5-3.0 h to dry from 15 to 9.8 per cent wb.

Re-circulating type paddy husk fired dryer

It consisted of a re-circulating type dryer coupled with IRRI type husk-fired furnace. A vibrating feeder drops the husk continuously in the combustion chamber through the grate and hopper. The blower draws the hot air through an opening and re-circulates it through the grain. The unit has been successfully applied to a rice mill.

Wind Power

It is a prominent source for water pumping, threshing, chaff cutting, grinding of grain, other agriculture applications and power generation in the potential wind velocity areas, which produces no pollution and environmental hazards. It is estimated that there exists a potential of 20000 MW power from this non-polluting source of energy in India. Starting from VII Plan period we have achieved installation of 793 water pumping units beside, the wind farms 90 per cent of these are in private sector, leading state is Tamil Nadu. small aero-generator systems with an aggregate capacity of 112 kW have been installed.

The concept of harnessing wind has been accepted globally with USA leading in setting up of single power plant of 107 MW installed at Buffalo Ridge in Minnesota. It consists of 143 turbine of 750 kW each.

The wind energy is successfully used in the field in India. The devices used are as follows:

Wind Pump

The sizes of wind pumps currently available range from 1 to 8 m rotor diameter. The pumping height and average wind speed influenced the average power output that can range from a few watts to about 1 kW. For higher power demands, wind electric pumping systems (WEPS) can be applied, incorporating a wind generator (available in larger diameter) driving an electronic motor pump combination. At higher power output levels (10 kW or more), the pumping system could be integrated with a small electric grid, supplying electricity for other purposes in agriculture. For average rural Indian applications, the daily output ranges from 1.5 to 500 m^3 at a head of 20 m or roughly from 0.1 to 30 kWh per day. The reasonable costs of pumping water run up to Rs. 20 per m^3. The pumps are available which can be operational at wind speeds of 5-6 km per hour and more. The application of wind power meets the irrigation schedule of crop. The high level storage tank can be built to collect water for irrigation schedule.

Power generation from wind

Wind energy can be successfully tapped in potential rural wind areas for generation of electricity. Currently wind generated power accounts for about 4500 MW of installed capacity worldwide. In India, an aggregate capacity of more than 1500 MW has already been installed and projected addition of 500 MW per year is envisaged. This is a sustainable energy source.

Wind farms, which constitute a cluster of grid connected wind electric generators of 250-750 kW aero-generators, have proved to be a feasible method of power generation on a large scale. It is well suited in locations where the annual average wind speed is at least 18 km/h or the energy content is above 2000 kWh/m^2/year. As wind farms need large open area (8-10 hectares/MW), the availability of land in windy regions is extremely important. But within a wind farm, only 5-10 per cent of the land area is actually required for installation of the wind electric generators and roads, etc. the remaining land can be put to agricultural productive uses such as orchard, crop growing, cattle grazing etc.

The average capital cost of a wind farm project works out to Rs. 5 to 6.0 crore per MW which is fairy comparable with cost of setting up of conventional fuel based power plants. Based on this investment and normal methods of cost calculation, the average cost of electricity generation in wind power projects is in the range of Rs. 2.25 to 2.27 per unit, depending upon the site.

Government of India has made provisions of subsidy for setting up of wind farm commercially and also for specific categories of users including agricultural use. Commercial organisations including agro-industries and professionals using wind electricity for their on going plant can claim 100 per cent depreciation in the first year of the installation. Low interest finance can also be availed from Indian Renewable Energy Development Agency for setting and to promoting manufacture and utilisation of wind energy gadgets. Many state governments has announced the wind power policy which includes, the sale of power generated from the wind farm to SEBs or transmission through SEB lines to the place of use by the owner of the wind farm or even banking with SEB besides sale to the third party. The setting up of wind energy based power plants are covered under the National Programme of electrification of 85,000 un-covered villages and the work is under way in private sectors with agreement to buy back the power by SEBs.

The import of wind energy based gadgets is also easy such as import of aero generator; control systems and materials are covered under the open general licence. Further, imports at concessional rates of customs duty are permitted to the manufactures in the country.

Hydro power

The history of hydro power in India dates back to end of 19th century when 130 kW capacity power plant was set up in Dehradun valley. The technology has been in use world wide since 12th century. It is an environmentally friendly, multipurpose application and site specific source requiring a perennial stream of water. The technology for the commercialisation is available and order for the turn key installation depending on the head and quantity of the water can be given. As of today India has the installed capacity of 21000 MW (about 22 per cent of the total installed capacity) with additional potential of more than 50000 MW of power from this source of which about 10000 MW is the mini and micro alone. The long gestation period and resistance from the environment activists is another important issue before taking up the crash plan of harnessing this natural source.

A commercial wind power project at Jogimathi in Karnataka.

IREDA-financed 4.90 MW wind farm at Vankusawade village, district Satara, Maharashtra.

It has been recognised that small hydro projects can play critical role in improving the overall energy scenario of the country, particularly of remote and in accessible rural areas. Due to increasing environmental consideration there is only a limited scope at present of setting up large hydro-electro projects. The total installed capacity of small hydro power projects up to 3 MW has increased four fold from about 63 MW to 240 MW during the last 12 years. SHP projects up to 25 MW are being covered now. This is an appropriate solution for sustainable power supply in potential rural areas.

Hydel Power

Wood and other biomass

Biomass is the widely accessible energy source for domestic and other agricultural applications. About half the world population uses it for cooking and will continue to do so in rural areas in India for next many decades. With per capita wood consumption of 180 to 240 kg/year a significant proportion of it goes for domestic uses. The Photosynthesis of trees is the most natural way to store solar energy and planting trees is one of the few truly effective ways of mitigating climate change, including the greenhouse effect. In order to analyse the GHG emission from wood fuels, a simplified carbon cycle works in the nature. This has resulted in forming forest policy of India with statutory requirement of 33 per cent areas under forest we hardly have 15 per cent area under plantation.

When trees are used as fuel, the combustion produces carbon emissions, but as long as trees are planted or naturally reproduced at the same rate as they are burnt, the carbon level, in principle, is kept in balance assuming that combustion is complete. Incomplete combustion of wood fuel, like all other type of fuels, does not only result in emission of CO_2, but also other GHGs, such as CH_4, N_2O, CO and other Non-Methane Hydrocarbons (NMHC), which cannot be absorbed by trees. In a wood stove with 90 per cent nominal combustion efficiency (30 per cent of overall efficiency), about 450 g carbon/kg of dry wood fuel is emitted as CO_2 and 50 g of carbon is emitted as CH_4, NMHC, etc. (Dry wood fuel mostly contains 50 per cent carbon). The gases like CH_4, NMHC, etc. have a much greater potential to contribute to global warming than CO_2. Although their warming effect will reduce over time, the potential can still be significant even in 100 years. Thus, when low efficiency devices are used, the non-CO_2 emissions become the main concern for environmental degradation in the case of wood fuel.

The technologies have been developed, established and commercialised for production of power from wood and other biomass using the thermal and biomethanation routes, which are most appropriate for decentralised generation of electricity in rural and remotely locate areas. The technologies are specially suitable for decentralised power generation and can be linked to wood production through energy plantation on waste land, harvesting, processing, conversion and conservation. This has been successfully demonstrated and set up in many states in India and other European countries.

Power Generation from Biomass

The biomass is available in rural areas in variety of forms. There are two possible routes for power generation, which can be employed for power generation in decentralised manner. These are as below:

1. Dendro Thermal Power Generation (D.T.P.G.)
2. Gasifier based power generation (G.P.G.)

Dendro thermal power generation

It basically involves, combustion of biomass externally. The thermal energy is converted into shaft power either directly or through various inter-mediate stages of conversion, involving steam production or the vapourisation of organic fluid.

Basically it consists of the following components:

1. Dryer
2. Boiler
3. Steam Turbine
4. Condenser
5. Generator

The dryer is used to reduce the dampness of the uneven wood to a lower level. In the dryer a part of the flue gases from the boiler, supplies the drying energy. The dried wood is fed into the boiler. It is then burnt in suspension in the boiler to raise a high pressure steam.

As far as power generation from Dendro Thermal based power generation is concerned it makes use of three commonly available thermodynamic cycles, i.e. Brayton, Stirling or Rankine cycles. In simple fashion, heat of combustion gases can be used to run gas turbine for power generation through Brayton cycle or alternately it can pass through heat exchanges for exciting a working fluid and finally to run a gas engine through a Stirling cycle. The heat of combustion gases can be used to generate steam vapour and to use it in steam/vapour engine or steam/vapour engine through Rankine cycle.

The high-pressure steam in turn drives a steam turbine in Rankine cycle route.

The gas or steam turbine drives the alternator or generator. The cooling system uses a condenser; the supply of cooling water is about 50 times that of the steam to be condensed. In case of water shortage a cooling tower can be added but it will consume about 2.5 per cent of the energy produced by the power station (for circulating pumps and fans).

Biomass gasification

In the gasification process, burning solid biomass with restricted air supply forms combustible gases. The process of gasification is carried out in a reactor. This is also known as generator or gasifier. There are three types of reactors on the basis of method of air supply. These are down draft type, up draft type and cross draft type. In the reactor the reactions at high temperature between oxygen in the air and solid fuel occur in the combustion zone to form carbon dioxide and water vapour. If there is a surplus of solid fuel, carbon dioxide and water vapour from combustion zone can be passed through glowing layer of charcoal and reduced to carbon monoxide and hydrogen in the region known as reduction zone

Gasifier based power generation

The gasifier based power generation system consists of following components:

1. Feed preparation unit
2. Gasifier
3. Cleaning and cooling unit
4. An internal combustion engine/alternator set
5. Switch gear necessary for power transmission.

The wood or the agricultural residues available in rural areas are cut into proper size. In case of some agricultural residues, they may have to be briquetted. The gasifier accepts wood chips, agricultural residues in shredded or briquetted forms. The biomass undergoes pyrolysis, oxidation and reduction and produces producer gas having low calorific value of 1000 - 1200 kcal/m^3. Carbon monoxide, hydrogen and methane are the main combustible components of the producer gas.

500 KW biomass gasifier project at Thiruvottiyur in Tamil Nadu.

The basic application modes of biomass gasification available in India are as follows:

(a) **Power Generation for Decentralised use:** Wide range of outputs (from 3 KW to 500 KW or more)

Salient Features:

- Use of diesel engine in dual fuel mode.
- On-line change over from 100 per cent diesel mode to dual fuel mode or *vice versa*.
- Specific fuel consumption of less than 100 cc of diesel and 1 kg of biomass per kWh.
- Governing (i.e. voltage and frequency control) fully comparable to DG sets.
- Standard configurations for stand-alone operation, operation through a change over switch or in grid paralleled mode

(b) **Irrigation/other mechanical modes:**

(i) Standard rating of 5 HP and 10 HP.
(ii) Other ratings as needed.
(iii) Unattended operation; refilling once in eight hours.
(iv) Diesel replacement of more than 75 per cent with controlled operation.
(v) Free mounting units also available.

(c) **Direct thermal applications:**

(i) Output ratings of 15,000 Kcal/h to 1.25 million Kcal/h.
(ii) Wide range of applications in industry, commerce, institutions etc. for boilers, kiln, dryers, ovens, furnaces, institutional cooking etc.
(iii) Flame temperature up to 90°C.
(iv) Excellent control over flame temperature, flame length etc.

Biomass based sterling engine

The Indian farmer, on an average, is using over 2000 MJ of energy in the form of fertilizer, chemical, mechanical operations, and electricity and diesel oil to produce one tonne of food grains. This sector is emerging as an important consumer of commercial energy Further, if we resolve energy available for crop production, major portion of energy goes in irrigation pump sets, which are mostly diesel fuel-based. The hot air cycled Sterling Engines available in the range of power required for the pumping the water are being manufactured in India. It is essentially a heat engine and makes use of biomass as fuel. The engine can be used for a variety of purposes. At CTAE this engine was mounted on a mobile chassis coupled with auto cooling system converting existing stirling engine for on-farm application, such as threshing, water pumping, chaff cutting, etc.

Biogas Technology

Biogas is a result of anaerobic fermentation of biomass. It is a gaseous mixture containing about 50 to 60 per cent methane a high value fuel, 10 to 35 per cent carbon dioxide and traces of other gases such as ammonia, hydrogen sulphide, oxygen etc. Cow dung is one of the most important and widely used biomass for the biogas production. The dung may be supplemented with other wastes like human excreta, sheep and poultry dropping camel and horse dung etc.

The biogas system besides providing domestic fuel at almost negligible cost using waste biomass or dung, it does not loose its nutritive value and the nitrogen content of the slurry goes up. Government of India has been stressing on the need for setting up more biogas plants in the country and has been offering subsidies for setting up the plants. The biogas can also be used for lighting, running pumps and other agricultural machineries by substitution of diesel.

The design and construction of a biogas plant is simple. The construction of the plant, however, calls for the services of a mason, who is trained in the setting up of such plants, to ensure that the construction is done as per design and other norms. There is an estimated potential of 12 million biogas plants against which about 3.28 million family sized plants have been set up so far.

Importance of biogas plant slurry

The biogas plant whether a family size or community size, has a distinct advantage of providing a nutritive digested sludge with high manurial value besides solving the problem of rural energy in domestic and agriculture sectors. Since the sludge is of biological origin, it contains most of the plant nutrients including macro and micro nutrients essential for plant growth. The nitrogen is considered to be of a particular importance due to its vital role in plant nutrition and growth. The digested sludge contains nitrogen (1.7-2.0%) mainly in the ammonical form. The applications of the digested sludge to crops serve dual purposes, both as a soil conditioner and a fertilizer. The humus available in sludge also contains less pathogenic organisms and weeds seeds than untreated animal excreta. Under tropical conditions, addition of organic manure to soil is extremely important in improvement of soil and its productivity. Hence, the effective and efficient use of digested sludge and reuse of water contained in it will have to be integrated with production of energy in order to make maximum utilisation of available resources. However, due to high water content digested sludge poses various problems of handling which require due attention for its better utilisation. The biogas plants set up so far have helped in producing 430 lakh tonnes of manure equivalent to 9.5 lakh tonnes of urea per year.

New Technologies for Sustainable Power Supply to Agriculture

Solar Hydrogen Power

Hydrogen is the cleanest fuel in the nature. The hydrogen as an energy carrier can monitor almost each and every application in the world. The combination of solar energy and the hydrogen economy should be viewed with exceptional interest. Since vegetable oils produce higher smoke emissions, dual fuel operation can be adopted for improving their performance. Alcohols have been widely used as primary fuels in dual fuel engines. However, dual fuel operation with alcohol induction results in higher hydrocarbon and carbon monoxide emissions. Higher viscosity and density of vegetable oils lead to slow combustion and hence the performance becomes inferior. Use of hydrogen, due to its high flame velocity can enhance the combustion rate of vegetable oils and reduce emissions.

Duel fuel operation normally poses problems of low efficiency when the concentration of the inducted fuel is low. This is because the lean mixture of the inducted fuel with air does not burn well. Use of fuels with wide flammability limits and high flame velocity can overcome such problem in dual fuel engines. Thus hydrogen can be used in a dual fuel engine as the inducted fuel. The high auto ignition temperature makes it knock resistant. Since hydrogen has no hydrocarbons it reduces hydrocarbon and carbon monoxide emissions.

Institutional biogas plant in use at Gurdwara Bhudda Sahib, district Patiala, Punjab.

The Boeing Corporation is working on a solar plant for the thermo-chemical decomposition of water. Given efficiency of the order of 50 per cent for this plant, the specific cost of the plant is estimated to $200-250/kW. The laboratory of the Public Service Electric & Gas Co. is testing an experimental 12.5 kW plant Hydrogen stored at 169 atm is used following reduction to atmospheric pressure in a fuel cell. The hydrogen power production system from fuel cell technology transform chemical energy directly to electrical technology. The various type of fuel cell, i.e. Alkaline, Molten Carbonate, Solid Oxide, Phosphoric acid and Solid Polymer Electrolyte (SPE) based systems are researched. With theoretical efficiency of 90 per cent almost 50-60 per cent have been achieved with Phosphoric acid and SPE base fuel cell respectively.

Fuel cells

Fuel cells using phosphoric acid (85-100% H_3PO_4) as the electrolyte operate in the temperature range of 160-210°C. Platinum based catalysts are used and the cells run on air and hydrogen produced from various liquid or gaseous fuels or stored in cylinders or metal hydrides. Output capacities range from few kWs to MWs of power range. These fuel cells can be utilized in a wide variety of applications including vehicular portable or remote power; central station and dispersed utility power; on-site integrated energy systems; and industrial cogeneration of heat and electricity.

New Fuel Cell

The Berlin Energy Utility, Bewag, launched a new fuel cell project in mid-June 2002. A stationary plant with a zero emission proton exchange membrane technology produces electricity and heat. With an installed electric output of up to 250 kW and a heat output of about 230 kW, the plant is the first of its kind in Europe. It was developed by the Canadian company, Ballard Power Systems, which claims to be the world leader in developing, manufacturing and marketing fuel cells for use in agriculture, transportation, electricity generation, portable power, and other products. Frankfurt-Main-based Alstom Energietechnik GmbH products and markets the technology in Europe.

The plant will be fuelled by natural gas to produce the necessary hydrogen. The oxygen is freely available from the air. Additionally, 'solar' hydrogen will be used in the fuel cell installation, to be produced by a 10 kW photovoltaic installation on the roof of the Treptow distant heating plant and a linked electrolyzer, a technical facility for splitting water into hydrogen and oxygen.

In several years of trial operation, the demonstration plant is to produce findings about the economic viability of this technology. The aim is to identify early on the possible applications and market potential of the fuel cell for decentralised energy supplies. Partners with Bewag in the project are hamburgische Electricitats-Werke AG, Electricite de France, Preussen Elektra Aktiengesellschaft, and VEGA Vereinigte Energiewerke Aktiengesellschaft. Planning and erection of the plant require an investment of 3.54 million dollars.

About 40 per cent of the funding is a subsidy from the European Union. Attached to the plant is a 'Fuel Cell Innovation Park', an information and discussion forum that aims to inform about all aspects of current and future energy supplies.

Solar chimney

Solar chimney power plant is an effective system of large-scale power generation system exceeding 1000 MW. Solar chimney works on the principle of "hot air rise" and very simple, reliable and environment friendly technology. Air heated by solar radiation under a low circular glass roof open at the periphery; this and the natural ground below it form a hot air collector. In the middle of the roof is a vertical chimney with large air inlets at its base. The joint between the roof and the chimney base is airtight. As hot air is lighter than cold air it raises up the chimney. Suction from the chimney then draws in more air from the collector and cold air comes in from the outer perimeter. The solar radiation thus causes a constant up draught in the chimney. The energy thus contained is converted into mechanical energy by pressure-staged wind turbines at the base of the chimney and into electrical energy by conventional generators. As the heat under the glass roof is constantly drawn out through the chimney a "greenhouse effect" with stabilised and even temperature conditions is created on part of land underneath. As the electricity is available on site, water can be pumped from bore wells to support agricultural activity. The single solar chimney with a suitably gazed roof area and a high chimney can be designed to generate 100 to 200 MW and power production cost comes around Rs. 2.96 kWh

Solar chimney operates even on diffused radiation since it is dependent on heat derived from sun permitting 24-hour operation thus achieving high plant load factors. Large solar chimney plant can produce 10-12 per cent of their energy during hours of complete darkness. No extra fuel is required to run the plant. Electricity thus produced can be directly fed to public grid by transformer. The thermal inertia of solar chimney plant is also safe in comparison with wind parks and photovoltaic plants. A solar chimney/Neptha based cycle plant of 200 MW capacity is under installation in desert district of Jodhpur in Rajasthan.

Solar generator

Australian technology firm, Orion Energy Management Pvt. Ltd. is to launch its hybrid solar turbine generator system, based on an organic Rankine cycle. Unlike solar panels that generate electricity using visible light, this system captures heat using a solar collector and converts it into electricity through a micro turbine generator.

With far lower operating costs than diesel generators, a fraction of the installation cost of solar photovoltaic systems and wider applicability than wind turbines, Orion expects significant interest from Australia's numerous operators of remote area power systems. Unlike traditional electricity, which is generated at a low frequency making it difficult to transport, the solar turbine generator can produce electricity at an incredible 600 Hz, making it more efficient to transmit over long distances and ideal for remote locations. Other target markets include eco-friendly residential developments and companies that want to minimise greenhouse gas emissions. The system was developed jointly with the UK Company, TTL dynamics. TTL Dynamics manufacturers the turbine blades and control electronics while the rest of the unit and solar collection troughs are manufactured in Australia.

Orion Energy Management is offering 6, 15, 25, 50, 100, 300, 400, 500, and 600 kW units for sale. The units generate electricity at 48 V (415 V, 50 Hz on larger units) and are matched with an inverter that suits the individual application. Any excess electricity generated can be stored or sold back to the grid.

The hybrid solar turbine is also readily adapted to recover waste heat from industrial processes for electricity generation. It can also receive supplemental fuelling using any heat source, ensuring electricity is provided 24 hours a day, 365 days a year in colder climates. This is a very cost effective and reliable technology, says Stephen Riddell, the Chief Executive Officer of Orion Energy Management. Rather than fighting the environment, the solar turbine takes full advantage of Australia's harsh climate, extracting as much useful energy as possible with current technology. It makes environmental and economic sense for a wide array of applications.

Energy Issues Before Agro Industries

Pulp and paper industry

As estimated around 4.0 million tonnes of total paper is produced per annum by around 400 mills in India consuming more than 10 million tonnes of raw material. In case of large paper mills having chemical recovery system (which contributes 30% of the total production only) 12 per cent of the raw material used ends up as waste mostly as inorganic and non-combustible. However in small and medium size mills based on agro residues (which contributes 36% of the total paper production), due to absence of chemical recovery system the quantity of waste generated is quite high (around 60%) of the raw material consumption.

The other waste streams are treated by conventional activated sludge process in large paper mills. The small scale pulp and paper mills discharge their black liquor along with other waste steams as most of them don't have chemical recovery system mainly due to small scale of operation and requirement of high capital investment. The discharge of black liquor results in loss of valuable biomass as well as problems in treatment by conventional activated sludge treatment process. With increase in activism of environmental regulatory authorities for compliance to discharge norms, pulp and paper mills specially small scale are looking for techno-economical methods for effluent treatment for survival and sustainability. It is in this perspective Biomethanation Technology offers a scope to address these issues in a cost effective manner to a certain extent. In recent times bio-energy recovery and its effective utilisation through biomethanation has gained importance primarily because the process helps in reduction of pollution load along with the added advantage of cogeneration of biogas.

A High Rate Demo Biomethanation Plant based on upward Flow Anaerobic Sludge Blanket (UASB) technology has been set up at M/s Satia Paper Mills Ltd., Ms. Satia Paper Mills Ltd., Muktsar, Punjab for treatment of agro residue black liquor with financial assistance from Ministry of Non-Conventional Energy Sources (MNES) under a UNDP/GEF Project. The commissioning activities of the demo plant were completed under technical guidance of Central Pulp and Paper Research Institute (CPPRI), which played an important and pivotal role in selection of technology, installation and commissioning of demo biomethanation plant. Two number of UASB reactors (each of capacity 2623 m) handle a total organic waste of 53 ton/day generated by the mill. The influent is fed at the bottom of the reactor through a special distribution system, which ensures proper and uniform contact between influent and active biomass present inside the reactor. As the influent rises through the sludge bed, the anaerobic microbes convert the organic matter present in the waste water into biogas, which provide a natural mixing of influent and biomass as it moves upwards. The unique three-phase separator is provided at the top of the reactor, separates biogas and sludge from the effluent. The treated effluent overflows via gutters, a part of which re-circulates to buffer tank and a part is discharged to the drain.

Sugar industry

The press mud (also called filter cake) is a solid waste, generated on clarification of cane juice before its concentration and sugar crystallisation. It is a soft, spongy, lightweight, amorphous, dark brown to black coloured material. It generally contains 60-85 per cent moisture (wb); the chemical composition depends on cane variety, soil condition, nutrients applied in the field, process of clarification adopted and other environmental factors. Due to sugar and other organic constituents,. the press mud emits obnoxious odour causing environmental pollution. The press mud at many places, is being used as a fuel. The possibility of using a mixture of filter cake and bagasse in different proportions has been studied to use the mixture as a fuel in the boilers for the generation of steam. It can be burnt directly in the form of briquettes. On burning, it emits toxic gases SO_2 and SO_3, which pollute the environment. Briquettes of press mud when used in boiler as a fuel, it forms clinkers.

The present methods for disposal of press mud are not economically viable and pollute the environment. As it contains appreciable proportion of biodegradable organic matter, it has very good potential for the production of biogas. The press mud used for generation of biogas contained about 77 per cent volatile solids with the C/N ratio of 14. The organic matter present in the press mud consisted mainly of cellulose 11.4 per cent, hemicellulose 10 per cent, lignin 9.3 per cent, protein 15.1 per cent was 8.4 per cent and sugar 5.7 per cent. It also contained various micronutrients. It is an excellent material for biogas production through the modern fast reactors, serving dual purposes making available power and controlling environmental pollution.

Incineration

Incineration is a process of controlled combustion for burning solid, liquid and gaseous combustible wastes to gases and residue containing non-combustible material. During combustion, moisture is vapourised whereas the combustible portion is vapourised and oxidised. Carbon dioxide, water vapour, ash and non-combustibles are the end products. The heat produced is recovered and used for heating water and generating electricity using Rankine's cycle in steam turbine. Though incineration is not a complete method of disposal, its main advantage is that it produces a residue that is substantially reduced in volume and may be relatively inert. However, incineration process should be considered as a possible option only after complete economic and environmental impact analysis in comparison with other methods of treatment. In conditions where wastes are too low in calorific value, high in moisture content, and capital and operating costs are likely to be beyond sustainable limits of the cities, incineration is definitely not suitable.

Refuse fuel for power generation

The main purpose of the refuse-derived fuel (RDF) method is to produce an improved solid fuel or pellets from refuse originating from households, commerce and industry. The material used in RDF production is mechanically separated from the refuse. The overall process for treating waste under this method is as follows: (a) all waste is initially shredded, (b) light waste materials are then separated, (c) separated waste materials are dried, and (d) dried materials are compressed into pellets. Based on an analysis of refuse composition, the RDF fraction will normally amount to approximately 5 to 10%. Refuse from some districts, however, will contain more light materials, thus making the RDF fraction slightly richer (approximately 10 to 20%). The RDF produced is normally used by local industries, heating plants or power plants.

Bio-diesel—an alternative diesel fuel

Many vegetable oils, animal fats and recycled cooking medium can be transformed into bio-diesel and there are many ways to do it. Oils and fats are composed of triglyceride chemical compound of fatty acids, glycerin and other minor components. Oil is combined with base catalysts such as sodium or potassium hydroxide, in the presence of excess alcohol to bond the fatty acids to the alcohol to produce bio-diesel. Once the methyl alkyl ester (bio-diesel) is extracted and washed making it safe for use in engines, the residual glycerin can be sold to the chemical suppliers. The process is very efficient yielding comparatively large amount of bio-diesel (80 to 90%) and comparatively small amount of residual product (glycerin). The process yield virtually nothing that could be called hazardous waste and can be conducted with very basic facilities without sophisticated manufacturing hardware, skilled labour or specialised technical support.

Safer and cleaner fuel

- Bio-diesel offers fleet operators, a safer, cleaner alternative to petroleum diesel.
- Bio-diesel is recognised as an alternative fuel. In its neat form and also in blends of 20 per cent or more with petroleum diesel the US Department of Energy has acknowledged bio-diesel as an alternative fuel.
- Bio-diesel operates in conventional CI engine from light to heavy duty, just like petroleum diesel. No engine modifications are required, bio-diesel maintains the pay loads capacity and range of diesel.
- Bio-diesel cuts down on targeted emissions. Bio-diesel used in 20 per cent blends with diesel and a catalytic converter will cut air pollution. Particulate matter is reduced by 31 per cent carbon monoxide by 21 per cent and total hydrocarbons by 47 per cent. Bio-diesel used in a blend will also reduce sulphur emissions and aromatics.

Using 100 per cent bio-diesel further reduces emissions and carcinogenic compound.

- Bio-diesel has a higher flashpoint than regular diesel fuel. It is classified as non-flammable by NFPA and is not required to carry a hazardous material label when being shipped.
- Bio-diesel increases lubricity to traditionally high sulphur diesel fuel levels.
- Bio-diesel is user friendly. The use of bio-diesel and blends results is noticeable reduction in exhaust odour with no irritation of eyes. Since bio-diesel is oxygenated, diesel engines have more complete combustion than using petroleum fuel.
- Bio-diesel has cetane rating slightly higher than diesel.

Out of all alternative fuel options for diesel, vegetable oils offer an advantage because of comparable fuel properties with diesel and can be substituted between 20-100 per cent depending upon its processing, The major advantages of vegetable oils as a diesel fuel are:

- Technologies of extractions and processing are very simple as conventional equipment requiring low energy input such as ghani in rural areas, can be successfully used.
- The byproduct left over is rich in protein and can be used as animals feed, fertilizer or solid fuels.
- Wide ranges of climatic conditions are tolerable for production of oil plants.
- On farm production of power is possible.
- Agro forestry that has bearing on energy balance in the eco-system can be developed.
- Physical nature being liquid ensures easy portability and free from handling hazards.
- Vegetable oils are renewable in nature.

Dr. Rudoff Diesel first develop the diesel engine in 1895 with the full intention of running it on a variety of fuels including vegetable oils. Dr. Diesel demonstrated his engine at the World Exhibition in Paris in 1900 using peanut oil as fuel. In 1911 he stated, the diesel engine can be fed with vegetable oils and would help considerably in the development of agriculture of the countries, which use it. In 1912 Diesel said, the use of vegetable oils for engine fuels may seem insignificant today but such oils may become in course of times as important as petroleum and the coal tar products of the present time.

Since vegetable oils produce higher smoke emissions, dual fuel operation can be adopted for improving their performance. Alcohols have been widely used as primary fuels in dual fuel engines. However, dual fuel operation with alcohol induction results in higher hydrocarbon and carbon monoxide emissions. Higher viscosity and density of vegetable oils lead to slow combustion and hence the performance becomes inferior. Use of hydrogen, due to its high flame velocity can enhance the combustion rate of vegetable oils and reduce emissions.

It has been reported by the researchers that extended operation of diesel engine on vegetable oils creates problem of injector choking, dilution of engine oil, deposits on engine components etc. The high acid value and presence of gums/wax etc. adversely affects the engine performance. To overcome these problems different technologies like cracking of plant's oils, heating and blending with diesel or alcohol and chemically transforming the vegetable oils thereby preparing Easters (Bio-diesel) by transesterifications process were investigated.

Duel fuel operations normally poses problems of low efficiency when the concentration of the inducted fuel is low. This is because the lean mixture of the inducted fuel with air does not burn well. Use of fuels with wide flammability limits and high flame velocity can overcome such problem in dual fuel engines. Thus hydrogen can be used in a dual fuel engine as the inducted fuel. The high auto ignition temperature makes it knock resistant. Since hydrogen has no hydrocarbons it reduces hydrocarbon and carbon monoxide emissions.

Commercialisation of Renewable Energy Sources in farming areas

The future use of renewable energy sources in rural areas for sustained power supply will depend on the commercialisation of the technologies. The efforts have already been started by targeting electrification of 85000 remotely located villages by renewable energy sources, thus making it a marketable technology through the use of sales outlets, after sales service, cost effective and confidence building of the users. The direct and indirect benefits from these energy sources make them comparable with the conventional energy sources. The time is not far off when these sources will turn every farm and house as power station, every industry as a power plant to meet their own energy requirement.

Conclusion

The extensive use of Renewable Energy Sources to complement the existing energy sources is an option to sustainable energy flow in rural areas. The control of the environmental pollution, which is likely to reach a new height in the time to come can also be achieved by these technologies. The cost of power generation from these sources is comparable if the environment cost is also accounted for. Adequate research and production facilities are necessary for making them cost effective. This will help us leaving the precision ênergy sources for our future generation also, which is not possible otherwise.

REFERENCES

1. Proceeding of Commercialisation Aspect of Renewal Energy Sources, 2000, CTAE Udaipur, India.
2. Proceeding of International Conference of Techno-Commercial Aspects of Decentralised Approach in Waste to Energy, 2002, MERC, Jaipur, India.
3. Singh, Harpal and Alam, A. *Crop Drying and Dryers*, Status Paper of AICRP on Utilisation of Renewable Energy Sources in Agriculture and Agro Based Industries.
4. Mathur, A.N., *Renewable Energy for Rural Development to Protect Environmental Pollution from Energy Sources*, Paper presented at National Confrence on Advances on Solar Energy Technologies.
5. Mathur, A.N., *Role of Renewable Energy in 21st Century*, paper presented at National Workshop held at Babasaheb Naik College of Engineering, Pusad, India, 2001.
6. pAnnual Report of Ministry of Non-Conventional Energy Sources, Government of India, 2001, New Delhi, India.

12

Impacts, Adaptation and Mitigation of Climate Change in Indian Agriculture

J.S. SAMRA

Introduction

Indian agriculture has provided food, feed, nutrition, employment and environmental securities to the ever increasing population of human beings and livestock. Food production in India increased spectacularly due to the Green Revolution from 69 million tonnes in 1965 to 211 million tonnes in 2002 and the mean cereal productivity increased from less than 1.0 t ha^{-1} to almost 3.0 t ha^{-1}. This was largely the result of area expansion, large-scale cultivation of new high-yielding semi-dwarf varieties, increased application of irrigation water, fertilizers and other inputs. Today, India is having surplus food stocks of 65 million tons. The very severe drought of 1987 in India could be managed easily without any problem of food security because of the enabling policy of establishing buffer stocks. Similarly, another drought of 1999-2000 in the states of Gujarat and Rajasthan, although created water scarcity but massive public distribution of food ensured that relatively few went hungry to the bed.

The rapid and unabated increase in population implies a greater demand for food. By 2020 the demand for rice and wheat, the predominant staple foods, is expected to increase to 122 and 103 Mt, respectively, assuming medium income growth (Table 12.1). The demand for pulses, fruits, vegetables, milk, meat, eggs and marine products is also projected to increase very sharply. This additional food will have to be produced from the same or even a shrinking land resource base.

Table 12.1: Demand of food in India for 2010 and 2020 assuming a 5 per cent GDP growth at constant prices (Adapted from Kumar, 1998)

Items	*Production (million tons)*	*Projected demand of food (million tons)*	
	1999-2000	*2010*	*2020*
Rice	85.4	103.6	122.1
Wheat	71.0	85.8	102.8
Coarse grains	29.9	34.9	40.9
Total cereals	184.7	224.3	265.8
Pulses	16.1	21.4	27.8
Food grains	200.8	245.7	293.6
Fruits	41.1	56.3	77.0
Vegetables	84.5	112.7	149.7
Milk	75.3	103.7	142.7
Meat and eggs	3.7	5.4	7.8
Marine products	5.7	8.2	11.8

The perceived gradual increase in environmental degradation, early signs of which are becoming visible in areas that benefited largely from the Green Revolution technologies, is further adding to the worries of food planners. There is now great concern about declining soil fertility, change in water table depth, rising salinity, resistance of harmful organisms to many pesticides and degradation of irrigation water quality, especially in north-western India. Nutrient removal by crops over time has exceeded application of N, P and K by about 10 million tonnes/annum. Consequently, farmers now have to apply more fertilizers to realize the same yield as achieved 20-30 years ago. These are signs of unsustainability or fatigue that must, at least partly, be attributed to the deterioration of resource quality.

The introduction of canal irrigation in India salinized about 3.4 million hectare land of the country. Aphids, stem borers and *Heliothis armigera* have shown increasing damage to the rice-wheat system. False smut, sheath rot, sheath blight and grain discoloration in rice have also increased. Similarly, foliar blights, head scab and Karnal bunt have appeared more frequently in wheat. The weed *Phalaris minor* developed resistance to most herbicides in large areas under rice-wheat rotation and is a real threat to wheat production.

The rapid increase in the number of tubewells during the last three decades in north-western India and other regions over-exploited groundwater in many blocks, leading to declining groundwater levels. In 80 per cent geographical area of Punjab, water tables declined significantly during the last three decades in most districts.

In the 21st century, one of the great challenges for India is, therefore, to ensure that food production reduces poverty and enhances environmental preservation. The sustainable agriculture development may have to consider two additional important global drivers of change in agriculture in the coming decades—globalisation and climate change. The on-going globalisation process and economic reforms are likely to force many countries, including India, to make structural adjustments in the agricultural sector. Agriculture has to become more competitive, efficient and perform without subsidies that are being phased out.

Assessment of Impacts

Prospects and problems of increasing food production are becoming compounded by the recent man-induced changes in the climate of the earth or in global warming. Increase in the atmospheric temperature due to enhanced levels of carbon dioxide (CO_2) and other greenhouse gases, uncertainty of rainfall, intensive climatic extremes such as droughts, floods, rainfall distribution and snowmelt are some of its consequences. The 1990s was, on an average, the warmest decade of the earth since the beginning of instrumental measurements of temperature in 1860. Similarly, the 1900s was the warmest century during the past 1000 years. The Inter-Governmental Panel on Climatic Change (IPCC) of the United Nations in its recent report has projected that the globally averaged temperature of the air above the earth's surface would rise by 1.4-5.8°C over the next 100 years. CO_2 levels are projected to increase to 388-399 ppm by 2010-2015 from the current (2000) level of approximately 370 ppm (Watson, 1995). For South Asia, the area-averaged annual mean warming by 2020 is projected to be between 1.0 and 1.4°C and between 2.23 to 2.87°C for 2050 (Watson, 1998).

These changes could considerably affect the food supply and access through their direct and indirect effects on crops, soils, livestock, fisheries and pests. Increase in atmospheric CO_2 promotes the growth and productivity of C3 plants. Higher temperature, on the other hand, can reduce crop duration, increase crop respiration rates, alter the equilibrium between crops and pests, hasten nutrient mineralisation in soils, decrease fertiliser use efficiencies, and increase evapotranspiration. The environmental changes, particularly higher temperature and sea level rise could also affect fisheries directly and indirectly through the availability of feed. Expansion of sea may call upon human resettlement/relocation with a host of social consequences (Aggarwal and Sinha, 1993).

Indirectly, there may be considerable impact of climatic change on agricultural land use due to snow melt, redistribution of water altered frequency and intensity of inter and intra-seasonal droughts/floods, soil organic matter transformations, soil erosion, decline in arable areas (due to submergence of coastal lands), and availability of energy. Several important socio-economic determinants of food supply such as government policies, capital availability, prices and returns, infrastructure, land reforms, and inter and intra-national trade are also expected to be influenced and altered by environmental change.

Thus, there is a tremendous challenge to develop technologies for combating adverse impacts of climatic changes on food production in the coming decades. Poverty reduction and food security represent major challenges to mankind in the new millennium. We require anticipatory research to formulate integrated agricultural development plans for future that will maximise food production, minimise environmental degradation and internalize socio-economic benefits.

Quantifying Recent Changes in Weather

Analysis of long-term changes in rainfall quantum across individual meteorological sub-divisions is quite revealing. There are regions which have recorded increase or decrease of annual rainfall on a long-term basis (1871-1999) and north-eastern shifts in the surplus rainfall zones during the last four decades as compared with the long-term means across the sub-divisions (Fig. 12.1). The spatial trend pattern during the last four decadal period (1961-1999) indicates a decreasing trend in western parts, most southern parts and central parts of India. An increasing trend is seen along the eastern coast and also in north-western parts especially Punjab and western Rajasthan. However, the highest increasing trends were seen in Gangetic West Bengal (26%) and Sub-Himalayan West Bengal (14%). This shift can have significant implications on the changes in crops and cropping patterns across these regions.

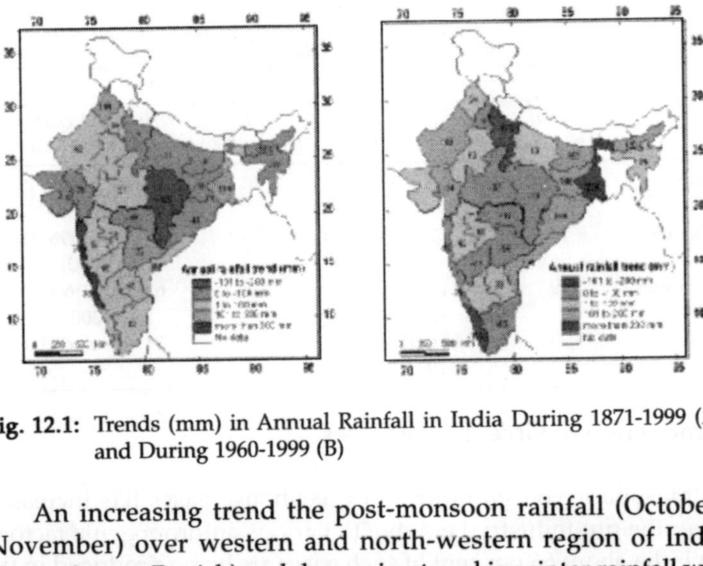

Fig. 12.1: Trends (mm) in Annual Rainfall in India During 1871-1999 (A) and During 1960-1999 (B)

An increasing trend the post-monsoon rainfall (October-November) over western and north-western region of India (Saurashtra to Punjab) and decreasing trend in winter rainfall was observed. Also many of the northern regions of India experienced an increase in minimum temperatures during the *rabi* cropping season. All these factors exhibit a significant impact on the crop production in the *rabi* season. Similar analysis from the scarcity zone of Maharashtra (e.g. Rahuri and Sholapur) showed increased trend in annual rainfall and *rabi* (winter) minimum temperatures. Analysis of occurrence of moderate and severe droughts in the Indian arid zone by Central Arid Zone Research Institute, brought out an increase in moderate to severe droughts (Mooley and Pant, 1981) in the last decade (1991-2000) compared to the earlier period in the last centuries (Table 12.2). Similar studies carried out on the rainfed region of eastern India revealed higher drought frequency in Uttar Pradesh, Chhattisgarh and Bihar compared to Orissa and West Bengal. Probability analysis showed that drought is more prominent in that regions especially during the reproductive phase of the rainfed rice crop adversely affecting its rice productivity. These analysis also proved that short-term climate variability is of greater concern as its influence on food security is more vital.

Table 12.2: Frequency of Moderate and Severe Droughts in the Indian Arid Zone

District	*Intensity of drought (No. of years)*			
	Moderate		*Servere*	
	Total (1901-2000)	*In last decade (1991-2000)*	*Total (1991-2000)*	*In last decade (1991-2000)*
Barmer	14	1 (1997)	20	4 (1991, 1998, 1999 and 2000)
Bikaner	19	2 (1993 & 1997)	19	4 (1991, 1998, 1999 and 2000)
Jaisalmer	19	3 (1991, 1993 & 1994)	28	6 (1992, 1994, 1997-2000)
Jodhpur	23	4 (1991, 1993, 1997 & 1998)	14	2 (1999 and 2000)

Production of Greenhouse Gases

Atmospheric concentrations of greenhouse gases has increased over the pre-industrial era due to various anthropogenic factors. In India about 66 per cent of such gases are being produced in the industrial sector and agricultural activities are contributing about 34 per cent only. Apart from that many agricultural systems or practices also act as sink (absorber) and sequestration or mitigation can be linked to trade in emission gases. Rice fields and livestock were alleged to produce excessive methane and nitrous oxide whereas many other gases were contributed by the burning of fossil fuels. Anaerobic conditions of puddle rice field, continuous ponding of water, high organic matter content, application of undecomposed manures, green manuring and incorporation of crop residues were some of the causative factor (Aggarwal *et al.*,

2000). Results of an internationally coordinated project revealed that methane emission rates in rice field of Indian soil were far less as compared to other Asian countries (Table 12.3).

Table 12.3: Methane emission from rice fields at different centres of UNDP-IRRI programme under a reference treatment (cultivar IR 72 under continuous flooding)

Expermental Site	*Seasonal methane (g/m²)*	*Organic carbon (%)*
Irrigated Rice		
Hangzhou, China	16.6	1.9
Beijing, China	5.0	0.99
Maligaya, Philippines	24.4	1.32
New Delhi, India	1.7	0.41
Rainfed		
Jakenan, Indonesia	17.1	0.48
Los. Banos, Philippines	7.5	1.2
Cuttak, India	4.0	0.36
Deep water		
Prachinburi, Thailand	10	0.54
Average	9.48	0.9

Source: Terminal Report UNDP/GEF, 1999.

CO_2 Enrichment Studies

Innovative approaches for conducting long-term experiments have been developed to investigate the impact of rising atmospheric CO_2 on crops. Free Air CO_2 Enrichment technology (FACE) was developed in collaboration with NPL and Italian group of scientists at IARI, New Delhi. It consists of 8m-diameter octagon shaped ring wherein CO_2 concentration is regulated on the basis of wind speed and wind direction by PC based controller and PiD valves.

Several studies have been conducted in open top chambers and using FACE technology. The highlights of its results are:

- Water stressed Brassica plants responded to elevated CO_2 ameliorating the adverse effects of moisture deficit on photosynthesis, growth, nutrient balance, anatomical microstructures of leaves and water relations.
- The photosynthetic response of Brassica oxycamp hybrid to elevated CO_2 was similar to its one parent B. campestris

whereas the other parent B. oxyrrhina did not respond to elevated CO_2.

- Stress induced adverse effect on grain carbohydrate and oil content of Brassica juncea were reduced under elevated CO_2.
- Rice cultivars 'Pusa Basmati-1' and 'P-677' responded to the elevated CO_2 by an increase in their grain yield due to greater number of tillers and grain per plant.

A South Asian CO_2 crop research network of Bangladesh, India, Nepal, Pakistan and Sri Lanka has been established. Multi-country, multi-disciplinary experiments on rice using common protocol are currently in progress in all these countries.

Development of Impact Assessment Simulation Models

The interaction effects of CO_2, rainfall and temperature can also be best studied through the use of crop growth simulation models. However, most of the existing crop models are too complex with large input data requirement, cannot be easily integrated in the application, and are not very user-friendly (Kropff *et al.*, 1996). Preliminary results have also indicated that some of them do not perform very well. A key reason is that these models do not consider growth and yield loss due to insects, weeds and diseases, common in tropical and subtropical regions. To overcome these limitations, Indian Agricultural Research Institute, in collaboration with scientists of ICAR and Universities have developed InfoCrop, a decision support system. Current version of InfoCrop deals with chickpea, cotton, groundnut, maize, mustard, pearl millet, pigeon pea, potato, rice, sorghum, soybean, sugarcane and wheat.

Adaption and Mitigation Options

There are several options which help in adaptation and mitigation of the adverse impacts of climate change to agricultural production and improvement of the carbon stocks. Some of the successful adaptation strategies are discussed below:

Management of rice fields

It has been stated earlier that methane production rate in India is very less as compared to South-east Asia. Alternate wetting and drying cycles in rainfed rice ecologies as well as intermittent application of water in irrigated eco-systems are re-deeming feature of the current rice production systems of India. Many designed experiments have revealed 28-30 per cent of reduction in methane gas liberation due to intermittent irrigation (Sinha, 1995). Bed planting experiments being carried out will further reduce the methane production rates. Organic carbon status of Indian soils is low and residues are being removed as feed for cattle, bedding material and wrapping/packaging material.

Integrated watershed management

Excessive biotic and abiotic interferences have caused considerable degradation of our natural resources. Demands on land, water and vegetation are increasing day by day due to demographic pressure. About 50 per cent of the total geographical area of the country is affected by different manifestations of land degradation. Rise in water table, salinization, frequent occurrence of floods and droughts and other environmental degradation problems are matters of serious concern in current as well as future global warming scenarios. About 50 per cent of the Indian agriculture shall continue to remain rainfed even after realizing full irrigation potential. Excessive soil erosion in the catchments of hydro electric reservoirs, unscientific management of mined areas, landslides, ravines and other human-induced activities are the major constraints in environmental stability. These constraints are likely to become more visible in global change scenarios of increased droughts and floods.

Watershed Management (WSM) has been found to be a well accepted single window and sound strategy for efficient management of land, water and vegetation resources through community participation for sustainable productivity. Recently evolved participatory processes however made it demand-driven programme. These programmes yield multiple benefits such as sustainable production, resource conservation, ground water recharge, drought moderation, employment generation and social equity. A consistent increase in the production of food grains, fruits as well as milk, and decline in runoff, soil loss and dependency on forest for fodder and fuel wood was noticed even after withdrawal of active intervention phase in the Fakot watershed project initiated in 1974 (Table 12.4).

Table 12.4: Production and protection impact of watershed management programme during pre-project, active interventions and after withdrawal of interventions (Fakot, Uttaranchal hills, area—327 ha)

Product	*PPP*	*Average of*	
	(1974-75)	*IP (1975-86)*	*PIP (1987-95)*
Food Crop (q)	882	4015	5843
Fruit (q)	Negligible	62	1962
Milk ('000 Rs.)	56.6	184.8	237.6
Floriculture ('000 Rs.)	Nil	Nil	120.0*
Cash crops ('000 Rs.)	6.5	24.8	202.5
Animal rearing	Heavily grazing	Partially grazing	Stall feeding
Dependency on forest fodder (%)	60	46	18
Runoff (%)	42	18.3	13.7
Soil loss (t/ha/annum)	11	4.5	2.0

Note: PPP: Pre-Project Period, IP: Intervention Phase, PIP: Post-Intervention Phase.

* Community diversified into Floriculture in *1994*.

Pilot projects have been undertaken by CSWCRTI, Dehradun, for rehabilitation of highly degraded lands through bioengineering measures. Nalotanala landslide project on Dehradun-Mussoorie highway, Sahastradhara mine-spoil rehabilitation project and Bainkhala torrent control project are some such projects with successful stories of technology. The highly degraded mine-spoil and landslide slopes were treated with small engineering structures such as loose stone/gabion check dams, contour trenches, wattling, geo-jute etc. and planted with suitable vegetative species (Samra and Narain, 1999). The bio-engineering technology not only rehabilitated the area but also considerably improved the water availability and its quality and, in turn the vegetation resource in the area for use by the local community. For example, the reclamation measures in the landslide and mine spoil affected watersheds rejuvenated the water springs with sustained water yield even during dry season (Tables 12.5 & 12.6).

Table 12.5: Effect of bio-engineering measures on landslide stabilization [Nalota Nala (60 ha), Uttaranchal Hills, treated since 1964]

Description	*Before Treatment (1983)*	*After Treatment (1996)*
Runoff mm	55	38
Dry weather flow, days	100	250
Sediment load, ton/ha/year	320	5.5
Vegetation cover, per cent	<5	>95
Nala bed slope per cent		
Lower reach	12	7
Middle reach	23	14
Upper	54	44
Toe cutting	Severe	Nil

Table 12.6: Impact of rehabilitation on mine-spoiled watershed at Sahastradhara (64 ha), Doon Valley, Uttaranchal hills

Particulars	*Before Treatment (1983)*	*After Treatment (1996)*
Debris outflow, t/ha/year	550	8
Monsoon runoff, %	57	37
Lean period flow, days	60	240
Vegetation cover, %	10	80

Ground water recharge is one of the important adaptation to moderate floods and droughts scenarios going to be created due to anticipated climatic changes. Rise in water table with ground water recharging adoptions was found spectacular in low rainfall regions, which was as high as 2.0 m in some cases (Table 12.7). Highly erratic and uneven distribution of rainfall both spatially and temporally is and would be the major factor for lower production in the rainfed areas. Watershed management technologies are known to bring stability to such regions. Per cent yield reduction in the drought year of 1987 was significantly less in the well managed watersheds as compared to unmanaged watersheds in different agro-ecological regions of India. Integrated development of watersheds significantly reduced runoff and soil loss (Table 12.8), which helped in moderating the effect of floods in the downstream reaches and improved *in situ* moisture conservation for increased biomass production. Following on the tremendous success of such projects, the Government of India launched a massive programme of National Watershed Development in the country during 1991 and made demand-driven by adopting the concept of people's participation since 1995.

Table 12.7: Effect of watershed management strategies on ground water recharge in different regions of India

Watershed	*Surface storage capacity created ha-m*	*Observed rise in ground water table m**
1. Bazar-Ganiyar (Haryana)	79.0	2.0
2. Behdala (H.P.)	18.0	1.8
3. Bunga (Haryana)	60.0	1.8
4. Chhajawa (Rajasthan)	20.0	2.0
5. Chinnatekur (A.P.)	5.6	0.8
6. GR Halli (Karnataka)	6.8	1.5
7. Joladarasi (Karnataka)	4.0	0.2
8. Siha (Haryana)	42.2	2.0
9. JNU and IIT, Delhi	0.46-2.218	0.8-9.9 (in 75 ha area)
10. Basaltic Formation of Central Maharashtra	Percolation structures	2.5
11. Coimbatore (T.N.)	Percolation ponds	1 to 2.5
12. Anantpur (A.P.)	Water harvesting structures	2.0 to 3.0
13. Parbhani (Maharashtra)	Nala bund, gully plugs	0.3 to 2.5
14. Tejpur (U.P.)	Four check dams 56 ha-m	3.7 metres
15. Kutch (Gujarat)	58 check dams, 48 percolation tanks 2 subsurface dams, 39 rechargeable wells	6 (in 3301 ha)
16. Jalgaon (Maharashtra)	6 percolation tanks	1 to 5
17. Amravati (Maharashtra)	3 percolation tanks	4 to 10 (in 280 ha)
18. CSIO (Chandigarh)	Injection of Roof Harvested water	2
19. IIT, Delhi	Two injection wells	0.29-0.87
20. President Estate, Delhi	Dug wells	2.58
21. Shram Shakti Bhawan Delhi	Lateral shaft with Bore well	1.43 to 2.15

* Difference between pre-project and post-project water table.

Table 12.8: Impact of integrated watershed management practices on runoff (flood moderation) and soil loss (enthronmental indicator)

Watershed	*Runoff as % rainfall*		*Soil loss (tons/ha)*	
	Pre-treatment	*Post-treatment*	*Pre-treatment*	*Post-treatment*
Bazar-Ganiyar (Haryana)	42.0	14.2	11.9	2.5
GR Halli (Karnataka)	14.0	1.3	3.5	1.0
Behdala (H.P.)	30.0	15.0	12.0	8.0
Joladarasi (Karnataka)	20.0	7.0	12.0	2.3
Una (H.P.)	30.0	20.0	12.0	10.0
Sukhana lake	29.0	7.0	140.0	18.0
Nalota Nala	55.0	38.0	320.0	5.5

Resource conservation technologies

Recent researches have shown that surface seeding or zero-tillage establishment of upland crops after rice gives similar yields to that planted under conventional high tillage over a diverse set of soil conditions. This reduces costs of production, allows earlier planting and thus higher yields, reduces weed growth, the use of greenhouse gases producing fuel and steel for tractor parts, and improves efficiency of water and fertilizers. In addition, such resource conserving technologies restrict release of soil carbon thus mitigating increase of CO_2 in the atmosphere. It is estimated that zero tillage saves 29.9 litres of diesel as compared to the conventional tillage. This leads to 77.7 kg/ha/year reduction in CO_2 production (assuming 2.6 kg of CO_2 production/litre of diesel burnt). It is estimated that if the entire wheat sowing in rice-wheat area (10.5 Mha) is done by zero tillage, 314 million litres of diesel will be saved and 816 million tons of CO_2 production will be avoided.

The raised bed planting system is another alternative crop management in rice-wheat systems. The practice saves nearly 30-50 per cent of the irrigation water compared to flat planted rice. Improved fertilizer efficiency through easier deep placement, the ability to weed mechanically make it environmentally benign. When permanent beds are used with minimal land preparation, this system adds the benefit of zero-tillage and improved soil physical structure to overall system productivity. Strip tillage is also a form of conservation tillage. Here also, wheat is sown directly, after harvest of rice, without any field preparation. Strip till drill used for this purpose prepares a 10cm wide strip of land, seed and fertilizer is placed simultaneously and 12.5cm wide strip of land remains undisturbed between two rows. The savings under strip till drilling compared to conventional sowing, and comparison of yields and economic returns are presented in Table 12.9. It is evident from these tables that strip till drilling saved around 70 to 80 per cent time, labour, diesel, energy (production of greenhouse gases) cost, and was economical compared to conventional sowing of wheat after harvest of rice.

Table 12.9: Comparison of Yield and Economic Returns under different Planting Methods of Wheat (2001-02) at PDCSR, Modipuram

Planting method	*Yield (t/ha)*		*Cost of Production*	*Net returns*	*Benefit: Cost*
	Grain	*Straw*	*(Rs./ha)*	*(Rs./ha)*	*Ratio*
Bed Planting	5.01	6.91	13,480	27,256	3.02
Conventional sowing	5.04	7.26	15,580	25,832	2.66
Strip till drilling	5.67	7.82	13,910	32,192	3.31
Zero till drilling	5.06	7.03	14,010	27,204	2.94

Enhanced carbon sequestration

Indian soils (sink) are largely carbon-depleted but can be brought back to their native carbon-carrying capacity by reforestation. The current stock of organic carbon in Indian soils (24.3 Pg) can be increased to 34.9 Pg, the difference representing the potential for sequestering additional carbon in soils. It is estimated that reforestation of 35 million ha of wastelands with suitable tree and grass species can sequester 0.84 and 1.06 Pg of carbon in vegetation and soil respectively.

Several studies have been initiated at many places to determine the effect of various agricultural management strategies such as zero tillage, mulching, incorporation of green manure and crop residues, silvi-pastoral systems and watershed management on enrichment of soil carbon.

Carbon sequestration through agroforestry/farm forestry

The prominent role of forestry and agroforestry systems in carbon sequestration has increased global interest in these land use options to stabilize greenhouse gases emission. Agroforestry system especially agri-silvicultural system can be carbon sinks and temporarily store carbon, while other systems (ruminant based) are purely greenhouse gases emission systems. In one of the studies in Uttar Pradesh, approximately 20 million tonnes of carbon has been estimated to be sequestered by the farm forestry plantations. The carbon sequestration potential for agroforestry practices is quite variable, depending on choice of trees and associated crops, the planting density and production/objective of the system. This is a potential option to add trees on the farmlands, alone or in association with crops. Table 12.10 summarizes these components.

Table 12.10: Components of forestry options

Options	*Land category*	*Potential area (million hectares)*	*Carbon pool (tons per hectare) at the end of 40 years*
Management	Dense forest	15.50	77
Enhanced regeneration	Marginally degraded land	9.42	171
	Totally degraded land	12.57	138
Plantation on private lands (including agroforestry/ farm forestry plantations)	Marginal farmlands and non-forest degraded land	24.17	83

Source: ADB, 1998.

The farmers owing to the added economic returns have almost accepted this new land management concept. This helps in making the agriculture sustainable too. The annual rate of growth of the forest trees on farmlands or under various agroforestry systems is comparatively higher than that under forests due to better management practices. This accelerates the wood production per unit area in a unit time.

Integrated Approach for Sustainable Development

To address multifarious challenges of sustainable development in context of future climatic change, agricultural planning has to ensure sufficient food production, employment generation and rural income without increasing the risk to the environment. It is generally difficult to identify such strategies when there are such potentially conflicting objectives. Information, therefore, needs to be generated to determine the consequences and trade-offs of different sets of policy aims on agricultural production and sustainability. Identification of economically viable optimal solutions should be based on consideration of the biophysical potential of the resources available and the socio-economic constraints.

A decision support system (DSS) has been developed at Indian Agricultural Research Institute to explore the window of opportunities for land use planning and food security of a region by integrating natural resource inventory, biophysical simulation of agricultural production potential, and socio-economic goals and constraints. This involves the use of GIS, remote sensing,

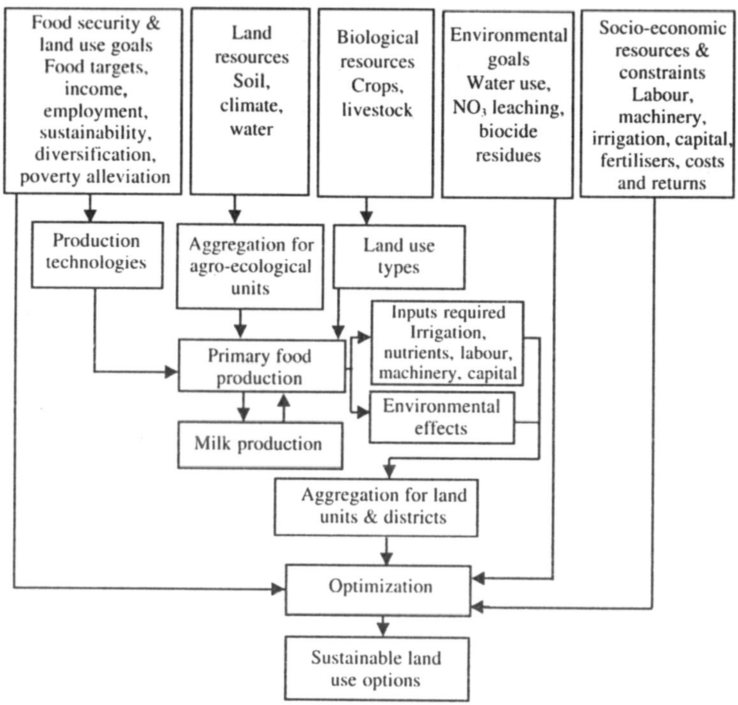

databases, surveys, crop and livestock models, and an optimisation model. The elements of the methodology are described in Fig. 3. The DSS involves close interaction with the stakeholders. The framework has been illustrated for the state of Haryana. Efforts are now being made to upscale this for the national level as well as to down scale this to the village and farm level.

REFERENCES

Aggarwal, P.K. and Sinha, S.K. (1993). Effect of probable increase in carbon dioxide and temperature on productivity of wheat in India. *Jour Agric Meteorol*, 48: 811-814

Aggarwal, P.K. and Talukdar, K.K. and Mall, R.K. (2000). "Potential yields of rice-wheat system in the Indo-Gangetic plains of India". Rice-Wheat Consortium Paper Series 10, New Delhi, India. RWCIGP, CIMMYT. p. 16.

Kropff, M.J., Teng, P.S., Aggarwal, P.K., Bouman, B., Bouman, J. and van Laar, H.H. (Eds.) (1996). *Application of Systems Approaches at the Field Level*. Volume 2. Kluwer Acad. Pub., Netherlands, p. 465.

Kumar, P., (1998). *Food Demand and Supply Projections for India*. Agricultural Economics Policy Paper 98-01. New Delhi: Indian Agricultural Research Institute, New Delhi.

Mooley, D.A. and G.B. Pant. (1981). Droughts in India over the last 200 years, their socio-economic impacts and remedial measures for them. In: *Climate and History—Studies in past climates and their impacts on man*. TML Wigley *et al.* Eds. Cambridge Univ. Preess. pp. 465-77.

Samra, J.S. and Pratap Narain. (1999). Soil and Water Conservation *in Fifty Years of Natural Resource Management Research*, Indian Council of Agricultural Research, New Delhi, pp. 145-76.

Sinha, S.K. (1995). Methane emission from rice padies: excellent methodology but poor extrapolation. *Curr. Sci.*, 68: 643-46.

Watson, R.T., Zinyowwerea, M.C. and Moss, R.H. (Eds). (1995). *Climate change 1995, impacts, adaptation and mitigation of climatic change: Scientific technical analysis*. IPCC II Report. Cambridge University Press, p. 880.

Watson, R.T., Zinyowera, M.C. and Moss, R.H. (Eds). (1998). *The regional impacts of climate change. An assessment of vulnerability*. IPCC II Report. Cambridge University Press, p. 517.

13

Role of Urban and Peri-Urban Agriculture in Sustainable Development of a Metropolitan City

A Case of Delhi

MADHUSREE MAZUMDAR

THE CONCEPT

Introduction

The process of urbanisation brings along with it a series of changes, both within and around a city, that initiate consequential developments, in the case of metropolitan city growth, there is a fast intrusion of urban activities into the agricultural landscape of the peri-urban areas, from the spill over of the expanding city population caused by rapid urbanisation, that changes the occupational structure and the landuse pattern of the urban fringe, creating both positive and negative impacts on agricultural practices. While the physical expansion of the city reduces the proportion of land under traditional agriculture and the grain crops, population growth enlarges the urban market, which gives a boost to the production of horticultural and other perishable food products as an economic activity in the urban and the peri-urban areas, to benefit from the proximity to the city's market.

Within the city, urban growth generates a wide range of employment that helps in improving the urban economy. But it also brings along with it physical congestion that manifests into the negative features of housing, utility and infrastructure shortages that cause pollution and instantiation, leading to innumerable public health problems. Moreover, the city becomes congested, when the open "lung" spaces are devoured by the increasing number of buildings and non-agricultural activities to contain the ever-expanding population, which tends to eliminate the greenery/vegetation that contributes to the assimilative capacity, thereby reducing the city's capacity to absorb waste. It also spoils the city's aesthetics.

In India, this deterioration in the quality of urban life is further accentuated by a continuous influx of uneducated and unskilled migrants (in search of employment) from the rural areas, who add to the woes of urban settlements by putting more pressure on the urban system through their informal existence and employment that avoids taxation and thereby their contribution to the city's maintenance revenue. However, some of these unemployed migrants with agricultural backgrounds, take to urban agriculture (UA) by cultivating the marginal/unused lands within the city, while awaiting regular employment and until such time till they acquire the technical skills of non-agricultural jobs. It has been observed that this process of income generation not only helps the low-income groups to earn a living, it also assists households to enhance the food security, either through an increase in income, or through additional nutrition derived directly from the use of the produce. Moreover, UA helps cities to improve its aesthetics and their waste assimilative capacity, both of which are highly valuable for a good quality of life.

Therefore, in the present day context of increasing urban poverty and pollution caused by rapid urbanisation, UA is being considered as a benefactor to city management: in growing more food for the ever expanding urban market, solving some of the unemployment/poverty problems by supplementing household income and/or food and by improving the environment through a natural process of assimilation by using solid and liquid waste (generated within a city) to promote horticulture and pisciculture. Moreover, UA makes good use of the underutilized, unutilized and all marginal lands within cities, thereby adding more value to such land. It is, therefore, hoped that all such measures will lead to poverty alleviation, improved socio-economic conditions and a better urban environment. A parallel phenomenon that is growing along with the cultivation of horticultural products in and around cities is the home processing and street vending of food as an income earning activity, and is, therefore, included in UA.

The Habitat II Conference of 1996 recognized urban agriculture as a realistic and desirable land use option in urban areas and as an integral part of the urban system. Urban agriculture was acknowledged for its potential role in increasing food security, employment and income generation, poverty alleviation, community resource development and conservation, waste management and environmental sustainability. The World Food Summit (FAO, 1996) had also recommended the inclusion of urban agriculture as a component in the food and nutrition policies. It is estimated that by the year 2005, 25-30 per cent of the world food production will be from urban areas, including nearly half of all vegetables, fish, meat and dairy products that are consumed in cities (Jac Smit, 1996).

India is self-sufficient in terms of food grain production for the country as a whole (*Times of India*, February 1999). But the World Bank reports that pockets of urban concentrations suffer from calorie deficiency more than their rural counterparts. Infact, urban dwellers pay much more for their food than the rural people. Therefore, a very large proportion of the income of the urban poor is spent on food. The UNICEF tells us that one-sixth of the world population suffers from inadequate diet. The UNCHS projects that between 1990 and 2020, urban population will increase from 45 per cent to 65 per cent (Jac Smit, 1996) of the total world population. Such effects of rapid urbanisation has led to a growing consciousness to utilise the marginal lands within cities and in peri-urban areas that otherwise lie fallow, to augment household income and nutrition by promoting urban agriculture, especially the highly priced and/or perishable products that can be cultivated intensively in small plots of land.

By definition, urban and peri-urban agriculture is food and fuel grown in and around cities directly for the urban market. It means growing crops, raising livestock or otherwise harvesting edible produce (for humans and animals) in urban spaces, or areas adjacent to it, for sale within the city. It also includes cultivation of crops and animal husbandry on roadsides, along railroads, in gardens, backyards of houses, on rooftops, within utilities rights of way, in vacant plots of industrial estates, on the grounds of large institutions and along rivers (often using recycled urban solid and liquid organic wastes as resources); aquaculture in tanks, ponds and rivers; orchards and vineyards and street trees and even floriculture, food processing and food vending within the confines of the city or in the periphery.

Urban agriculture normally produces goods for the daily urban market. It does not specialize in cereal crops. But that does not mean that UA does not cultivate grain crops at all. For instance, fields of mustard, wheat and millets are visible on the floodplain of the river Yamuna in Delhi, though water melons, flowers, spinach and vegetables are more common. These vegetables are sold in the informal "farmer's markets", close to their areas of cultivation. UA is typically intensive cultivation of high yielding crops, producing 3 to 15 times as much per hectare than common rural methods, dominated by vegetable crops. It is considered to be more organic and sustainable than rural agriculture for two reasons: first, because the urban waste which is used as fertiliser is more abundant than rural waste and second, because the urban farmer's labour intensive methods use less land and water per unit of production than when agriculture is carried out as an industry (Jac Smit,1996).

The scale of urban agricultural production in the world is far above common perceptions. It was estimated that in 1993 between 15 to 20 per cent of the world's food was produced in the urban areas (Jac Smit,1996). The project, "Cities Feeding People", (IDR, 1991) Cites how Chinese cities are self-sufficient in perishable food crops and how UA is spreading in Asia. Ganapathy (1983) mentions that only 6 sq. metres of area can produce all the vegetables needed for a family of four. Other studies also indicate nutritional self-reliance.

Apart from promoting market gardening, livestock production and aquaculture that augment the food supply of a city, urban agriculture (which includes the growing of trees) can also contribute to the quality of the urban environment as an excellent assimilator of solid, liquid and gaseous waste. It can even help to reduce the cost of waste processing through the use of recycled solid and liquid organic waste that not only helps to fertilise the soil for UA, but is also a good management practice that can augment the cost of waste processing and disposing by the municipality through the sale of manure to the city farmers. City management, therefore, has the twin benefits of fertiliser production and cost reduction from the use of city waste for UA. Urban Development Authorities that undertake avenue plantations, development and maintenance of parks, institutional areas and green belts, nursery raising, etc. to improve the city's environment and the assimilative capacity and aesthetics, can also make use of such benefits to reduce the overall cost of city maintenance.

Practising UA is also a very efficient way of managing land. It utilises "idle" space under public possession or not suited for building; lands that can have an interim use while awaiting the assigned development within a city or in the periphery and community lands and household yards that can be utilised for vegetation (often as a pastime or for aesthetics), thus bringing value to the otherwise unused land, even if it is of a temporary nature, thereby contributing to the city's economy. By doing so, UA reduces the public costs of land maintenance and simultaneously yields benefits from the productive use of land.

There is also a belief that there can be a major reduction in the cost of food production from the savings on refrigeration and trucking, which is not required if perishable food is grown within short distances from the consumers. Besides, the entry of less number of trucks into the city may also mean a saving of energy and a reduction in air pollution from motor vehicles. Less number of vehicles also mean less pressure on the city's infrastructure and maintenance costs. Therefore, the positive externalities arising from UA are many: the improvement in the air assimilative capacity, the use of recycled bio-degradable waste that helps in reducing the solid waste management cost and at the same time helps in enriching the soil, the use of liquid waste after an initial treatment, economic use of valuable under-utilised urban land and the enhancing of the aesthetics of open areas used as lung spaces within cities. Thus, metropolitan cities of developing countries, in their quest for management solutions, are looking upon urban and peri-urban agriculture as a panacea for many of their urban ills. Hence urban agriculture, of late, is being recommended as a good management practice for cities, to bring about social and economic change and physical environmental improvements. In a country like India where almost 60 per cent of the population lives in large cities (of more than one lakh population) and about

30-40 per cent of a city's population is in slums, UA can assume importance as a catalyst for environmental improvement, employment generation, and poverty alleviation.

Therefore, even though agriculture and urbanisation are seen as typically conflicting activities, UA is increasingly being recognised as a realistic and desirable landuse option in urban areas and as an integral part of the urban system. Hence, interest in UA is growing very rapidly. There are numerous examples of urban farming throughout the world, in countries like the USA, Canada, China (with roughly 40 per cent of the urban jobs in agriculture). Hong Kong, Singapore, Papua New Guinea, Zambia, Kenya, Mozambique (the capital Maputo has 30 per cent in UA), etc. which testify the benefits derived from UA. In Berlin as many as 50,000 persons rent land to produce crops. In Dar es Salaam 68 per cent of the city workers produced food in 1988. The common belief is that the future of UA is in Asia. Rightly so, as urbanisation is more rapid in the Asian countries today, than in the West (Internet Information, 1998).

But it is to be remembered that UA is transient in character, as it is practised mostly on marginal/underutilised/transitional lands. Therefore, urban developments can obliterate such agriculture both within the city, as well as in the peri-urban areas. On the periphery of a city, UA can be pushed farther away from the centre of the city because of urban expansion. Therefore, what is more important in city management is the phenomenon of UA, rather than its spatial ramifications. For neither can city limits remain constant, nor can UA be restrained by spatial determinism. What needs to be emphasised about UA is that as a concept it is very different from the traditional crop cultivation, even though it is developing as an economic activity.

At a time when sustainable development is a global quest, city improvement through agriculture can become an additional instrument for attaining sustainability. It is being increasingly recognised that economic development has to be balanced by social development. Both stand to gain in urban agriculture, which improves income and promotes community resource development. However, it is to be noted that no city can be self-sufficient in food in absolute terms, as cities are concentrations of non-agricultural economic activities and therefore, depend on rural agricultural productivity for sustenance. At the same time, no agriculture can survive without an urban market.

This paper will study the concept, characteristics and practices of UA and examine the newly found role of urban agriculture in city management, pertaining to landuse planning, aesthetics, employment generation, poverty alleviation, food security, waste assimilation and the socio-economic changes and identify the stakeholders influencing UA and city management. It will then assess the status of UA in Delhi *vis-a-vis* city development and find out the influence of urbanisation on UA and *vice versa*. Finally, the study will discuss the attention given to UA by the Indian plans and policies to improve the urban environment.

Development of UA

Historical development of UA reveals that it is a global phenomenon. The traditional practice of UA came to supplement the family diet. It was developed with the help of recycled biological waste that could be used for small farms demanding low investments and operating costs. UA was initially a twin process of market gardening and waste assimilation. The Chinese cities are the best examples of highly productive urban waste recycle technology for agriculture. In fact even today this technology is being practiced in cities like Hong Kong, Singapore and many other Asian cities. In the wetlands of Kolkata (erstwhile Calcutta) sewage is being recycled for aquaculture from which the city raises one-third of its demand for fish (Ghosh and Furedy, 1983). Moreover, human waste is also being used for renewing the soil fertility to grow vegetables in China and Kolkata.

In the initial years of development UA was basically a concept of poverty alleviation. But subsequently the focus widened to include many environmental and socio-economic issues of urban management. However, while in the East it is mostly associated with employment generation and public health concerns, in the West UA is considered to be more recreational, with home and community gardens supplementing the family diets and at the same time providing leisure. The main driving force behind the development of UA in India is the market value of agricultural products and its income earning capacity. In developing countries UA is being considered as a panacea for creating employment and food security. It has still not been seriously considered for urban planning, as city planners and policy makers have biases in using urban land and water bodies in and around cities for UA. Planners attach a higher value to urban land supporting housing and industries, than agriculture. In a city, every piece of land is intensively used for non-agricultural activities; though some of the more recent policies on environment are trying to promote urban forestry to increase the air assimilative capacity within cities.

In European countries like Holland and UK, UA has always been an element of urban planning, although mainly with a narrow conception: home gardening. However, the concept of "local initiatives" emerging from the Rio Conference has stimulated many countries to promote UA for multifunctional use of urban spaces, combining recreation, production and environmental functions. UA is also being suggested to strengthen rural-urban linkages, of which UA could be a part. Also, the economic role of green spaces within cities is now being valued much more after the UNCED conference of 1992.

In Eastern Europe, the spontaneous development of UA is dramatic since the collapse of the collective doctrine. Where the formal sector production is stagnating and incomes of urban people are declining, the interest in urban farming activities is booming in a large number of countries and cities. As in the developing countries, UA is considered here for employment substitution in the absence of organised sector jobs (Internet, 1998).

Farming techniques too have got diversified over the years into hydroponics (using combinations of nutrient solutions in limited household space), rooftop gardening, shelf poultry and mushroom culture and many other innovative ways of producing more food in limited (urban) space, where land is a scarce resource. To cite an example, Delhi has a Kitchen Garden Association for amateur growers, to learn about the techniques and cultivaars appropriate for cities.

UA has had plenty of support from the "development cooperatives", like the UNICEF, FAO, IDRC, World Bank, OXFAM, ADB, ODA, GTZ, UNDP, USAID and CARE. As a result, the developed countries witnessed a resurgence of farming in the cities in the 1970s (Jac Smit, 1996). The most typical activities those days were home and school gardens. The UNICEF, FAO and many aid organizations supported community gardens, with the prime objective of improving the family diet. Unfortunately, most of these programmes failed because of local preferences and priorities.

In the 1980s a crucial role was played by the "Food Energy Nexus" project of the United Nations University to promote UA. The IDRC too got engaged in a large number of studies on urban food distribution systems and food security and the use of waste as a resource for UA. The USAID supported the Street Food Project, emphasising the importance of locally produced informal marketing of food products. The UNDP too started the Healthy Cities project, integrating some aspects of UA. This programme is still continuing.

The support for UA continued in the 1990s as well. In 1992 the UNDP established the Urban Agriculture Advisory Committee, which in the following year led to the establishment of the Support Group on Urban Agriculture (SGUA) with the participation of various agencies and stakeholders. The SGUA subsequently established the Global Facility on Urban Agriculture (GFUA) in 1996 to stimulate activities in UA by the national and local governments, NGOs, and agencies for international and bilateral development cooperation and the direct involvement of the local stakeholders (urban farmers, neighbourhood organisations, small entrepreneurs, etc.). The GFUA seeks to counteract roadblocks to UA and intends to actively support innovative action and research.

The Agenda 21 of the Rio Conference also emphasised the need for innovative and integrated strategies in urban landuse planning that took into account environmental and social issues and employment for the urban poor, especially small scale food production and food processing. Agenda 21 also recommended more funds for innovative research in re-cycling and re-use of urban waste, all of which are very conducive for UA. Hence UA is gaining importance today in the context of "sustainable habitat" and "ecological cities".

Thus, an overall experience has been that UA is being favoured for its multiple use of urban space in the developed countries and because of the possibility of decentralisation of urban waste management, whereby waste can be turned into resource at the local level. In the North, UA is also given importançe for conserving energy and preventing pollution. In the developing countries, UA is prized for generating employment, supplementing household income and contributing to food nutrition and easy accessibility of food for the poor. Here waste assimilation and pollution control is only an externality. Hence UA is being encouraged in the South as an economic activity, much more than in the North.

UA in Asia and other developing countries is being practised to resolve local issues and problems. While in some countries the local government has taken the responsibility of promoting/ encouraging UA to solve some of their management and economic constraints, in others UA is purely a local initiative to cope with poverty, waste management and aesthetics. With rapid urbanisation and population expansion, Asian cities are increasingly adopting different UA strategies to solve the basic problems of poverty, employment and waste assimilation like in Lea (Papua New Guinea), Shanghai, Hong Kong, Singapore, Metro Manila, Dar es Salaam Inner City and many more cities.

In India, urban agriculture is being practised by various actors with different intents. The garbage farms of Kolkata and the vegetable plots on the narrow strips of land along the railway lines in Mumbai are developed by growers and slum dwellers for commercial purposes. For the fisheries of Kolkata the sewage lagoons satisfy one-third of the city's market demand for fish. In India most of the small scale dairy enterprises (that supplement the public provision of milk) and the poultry units are developed in and around cities. Again, organisations like the COCO in Bangalore and Mother Dairy in Delhi, collect and market the products through consumer outlets. Moreover, individual households also grow vegetables, fruits, trees and flowers in backyard gardens and/or rooftops for home consumption.

The Potential Role of Agriculture in City Management

A study of the definition, concept, characteristics, practices and the possible benefits of UA lead to envisaging a multi-dimensional role of UA in city management. As mentioned earlier, the different sectors of development that can be promoted by UA are: food security, poverty alleviation, employment, economic development, community participation and social upliftment, land use planning and land regeneration, assimilation of solid, liquid and gaseous waste, environmental change including microclimate and aesthetics and recreation. However, the potential of UA to improve the city's economy and environment, as also the socio-economic status of the citizens from employment in UA and better access to food and nutrition and thereby a good quality of life, is intimately connected to the process and extent of urbanisation, its impacts and the methods used for city management. Effective practice of UA will depend upon factors like the nature of city growth and administration, plan-provisions for urban expansions that influence land use and activity zones, the institutional support available, the city's economy including the extent of poverty and unemployment, the quantity and quality of infrastructure support and so on. To consider all these, a systematic approach will have to be adopted to integrate them into an efficient city management plan, including an environment management system. A brief idea as to how UA can help in the different aspects of city management and human welfare is given below.

Food Security

Urbanisation creates a demand for both the quantity and the quality of food. A logical phenomenon is that the demand for any food item increases with population expansion. Moreover, metropolitan cities tend to diversify needs because of their large population base and the exposure to a variety of cultures. Hence with large concentrations of population, cities form lucrative markets for farmers and traders. Two advantages derived by agriculture within cities are an abundant supply of labour and a ready urban market. This phenomenon follows the simple demand-supply logistics that help in determining the nature of UA. Some of the foodstuffs in demand are of high value, from which farmers can earn large profits. The demand for special food items in metropolitan cities is changing the pattern of agriculture in and around them. For example, the cultivation of mushrooms, strawberry, broccoli etc. is gaining grounds in the Indian metropolitan cities, to cater to a newly created market supported by the diverse culinary arts that have invaded these cities. India is self-sufficient in terms of food grains that are grown in the rural areas. Hence cities produce high value vegetables, fruits, livestock, fish and other perishable products that are difficult to transport from a distance. Given official support, UA can help in supplying food to urban dwellers in many ways: (i) as income to buy food (perhaps of better quality and quantity), (ii) provide more nutrition from the direct use of UA products, (iii) provide highly perishable foodstuffs that are also highly priced, and (iv) offer a range of exotic food products that have developed with modernisation.

Poverty Alleviation

In India, where rural to urban migration, in search of jobs, is a common practice, UA works as a surrogate employment until such migrants get absorbed into the formal job market. It has been observed that agriculture is considered to be a temporary solution because of its low value in the job market, where skilled jobs are better paid. The value estimation is done in the context of the fact that agriculture is generally not permitted in land that is put to urban use. Therefore cultivation of crops is transitional and impermanent and is not considered as a stable job opportunity and a permanent solution to unemployment. For, UA has always been considered by economists as an externality. Therefore not much attention is given or investments made for agriculture within a city by the planning/development authorities. However, it certainly covers a risk for the poor.

Employment

As the market for food expands, the scope for employment is bound to rise. The issue here is whether employment in the food industry should also be included in UA. If the term UA is used in a broad sense, then food processing within the city can be considered as UA (as discussed in the Introduction). However, even if only the growing of food products is considered to be UA, employment in UA will still indicate a rise over the years because of the sheer need to provide more for a growing population.

The growing of food crops within the city by the poor and the marginal workers add to the job opportunities of the poor, who do not have to invest on land as UA is carried out mostly on marginal lands or as a transitional occupation. But to provide for a growing population, UA is carried out as a business proposition, especially for the highly perishable products that need to be raised close to the market. As mentioned earlier, such products earn large profits for traders and agriculturists and employs both the rich and the poor.

Economic Development

Though agriculture is a contradiction to urban activities, producing food within the city is supposed to improve the food security situation, as cities can become more self-reliant. This does not mean that food cannot be obtained from distant sources. Ideally, if a city is able to supply large proportions of its needs in vegetables, fruits, livestock and fish (that is, those food items which are highly perishable) from within its own precincts, it inculcates a capacity to conserve energy by shortening the distance between the points of production and consumption, saves on storage and transport losses, avoids pollution from vehicular movement (that otherwise leads to health and crop losses) and promotes employment and economic self-sufficiency. The additional urban production improves the accessibility to food or income for the poor urban families and often brings down the costs of food. Saving on food expenditures translate into a significant portion of the family income becoming available for other non-food expenditures. Urban agriculture cannot only reduce dependency on inputs from outside the city, but also generate more efficient use of resource flows within the city, and bring about reduction and re-use of waste flows (water and biodegradable solid waste) whenever possible.

Besides providing affordable food to the citizens, UA fosters other factors like proximity to markets and consumers, efficient use of land and urban solid and liquid waste, management of animal waste, reduction of public costs for land maintenance or municipal services and employment generation for the poor and/ or the marginal workers, all of which promote overall development and thereby the city's economy. In fact, UA has already been acknowledged for its potential role in increasing food security, employment and income generation and environmental sustainability in Habitat II at Istanbul in June 1996.

Community Participation and Social Upliftment

It has been observed that in cities, which otherwise inculcate heterogeneity, farming helps in community development and building a self-sufficient system of growth by organising homogeneous groups. Besides, farming as an exercise is beneficial for physical and mental health (Joe Howe & Paul Wheeler, 1999).

Farming also supplements income and the family diet and thereby fosters socio-economic upliftment.

Landuse Planning and Land Regeneration

Urban agriculture *per se* is a paradoxical phenomenon; for conceptually agriculture is the prerogative of the rural areas and its inclusion in the urban development plans is considered to be backward (Yeung, 1985). Hence, in India, practically all development assistance for agriculture and forest is mostly confined to rural programmes. Thus urban agriculture is deprived of any plan support (in India) and is considered to be an incompatible landuse, unless used as buffer zones between built areas for assimilation of pollution, especially in the form of lung spaces. Within a city the maintenance of parks and roadside trees is normally the responsibility of the horticulture department of the municipality or that of the development authority. However, within the city urban forests are said to "absorb" pollution much better than agricultural/horticultural crops. Hence, its promotion within the city needs proper examination of land values and benefits, for economic viability.

Assimilation of Solid, Liquid and Gaseous Waste

As cities grow, chances of environmental deterioration rise with population congestion. In the metropolitan cities of India there is a virtual breakdown of the infrastructure system because of the overuse of utilities without augmenting them with population expansion. As a result, pollution is rampant. For example, in Delhi the MCD collects only 70 per cent of the municipal waste (NIUA, 1998). Moreover, with the expansion of the city size, a large number of vehicles are added every year, which creates heavy pollution. In Delhi, pollution from motor vehicles contributes about 64 per cent of the total air pollution.

UA contributes towards improving the air quality of a city by enhancing its assimilative capacity through city/social forestry and/or by developing other green spaces that would act as lung spaces for congested conditions/areas. A study by CPCB explains how "jamun" trees are good assimilators of lead from the air (CPCB, 1984). The recent inclusion of a list of trees, in the revised

Master Plan of Delhi, to be appropriately grown in the different parts of the city based on soil and climatic conditions, indicates the recognition by city planners of the importance of trees in enhancing the assimilative capacity of air. It is said that a sugar maple tree along a roadway removes in one growing season 60mg of cadmium, 140mg of chromium, 820mg of nickel and 5200mg of lead from the environment. In fact UA can use pollution resistant species of vegetation to improve the air and the soil quality. Moreover, there is 7db noise reduction per 100ft of forest due to trees reflecting and absorbing sound energy.

Environmental Change, Including Microclimate

Since UA helps in digesting waste, environmental conditions are bound to improve. UA contributes to environmental change in several ways: by encouraging the use of partially processed solid and liquid biodegradable waste and by assimilating air pollution with the help of trees. Temperatures tend to reduce with the growth of trees, which also act as a windscreen when the wind velocity is high. UA also takes care of public health concerns. Moreover, by providing employment, it improves the socio-economic conditions of the poor that lead to a better quality of life.

Aesthetics and Recreation

Home gardening has the twin benefits of recreation and food security. A common example of it is the allotment gardens of UK and USA that develop into recreational activity promoting public health. Landscaping and gardening of public spaces is also very pleasing. It can be done within institutional campuses, in residential neighbourhoods, along roads and open spaces for beautification. The city government often undertakes the planting of trees or development of gardens, which forms part of UA. Thus UA can beautify a city, as well as contribute to recreational facilities.

The Stakeholders

The role of any planning or management "instrument" (if UA is to be considered as one) cannot be assessed without understanding the involvement of the stakeholders in the process of development. Moreover, the role will depend upon the issues to be resolved. In India, any development normally involves many agencies of management and administration. As a result, overlapping and duplication of work is a much repeated accusation for urban management, where because of the enormity of the task, a range of organisations are set up to take care of different aspects of development. Often the duties of these organisations are not very well defined, to avoid duplication and conflicts. Hence, it is important to clarify the role of the various agencies and the stakeholders in attempting to understand what the management process would culminate to be, in the development and practice of UA. Placed below is a table giving the details of the involvement of the different stakeholders in UA, to ruminate over the existing status to assist future decisions.

Table 13.1: Stakeholders for UA

Role in City Management	*Actors*	*Beneficiaries*
Food Security	Poor citizens. Farmers (in agriculture & allied activities), neighbourhood organisations, small entrepreneurs	Entrepreneurs, Traders, Employees, Consumers (especially low income groups), the State
Poverty Alleviation	Poor Migrants, Marginal Workers, Farmers, Unemployed	The Poor, City, State
Employment	Farmers, Providers, Entrepreneurs, Traders, Food Industries	Poor, Unemployed, City, State
Assimilation of Waste	Municipality, Pollution Control Boards, Department of Industries, Farmers	Municipality, Farmers, Citizens
Landuse Planning	Town Planning, Development Agencies	City Managers, Residents
Economic Development	Business (producers, retailers, wholesalers), Farmers	Low Income Groups, City, State
Social Change	Farmers, Unemployed, Poor Migrants	Communities, Local Government
Aesthetics	City Planners, Households, Municipality, Institutions	City Managers, Citizens

For any policy change to take place to promote UA, all the actors mentioned below will have to be involved. Besides, beneficiaries too need to understand their role in supporting UA.

For ultimately it is the community/actors who will have to support a new phenomenon that is being introduced, if they are to benefit from it.

The Issues

The two dominant issues emerging out of debates regarding UA as an instrument for planning and management are:

- Who benefits from UA as (i) a source of food security, (ii) as an urban industry, (iii) as a landuse option, (iv) as a method of waste management, (v) as a devise for pollution control and (vi) as an environmental intervention?
- How significant are these benefits? To which extent does it contribute to city development and management?

Moreover, if UA is to be regarded as a planning or a management instrument, then whose responsibility should UA be? Should it be the concern of the Department of Agriculture, or must it be administered by the municipality? Besides, if UA is to benefit different aspects of management, what kind of institutional arrangement should be made?

There is a long list of benefits that accrue from UA, such as efficient and economic use of marginal lands within cities, enhancement of aesthetics, increase in the waste assimilative capacity, employment and income generation, making waste processing more cost-effective, improving the overall environment and so on. But it is not to be forgotten that UA can also create problems like uneconomic use of land, incompatible use of urban land, contamination of the soil from fertilizers leading to pollution of the underground water, contamination of crops from urban air pollution, shortage of water for irrigation and so on.

Hence, the planning issues raised are:

- What should be the nature and extent of UA to be carried out within cities?
- What is the extent of succour brought to the poor in terms of income or food security?
- FAO (1996) estimates that by the year 2005, 25-30 per cent of the world's food production will be from urban areas.

Judging by such estimates, how dependable is urban agriculture for attaining self-sufficiency in food for cities, especially when it is of a transient nature.

- Is UA significant enough to influence food import regulations?
- Should sale of products be restricted to the city only, as per the definition of UA?
- Does UA actually reduce the cost of waste management or land management?
- Does UA help in reducing food prices by saving on fuel, refrigeration and transportation, or is it a myth?
- Is UA a good substitute for other urban jobs?
- Should UA compete with other industrial categories if it is to assume a socio-economic role?

Much of the benefits from UA will depend upon the strategies adopted for environment management. If UA is to be used as an instrument of planning, UA will have to evolve methods and practices conducive to city management and to improve the quality of life for the citizens. However, the anticipated benefits from UA are still required to be proved in India.

THE CASE STUDY OF DELHI

Population Distribution and Expansion

A case study of Delhi gives a brief insight into the nature of UA that develops in an Indian metropolis with urbanisation. While facts and figures reflect the status, much depends on policies, plans, physiography, location and the infrastructural support given to the city.

Delhi is the third largest city and the capital of India. The Union Territory of Delhi (DUT) has a population of 12,791,458 (2001 census), spread over an area of 1483 sq.kms. The city has been a focal point of politics and administration from historical times. Modern Delhi is the ninth capital after Indraprastha, Mehrauli, Lalkot, Siri, Tughlaqabad, Firozabad, Shahjahanabad and New Delhi. Along with the changing status, the city's area has been redefined by each ruler. Today, Delhi has grown so large, that it not only encompasses all the capitals of the past, but it has even expanded beyond them. Delhi has been growing at an average rate of 50 per cent per decade since Independence (Table 13.2). This pace has been too fast for the Municipal Corporation of Delhi (MCD) to manage the city. Of the three local governments that constitute Delhi, the New Delhi Municipal Committee (NDMC) and the Cantonment Board were able to cope with the population increase because of the restrictions they impose on migration. As a result of this regulation, MCD had to take the population pressure that created the demand for infrastructure that could not be met because of resource constraints and due to the enormity of the task.

Delhi has spread on all sides because of its inland location, with no physical barriers preventing its growth. As a result, the city forms the core of the different administrative jurisdictions that were drawn with time to facilitate urban management (Map). Despite provisions made (in the form of the DMA and the National Capital Region) to de-densify Delhi, 90 per cent of the urban population still lives within the National Capital Territory (Table 13.3), which is proper Delhi. However, the process of dispersal has just begun. Though the total volume of urban population is still increasing, its proportion to the NCT is on the decline. Such a phenomenon indicates suburbanisation. In the case of Delhi, the suburbs are growing in the adjoining areas of U.P. and Haryana, especially in and around the towns of Ghaziabad, NOIDA and Gurgaon. Indicators of congestion reveal densification

Table 13.2: Decadal Variation in Population of the DUT

Year	*Population*	*Decadal Variation*	*Percentage Decadal Growth*
1901	405819	–	–
1911	413851	8032	1.98
1921	488452	74601	18.03
1931	636246	147794	30.26
1941	917939	281693	44.27
1951	1744072	826133	90.00
1961	2658612	914540	52.44
1971	4065698	1407086	52.93
1981	6220406	2154708	53.00
1991	9420644	3200238	51.45

Source: NIUA: Urban Environmental Maps, 1994.

Table 13.3: Urban Population of Delhi

Year	*Urban Population*	*Percentage to Total*	*Percentage Increase*
1901	214115	51	-
1911	237944	56	11
1921	304420	62	28
1931	447442	70	47
1941	695686	76	55
1951	1437134	82	107
1961	2359408	88	64
1971	3647023	90	55
1981	5768200	93	58
1991	8427083	90	46

Source: Government of National Capital Territory of Delhi, 1997. (Please note that since the source of the above data is different, there is a slight variation from the census figures.)

of Delhi, Gurgaon and Faridabad, pointing to an ongoing process of rapid urbanisation of the DMA.

Rural-Urban Fringe of Delhi and Urban Agriculture

As a result of the incessant flow of people into the city, leading to an expansion of the urban areas, the rural areas are decreasing. But interestingly enough, the rural population is not declining. In fact, statistics indicate a rise in population congestion even in the rural areas of the NCT. But the congestion in the rural areas of the adjoining districts of Delhi is reducing, indicating a rural to urban migration from the neighbouring districts into Delhi.

The rural-urban fringe of Delhi is not a concentric zone around the city, but is polygonal in shape, following the axial transportation routes (S. Nangia, 1976). But while in 1976 this fringe was 17 km. away from the city centre, in 1998 it was 25-40 km. away. The fringe is also influenced by the nature of the urban developments in the different directions. The physiography too determines the extent and form of the rural-urban fringe, such as the lowlying and floodable areas in the eastern part of the Yamuna river, the salt pans/sand dunes and depressions of the west and the south-west and so on. A survey conducted by SEED (an NGO) identifies a peri-urban belt where 20-40 per cent of the population is engaged in agriculture. The proportion of agriculture employment is influenced by the distance from the city core and the available transportation facilities.

The Master Plan of Delhi-2001 suggests a two-pronged strategy to accommodate the 12.2 million population estimated for the year 2001: one is to increase the population holding capacity of the area within the urbanisable limits of 1981; and the other is to extend the urbanisable limits further. While the existing urban limits (DUA-81) are estimated to accommodate about 8.2 million people, the balance population will require an additional 18,000-24,000 ha. Hence to accommodate the growing urban population the adjoining rural areas will have to be included within the city. However, with the recent decision taken to increase the area of the NCR (The Times of India) such predicaments can be taken care of.

Urban agriculture is a paradoxical phenomenon. Since agriculture is the prerogative of the rural areas, practically all development assistance for agriculture and forest is confined to rural programmes. However, in the Master Plans of Delhi (in both the original and the revised), provision for agriculture does exist. The Master Plan proposes a system of linked open spaces and district parks, including existing orchards and fruit gardens which should be interconnected by green linkages and smaller local parks penetrating through residential and work areas. But this has been done only with a view to providing "lung" spaces.

The Zoning Regulations have also permitted the development of non-commercial farms, agricultural gardens, nurseries and greenhouses in "residential" zones for the purpose of providing buffer zones between the city and its agricultural surroundings, to protect the area from pollution (in Use Zone A.1). Besides, an Agricultural Green Belt has been proposed for Delhi, with permission for uses such as: agriculture, horticulture, dairy, poultry, farming, dairying and milk chilling centres, piggery, nursery, forest, orchards, farm houses and their accessory buildings and uses within one-acre plot area (Use Zone A.2). But though the Master Plan permits only non-commercial use in the Use Zone A.1, market gardening and cultivation of rare species of vegetables, flowers, etc. are often carried out for commercial purposes, thereby promoting UA. Farmhouse market gardening very often supply the urban market with exotic items that are also highly perishable. Hence growing of such horticultural products are beneficial for the urban market.

Landuse

With increasing population, more land is being transferred to non-agricultural use. The area under such use has risen from 34,207 ha in 1970-71 to 57,791 ha in 1993-94, indicating an increase of about 69 per cent in a period of almost 25 years (Table 13.4). There is also an increase in the barren uncultivable land over the years, which normally occurs because of building construction and seepage of pollutants. It has been observed that pollution from urban use often renders cultivable land unfit for crops. If care is taken to protect such land from deterioration, it can be temporarily used for UA, while waiting to be developed.

There was a massive rise (of about 222 per cent) in the cultivable wasteland between 1970-71 and 1993-94 indicating that the newly acquired agricultural land for urban development is often left fallow for a long time and is not put to good economic use. It is actually this land that can be used for urban agriculture while waiting to be developed. In fact, even the fallow lands within the city can also be used after enriching the soil, until such time when development takes place. The dilemma here is more with regard to administration, as the agencies to which such land may belong may not be in a position to lease out the land. Of course, it is not uncommon for such land to be put to agriculture, especially if the land belongs to public sector undertakings. But formal records of such use are rare. However, in many cities this land is leased out to the original farmers from whom the land had been acquired, in order to raise the productivity of the land while in waiting. It also helps in employing people.

A decrease in the total crop area and the net sown area is also indicative of the gradual devouring of the cultivable land for the purpose of urban development. A decline in the area sown more than once (which indicates intense use of land) also points to a deterioration of the soil conditions, or a change in the soil structure, as a result of which farmers are unable to cultivate throughout the year. However, with efforts made to increase the area sown more than once by enriching the soil, UA can be promoted. The forest cover and the pastures, that are also declining with rapid urbanisation, can be improved and made more useful by planting such species of trees that will improve the waste assimilative capacity.

Table 13.4: Utilisation of Land in Delhi

(in hectares)

Land Classification	*1970-71*	*1980-81*	*1985-86*	*1986-87*	*1987-88*	*1988-89*	*1989-90*	*1990-91*	*1991-92*	*1992-93 (P)*	*1993-94 (P)*
Area According to village papers, Professional Survey	147612	147488	147488	147488	147488	147488	147488	147488	147488	147488	147488
Forests	1143	1434	1561	1561	1561	1561	1561	1561	1561	1561	1181
Area not available for cultivation	47314	52077	71330	68043	68310	69629	72191	74248	74953	78546	77279
(a) Land put to non-agricultural uses	34207	34248	60435	57662	57332	59930	62369	64562	63923	62962	57791
(b) Barren uncultivable land	13107	17829	10895	10381	10977	9699	9822	9687	11030	15585	19488
Other uncultivated land excluding fallow land	3602	2719	5456	11580	11244	11400	12523	12864	10074	11708	11387
(a) Permanent pastures and other grazing land	402	864	696	746	746	746	746	746	746	64	63
(b) Land under misc. tree crops	41	1064	1225	887	887	887	1267	1267	1470	1143	1143
(c) Cultivable waste land	3159	791	3535	9947	9610	9767	10510	10850	7858	10501	10181
Fallow land	15043	32707	12816	10112	15898	15258	12864	12864	11870	11800	11550
Net area sown	80510	58551	56324	56192	50474	49640	48349	48357	49030	43874	46091
Area sown more than once	36075	29048	25053	30381	18937	247447	22903	27882	16543	8196	14766
Total crop area	116585	87599	81377	86573	69411	77087	71252	76237	65573	52070	60857

(P) Projected

Source: District Census Handbook, 1991 and Delhi Statistical Handbook, 1995.

Map—Policy Zones

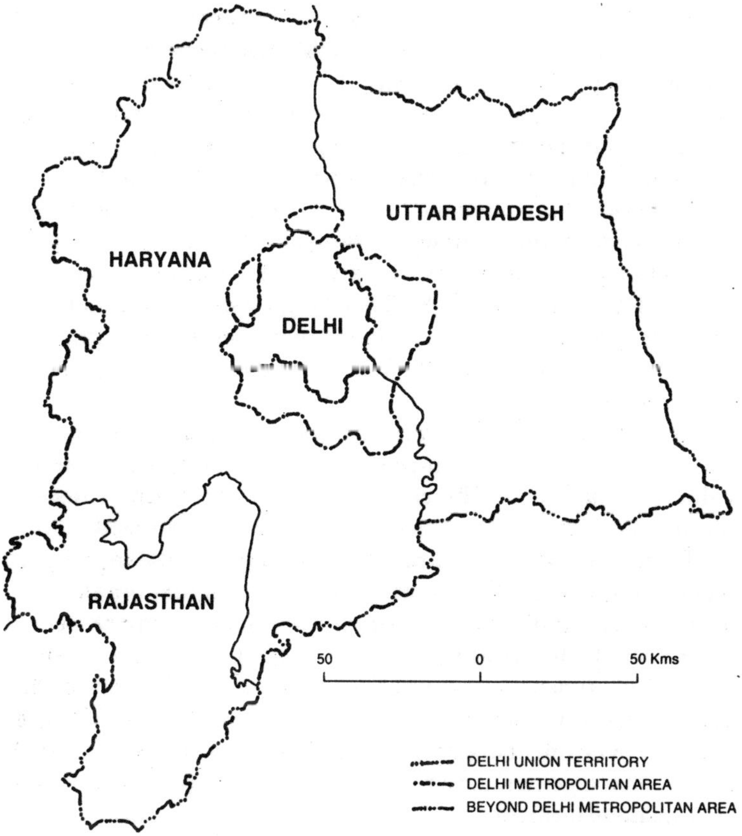

Agriculture

The NCT in 1994 had 60857ha of cropped area (latest data available), which was 41.26 per cent of the surveyed area of 147488ha. Within the overall urban landuse there were also the forest lands, pastures, areas with trees, fallow lands and the cultivable waste lands that are very often used for UA. These added up to another 16.35 per cent of the NCT. Besides, there are the water bodies and the vacant lands that can be used for UA. In fact apart from the cropped area, agriculture can also be practiced in the fallow, waste and vacant lands, thereby increasing the total area under agriculture. However, an estimate published by *The Times of India* on December 15, 1997, said that only about 1.2 per cent of the city's total income is generated on the farms. Given the proportion of land that can be used for UA, the income from such activity would be much more. The newspaper report also said that land under agriculture in Delhi is diminishing rapidly and is now almost half of what it used to be two decades ago. Table 13.4 also supports this statement. However, agriculture is by no means a closed chapter for the city government, which has embarked on a project to promote medicinal and aromatic plants in what is "rural" Delhi (SEEDS, 1998). These high value products have a thriving export market. Indian medicinal herbs are fetching fancy prices in the global market. The city government is probably concerned about the fact that unless farmers are assured of high returns, they would be inclined to sell off their lands for urban use that would fetch them premium prices because of the high value of urban land. The crucial boundary for change rests on productivity. If urban activities generate better revenues, then rural land is transformed into urban. That would mean more pressure on civic amenities, a larger army of jobless population and more shortages of utilities leading to more pollution and environmental deterioration. To avoid this situation, it is wise to produce high value crops that would strengthen the household income of the agriculturists and improve the city's economy. In fact, in this case, the city government appears to be enterprising enough to use UA as a means to generate more revenues for the city. Such a scheme also sustains farmers.

The crops that are generally grown in and around Delhi are:

1. wheat	6. bajra (millet)	11. potato	16. brinjal
2. spinach	7. rice	12. onion	17. coriander
3. moong	8. jowar (millet)	13. radish	18. mint
4. mustard	9. milk	14. flowers	19. turnip
5. sugarcane	10. tomato	15. cauliflower	20. gourd

Though foodgrains are grown, it is the horticultural products that are predominant. But comprehensive data on it is not available. There is no specific pattern regarding the area and production of the crops that are cultivated. A general observation is that the areas under different crops are not influenced by population expansion. However, there is an increase in the yield over the years. This certainly indicates an improvement in technology.

Most of the land holdings are of 1-2 and/or 2-3 hectares in size. The predominant pattern prevailing is that of small land holdings. The numbers of land holdings decrease with increase in size. Hence, the proportions of area in the larger categories are less than those in the smaller categories.

Two types of marketing systems are found in and around Delhi for horticultural products. The formal marketing system consists of three agencies, the Vegetable Traders Association, the Mother Dairy and the NAFED. These deal mostly with wholesale trade. Each has its own functional identity. While the Vegetable Traders Association is totally private in character, the Mother Dairy is a semi-government organisation, where products are bought directly from the producers and sold to the consumers through booths. NAFED on the other hand is a central agency dealing in minimising price levels. NAFED protects the interests of both the consumers and the producers.

The marketing channels for the small producers are somewhat different. They either sell their produce to the pre-harvest contractors and to nearby big producers, or even to local retailers. They normally avoid the transport cost that works out to be very high because of proximity. Hence they prefer to sell their produce to local contractors, merchants, or retailers to save on time, money and energy (Bharadwaj *et al.*, 1998). They are also not given the "*mandi*" facilities. Hence they often sell their produce informally within the city.

Delhi procures milk from different sources, such as the Mother Dairy, Delhi Milk Scheme (which are the two major suppliers), milk supplied by other states under different brand names like Saras, Paras, Nanak, Parag, etc. and the local small and marginal farmers doing animal husbandry. Generally, the procurement of milk is less than the demand. This gap is often met through the import of powder milk. Delhi's demand is roughly 25 lakh litres per day. The Mother Dairy and the Delhi Milk Scheme meet only 40 per cent of the city's requirement. The rest is met from local and other sources. The local milk/dairy industry is generally handled by marginal workers/farmers. The Department of Animal

Husbandry of the government has several schemes to promote and monitor the provision of milk and milk products. But most of these schemes are on a national basis. The government has also built good research institutions for dairy development all over the country.

Marketing of flowers follow a pattern akin to that of vegetables and fruits. But the entire marketing process is informal and thereby less regulated. The place for whole sale markets are self-determined by the traders (for example, in front of the State emporiums in Baba Kharak Singh Marg, Mehrauli, Janpath, etc.). Normally the agents bring the flowers from all over India, from where they are sold to retailers/wholesalers through another set of agents and middlemen. Being informal, there are no stalls assigned to the agents. Local flowers are present in very small quantities. Most of the flowers come from outside Delhi. Hence it is difficult to estimate the contribution of flowers from within Delhi.

Employment in Agriculture

The overall employment in Delhi is higher by 2-3 percentage points than the surrounding districts, because of better employment opportunities in the metropolis. However, the rural-urban bifurcation of the total workers indicates a reverse pattern for Delhi *vis-a-vis* the neighbouring districts. While urban workers are more in the capital, the adjoining districts have more of rural workers. It indicates that peri-urban Delhi is to a large extent agrarian, with a distance decay function influencing urban development (Nangia, 1976; Dwivedi, 1998). But a change is coming with time in the districts of Faridabad and Ghaziabad, where the proportion of urban workers is increasing (Table 13.5). These two districts have had considerable urban developments following the rapid urbanisation of Delhi. Gurgaon is also picking up in urban development.

An analysis of the industrywise employment data on agricultural activities (like cultivators, agricultural labour and those employed in livestock rearing, forestry and fishing) reveal a higher proportion of agricultural workers in Delhi than in the surrounding towns (Table 13.6). Such a pattern develops to serve a large urban market. The rising proportion of urban agricultural workers indicates the practice of urban and peri-urban agriculture, which is on the increase in the capital. This feature can be interpreted in many ways, such as:

- the need for more agricultural products because of an increasing demand from a larger market caused by urbanisation and concentration of people (especially livestock rearing for purposes of milk and meat).
- the increasing need for the employment of marginal/ unemployed workers to augment family income (indicating higher cost of living in cities).
- more rural-urban migration leading to extension of rural activities in the city.
- increasing poverty, unemployment and food insecurity leading to cultivation of even the marginal lands.
- lack of organised employment in large cities, forcing people to take up informal employment.

Though certain kinds of animal husbandry are prohibited in the city, it is actually the city that has more requirements for animal products than the countryside. This is evident from the fact that in the districts that are urbanising very fast, such as Faridabad and Ghaziabad, urban livestock workers are more. In fact Delhi has the highest figure in this category.

It is understood that rural areas will have more agriculture; though a receding trend of agricultural labour in the rural areas does indicate increasing migration. But a receding trend of cultivators, which is the case in the adjoining districts, would mean a structural change in employment because of urbanisation.

Female workers are increasing with time. Particularly in Delhi there is a sizeable increase in female workers as cultivators and in livestock rearing. Livestock rearing has become a common practice because of the growing urban market. This is an indication of the development of entrepreneurship, as in the urban areas certain types of agricultural activities take the form of business.

While concluding this section it can be said that an overall structural change in agricultural employment is taking place with urbanisation. Urban agriculture is becoming popular with urbanisation because of an expanding urban market. With the increase of cultivators in Delhi, with only the marginal lands being

Table 13.5: Main Workers with Rural-Urban Bifurcation

Name of Districts	Total (% to total population)			Rural (% to total workers)			Urban (% to total workers)		
	1971	1981	1991	1971	1981	1991	1971	1981	1991
Delhi	30.21	31.93	31.51	9.07	6.49	9.19	90.93	93.51	90.81
Sonepat	–	28.22	29.21	–	82.34	78.00	–	17.66	22.00
Rohtak	23.66	26.71	2931	83.83	80.41	80.30	16.17	19.59	19.70
Gurgaon	26.12	27.79	27.75	80.29	80.70	79.66	19.71	19.30	20.34
Faridabad	–	29.43	28.71	–	54.92	49.53	–	45.08	50.47
Ghaziabad	–	27.46	27.23	–	64.91	53.29	–	35.09	46.71

Note: (–) Not available.
Source: Census of India.

Table 13.6: Urban Agricultural Workers

(*Percentage to Sector Total*)

Name of Districts	Cultivators			Agricultural Labours			Livestock, Forestry and Fishing		
	1971	1981	1991	1971	1981	1991	1971	1981	1991
Delhi	16.08	20.74	25.63	23.60	29.58	31.04	87.04	–	77.23
Sonepat	–	1.85	2.65	–	4.51	8.78	–	–	17.52
Rohtak	2.56	3.13	2.78	3.52	4.84	8.53	16.61	–	39.19
Gurgaon	2.22	2.80	2.33	4.88	7.15	7.26	11.33	–	8.80
Faridabad	–	6.34	5.31	–	8.29	10.87	–	–	53.93
Ghaziabad	–	4.54	8.73	–	9.60	12.96	–	–	42.88

Note: (–) Not available.
Source: Census of India.

cultivated and with the provision made by the Master Plan for farm houses in the peri-urban areas of the city, along with permission to carry out some urban-oriented agricultural practices such as market gardening and animal husbandry, there is a clear indication that the need to practice UA with urbanisation is being gradually accepted in cities. The issue here is not just of growing crops. New forms of agriculture, which manifests as business propositions, are also being considered.

Another feature which is prominent is the increasing number of female workers with time. This is also an outcome of urbanisation, which leads to improvements in technology, knowledge and awareness. Besides, urbanisation also brings about higher costs of living to attain a better quality of life, for which more income is required. Hence more female workers are compelled to be inducted into the workforce with time.

The third important feature that is being revealed is the development of livestock rearing for meat and milk production for the growing urban market (Table 13.7). This is mostly to be found in the peri-urban areas.

Table 13.7: Livestock in Delhi

Description	*Total Livestock*						
	1961	*1966*	*1972*	*1977*	*1982*	*1987*	*1992*
Cattle	93978	81667	67919	48290	52109	56228	40101
Buffaloes	100082	103826	128205	108924	177600	218515	248660
Sheep	9560	5749	4434	9276	2833	5416	198
Goat	18882	13266	11918	19869	14370	12147	16225
Pigs	12631	10797	10889	10489	21568	26946	11996
Poultry	62757	129417	303529	216911	218698	300820	301050

Source: Statistical Abstract 1977-1996, Directorate of Economics & Statistics, Delhi.

The issue, therefore, is of diversification of agricultural activities with urbanisation. The need is for a variety of products because of a growing market. As urbanisation continues, more attention is necessary for food production. While grain crops demand a specific focus, horticultural and other food products seek a different kind of attention that is market related. Within a city this entire phenomenon also influences the socio-economic and the environmental conditions.

Demand for Utilities and Infrastructure

With the rise in the population, the demand for infrastructure has also increased in Delhi. Areal and population growth demand infrastructure provision of two kinds: upgradation of the existing utility systems for higher capacity and additional developments in the newly urbanised zones/areas. Normally a percapita standard is used to provide the basic utilities and infrastructure. Unless replenished, a shortfall occurs in the percapita utilities with population expansion. For example, Delhi is unable to supply the required amount of water to its citizens. As per the norm (of 318 lpcd) Delhi falls short of 1350 mld of water for an estimated population of 12.5 million (Table 13.8).

Table 13.8: Water Supply in Delhi

		1996-97	*1997-98*
I.	Total Water Produced (Mld)		
	Total	2610	2620
	a. Surface	2315	2315
	b. Ground	295	305
II.	Total Piped Water Supplied (Mld)		
	Total	1255	1175
	a. Domestic	1076	969
	b. Industrial	41	42
	c. Commercial	135	165
	d. Standpost	–	–
	e. Others	3	2
III.	Unaccounted Water (Mld)	1064	1112
IV.	Per Capita Norm		318 (lpcd)
V.	Per Capita Supply (for 12.5 million projected population of 1999)		210 (lpcd)
VI.	Per Capita Shortage		108 (lpcd)
VII.	Total Shortage	–	1350 (mld)

Source: Data collected for an ongoing NIUA Project on Status of Water Supply, Sanitation and Solid Waste Management in Class I & II Cities/Towns of India, Delhi Jal Board, New Delhi.

The rise in the metered connection of water supply also reflects the rise in the demand. Similarly, the increase in the registered vehicles can act as a surrogate variable to indicate the possible rise in the pollution, given the technology that is being used in India. Again, an increase in the length of roads is also an indication of the rise in the demand for such infrastructure. Another surrogate variable for pollution (for both air and water) could be the number of industries that is increasing with population and time. In fact, increase in urban activities and shortage of infrastructure can lead to a lot of pollution, unless controlled by advanced technology and/or regulations.

Pollution Levels in Delhi

The main sources of pollution in Delhi are industrial, domestic and vehicular waste. In 1991, 64 per cent of the air pollution in Delhi was from vehicular emissions (Table 13.9). To mitigate such pollution, efficient pollution prevention technology will have to be used in the manufacturing of motor vehicles. Also, restrictions will have to be imposed on the use of certain types of fuel like

Table 13.9: Sources of Pollution in Delhi (*In percentage*)

Source	*1970-71*	*1980-81*	*1990-91*	*2000-01 Projected*
Industrial	56	40	29	20
Vehicular	23	42	64	72
Domestic	21	18	7	8

Source: White Paper on Pollution in Delhi with an Action Plan, Ministry of Environment and Forests, GOL New Delhi.

unleaded petrol, diesel, etc. Of late Delhi has put a restrain on the use of cars without Euro I standards of pollution control. As the population increases, there is bound to be more cars on the roads. Therefore preventive measures will have to be adopted to control pollution. The increase in the solid waste collection also indicates increased waste generation with population expansion. The gap between the demand and supply of services is crucial. On it depends the extent of pollution the city faces.

Statistics indicate that pollution is on the rise with increasing urbanisation in Delhi. This is true for air pollution, garbage generation, the pollution load of the river Yamuna in Delhi and the incidence of diseases resulting from the shortage of utilities and basic services.

When appropriate and adequate infrastructure and technology are not provided with the rise in population, pollution tends to increase. This can be injurious to human health, animals and plants. For example, lack of sanitation facilities can cause diseases like cholera, hepatitis or gastroenteritis.

Chart 13.1: Vector/Water-borne Diseases in Delhi

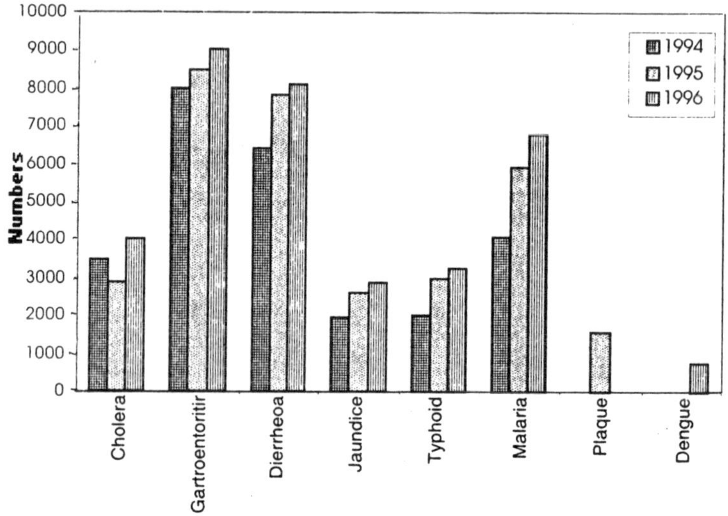

Source: Basu, Soma (1997); Pollution Capital, The Hindu Survey of the Environment.

Again, inappropriate or crude technology in industries and motor vehicles can lead to air pollution causing human discomfort, as is happening in Delhi with the rise in the respiratory diseases. Scientific studies have indicated that pollution has a deleterious effect also on crops (Sinha: undated).

Often management strategies play an important role in reducing pollution. For example, a study was done in 1985 by the CPCB to assess the impact of autoexhaust lead pollution on the roadside vegetation of Delhi. The concern was that the lead added in the petrol to improve the antiknock property is emitted as particulate matter, of which the roadside soil and vegetation are the immediate receptors. The study suggested that trees resistant to lead should be planted. Thus UA can help in management strategies to reduce pollution and improve the urban environment.

APPLICATION

Plans and Policies Supporting Urban Agriculture

A review of the plans and policies has revealed that UA has so far not been taken up seriously in India as a mode of city management or for promoting employment, or even for poverty alleviation. Neither have the benefits of UA been understood, recognised, or practised in pollution abatement or health care. There is no direct reference made in the plans on the promotion of UA, except in the Sixth Plan which proposes to improve agriculture, including horticulture in and around cities, from the point of view of building a national food security system. However, there was a mention of public policy measures that would stimulate production by small and marginal farmers. The Sixth Plan also suggested the use of marginal lands, without mentioning its rural/urban identification. The Plan also mentioned that the aim of landuse planning should be to optimise opportunities for gainful employment. The proposal was for a systems approach to agricultural production, conservation, consumption, and trade. However, this strategy was meant to be adopted in general for all types of agriculture and was not specifically for cities only.

Conservation policies have emphasised the protection and promotion of greenery and bio-diversity in and around cities. The focus is on prevention of pollution and waste assimilation. It does not mention UA directly. Development of city parks from the viewpoint of creating and maintaining lung spaces in the context of physical planning of urban settlements has also been considered. Social forestry is today a popular phenomenon to increase the assimilative capacity of air. But UA as a panacea for socio-economic problems has never been formally considered so far. The inclusion of Zones A. 1 and A.2 in the Master Plan of Delhi, which constitute a green belt, has been mostly to avoid incompatible industries (that require plenty of space or created some nuisance in congested surroundings, such as dairying) from being located within the city. At the same time these zones are to act as a buffer between the urban and the rural and absorb those rural industries that cater to metropolitan requirements. However, the mandatory requirement of EIA since 1994 has made some improvements in our thinking on the protection of forests, agricultural lands, green belts and other natural elements.

The Need for Urban Agriculture (in Delhi)

Like all metropolitan cities, Delhi is growing very rapidly. The catalyst came in the form of the country's partition at the time of Independence, when refugees migrated to the city from western Punjab. Since then Delhi has been growing steadily at the rate of about 50 per cent per decade.

In the initial years of the "independent" rule, most of the employment generated were tertiary activities related to the country's administration. Subsequently more jobs had to be created for the increasing population, which were generally in trading, small scale industries and services. But it was soon realised that to sustain the city, large industries should be set up to increase economic productivity. Though initially the industries were located within the city, like the DCM, as also the small scale industries, with time the large industries were being located away from the city centre to avoid pollution, as planners had by then become conscious of environmental pollution resulting from certain types of developmental activities. However, the small scale industries continued to be within the city. But today, even those are being removed outside the city (as per the Supreme Court orders), as the combination of population growth and industrial growth is leading to severe pollution from congestion and waste generation. Newspaper reports declare Delhi to be the fourth most polluted city in the world (*The Times of India*). Therefore, technology changes have been suggested to control pollution. Besides, good management strategies are also being sought after to prevent pollution and to improve the city's environment.

Given the existing conditions, a possible management strategy could be to promote UA in order to improve the environment and the economy. Moreover, the benefits of UA for city management have already been discussed in the first section of this paper. Since no management tool is singularly used for solving only one problem, efforts can be made to derive multifarious benefits by making the maximum use of a tool. A study of the concept and role has shown that UA cannot only reduce pollution by digesting waste which will improve the natural assimilation capacity, but that it can also alleviate poverty and improve the city's finances by creating employment. Besides, UA can improve the food security, generate income from more productive use of land, reduce the maintenance costs and make the city more beautiful: all of which will raise the quality of life.

Data on the infrastructure of Delhi indicate the nature and magnitude of the shortages in the utilities and the built environment. As often discussed, deterioration of environment is caused either by overuse of resources that cause pollution or from poverty, which is an outcome of shortages. Incidences of diseases indicate the manifestations of insanitary conditions within cities. Hence utilities need to be upgraded with time to meet the demands of the increasing population.

The existing peri-urban areas of Delhi point to a diminishing size of the open areas earmarked for the purpose, which would either act as a buffer for the city, or as lung space for the people to breathe freely. But as has been mentioned earlier, peri-urban areas are transient in nature and keep shifting away from the main city centre. As a result, the peri-urban areas of Delhi are merging with those of the neighbouring towns and cities. The expansion of Delhi arid its surrounding towns are virtually filling in the rural areas between the cities and advancing towards the creation of a large conurbation. Under the circumstances, UA would be very helpful to recreate open lung spaces for the people to breathe some fresh air and act as buffers. As Lewis Mumford had said, "the most important public task, around every growing urban centre, and far beyond, is to preserve permanent open areas, capable of being maintained for agriculture, horticulture and related rural industries". His vision was that such areas would bring succour to the urban dwellers living in cramped conditions within cities. He also thought that such areas would prevent the coalescence of one urban unit with another (Mumford, 1986).

With more land being transferred to non-agricultural use over the years, there is an increase in the built area and a reduction in the total cropped area. But there are also some cultivable wastelands that have been kept vacant (in Delhi), which can be used for UA. The area sown more than once has also declined, indicating a reduction in soil fertility; for urban development results into severe soil deterioration. Changes in the soil structure prevent farmers from cultivating throughout the year. The changing landuse and the soil structure promote intensive agriculture (often with fertilisers that spoil the soil) in order to meet the demand-supply gap of the growing urban market and to reap higher benefits (which is very urban in its characteristics). Landuse options indicate that a sizeable amount of UA can be carried out in Delhi. However, the nature of agriculture will be of short-term benefits.

The development of UA is guided by the physiography of the city-region and the pattern of urbanisation. For example, since urbanisation in the east of Delhi is more intense, developing along the lines of transportation, UA has developed more towards the west. Again, soil conditions promote better agriculture in the west. But there is no definite pattern of UA in and around Delhi. There are immense data constraints regarding UA, as all such information is maintained only at the district level and not at the city level. Hence for analysis, districts adjacent to Delhi were considered, especially in diagnosing peri-urban patterns.

Considering the size of the population, very little of UA is carried out in and around Delhi. As mentioned earlier, only 1.2 per cent of Delhi's income is generated on the farms. Besides, a very small percentage of the total workers are employed in agriculture. The land holdings are also very small, ranging between 1-3 hectares. Some cereals and vegetables are grown. There are also some fruits grown, of which the larger share comes from Haryana. But what is more important is the marketing of fruits and vegetables. Delhi being a regional centre, most of the produce from the surrounding areas is brought to Delhi, before being redistributed. Hence, marketing strategies are very important for UA. The contributions of the local farmers are very important for meeting the deficits created by the gap between the demand and the supply. Sometimes the market regulations prevent the local fanners from directly marketing their produce in the local market. They have to route their sale through the wholesale markets or the *mandis*. However, whatever be the quantity and the quality of agricultural produce, it is very pleasant to see green fields of crops and vegetables in the Yamuna river floodplain, often interspersed by flowers that are grown for the urban market. Besides, adding to the food security of the city and providing employment to the poor, these fields of crop cultivation are aesthetically welcoming and contributes to the landscape.

With the help of the local government and other development agencies, more trees are being grown in Delhi in recent times. Landuse data points to an increase in the area under trees. The revised Master Plan of Delhi has worked out a list of trees suited to the different parts of the city, based on climatic and appropriate soil conditions and a selection of species that will help to improve the urban environmental conditions. All this has happened with the recent consciousness on resource conservation, environmental management and sustainability.

Agricultural practices indicate a changing pattern of agriculture with urbanisation. A change can also be found in the employment pattern, though UA has still not been able to create a niche around Delhi or in the Indian metropolises, as it is in Hong Kong, China or Singapore. Moreover, the plans and policies do not directly support UA. A review of the plans reveals an emphasis on the provision of utilities and housing in urban areas to prevent or reduce pollution. It does not consider UA as an instrument for the reduction of pollution. However, of late, the assimilative capacity of social forestry is gaining importance.

Policies that can influence or promote UA, such as the Pollution Abatement, Siting of Industries and the National Conservation Strategy only support pollution prevention in cities by dispersal of industries and conservation of the biodiversity and the ecology. However, efforts to do so do not ensure the development of UA. Only the so called Landuse Policy tries to promote soil conservation and increase soil productivity that helps agriculture. But even this policy does not directly propagate UA for city or peri-urban management.

Despite the Seventy Fourth Amendment of the Indian Constitution that propagates environmental improvement within cities, the local government's involvement in agriculture is negligible. It is only confined to leasing out some of the vacant lands, or the trees producing cash crops, like the long staple cotton (semur) or the fruit bearing trees like tamarind or "jamun" and/ or the development of nurseries, though the DDA and the municipalities do have their horticultural departments. Given the multifarious role of the UA, it is to the advantage of the city managers to promote UA.

Conclusion

It has been noticed that urbanisation brings along with it a resurgence of agriculture, but with a difference. As cities expand

and the needs increase, the range of economic activities widen. The snowballing effect that fosters population expansion demands more food, stimulating the development of UA. In the metropolitan cities of developing countries, this diversification brings about varied lifestyles, ranging from an extension of the rural life to the most sophisticated standards of modern living and agribusiness. The wide range of lifestyles generates diverse food requirements, which UA tries to satisfy through the city's large and varied urban food market.

However, UA is not just crop cultivation of the type common in rural areas. It caters to very special and stylised needs of the urban milieu. Of course, there is also the sheer necessity to provide for a large population as well. Therefore, rapid urbanisation is bringing back to the cities a type of agriculture that is more conveniently practiced to cater to the city's population. While doing so, UA helps the city to solve some of its socio-economic and management problems, as mentioned in an earlier section of this study. Some typical examples of urban agriculture include:

- fish and other aquatic products harvested from tanks, ponds, rivers, sewage lagoons and estuaries.
- horticulture on excess vacant space at large facilities, principally dedicated to other activities (like airports, factories, etc.).
- chicken, rabbits, guinea pigs raised in bookshelf cages hung on walls.
- vegetables grown in hydroponics solution on roofs, patios and stairways.
- market gardens on vacant plots, in the green wedges between urbanised corridors or along highways/railroads in peri-urban areas.

Urban farming is perforce intensive, making the best use of space, with a predominance of shorter-cycle, higher-value market crops. It utilises multi-cropping and integrated farming techniques and makes judicious use of both vertical and horizontal space.

An examination of the contribution of UA towards sustainable development indicated a multi-sectoral role of UA in city management. However, UA focuses mainly on environmental improvements, food security and socio-economic development, all of which promote a good quality of life. Its benefits to the poor are crucial to city development and thereby city management, as providing for the poor has different economic and management connotations. However it was found that the exact estimation of the quantity and quality of environmental improvement (in Delhi) was hard to achieve for want of quantitative data, as UA is more informal than formal, as a result of which records are not maintained. Moreover, since agriculture is opposed to "urban", plans and policies related to city development do not support such activities; though records of land utilisation mentioning the area under crops or multiple cultivation (in Delhi) do indicate an agreement with the phenomenon. But the market mechanism for selling vegetables, fruits, flowers and milk (in Delhi) revealed an absence of any supportive system for the small and marginal farmers commonly engaged in UA.

Even though informal economic activities contribute to the city's economy, the revenues generated do not necessarily add to the municipal coffers, as it operates outside the tax structure. While such employment may be beneficial for the poor, generation of these jobs creates management problems in the absence of a planned support system. Yet improving the economic conditions of the poor enhance both the city and the state income. This conflicting position of employment creation *vis-a-vis* lack of tax support is a continuing dilemma faced by the planners in India, which can only be resolved through policy and legislative changes.

There is again a need to know how much a city can save on the cost of city maintenance through UA: such as the cost of maintaining fallow or marginal land, the roadside trees, garbage collection and disposal, sewage water treatment and disposal, prevention of air pollution, etc. All these along with income from UA add to the actual monetary benefit the city enjoys from UA. To this should be added the benefits of social upliftment: such as improved education, prevention of crime because of gainful employment, community participation that helps local administration, improvements in public health conditions resulting from waste digestion, prevention of epidemics and the like, all of which reduce the cost of city management by avoiding difficulties and expenditures arising from its absence. Each of these sectoral assessments will be an exercise by itself, if detailed analysis is done of the effects of UA on the city. Such an analysis could not be done for Delhi for want of appropriate data and time.

What has never been considered is the beneficial role of UA in poverty alleviation and social development. This needs more thinking. The fact remains that rural is divorced from urban and that rural activities within a city is incompatible to the very concept of urban, which emphasises on non-agricultural activities and a life that is far removed from the soil. Therefore, should such activities be permitted within cities? Or to which extent can UA be practiced? Urban planners are biased against the use of land and water bodies in and around cities, for UA. They attach more value to land supporting housing and industries than agriculture. Besides, water in the urban areas is often a scarce resource/utility.

The promotion of UA as a business proposition by the rich and as an instrument of poverty alleviation for the poor would mean both a social and an economic upliftment. However, the crucial decision of accepting or rejecting UA rests with the city government. How far it will help in city management will have to be examined sectorwise, to weigh the benefits it will accrue to the city. Thus development of UA will need further research. Though present in a limited way, UA has now acquired new dimensions with rapid urbanisation, especially in a country like India where 30-40 per cent of the population of the metropolitan cities live in slums and suffer either from unemployment or from low income, both of which lead to shortage of money to buy food.

The case study of Delhi has brought out the redeeming features of UA *vis-a-vis* pollution, congestion, shortage of utilities/infrastructure with urbanisation. Though results of the strategies adopted for UA could not be measured quantitatively, facts and figures leaned heavily towards the acceptance of UA in improving the city's environment and food security. The issue that has emerged is not of a choice for UA in cities, but of the inevitable/spontaneous development of UA with urbanisation. The dilemma is with regard to the lack of institutional support to be given to UA.

The basic question is, whose responsibility should UA be? The nature of responsibility ranges from allocation of land, to provision of water, to building up of a market system, to selling of agricultural produce, to pollution control and the planting of appropriate trees, to improvement of the assimilative capacity of the natural elements and so on. In 1983, Ganapathy had argued that the State alone is not sufficient to promote UA in the Indian cities. To make it successful, commitments at the local level are also required; which would mean decentralisation and complete involvement of the community. He argued that "an important policy goal in urban agriculture will be to develop a contextually relevant optimal balance of power between community, state and the market place." State support would be encouraging by way of research, development impetus to local planning, provision of inputs and formulation of legislation. It can act as a negotiator whenever there is conflict in the usage of urban space. Ganapathy, however, felt that with the high land prices and the demand on limited land resources, urban agriculture cannot be economical on a large scale. Access to land is an important factor for urban agriculture and its availability to urban poor is crucial. Yet, land use planning and policy-making do not often address this issue from the standpoint of the urban poor (Yeung, 1985).

With the 74th amendment of the Indian Constitution, the municipality now forms the third tier of the government to manage cities in a decentralised form, at the local level, so that people's priorities can be given a hearing. Hence the importance of UA will depend upon the decisions taken at the local level, even though the phenomenon is showing signs of globalisation. That is, even though the issue affects cities all over the world, practice of UA has to be location specific. In India the recent introduction of "urban forestry, protection of environment and promotion of ecological aspects" as a responsibility of the municipality as mentioned in the Twelfth Schedule of the Constitution will help to facilitate the practice of UA by giving it a legal connotation. This privilege was absent in the past. Thus UA need not necessarily be an informal activity anymore. However, the focus for further studies will have to be on the main issues of urban management, depending upon their relevance.

As for the peri-urban areas, expansion of the city into the fringe farmlands is reducing traditional agriculture. But since peri-urban areas are belts of perpetual conversion of rural land into urban, transformation of agricultural activities into non-agricultural occupations (that is, from green to brown landuse) is inevitable. At the same time these zones are gaining in horticulture, floriculture, pisciculture, livestock rearing and so on, which produce high value components of food for the urban markets. In fact, Master Plans (as in Delhi and many other cities) are gradually including such usage around cities. Therefore, an appropriate mix of UA and urban development would be more acceptable for city planning, rather than a total change from rural to urban. As Lewis Mumford had visualised almost half a century ago, that "in cities of the future, ribbons of green must run through every quarter, forming a continuous web of garden and mall, widening at the edge of the city into protective greenbelts, so that landscape and garden will become an integral part of urban no less than rural life, for both weekday and holiday uses." It is hoped that with UA such needs will be met.

Yet despite all benefits, UA is little understood. Urban farming is often considered as "kitchen gardening", or marginalised as leftover rural habits. The benefits of UA are lost behind myths that emanate from cultural, planning and policy biases. It is necessary to identify and address the myths surrounding UA to recogise its potential. However, the contribution of UA would be more beneficial in poor/developing countries with threats of unemployment and food insecurity.

REFERENCES

Bhardwaj, S.P. *et al.* (1998) Marketing of Fruits and Vegetables in Delhi Market with reference to Small and Marginal Farmers, *Proceedings of the National Seminar on Problems of Small and Marginal Farmers in Marketing of Fruits and Vegetables,* organised by Fanners Education and Welfare Society, New Delhi, pp. 48-53.

Central Board for the Prevention and Control of Water Pollution (1984) *Impact of Autoexhaust Lead Pollution on Vegetation in Union Territory of Delhi,* Central Board for the Prevention and Control of Water Pollution, New Delhi.

Dwivedi, Jyotsna (1992) *Rural-Urban Fringe in Indian Cities: A Case Study of Varanasi,* Unpublished Ph.D. Thesis in Geography Submitted to Benares Hindu University.

Howe, Joe and Paul Wheeler (1999) Urban Food Growing: The Experience of Two UK Cities, *Sustainable Development* 7, pp. 13-24.

Institute of Wetlands Management and Ecological Design, Calcutta (1996) Integrated Study on Wetland Conservation and Urban Growth: A Case of Calcutta's Wetland, in HSMI (HUDCO) and IHS (Rotterdam); *Urban Environmental Management: The Indian Experience,* New Delhi.

Mumford, Lewis (1968) *The Urban Prospect,* Harcourt, Brace and World.

Nangia, S. (1976) *Delhi Metropolitan Region: A Study in Settlement Geography,* K.B. Publications, New Delhi.

NIUA (1998) India's Urban Sector Profile, Research Study 61, National Institute of Urban Affairs, New Delhi.

SEEDS (1998) *Baseline Information Survey,* ICCET/IIED, London and SEEDS, New Delhi.

Sinha, Dr. Prabhas C. (undated) *Impact of Air Pollutants on Crop Yields in India: A Policy Review,* WWF, New Delhi.

Smit, Jac (1996) Urban Agriculture: Green and Healthy Cities, *Global Facility for Urban Agriculture.* http://www.citvfarmer.org/ourplanetJS.html, February 1998.

Smit, Jac (1996) *Urban Agriculture: Food, Jobs and Sustainable Cities,* UNDP, Publication Series for Habitat n. Volume One.

Smit, Jac (1998) Urban culture, Bulletin (May), *City Farmer,* Canada's Office of Urban Agriculture, file:///C|/WINDOWS/TEMP/iacmav98.htmL May 5, 1998.

Town and Country Planning Division; *Masterplan of Varanasi-2011,* Government of Uttar Pradesh, Varanasi.

Yardi & Soree (1997-98) *Urban Agriculture Information, Documentation and Action Project,* New Delhi.

Yeung, Yue-man (1985) Urban Agriculture in S.E. Asia: A Substantive and Policy Review, *Occasional Paper No. 81,* Paper prepared for the Food-Energy Nexus Programme of the United Nations University, Tokyo.

14

Agricultural Informatics and Communication Network (AGRISNET)

An ICT Infrastructure to Usher in Digital Opportunities for Sustainable Agricultural Development in India[1]

M. MONI

Introduction

Agriculture has undergone several fundamental changes during the 20th century, including extensive dependence on farm machinery, intensive fertiliser and agrochemical management, crop breeding, high yielding hybrid varieties, and genetic manipulation. Farming systems are continuing to change in response to economic, technological and social trends. Though many parts of India have been blessed with excellent agro-climatic and water resources, these parts have a very low productivity. The growing demand for food grains, vegetables, fruits, milk, poultry and meat as well as cash crops present greater and newer challenges to agriculture. At the end of the 20th Century and beginning of the new millennium, the agricultural enterprise stands at a technological crossroads.

The global environment arising out of the World Trade Organisation (WTO) poses challenges, which must be addressed *to render* Indian Agriculture *competitive, sustainable, viable* and *equitable*[2]*. Till the harvest, agriculture is the state subject and afterwards,* *it becomes a commodity of global trade.* The Tenth Plan Approach Paper of the Planning Commission has called for an economic growth target of 8 per cent during the plan period, with emphasis on second generation reforms, reduction in subsidies and hard economic decisions to raise resources for increased investment and prune non-plan expenditure. Pursuit of a strategy for achieving an economic growth rate of 8 per cent during the Tenth Plan period, calls for bold departures from existing policies[3], among the major sectors, in Agriculture and Land Management sector.

Due to ever increasing population pressure and shrinking natural resources, increase in food productivity has to come necessarily through higher and efficient use of inputs like quality seeds, fertiliser and water. Availability of timely and adequate information on these critical inputs is the pre-requisite for sustainable high productivity and food security in the country. Sustainable Development depends on the judicious use of Natural Resources, i.e. Soil, Water, Livestock, Plant Genetic, Fisheries, Forestry, Climate, Rainfall and Topography, in a acceptable technology management framework under the prevailing socio-economic infrastructure.

Developments in enabling technologies such as Information and Communication Technology (ICT), Geographical Information System (GIS) Technology, and Global Positioning System (GPS), Supervisory Control And Data Acquisition (SCADA) Technology, facilitate "Informatics Led Agricultural Development" which will be a step towards precision agriculture and enhancement of quality of life of the farming community in India. "Informatics led Agriculture Development" will require a sophisticated Information and Communication Technology (ICT) network, facilitating an integrated approach of "Internet Technology" and sustainable "Agricultural, Rural and Backward Area Development" with its farm and non-farm linkages for sustainable livelihood of rural people.

India is fast moving into being an information and knowledge society — especially with the emphasis on Information Technology (IT) and "transparent" e-governance. E-governance is the development, deployment and enforcement of the policies, laws, and regulations necessary to support the functioning of a digital society and economy, as well as e-government. Developments in e-Governance provide opportunities to harness the power of

Information Technology (IT) to make the business of governance inexpensive, qualitatively responsive, and truly encompassing. Emergence of Information Technology on the national agenda and the announcement of IT policies by various State Governments have recognised the "Convergence of Core Technologies and E-Governance" as the tool for sustainable development and globalisation of economy. An agrarian society needs "a-governance" (agriculture-governance) to make India a first-rate economy.

This proposal also reviews government initiatives in establishing Information and Communication Technology Network (ICT): AGRISNET—to usher in "digital opportunities for sustainable agricultural development". This will facilitate new opportunities for public administrations to work in close partnership with the private sector to develop online systems that respond directly to the needs of farmers and businesses through "Agri-clinics". Digital opportunities include government portals, digital communities, and e-Government Framework. This is likely to be the largest sharable Internet Portal in the world, for agricultural sector in India, on NICNET having more than 10,000 nodes to government itself. In view of the on-going macro-level economic reforms (and of course, globalisation of the Indian Economy), implementation of WTO's Agreement on Agriculture (AOA) and grassroots level decentralisation, AGRISNET has the potential to usher in "a-Governance" in the country.

Impact of ICT Diffusion on Economic Growth and Sustainable Development

Economic growth and industrial growth of India are dependent on production and productivity in agriculture. Hence, any change in its structure is likely to have a corresponding impact on the existing pattern of social equity. Various research studies and policy papers highlight that the Indian Agricultural Sector faces resource constraints, infrastructure constraints, institutional constraints, technology constraints, policy induced limitations and implementation hurdles. Generation and Transfer of Technology have become very crucial the World over. Investment made in technology generation must be informed to potential users of that technology if they are to succeed in accelerating agricultural and allied production, in creating more jobs, and in improving the standard of living of the rural millions. Research, Education, Extension and Training are considered as the basics of sustainable agriculture and rural development. Instant access to information on the availability of inputs, financial resources, technological innovations and changing market conditions are critical to the viability of rural economy.

Information and Communication Technologies (ICT) are primarily enabling technologies and form part of the infrastructure sector of a modern economy. The diffusion of ICT throughout all industries is, therefore, far more important than the production of ICT industries *per se*. ICT diffusion derives economic force from the complementary development of a knowledge-intensive society.[4] In the present "crucial decade" of this millenium, a high rate of investment in Information Technology capital and a supportive environment are expected to achieve "digital economy". Its rapid growth, however, depends on:[5]

- A higher rate of productivity growth related to investment in Information Technology;
- A rise in Total Factor Productivity (TFP) growth due to Information Utilisation across the economy and resulting in "spill-over" effects;
- An increase in factor utilisation; and
- A decline in the non-accelerating inflation rate and rate of unemployment.

Various study results strongly support that the "payoff" effect of ICT on economic growth can be achieved only through a robust National Information Infrastructure (NII), i.e. AGRISNET for the agricultural sector, that supports ICT adoption and application. Distributed databases are the converging point of networking the database technologies to bring "Power to the People" for planning and bringing in responsive administration (e-Governance) in developing countries.

Reaching the Unreached—the rural area—is the corner stone of Rural Development. The emerging new paradigm for International Cooperation on Sustainable Development demands "Informatics" as the appropriate tool for sustainable development, aiming at economic, social and cultural development of "rural" and "remote" regions and countries. Harnessing the information revolution for economic development, social cohesion and poverty alleviation in the 21st century is the theme for various National and International Conferences. The prime objective of the Digital Task Force of the G-8 Countries and the UN ICT Development Programme Task Force is to understand the digital divide issues of the developing countries and then to come out with strategy to support those nations to bridge the same.[6] The UNESCO report says "Information and Communication Technologies (ICTs) have the potential to dramatically reshape and transform the ways in which people organize their lives, interact with each other and participate in the various spheres of society."[7]

Fusion of Information Technology, BioTechnology, GIS Technology, Remote Sensing Technology, Global Position System (GPS) Technology, and Environment Technology is expected to bring in the required science and technology inputs for regional and rural development in the country. Information and Communication Technology (ICT) and Bio Technology (BT) are quintessential "drivers" of globalisation of economy, with their complementarities of liberalisation, privatisation, and tighter IPR. Internet Commerce (or e-Commerce) is growing fastest among businesses and facilitate companies to integrate and maximise changes (i.e. restructuring, business-process standardisation, enterprise resource planning, etc). Relationship between Informatics and Productivity is defined as follows:

Hypothesis

- "Good Communication System and Information System reinforces commitments to Productivity" holds good.
- "There exists a complementarity relationship between Sustainable Development and Productivity."

The central issue in agricultural development is the necessity to increase productivity, employment and income for poor segments of the agricultural population of whom the small and marginal farmers constitute a sizeable portion. Man, Land and Natural Resources supported by the Land had intrinsic and dynamic relationship. Farmers, more than any other profession, have intimate relationship with the land. There is tremendous spatial variability in farmland, and farmers need to understand the effects that the spatial variability will have on their crops and livestock. This means that a "rural renaissance through a spatially oriented strategy of development: Auto-Kinetic Development"[8] is inevitable. The NAP-2000 accorded high priority to evolve location-specific and economically viable improved varieties of agricultural and horticultural crops, livestock species and aquaculture as also conservation and judicious use of germplasm and other bio-diversity resources. It also envisages safeguarding the interests of the poor and the vulnerable groups. Gujarat's "Agrovision-2010" also envisages "Agri-ports" and "Agri-parks" to strengthen agriculture.

Precision Farming is one of the most scientific and modern approaches to sustainable agriculture that has gained momentum towards the end 20th century. Precision farming is essential for serving dual purpose of enhancing productivity and reducing ecological degradation. Despite potential of economic and ecological benefits, adoption of precision technologies is very slow through out the world. Agricultural economists have not deemed it necessary to accord "farm management and development of sophisticated management system" a high priority.[9] Precision Farming, though in many cases a proven technology, is still restricted to developed (America and Europe) countries, and has limited implementation in Asian countries in view of the following:

- Small land holdings,
- Cost-benefit aspect of Precision Farming System,
- Heterogeneity of cropping system,
- Lack of local technical expertise, and
- Knowledge and technological gaps.

Out of these, the two major problems for implementing Precision Farming in India are small land holding and cost of Precision Farming System. In India, about 57.8 per cent of operational holdings have size less than 1 hectare. With this field size, and the farming being mostly subsistent farming, it is difficult task to adopt the techniques of Precision Farming at individual field level. In view of this, Precision Farming can be adopted as "Information Based Agricultural System" in Agro-Ecological Units. The objective will be to engage in a meaningful continuous dialogue with the external environment in the changing scenario and to have on-line and real time system of "Agriculture on-line" capacity to analyse the signals emanating from the farms and the markets for the benefit of the farmers.

The National Agricultural Policy-2000 (NAP-2000) envisaged application of frontier technologies, viz. Information technology, bio-technology, remote sensing technology, pre-post-harvest technology, energy saving technology, technology for environmental protection, through national research system as well as proprietary research. Karnataka State Agricultural Policy (1995) and Gujarat State Agricultural Policy (2000) "Agrovision-2010" have envisaged Information Technology applications to globalize their agricultural sector in a big way. These technologies have many potential applications spanning the breadth of the agricultural industry, at all scales of organisation from farmer to cooperative and professional bodies, from farm machinery vendors, fertiliser and chemical companies, insurance, regulators, and commodities, to agronomists, consultants, and farm advisers. The proposed strategy reinforces commitment for higher agricultural productivity in India, which has been blessed with excellent agro-climatic conditions and water resources. This "informatics-led development" in Agricultural Sector provides enough scope for reduction of new risks of marginalisation and vulnerability of small farmers, in view of the two on-going processes (i) economic reforms and liberalisation (1991) and WTO/GATT Agreements (1994) at macro level, and (ii) decentralization reforms at micro level, operating in India. A journey "from digital divide to digital opportunities for sustainable development" has thus begun in the beginning of the 21st century.

From Digital Divide to Digital Opportunities for Sustainable Agricultural Development

Agricultural sector is the mainstay of Indian rural economy as well as the largest private sector in the developing economies, around which socio-economic privileges and deprivations revolve. Taking the benefits of new technologies to the economically and socially disadvantaged sections of the rural populations, is thus, a prerequisite for promoting a new paradigm of rural development, based on concurrent and integrated attention to the imperatives of ecology, economics, employment, and equity (Swaminathan, 1993).[10] The Central Ministry of Agriculture (MOA) is responsible for implementation and formulation of national policies and programmes to achieve agricultural growth through optimum utilization of the land resources, water, soil, plant, fisheries, and livestock resources. Government of India implements the following agricultural related schemes (whether Watershed based or Agro-climatic region based) in the country, which deal agricultural resources information for Planning and Development:

1. Agro-climatic Regional Planning (ACRP) Project
2. Agro-Ecological Mapping Project of the National Bureau of Soil Survey & Land Use Planning (NBSS&LUP)
3. All India Soil and Land Use Survey (AISLUS)
4. Early Warning System of Agricultural Situation in India
5. Forecasting of Agricultural output using Space, Agro-meteorology and Land based observations (FASAL) Project
6. Land Records Computerisation Project
7. National Agricultural Research Project (NARP)
8. National Agricultural Technology Project (NATP) to strengthen research-extension-farmer (r-e-f) linkage
9. National Watershed Development Programme for Rain-fed Areas (NWDPRA)
10. Soil and Water Conservation Programmes
11. Drought Prone Area Development Programme
12. Desert Development Programme
13. National Wastelands Development Programme
14. Integrated Mission on Sustainable Development (IMSD) Programme
15. Agriclinics and Agribusiness centres to advise farmers for better farming

The Department of Agriculture and Cooperation (DAC) has desired to build up an ICT (Informatics) Network: "AGRISNET – A NICNET Based Agricultural Informatics & Communication

Network" [NIC98][11], to utilise "digital opportunities" for sustainable development. This ICT network has envisaged to facilitate an integrated approach of "Internet Technology" and "Sustainable Agricultural and Rural—Backward Area Development" with its farm and non-farm linkages for sustainable livelihood. This ICT Network will have 7/24 infrastructure facilities in all 35 State/UT Agriculture Departments, 600 District Agriculture and Cooperation Departments, and 6000 Block Agricultural Offices, to strengthen "ICT led Agricultural Development" in the country. Development block is the smallest agricultural development support unit. The proposed AGRISNET Nodes in States and NCT/UTs are expected to facilitate "Agricultural Informatics and Communication", for strengthening agricultural development strategy, in the areas of:

1. Development of natural resources and protection of environment (development of land and water resources, protection and conservation of bio-diversity, and protection of environment)
2. Food and nutritional security
3. Diversification of Agriculture (Horticulture, Floriculture, etc.)
4. More efficient management of inputs (seeds, fertilisers, plant protection and mechanisation)
5. Development of rural infrastructure (rural roads, irrigation, and power)
6. Marketing and value addition (rural markets, post-harvest management, agro-processing)
7. Revitalisation of cooperative institutions
8. Improving rural credits
9. Research, education and extension
10. Human Resources Development (farmers and agricultural labourers, NGOs, and Panchayati Raj Institutions)
11. Trade and export promotion
12. Land Reforms
13. Enabling environment for higher agricultural growth
    - (a) Relaxation of restricting controls and regulations
    - (b) Parity with Industry
    - (c) Increased private-public partnership
    - (d) Agricultural taxation

14. Risk management
    (a) Crop insurance
    (b) Remunerative price
    (c) Capital formation
    (d) Targeted subsidies

In addition, this ICT Network will facilitate agribusiness partners (agricultural input industries, food processing industries, agricultural marketing and international trade organizations, rural finance institutions and development institutions and voluntary organizations engaged in rural development and others) interact with each other for sharing information and decision making on subject of their concern.

Global competition and new technologies are forging new relationships within, and between, different layers of agribusiness, transforming the industry from a chain to a complex web. Internet Commerce (or e-Commerce) is growing fastest among businesses and facilitate companies to integrate and maximise changes (i.e., restructuring, business-process standardisation, enterprise resource planning, etc). The Industry developments provide an insight into trends, potential impacts and prospects, as given below:

- e-marketplace/Neutral e-Hub
- e-distribution sites/Distributor model
- e-procurement sites/Aggregation model

This ICT Network is a "farmer-centric" project (Fig. 14.1) with a view to integrate government functions (G2G), to integrate agri-business partners (B2B), to connect farmers (C2C), to empower employees, and to enhance government productivity, value and financial services. The goal of this scheme is to deliver coherent and integrated solutions (best practices, experiences and global solutions) for sustainable agricultural development.

The ICT Network, AGRISNET, envisages to take advantage of convergence of technologies and services sectors, for promotion of "e-governance" (digital governance) in the agricultural sector, with the emerging killer applications: unified messaging, collaborative data sharing (e-commerce and data warehousing), network security and information security to facilitate e-solutions, video streaming and conferencing, unified Internet multimedia service, ultra high speed internet service, and expertise content service. In addition, National Level Portal will have information to facilitate formulation strategies and policies for the Central Government, where as the state level portal will be "state-specific", district level portal will be "district-specific", and block level portal will be "block-specific". State Agricultural Universities, Agricultural Colleges, State Agriculture Departments, Agricultural Financial Institutions, Indian Council of Agricultural Research (ICAR) Institutes, Central Agricultural Departments, and Departments of Geography will provide the content for these Portals. The following informatics sub-networks will strengthen these portals:

- FERTNET — Fertilizer Informatics Network
- APHNET — Animal Production and Health Informatics Network in India
- HORTNET — Horticulture Informatics Network
- PPIN — Plant Protection Informatics Network
- VISTARNET — Agricultural Extension Informatics Network
- ARISNET — Agricultural Research Information System Network
- CROPSNET — Crops Informatics Network
- FISHNET — Fisheries Informatics Network
- SEEDNET — Seed Informatics Network
- ACIN — Agricultural Credit Informatics Network
- AGMARKNET — Agricultural Produce Marketing Informatics Network
- AgriES — Agricultural Economics & Statistical Informatics Network
- LISNET — Land Information System Network to strengthen Soil, Water and Nutrient Management Research and Development in India
- NDMNET — Natural Disaster Management Knowledge Network in India
- Weather — Weather Resource System of India

To strengthen these informatics sub-networks, AGRISNET

Nodes will be established at national, state level, district level, and block level, with Internet/Intranet gateway at national level and regional level (grouping of states).

The small farmers need access to best practice in precision farming, affordable credit, farm inputs and modern equipments in order to increase productivity. This will have the role model of "Agri-Clinic" and "Agribusiness centre" which can be established at even below block level (i.e. Village level). "Agri-Clinic" and "Agribusiness Centre" will be set up outside the Government set up to facilitate unemployed agricultural graduates to generate income and employment through "knowledge services" for farmers. The emerging technologies on "last mile" problems provide required technology solutions to establish "Agri-Clinic" and "Agribusiness Centre" at sub-district levels.

Emerging Digital Communication Technology for "last-mile" solutions

About 99 per cent of the districts have Optical Fibre Network (OFN) providing desired bandwidth for Internet connectivity for e-Commerce and e-Governance applications in the country. Out of 6000 development blocks, about 50 per cent blocks have access to OFN for Internet Access. Only 5900 Blocks have Subscribers Trunk Dialing (STD) facilities, which can be utilised for Internet access. As of now, only 200,000 Villages have Wireless in Local Loop (WLL) Technology/ PSTN facility that can provide 14.4 KBPS for data access. BSNL (Bharat Sanchar Nigam Ltd.) utilises WLL (Codect) Technology in metropolis only. Availability of electricity at block/Village level is the real problem, which is essential for operating AGRISNET Nodes. About 60,000 Villages (Andhra Pradesh—6000, Madhya Pradesh—14000, Chhattisgarh—5000, Rajasthan—16000, Maharashtra—11000) may not have any access to data/voice facility in near future, as the Private Licence Holders did not fulfil the commitments. BSNL have planned to establish VSAT based telephone facilities in these villages.

Bridging "the last mile" involves technology, economics and geography. The Home Network of the Future will ultimately serve a multitude of appliances with a voracious appetite for content, for which the obvious answer is "broadband connections covering the last segment of the data pipeline", known as "the last mile".

The available technologies for transmission are Wireless Technology and Dial-Up Connection. One of the major problems with the Wireless Technology is how to deal with the high rate of packet loss. Millions of dial-up users are tired of sluggish connections and hence the market is there for broadband—in one form or another. The emphasis on full Internet Protocol (IP) interoperability has been important, as the backlash has already begun against the lighter-weight Wireless Applications Protocol (WAP). The National Task Force on Information Technology and Software Development (1998) recommended the "last mile" linkage either by "fibre optics" or by "radio communication" for IT Applications Services Providers (ASPs), Internet Services Providers (ISPs), and IT Promotional Organisations, with the aim to "boost efficiency and enhance market integration", through Internet/Intranet, for sustainable regional development.

The logical way to network ever-increasing number of households is to use the already existing Wire Media and state-of-the-art Wireless Media, which are discussed below:

- *Cable TV network* (in place) for high speed Internet Access (2 Mbps up-link & 50 Mbps down-link on a single TV Channel of 6 MHz) and Video Conferencing;
- *Telephone Network* for high speed (8 Mbps/768Kbps) internet access, e-commerce and Video Conferencing (using ADSL System) ;
- Home Power Distribution Wiring for Internet Services and Utility Metering (speeds of up to 2.5 Gbps) ;
- *BlueTooth Technology* for transmission of voice and data at a low-power and low-cost reliable link between computers, printers, mobile phones, LAN/WAN etc.;
- *Free Space Optics (FSO)*: Free Space Optics (FSO) uses laser or light pulses to send packetised data in terahertz (THz) spectrum range. Air (not fibre) is the transport medium. It supports data transfer at the rate of 622 Mbps (OC-12) to 1555 Mbps (OC-3), low-cost, and can be deployed very fast;
- *Local Multipoint Distribution System (LMDS)*: LMDS, like cellular technologies, is point-to-multipoint and viewed as a future component in the convergence of data and telephony services. LMDS is a broadband microwave

wireless transmission, direct from a local antenna to homes and business units, within a Line-of-Sight radius. LMDS offers a bandwidth of up to 1.5 Gbps downstream to users and 200 Mbps upstream from the users;

- *Multichannel Multipoint Distribution Services (MMDS)*: MMDS is a wireless cable and operates in the UHF portion of the radio spectrum between 2.1 and 2.7 GHz, which is a substitute for conventional Cable TV. An MMDS network can provide high speed Internet Access, telephone/fax, and TV together, without the constraints of Cable connections.

FSO is a very cost effective local access alternative to Technologies such as: DSL, Cable Modem, Local Multi-Point Distribution System (LMDS), and Multichannel Multipoint Distribution Service (MMDS). FOS works in unregulated frequency spectrum (THz) and does not interfere with other transmissions or is fairly difficult to intercept. The "Wireless-in-Local-Loop (WLL)" also offers a technological solution for the present-day last mile problems, provided there is a clear Line-of-Sight (LOS). Broadband Satellite Technology has emerged as a cost-effective technology to solve both "first-mile" and "last-mile" problems.

Broadband Satellite Technology: A state-of-the-art and cost-effective Technology Broadband Solution to establish AGRISNET in the Country and Solution for First-Mile and Last-Mile problems

AGRISNET is a NICNET based Agricultural Informatics and Communication, to utilise digital opportunities for sustainable agricultural development in the Country. Under this project, it is envisaged to link 35 State/UT Agriculture Departments, 35 State/UT Cooperation Departments, 600 District Agriculture and Cooperation Departments, 6000 Block Level Agriculture Departments. AGRISNET will take advantage of convergence of technologies and services sectors for promotion of e-governance in the agricultural and cooperation sector, by incorporating applications like unified messaging, collaborative data sharing, network security, Video streaming and conferencing, expert content service, etc. In addition, AGRISNET will facilitate national level, state level, district level, and block level portals and solutions in respect of agricultural sector for (a) integrating government functions (G2G), (b) integrating Agri-Business Partners (B2B), (c) empowering employees (B2C), (d) Connecting Farmers (C2C), and (e) Enhancing business productivity and financial services.

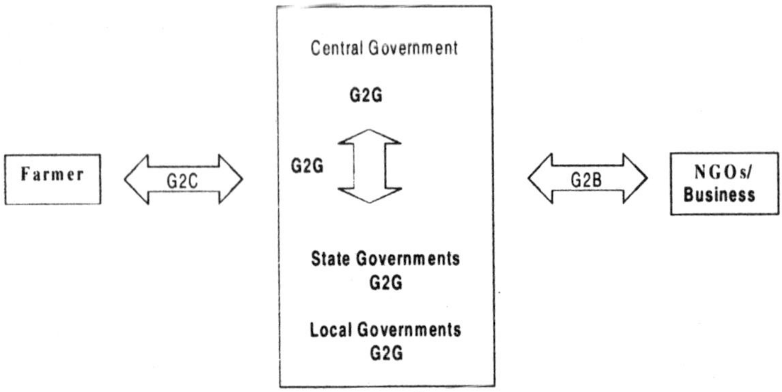

Fig. 14.1

In e-governance, "electronic" means support and stimulate good governance. E-governance will mature according to the following four phases (Gartner Report):

- Information → Presence : Web sites
- Interaction → Intake processes : e-mail, serach engines, download forms and documents
- Transaction → Complete transactions : Network and information security
- Transformation → Integration and change : Virtual counter

Satellite is an attractive solution for high broadband Internet access, both the First Mile (Backbone) and the last Mile. Satellites have been most successful in distributing information over very large geographical areas using a single transmission. With services such as television broadcasting, data broadcasting, digital messaging, enterprise virtual private networks (VPNs) and point-to-point Telecom-Datacom services, traditional bent-pipe satellites have played a significant role in our daily lives. A new generation of application needs, higher throughput requirements and communication demands are changing the way satellite systems are designed, implemented and operated. New architectures and system networking concepts are being implemented to make satellite systems capable of addressing these new market demands.

Broadband Satellite System (BSS) is the revolutionary satellite based IP solution built upon a new geo-stationary satellite technology, which enable large bandwidth capacity improvement unprecedented in the current satellite technology. BSS is a cost-effective, total solution for "last-mile" broadband communication that gain its competitiveness with other existing terrestrial last-mile broadband solution, i.e. xDSL and Cable Modem. The space segment facilitates (a) multiple "cellular" spot beams—increase bandwidth from frequency reuse, and (b) dynamic power management—increase on-board power efficiency and excellent link availability for each beam. The ground segment facilitates (a) dynamic bandwidth management, (b) new coding and modulation, and (c) new network protocol and management. Various application and services supported by BSS are internet access, distance learning, desktop multimedia, image networking, transaction services and high speed data, teleconferencing, telecommuting, telemedicine, video conferencing, video telephony, broadcast TV, etc. A VSAT based countrywide network creates a highly reliable, error free and flexible information highway compared to the terrestrial alternatives available in the Country. It provides a service free from the "last-mile" problems, as the VSAT is located at the users premises and hence the problem of data arriving from public switching networks (in the case of terrestrial links) is avoided. According to Pioneering Consulting, a leading market research firm, there will be nearly 40 million users for satellite broadband worldwide by 2007.

There are four basic technology categories that form the basis for the various satellite broadband service offerings: Ku-band FSS, bent pipe Ka-band, on-board processing Ka-band and L-band MSS. The first generation services that are now in place use existing Ku-band fixed satellite service (FSS) satellites for two-way connections. Using FSS, a large geographical area is covered by a single broadcast beam. Satellite Broadband System uses (a) Digital Video Broadcast-Return Channel via Satellite (DVB-RCS) Technology which is an open standard, and (b) iPSTAR Technology which is a proprietary system increasing the two-way traffic by applying a broad beam forming system to provide a smaller coverage similar to the terrestrial cellular concept.

2-way Broadband Satellite Technologies

Satellite Broadband Technology Category	*Representative Offerings*	*Capacity (per system)*
Ku-band (FSS)	DirecPC/ DirecWay, StarBand, SkyBridge	500 Mbps
	iPSTAR	40 Gbps
Ka-band (bent pipe)	WildBlue, Astra-BBI, iPStar	30 Gbps
Ka-band (on-board processing)	Astrolink, SpaceWay, Teledesic	30 Gbps
Mobile (3G MSS) (L-band)	Inmarsat's B-GAN, New ICO	100 Mbps
Airplane (Ku-FSS)	Connexion	500 Mbps

The Central Data Centre (DC) will be at Delhi, which will house the Applications servers and the Portals (Commodity Portals, Inputs Portals, Natural Resources Portals, Prices Portals, Decision Support Systems Portals, etc.). Data centres will be established at State/UT Agriculture Departments, State/UT Cooperative Departments, District Agriculture Departments, District Cooperative Departments, and Block Agriculture Departments. Since Agri-Clinics and Agri-Business Centres are envisaged to set up in the private sector, the private entrepreneurs will be permitted to have the benefits of VSAT Technology. The Project activities include establishment of network infrastructure and network services, development of applications services and content ASP, support services for establishing AGRISNET Nodes at Agri-clinics and Agri-business centres, and human resources development programmes.

Conclusion

The Ministry of Agriculture (MOA) is responsible for implementation and formulation of national policies and programmes to achieve agricultural growth through optimum utilization of the land resources, water, soil, plant, fisheries resources, and livestock resources. Given its endowment with regional diversities (Agro-climatic regions, Agro-ecological regions, Human resources (Population density), Level of investments in rural infrastructure, and Level of investment in technology) for its uneven "economic and agricultural" development, Indian Agriculture is faced with a great diversity of needs, opportunities and prospects.

India is fast moving into being an information and knowledge society—especially with the emphasis on IT and "transparent" e-governance. An agrarian society needs a-governance (agriculture-governance) to make India a first-rate economy. The fusion of information technology, biotechnology, environment technology, GIS technology, and remote sensing technology is expected to bring in the desired S&T inputs for sustainable agricultural and rural development. As a step towards "reaching" technology to the Small Holders (Resource-Poor-Farmers) of the Country, the Central Ministry of Agriculture have taken initiatives to build up an Informatics Network—AGRISNET : Agricultural Informatics and Communication". This ICT Network envisages to facilitate an integrated approach of "Internet Technology" and "Sustainable Agricultural, Rural and Backward Area Development" with its farm and non-farm linkages. Developments in enabling technologies such as Information Technology (IT), Geographical Information System (GIS) Technology, and Global Positioning System (GPS) Technology facilitate "Informatics Led Agricultural Development" which will be the step towards precision agriculture or site-specific agriculture in India.

These technologies have many potential applications spanning the breadth of the agricultural industry, at all scales of organisation from farmer, to cooperative and professional bodies, from farm machinery vendors, fertiliser and chemical companies, insurance, regulators, and commodities, to agronomists, consultants, and farm advisers. This facilitates farming systems to change in response to economic, technological and social needs. The proposed strategy reinforces commitment for higher agricultural productivity in India, which has been blessed with excellent agro-climatic conditions and water resources.

This "informatics-led development" in Agricultural and Rural sector provides, enough scope for reduction of new risks of marginalisation and vulnerability of small farmers, in view of the two on-going processes (i) economic reforms and liberalisation (1991) and WTO/GATT Agreements (1994) at macro level, and (ii) decentralization reforms at micro level, operating in India. Hence the AGRISNET, which is an Agricultural Informatics and Communication Network to usher in Digital Opportunities for Sustainable Agricultural Development in India, is expected to provide the necessary impetus for "agricultural governance" in the country. This will facilitate new opportunities for public administrations to work in close partnership with the private sector to develop online systems that respond directly to the needs of farmers and businesses through "Agri-clinics" and "Agri-Business Centres".

NOTES

1. Theme Paper presented in the International Conference on "Sustainable Agriculture, Water Resources Development and Earth Care Policies", 18-20, December, 2002 organised by Bhoovigyan Vikas Foundation, New Delhi.
2. Speech of the Union Minister of Agriculture, Conference of Chief Ministers on WTO/Agreement on Agriculture and Food Management, May 21, 2001, New Delhi.
3. Government of India (2001): "Approach Paper to the Tenth Five Year Plan (2002-2007)", Planning Commission, New Delhi, September 2001.
4. Eunice Wang (1999): ICT and Economic Development in Taiwan : Analysis of the Evidence", *Telecommunications Policy*, 23(3,4), April/ May 1999, pp. 235-43.
5. M.Moni (2000): "New Productivity Paradigms and Strategies in the e-Age—Government Initiatives on IT-led Development in India", International Conference on Productivity in the e-Age, Asian Productivity Organisation, 22-24 November 2000, New Delhi.
6. Government of India (2001): Tenth Five Year Plan—Information Technology Sector (2002-07)", Ministry of Information Technology, New Delhi.
7. UNESCO (1996): UNESCO Report (CII-96/WS/6) on "Information and Communication Technologies in Development".
8. Sundaram, K.V. (2001): "Rural Renaissance through a Spatially Oriented Strategy of Development", 23rd Indian Geography

Congress, December 28-30, 2001, Dr. H.S. Gaur University, Sagar (Madhya Pradesh), India.

9. David Zilberman (1996): "Comments on Precision Agriculture", presented at Workshop on Remote Sensing of Agriculture in the 21st Century, University of California, Davis, CA (USA), 1996.
10. Swaminathan, M.S. (1993): "*Information Technology: A Dialogue*", (Ed), Macmillan, Chennai, India.
11. [NIC98]—Proposal for "NICNET based Agricultural Informatics and Communication" (AGRISNET) to facilitate Higher Sustainable Agricultural productivity and establish "Indian Agriculture on-line" in the Country", May, 1998, Agricultural Informatics Division, National Informatics Centre, Government of India.

Part IV

Policies for the New Millennium

15

Policies for Access, Equity and Equality

Physical Resources and Human Resources

R.S. DESHPANDE, L. VENKATACHALAM & A. NARAYANAMOORTHY

Introduction

The concept of equity implies that ideally everyone should have a fair opportunity to attain their share of benefits generated by public goods and that no one should be deprived of their own share during the course of accessing such benefits. This stems from the fundamental Pareto optimality principle, which states that a policy change may result in enhancing the welfare of a few but should not affect the welfare of any other person. Pareto optimality largely concerns with efficiency alone since it does not talk about two things: (i) who should benefit; and (ii) what is the distribution of benefits among the beneficiaries. Moreover, the Pareto optimally in principle does not hold true in real world situation because, many policies result in making somebody better-off only by making somebody else worse. However, the usefulness of Pareto optimality principle lies in the fact that it provides insights into three fundamental questions, namely access, equity and equality in the process of resource sharing.

Equity has a primary determinant in use of service by those who need them most. Other factors such as income, location of residence and so forth should not play an important role in selecting who receives the benefits and who does not. Access to basic services would be equitable if and only if, there are no information barriers, financial barriers, or supply constraints that prevent access to a reasonable or basic minimum availability of services. Equity concepts derive from and relate to a number of political philosophies, namely (i) equalising individual net benefits or opportunities for such benefits; (ii) provision of distribution of basic services according to entitlement; (iii) providing a decent minimum basic services, (iv) utilitarianism, or maximising aggregate gain with resources; (v) the Rawlsian maximum, or maximising the position of the least well off; and (vi) providing for envy free allocations.

Equality involves a further extension. It means that everyone should be treated at the same level in access to resources. In practice, treating everyone at the same level does not always take care of their needs and thereby leading to unequal access and opportunities. The term equality also ignores other kinds of political, economic, social and institutional background as well as the physical inability of different kinds of people in the society. This implies that in the process of achieving equality and to meet the needs of different individuals, we have to take into account many factors. Therefore, equity and equality in terms of access to the basic amenities always involves policy issues. The most important question one needs to address here relates to framing the policies in such as way that the equity and equality could be achieved in right perspectives taking into account the variables that matter. The question is more complex when we consider the physical, human and natural resources.

In this paper, we are addressing to the issues relating to access, equity and equality in physical and human resources. Among the physical resources land, water and infrastructure are important from the point of connectivity between access, equity and equality, whereas human resources find an important place in the context of end result. Access or availability indicates the means whereas the equity and equality are the terminating points of a policy frame in any welfare state. The paper initially deals with human and infrastructure followed by land and water resources. We have ended with the policy implications after analysing the present status of access, equity and equality.

Human Resources

In the context of human development, education and health play a dominant role in enhancing the quality of human capital. The sustainable improvement in individuals' well-being is enhanced by education and supported by a good quality of life. A study using data from 88 countries for the period 1960-63 and 1970-73 found that a 10 per cent increase in the literacy level had resulted in 8 per cent increase in the real GDP of the countries. Another study using data from 66 middle and low income countries found that a one per cent increase in the primary enrollment ratios would lead to 0.035 per cent increase in the per capita income (see GOI, 2002). The importance of education as a fulcrum of human development is amply demonstrated by the National Human Development Report, 2001.

Here a major question to be addressed is whether the inequality depends on the level of education. Studies in the past revealed that the countries with more inequality in income were those countries whose literacy level was also low. It has been noticed that effective implementation of primary education at the lower level of development in an economy would make the Kuznet's hypothesis invalid because literacy will have an income augmenting feature. In Indian context, despite the failure in universal education, progress in literacy is quite commendable (Table 15.1). It will not be exaggeration if we term literacy as a leading variable in India's achievements under HDI framework.

Table 15.1: Trends in Human Development Indicators

Year	*Life Expectancy at Birth (Years)*	*Death Rate (90)*	*Infant Mortality Rate (Per 1,000)*	*Literacy Rate (%)*
1951	32.1	27.4	146	18.3
1961	41.3	22.8	146	8.3
1971	45.6	14.9	129	34.5
1981	50.4	12.5	110	43.6
1991	59.4	9.8	80	52.2
1996	62.4	9.0	72	na
1997	na	8.9	71	62
1998	63.4	8.5	60.81	65.38

Source: Economic Survey 1999-2000, Government of India.

It should also be noted that the education in our country is given as a fundamental right by the Constitution but we are yet to achieve the goal of universal primary education. This is not only due to various lacunae in the policies but also an issue that arises from the existence of asymmetric information between the government and the citizens over different kinds of rights. Even though education has been made a fundamental right, the existence of asymmetric information and proper utilisation of the benefits has always caused obstacles in attaining the goal. The major implication of this argument is that access to education especially by the poorer section of the society depends mainly on their access to basic level of information about their rights. A vicious circle characterised by lack of access to information leading to lack of education which in turn leads to lack of access to information has called for a right kind of intervention that could break the vicious circle. In other words, the right for information should be the first step towards achieving the universal primary education in an equitable manner. In many parts of the country, measures to increase the enrollment and reduce the absenteeism in primary schools could not adequately address these kinds of issues because, still the root cause of the problem in the form of general poverty persists everywhere. Hence, one of the ways in which the vicious circle could be dealt with is providing opportunity to access information.

Apart from the access to information, existence of general poverty is another area which deprives many in this country of their basic right to education. The poverty emanating from larger household size and lack of natural or financial resources, prevent the children of the poorer section of the households from accessing of even primary education. Poverty and lack of access to education has a close connection with degradation of natural resources. In many of the African and sub-Saharan countries, as well as in some of the Asian countries, the vicious circle of poverty is caused mainly by the degradation of natural resources. When the households depend largely on the natural resources for their subsistence, degradation of these resources requires many hands to earn at the household level. For instance, when fuel-wood, fodder and potable water become scarce, at that time limited number of labour within the household is insufficient to bring adequate amount of income and therefore, children are deprived from getting to schools. This implies that lower the access to basic resources, higher will be the burden on the state in attaining the goal of universal primary education. The right kind of government intervention here would be to ensure the households to have access to adequate amount of natural resources in a sustainable and equitable manner.

The policy for health involving provision and access to health, providing access to health care facilities in an equitable and efficient manner is confronted with score of difficulties. Achieving 'equity' in the provision of health care facilities is an inevitable goal of health policies for any state. Achieving the progress in health care sector depends mainly on how the health care facilities are equitably distributed among different social groups. Equity here refers to horizontal and vertical equity and therefore, equity is an integral part of redistribution of income among different individuals especially in terms of accessing the health care facilities.

The health sector policies in our country lack an integrated approach in fulfilling the overall objective of providing access to healthcare facilities to all social groups. One of the important aspects to be noted here is that health of the households is not only dependent on the health care facilities available directly to them but also on other types of constituents of health *per se* such as the sanitation facilities, the quantity and quality of drinking water, etc. (Tables 15.1 and 15.2). It should be noted that in India, there exists lot of variation in terms of access to sanitation facilities both within the states as well as across the states. As per the 1991 population census, only around one-fourth of the households in this country had toilet facilities. The situation in rural areas was worse with only around 10 per cent of the households having access to wastewater discharge facilities in the premises of their households. A wide variation in the access to sanitation facilities has been found across different states in the country. The sewage water contaminating the local drinking water sources, in many cases, further causes deterioration of the existing health related problems among the rural poor and urban slum dwellers. According to World Health Organisation, around 70 per cent of the common diseases in developing countries are caused mainly by the contaminated water. The underlying policy implication is that provision of good quality drinking water and sanitation facilities itself will improve the health status of the people tremendously and therefore, the existing health policies should be expanded to cover the negative consequences of not providing good quality drinking water and sanitation (Table 15.2).

Table 15.2: Infrastructure Availability for Weaker Section-1991

	Scheduled Caste			*Scheduled Tribe*			*Others*		
	Total	*Rural*	*Urban*	*Total*	*Rural*	*Urban*	*Total*	*Rural*	*Urban*
Percentage of Households having safe drinking water	63.60	59.84	80.59	43.21	41.11	65.71	64.10	56.40	81.99
Percentage of Households having Toilet facilities	11.16	5.15	38.28	7.22	4.10	40.68	28.63	11.52	68.33
Percentage of Households having both Safe Drinking Water and Toilet facilities	8.61	3.35	32.34	3.35	2.02	28.16	22.13	6.73	57.92

Source: Census of India: 1991.

One of the questions often confronted by the policy-makers is to arrive at the process of getting out of 'low-level equilibrium trap' that challenges sustainability as well as efficiency of many of the water supply and sanitation programmes. This low level of equilibrium trap is characterised by lower generation of revenue, which leads to poor quality services. This in turn leads to low level of preferences, which thereby causes to low level of willingness to pay and finally leads to low level of revenue. Many of the studies conducted by donor agencies found that reliability of water supply and sanitation services play an important role in achieving the sustainability of these services. However, the sustainability as such depends on the availability of the financial resources to the implementing agencies. Apart from the schemes that are sponsored by the international donors, implementation of other schemes depends mainly on their own resource base and therefore, the policy makers have to find out new sources of revenue. One of the major sources of revenue is the user-fees collected from the users. However, it is found that the existing level of user fee in many cases is *not* adequate to cover even the cost of providing these services.

However, the sustainability, equity and equality depend mainly on one particular aspect, namely efficiency. Efficiency is a driving force that, to some extent, helps to achieve equity and equality especially in the area of access to basic amenities such as health care facilities, water supply, sanitation, etc. For instance when financial efficiency is achieved through increased tariff rate, more number of users including the poor of the society could be covered by the services which will maximize the overall benefits. When it comes to the question of payment to the service enjoyed by the users, the policy makers always encounter with a question, namely whether the poor should also pay for the services so that the equity and equality in payment should be achieved. This is a subjective question which falls beyond the purview of economics. Moreover, the government intervention with the underlying welfare state principal should ensure that the poorer section gets the benefits of the services in an equitable manner. However, one of the important questions that we need to ask is whether or not the poor is willing to pay for the basic services that they enjoy. The answer to this question comes clearly from the findings of empirical studies in the area of water supply, sanitation and health conducted during the past three decades in various developing countries especially by the World Bank and other organizations. The findings of these studies suggest that the willingness to pay for basic services are not influenced by the income and therefore, even the poorer section of the society is also willing to pay for the services they enjoy. This means that there are so many other factors which influence the households' willingness to pay and the policy makers have to take into account these factors while formulating policies on provision of local public goods. The factors influencing the household's willingness to pay includes reliability of the service, level of education, nature of the service at present, gender, etc. Hence, the question of equity concerns are very much embedded in understanding the preferences of the households for different levels of services of basic amenities.

The path of human development goes through education (literacy), health standards (IMR) and the sources of income. As stated by the architects of the Human Development Index (HDI), it represents the end result of measuring the impact of policy intervention in the process of development. We can see the case of India in the context of last decade that the country changed significantly from where it began. The credit of achievement should go to literacy but it is also true that the other two vanguards could not keep pace with the third component (Table 15.3 and Fig. 15.1, on the progress of HDI). There are of course, on different circumstances across states. The Planning Commission of

Table 15.3: Trends in Human Development Index—India

Year	1975	1980	1985	1990	1992	1995	1998	1999	2000
HDI	0.407	0.434	0.473	0.511	0.382	0.545	0.563	0.571	0.577

Source: Human Development Reports, UNDP for various years.

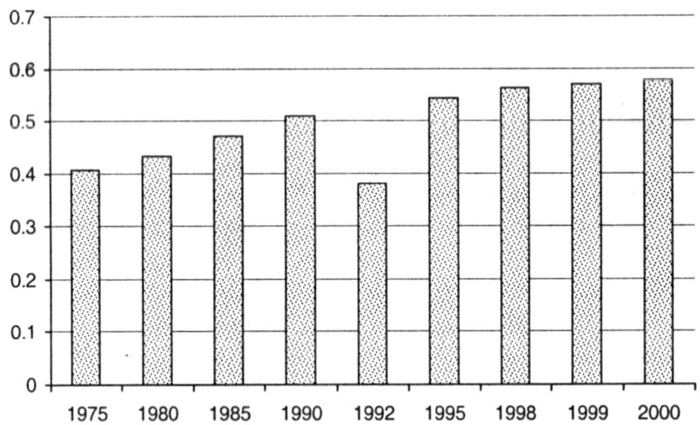

Fig. 15.1: Human Development Index

Government of India has recently prepared the Human Development Index (HDI) for some of the major states in India. Following the UNDP methodology, four different indicators closely linked to level of access to education, health and economic freedom had been used to develop the HDI across states. Life expectancy at age 1 and Infant Mortality Rate, literacy rate 7+ and intensity of formal education, per capita real consumption expenditure adjusted for inequality and worker-population ratio in case of gender equality index are the indicators used in the Planning Commission's exercise.

Table 15.4: Human Development Index for Major States in India-combined

States	*1981*		*1991*		*2001*	
	Value	*Rank*	*Value*	*Rank*	*Value*	*Rank*
Andhra Pradesh	0.298	9	0.377	9	0.416	10
Assam	0.272	10	0.348	10	0.386	14
Bihar	0.237	15	0.308	15	0.367	15
Gujarat	0.360	4	0.431	6	0.479	6
Haryana	0.360	5	0.443	5	0.509	5
Karnataka	0.346	6	0.412	7	0.478	7
Kerala	0.500	1	0.591	1	0.638	1
Madhya Pradesh	0.245	14	0.328	13	0.394	12
Maharashtra	0.363	3	0.452	4	0.523	4
Orissa	0.267	11	0.345	12	0.404	11
Punjab	0.411	2	0.475	2	0.537	2
Rajasthan	0.256	12	0.347	11	0.424	9
Tamil Nadu	0.343	7	0.466	3	0.531	3
Uttar Pradesh	0.255	13	0.314	14	0.388	13
West Bengal	0.305	8	0.404	8	0.472	8
All India	0.302		0.381		0.472	

Source: National Human Development Report-2001, Planning Commission, Government of India.

Based on the HDI, different states are ranked according to their performance in the indicators mentioned above. It should be noted that the BIMARU states where the population is considered to be the major problems are ranked above 12 (out of fifteen) which means that they are performing very poorly in terms of empowerment of human capita, compared to other states. Kerala, which has attained 100 per cent literacy and extended health care facilities to a larger percentage of the households ranks first, followed by Punjab. In the case of Punjab, the economic empowerment in terms of increased per capita income facilitates the people to access good quality health care facilities and education. In the case of remaining states which carry single digit ranking, the performance of HDI is explained by many different factors. It should be noted that in Maharashtra and Gujarat, the industrialisation contributes to the higher level of per capita income which in turn provides means for accessing education and health. In the case of Haryana, it is both agricultural growth and industrialisation that explain the level of attainment of human development. Though the growth of industrialisation and agricultural development are not that much high compared to some of the northern states, the three southern states, namely Karnataka, Tamil Nadu and Andhra Pradesh perform well in terms of human development because of various other factors such as good governance, population control, better access to education and other infrastructure, etc. It should be noted that the HDI developed by the Planning Commission and used to rank the states is not quite comprehensive since it includes only four variables in it. However, in future, the HDI should incorporate more number of other variables such as per capita availability of potable water, level of access to sanitation facilities, etc.

Access, Equity and Equality in Land Resources

Land is the major natural resource in any developing nation and India is not an exception. Equity and equality in land distribution is one of the main objectives of land policy since independence. Land policy in India has been under discussion even prior to independence and especially following the infamous Deccan Riots. One of the important issues on which the peasants backed the independence movement was the land to the tiller policy promised by the then Congress party. In order to keep the promise Congress party appointed a Committee, under the Chairmanship of Late Shri J. C. Kumarappa to look into the problem of land distribution. The Kumarappa Committee gave its report and it was during that time the discussions on land reforms began world over in different countries. There were three important issues confronting the policy makers then. First, land was concentrated in the hands of a few and there was a proliferation of intermediaries who had least interest in self-cultivation of land. Naturally leasing-out land was a common practice. This had affected efficiency as well as distribution. Second, the tenancy contracts were expropriative in nature and the tenant exploitation was ubiquitously prevalent. Land market did not provide open access. Third, the records of land were in extremely bad shape giving rise to large number of litigations. All these factors reflected inequity in ownership and access to land resources.

Historically, India's land revenue system emerged from the Mughal rule, the only rulers then who had control over larger area of the country. Over the years land policy manifested through two different administrative regimes, namely the Mughal System and the British Indian administrative system. Therefore, India had a curious admixture of different processes in land administration. Akbar's attempt to replace the system of assigning revenue of specified areas to officers as their pay by cash salaries, had a very limited success and totally lapsed during the following regimes [Dharmakumar (Ed), 1970]. Two important players dominated the agrarian relations, namely the *ryot* (peasant) and the *Zamindar* (land master) and the State dealt with these to the advantage of optimising revenue. As Sir John Shore explained, "The relation of a *Zamindar* to government and of a *ryot* to *zamindar* is neither that of a proprietor nor a vassal but a compound of both. The former performs acts of authority unconnected with property rights. The latter has rights without real property and the property of one and the rights of the other are in a measure held at discretion" (Quoted in Dharmakumar, 1970; p. 13). During the Mughal period land policy was formulated in clear terms, as land was the major source of revenue. Land policy was more synonymous to land revenue policy. The Adilshahi in the Deccan region of the country and the Mughals from Delhi established a systematic network of land revenue collection through various designated officers. *Marathas* followed this system in western India. In the South the kingdom of Vijayanagaram, Mysore State and the governments of Travancore and Cochin had the *Ryotwari* system in line. Despite the four variants the land policy and revenue system had worked effectively for quite sometime till the British came into power in the country. The British rulers continued with the existing land revenue policy and procedures with a few but significant modifications. British India had typically areas with different agrarian relations and the shades ranged from a complete feudalistic production relations to the *Ryotwari* system (peasant proprietorship). From the north beginning with the Awadh and the *Khalasa* system of land policy in Punjab to the *Zamindari* and *Mirasdari* systems of Central and the *Ryotwari* of the south. Each of these systems dictated a differential emergence of land policy across the country during British regime and surprisingly even in independent India. A review of various document reveal various shades of the emergence of land policy in the country across the provinces (states). This indicates a myriad of the agrarian relations in India, varying from peasant proprietorship to a pure land-lord serf kind of relationship. At the time of independence India had a major challenge to set right the agrarian structure as promised during the struggle of independence. Therefore, the first task before the first Indian parliament was to address the land policy. The driving force of this policy frame was to ensure equitable distribution and free access to land market. Keeping in tune with this theme, the Constitution of India while recognising the need to bring about land reforms in the country provided under Article 39 of the following:

(*i*) That the ownership and control of the material resources of the country should be so distributed as best to serve the common good, and
(*ii*) That the operation of the economic system does not result in concentration of wealth and means to production to the common detriment.

This particular article of the Indian Constitution was the basis for thinking on the redistribution of land and consequently land reforms in the country. Under the Constitution of India, the States are assigned responsibility of land administration and land reform, whereas, at national level the Department of Land Resources in the Central Ministry of Rural Development has a mandate to address land administration and land policy issues.

Broadly there are three significant phases that mark the changes in the land policy in India. Though the theme changed during the five decades the core issues are still revolving around the just distribution of land resources. Land reforms and community development came more or less together and these interventions were meant to provide means of production to the millions of poor who were either lacked access to resources or did not have the required know-how to use them. Initially policy was focused more on bringing under efficient cultivation the land that was left unused. Reforms focused on taking away the land rights of the intermediaries who held large share of the land resources. Close on the heels were the tenancy reforms that began on the hypothesis of 'tenant efficiency' and an expected increase in the capital formation due to tenancy legislations. In addition to these economic goals, the tenancy reforms were taken as an intervention to provide the right to land to the tenant who were always at a receiving end. Access to cultivated land was the focus. Thus abolition of intermediaries and tenancy reforms formed the first phase of reforms. The ceiling on land holding followed this. These were addressed to reduce the concentration of wealth in the hands of a few and providing means of living to others. Second important intervention came in the form of the area-based programmes like Drought-prone Area Programme and Desert Development Programme. Both the programmes focused on augmenting the land resources in these ecologically fragile regions and to provide employment opportunities to the inhabitants. The third important land policy intervention came from the policy emphasis on soil and water conservation through a massive watershed development programme. This programme ran parallel to the Wasteland Development Programme that intended to restore the ecology and environment in drought prone areas.

Abolition of intermediaries was taken to bring under cultivation the unused land and providing access to land to the landless. This component of the reform was quite successful but could not eliminate the intermediaries who were unrecorded. Therefore, the success was confined to only selected regions. The major aspects of tenancy reforms included security of tenure, termination of tenancy, resumption for personal cultivation by the landlord, regulation of rent, and confirmation of ownership rights. Various state laws were enacted between 1960 and 1972. These differed across the states and territories. Owing to the diverse and complicated nature of social and agrarian structure in the countryside, no uniform legislations could be enacted across the states in the country. The consensus on the policy of tenancy reforms favoured neither complete expropriation of landlordism nor favoured interest of the tenants. In the national guidelines the following measures were communicated to the state governments for incorporating in the State level legislation:

(i) Security of the tenancy to be conferred on the actual cultivator.
(ii) Fair rent to be fixed between 1/4th and 1/5th of the gross produce.
(iii) Landowners may be permitted to cultivate land for the personal use.
(iv) The surrender of the tenancy rights with mutual consent.
(v) In respect of some of the area, the landlord tenant nexus to be ended and the tenant cultivator be brought directly under the contact with the state.
(vi) The disabled persons, the defence personnel and such exemptions be provided.
(vii) The term personal cultivation be clearly defined if land were to be resumed for cultivation.
(viii) Correct the record of tenancy and abolish oral tenancy all together.

Table 15.5 shows the changes in land leased in by various groups of cultivators. During the three decades, it can be observed that the concentration of leasing land is higher in the higher size classes. This provides an empirical evidence to the reverse tenancy hypothesis. But overall, the incidence of tenancy has reduced. The experience across States however differs significantly.

Table 15.5: Changes in Leasing of Land in India: 1961 to 1991

(*% of total*)

S. No.	*Farm category*	*1961-62*		*1970-71*		*1980-81*		*1990-91*	
		No. of Holdings	*Area*	*No. of Holdings*	*Area*	*No. of Holdings*	*Area*	*No. of Holdings*	*Area*
1.	Marginal	24.1	16.6	27.0	18.9	14.4	9.7	9.3	8.7
2.	Small	25.1	14.0	27.8	14.6	17.9	8.5	14.9	8.5
3.	Semi-Medium	23.6	11.7	24.8	11.7	15.9	7.3	12.2	7.4
4.	Medium	20.5	9.6	20.9	8.7	14.5	6.6	13.1	6.9
5.	Large	19.5	8.3	15.9	5.9	11.5	5.3	16.7	11.4
6.	All Sizes	23.5	10.7	25.7	10.6	15.2	7.2	11.0	8.3

Source: National Sample Survey Organisation of India, Report No. 407 of 48th Round, 1995, pp. 28-29.

Table 15.6: Distribution of Operational Holdings and Area: All India

(*% of total*)

S. No.	*Category of Holding*	*1970-71*		*1980-81*		*1985-86*		*1990-91*	
		No. of Holdings	*Area*	*No. of Holdings*	*Area*	*No. of Holdings*	*Area*	*No. of Holdings*	*Area*
1.	Marginal (Less than 1 ha)	50.6	8.9	56.4	12.1	57.8	13.4	59.4	15.0
2.	Small (1 to 2 ha)	19.1	11.9	18.1	14.1	18.4	15.6	18.8	17.4
3.	Semi-Medium (2 to 4 ha)	15.2	18.5	14.0	21.2	13.6	22.3	13.1	23.2
4.	Medium (4 to 10 ha)	11.2	29.7	9.1	29.6	8.2	28.6	7.1	27.1
5.	Large (Above 4 ha)	3.9	30.9	2.4	23.0	2.0	20.1	1.6	17.3
	Total (No. of holdings in Millions Area in ha.Millions)	70.5 (100.0)	162.1	88.9 (100.0)	163.8 (100.0)	97.2 (100.0)	164.5 (100.0)	106.6 (100.0)	165.5 (100.0)

Source: Agricultural Statistics at a Glance, Directorate of Economics and Statistics, Govt. of India, for various years.

The land distribution at the time of independence was extremely skewed and 53 per cent land was held by 7 per cent large holdings, whereas 28 per cent of sub-marginal and marginal holdings owned about 6 per cent area (see the figures giving distribution). The land distribution even within the States was also quite skewed and that can be seen from the Lorenz ratios of 1952-53. The ceiling on land holding was felt essential out of three economic compulsions. First, there was a strong argument about inverse size-productivity relationship. Thereby hinting that the aggregate production efficiency gets hampered due to land locked under large holdings. Second, it was believed and supported with evidence that large holders of land leave land fallow thereby leaving land unused. Third, there were large population of land-based poor who wanted to have land as an economic resource for their livelihood. The surplus land could be distributed to such poor people. Finally, the general position in favour of the ceiling was based only on the concentration of social justice and equity and not on the grounds of increasing production and developing agriculture.

Table 15.7: Trends in Distribution of Operational Holdings in Rural India: Major States

(Area % to total)

States	*Sub-Marginal Holdings*	*Marginal Holdings*	*Large Holdings*
Andhra Pradesh	2.96	14.58	21.41
Assam	7.50	26.74	5.28
Bihar	8.27	20.74	11.62
Gujarat	1.29	5.82	44.27
Karnataka	1.12	8.44	34.76
Kerala	23.24	30.03	4.63
Madya Pradesh	0.67	6.03	35.04
Maharashtra	0.75	5.91	38.81
Orissa	3.83	18.27	9.92
Punjab	1.21	4.99	37.69
Rajasthan	0.83	4.73	55.62
Tamil Nadu	7.55	21.39	9.28
Uttar Pradesh	5.39	19.57	10.90
West Bengal	11.83	28.15	1.52
All India 1953-54	1.07	3.36	53.41
1971-72	1.69	7.53	39.17
1991-92	3.32	12.28	28.16

Source: Report on Landholdings (4 &5) 8th Round1953-54, NSS Report No. 66, Report on Some Aspects of Landholdings; 26th Round 1971-72, NSS Report No. 215. Report on Some Aspects of Operational Holdings (1); 48th Round, 1991-92, NSS Report No. 407.

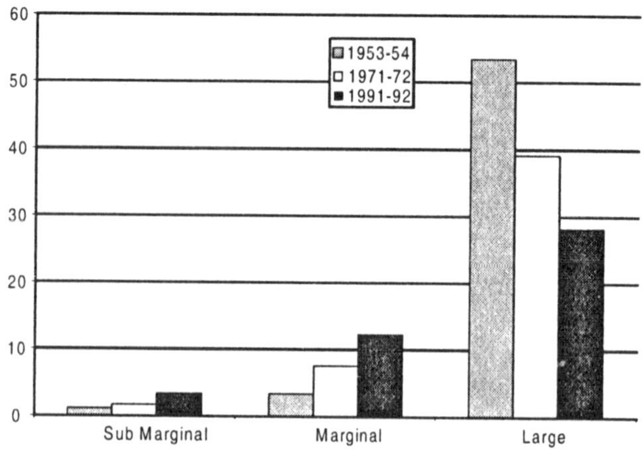

Fig. 15.2: Distribution of Land Holding in India

The ceiling laws were enacted and enforced into phases first beginning at 1960 and the second at 1972. The loopholes that existed in the first phase of legislations were corrected during the second phase. Among the major loopholes that existed in the ceiling acts of various states included the high ceiling limits, retrospective transfers, large number of exemptions, and the basis of fixation of ceiling limits. The national guidelines were prepared during the Chief Minister's conference held in July 1972. But all the states modified or used their own laws which were enacted earlier. Probably the guidelines were too flexible and accommodative to cover the variations in the state specific legislations. Among various factors that featured the debate were the definitions of family, transfers, and standard holding, ceiling area and exempted categories. All these matters complicated the process of implementation.

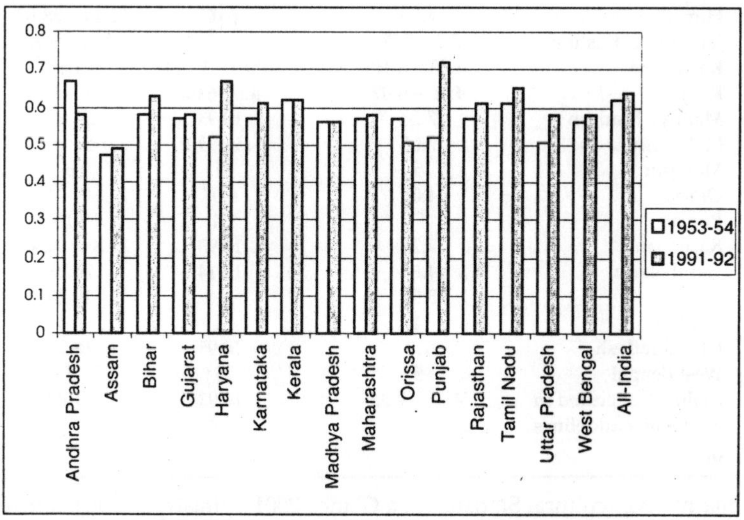

Fig. 15.3: Distribution of Land Holdings: Gini Ratios.

The distribution of land holdings as reflected by the index of inequality (Gini Ratios) indicates increased inequality between 1953-54 and 1991-92. This is certainly due to the fact that large holdings are declining at a fast rate. But at the same time there is tremendous increase in the marginal and sub-marginal holdings. Abolition of intermediaries and ceilings on the land holdings have contributed to this trend significantly. One can however note the differential impact across the states. Therefore, the Gini ratios are different in the magnitude as well as direction of change. The state legislations more or less conformed to the national guidelines so far as fixation of the ceiling limits and distillation of surplus land are concerned.

Table 15.8: Ceiling Limits on Land Holdings of Different States

(*In hectares*)

States	Irrigated Land with two crops	Irrigated Land with one crop	Dry Land
Andhra Pradesh	4.05 to 7.28	6.07 – 10.93	14.16 – 21.85
Assam	6.74	6.47	6.74
Bihar	6.07 to 7.28	10.12	12.14 – 18.21
Gujarat	4.05 – 7.28	6.07-10.93	8.09 – 21.85
Haryana	7.25	10.9	21.8
Himachal Pradesh	4.05	6.07	12.14 – 28.83
Jammu & Kashmir	3.6 – 5.06		5.95 – 9.20
Karnataka	4.05 – 8.10	10.12 – 12.14	21.85
Kerala	4.86 – 6.07	4.86-6.07	4.86 – 6.07
Madhya Pradesh	7.28	10.93	21.85
Maharashtra	7.08	10.93	21.85
Manipur	5	5	6
Orissa	4.05	6.07	12.14 – 18.21
Punjab	7	11	20.5
Rajasthan	7.28	10.93	21.85 – 70.82
Tamil Nadu	4.86	12.14	24.28
Sikkim	5.06		20.23
Tripura	4	4	12
Uttar Pradesh	7.3	10.95	18.25
West Bengal	5	5	7
Ceiling Suggested in National Guidelines of 1972	4.05 – 7.28	10.93	21.85

Source: Agricultural Statistics at a Glance-2001, Ministry of Agriculture and Cooperation, Govt. of India, New Delhi.

The entire emphasis of ceiling on land holding was to detect surplus land which was above economic holding size, acquire that and redistribute it among the landless who require such economic base. However, among the measures taken for efficient utilisation of land resources this component failed on both counts, namely acquiring the surplus land and as the acquisition was meagre the distribution was also insignificant. A government document accepts that "It is widely recognised that the chief reason for the poor implementation of land reforms has been the lack of political will. It would not be surprising to expect so, if we appreciate the realities of the rural situation and development of Indian politics" (quoted in Rao, 1990). Even the micro level studies noted that land tribunals' functioning was not very transparent and doubts were raised about the functioning of the non-official members (Thimmaiah and Aziz, 1983). Despite the limited success in redistribution of surplus agricultural land, ceiling laws have succeeded in keeping a check on concentration of land in the hands of a few. The surplus land distributed does not form even 2 per cent of the total net operated area. Large number of experts now agree that implementation of ceiling laws especially possession and redistribution of surplus land is no longer an option for engendering social equity.

Political Economy Aspects of Land Issues

In India land has always been associated with the social status and historically remained to be in the control of land associated groups. Social stratification is quite strong in India and this is based on Caste system. The main caste groups are *Brahmin, Vaishya, Kshatriya* and *Shudra*. The castes are associated with specific works and hence one can group them in to land associated and others. The land-associated castes are usually the traditional cultivators. The social structure in terms of caste itself was geared to the required segregation between the groups associated with cultivation, trade, teaching along with priestelyhood and other services. This segregation of social structure was associated not only with political base but also with the land ownership pattern in the country. The power nexus derived a good advantage from this social segregation and therefore the emergence of political power in the country can be easily associated with caste groups. Land reforms were taken as the first initiative and to keep the commitment made by the Indian National Congress (the then leading political party) during pre independence movement. The caste groups that were land associated shared the political power and hence the very interests of those responsible for law making were tied with the implementation of the law. Naturally the law was not accompanied by proper implementation. The *Shudras* who were later grouped into Scheduled Castes and Scheduled Tribes groups under the Constitution of India happen to be the weakest economic group and had least access to land.

In the course of last five decades all social groups have confronted the process of shrinking of holding size but the weaker sections suffered it more acutely. It must be noted here that the Scheduled Castes and Scheduled Tribes are the groups that also have the highest concentration of poor in India. What comes out of the data on land holdings of these groups is the sharper marginalisation of these groups.

Table 15.9: Distribution of Ownership Holding among Weaker Sections.

Size Classes	*Scheduled Caste*		*Others*	
	1982	*1992*	*1982*	*1992*
Landless	12.61	13.34	10.18	9.85
Marginal	72.41	72.91	52.20	53.95
Small	8.40	7.85	16.09	13.58
Semi-medium	4.52	3.86	12.05	10.08
Medium	1.80	1.83	7.66	11.48
Large	0.26	0.21	1.82	1.06
Total	100.00	100.00	100.00	100.00

Source: NSS, Land Holding Survey 1982 & 1992, CSO, Delhi.

It can be observed from Table 15.9 that the share of land holdings belonging to Scheduled Castes is declining at a sharper rate than the trend among others. Thus marginalisation process is a clear phenomenon and clearly depicts shrinkage in access to land. Furthermore, their participation in the land lease market is also marginal and largely with small fragments of land. Only 82 thousand hectares were leased-in by the cultivators belonging to Scheduled Castes in the year 1990-91, which is about 0.62 per cent of their total operated area. Even out of this, more than 34 per cent comes under the marginal farmers' group. Clear evidence thus suggests that this group suffer on count of access and equity. The tenancy contracts are generally in terms of share of produce or fixed money rent. The number of holdings under the group of marginal farmers is increasing and that under the size group of large holdings is declining. But the increase in the number of marginal farmers belonging to Scheduled Castes is much faster than in the other Social Groups. Another, most pertinent observation from this table is the group of farmers having small size of holding, belonging to Scheduled Castes, has declined, whereas, the small size of holding has shown an increase among the other Social Groups. This gets clearly reflected in the average size of holding. It is quite alarming that the land base of the rural poor has been sharply declining.

Land—Poverty and Policy Issues

The nexus between the land policy initiatives and growth is quite clear. Though one cannot implicate one to one correspondence between land policy and growth the available evidence is significant enough to suggest such nexus. A paper by Besley and Burgess gave a robust evidence of a link between poverty reduction due to tenancy reforms and abolition of intermediaries. They also inferred that land reforms also benefited the landless (Besley and Burgess, 2000). In this context V.M. Rao's observation is quite pertinent. He wrote "This identification is based on three premices about the role of land reforms and common lands in the emerging development strategy. First, they have to serve as a link helping integration of growth policies with poverty alleviation programmes. Such integration is necessary to focus the development strategy as a whole—and not merely the individual schemes and programmes—on the rural labourers and poor. Second, at the ground level, land reforms and improved access to common lands need to be part of a package of measures specifically designed to the requirement of different sub-groups of rural labourers and poor. Third, the ultimate goal of land reforms and other structural reforms is to promote the emergence of a viable and modernised peasantry consisting of small farmers and providing as much room as possible for the landless to enter the peasant sector" (Rao, 1990). Therefore, land policy though looks distanced from the direct impact on the rural poverty has a significant influence on it.

Land policy intervention and their perceived impact can be located in five different perspectives. The process of land distribution and land access policies have a poverty alleviating impact. But the intensity depends upon the process of implementation. Equity or conflict resolution is another dimension of land policy. It was noted that this goal is achieved to a large extent. The other three aspects, namely environmental management, sustainable economic growth and production efficiency show mixed impact (Table 15.10).

Table 15.10: Policy Interventions and their Perceived Impact

Policy Interventions	*Poverty Alleviation*	*Conflict Management/ Equity*	*Environ-mental Management*	*Sustainable Economic Growth*	*Prod-uction Efficie-ncy*
Abolition of Intermediaries	Neg	Sig	Par	Sig	Sig
Tenancy Reforms	Sig	Sig	Neg	Par	Sig
Ceiling on Size of Holding	Sig	Sig	Neg	Sig	Par
Consolidation of Holdings	Neg	Neg	Par	Par	Sig
Computerisation of Land Records	Neg	Sig	Neg	Neg	Par
Drought prone Area Development Programme and Desert Development Programme	Par	Neg	Sig	Sig	Par
Waste Land Development	Par	Neg	Sig	Sig	Rar

Note: Impact levels are perceived as Sig—Significant, Par—Partial, Neg—Negligible

The policy interventions in India's Land Policy during the last five decades could be seen from the point of view of their impact on various parameters. These were looked from the point of view of the impact on alleviation of poverty, conflict management and equity, sustainable economic development, environmental impact and production efficiency. It was noted that the interventions have varying impact across the States and depending up on the agrarian situation. Among the policy options discussed in the recent past roll back land ceiling laws assumed prominence. It is argued that the ceiling limits do not provide for a viable land size for a family.

As there are no limits on investment in other sectors why agriculturist should face a restriction on increasing the size of holding. Economically viable size of holding is the crux of present crisis. But given the present political and administrative climate in the country this seems to be a difficult option. Where efficiency of small and large farms is found more or less equal, it is necessary to allow size of holding which can generate the investable capital in agriculture sector. The second policy option discussed strongly in a countrywide debate is the desirability of making legal the agricultural tenancy and renting in land. Among the arguments put forth the pro-poor impact of legalising the tenancy has gained ground. It is felt that majority of the beneficiaries will be smaller marginal farmers. Presently there's no protection to the tenant as well as to the landlord.

Towards a Land Policy and Land Use Monitoring Framework

(*i*) The concept of land reforms may have to be reviewed in line with the concepts of New Economic Policy. Although abolition of tenancy has been ideal among the land reform instruments, it is debatable whether the tenancy can ever be entirely abolished even when the man-land ratio in agriculture is favourable for its abolition. Variety of circumstances may necessitate its continuance to some extent in all situations. Even if the redistribution of land is carried out, every rural family cannot possibly be given a piece of land sufficient to provide subsistence. In the short run, only a realistic course of policy is to recognise the inevitability of some tenancy and to legalise and promote the most productivity oriented form of tenancy and not to attempt to outlaw it. Empirical research is required to determine the precise manners in which alternative tenancy arrangements effect input use and productivity.

(*ii*) The classification and maintenance of land records of rights should be given high priority and land records should be constructed before any field level investment planning is taken up in the micro-watersheds. The land use planning recognises the capability of land resources for alternative uses, but their social benefit-cost calculations vary depending on the ownership. For this reason, a clear demarcation of biosphere reserves, production forests, community lands, urban green belt and private level on a priority basis.

(*iii*) The State Land use Boards are organised in some of the states but these do not function effectively as a coordinating and supervising agency of the State Government in ensuring land resources management, development, and conservation. The Land Use Boards should have technical and managerial staff of proven ability to prepare annual action plans for training of extension personnel and coordinate different departmental activities in the implementation of the action plans for agricultural development. The Boards should also function as a regional resource centre for management of the Production Management Information System (PMIS) at the State level.

(*iv*) The Panchayat Raj Institutions should be the grassroots agency for developing the operational (investment) plans for promoting the desired land use at the micro-watershed level.

(*v*) It is necessary to decentralise land revenue administration and the social development programmes like drinking water, primary education, and health care to a constitutional self-government closer to the people. For this purpose adequate financial autonomy has to be ensured to the proposed on Panchayati Raj Institutions and an adequate law and order machinery that should go with it if it is to function effectively as a constitutional third tier of government for micro-ecology development through land use planning.

(*vi*) For effective land use, capability classification of the FAO system of land evaluation has to be preferred to USDA system. The land use survey organisation should be decentralised to district or even taluk level to suggest most appropriate land use and a data card maintained for each holding.

(*vii*) Environmental protection laws which relate to acts as cutting trees should be made more stringent and the growth of the appropriate species on land should be supported by incentives in favour of growing the recommended crop or trees and disincentives for departures from recommended land use. Such a package of incentives and disincentives should be carefully worked out.

(*viii*) The watershed development programme should be implemented in three phase, namely resource conservation, resource development and resource utilisation with human interface. The programme should ensure farmers participation in the development activities including in its financial components. This will ensure equity and access to better quality of land resources.

(*ix*) Instead of Government incurring the expenditure on development of waste lands, the responsibilities should be left to the farmers under the technical prescription of the Department of Agriculture. If the farmers do not undertake the presented advises, it has got to be undertaken by the Department and the cost should be treated as a loan at nominal interest rate.

Equity Aspects of Indian Irrigation

Irrigation constitutes the main component of water use in rural areas. The question of access, equity and equality in water resources gets directly to the use of irrigation water. Though area under irrigation has increased considerably over the years in India, an important issue of who is benefited among the farmers from irrigation expansion is not adequately addressed covering relatively larger period. In order to make proper planning for irrigation development in the future, there is a need to find out answers to the questions such as: Has the expansion of irrigation benefited small farmers? Have the inter-class differences in irrigation widened or narrowed? What is the regional (state) distribution of irrigation by farm size? Keeping this in view, an attempt is made in this section to find out the irrigation development by farm size. Agricultural Census of India has been publishing sourcewise irrigation data by farm size once in five years since 1970-71. Currently data are available for five time points: 1970-71, 1976-77, 1980-81, 1985-86 and 1990-91. These data provide good basis to ascertain access and equity in distribution of irrigation.

Surface Irrigation Development by Farm Size

Though the area under irrigation has increased significantly since independence, the growth rates in the expansion are not the same across different size group of farmers. In view of this, we have made an attempt to analyse the development of irrigation across different sources by farm size. Development of surface sources like canals and tanks by farm size is the major source of irrigation. Area under canal and tank irrigation by farm size for five time points is presented in Table 15.11. Our aim here is not only to find out the growth of irrigation by farm size but also to study the inter-class variation over years. Canal irrigation, which is predominantly controlled by the government agencies, has increased from about 12.17 mha in 1970-71 to 15.67 mha by 1990-91, with a growth rate of 1.27 per cent per annum at the national level. However, the growth is not the same among different size class of farmers. While the area under canal irrigation increased at a rate 3.24 per cent per annum among the marginal farmers, the same declined at a rate of 1.15 per cent among the large farmers. In fact, the growth of canal irrigation is inversely related with farm size between 1970-71 and 1990-91. The marginal size group has not only gained considerably in terms of growth of area under canal irrigation but also gained in terms of percentage to total canal area when compared with the other groups. This disproves the common argument that the canal irrigation benefits mostly the large and resourceful farmers. But such disapproval has to be read with the fact that holding size is always small in the assured irrigated area. The inter-class difference in area under canal irrigation has declined only marginally between 1970-71 and 1990-91, which is shown by coefficient of variation (CV).

Unlike canal irrigation, tank irrigation, which is a user-friendly and low cost source of irrigation, has declined at a rate of 0.85 per cent per annum between 1970-71 and 1990-91, at the national level. However, tank area has increased at a rate of 1.22 per cent per annum among the marginal farmers during this period. Except in the group of marginal and small farmers, the area under tank irrigation has declined among all other size groups. Since the reliability of tank irrigation has declined over the years due to various reasons, farmers belonging to semi-medium, medium and large, who are relatively rich, may have gone to other sources like groundwater irrigation. As a result, area under tank irrigation may have declined among these groups of farmers. Since the marginal farmers are poor and they cannot afford to have other sources like groundwater, their area under tank has been increasing over the years, despite persistent decline in area under tank irrigation at the national level.

Groundwater Irrigation Development by Farm Size

The growth of area under groun dwater irrigation is entirely different from the growth pattern seen in surface irrigation sources. Not only the total area under groundwater irrigation has increased considerably between 1970-71 and 1990-91 but a positive growth has been seen across all size group of farmers (see, Table 15.12). Area under groundwater irrigation is seen to have increased at a rate of over 5 per cent per annum among the marginal and small size groups, whereas the same increased only at a rate of 2.87 per cent and over one per cent respectively among the medium and large size group. A uniform growth of groundwater irrigation taken place across different size of farmers has also reduced the inter-class variations considerably between 1970-71 and 1990-91.

While looking at the area under groundwater irrigation separately by wells and tube wells, we could see different kinds of growth pattern among various categories of farmers. Although area under tube wells has increased considerably among all categories of farmers over the last twenty years, the same trend is not seen with area under well (dug) irrigation. Area under wells registered a marginal increase of 0.94 per cent per annum among the marginal size group, while the same recorded a negative growth of 0.20 per cent among the large size group during the period 1970-71 to 1990-91. We have expected that due to rapid expansion of tube well technology, area under wells would have declined among all categories of farmers. However, against our expectation, it increased at a rate of nearly 2.50 per cent per annum among the small and semi-medium category of farmers. Though there are differences in growth rate between wells and tube wells, not only the area under groundwater (wells + tube wells) has increased over 5 per cent per annum among the marginal and small category farmers, but their share in the total groundwater area has also increased considerably during the last twenty years period considered for the analysis.

Net and Gross Irrigated Area by Farm Size

After having analysed the sourcewise development of irrigated area by farm size, we have made an attempt to study the trends in net and gross irrigated area. Table 15.13 presents the net and gross irrigated area by farm size for all five time points. It is clear from the table that net irrigated area recorded a growth rate above 3 per cent per annum among the marginal and small size category of farmers during the period 1970-71 to 1990-91. However, at the same time, net irrigated area recorded a negative growth of 0.13 per cent per annum among the large size farm category. As observed in canal and groundwater area, the growth of net irrigated area is found to be inversely related with the size of farm in net irrigated area between 1970-71 and 1990-91. The share of irrigated area of marginal and small farmers to total net irrigated area has also improved considerably during this period. The growth pattern of gross irrigated area across farm size is similar to the pattern observed in the net irrigated area. The only major difference between the net and gross irrigated area is that the growth of gross irrigated area recorded at a rate 0.68 per cent per annum among the large size category, but it was found to be negative in the net irrigated area. This indicates increase in cropping intensity among the larger size of holding compared to the other groups.

Apart from analysing the absolute area under irrigation by farm size, there is also a need to compare the irrigated area in relation to cultivated area. In fact, percentage of irrigated area to net sown area or gross cropped area is considered to be one of the appropriate indicators for judging the irrigation development by farm size. Table 15.14 presents percentage of irrigated area to net sown area by farm size for all five time points. It is evident from the table that percentage of NIA to NSA is inversely related with farm size in all five time points. While the NIA to NSA was 43.6 per cent among the marginal size farmers, the same was found to be only half of this amount among the large size category in 1990-91. The size effect certainly plays a dominant role. The same trend is observed at all other four-time points as well. However, the

Table 15.11: Area Under Canal and Tank Irrigation by Farm Size: 1970-71 to 1990-91.

Major Size Classes	*Canals*					*ACGR (%)*	*Tanks*					*ACGR (%)*
	1970-71	*1976-77*	*1980-81*	*1985-86*	*1990-91*		*1970-71*	*1976-77*	*1980-81*	*1985-86*	*1990-91*	
1. Marginal	1,769	2,234	2,696	3,095	3,348	3.24	737	742	941	805	940	1.22
(< 1 ha)	(14.53)	(18.43)	(18.76)	(20.49)	(21.37)		(21.00)	(23.25)	(28.24)	(28.92)	(31.79)	
2. Small	1,991	2,268	2,656	2,865	3,061	2.17	668	627	742	636	682	0.10
(1-2 ha)	(19.14)	(18.71)	(18.48)	(18.96)	(19.54)		(19.03)	(19.64)	(22.27)	(22.84)	(23.06)	
3. Semi-medium	2,714	2,909	3,360	3,514	3,645	1.49	800	730	753	638	654	–1.00
(2-4 ha)	(26.09)	(24.00)	(23.38)	(23.26)	(23.27)		(22.79)	(22.87)	(22.60)	(22.92)	(22.12)	
4. Medium	3,477	3,197	3,778	3,775	3,851	0.51	828	732	636	509	503	–2.46
(4-10 ha)	(33.42)	(26.37)	(26.29)	(24.99)	(24.58)		(23.59)	(22.93)	(19.09)	(18.28)	(17.01)	
5. Large	2,221	1,515	1,883	1,858	1,762	–1.15	477	361	260	196	178	–4.81
(>10 ha)	(21.35)	(12.50)	(13.10)	(12.30)	(11.25)		(13.59)	(11.31)	(7.80)	(7.04)	(6.02)	
All Total	12,172	12,123	14,373	15,107	15,667	1.27	3,510	3,192	3,332	2,784	2,957	–0.85
	(100.00)	(100.00)	(100.00)	(100.00)	(100.00)		(100.00	(100.00)	(100.00)	(100.00)	(100.00)	
CV	27.94	27.04	25.29	24.51	26.26		19.95	25.37	37.87	40.85	47.25	

Notes: ACGR—Annual Compound Growth Rate is 1990-91 over 1970-71; CV—Coefficient of Variation; Figures in brackets are percentage to total area.

Source: GOI, *All India Report on Agricultural Census* (various years), Ministry of Agriculture, Government of India, New Delhi.

Table 15.12: Area Under Groundwater Irrigation by Farm Size: 1970-71 to 1990-91.

(*Area in '000 ha*)

Major Size Classes	*Wells*					*ACGR (%)*	*Tube wells*					*ACGR (%)*
	1970-71	*1976-77*	*1980-81*	*1985-86*	*1990-91*		*1970-71*	*1976-77*	*1980-81*	*1985-86*	*1990-91*	
1. Marginal	842	806	858	885	1,015	0.94	677	1,270	1,793	2,579	3,319	8.27
(< 1 ha)	(12.63)	(13.06)	(12.25)	(15.41)	(11.17)		(13.98)	(21.24)	(18.59)	(19.54)	(22.59)	
2. Small	975	904	1,036	1,136	1,611	2.54	742	1142	1698	2457	3013	7.26
(1-2 ha)	(14.62)	(14.65)	(14.79)	(19.78)	(17.73)		(15.32)	(19.10)	(17.60)	(18.61)	(20.51)	
3. Semi-medium	1459	1390	1647	629	2311	2.33	1159	1519	2341	3266	3555	5.76
(2-4 ha)	(21.88)	(22.53)	(23.51)	(10.95)	(25.43)		(23.94)	(25.40)	(24.27)	(24.74)	(24.20)	
4. Medium	2036	1973	2254	2035	2845	1.69	1535	1553	2661	3526	3442	4.12
(4-10 ha)	(30.53)	(31.98)	(32.18)	(35.43)	(31.31)		(31.70)	(25.97)	(27.58)	(26.71)	(23.43)	
5. Large	1357	1097	1210	1058	1305	–0.20	729	496	1154	1373	1364	3.18
(>10 ha)	(20.35)	(17.78)	(17.27)	(18.42)	(14.36)		(15.06)	(8.29)	(11.96)	(10.40)	(9.28)	
All Total	6669	6170	7005	5743	9087	1.56	4842	5980	9647	13201	14693	5.71
	(100.00)	(100.00)	(100.00)	(100.00)	(100.00)		(100.00)	(100.00)	(100.00)	(100.00)	(100.00)	
CV	35.16	38.04	39.94	46.35	41.25		38.32	35.72	30.42	31.80	30.74	

(*Contd.*)

Table 15.13: (*Contd.*)

(*Area in '000 ha*)

Major Size Classes	*Total Wells*					*ACGR (%)*
	1970-71	*1976-77*	*1980-81*	*1985-86*	*1990-91*	
1. Marginal (< 1 ha)	1,519 (13.20)	2,076 (17.09)	2,651 (15.92)	3,464 (18.29)	4,334 (18.23)	5.38
2. Small (1-2 ha)	1717 (14.92)	2046 (16.84)	2734 (16.42)	3593 (18.97)	4624 (19.44)	5.08
3. Semi-medium (2-4 ha)	2618 (22.74)	2909 (23.94)	3988 (23.95)	3895 (20.56)	5866 (24.67)	4.12
4. Medium (4-10 ha)	3571 (31.02)	3526 (29.02)	4915 (29.52)	5561 (29.35)	6287 (26.44)	2.87
5. Large (>10 ha)	2086 (18.12)	1593 (13.11)	2364 (14.20)	2431 (12.83)	2669 (11.22)	1.24
All Total	11511 (100.00)	12150 (100.00)	16652 (100.00)	18944 (100.00)	23780 (100.00)	3.69
CV	35.77	31.90	32.53	29.92	29.97	

Notes: ACGR—Annual Compound Growth Rate is 1990-91 over 1970-71; CV—Coefficient of Variation;Figures in brackets are percentage to total area.

Source: GOI, *All India Report on Agricultural Census*,(various years), Ministry of Agriculture, Government of India, New Delhi.

Table 15.14: Area Under Net and Gross Irrigation by Farm Size: 1970-71 to 1990-91

(*Area in '000 ha*)

Major Size Classes	*Net Irrigated Area*					*ACGR (%)*	*Gross Irrigated Area*					*ACGR (%)*
	1970-71	*1976-77*	*1980-81*	*1985-86*	*1990-91*		*1970-71*	*1976-77*	*1980-81*	*1985-86*	*1990-91*	
1. Marginal (< 1 ha)	4,393 (15.09)	5,606 (18.79)	6,872 (18.67)	8,062 (19.92)	9,457 (20.69)	3.91	5,390 (15.09)	6,693 (18.88)	8,467 (17.88)	10,659 (20.03)	13,215 (21.43)	4.59
2. Small (1-2 ha)	4,741 (16.29)	5,425 (18.18)	6,618 (17.98)	7,656 (18.92)	9,085 (19.88)	3.31	5,833 (16.33)	6,419 (18.11)	8,193 (17.31)	9,970 (18.73)	12,075 (19.58)	3.71
3. Semi-medium (2-4 ha)	6,604 (22.69)	7,133 (23.91)	8,713 (23.67)	9,684 (23.93)	10,971 (24.00)	2.57	8,147 (22.81)	8,622 (24.32)	11,201 (23.66)	12,821 (24.09)	14,505 (23.52)	2.93
4. Medium (4-10 ha)	8,332 (28.63)	7,980 (26.75)	9,873 (26.83)	10,360 (25.60)	11,286 (24.69)	1.53	10,231 (28.64)	9,447 (26.65)	13,158 (27.79)	13,551 (25.46)	14,866 (24.11)	1.89
5. Large (>10 ha)	5,037 (17.31)	3,693 (12.38)	4,727 (12.84)	4,700 (11.62)	4,905 (10.73)	-0.13	6,116 (17.12)	4,268 (12.04)	6,325 (13.36)	6,227 (11.70)	6,998 (11.35)	0.68
All Total	29,107 (100.00)	29,837 (100.00)	36,803 (100.00)	40,462 (100.00)	45,704 (100.00)	2.28	35,717 (100.00)	35,449 (100.00)	47,344 (100.00)	53,228 (100.00)	61,659 (100.00)	2.77
CV	28.15	27.80	27.06	27.20	27.89		28.33	28.62	28.50	27.04	25.78	

Notes: ACGR—Annual Compound Growth Rate is 1990-91 over 1970-71; CV—Coefficient of Variation; Figures in brackets are percentage to total area.

Source: GOI, *All India Report on Agricultural Census*, (various years), Ministry of Agriculture, Government of India, New Delhi.

growth in share of irrigated area is almost positively related with the farm size. For instance, while the growth of percentage of irrigated area recorded a growth rate of 2.78 per cent among the large size category, the same was only 1.28 per cent per annum among the marginal size farmers between 1970-71 and 1990-91.

Table 15.15: Percentage of Net Irrigated Area to Net Sown Area

Size Classes	*1970-71*	*1976-77*	*1980-81*	*1985-86*	*1990-91*	*ACGR (%)*
1. Marginal (< 1 ha)	33.8	37.5	40.2	42.8	43.6	1.28
2. Small (1-2 ha)	27.9	30.6	32.7	34.3	35.7	1.24
3. Semi-medium (2-4 ha)	25.2	26.6	29.3	30.7	32.8	1.33
4. Medium (4-10 ha)	20.4	20.3	24.2	26.1	29.7	1.90
5. Large (>10 ha)	13.0	12.4	16.3	18.8	22.5	2.78
All Size Class	21.4	23.2	26.9	29.4	32.6	2.13
CV	32.64	37.74	31.46	29.38	23.61	

Notes: ACGR—Annual Compound Growth Rate is 1990-91 over 1970-71.

CV—Coefficient of Variation.

Source: GOI, *All India Report on Agricultural Census* (various years), Ministry of Agriculture, Government of India, New Delhi.

This is entirely different from the results arrived using (absolute) area under irrigation. On the whole, what is clear from the above is that though the growth of area under irrigation across different sources is inversely related with the farm size category, the growth of percentage of irrigated area to net sown area is positively associated with the farm size category. In other words, access to the sources of irrigation has been free, however distribution generates the problems about equity. The access as well as equity in irrigation is governed mainly by the ownership of land and land based assets. However, as irrigation brings down the economic viability threshold on the scale of land holding, the small and semi-medium farmers get larger benefits.

Irrigation expansion by farm size across states

Access, equity and the impact of irrigation varies across regions in the country. From the policy viewpoint it is pertinent to analyse these aspects across states. Since the agro-climatic conditions in each state are different, the results arrived at the national level in respect of irrigation expansion by farm size may not be the same with the states. Therefore, we have made an attempt to study and compare the irrigation development by farm size across the states by taking data covering two time points: 1970-71 and 1990-91. Our main objective here is to study the growth pattern of different sources of irrigation by farm size. Table 15.15 presents statewise and sourcewise area under irrigation by farm size for two time points mentioned above. Looking first into the growth pattern of canal irrigation by farm size across the states, it is seen that out of 15 states considered for the analysis, except five states (Jammu and Kashmir, Kerala, Punjab, Tamil Nadu and West Bengal), the growth of canal irrigated area is inversely related with the farm size in all other states between 1970-71 and 1990-91. Both in Punjab and Tamil Nadu, which have relatively more area under canal irrigation, the area under canal irrigation declined at a rate of over 3 and 6 per cent per annum respectively among the marginal size category.

The growth pattern of tank irrigation is not uniform across different farm size groups and states. Since tank irrigation is an important source in South Indian states, a specific look at Andhra Pradesh, Karnataka and Tamil Nadu provides some clues. Even in these three states, the growth pattern of tank irrigation is found to be different. The growth of area under tank irrigation is found to be inversely related with the farm size in Andhra Pradesh, but a mixed growth pattern is seen across farm size in Tamil Nadu. One thing is clearly emerging out from Table 15.16 is that the area under tank irrigation recorded a positive growth in majority of the states among the marginal farmers category between 1970-71 and 1990-91, as noticed at the national level.

Unlike tank irrigation, a positive rate of growth in area under total well irrigation is observed across farm size in most of the states, as observed at the national level. The growth rate of total well irrigation is inversely related with the farm size in almost all the states, except in Orissa and Punjab. While the growth rate of total well irrigation is positively related with the farm size in Punjab, the same has declined in all categories of farm size, except semi-medium, in Orissa.

Although there are differences in growth rates of each source

Table 15.16: Statewise and Sourcewise Area under Irrigation by Farm Size: 1970-71 and 1990-91

(*Area in '000 ha*)

State	*Farm Size*	*1970-71*						
		Canal	*Tank*	*Well*	*T.well*	*Total well*	*NIA*	*GIA*
(1)	(2)	(3)	(4)	(5)	(6)	(7)	(8)	(9)
1. Andhra Pradesh	< 1 ha	277	209	39	5	44	547	653
	1-2 ha	270	182	51	6	57	526	626
	2-4 ha	329	218	80	10	90	665	793
	4-10 ha	369	259	120	14	134	799	956
	> 10 ha	185	217	110	11	121	533	635
	Total	1,430	1,085	400	46	446	3,070	3,663
	CV	24.27	12.73	44.29	40.23	43.78	19.21	19.40
2. Bihar	< 1 ha	146	15	53	50	103	414	484
	1-2 ha	141	13	39	43	82	368	435
	2-4 ha	211	26	55	69	124	551	651
	4-10 ha	254	32	46	76	122	588	709
	> 10 ha	155	19	20	46	66	324	403
	Total	907	105	213	284	497	2,245	2,682
	CV	27.19	37.65	33.14	25.98	25.39	25.67	25.31
3. Gujarat	< 1 ha	11	2	23	3	26	41	43
	1-2 ha	19	2	54	7	61	85	90
	2-4 ha	38	4	130	14	144	193	203
	4-10 ha	72	7	315	21	336	428	454
	> 10 ha	37	5	232	9	241	289	306
	Total	177	20	754	54	808	1,036	1,096
	CV	66.45	53.03	81.01	64.28	79.21	75.62	75.88
4. Haryana	< 1 ha	27	0	5	19	24	52	71
	1-2 ha	60	0	11	40	51	113	152
	2-4 ha	149	0	23	99	122	277	374
	4-10 ha	366	0	40	206	246	624	836
	> 10 ha	331	0	21	148	169	511	680
	Total	933	0	100	512	612	1,577	2,113
	CV	83.00	0.00	66.90	75.13	73.34	78.52	78.16
5. Jammu & Kashmir	< 1 ha	116	1	0	1	1	120	138
	1-2 ha	64	0	0	0	0	66	77
	2-4 ha	59	0	0	0	0	60	74
	4-10 ha	24	0	0	0	0	24	29
	> 10 ha	3	0	0	0	0	4	5
	Total	266	1	0	1	1	274	323
	CV	81.21	223.61	0.00	223.61	223.61	81.26	79.12
6. Karnataka	< 1 ha	52	50	15	0	15	128	154
	1-2 ha	73	60	24	0	24	174	212
	2-4 ha	106	81	40	0	40	254	313
	4-10 ha	139	91	62	0	62	324	396
	> 10 ha	97	45	56	0	56	220	287
	Total	467	327	197	0	197	1,100	1,362
	CV	35.43	30.40	51.07	0.00	51.07	34.13	34.24

(*Contd.*)

Table 15.16: (*Contd.*)

State	Farm Size	1970-71						
		Canal	Tank	Well	T.well	Total well	NIA	GIA
(1)	(2)	(10)	(11)	(12)	(13)	(14)	(15)	(16)
7. Kerala	< 1 ha	21	14	11	1	12	58	78
	1-2 ha	228	7	7	1	8	48	70
	2-4 ha	27	5	6	1	7	52	76
	4-10 ha	10	3	3	0	3	20	29
	> 10 ha	2	0	1	0	1	5	7
	Total	288	29	28	3	31	183	260
	CV	166.23	90.74	68.70	91.29	69.75	62.59	61.79
8. Madhya Pradesh	< 1 ha	61	7	24	1	25	97	99
	1-2 ha	86	14	41	2	43	147	151
	2-4 ha	148	23	90	2	92	274	281
	4-10 ha	232	44	202	3	205	508	528
	> 10 ha	175	41	189	3	192	439	451
	Total	702	129	546	11	557	1,465	1,510
	CV	48.97	63.18	75.60	38.03	74.80	60.97	61.44
9. Maharashtra	< 1 ha	17	15	28	0	28	70	78
	1-2 ha	28	27	54	0	54	121	133
	2-4 ha	47	44	123	0	123	233	257
	4-10 ha	75	64	277	0	277	440	484
	> 10 ha	54	45	257	0	257	371	405
	Total	221	195	739	0	739	1,235	1,357
	CV	51.28	48.07	77.43	0.00	77.43	64.02	63.77
10. Orissa	< 1 ha	113	27	2	2	4	154	3
	1-2 ha	158	22	6	3	9	201	3
	2-4 ha	116	37	2	2	4	165	3
	4-10 ha	105	37	2	3	5	152	3
	> 10 ha	22	26	0	2	2	54	1
	Total	514	149	12	12	24	726	13
	CV	48.29	22.93	91.29	22.82	53.93	37.64	34.40
11. Punjab	< 1 ha	74	0	23	58	81	156	248
	1-2 ha	123	0	31	110	141	266	416
	2-4 ha	269	0	51	267	318	581	899
	4-10 ha	528	0	63	528	591	1,127	1,697
	> 10 ha	391	0	25	295	320	718	1,024
	Total	1,385	0	193	1,258	1,451	2,848	4,284
	CV	67.78	0.00	45.53	73.30	68.52	67.77	66.55
12. Rajasthan	< 1 ha	14	17	71	2	73	105	119
	1-2 ha	34	26	125	4	129	194	215
	2-4 ha	104	41	243	9	252	405	444
	4-10 ha	341	51	411	18	429	834	904
	> 10 ha	469	26	905	10	915	817	912
	Total	962	161	1,755	43	1,798	2,355	2,594
	CV	105.02	42.21	95.73	72.43	94.32	72.51	72.17

(*Contd.*)

Table 15.16: (*Contd.*)

State	Farm Size	1970-71						
		Canal	Tank	Well	T.well	Total well	NIA	GIA
(1)	(2)	(3)	(4)	(5)	(6)	(7)	(8)	(9)
13. Uttar Pradesh	< 1 ha	482	89	416	519	935	1,604	1,804
	1-2 ha	514	72	364	504	868	1,532	1,747
	2-4 ha	665	68	409	656	1,065	1,873	2,161
	4-10 ha	631	42	298	633	931	1,661	1,927
	> 10 ha	216	11	60	191	251	500	573
	Total	2,508	282	1,547	2,503	4,050	7,170	8,212
	CV	35.32	53.99	47.56	37.09	39.58	37.47	37.66
14. Tamil Nadu	< 1 ha	991	236	125	8	133	597	817
	1-2 ha	201	180	162	9	171	557	758
	2-4 ha	208	182	199	12	211	606	814
	4-10 ha	165	151	190	13	203	523	689
	> 10 ha	56	55	77	5	82	196	250
	Total	1,621	804	753	47	800	2,479	3,328
	CV	116.50	41.44	33.36	34.14	33.34	34.46	35.77
15. West Bengal	< 1 ha	94	52	3	5	8	172	224
	1-2 ha	127	59	4	9	13	219	277
	2-4 ha	162	69	4	12	16	265	326
	4-10 ha	101	43	1	9	10	165	203
	> 10 ha	4	2	0	1	1	27	10
	Total	488	225	12	36	48	848	1,040
	CV	60.17	57.46	75.69	59.25	59.20	52.66	57.98

Table 15.16: (*Contd.*)

State	Farm Size	1990-91						
		Canal	Tank	Well	T.well	Total well	NIA	GIA
(1)	(2)	(10)	(11)	(12)	(13)	(14)	(15)	(16)
1. Andhra Pradesh	< 1 ha	586	365	147	66	213	1,208	1,506
	1-2 ha	444	279	203	73	276	1,043	1,252
	2-4 ha	436	268	243	93	343	1,090	1,289
	4-10 ha	328	213	226	100	266	911	1,053
	> 10 ha	80	70	90	40	462	295	326
	Total	1,874	1,195	909	372	1,560	4,547	5,426
	CV	50.31	45.62	34.56	31.93	30.69	39.54	41.82
2. Bihar	< 1 ha	406	49	84	315	399	1,137	1,194
	1-2 ha	194	23	44	196	240	599	702
	2-4 ha	262	36	52	249	301	758	929
	4-10 ha	168	19	42	154	196	482	696
	> 10 ha	40	6	15	31	46	113	188
	Total	1,070	133	237	945	1,182	3,089	3,709
	CV	62.68	61.92	52.23	56.56	55.36	60.72	49.98

(*Contd.*)

Table 15.16: *(Contd.)*

State	Farm Size	1990-91						
		Canal	Tank	Well	T.well	Total well	NIA	GIA
(1)	(2)	(10)	(11)	(12)	(13)	(14)	(15)	(16)
3. Gujarat	< 1 ha	38	1	71	42	113	157	184
	1-2 ha	72	2	184	88	272	359	412
	2-4 ha	113	3	324	139	463	602	692
	4-10 ha	115	5	463	146	609	758	880
	> 10 ha	25	2	133	34	167	201	239
	Total	363	13	1,175	449	1,624	2,077	2,407
	CV	57.18	58.33	67.22	58.35	63.92	62.33	61.91
4. Haryana	< 1 ha	97	0	1	122	123	223	405
	1-2 ha	163	0	2	198	200	368	586
	2-4 ha	292	0	7	389	396	698	1,210
	4-10 ha	479	0	4	509	513	1,003	1,565
	> 10 ha	275	0	1	263	264	540	664
	Total	1,306	0	15	1,481	1,496	2,832	4,430
	CV	55.87	0.00	84.98	52.03	52.10	53.40	54.62
5. Jammu & Kashmir	< 1 ha	72	1	0	1	1	110	158
	1-2 ha	58	1	82	1	83	170	125
	2-4 ha	57	1	0	1	1	86	122
	4-10 ha	24	0	0	0	0	35	52
	> 10 ha	6	0	0	0	0	7	13
	Total	217	3	82	3	85	408	470
	CV	63.01	91.29	223.61	91.29	217.05	78.42	63.31
6. Karnataka	< 1 ha	130	53	35	12	47	251	290
	1-2 ha	181	63	20	26	46	332	451
	2-4 ha	235	69	116	39	155	515	601
	4-10 ha	253	66	152	45	197	578	665
	> 10 ha	83	25	79	25	104	238	273
	Total	882	276	402	147	549	1,914	2,280
	CV	40.28	32.47	68.42	43.99	60.57	40.58	38.89
7. Kerala	< 1 ha	34	27	48	2	50	140	204
	1-2 ha	22	10	235	1	236	285	88
	2-4 ha	18	7	13	1	14	51	61
	4-10 ha	9	4	5	0	5	23	30
	> 10 ha	1	3	5	1	6	13	16
	Total	84	51	306	5	311	512	399
	CV	74.99	95.91	161.39	70.71	158.97	111.02	93.77
8. Madhya Pradesh	< 1 ha	183	12	93	9	102	315	327
	1-2 ha	264	18	294	25	319	646	611
	2-4 ha	390	26	407	55	462	965	1,016
	4-10 ha	490	36	638	135	773	1,447	1,492
	> 10 ha	287	21	366	131	497	930	965
	Total	1,614	113	1,798	355	2,153	4,303	4,411
	CV	36.90	40.02	54.77	83.06	57.25	48.72	50.00

(Contd.)

Table 15.16: (*Contd.*)

State	Farm Size	1990-91						
		Canal	Tank	Well	T.well	Total well	NIA	GIA
(1)	(2)	(10)	(11)	(12)	(13)	(14)	(15)	(16)
9. Maha-rashtra	< 1 ha	77	18	127	0	127	263	300
	1-2 ha	117	28	0	1	1	204	557
	2-4 ha	116	28	410	2	412	616	684
	4-10 ha	70	22	406	2	408	540	602
	> 10 ha	12	5	118	0	118	145	162
	Total	392	101	1,061	5	1,066	1,768	2,305
	CV	54.81	47.02	87.48	100.00	87.43	59.61	47.79
10. Orissa	< 1 ha	199	26	2	1	3	246	350
	1-2 ha	226	27	3	2	5	283	390
	2-4 ha	218	32	5	1	6	281	355
	4-10 ha	110	22	4	1	5	153	189
	> 10 ha	20	9	1	0	1	33	36
	Total	773	116	15	5	20	996	1,320
	CV	57.12	37.50	52.70	70.71	50.00	53.64	56.55
11. Punjab	< 1 ha	39	0	0	104	104	144	275
	1-2 ha	85	0	1	205	206	294	554
	2-4 ha	199	0	1	552	553	761	1,486
	4-10 ha	474	0	1	992	993	1,489	2,855
	> 10 ha	384	0	0	578	578	975	1,887
	Total	1,181	0	3	2,431	2,434	3,663	7,057
	CV	79.64	0.00	91.29	72.26	72.21	73.84	73.82
12. Rajasthan	< 1 ha	46	10	104	30	134	194	251
	1-2 ha	100	16	214	51	265	388	462
	2-4 ha	244	24	432	91	523	802	975
	4-10 ha	633	29	702	133	835	1,511	1,903
	> 10 ha	401	11	440	51	491	909	1,172
	Total	1,424	90	1,892	356	2,248	3,804	4,763
	CV	83.75	45.98	61.08	57.59	59.82	67.24	68.13
13. Uttar Pradesh	< 1 ha	1,052	22	48	2,083	2,131	3,279	5,271
	1-2 ha	797	55	64	1,719	1,783	2,686	3,949
	2-4 ha	767	11	59	1,621	1,680	2,503	3,533
	4-10 ha	522	5	37	1,087	1,124	1,677	2,151
	> 10 ha	98	1	10	188	198	303	450
	Total	3,236	94	218	6,698	6,916	10,448	15,354
	CV	55.60	115.59	49.26	54.93	54.57	55.10	59.91
14. Tamil Nadu	< 1 ha	255	287	211	48	259	816	872
	1-2 ha	182	1	211	37	248	439	624
	2-4 ha	163	111	200	37	237	517	586
	4-10 ha	119	70	147	31	178	369	411
	> 10 ha	43	25	45	12	57	126	136
	Total	762	494	814	165	979	2,267	2,629
	CV	51.46	114.74	43.60	40.14	42.73	55.14	51.93

(*Contd.*)

Table 15.16: (*Contd.*)

State	Farm Size	1990-91						
		Canal	Tank	Well	T.well	Total well	NIA	GIA
(1)	(2)	(10)	(11)	(12)	(13)	(14)	(15)	(16)
15. West Bengal	< 1 ha	90	66	41	473	514	856	1,534
	1-2 ha	88	0	53	382	435	685	1,216
	2-4 ha	61	38	42	273	315	538	858
	4-10 ha	17	11	16	90	106	174	249
	> 10 ha	0	0	0	2	2	3	5
	Total	256	115	152	1,220	1,372	2,256	3,862
	CV	80.21	124.43	71.49	80.57	78.88	78.65	83.08

Table 15.16: (*Contd.*)

State	Farm Size	ACGR: 1990-91 over 1970-71						
		Canal	Tank	Well	T.well	Total well	NIA	GIA
(1)	(2)	(17)	(18)	(19)	(20)	(21)	(22)	(23)
1. Andhra Pradesh	< 1 ha	3.82	2.83	6.86	13.77	8.20	4.04	4.27
	1-2 ha	2.52	2.16	7.15	13.31	8.21	3.48	3.53
	2-4 ha	1.42	1.04	5.71	11.80	6.92	2.50	2.46
	4-10 ha	-0.59	-0.97	3.22	10.33	3.49	0.66	0.48
	> 10 ha	-4.11	-5.50	-1.00	6.67	6.93	-2.91	-3.28
	Total	1.36	0.48	4.19	11.02	6.46	1.98	1.98
	CV							
2. Bihar	< 1 ha	5.25	6.10	2.33	9.64	7.01	5.18	4.62
	1-2 ha	1.61	2.89	0.60	7.88	5.52	2.47	2.42
	2-4 ha	1.09	1.64	-0.28	6.63	4.53	1.61	1.79
	4-10 ha	-2.05	-2.57	-0.45	3.59	2.40	-0.99	-0.09
	> 10 ha	-6.55	-5.60	-1.43	-1.95	-1.79	-5.13	-3.74
	Total	0.83	1.19	0.54	6.20	4.43	1.61	1.63
	CV							
3. Gujarat	< 1 ha	6.39	-3.41	5.80	14.11	7.62	6.94	7.54
	1-2 ha	6.89	0.00	6.32	13.49	7.76	7.47	7.90
	2-4 ha	5.60	-1.43	4.67	12.16	6.01	5.85	6.32
	4-10 ha	2.37	-1.67	1.94	10.18	3.02	2.90	3.36
	> 10 ha	-1.94	-4.48	-2.74	6.87	-1.82	-1.80	-1.23
	Total	3.66	-2.13	2.24	11.17	3.55	3.54	4.01
	CV							
4. Haryana	< 1 ha	6.60	0.00	-7.73	9.74	8.51	7.55	9.10
	1-2 ha	5.12	0.00	-8.17	8.33	7.07	6.08	6.98
	2-4 ha	3.42	0.00	-5.77	7.08	6.06	4.73	6.05
	4-10 ha	1.35	0.00	-10.87	4.63	3.74	2.40	3.18
	> 10 ha	-0.92	0.00	-14.12	2.92	2.26	0.28	-0.12
	Total	1.70	0.00	-9.05	5.45	4.57	2.97	3.77
	CV							

(*Contd.*)

Table 15.16: (*Contd.*)

State	Farm Size	ACGR: 1990-91 over 1970-71						
		Canal	Tank	Well	T.well	Total well	NIA	GIA
(1)	(2)	(17)	(18)	(19)	(20)	(21)	(22)	(23)
5. Jammu & Kashmir	< 1 ha	-2.36	0.00	0.00	0.00	0.00	-0.43	0.68
	1-2 ha	-0.49	0.00	0.00	0.00	0.00	4.84	2.45
	2-4 ha	-0.17	0.00	0.00	0.00	0.00	1.82	2.53
	4-10 ha	0.00	0.00	0.00	0.00	0.00	1.90	2.96
	> 10 ha	3.53	0.00	0.00	0.00	0.00	2.84	4.89
	Total	-1.01	5.65	0.00	5.65	24.87	2.01	1.89
	CV							
6. Karnataka	< 1 ha	4.69	0.29	4.33	0.00	5.88	3.42	3.22
	1-2 ha	4.64	0.24	-0.91	0.00	3.31	3.28	3.85
	2-4 ha	4.06	-0.80	5.47	0.00	7.01	3.60	3.32
	4-10 ha	3.04	-1.59	4.59	0.00	5.95	2.94	2.63
	> 10 ha	-0.78	-2.90	1.74	0.00	3.14	0.39	-0.25
	Total	3.23	-0.84	3.63	0.00	5.26	2.81	2.61
	CV							
7. Kerala	< 1 ha	2.44	3.34	7.64	3.53	7.40	4.50	4.92
	1-2 ha	-11.03	1.80	19.21	0.00	18.44	9.32	1.15
	2-4 ha	-2.01	1.70	3.94	0.00	3.53	-0.10	-1.09
	4-10 ha	-0.53	1.45	2.59	0.00	2.59	0.70	0.17
	> 10 ha	-3.41	0.00	8.38	0.00	9.37	4.89	4.22
	Total	-5.97	2.86	12.70	2.59	12.22	5.28	2.16
	CV							
8. Madhya Pradesh	< 1 ha	5.65	2.73	7.01	11.61	7.28	6.07	6.16
	1-2 ha	5.77	1.26	10.35	13.46	10.54	7.68	7.24
	2-4 ha	4.96	0.61	7.84	18.02	8.40	6.50	6.64
	4-10 ha	3.81	-1.00	5.92	20.97	6.86	5.37	5.33
	> 10 ha	2.50	-3.29	3.36	20.78	4.87	3.82	3.88
	Total	4.25	-0.66	6.14	18.97	6.99	5.54	5.51
	CV							
9. Maharashtra	< 1 ha	7.85	0.92	7.85	0.00	7.85	6.84	6.97
	1-2 ha	7.41	0.18	0.00	0.00	-18.08	2.65	7.42
	2-4 ha	4.62	-2.23	6.20	0.00	6.23	4.98	5.02
	4-10 ha	-0.34	-5.20	1.93	0.00	1.96	1.03	1.10
	> 10 ha	-7.24	-10.40	-3.82	0.00	-3.82	-4.59	-4.48
	Total	2.91	-3.24	1.82	0.00	1.85	1.81	2.68
	CV							
10. Orissa	< 1 ha	2.87	-0.19	0.00	-3.41	-1.43	2.37	26.87
	1-2 ha	1.81	1.03	-3.41	-2.01	-2.90	1.73	27.55
	2-4 ha	3.20	-0.72	4.69	-3.41	2.05	2.70	26.96
	4-10 ha	0.23	-2.57	3.53	-5.34	0.00	0.03	23.02
	> 10 ha	-0.48	-5.17	0.00	0.00	-3.41	-2.43	19.62
	Total	2.06	-1.24	1.12	-4.28	-0.91	1.59	25.99
	CV							

(*Contd.*)

Table 15.16: *(Contd.)*

State	Farm Size	ACGR: 1990-91 over 1970-71						
		Canal	Tank	Well	T.well	Total well	NIA	GIA
(1)	(2)	(17)	(18)	(19)	(20)	(21)	(22)	(23)
11. Punjab	< 1 ha	-3.15	0.00	0.00	2.96	1.26	-0.40	0.52
	1-2 ha	-1.83	0.00	-15.78	3.16	1.91	0.50	1.44
	2-4 ha	-1.50	0.00	-17.85	3.70	2.81	1.36	2.54
	4-10 ha	-0.54	0.00	-18.71	3.20	2.63	1.40	2.64
	> 10 ha	-0.09	0.00	0.00	3.42	3.00	1.54	3.10
	Total	-0.79	0.00	-18.80	3.35	2.62	1.27	2.53
	CV							
12. Rajasthan	< 1 ha	6.13	-2.62	1.93	14.50	3.08	3.12	3.80
	1-2 ha	5.54	-2.40	2.72	13.57	3.67	3.53	3.90
	2-4 ha	4.36	-2.64	2.92	12.26	3.72	3.48	4.01
	4-10 ha	3.14	-2.78	2.71	10.52	3.39	3.02	3.79
	> 10 ha	-0.78	-4.21	-3.54	8.49	-3.06	0.53	1.26
	Total	1.98	-2.87	0.38	11.15	1.12	2.43	3.09
	CV							
13. Uttar Pradesh	< 1 ha	3.98	-6.75	-10.23	7.20	4.21	3.64	5.51
	1-2 ha	2.22	-1.34	-8.32	6.33	3.66	2.85	4.16
	2-4 ha	0.72	-8.71	-9.23	4.63	2.31	1.46	2.49
	4-10 ha	-0.94	-10.09	-9.91	2.74	0.95	0.05	0.55
	> 10 ha	-3.87	-11.30	-8.57	-0.08	-1.18	-2.47	-1.20
	Total	1.28	-5.34	-9.33	5.04	2.71	1.90	3.18
	CV							
14. Tamil Nadu	< 1 ha	-6.56	0.98	2.65	9.37	3.39	1.57	0.33
	1-2 ha	-0.50	-22.87	1.33	7.32	1.88	-1.18	-0.97
	2-4 ha	-1.21	-2.44	0.03	5.79	0.58	-0.79	-1.63
	4-10 ha	-1.62	-3.77	-1.27	4.44	-0.65	-1.73	-2.55
	> 10 ha	-1.31	-3.87	-2.65	4.47	-1.80	-2.18	-3.00
	Total	-3.70	-2.41	0.39	6.48	1.01	-0.45	-1.17
	CV							
15. West Bengal	< 1 ha	-0.22	1.20	13.97	25.54	23.14	8.35	10.10
	1-2 ha	-1.82	0.00	13.79	20.61	19.19	5.87	7.68
	2-4 ha	-4.77	-2.94	12.48	16.91	16.07	3.60	4.96
	4-10 ha	-8.52	-6.59	14.87	12.20	12.53	0.27	1.03
	> 10 ha	0.00	0.00	0.00	3.53	3.53	-10.40	-3.41
	Total	-3.17	-3.30	13.54	19.26	18.25	5.01	6.78
	CV							

Notes: ACGR—Annual Compound Growth Rate in per cent;
T.well—Tube wells;
NIA—Net Irrigated Area;
GIA—Gross Irrigated Area;
CV—Coefficient of variation.

Source: GOI, *All India Report on Agricultural Census* (various years), Ministry of Agriculture, Government of India, New Delhi.

of irrigation across farm size in different states, the growth rate of net irrigated area (NIA) and gross irrigated area (GIA) show an uniform pattern in majority of the states. Except in Jammu and Kashmir, Kerala and Punjab, the growth rates of net as well as gross irrigated area are inversely related with farm size in all other states. Unexpectedly, both in Jammu & Kashmir and Punjab, the growth rate of net irrigated area as well as gross irrigated area are positively associated with the farm size. In Kerala, no clear trend is observed between the growth of irrigated area and the farm size.

On the whole, the following points emerge out from the analysis of irrigation development by farm size carried out using Agricultural Census data covering five points of time—1970-71, 1976-77, 1980-81, 1985-86 and 1990-91:

— In absolute term, the growth of area under all major sources of irrigation recorded relatively at a higher rate among the marginal size group when compared to all other group of farmers between 1970-71 and 1990-91.

— The growth rate of area under all major sources of irrigation is found to be inversely related with the farm size between 1970-71 and 1990-91. This is observed even in area under groundwater irrigation, which is a costly source of irrigation.

— The share of area of marginal and small farmers in the total area of all the major sources of irrigation has improved considerably between 1970-71 and 1990-91. At the same time, the share of medium and large farmers has declined in all the major sources of irrigation.

— The growth rate of both net as well as gross irrigated area is found to be inversely related with the farm size between 1970-71 and 1990-91.

— The percentage of net irrigated area to net sown area is found to be much higher among the marginal and small size group when compared to the medium and large size group in all five-time points. However, the growth of percentage of net irrigated area to net sown area is found to be positively related with the farm size.

— As observed at the national level, the growth rate of all the major sources of irrigation is found to be inversely related with the farm size in majority of the states between 1970-71 and 1990-91. The same trend is observed in net and gross irrigated area as well. However, both in Jammu and Kashmir and Punjab, the growth rate of net as well as gross irrigated area is found to be positively associated with the farm size. Surprisingly, in Tamil Nadu, both net as well as gross irrigated area registered a negative growth rate in all size groups except marginal group between 1970-71 and 1990-91.

Policy Options for Irrigation

— In order to enhance access, equity and equality in irrigation sector it is necessary to attend urgently to the institutions governing distribution of water and controlling the water policy in the country. We have had recently Water Policy which incorporates a keen concern about the distribution of water resources as well as attends to the economic viability of water supply systems. Therefore, distribution, economic viability and efficiency will have to be the three important counters that need to be attended at macro level.

— It is essential to draft a plan for enhancing efficiency in distribution in all the command areas as the problems of distribution are area specific in nature. A guideline plan can be given to all the command area authorities to chalk out their independent plans. Basin-wise approach needs to be followed in such planning. Effective utilisation of the generated potential is an important aspect of irrigation reforms.

— The argument, about enhancing water rates, is well taken and needs to be pursued on policy front, however, the water rates should bear proportion to net revenue generated (excluding cost towards irrigation) rather than the gross revenue generated as suggested by many others. Similarly, the argument about covering the operation and maintenance cost through Water Rates is acceptable, if and only if such costs are marked determined and exclude all wasteful expenditure by the irrigation department.

— It is also feasible to apply differentiated Water Rates so that the weaker section among the cultivators pay lower rates as compared to the economically strong classes. Water Users' Associations should also take this aspect into consideration.

— It is essential to prepare basin-wise detailed plan for inter-basin and intra-basin use of water resources, viability of intra-basin projects and plans for the future operation and maintenance costs need to be always ready. Intra-basin transfer of water should receive priority over inter-basin huge projects. Autonomous basin development boards are strongly favoured but these should self-financed. There should not be any support from the State in order to run the distributaries as well as the irrigation systems in each of the basins.

— As regards the groundwater utilisation it is essential to promote a proper legal framework in the light of the Water Users' rights. Specific schemes should be undertaken to supplement water recharge zones in gray and dark blocks.

— In the sector of the tank irrigation World Bank has aided a few projects for revitalising this source of irrigation with the help of peoples' participation. If these schemes are successful then it would be imperative to take up replication of such schemes in different states.

Conclusions

In a long term development perspective, the access and distribution of resources assumes great importance. Market mechanism is one of the tools of distribution but the end result of such over dependence on the market may not yield socially desirable results. Such process may not also be welfare augmenting. This process has always the danger of increasing concentration of resources in the hand of a few. Therefore, policy intervention on the part of the state is required. In a similar vein even over-dependence on the state may also cause severe inefficiencies. Therefore, the policy initiatives have to be planned keeping in view the positive impacts of these institutions. In this paper we tried to ananlyse access, equity and equality in distribution of infrastructure, human resources, land and water. We have pointed out the existing problems in access, present distribution pattern and the constraints in distribution. The paper finally offers suggestions for an equitable and welfare augmenting resource distribution in the context of the human resources, land and water resources.

REFERENCES

Aziz, Abdul and Sudhir Krishna (1997). *Land Reforms in India: Karnataka Promises Kept and Missed*, Sage, New Delhi.

Besley, Timothy and Robin Burgess (1998). Land Reform, Poverty Reduction and Growth: Evidence from India, *The Quarterly Journal of Economics*, May.

Burns, Tony and R.S. Deshpande (2001). *Karnataka Rural Policy Review: Land Administration*, Agricultural Development and Rural Transformation

Chadha, G.K., Sucharita Sen and H.R. Sharma (2002). Land Resources in India Agriculture: Policy, Use and Future Strategic Choices, A Report for the Millennium Study on Indian Agriculture, New Delhi.

Deshpande, R.S. and K.V. Raju (2001). Rural Policy for Growth and Poverty Reduction, Agricultural Development and Rural Transformation Unit, Institute for Social and Economic Change, Bangalore.

Deshpande, R.S. (1998). Land Reforms and Agrarian Structure in Maharashtra. *Journal of the Indian School of Political Economy*, Vol. 10, No. 1.

Deshpande, R.S. and A. Narayanamoorthy (2001). Issues Before Second Irrigation Commission of Maharashtra, *Economic and Political Weekly*, Vol. XXXVI, No.12, March 24.

Dharma Kumar (1970). *The Cambridge Economic History of India*: Vol. 2, C 1757-1970, Orient Longman, New Delhi.

Govt. of Karnataka (2001). *Perspective Land use Plan for Karnataka-2025*, Institute of Agriculture Technology, State Land Use Board, Govt. of Karnataka, Bangalore.

Govt. of India (Various Years). *Economic Surveys*, Ministry of Finance, New Delhi.

Govt. of India (2000b). *Land Use Statistics and A Glance, 1995-96 and 1996-97*. Ministry of Agriculture, New Delhi.

Rao, V.M. (1990). *Land for the Poor: A Policy Perspective for Land Reforms and Use of Common Lands*, National Commission on Rural Labour, Study Group on Land Reforms and Common Property Resources, July.

Rao, V.M. (1992). "Land Reform Experiences: Perspective for Strategy and Programmes", *Economic and Political Weekly*, June 27.

Sinha, B.K. and Pushpendra (2000). *Land Reforms in India: An Unfinished Agenda*, Sage, New Delhi.

Thimmaiah, G. and Abdul Aziz (1983). The Political Economy of Land Reforms in Karnataka—A South Indian State, *Asian Survey*, Vol. XXIII, No. 7, July.

16

Social and Economic Equity, Poverty Reduction and Employment Generation

K.V. RAMAN

Poverty and chronic deprivation have long been a tragic aspect of human society. Poverty, however, is neither natural nor inevitable. In modern economics, large-scale poverty imposes an enormous economic loss, wasting the talents and energies of hundreds of millions of men and women, diverted from socially productive activities that could create wealth for society, to the struggle for mere survival. Poverty is defined as the inability of an individual to secure a normative minimum level of living.

Nobel Prize laureate Amartya Sen in his interesting article "*Hunger and Public Action*" (1989) has analysed the causes of famines and observed cases in which people starved to death in spite of food availability—because they had no "entitlement".

> "What we can eat depends on what food we are able to acquire. The mere presence of food in the economy, or in the market, does not entitle a person to consume it. In each social structure, given the prevailing legal, political and economic arrangements, a person can establish command over some alternative commodity bundles... [i.e.] this person's entitlements. A person's entitlements depend on what she owns initially and what she can acquire through exchange. For example, a wage labourer owns her labour power, and by exchanging that for a wage... she acquires some money, which she can exchange for some commodity bundle or other...."

Besides the economic criteria of income, poverty has many other important dimensions. Probably Dr. Amartya Sen's definition of poverty is the most appropriate and acceptable one, which is that poverty, is the deprivation of basic capabilities. Dr. Sen argues that every person should have the substantive freedom to lead the kind of life he has reasons to value. Inadequate income is one of the principal reasons for a person's capability deprivation. Sen distinguishes the standard income-based poverty approach from his proposed 'capability perspective' because capabilities are seen as intrinsically important whereas income is instrumentally significant. In order to eradicate poverty something more than income is necessary and that is the opportunity to develop one's basic capabilities which include opportunities for education, health care, sanitation, nutrition, clean drinking water, housing, etc. *dication of poverty*, improvement of the economic status and quality of life of the people, employment generation that will increase purchasing power, increased industrialization and modernization of our industries, technological upgradation, green peace programmes involving environmental protection and sustainability, and more importantly harmonization of all these factors in the general development scenario, are our primary concern.

The strategies and policies, developed by the planners and policy-makers, adopted two approaches, one focusing on the overall economic development (through percolation/Trickle Down/Spread Effect) and another poverty alleviation (direct intervention). Though these approaches reinforce each other, there was no effort to integrate them. While eradication of poverty has been a recurrent theme in all the Five-Year Plans, the proportion of those living below the poverty line has not decreased appreciably. On the other hand, the number of those below the poverty line in absolute terms has increased. This is a matter of serious concern. Mere formulation of a large number of programmes can be at best temporary; they create conditions so that the programme can be phased out and more lasting solutions like employment opportunities and transformation of the rural society are brought out. The argument is that a good growth rate over a reasonable time frame can have a trickle down effect, down to the lowest layers of poverty. Our own experience in this country as well as many others in the world show that this is not necessarily correct.

Agricultural growth is an important factor in poverty reduction, especially in agrarian economies like ours. However, detailed analysis by economic experts indicates that agricultural development may be a necessary, but not a sufficient condition for eradication of rural poverty. On the basis of the available data, it is possible to infer that agricultural growth cannot always be relied upon as a major strategy for poverty alleviation under all situations. What is important is that the growth process has to be more broad-based involving the participation of small and marginal farmers, tenants and agricultural labourers through various institutional reforms. Factors like (i) growth in real wages, (ii) growth of real employment in the organised non-farm sector, (iii) poor people's increased access to land (iv) increased access to subsidised food and (v) increased expenditure on IRDP and employment programmes under some situations help reduce rural poverty. In fact, there cannot be a single planning strategy for poverty alleviation. It has to be location specific, depending on the need and objectives of the programme, as well as the socio-economic and ethno-cultural situation of each region.

Fifty years of development experience in our country have yielded some valuable and critical lessons:

1. Macroeconomic stability is an essential prerequisite for achieving growth needed for development.
2. In largely agrarian societies like India, economic growth should ensure employment generation.
3. Growth does not trickle down; development should address human needs directly.
4. No one policy will trigger development; a comprehensive approach is needed.
5. The development orientation should be sustainable.
6. Sustained development should be rooted in processes that are socially inclusive and responsive to changing circumstances, where local empowerment and institutions matter.

Agenda 21, the action pathway for sustainable development clubbed sustainable agriculture and rural development under one head in its Chapter 14. This clearly brought out the holistic interpretation of sustainable agriculture as a development paradigm, not only with production targets but also with the socio-economic and cultural aspirations of the rural population. The majority of the poor in the world live in these rural areas, whose toils which has taken on itself not only to feed the world, but also comprise of with sub-optimal access to the food that is produced in the neighbourhood.

Access to sustainable livelihoods for all is a gateway to sustainable development. Providing adequate and appropriate livelihood opportunities is one of the key factors for sustainable alleviation of poverty. No discussion on livelihood opportunities will be complete without an analysis of productive employment opportunities. Employment programmes, if well designed with sufficient thrust incorporating a guarantee (unlike the lean season focus as of now) of round the year employment to the poor, can have a major impact as the State's responsibilities of providing 'poverty-subsidies' get reduced. Wage employment programmes are self-targeting in nature and therefore, are more effective in reducing poverty. Emphasis on improving the rural resources and infrastructure can have a strong, positive impact on poverty reduction. The problem of eliminating hunger, reducing poverty, enhancing livelihood opportunities and improving the quality of life requires the understanding, inventiveness, and interaction of farmers, industrialists, agricultural scientists, educators, environmentalists, health care workers, and policy makers, who share a commitment to development and change.

A livelihood is sustainable when it can cope with and recover from stresses and shocks, maintain or enhance its capabilities and assets, while not undermining the natural resource base. In other words, sustainable livelihood should include gainful employment, which is ecologically conserving, economically efficient, and socially equitable. Income-generating employment is the most fundamental and basic component of what a livelihood is, because the latter includes several other additional parameters, both tangible and intangible, which are essential for human development. The tangibles are generally accessible with money, while the intangible ones like the sense of well-being, happiness, self-esteem, security etc. need additional conditions regarding societal structure, values and individual attitudes.

Scoones (2000) recognized five key elements as directly related to sustainable livelihoods, the first three focusing on livelihoods linking concerns over work, employment, poverty reduction, well-being and capabilities, and the last two adding the sustainability dimension.

1. Creation of working days: Creation of a gainful employment for a certain portion of the year—either on on-farm or off-farm, so that they get an economic income to meet their daily requirements of food and other expenses.
2. Poverty reduction based on income or consumption levels, which addresses issues of poverty and inequality.
3. Well-being and capabilities, which encompasses far more than the material concerns of food intake or income. This will include such diverse factors as self-esteem, security, happiness, stress, empowerment etc.
4. Livelihood adaptation, vulnerability and resilience which includes the ability to be able to cope with and recover from stresses and shocks, coping with temporary adjustments in the face of change or adapt to longer term shifts in livelihood strategies.
5. Natural resource base sustainability.

About 70 per cent of the 1,006 million people in India live in the rural areas and derive their livelihoods directly or indirectly from the 329 million hectares of land resources. Small and marginal farmers dominate Indian agriculture. Of the total number of farming families, more than 78 per cent are small and marginal with less than two hectares of farming land. They cultivate about 32 per cent of the arable land. There are over 111 million cultivators, who are further supported by over 75 million landless workers. Agriculture will be the primary absorber of this workforce, and this situation is not likely to change much in the foreseeable future. The availability of employment in this important sector throughout the year is dismally poor. Except in about 53.5 million hectares of the irrigated arable land, where the conditions may be marginally better, 90 m ha of rainfed arable lands hardly provides 100 days of employment in the year. It is interesting to note that this land area still produces 90 million tons of food grains out of about 200+ million tons that we produce; however, since the activity is highly seasonal, the availability of on-farm work is irregular and uncertain.

It has been estimated that at the national level, the average days worked per adult wage earner in the agriculture wage work is 137 (145 for male and 124 for female). This figure varies very widely depending on the region and the nature of agriculture that is practiced. Thus, in the arid and semi-arid regions with limited rainfall, the work available is highly seasonal and is limited in extent. For example, in Rajasthan, agricultural work is available only for 53 days in a year, while it is about 190 days in the North East Region.

Livelihood security will have to be provided to this huge workforce. Since crop-based agriculture alone cannot support them, it is necessary for agricultural labour to look for additional income-generating opportunities. Multiple livelihood opportunities, if developed at the farm/community level, help to increase the number of employment days, diversify activities, enhance total income and minimize risks. This is especially true for women who perform multiple tasks at the farm level. The ability to pursue different livelihood strategies is dependent on the basic Natural resources available in the region and social, tangible and intangible assets that people have in their possession. These include (a) Natural capital of soil, water, air, genetic resources etc. and environmental services (hydrological cycle, pollution sinks etc.) from which resource flows and services useful for livelihoods are derived. (b) Economic or financial capital including cash, credit/debt, savings, and other economic assets, as well as basic infrastructure and production equipment and technologies which are essential for the pursuit of any livelihood strategy. (c) Human capital—the skills, knowledge, ability to labour and good health and physical capability important for the successful pursuit of different livelihood strategies. And (d) Social capital or the social resources upon which people draw when pursuing different livelihood strategies requiring coordinated actions. In order to create livelihoods, therefore, people must combine the 'capital' endowments that they have access to and control over.

Providing Multiple Livelihood Opportunities

All efforts in overcoming poverty at the micro level of the household has to be essentially by the committed efforts of the people themselves, though assisted by community at large. Since most of the ultra-poor are either landless workers or people with very small land holdings that are not economically viable, income enhancement can arise only through multiple livelihood opportunities. These include:

(a) Primary value addition of commodities at the household level like production of semi-processed foods, pickle making, sun drying and packaging etc.
(b) Utilization of locally available resources like paddy-straw for mushroom growing, sericulture, goat rearing, dairying and milk production, backyard poultry for eggs and meat.
(c) Horticulture that includes production of fruits and vegetables.
(d) Floriculture, including production of flowers for domestic market as well as export.
(e) Aquaculture including integrated fish farming and utilization of Community ponds and proper use of marine wealth.
(f) Effective use of common property resources, use of waste and degraded lands, specially community ponds for community aquaculture.

Most of the above activities require only the relatively small external financial input, but in terms of income, provide attractive returns. Micro-credit need to be provided for this activity to initiate action. However, what is probably most important is, ensuring adequate market opportunities for these products, since individual efforts at marketing will not only be difficult and unsuccessful, but also, exploitative of the farmer.

Productivity Improvement in Agriculture

The primary requirement for improving agrarian economy and alleviation of rural poverty is increasing agricultural production and productivity. As discussed earlier, the country achieved remarkable improvement in production and productivity of food grains, thanks to the revolutionary technologies that the advent of the Green Revolution witnessed. However, there is still a wide gap between potential yields and actual yields at the field level. It is possible to close this by adopting even the existing technologies more extensively and making use of new and emerging technologies. The Vision 2020 document of the Ministry of Agriculture, Government of India, outlines the strategy under two initiatives: (a) consolidating the gains already made; and (b) planning for and making new gains. A number of interventions to utilize the untapped potential are suggested and it may not be necessary to outline them all here. Suffice to say that we can have immense optimism in our hopes for the future, as the following table will show. Increased agricultural production will activate a chain of activities towards increased income and employment opportunities.

Proposed intervention/Untapped potential	*Expected additional production*
Enhancing fertilizer use efficiency	30 million tonnes
Water management including drainage	30 million tonnes
Soil health care including reclamation of salinity/acidity/alkalinity	40 million tonnes
Realignment of cropping patterns on ecological principles	30 million tonnes
Regain productivity of command areas of wells and tanks, and small and medium irrigation projects	120 million tonnes
Total increase in production expected from all the above interventions	250 million tonnes

Source: Sankaran A., Unpublished-1999.

The above interventions proposed are in terms of Natural Resources Management. Technological advances in other areas like biotechnology, genetic improvement, integrated pest management, better storage and processing—all these hold promise of increased total production, which in turn generates additional entrepreneurial activities. It is this optimism and hope that make us venture to propose an integrated development plan for the rural areas.

Technology is a necessary resource for sustainable agricultural development. For technologies to be sustainable ecologically conserving, environmentally safe, economically efficient, and socially equitable. In addition, in the context of the recent 'energy' considerations, they should also be energy-efficient, and have low energy requirements. Recent advances in science and technology, biotechnology, information and communication systems and advanced materials can bring about a technological transformation in the rural areas. It is true that modern information and knowledge-based production technologies are far less energy and material intensive, less polluting and economically efficient, and can add sustainability and social equity to rural production systems of different categories.

Agricultural sector, which includes forestry and animal husbandry, has a fairly high potential for proving job opportunities if the innovative techniques for improving land and agricultural production are adopted. Soil and water conservation, tank development, afforestation, horticultural development etc. have such immense potential. I had the privilege of developing a Consultancy Paper on "Social Security and Employment" for the National Commission to Review the Working of the Constitution (more popularly known as Justice Venkatachalaiah Commission). Since poverty alleviation, livelihood opportunities and gainful employment are closely linked, a suggestion whether "Right to Employment" should be guaranteed under the Constitution as a Fundamental Right, was being considered. Employment/ Unemployment in the country, seasonal nature of agricultural work, the impact of introducing newer agricultural technologies including crop diversification, cost of production and a host of several associated issues were analysed systematically and some conclusions drawn. How these issues were handled globally and in the different countries in this region, were also considered, mainly to get an insight into the problem.

The opportunities for livelihoods can be broadly divided into on-farm and off-farm agriculture and related activities like animal husbandry, poultry, horticulture, agroforestry, etc. and non-farm activities not concerned with agriculture. Rural livelihood strategies can be composed in a number of ways, both singly and multiply. Some of the more common pathways are:

- Agricultural intensification and allied activities like horticulture, animal husbandry, social forestry, sericulture, etc. both on-farm and off-farm.
- Utilization of natural resources (common property) including wastelands.
- Non-farm activities in the services sector, retail trading, transport, restaurant, catering, sanitation etc.
- Social institutions and networks like schools, hospitals, credit services, vital information services for marketing, local weather etc.
- Development of activities like road laying, canal digging, desiltation of waterways, construction activities.
- Primary and secondary processing of agricultural and allied activities, production of bio-fertilizers, bio-pesticides etc.

Most of the poor do not have access to formal sector

employment. They have to forge their livelihoods in the private and non-formal sectors.

The total number of additional jobs that will be created as a result of bringing in some changes in current agricultural scenario were calculated, and summarized in the Table below:

Summary Table Indicating Additional Jobs that would be Created

Sl. No.	*Enterprise*	*Jobs Created*
1.	Productivity Improvement in Agriculture	7,000,000[1]
2.	Integrated Horticulture	
3.	Floriculture	6,327,000[1]
4.	Medicinal Plants Production	
5.	Production of Seeds and Planting Materials	
6.	Animal Husbandry Programmes	13,700,000[5]
7.	Integrated Programme of Intensive Aquaculture	1,117,500[1]
8.	Sericulture	700,000[1]
9.	Afforestation and Wasteland Development	50,000,000[3]
10.	Soil And Water Conservation	
11.	Water Conservation and Tank Rehabilitation	1,000,000[2]
12.	Compost Preparation, Vermiculture and Organic Farming	5,00,000[4]
13.	Establishment of Agro-Industrial Complexes	1,000,000[1]
	Total	About 80 million additional jobs

Source: Estimates by G. Rangaswami for the International Commission on Peace and Food *"Prosperity 2000"*. Bharatiya Vidya Bhawan.

From Estimates included in the EEC documents.

From NCEAR estimates.

From Experiences in the Biovillages program at Pondicherry.

From NDDB Estimates.

Providing for social and economic equity in our planned efforts towards poverty reduction through economically rewarding and ecologically compatible agriculture is a challenging task. Income enhancement through multiple livelihood opportunities coupled with sustainable agriculture will be a means of combating the problem. Success stories on a limited scale show the pathway but determined action with committed people is needed for replicating these successful experiences.

17

A Development Perspective for Punjab

Managing Carrying Capacity Towards Sustainability

GOPAL KRISHAN

While enunciating a development perspective for Punjab, an essential prerequisite is to spell out the vision of Punjab—the kind of economy, society, polity and ecology envisaged for it, over a given period of time. This style of dealing with the issue is strikingly different from the usual practice wherein the future agenda is set in the light of the evolving scene, particularly with reference to problems that have emerged on the way. The intention is to define and work out a feasible dream for the state and thus go beyond the conventional diagnostic and curative approach.

In its bare essentials, the state has to be not only efficient and progressive economically, just and harmonious socially, democratic and participatory politically, friendly and prudent ecologically, aesthetic and functional spatially, but also civil and sustainable systemically. In this light, one can envision Punjab eventually as a region which is suburban, displaying a continuum of rural and urban, agriculture and non-agriculture, with a hierarchy of settlements interlinked by a free-flowing transport network; thereby serving as a platform for what is envisioned. Herein symbolically the role of a development architect, social scientist and a professional practitioner gets entwined. Things would have been easy if Punjab were a clean slate to work on. Certainly it is not. This poses a real challenge. The evolved scene has to be redesigned and reconstructed rather than built anew.

Punjab acquired its present form in 1966 after having undergone three reorganisations of its territory not only in this year but also earlier in 1947 and 1956. Situated in the north-western part of the country and bordering with Pakistan, the state occupies a position of great strategic importance. Triangular in shape, it covers an area of 50,362 km^2. The 2001 Census of India recorded its population as 24.2 million, distributed amongst 12,729 villages and 157 towns.

The Context

Some salient features of Punjab may be recapitulated. The state enjoys highest per capita income in the country (Rs. 23,043 against the national average of Rs. 15,562 in 1999-2000), and is highlighted as a model of agricultural development. Here poverty is not an issue; achieving a higher level of economic well-being is! People here can move to a greener pasture anywhere in the world if the opportunities at home are not attractive enough.

Such was the stimulus which motivated many a native of Punjab to migrate not only to other parts of India, as diverse as newly reclaimed agricultural lands, lucrative urban places or remote forested areas, but also to emigrate to several foreign countries including, the United Kingdom, Canada, United States, Australia and Middle East, among others. This exposed them to the ethos of the developed world. No wonder, the popular development perspective seeks transformation of the state in the mould of a western country. An oft-repeated self-question is: why cannot Punjab be like the United States or United Kingdom or like Israel or Denmark among the smaller countries? They believe that the state has all the potential for evolving in that direction and it is the obligation of the government to harness this.

One peculiar feature of the development process in Punjab may be underlined: as soon as a new growth activity is initiated, it picks up momentum, and reaches a plateau rather too soon. A question mark on the state's 'carrying capacity' is implicit. The green revolution is one such case. It made a beginning in 1966; by 1985, it had reached a saturation level and has been seeking a new direction, which is more remunerative than the wheat-rice rotation regime. Not much success has been met on this count. Water depletion in the tube well irrigated lands and waterlogging in the canal irrigated ones have emerged as serious problems. Sustainability of the development process and providing new channels for its flow are the crux of the matter. This cannot be ignored as a parameter of the development perspective.

A newly acquired economic well-being soon gets translated into an aspiration for living in an upgraded habitat. One of the most visible outcomes of the green revolution is a remarkable transformation of village settlements, particularly by way of conversion of *kutcha* houses into *pucca*. In urban places too, a well-designed house located within a modern locality, has become a priority. An urge to live in standard houses with clean and green surroundings has been ignited. Quality habitat, thus, claims inclusion as an imperative in scheme of things.

A statement on development perspective for the state will not be complete if we do not take care of the globalised psyche of its people. Punjab is an anomaly to the students of migration studies. Though well placed economically, it remained a net outmigration state till the last decade in its recent history of a century. Though not a coastal state, it has recorded large scale emigration too. Punjab is an extrovert entity, actively interacting with areas all over the world at large. This global dimension of the state has to find a place in any formulation of a development perspective for it.

Finally, as rightly perceived, Punjab is eulogised for the progressive outlook, great dynamism, and exceptional enterprise of its people. It has a fairly laid out infrastructure base also. In that light, virtually any problem it faces or any situation which constrains its development can largely be attributed to a management failure. People opine that Punjab can be a model state simply if its political and administrative train is on the right track. Thereby, 'good governance' is underlined as the most critical aspect of its development scene. It is deemed basic to the actualisation of all other development perspectives.

What should be the time frame for the realisation of the development perspective visualised for Punjab? The faster it is the better for the people but time targets have to be assigned. In the medium term, it could be placed at 1 November, 2016 when Punjab would be celebrating the golden anniversary of its formation; on the short term, it can be placed at 31 March, 2007 when the Tenth Plan gets completed; and as a relatively long term scenario, it can be dated as 31 December, 2020 in the spirit of a new vision. These three datelines can adopt evolving development dimensions as their top priority: financial recovery as the necessary base (2007); human development (education and health) by 2016; and habitat (environment) by 2020.

Perspective of Five Year Plans

Let us review as to what has been the development perspective of the successive state plans (Government of India, 1969 to 2002). Which were the sectors listed as priority? Which strategies were deemed as most effective for the purpose? Answers to these questions are necessary as the state has invariably played a pervasive and ubiquitous role in determining the content, pace and quality of the development process. The intentions of the government can be discerned from the pages of plan documents.

The formation of Punjab in 1966 synchronised with the ushering in of the green revolution. By that time, the state had carried out consolidation of landholdings over its entire space, 59 per cent of the net area sown had been brought under irrigation, virtually all the villages had been covered by agricultural credit societies, the Mandi (Market) Township Act had come into force to facilitate the disposal of agricultural produce, and benefits accruing from research and extension activities of the Punjab Agricultural University, Ludhiana, had started making an impact. A stage for putting the state on a fast track to agricultural and rural development had been set.

The years 1966-69 were a phase of Annual Plans, during which the state received special funds for its transformation into a veritable 'bread basket' for the country facing a prolonged and massive food-deficit. Two consecutive drought years of 1964-65 and 1965-66 had worsened the situation in India. This gave Punjab an opportunity to prove its mettle. It met the challenge by way of contributing 61 per cent of wheat and 8 per cent of rice procured for the public distribution system at the national level in 1968-69.

The Fourth Plan (1969-74) document highlighted that the state could take pride in having saved the country from a grave food crisis; and for having successfully stabilised for itself the strides made in the green revolution. Its efforts at diversifying the economy towards industrialisation were yet to make an impact. Inadequacy of finance, shortage of raw materials, and gap in power supply, to the extent of less by one-third of demand, were adduced as the factors responsible.

Taking a cue from above, the Fifth Plan (1974-79) aimed at a bold programme of 'industrialisation and development of infrastructure' so as to accelerate the pace of economic growth. Massive investment in power was deemed as essential. The assessment was that ultimately it was industry which could reduce the disparity in development level of different parts of the state.

The Sixth Plan (1980-85) introduced a new idiom seeking transformation of Punjab into a 'model state' during the next ten years. The main components of such a vision included diversification of the economy in favour of industry; generation of jobs for the unemployed and underemployed; reduction in regional, rural-urban and caste-based disparities; and improvement in the overall quality of life. All this was to be achieved through an accelerated rate of economic growth, an efficient and honest administration, and a decentralised pattern of planning and development.

The Seventh Plan (1985-90) promised 'growth with justice'. A major thrust was envisaged for correction of distortions that may have crept in during the preceding plan periods. These included, for example, reclamation of degraded agricultural land, extension of irrigation in the submontane and other backward tracts, improvement in delivery of educational and health facilities, and promotion of industry, particularly in border districts. Augmentation of power supply and initiation of environmental improvement schemes were listed as priorities. The two annual plans, during 1990-92, carried forward the ongoing development schemes apart from initiating some new ones, as financed by the Central Government.

'Generation of additional employment' was adopted as the core concern of the State's Eighth Plan (1992-97). Three border districts of Gurdaspur, Amritsar and Firozepur, victim to a greater degree of statewide militancy during the eighties, were in special focus. Again 'promotion of industry' was identified as an effective route to the realisation of this objective. Diversification of agriculture, in general, and of the cropping pattern, in particular; improvement of human resource through education, health and training; and extension and modernisation of basic infrastructure were among the other tasks listed. In respect of institutional reforms, decentralised planning at the district level was to receive a further impetus; private investment was to be encouraged in all sectors, and viability of the public sector undertakings was to be ensured.

The Ninth Plan (1997-2002) enumerated the following as the broad lineaments of its strategy: vigorous thrust to agriculture and rural development; a great push to irrigation and power sectors; improvement in quality of life in both villages and towns; creation of additional employment opportunities; and social justice for the disadvantaged. Micro-level planning was to receive special attention, more so in the border districts.

The Tenth Plan (2002-2007) strategy is virtually an iteration of what was contemplated in the Ninth Plan. Diversification of agriculture as also of the cropping pattern has been projected as the measure to meet the challenge posed by the stipulations of the W.T.O. Various development projects, such as Integrated Watershed, Health Care Systems, and Water Supply and Environmental Sanitation, aided by international agencies, are to continue.

An overview of the plan documents leads one to the following conclusions:

— Perspective and strategies indicated for various plans remained virtually the same: diversification of economy towards industry, of agriculture towards non-farm activities, and of the cropping pattern away from the stubborn wheat-rice rotation; irrigation and power as the mother sectors; and unemployment as the main challenge.

— Theoretical underpinnings of the plan documents remained unspelt. Only the Sixth Plan projected a vision of making Punjab a 'model state'. Instrumentalities indicated were a reformed administration and decentralised planning, with a flavour of good governance.

— The successive plan proposals, by and large, echoed the issues highlighted at the national level. Specificity of the state level concerns was not projected in a bold manner. The plan documents were drafted with a bureaucratic mind; the input emanating from the research institutions and university academics was meagre.

— Sub-plans for the backward areas, including the submontane tract, floodplains and border districts found special place in the documents. This is as it should have been. It is, however, not clear as to how these sub-plans were integrated with micro-level planning.

— Expenditure exceeded outlay during most of the plan periods. The state could arrange additional resources from the Planning Commission or was able to mobilise these at its own level. The Ninth Plan was an exception when expenditure incurred was only 77 per cent of the approved outlay. Irrigation and power accounted for about one-half to over two-thirds of the expenditure under various plans. Ironically, both were losing sectors financially, under the twin effect of subsidies involved and pilferage.

The sectoral affairs of the state reflect and mirror the implementation of plan provisions. It is necessary to review the situation in each case and to enunciate specific development perspectives. This is precisely what follows in the ensuing section.

Sectoral Perspectives

Economic Growth and Regional Disparity

Most worrisome feature of Punjab economy today is the drop in its annual growth rate: from 5.3 per cent during 1980-81 – 1990-91 to 4.7 per cent during 1991-92 – 1997-98. By comparison, growth rate at the national level moved up from 5.6 to 6.9 per cent during the same period. In sympathy, the annual increase rate of the State's per capita income also came down from 3.3 to 2.8 per cent.

A perusal of relevant data shows a regular decline in the agricultural growth rate of Punjab since 1985. The state's share in the contribution of wheat to the Central pool declined from 45 per cent in 1980-81 to 36 per cent in 2000-01, and that of rice from 73 to 58 per cent during the same period. The livestock sector, which was earlier having an upswing, has been decelerating since 1997. The same is true of the manufacturing sector. Electricity generation rate also suffered a decline after 1990. Construction, transport, and trade sectors did display some buoyancy. On the whole, the nineties emerge as a difficult phase for Punjab economy. Why did things come to such a pass?

The unhappy downward turn of Punjab economy can be

traced to 1984-85, when it became a 'revenue deficit state' from the status of a 'revenue surplus one' (Government of Punjab, 2002 June, p. 3). The Government of Punjab attributes this to 'an ever increasing salaries and wage bill of the employees (particularly since implementation of the Fifth Pay Commission recommendations), mounting debt burden, heavily subsidised social sector (education and health) and economic services (irrigation and electricity), slow growth of revenue, and loss making public sector undertakings' (Government of Punjab, 2000 March, p. 11). Both the imposition and collection of taxes had been adversely affected by the difficult political situation during the eighties. This was more so during the prolonged phase of President's rule when the caution was not to create any situation that could add fuel to fire. During the tenure of elected governments, 'subsidies on populist lines' made their own contribution to worsening the situation. Meanwhile fiscal deficits of the public sector undertakings were also mounting and adding to the financial misery of the government. The recourse followed was to go in for public borrowing in a big way in place of curing the malaise. Interest payment as percentage of revenue moved up from 16.8 in 1990-91 to 29.4 in 2000-01. This was the highest for any major Indian State; the all-India figures were 13.1 and 17.6 per cent respectively. Investment on development suffered badly. The development expenditure as percentage of the total expenditure had a steep fall from 71.9 in 1980-81 to 54.5 in 1997-98, and further down to 46.5 in 1998-99. Implications of all this for the state's economic growth rate are not difficult to understand.

The fiscal programme of the Punjab Government envisages an annual economic growth rate of 5.5 per cent during the Tenth Plan, at constant prices. With the current population increase rate being about 1.8 per cent, the annual rise in per capita income would be of the order of about 3.7 per cent. The Planning Commission expects Punjab to achieve a higher annual growth rate of 6.4 per cent (agriculture 4.1 per cent, industry 8.1 per cent and services 8 per cent). This calls for a greater effort than the state had assigned to itself. The government proposes to stimulate the economy by correcting the fiscal imbalance, and thereby making available a larger share of the budget for development. Major steps contemplated include: reforms in the area of sales tax; revision of user charges in respect of transport, irrigation, higher/professional education, secondary/tertiary health care, and drinking water supply; and gradual privatisation of public sector undertakings.

Mercifully, the picture of Punjab as a relatively prosperous and progressive state still persists in the popular mind. As noted earlier, there are valid reasons for this. This must not lead one to believe that there are no regional disparities within; these are rather striking, as measured by any set of economic and social indicators (Gosal and Krishan, 1984). In specific, the central belt of Punjab, covering Amritsar, Kapurthala, Jalandhar, Ludhiana, Fatehgarh Sahib and Patiala districts, is relatively the most developed. It is characterised by a very progressive agriculture, significant concentration of industry and a high level of urbanisation. The Amritsar-Delhi railway track and the Grand Trunk road form the economic backbone of this zone and provide it with the necessary dynamism. The north-eastern zone, comprising Gurdaspur, Hoshiarpur, Rupnagar and Nawanshahr districts, is comparatively the least developed. This is attributed to its dissected and undulating topography, small size of landholdings, and relative isolation of some of its parts. The scene is, of course, now changing for the better, with the World Bank sponsored Kandi Area Integrated Watershed Development Project being underway, industry coming in a significant manner in Hoshiarpur and Ropar districts, and infrastructure getting greatly strengthened in areas around Chandigarh. The south-western zone, comprising Firozpur, Moga, Muktsar, Faridkot, Bathinda, Mansa and Sangrur districts, are acquiring new dimensions of development. It has made noticeable progress in agriculture. Industry is also picking up. The most important factor accounting for its agricultural advancement has been the relatively large size of landholdings, promoting mechanisation. Industrial development is facilitated by availability of agricultural raw materials, particularly cotton and rice.

Within this broad framework of regional disparities in Punjab, the government has identified three kinds of backward areas in the physical structure of the state; the hilly and foothill Kandi tract; the floodplains of the Ravi, Beas, Satluj and Ghaggar, and the border belt. Each of these suffers from its own specific physical and locational problems. The Kandi tract has an undulating and degraded topography; the floodplains are not free from the fury of river-waters during the rainy season; and the border belt with

Pakistan is most distant from the state capital and is in the nature of a typical neglected periphery. Special attention to such problematical areas is in order.

Rural Development and Agriculture

Among the Indian States, Punjab holds a place of pride for its outstanding achievements in rural development. A healthy mix of environmental, institutional and technological factors explains this scenario evolving since independence and picking up pace since the state's reorgnisation in 1966. The most striking feature of the Punjab model is the government's manysided participation in the development process (Chadha, 1986, p. 338). Imbedded in the scheme of things was the adoption of agriculture as the lead sector not only in consonance with the physical attributes of the state but also as a response to the national demand for food. The fact that the political power in the state has consistently been rural based and drawn from a farming background, rural development and agriculture were to remain a priority. Not only that. A right sequence of policies was followed for the purpose. Beginning with consolidation of landholdings, followed by reclamation of new agricultural lands and synchronous extension of irrigation through Bhakra canals, and the process being further strengthened by the green revolution strategy of biochemical inputs (high yielding variety seeds, chemical fertilizers and irrigation) and mechanical inputs (tractors, thrashers and harvestor-combines), Punjab agriculture continued making rapid strides over the years. The agrarian structure characterised by middle level peasantry, with landholdings of two to four hectares, and predominance of owner cultivators, was no less important a factor for the success of this process. Exogenic factors also played a role in modernisation of Punjab agriculture. Exposure of the state to external influences through emigration to foreign countries, migration to other parts of India, and tradition in army service had at least a three pronged effect: brought in remittances which were used for augmenting agricultural infrastructure at the household level, reduced pressure on agricultural land, thereby saving the landholdings from getting very small; and stoked a tendency towards achieving higher levels of opulence.

Most important to the whole process was the government's

thrust on rural agricultural development. The main components of the strategy included: extension of irrigation, rural electrification, rural link roads, rural focal points providing a variety of services, closely spaced agricultural market centres and above all an assured provision of credit and agricultural inputs. Widespread infrastructure, which could boost agriculture, was made available. As a part of the national policy, the minimum support price for wheat and rice, the state's two major crops, played a significant role in sustaining agricultural development, and thereby raising rural incomes. In 1999-2000, only six per cent of rural households in Punjab were below the poverty line, as compared with 27 per cent in rural India.

The emerging scene of rural Punjab, and within that of agriculture, is not free from some serious concerns. Notwithstanding a commendable quantitative expansion of a variety of services, notably schools/colleges, dispensaries/hospitals, veterinary centres, electrification, link roads, and focal points, the quality of service provided in every case is far from satisfactory. Schools and dispensaries do not function properly, electricity suffers frequent breakdowns, link roads are not well maintained, and several of the focal points are non-functional. Upgradation of quality in service provision is now the greatest challenge for any effort at improving the situation in rural Punjab.

On the agricultural front, the persistence of wheat-rice rotation, despite efforts at promoting diversification of the cropping pattern, is causing a serious damage to the state's natural resource base. Rice, in particular, is a water-intensive crop and is not eco-friendly for Punjab. Its popularity, however, could not be contained for it is not only a lucrative crop but also an assured one in returns. The consequence is there for everyone to see: water-table depletion in tube well irrigated areas and waterlogging in canal irrigated ones. The question remains: how to wean the Punjab farmer away from the wheat-rice rotation. A serious call to this effect was made as early as in 1986. The situation evolved to the contrary, with the rice area increasing from 1.7 to 2.6 million hectares, and wheat area from 3.2 to 3.4 million hectares during 1985-86 to 2000-2001. Short term private economic gains are ignoring the long term extensive ecological damage.

'Precision diversification based on local agro-ecological conditions in different parts of Punjab', is now being recommended. In simple words, rice is to be shifted from tracts 'where sandy and loamy soils predominate'. Production of basmati rice, which is less water-intensive, should be encouraged through assured support price. At least 20 per cent of the area under wheat and rice should be shifted to some other crops such as maize, oilseeds, sugarcane and fruits/vegetables or other farm enterprises (Johl and Ray, 2001, p. 251). The corporate sector, in linkage with farmers' associations, should be asked to not only improve quality of agricultural products but also promote agro-processing industry.

Despite a visible improvement in the quality of life in Punjab villages, particularly by way of conversion of *kutcha* houses into *pucca* ones, much remains to be done for environmental improvement of the rural habitat. Introduction of 'Unnat Gram' scheme by the Punjab Government, during the Eighth Plan, was one creditable effort in this direction. Pavement of streets, construction of drains, disposal of sullage water, metalling of *phirnis*, and provision of water borne latrines in each house were the main planks of this scheme. Shortage of funds permitted only a limited success. In that context, the old *abadi* part of every village is invariably too congested, poorly maintained and ecologically deficient. A culture of healthy living needs to be promoted. Upgradation of the quality of rural habitat remains an unfinished agenda item on the development chart of the state. An effective course would be to pool the available funds under all the district level schemes and disburse these by way of following a policy of 'one village, one scheme' at a time. As at present, funds are spread too thin to cover a number of schemes in a village.

Towards that goal, it is suggested that a scheme of planned rural residential colonies be formulated and implemented at the focal points, to begin with. Each of these colonies could be designed for about 200 or more housing units of varying sizes, depending upon the demand at each site, with provision for expansion in future. The locality must become a model in house design, provision of services, and overall maintenance. A component of commercial outlets could be included as a part of the scheme, and thereby cross-subsidise the residential component. The scheme is visualised as self-financing.

It may not be known to many that the proportion of the scheduled caste population at around one-third in the total is the highest in Punjab among Indian states. This section of society is characterised by a significantly higher birth rate, lower literacy rate, and less incomes/wages. The pregnancy rate, that is percentage of eligible women pregnant at anytime, is 6.1 in the case of scheduled castes as compared with 3.5 for the rest of the population. Most of them may be above the poverty line, but in comparison with other sections of society, their economic upliftment remains a task to contend with. Family planning, education and health are the major issues in their case.

Putting things together, enhancement of the economic wellbeing already achieved, upgradation of the quality of life, improvement of the habitat, care of the scheduled castes, and preservation of the natural resource base emerge as the main assignments in the context of rural Punjab. The priorities for the government get defined. An active involvement of the corporate sector and non-government organisations (NGO's) can be an effective measure for the purpose. They can play a role in generating awareness about the development programmes and schemes launched by the government; imparting training to the youth for self-employment; managing natural resources; and promoting education. The corporate sector can, in addition, assist in marketing of agricultural produce, and providing employment to the youth trained by them for a given vocation.

Above all, an effort can be made, on organised lines, to involve non-resident Indians (NRI's) for the development of their native villages. Emigration from several parts of Punjab has been an ongoing process for long, and many emigrants have garnered big fortunes at their new abodes. The willing ones among them can be encouraged, facilitated and given incentives for adoption of their native places for upgradation into 'model villages'.

Urban Development and Industry

With 34 per cent of its total population living in towns/urban agglomerations in 2001, as compared to 27.8 per cent at the national level, Punjab is one of the more urbanised States of India. The state's 8.3 million urban population is distributed amongst 157 towns/urban agglomerations—139 statutory and 18 Census ones. Fourteen towns/urban agglomerations have a population of at least one lakh each, and together account for 58.4 per cent of the total urban population. The urban growth rate of Punjab, 37.6 per cent during the nineties was significantly higher than 29 per cent at the national level. The experience at the international level suggests that urbanisation gets a momentum in regions after they became 30 per cent urban and simultaneously achieve a per capita income of U.S. $ 500. Punjab has been one such case since 1991. Projections are that the state would become urban majority by 2020. This would reverse the popular image of Punjab as a predominantly rural case. The implication is that urban issues are going to gradually assume greater importance. A change in the thrust of policy would be inevitable.

Some redeeming features of the Punjab's urbanisation are worthy of note. Towns are almost uniformly distributed and closely spaced; their average spacing is about 20 km and this figure is the lowest for any state, barring Kerala and Goa. Impact of agricultural development and associated agro-based industry is evident.

As an outcome of this, Punjab is distinguished by a strong urban-rural linkage and narrow urban-rural gap. In fact, average assets per household in rural areas were recorded as double of those in urban places. The proportion of population below the poverty line at around 6 per cent is virtually the same in rural and urban areas. An urban-rural continuum has been taking shape, which is most manifest in the corridor development along the roads connecting big cities, such as Ludhiana, Jalandhar and Amritsar. A tendency among several agricultural landowning households to raise an additional establishment in a nearby town to avail of better facilities and services is observed. This is giving rise to a class of people whose economic interests are partly rural and partly urban.

Despite some efforts at control, much of the physical growth of towns has been taking place in a haphazard manner. Not only cities but also small and medium towns are subject to this malady. A change in morphology of all types of towns became necessary to meet the increased demand for space for new land uses, for relocation of facility points to alternative sites, and for coping with the fast increasing number of motor vehicles on the road. The response is visible in the emergence of new residential colonies, resiting of old grain markets and bus stands, and laying out of bypasses to divert inter-town traffic.

Illegal encroachment on land is a pervasive malady in all towns. The affected localities could be commercial, residential, institutional, industrial, for that matter any. One manifest expression of this tendency is the proliferation of slums mostly on public land. In 2001, the slum population accounted for about one-fifth of the total living in towns, each with a population of 50,000 plus.

While slums are an index of scarcity of formal housing at an affordable price, inadequacy of several other basic urban services is no less glaring. Even in the four municipal corporations of Ludhiana, Amrtisar, Jalandhar and Patiala, nearly one-third of the population has no access to safe water supply and more than one-half have to go without the facility of sewerage. In 32 nagar panchayats, safe water supply is not available to more than one-half of the population and 95 per cent are not covered by sewerage facility. No less than 40 per cent of roads and streets in Punjab towns require extensive repairs. This is the scene of the quality of life in towns of the most prosperous state of India!

Financial crunch, which the urban local bodies are facing, is at the root of this sorry state of affairs. An extremely low recovery rate of user charges is one major bane of this situation. The aggregate income of urban local bodies from water supply and sewerage charges during 1996-2001 was only Rs. 2 billion as against the projected figure of Rs. 13.5 billion, that is hardly around 15 per cent. Even if only the operation and maintenance cost is taken into account, this percentage would rise to just 47. Actual expenditure on provision of all obligatory services was found to be only around 40 per cent of what was projected, with serious implications for both quantity and quality.

What is the way out? Quality of life in the towns of Punjab calls for an immediate attention. This requires not only a massive input of financial resources but also a serious reform in management. Towards that goal, an effective implementation of the Nagarpalika Act is imperative. Devolution of decision making and financial powers to urban local bodies has so far been hesitant and piecemeal. Parallel functioning of the state apparatus and the elected body in managing urban affairs is replete with problems of coordination in every town.

Urgent reform in management of municipal finances is imperative. Most essential is to rationalise rates of user charges and improve their collection. Selective involvement of the private sector on the lines of 'water supply and sewerage project at Tirupur (Tamil Nadu), 'maintenance of streetlighting, solid waste removal and local transport etc.' at Rajkot (Gujarat), 'solid waste management' at Hyderabad, and 'preparation, distribution and collection of bills' at Ludhiana, can help in reducing the administrative and financial burden on urban local bodies, in addition to improving the quality of the service provided. Floating of municipal bonds to finance urban infrastructure, as has already been done by Ahmedabad, Bangalore, Hyderabad and some other municipal corporations, is still another way of augmenting the financial resources of urban local bodies. Involvement of 'community based organisations' is also valued today as an effective strategy towards coverage and quality of service provision.

Perspectives on urban development vary. Some express their preference for aesthetics of the city by way of its beautification in diverse ways. Another paradigm shifts in favour of 'healthy cities' providing high quality services. Still another view cherishes cities as dynamic economic entities, attracting a variety of activities, generating employment and incomes, and yielding revenues for their proper maintenance. A perspective for Punjab towns can be on similar lines: well designed in physical layout, equipped with a delivery system of quality services, and promising ready employment, through industry in particular.

The industrial structure of Punjab has remarkably expanded in size, diversified in composition, and dispersed over space since 1966. Even during the politically difficult eighties marked by militancy, the state did not lose its industrial momentum. A long term view of 1966-2001 shows that the number of small scale units multiplied more than 25 times, from 8023 to 200603; and that of large and medium scale units by over 5 times, from 122 to 638. Growth of food processing, cotton ginning, hosiery knitting, metal processing, machine tools, transport equipment, and furniture production units has been phenomenal indeed. Both small and large/medium scale units have been dispersing not only to less industrialised parts of the state as a positive response to institutional incentives but also to rural areas wherever infrastructure and accessibility posed less problems. Around 60 per cent of the large/medium scale units in Punjab toady find a rural location, especially along the trunk rail and road routes and around big cities, such as Ludhiana, Jalandhar, Amritsar, and the Chandigarh Union Territory.

Nevertheless, regional disparities in industrialisation persist and their degree varies by the type of industry. Ludhiana, Patiala and Ropar districts account for one-half of the industrial production in the state. Industries using bulky raw materials, such as steel rerolling and metal products, or requiring specialised skill, such as hosiery, silk textiles and transport vehicles, showed a weaker tendency to disperse. On the other hand, direct consumer goods industries, such as food processing, electrical items, and furniture have dispersed widely. Notably the eastern part of the state today is overshadowing its western counterpart, which previously was more industrialised. This is a reversal of an established spatial pattern explained, among other factors, by the presence of a sensitive international border on the west and the location of the state's capital to the east.

Punjab cannot be described as industrially backward as was the refrain some twenty-five years ago but there can be no slowing down on this front; rather what is needed is an acceleration. This is necessary for hastening the shift from agriculture to non-agriculture by generating new employment opportunities and also for reducing regional disparities. What is required is a further strengthening of backward and forward linkages of industry with agriculture.

Such a scheme of things requires a 'SWOT' (strength, weakness, opportunity and threat) analysis of the industrial scene of Punjab. The state is strong in agricultural raw materials, infrastructure base, skilled labour, dynamic entrepreneurship, and high income/consumption level of the people. On the other hand, its weakness lies in a location on the border with an unfriendly country, a peripheral position distant from major national markets, absence of minerals, and relatively low industrial wage rates associated with the predominance of unorganised small scale units. A sizeable section of industrial labour here is migrant from the low income states, such as Uttar Pradesh and Bihar. They agree to work at low wages, and thereby establish an income threshold which does not find favour with the local labour. This is one of the reasons which discourages the local unemployed from seeking an industrial job. Nonetheless, opportunities for industry are rightly being extended through a variety of government incentives and concessions. But then the WTO has recently emerged as a threat to industry in the state. Punjab's industry is now facing a serious competition not only from within India but also from other countries.

Hence, as a perspective for an appropriate framework for accelerating the process of industrialisation in Punjab, three things become essential: (i) identification and prioritisation of those industries for which it is more advantageously placed; (ii) modernisation of the managerial style and upgradation of technological level of industry, presently entrenched in the culture of unorganised small scale industry; and (iii) provision of a special impetus to information technology, both as a strategy for employment generation, and for information dissemination for usage in industry at large. Industries for which the state is favourably placed include: liquor and malt, dairy products, leather goods, blankets, carpets and rugs, hosiery and readymade garments, cotton ginning, cotton textiles, chemicals, paper items, and wood processing.

Beyond this general overview, there are several other critical areas which need to be attended. The foremost one is to work for a coordinated development of large, medium, small and tiny industries. This can take several forms: (i) small scale industry producing component parts, as in bicycle industry, to be refurbished and assembled by large scale industry, or the other way round, as in the case of computer assembling; (ii) large scale industry helping the small scale industry in technological upgradation and human resource development by providing training facilities; and (iii) both large and small scale industries co-functioning in industrial parks, equipped with modern infrastructure facilities; both going in for cooperative marketing and ensure strict quality control; and both jointly running professional courses for training the educated unemployed.

The corridor industrial development, as proliferating along the trunk routes, calls for special attention. Although welcome as a dynamic feature of industrialisation, it is not without some attendant problems, particularly those pertaining to transport mobility, environmental quality, and service provision. Industry, along the transport routes, should be made to grow in the form of a cluster rather than a ribbon. Such clusters can be developed on planned lines, in proximity of railway stations on the route of the corridors. Each cluster can specialise in a particular kind of industry.

Finally, the basic issue is: how to make Punjab investment-friendly for industrial development? On strategic lines this question can be rephrased as: how to attract the prospective industrialist to the state? Involved here are not only factors of location of an industry but also the considerations of the quality of life at the place which may attract the industrialist. Therefore, the most effective strategy would be to raise new planned industrial towns in the proximity of Ludhiana, Jalandhar, Amritsar, Bathinda and Patiala. These should be equipped with first rate infrastructural facilities for industry and quality services for daily life. An uninterrupted flow of electricity is vital to such a scheme of things.

Employment

Providing gainful and high quality employment to the unemployed and new entrants to the labourforce is one of the main targets of the Tenth Plan. Although Punjab is relatively the most progressive and prosperous state of India yet it is not free from the twin maladies of unemployment and underemployment. A sizeable section of the agricultural population is being rendered surplus due to a regular decline in the size of landholdings in association with the rapid growth of population. The rural service and artisan castes are finding their vocations inadequate and less rewarding. The educated among the rural are generally keen to get an urban job. Things are no better in urban places where an increasing number of local unemployed is being joined by unemployed migrants from rural areas. The size of registers at employment exchanges is swelling.

The employment context of Punjab significantly changed after its reorganisation in the present form in 1966. Agricultural migration to newly reclaimed lands in other parts of India, which has been continuing since the closing decades of the nineteenth century, virtually came to a halt. Recruitment in defence forces was regulated on the basis of the share of the eligible population in different states in 1974 and this was to the disadvantage of Punjab. The number of ex-servicemen, seeking re-employment, is much larger than the new entrants to the defence forces. Meanwhile, the avenues of emigration to other countries remain regulated.

The National Sample Organisation recorded the unemployment rate of Punjab at 4.2 per cent in 1999-2000, as against 7.3 per cent in India. This rate has risen from 3.1 per cent in 1993-94. By that token, the number of unemployed in Punjab is estimated at nearly four hundred thousand. The number of the underemployed is placed at another half a million, going by the percentage of marginal workers at 5.4, as a recorded by the 2001 census.

The compound annual growth rate of employment in Punjab during 1997-2002 was only 0.7 per cent against the growth rate of the labourforce at 2.3 per cent. This growth rate of employment was the lowest for any State of India, and much below the national average of 2.4 per cent. A rule-of-thumb-estimate world suggest that economic growth rate should be three times the population growth rate if unemployment were to be taken care of. The annual economic growth rate of Punjab has been in the vicinity of 3 per cent during the nineties while population growth rate was around 1.8 per cent. That explains the rise in unemployment rate over the years, although at a moderate pace. It also suggests that the state must aim at an economic growth rate of at least 6 per cent if the stock and flow of unemployment is to be managed.

Unemployment in Punjab is essentially educated in nature—61.6 per cent being matriculate or above. Nearly one-fourth of them are technically or professionally trained, being diploma holders, engineers, trained teachers and doctors. Educated unemployment is growing faster in rural areas than in urban places.

Rising unemployment among educated rural youth is a serious problem facing Punjab. How to generate jobs and how to prepare them for self-employment, is the question to reckon with. The typical recommended line of action is diversification of agriculture in favour of dairying, pomi-culture, bee keeping and fishing. There is a fervent advice to 'emulate Denmark which during the late nineteenth century swiftly shifted from grain forming to dairying, piggery and poultry, as soon as Europe got flooded with grains from North America, Argentina and Baltic States' (Kahlon, 2001, p. 89).

As matters stand, it is most desirable that the pace of industrialisation must be accelerated. Incentives on this count have produced positive results and need to be continued. Small scale industry is to be preferred in view of its labour-intensive character.

With 20 per cent of total industrial investment, it accounts for 80 per cent of industrial employment in the state. As detailed above, its integration with large/medium scale industry is also very necessary.

For this, industry must find its rightful place in district planning. This requires a meaningful coordination between different government departments. For example, planting of trees by the Forest Department be linked with promotion of furniture manufacturing by the Industries Department, for its utilisation in local schools by the Education Department.

Though in an incipient stage today, the Information Technology (I.T.) industry has all the potential of rapid growth and can provide quality employment in large numbers. The manpower requirement for this industry during 2002-2007 has been projected at 99,000 (that is 6,000 in category A of software product and technology services; 16,000 in category B of I.T. services; and 77,000 in category C of I.T. enabled services). Now it devolves upon the Government of Punjab to provide for training this number of high quality manpower within a span of five years.

Construction is another activity which can generate jobs in bulk in both secondary and tertiary sectors. It will be most advisable to go in for a 'new city' project. This should preferably be located in the Doaba region but in close proximity to Ludhiana. It would attract large investment from the NRIs, offer jobs in thousands, apart from reducing the pressure on Ludhiana.

In addition, we may explore some additional avenues of employment in other spheres and in different ways. Considering the relative prosperity and lifestyle of Punjabis, there is considerable scope for promoting fast-food joints on modern lines. The private sector can additionally be harnessed for the provision of security, maintenance and local transport services on organised lines. In the primary sector, introduction of planters, transplanters and potato diggers may tempt even educated youth to join their family vocation. For the females, we could encourage part-time employment in such divisible jobs, as office work, teaching, and health services.

Above all, the employment exchanges should not remain simply the registration centres of the unemployed. They must do the job of data analysis and advice government on employment policy. On the other hand, the unemployed youth must have greater access to information about the kind of jobs available in the market, the level of education required in each case, and facility of loan if one opts to go in for self-employment. One potential skill in which the educated unemployed youth can be trained is 'rural marketing'. Creation of additional job in teaching will also help.

Education

It is a socio-economic anomaly that Punjab, which ranks first on per capita income, is tenth among Indian States in terms of literacy. Here is a case of incongruity between economic and social dimensions of development. At the 2001 census, 70 per cent of the Punjab's seven-plus population was recorded as literate as compared with 91 per cent in Kerala and 77 per cent in Himachal Pradesh. The all-India figure was 65 per cent.

A snapshot of education in Punjab is as follows:

— Practically every village in Punjab has a primary school, a middle school within 2 km, a high school within 2.5 km, and a senior secondary school within 7 km, thus exceeding the norms set by the Government of India. Of the nearly 4 million school children, 80 per cent attend government school, signifying the contribution of government to the spread of education. No less than 78 per cent of the children, who join a school, dropout by the time they reach senior secondary level, and one-half of those who appear in the matriculation examination, as regular student, fail to pass. This is a colossal waste of educational effort on any count!

— The fast growing popularity of private English medium schools, more so in rural areas, questions the quality of education provided by government schools.

— With 6 universities (two general, one technical, one medical, one veterinary, and one agricultural) and 287 colleges of all types, the state is well served by higher level educational and professional institutions. One-third of the colleges are located in rural areas. The number of graduate and post-graduate students approaches two hundred thousand, with females exceeding males. Scheduled Caste students account for about one-tenth of all students in colleges/universities while the scheduled caste population accounts for around one-third of the total.

— Government colleges make only about one-fifth of the 223 general category colleges in the state. The remaining are in private sector. Most of the engineering colleges are run by the private sector, and medical colleges by government.

— As much as 99 per cent of the primary education budget goes towards disbursement of salaries. The corresponding figures are 90 per cent for secondary education, 71 per cent for college/university education, and 66 per cent for professional institutions. Paltry sums are left for infrastructural facilities.

— The state outlay on education was 7.2 per cent of the total under the Fourth Plan (1969-74). It declined to 2.9 per cent in the Ninth Plan (1997-2002). In an effort to redress the aggravating situation, the Tenth Plan (2002-2007) proposals provide an outlay of 6.1 per cent for education.

Improvement in the quality of school education, particularly in rural areas, is the most critical issue in the sphere of education in Punjab. The state is saturated as far distribution of schools is concerned; it is the quality which is in short supply. The Punjab Education Policy 2000: Programme of Action demonstrates that the government is aware of the gravity of the existing situation. A variety of proposals to strengthen the infrastructure, upgrade the quality of teachers, and improve management of education in schools has been listed. This augurs well for the reform of school education in Punjab.

We may, however, review here a moot suggestion made as part of the state's new education policy. While the decision to restructure the present four levels of school education (primary, middle, high and senior secondary) to two levels (elementary and secondary) is most welcome, the proposal to upgrade every primary school to elementary school does not appear feasible. The purpose of education would be better served if a policy of consolidation rather than of expansion is followed. At the first stage, it would be advisable to upgrade only centrally located primary schools to the level of elementary schools, each of which is surrounded by three already existing primary schools. Only at a later stage, the decision about upgradation or continuation or closure of the remaining primary schools could be taken in the light of the experience gained.

Under the new dispensation, it would be advisable if the elected bodies, that is the village panchayats and nagarpalikas were asked to regularly monitor the functioning of the schools. The policy document is silent on this issue. Mention has been made of the village and town-level education development committees; absence of any reference to the elected local bodies is rather intriguing. In all fairness, involving the existing institutions is always better than creating new ones.

Punjab is no less happily placed in terms of the number of institutions of higher education, both general and professional. Again, while proximity is no issue, quality certainly is. Involved here are matters relating to infrastructural facilities, professional commitment of the teachers, and the desired culture of management. Faced with a severe resource crunch, the state government has recently been extending a wide space for the entry of private sector in higher education, more so in the professional field. To what extent promoting privatisation of higher education is desirable and what will be its eventual outcome is not easy to predict. Should we assume that there is little room for reforming higher education and making it cost-effective within the public sector? In any case, management of privatisation, particularly in higher education, is a serious obligation of the government. Equally important here is to understand that the quality of higher education and that of school education are interlinked. Teachers, of all disciplines and status, have to come through the channel of higher education and the quality of higher education is a function of the kind of students which school education produces. It is the quality of the teacher which ultimately determines the quality of the entire system.

Health

On almost all parameters, the health infrastructure in Punjab has expanded phenomenally since 1966. A new hierarchy of health outlets, including referral hospitals, community/primary health centres, sub-centres, mother and child care units, and family planning clinics has evolved in both rural and urban areas, through public sector. Along with, universities and public sector undertakings too provide health facilities to their employees.

No less spectacular has been the growth of health services in the private fold. Its participation is no longer confined to individual private clinics but extends also to hospitals, polyclinics, diagnostic centres, nursing homes and speciality premises. The organised private sector, in addition, caters to the health needs of its employees.

A perusal of data and information about the health sector in Punjab brings out the following facts:

- During 1966-2001, the number of health institutions in the public sector multiplied by 4.5 times, from 496 to 2229, and this rate of increase was three times faster in rural areas than in the urban. Most rapid growth took place during 1973-83 when a large number of sub-centres were opened all over the State. A kind of plateau was reached by 1985. The establishment of the Punjab Health System Corporation in 1996-97, through World Bank assistance, is a major development of recent years in this context.
- The availability of medical and paramedical personnel also recorded an impressive increase: the number of doctors per unit of population became twofold, of midwives six-eight times, and of nurses five times.
- Ironically, the quality of health services provided by the government has gone down drastically over the years. Only one-third of the outdoor patients now opt for a public health outlet, as compared with nearly one-half in India. It was a case of management failure. While the popularity of the public sector suffered, the private sector started flourishing.
- The average cost of outdoor treatment per occurrence of illness in private sector is one-third higher than in the public sector. The cost of hospitalised treatment is 2.5 times more expensive. The average cost of treatment per episode of illness in public sector is roughly one-third higher in Punjab than at the all-India level.
- The birth rate of Punjab at 21.5 per thousand in 1999-2000 was three times the death rate at 7.3 per thousand. For the

stabilisation of the size of population, a continued thrust on family planning is necessary.

— In the sphere of reproductive and child health, some dimensions remain worrisome: maternal mortality rate of 369 per hundred thousand women is four times that of Kerala; still birth rate at 10 per thousand is higher than the national average of 8; about 60 per cent of the deliveries take place at home; nearly one-fourth of the children born are underweight. No less than 41 per cent of women suffer from anaemia. Punjab's infant mortality rate at 52 is fortunately lower than India's 68.

— On nutrition, 15 per cent of adults in Punjab have been reported as obese. This percentage is 30 in the case of women, the highest for any state in the country. On the other hand, per capita calorie intake in the state declined by almost one-third during 1972-94, while it stayed static in India. Protein intake has come down but fat intake has risen.

The above discussion confirms that the situation is not happy on the health front in Punjab. The public sector is not delivering the service on desired lines. There is increasing disenchantment with its performance. The private sector is proving effective but is expensive for the poor. Preventive and emergency health services remain the domain of the public sector.

Affordability does not seem to be a major issue in the sphere of health care in Punjab. It is the access to and quality of service which is more critical. The public and private sectors need to define their respective roles in that light. A system can be evolved wherein the public sector concentrates more on primary health care, health education, sanitation, immunization, emergency services and specialised treatment and the private sector is encouraged and facilitated to take care of curative services. Equally crucial for the government is to manage the private sector properly through its mandatory registration, service monitoring, and fees regulation.

Infrastructure

As a base and concomitant of the development process, infrastructure is fairly well organised in both rural and urban segments of Punjab. On the score of infrastructure rating, the Centre of Monitoring Indian Economy has placed Punjab on the top; with an index which is almost twice of the national average. No less than 94 per cent of the net area sown here is irrigated, 75 per cent by tube wells and 25 per cent by canals. Virtually all the 12729 villages are not only electrified but also linked by a *pucca* road. The 144 regulated markets, for disposal of agricultural produce, are spaced at an average distance of 20 km from each other, and are attached to 519 sub-yards distributed all round. Over 40 per cent of the 2,575 bank branches in the state are located in villages. As many as 597 rural focal points are being developed to provide a variety of services to rural populace.

In overall terms, per capita consumption of electrical energy at about one thousand kWh in Punjab is the highest among all the states. The total consumption in 2000-2001 was 2717 MW; one-half thermal, one-fourth hydel, and the remaining one-fourth purchased from the national grid. Agriculture shared 29 per cent of the total consumption, industry 42 per cent, and domestic and other uses 29 per cent. Eighty-seven per cent of the households in the state have the facility of electricity. Demand for power is growing by 7 per cent annually. Transmission and distribution losses are placed at 17 per cent and non-technical losses at another 9 per cent. Losses of this nature, hidden in the free supply of electricity to agricultural sector, are not included in this assessment. Revenue per unit is Rs. 2.07 against the cost of Rs. 2.93, representing a subsidy of over 40 per cent.

Punjab is well served by a dense network of roads; 1.1 km for every one sq. km as compared with 0.4 at the national level. Road length, which was only six thousand km in 1965-66, had increased to fifty-five thousand km by 2000-01. Intrastate mobility is primarily by road; the most distant town is within six hours of bus journey from the state capital. High speed trains connect Punjab with all parts of the country. Amritsar is an international airport and Ludhiana a domestic one.

About twenty-six thousand public call/straight trunk dialling offices connect Punjab not only within but also nationally and globally. The 1.3 million connections give a telephone/population ratio of 5.5 per thousand persons as compared with 3.6 at the all-India level. Practically every panchayat in the state is connected by telephone.

All this is highly creditable. This quantitative scene is, however, not backed up by a quality culture. Electricity breakdowns are not infrequent; electricity in villages is available only for seven hours in a day; and electricity losses in transmission and distribution are huge. During the nineties, while the number of motor vehicles multiplied two times to almost three million, the road length got extended by hardly 20 per cent. Several roads require immediate widening or repairs or both. By comparison, while the quality of telephone service has vastly improved over the years, its quantitative coverage is far from complete. The waiting list for a phone runs into thousands.

Natural Resource Base

The natural resource base of Punjab—land, water and vegetation —is under great stress. No less than 85 per cent of the state's geographical area is under cultivation, of which 94 per cent is irrigated. Cropping intensity is as high as 186.

Around 40 per cent of the land is said to be degraded in varying degrees. Included herein are the gully or ravine lands in the north-eastern hilly and submontane region; soil-fertility depleted pockets in the central zone; waterlogged tracts in the south-western region; and marshy land along rivers and streams. Nearly 1.1 million tube wells (85 per cent in the rural and 15 per cent in urban areas), regularly suck underground water for irrigation, domestic, industrial and other uses. Nearly one-half of the development blocks (especially in the central zone where water table has gone down by 5 to 10 metres during the last 25 years) report over-exploitation of subsoil water. Hardly 3 per cent of the total area is under forest cover. Such a situation is a sad commentary on what is happening in an agriculturally progressive state, dependent highly on soil and water. Added to all this is the fact that almost 70 per cent of Punjab is prone to floods.

Considerable effort is being made by the Government of Punjab to redeem the situation. Watershed development projects have been undertaken in parts of the Kandi or submotane tract; wetlands are being raised on systematic lines in highly flood-prone areas; and waterlogging is being tackled in all seriousness in the south-western region. The situation in respect of depletion of underground water and fall in soil-fertility is aggravating in the wheat-rice rotation region, which covers almost one-half of the state's total area. Diversification of the cropping pattern is certainly a remedy; in addition the feasibility of developing tube well and canal irrigation as complementary to each other in the same area should also be explored.

Flood-proneness of a large part of the Punjab is paradoxical but is understandable when one realises that roads and canals at several places have been constructed against the grain of the land and thereby obstruct the natural flow of water. The drains, which are meant to flush out the rain water, are often poorly maintained, get choked and cause floods. These drains should not only be cleared of any obstructive material on a regular basis but also be provided with check dams placed across at a reasonable distance from each other. This will help in harvesting the rainwater, and thereby recharging the underground water.

Finally, to compensate for the gross inadequacy of forests in Punjab, agro-forestry and social forestry continue to be a viable proposition. Agro-forestry, involving judicious interculture of trees and crops, should be encouraged in flood-prone and waterlogged areas; and social forestry on *panchayat* lands. Government should prefer plantation of *sheesham* over eucalyptus along canals and roads. Since many saplings, planted by government agencies, get uprooted due to lack of proper care, it is essential to involve the local population in this task. Farmers, whose lands adjoin the plantation sites, may be asked to render the necessary care. Strategies, of course, will vary in accordance with local conditions.

On the whole, Punjab emerges as a grand success story. Despite the constraint inherent in its location on an international border with an unfriendly country and the challenge posed by militancy during the eighties, it has the highest per capita income in the country, was the first to work out the green revolution, and is now aheading towards a phase of large scale agro-industrialisation. Evolving in the mode of a 'culture of competition', the state is taking time to acquire a 'culture of cooperation'. Human development is yet to reach the expected level. For that matter, Punjab has not been in a position to realize its full potential.

Development Strategies

Good Governance

Where does the fault lie? One could single out the 'lack of good governance' as the real malefactor. A populist political culture, inefficient bureaucracy, sagging work culture, lack of necessary respect for law, and above all, systemic corruption are among the parameters describing such a situation. The malady may be nationwide but there is no reason that a progressive state like Punjab should have fallen in line. There are, at the same time, examples of Maharashtra, Karnataka and Andhra Pradesh doing much better in governance, at present.

How to remedy the situation? How to reinvent the government? What does good governance involve? In the final analysis, it stands for conduct of the affairs of the state in such a manner that it enhances the creditability of those who are at the helm of affairs at any level, which is cost and time-effective in responding to the needs and aspirations of the people, and which has civil society as its cherished goal. In addition, it has to promote economy, ensure equity, enhance ecology and provide security.

Three important observations will be in order here. First, the concept of governance is not understood properly in the developing countries where it is equated with the idea of 'control'. This is not the spirit of the term. Governance is a process by which 'a society solves its problems and meets its needs by using government as an instrument' (Osborne and Gaebler, 1992, p. 24). With government at the core, it encompasses the role also of the private sector, non-government organisations and individual households, and thereby involves people in its functioning a variety of ways. This contemporary liberal meaning of governance must be made a part of popular understanding. Secondly, the mindset of the personnel in the conduct of governance is also to be transformed. They are not to project themselves as providers and benefactors, as the case has been so far. They have to be in the service of the people. For that, they have to take some new lessons. The most important learning would be that 'good governance is driven by some grand mission rather than by rigid rules and regulations'. 'It decentralises any activity requiring management and pre-empts problems before these arise'. Above all, 'it empowers citizens in terms of control over their affairs and treats them as patrons by offering choices between a variety of services'.

Towards that end, the role of e-governance requires elaboration. This, of course, begins with networking of the administrative centres of all orders in the hierarchy. Equally essential is to net every panchayat and nagarpalika in the system of e-governance. No less necessary is it to make available details of development schemes, forms for availing opportunities offered by the government, and all other information of public interest on special websites designed for the purpose. Widespread training of a large number of personnel in computer use is a prerequisite of promoting such a culture of governance.

Above all, access to information is a condition of good governance, as a factor of empowerment of the people. It enables them to be subjects and not mere objects of development. It is in this context that I.T. revolution assumes tremendous significance, as an instrument of e-governance.

Empowering Local Bodies

How to involve all the stake holders in the grand task of good governance? The most effective strategy would be to strengthen the local level elected bodies. This calls for a genuine faith in the efficacy of the gram panchayats and nagarpalikas, as mandated by the 73rd and 74th Constitutional Amendments. Much remains to be done on this count in Punjab. A further necessary step would be to devolve to local bodies the 29 subjects earmarked for them in the sphere of service provision and development planning, as also to provide the necessary administrative and technical for the purpose. Local bodies, in their own turn, should feel obliged to do the following: (i) monitor the quality of services, such as school, dispensary, water supply, electricity and the link road, made available to their locality by the state government; (ii) highlight village problems, such as flooding, water logging, plant diseases, and lack of transport facility, so as to call attention of those who matter; (iii) prepare a blueprint of a development plan of their settlement; and (iv) take care of the natural resource base.

All this is easier said than done. This will not translate into a possibility, let alone be a reality, until the members of panchayats are made aware of their obligations and rights through well-designed training programmes on a continuing basis. The knowledge, technical skill and governance skill of the peoples' elected representatives have to be upgraded for ushering in a new era. The task is stupendous as it has to cover almost one hundred thousand persons of 12369 gram panchayats, 140 panchayat samitis, and 17 zila parishads in the state. The experience of the involvement of the Centre for Research in Rural and Industrial Development, Chandigarh, demonstrates the effective contribution that non-government organisations can make in this sphere.

Micro-level Planning

As a concomitant of political decentralisation at the grassroots level, a genuine thrust to micro-level planning, with a block or a district as the spatial unit, has to be an essential ingredient of any development strategy for Punjab. What is visualised is an integration of plans prepared for individual settlements, blocks and districts, through involvement of the stakeholders. This is not the practice at present. Planning and development still remain a government activity, by and large. As a result, the masses have acquired a state-dependency mindset to the exclusion of local enterprise and leadership. A call for a 'genuine' mode of decentralised planning is made here to reverse this tendency so that a more meaningful socio-economic transformation gets underway through peaceful means.

A micro-level plan is in the nature of a blueprint for action. In actual practice, it involves the following tasks: recommending location specific projects for filling spatial gaps in the distribution of infrastructure; suggesting ways to harness the potential and solve the problems of the micro-region; reviewing the ongoing schemes and indicating as to which should be made to continue or be modified, or even abandoned or which should be adopted as new; and identifying special areas of concern, such as backward villages, village common-lands, and land use in general. Such an exercise calls for a mapping of hazard prone tracts, the settlement system and the infrastructure base. It also demands an insight into the socio-economic life, political contours, institutional arrangements, aspirations and constraints of the people, among other things. It presumes a comprehensive and intimate knowledge and appreciation of local conditions.

Not much effort is visible on this front. The ground experience is that the Additional Deputy Commissioner, expected to take care of the development agenda, is often not given charge of the relevant subject, and the office of the block development officer, vital at the local level, is treated as a musical chair with the incumbents changing positions every year or two, on an average. A sense of continuity in development planning is simply lacking. To make micro-level planning effective, it is essential to follow the tenets of development administration. Matters would certainly improve if the Additional Deputy Commissioner is given charge of development administration, in the true spirit of the office, and a block is administered by an officer hailing from the Indian Administrative Services.

Administrative Area Reform

A close scrutiny of the administrative map of Punjab, down from the division to the district, tahsil and block level, shows some serious distortions in the organisation of administrative space. Currently, the state is organised into 4 divisions, 17 districts, 72 subdivisions, and 140 development blocks. In 1966, Punjab had 2 divisions, 11 districts, 37 subdivisions/tehsils and 117 development blocks. Despite some efforts at rationalisation, Firozpur district remains unwieldy and Kapurthala fragmented. Boundaries of three districts and seven subdivisions were tampered with to create Fatehgarh Sahib district. It covers an area which is not much bigger than that of an average subdivision in the state. A periodic administrative reform, not on an *ad hoc* but on comprehensive basis, emerges as imperative for the sake of both administrative efficiency and development administration.

There are some other issues to debate. Should the state continue with its existing system of divisions, districts, subdivisions or development blocks, or dispense with divisions and subdivisions and retain only districts and development blocks? What is the relevance of a division in a small state like Punjab? Do we need subdivisions when the average number of development blocks in a district is just eight? Multiplicity of tiers in administration generates confusion and creates delays (Krishan and Kant, 1998, p. 12).

There is still another moot point for deliberation. Should development blocks continue to remain exclusively rural, as they were originally designed, or should any town falling within their territorial jurisdiction be also included as a part of the block? The rationale of keeping rural and urban areas as separate in any scheme of things is difficult to justify in the present context. A serious difficulty is faced when one is preparing a block plan wherein towns are to be kept out of reckoning. This is not how ground realities operate. A block must cover both villages and towns located within its spatial parameters.

As a development strategy, there is still another way of reforming the administrative areas. Let the boundaries of the state assembly constituencies and those of blocks correspond with each other, and likewise those of parliamentary constituencies with higher order administrative units, such as divisions or a group of districts. An arrangement on these lines will render the desired congruence between political, administrative and developmental dimensions of the state at all levels.

Civil Society

To accomplish all this, and also as an ultimate goal in itself, Punjab must strive at evolving as a civil society. The basic strands of such a society include: a genuine faith in pluralism as inherent in every system; a reinvented democracy which is sensitive equally to aspirations of the minority as much of the majority; and the presence of all variety of civil groups which function not merely in their own interest but for a collective cause by way of influencing the decision makers. Civil society does not allow the government to be authoritarian but has no design on its part to be a 'political equivalent of the private sector'. Its aim is to transform differences into complementarities, competition into cooperation, and distance into proximity. Thereby, it ensures identity, dignity and liberty to every individual (Uberoi, 1999, p. 104). A 'humane future is envisioned', with the state as a more 'responsive than repressive' agent. Cultivation of appropriate 'cultural values and civic virtues' is basic to the attainment of such a goal.

Punjab, as a society, is marked by a significant degree of structural stratification and spatial segmentation. Structurally, it displays diversity in terms of religion (Sikh, Hindu, Christian, Muslim and others); caste (higher, peasant, artisan, service, and scheduled ones); and status (landowning or landless and native or inmigrants). The spatial parameter of distinction is represented by a urban and rural background, as also by the sub-regional identity of the Majha, Doaba and Malwa, on traditional lines. This is the context in which the question of civil society in Punjab is to be placed.

Punjab is the only Sikh-majority state of India. With 63 per cent of its population as Sikh and 34 per cent as Hindu, the state is bi-religious, since the two communiites have a common heritage, shared values, and common life practices. A tradition of honouring each other's religion always existed.

As a fact of history, the Hindus in Punjab were more urban-based, and the Sikhs concentrated predominantly in rural areas; the former more in trade and services and the latter in agriculture. Over time, a kind of complementarity and interdependence between the two took shape on economic lines. With the spread of education and recent acceleration in the process of urbanisation, accompanied by migration from villages to towns, the proportion of the Sikhs in urban places has been enlarging. They have been entering into services, trade, transport, industry and other urban vocations in an increasing number, particularly after the formation of Punjab in 1966. This has brought the two communities on a more interactive common space and mutual interdependence, a situation which can facilitate the formation of a civil society.

Both the Sikh and the Hindu communities have their caste divisions. The primary one is that between the Scheduled Castes and the non-scheduled ones. It is estimated that among the Scheduled Castes, who now account for around one-third of the state's population, more than one-half are Hindu and nearly one-half Sikh. They have to contend with common issues of economic upliftment and social mobility. The factor of religion gets diluted in their case. By bringing the two religious groups onto a common space, they simplify the task of working towards a civil society in the state.

A notable feature of the evolving scene of Punjab's demography is the sizeable inflow of migrants, from the Hindi belt, mainly as agricultural and industrial labourers. They are integrated economically with the native society, but to what extent are they socially linked is a moot question. Some chauvinists view this trend as disturbing for it will affect the electoral calculations of those with vested interest. Mercifully, such a feeling is not pervasive; certainly not expected on the part of a community which itself has sought new pastures not only within the country but also in foreign lands. The intention here is to indicate that we should try to cultivate desired perceptions on this count in the interest of the civil society that we envision.

An issue most critical to the creation of a civil society in Punjab is to render due status to women in overall scheme of things. Despite its impressive gains in economic development, exposure to the developed world, and spread of education, the society here is not as just to the fair sex, as much expected. By and large, a girl child remains unwelcome at birth and women face neglect and discrimination in various forms at different stages of their life. At the first post-independence Census of 1951, Punjab's sex ratio, which is an indicator of the very survival rate of the female, was hardly 854; even after half a century it improved to only 874 at the 2001 Census. These figures are much below the expected sex ratio-at-birth of around 950 and are a pointer to the higher mortality rate of females. Punjab's total fertility rate, representing the number of children a woman is likely to bear in her lifetime, was higher than the national average till 1971. In 1998-99, Punjab's female infant mortality rate at 65 was distinctly above the male infant mortality rate of 50.

Most worrisome is the recent rising incidence of female foeticide, estimated at around ninety thousand a year, in response to an easy accessibility to the pre-birth sound scanning technique. This is manifest in a sharp decline in the sex ratio of 0-6 age group from 875 to 793 during the last intercensal decade of 1991-2001. Urban places and rural areas do not differ much on this count, signifying that the practice of female foeticide is fairly widespread. This uncivil propensity, which is an evil device to marry family planning with son-craze, is unpardonable and poses a challenge that has to be met.

On the other hand, the emerging situation is not without some positive pointers. The 73rd and 74th Constitutional Amendments have mandated reservation of at least one-third of the seats in panchayats (rural) and nagarpalikas (urban). This has certainly changed things in favour of women as far as their political representation at the local level is concerned. The share of women among government employees is the state has also gone up from 14 per cent in 1981 to 17 per cent in 2001. Most notably, on the college and university campuses in the state, girls are now in majority.

Much remains to be done. A basic task is to instill the value of daughter in the son-crazy psyche of Punjab. One necessary step would be to make liberal education universal wherein gender sensitivity is convincingly ingrained as a part of learning. On pragmatic lines, the issue of status of women can be addressed to two strategies: (i) small family, wherein they do not bear large number of children restricting their mobility, and (ii) economic self-reliance, which gives them a greater leverage in taking life decisions. As such, promotion of family planning and generations of job opportunities for women emerge as viable measures towards creating the desired scenario.

What should be the strategy for the realisation of a civil society in Punjab? This goal will be best achieved if non-government organisations are encouraged to play a big role, especially in rural areas, by way of organizing people to solve their problems. Such groups tend to be plural in composition and are expected to imbibe values which are civic in nature. Non-government organisations, on their part, have to learn a great deal from missionary institutions to whichever religion these may belong.

In other words, while working towards the goal of designing a civil society, they must combine education, health, and human values as part of their activities. Secondly, in recognition of the fact that the Punjab society is highly materialistic and pragmatic, it will be necessary to demonstrate that a civil society is in their economic interest. They must feel convinced that a civil society is imperative for sustaining and protecting their relative prosperity. A cost-benefit analysis of conflict resolution in favour of civil society will change their perceptions on desired lines. Finally, it is not merely education but the quality of education, built through the input of dedicated teachers as a role model, which can facilitate this process. They are the ones who produce the decision makers, administrators, doctors, engineers, and teachers themselves, among others, and influence the overall value system of a society. Civil society must have the 'teacher' at the centre of its all strategic formulations.

Sustainable Society

Finally, any development strategy for Punjab has to incorporate the elements of environmental, politico-economic and socio-cultural sustainabilities. Environmental sustainability is assured if the inherent productivity of the ecosystem is not made to suffer any loss; rather it is enriched in terms of its constituents, individually and collectively. This is possible if the life support system is protected from contamination of water, degradation of land, depletion of soil fertility, removal of vegetation cover, pollution of air, and loss of biodiversity. From the viewpoint of econo-political sustainability, all such modes of production and political institutions are to be promoted which lead to a higher level of economic well being and allow people to participate in taking decisions which are relevant to their day to day life, to their mutual interaction, and to their integration with the wider global context. Socio-cultural sustainability is a function of the freedom which people enjoy in pursuit of happiness, harmony and justice, as also in fulfilment of life values they cherish.

Punjab is not in a comfortable situation on the question of multifaceted sustainability. Economic development has extracted a heavy ecological price; functioning of the politico-economic system is riddled with infirmities, and socio-cultural institutions are under the stress of moral collapse. The question of sustainability is rarely raised beyond its economic parameters. Ethical questions are described as lacking paragmatism. Traditional culture is seen as losing its sheen.

Concluding Remarks

The preceding discussion allows us to glean the main strands of development perspective for Punjab. These include: rejuvenation of the socio-economic dynamism of the state; improvement in the quality of life as well of habitat in both rural and urban areas; upgradation of the human resource base by improving the quality of educational and health services; diversification of the economy from agriculture to non-agriculture, of agriculture towards non-farm activities, and of wheat-rice rotation towards ecologically viable crop-combinations; and effective management of water and soil.

Additional issues pertinent to development perspective can be listed as: how to make Punjab investment friendly for industry? How the state should be meeting the challenges posed by globalisation of economy, labour replacing new technologies, and overproductive biotechnology? How to promote a culture of taking rational locational decisions, wherein economics leads politics rather than the other way round? How to transform Punjab into a prosperous, good-governed and civil society on a sustained basis. The analysis in this paper demonstrates that 'rejuvenation, quality and management' are the three key ingredients of reinventing Punjab today.

For years after independence, Punjab effectively demonstrated that it could lead in the mode of a model state in India. Today, it is craving to be led. The tide will turn only when leaders with foresight awaken the state from the slumber of past glory and create a space for new dreams to manifest.

Acknowledgements

This paper is a modified version of the two chapters on 'Development Perspective' and 'Strategy for Development' for Punjab, contributed by the author to the *Punjab Development Report*, prepared at the Centre of Research in Rural and Industrial Development (CRRID), Chandigarh, for the Planning Commission, New Delhi. Incorporation, in places, of some bold facts and information appearing in other chapters of the Report is duly acknowledged. Special thanks are due to providing the CRRID for an enviable opportunity of doing this assignment. A sincere gratitude is expressed for Dr. Anu Kapur, Reader, Department of Geography, Delhi University, Delhi, for going through the draft of the paper and giving highly useful suggestions. The author alone is responsible for the views expressed as also for any infirmity in the paper.

REFERENCES

Chadha, G.K. (1986), *The State and Rural Economic Transformation: The Case of Punjab*, 1950-85, Sage Publications, New Delhi.

Gosal, G.S. and Gopal Krishan (1984), *Regional Disparities in Levels of Socio-Economic Development in Punjab*, Vishal Publications, Kurukshetra.

Government of Punjab (1969-2002), *Five Year Plans, Fourth to Tenth*, Department of Planning, Chandigarh.

Government of Punjab (2000 March), *White Paper on the State's Finances*, Ministry of Finance, Chandigarh.

Government of Punjab (2002 June), *Medium Term Fiscal Program*, Department of Finance, Chandigarh.

Johal, S.S. and Ray, S.K. (2002), *Future of Agriculture in Punjab*, Centre for Research in Rural and Industrial Development, Chandigarh.

Kahlon, Gurbhagwant Singh (2001), *Dairying and Farm Diversification*, Punjab Institute for Sustainable Development, Ludhiana.

Krishan, Gopal and Surya Kant (1998), "Administrative Space" in J.S. Grewal and Indu Banga, *Punjab in Prosperity and Violence: 1947-1997*, K.K. Publishers, New Delhi.

Osborne, David and Ted Gaebler (1992), *Reinventing Government*, Prentice Hall of India, New Delhi.

Uberoi, J.P.S. (1999), *Religion, Civil Society and the State*, Oxford University Press, Calcutta.

18

Policies for Our Plundered Planet

Some Pathways to the Future

K.V. SUNDARAM

Introduction to the Focal Theme

A major objective of the Bhoovigyan Vikas Foundation (BVF) is to work towards the common goal of "Saving our Planet", through various activities designed to achieve Sustainable Development. It implies a deep concern for the Sustainable Development and management of our Natural Resources, with conservation and equity considerations. The objectives here are: (i) to widely disseminate and spread the message of Sustainable Development and living by creating the awareness, need and urgency for protecting the earth from the ravages of human action, and (ii) to promote the rational use of natural resources through planned practices of conservation and development. To achieve these objectives, policy guidance through carefully conceived Earth Care Policies is necessary, to design a realistic perspective plan for a new Global Society.

This paper is mainly confined to outline the contours of some priority policies and will not go into the details of the current state of environment, the problems emerging from Earth-Man interface and their various consequences, which call for urgent action along several fronts. It is assumed that these are fairly well known and they constitute the starting point for our discussion here. (For a shortlisting of the consequences of human action, see Appendix I).

The paper underlines the fact that humanity's stake in earth protection is enormous during the current century, as the sane earth care policies, necessary in this behalf, have been neglected too often in the past. The basic dilemma here is related to the two-way relationships between development and environment. The twin concerns in this relationship are:

- Environment without development would be life without opportunities.
- Development without adequate environmental protection would inflict serious environmental damage and destroy Earth's delicate natural balance and hasten its very end.

Our Focus

The focus of our discussion will be the Indian context, in relation to the changing global economy in the new millennium. Our country is blessed by the beauty of its vast and varied landscapes and the wealth of its natural resources. But with this blessing, comes the responsibility to ensure their preservation and a healthy environment, in a planet that should be livable and pleasant. In the new knowledge-based and technology-driven global economy, this can be achieved only by integrating our economic, environmental and social goals and policies with various levels of government, within our country and across the globe. These goals must be achieved in partnership with several stake-holders —governments, and the civil society; industries and business; academicians, researchers and technologists—who have the requisite perception, knowledge and expertise to steer the right course of action. In short, Caring for the Earth is everyone's business.

Our Strategy

Caring for the Earth falls between too many disciplinary stools and calls for broad and explicit strategies, encompassing a vast and wide spectrum of policies and programmes in numerous sectors of development. The policies and actions needed in this context have to be in the nature of "coordinated efforts", ranging from local to global. They must be conceived as an 'interlinked strategy', mutually supporting each other and aimed at the common goal of sustainable development. The Bhoovigyan Vikas Foundation's role will be one of encouraging our common concerns through motivation, stimulation, cooperation, teamwork, partnerships and shared values and advocacy of sustainable policies, ethics and practices and concretising these with empowered action. It hopes to gradually expand its horizon of action through continuous learning, by undertaking various assignments and special projects, through the training and development of its core professionals and constant interaction and networking with experts in various fields. The medium for such action will be through exchange of thoughts in Discussion Forums, Seminars, Colloquiums, Workshops and Conferences and networking its activities with professional and scientific institutions in India and abroad.

Earth Care Policies: its Strategic Directions

The issues to be addressed under the term, "Earth Care Policies", will cover a set of carefully conceived proposals for national strategies, plans and processes of development and promoting a value system enshrining the principle of sustainability over generations, of the planet's multitude of natural resources, including Land, Water and the Biospheric environment, with their numerous living species, including the humankind. This calls for an array of consistent, coherent and properly sequenced actions on multiple fronts by multiple organizations. This is no small task. The present paper will focus on some prismatic and targeted policies relating to those natural resources, which rank high among the Earth Care Priorities

This discussion is organised around the following major heads:

- International environmental concerns.
- The crisis of multilateralism.
- Environmental Degradation Sustainable National Resources Management.
- Sustainable Water Security.
- Sustainable Agriculture and Food Security.
- Earth Care policies for halting Land Degradation.
- Sustainable Forestry and Biodiversity.
- Sustainable Energy and Industry.
- Towards a 'Circular Model' of Materials Economy.
- Sustainable Rural Development Policy.

- Population and Carrying Capacity and Human Settlements Planning.
- Environmental laws and economic instruments for promoting sustainable development.
- The limited coverage of this paper.
- Towards a new paradigm of Caring for Mother Earth.

International Environmental Concerns

Beginning from the Stockholm Conference in 1972, the subject of Earth Care Policies has been addressed in successive global forums, to ensure that human progress should be sustained through sustainable development, 'without bankrupting the resources of future generations'. The Brundtland Commission Report on Environment and Development in 1987, which was followed by the United Nations Conference on "Environment and Development" in Rio de Janeiro in 1992 with its Agenda 21, and the recent World Summit on "Sustainable Development" at Johannesburg in September 2002, are significant milestones in the thinking about our "Common Future". They have all sought to advance our knowledge and ideas (at least in a conceptual sense), that would contribute to a style of development, that would be economically desirable, socially equitable and environmentally sustainable. Still in a practical sense, the developing and the developed countries are far from reaching these envisioned goals. On the contrary, there has been mounting evidence to prove that "our economic policies that have yielded the extraordinary growth in the world economy are the same ones that are destroying its support systems" (Lester Brown, 2001). The facts and figures thrown up by the World Watch Institute and the Earth Policy Institute are revealing. (For a snapshot of the criticalities facing our Planet in areas like Climate, Water and Biological Base, See Appendix–I). The complexity of the problems that we face in the beginning of this new century is quite perplexing and the need to act with greater determination, vigour and urgency has become more pressing. In this context, "the gap between what we need to do to arrest the environmental deterioration of the planet and what we are doing continues to widen. Somehow we have to turn the tide" (Lester Brown, 2001).

Since Stockholm, it has become clear that a holistic, cooperative multilateral and partnership approach needs to be taken relating to the multifarious aspects of our natural ecosystems—their structure, functions and diversity—with due deference to ethics, values and the promotion of justice and equity. To achieve practical success, we need to recast our programmes and efforts to deal with specific and focused issues. We need to deal not only with the domestic policies of 'local' concerns in regard to air, water pollution and chemical toxicity, but also with the interlinked issues demanding international concerns, like climate change, rising sea level, dying coral reefs and disappearing species. The magnitude of restructuring that is needed to meet these challenges and to advance towards these goals with commitment and dynamism is indeed frightening, as it needs increased national and international efforts for continued action at consensus building and global partnerships for sustainable development. Here there is no way, other than adapting our national and international policies and multinational cooperation strategies to the new challenges and realities of our present millennium. In this respect, humanity, now more than ever, truly stands at a defining moment in history.

The Crisis of Multilateralism

Among the International concerns aimed at multilateral efforts, a major one to be addressed is climate change. The air we breathe belongs to everyone, but the extent or 'space' to which it can be polluted by emissions like Carbondioxide (CO_2) and other greenhouse gases (GHG), is finite and limited. According to one estimate, India is now the World's fifth largest fossil fuel CO_2 emitting country, the emissions having grown at 6 per cent a year since 1950 (Karunakaran, 2002). The only solution by which the emissions could be contained within reasonable limits, will be by sharing this 'space' among all nations on some equitable basis. According to the "strategy of contraction and convergence", the rich countries should contract their emission levels, to a maximum extent (as they are the greatest polluters), while the poor countries may be allowed, (for the sake of developing their economies) to increase their emissions to a reasonable level. The per capita emission and the time for adjusting to safe levels of CO_2 concentration are matters to be negotiated internationally. This strategy will hopefully lead to a just and legally-binding framework for global safety and saving the world from a looming catastrophe. While some developed countries like Denmark, The Netherlands, United Kingdom and Japan have endorsed this principle of 'contraction and convergence' at the Kyoto discussions, some others like USA, who are the worst polluters, have not agreed to do so.

The World Summit on Sustainable Development at Johannesburg, which took place between August 26 to September 4, 2002, with some 21,000 delegates, including 104 Heads of State and Governments, also could not make much headway in this regard, excepting urging the countries who have not signed the Kyoto protocol to do so. Finally, the Johannesburg meet dealt with defining certain dead lines for some specific issues like sanitation and clean water, health, agriculture, environment, renewable energy and poverty. Ultimately, the summit ended as a compromise to accommodate the demands of a powerful few, at the cost of the many poor countries. It could not draw a road map for sustainable development. Despite its failure, multilateralism and global negotiations have to continue with hope against hope.

Following the World Summit, a ten-day Eighth Conference of the Parties (COP) to the United Nations Framework Convention on Climate Change (UNFCC) held its deliberations at New Delhi during September-November, 2002, intended to move ahead towards the substantive issues related to the Kyoto Protocol, following its earlier meetings at Bonn (Germany) and Marrakesh (Morocco). In the final Delhi Declaration, the Convention managed to achieve a degree of success on most of the contentious issues, except on the issue of future commitments. A positive progress was in regard to spelling out the concept of Clean Development Mechanism (CDM), by which developed countries can invest in emission-reducing projects in developing countries and thereby earn carbon credits. This summit has certainly paved the way for the ratification of the Kyoto Protocol by 96 countries, which account for a total of 37.4 per cent of the emissions. The process of multilateral negotiations is undoubtedly a complex and long drawn-out one. But ultimately, the dialogue should be able to bridge the differences between the developing and the developed countries, by the sheer compulsions for creating a livable planet. How this could be brought about is still a moot question. But the only increasing hope in my view, since we cannot afford the luxury pessimism, would be through a revamped and highly empowered United Nations Organisation. The tide in the affairs of 'Earth and Man' today beckons us for greater global cooperation and for more cooperative decision-making. Let me also remind the words of our first patron, the late Shri C. Subramaniam, "there is not much time left for the planet to be saved".

Environmental Degradation and Sustainable Natural Resource Management

Developing countries, who are highly dependent on primary production, rely heavily on the efficient and sustainable management of their resource base,—the land, water and the biosphere—which support these activities. A major requirement for formulating comprehensive Earth-Care Policies for halting environmental degradation is the need for a reliable database, which is a constraint in all developing countries. In the absence of such a database, policy decisions are always taken with 'optimal ignorance'. However, rapid advancement in the techniques of natural resource surveys and developments in Information and Communication Technology (ICT), Biotechnology, Ecotechnology and Geomatics (Spatial Informatics Technology), and their applications in planning through "fusion of technologies" has changed the context.

By leveraging these technologies for securing sustainable growth and competitive advantage for value addition, as well as for providing remunerative opportunities for the farmers and empowering them to capture the optimum value for their produce, it would be possible to elevate the Indian farmer and enhance his purchasing power and competitiveness to withstand the challenges of our new century. This must be recognized as the most important among our priorities in framing our Earth Care Policies in agriculture for the future. The policy dimensions in this context would be:

(*i*) Substantial increase in yields[1] which will enable higher farm incomes;
(*ii*) Diversification of land use to optimize farm income by better aligning of the produce with the needs of the market, both domestic and international;
(*iii*) Effective linkages with the food processing industry, to develop and market its value added products in the domestic and international markets;
(*iv*) Efficient aggregation mechanisms and logistics to service the requirement for high quality inputs and knowledge at the farm end on the one hand, and to assist in output marketing on the other, making cost of transactions and logistics internationally competitive.

In the above context of enhancing global competitiveness of Indian agriculture, four major problems needed to be addressed are:

(*i*) Impact of subsidies and incentive structures related to land use planning;
(*ii*) Neglect of the small producer;
(*iii*) Degradation of the resource base owing to short-sighted policies resulting in loss of soil resources and desertification;
(*iv*) Precision farming for productivity improvement, by adjusting farm practices to match the variations of soil and terrain across time and space, as well as ensuring the timeliness and the method of sowing, irrigation and other agricultural operations.

Earth Care policies in the agricultural sector would also require several other enabling requirements such as:

(*i*) Redirection of government effort;
(*ii*) Amendments in the legal framework;
(*iii*) Rationalisation of fiscal levies;
(*iv*) Mandatory packaging of food products; and
(*v*) Bringing together various stake-holders in the food supply chain and creating a "Partnership Web" for mutual benefit.

Sustainable Agriculture and Food Security

Globalization has brought to the forefront the challenges before Indian agriculture. These include increasing food production and productivity, poverty reduction, hunger elimination, employment generation and environmental protection. Demographically, most of the world's poor live in countries with rapidly growing population, where poverty and population growth are reinforcing each other. The Indian subcontinent, for example is adding 21 million people a year, the equivalent of another Australia. By mid-century, the population of India, which is already characterized as one of the hungriest among the nations is expected to include another 900 million people. According to present estimates, India has more than 90 million farms of less than 2 ha. Many experts have opined that unless cropland productivity is raised and the yield per crop increased, through multiplecropping agriculture, as practiced by traditional farming methods, with crop residues being fed to ruminants (to produce more meat and milk) and organic farming, by and large, replacing chemical fertilizers, the hunger problem of India and the persisting land degradation cannot be effectively tackled. Biotechnology's contributions are more likely to come in developing crop varieties that will reduce insecticide use, are more drought-tolerant, or are more salt-tolerant. If genetic engineers can breed salt-tolerant varieties, it would alleviate water shortages. In the other context of improving agricultural production and productivity, perhaps the largest question hanging over the future of Biotechnology is the possible long-term environmental and human health effects of using genetically modified crops. The question often raised is: Will it help us in finding sustainable development paths for sustaining the livelihoods of our rural poor? In our country, this problem could perhaps be effectively tackled through the excellent network of our national and state research centres, development of high yielding seeds, provision of better irrigation, the fostering of location-specific technologies and micro-level planning. Some success stories like the Biovillage experiment in Pondicherry by the M.S. Swaminathan Foundation, the VANRAI model of Mohan Dharia, the process of change effected in Ralegan Siddhi by Anna Hazare, the Bharatiya Agro-Industrial Foundation's (BAIF) model for sustainable livelihoods, the work of Ramakrishana Mission in rural areas are some examples. In all these cases, economic and social change through voluntary action by civil society participation has been a potent, combative and constructive force, laying the groundwork for building a better society. The biovillage concept of the Swaminathan Foundation addresses the ecological foundations for sustainable agriculture and providing sustainable livelihood opportunities. It is a pro-nature, pro-poor, pro-women development paradigm to sustainable agriculture and rural development. Bhoovigyan Vikas Foundation's advocacy of a model of auto-kinetic development, (Fig. 18.1) with its underlying concepts of enhancing "recycling ratios" in the village, establishing "integrated economic circuits" in village clusters and the promotion of agro-industries in accordance with the principle of subsidiarity, conforming to Christaller's concept of hierarchical planning of economic activities and social services is a further elaboration of these models, leading to holistic sustainable development, technological empowerment and social mobilization, operated on a 'village cluster planning' mode.

Some Postulates and Policy Dimensions

In our quest for sustainable agriculture, the following postulates and policy dimensions must be recognized:

- Ensuring food security;
- Increased access to land, water, fertilizers, pesticides, markets, infrastructure and other requirements;
- Organising the small farmers and the rural poor;
- Bureaucratic and extension reorientation;
- Working with community-based organisations and para professionals;
- Adopting the farming systems approach;
- Re-orienting the activities of small farmers' production systems, in order to assist them to mobilize capital through joint credit and other means to enable them to enter the market economy;
- Community management of common property resources;
- Encouraging non-farm activities to reduce poverty-levels

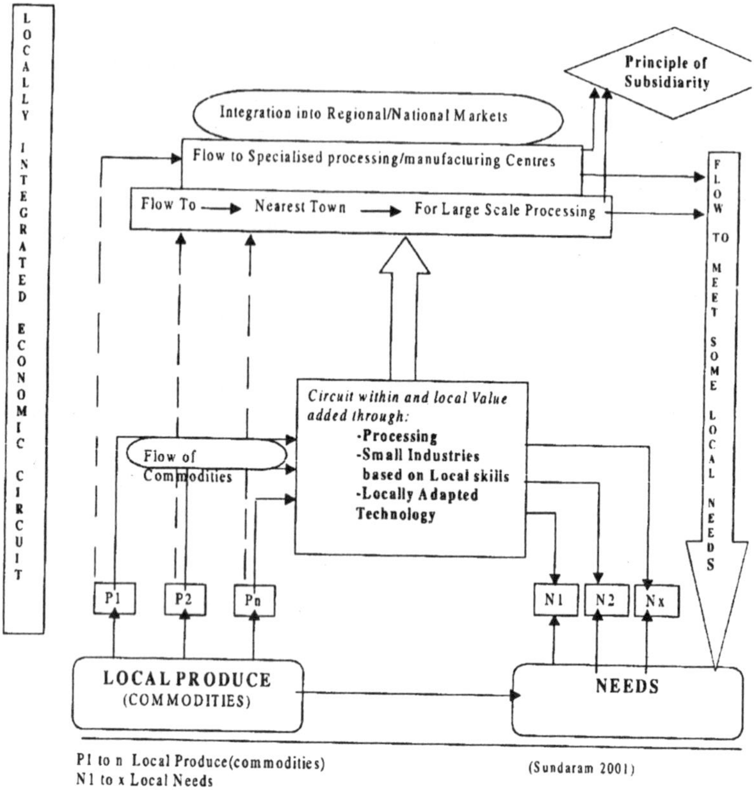

Fig. 18.1: Model of Autokinetic Development.

in rural areas both by way of contributing to the GDP as well as by increasing the employment potential to absorb surplus labour in the agricultural sector;

- Narrowing the rural-urban divide, as the benefits of better income growth during the 1990s seem to have benefited mostly the urban areas (Bhalla, 2000);
- Removal of Quantitative Restrictions (QR's) under the WTO regime, which allows artificially cheap commodities to enter domestic markets and destroy our farmers' livelihoods and incomes. The on-going economic reforms modelled on the so called "Washington consensus", would

> be totally irrelevant in our context. What is needed is a new agenda for development based on growth with social justice, recognizing the strengths and weaknesses of our rural agricultural system.

All the above postulates and policy dimensions of Sustainable Agriculture constitute a tall order, entailing a big bundle of "Earth Care Policies", which should be unambiguously formulated and rigorously implemented.

Another major Earth Policy consideration in the agriculture sector is meeting the challenge of land degradation. While the estimates of the magnitude of land degradation in India vary considerably, (ranging between 23% and 32.75% of the total geographical area of the country[2], it is definitely a challenging problem demanding urgent attention. According to Ravindra Babu, "Even if one million hectares of land are successfully treated every year, it would still take more than 50 years to recharge all the affected areas." With land degradation are the associated continuous geomorphic and anthropogenic processes like soil erosion, reduction in forest cover, over-exploitation of the ground water, changes in the cropping systems, loss of crop diversity and a rapidly growing population which impinge on the land, affect food security and threaten the livelihoods of millions of people.

Land degradation, particularly in dryland regions, is characterized by increasing conflicts between different users for control over farmland, water and pastures. More successful instances of combating land degradation comprise.of small scale programmes, based on simple technologies, developed with the full participation of local people and providing fairly immediate benefits to them. Earth Care policies must therefore confer special rights and responsibilities to manage natural resources by "local user groups".

In dryland regions again, food security and water security are often concomitant problems. These have to be addressed through both government as well as by local organizational efforts. Food security measures by government would include the implementation of efficient public distribution system and 'food for work' and other kinds of employment programmes, while community efforts would be by building "Food Banks" or "grain golas" and other cooperative methods. Water security measures would also require the attention by both government and local efforts. Lessons have to be drawn from small scale, locally appropriate water security projects initiated by NGOs and rain water-harvesting measures practiced in local areas by people, based on indigenous knowledge and traditional practices.

Sustainable Water Security

In the above context of agricultural planning, developing and managing our water resources on an integrated basis, in order to meet the present and future needs for agricultural production on a sustainable basis, bearing in mind the competing demands for limited water resources, the rational use of water and an efficient water management strategy have become critical issues. It is not too much to assert that high priority should be accorded in our policies to the adoption of urgent measures for soil and water conservation, within the framework of integrated land and water management, with due regard to long-term as well as short-term productivity.

The importance of water in Earth Care policies for sustainable development arises mainly from the problems of water scarcity, resulting from uncoordinated and badly planned land and water development as well as water quality, and degradation due to agricultural, industrial and municipal water pollution. The related issues on sustainable water resources development are the poverty, environmental degradation and population growth.

The following five priority areas for action are indicated for the development of water for sustainable agriculture (FAO):

(*i*) Efficient water use;
(*ii*) Waterlogging, salinity and drainage;
(*iii*) Water quality management;
(*iv*) Small-scale water programmes; and
(*v*) Scarce water resources management.

While the broad measures for alleviating the problems of scarce water management are generally known, the areas of conflict arise in the "frictional losses" in implementation, as government administration in federal countries are characterized by marked regional interests, the latest Cauvery issue in our country being an example. This is not the place for further analysis of this issue, as it is mixed up with legal issues and the approach of political economy. We shall, however, confine ourselves to some policy dimensions involved in water as a critical factor of life—sustaining resource—its quality, access, supply, management, treatment and disposal, all of which have a direct bearing on 'nutritional security'. In the definite movement in our changing times towards an ecology-oriented river management, re-naturalisation and conservation as well as progress towards a concept of ecologically and environmentally compatible form of drainage, the triangular relationship between the terms "Water, Protection and Human beings" stand out as one central concern in our Earth-Care Policy measures. More specifically, river water management, water supply both for drinking and irrigation and waste water treatment and disposal constitute the cardinal dimensions of a sound water-care policy. This will require main attention to the following earth care policies for sustainable water management:

(*i*) Exploration and data collection for assessing water availability from the point of sustainable yield;
(*ii*) Thrust on carrying out objective environmental impact assessment in regard to new projects and especially for evaluating the effects of deforestation, as they affect water projects and for enhancing experience and technology transfer among developing countries;
(*iii*) Instituting strict water use and conservation rules with legislative requirements and ensuring monitoring, evaluation and feedback systems on a long term basis;
(*iv*) Developing and implementing appropriate land use and environmental programmes in upper catchments; and
(*v*) Identifying and implementing appropriate environmental protection measures across the entire watersheds.

The normal practice of construction of water harvesting structures, such as check dams, etc., are costly in developing countries. Instead, promoting traditional water harvesting measures, e.g. farm ponds at strategic locations should be the preferred solution. In this context, the major thrust of the policy should be on enhancing the role of local communities in implementing and managing water developments.

In arid, semi-arid and drought-prone areas, besides the policy measures enunciated above, the emphasis should be on the optimization of water resources exploitation and raising the level of reliability of supplies through conjunctive use of surface and ground water and ensuring proper functioning of existing structures, conveyance systems and other assets through adequate maintenance and operation. Basic to all these measures would be by promoting beneficiary's participation in all aspects of water planning and management through Water User's Associations and Micro-level planning.

Since the introduction of the Eighth Five Year Plan in India (1992-1997), focus is shifting towards the watershed development and management programmes at the micro-level. The watershed, which is organically linked to the natural drainage system and hierarchically integrated from lower to higher order drainage networks, constitutes an ideal unit for conservation, upgradation and utilization of water resources and ensuring restoration of ecological balance in rainfed areas. Earth Care Policies in relation to watershed planning and development should address issues such as land owner's rights, conflicting issues like individual *versus* group ownership of resources and guidelines for adapting new or changing land use pattern. Such policies should focus on raising family income, increasing farm productivity, diversifying economic activities to provide better opportunity for earning livelihood. The emphasis should be on decentralization of decision making, so that the development plan would flow from user groups and associations, self-help groups and local people.

Needed a Multi-Pronged Strategy

To tackle the Sustainable Development of Agriculture, we need multi-pronged strategies and policies, not merely in terms of economic and technology innovations, but by adopting various other non-conventional methods to address the issues of food security, nutrition adequacy, rural income generation, provision of employment opportunity and removal of poverty. The major components of such a strategy, which must find a place in our Earth Policies are:

(*i*) An improved R & D system with a "Knowledge Information and Communication Systems Centre", installed in each village to bring extension services and knowledge dissemination concerned with developing techniques that would contribute to sustainable agriculture systems and providing easy access to all farmers—both knowledge and services;

(*ii*) Effectively operationalising the new concepts of participatory democracy, effective local governance and participation of the civil society and NGOs and new institutional arrangements to face the challenges of quality and competitiveness in this era of globalization and liberalisation;

(*iii*) Conceiving and devising new organisational receiving mechanisms and other changes to tackle the problem of our fragmented production base, operated by a large number of small farmers, with limited reach for modern technologies to overcome their biggest handicaps for competing in the export markets with the necessary capital and market intelligence. One of the methods would be to bring our corporate houses into agribusiness jointly with the producers (farmers);

(*iv*) Promoting increased 'localism' in the planning process of the agricultural sector and ensuring the greater involvement of local groups and the private sector to play a more active and instrumental role in agricultural development;

(*v*) Bringing about effective partnerships for synergised action among various stakeholders, for translating a strategy of efficient resource use and management. The partners would be individual farmers, interests groups, community-based organisations, captains of Industry and Trade, Panchayati Raj institutions and local leaders;

(*vi*) Adopting a research thrust on managing the factors of production and adapting individual technologies to suite location-specific peculiarities;

(*vii*) Changing our extension approach from a fragmented

message-based process to a broad-based 'farm management approach'. The shift should be from a 'contact farmer approach' to a 'group approach', which will promote social cohesion and collective action, essential for marketing, conservation and use of natural resources;

(*viii*) At the level of public policies, investments and services, the adaption of a 'convergence approach', by which all public investments in infrastructure—irrigation, power, transport, communication, storage etc. and provision of services—research, development of infrastructure and rural credit etc. can be brought together in mutually supportive and sequent actions to sustain the emerging market-led agricultural growth;

(*ix*) The widening of the scope of non-farm employment by attracting capital flow into the rural sector through an "auto-kinetic model" of rural development (see Fig. 18.1). This model will increase the value-added income of the village and establish a mutually supporting hierarchical mode of rural development, based on the Gandhian model, incorporating the "subsidiarity principle". In this way, an integrated approach of convergence of markets, jobs and investments would follow and rural-urban integration would be secured. Through 'micropolises' and rural service centres serving as nodal points for services and employment opportunities, a "Rurban Model of settlement pattern" would emerge;

(*x*) To enhance corporate capital investments in agriculture, restrictive land ceiling laws on dry lands, particularly waste lands must be revised.

Sustainable Forestry and Bio-Diversity

Since forests are important for climate regulation, flood control, soil conservation, water regulation, nutrient storage and recycling, fertilization, seed dispersal and recreation, which are all a basic part of any economy's support systems, policies for protecting forest products and services assume great importance in our strategies of caring for the Earth. Sustainable forestry practices can be achieved through:

(*i*) Maintaining the harvest of all products at sustainable levels by careful control of harnessing levels, timing and frequency;
(*ii*) Maintaining essential eco-system processes, e.g. by retaining continuous vegetation cover, returning nutrients to the soil etc.;
(*iii*) Maintaining biological diversity at eco-system, species and gene levels;
(*iv*) Satisfying the needs of the people living in and around the forests;
(*v*) Ensuring economic sustainability on the part of the forest user and on the part of governments.[3]

In the above context, the earth care policy framework for conservation of sustainable development of forests should include the following major ingredients:

(*i*) Halt inappropriate incentives like the subsidies, logging concession terms, tenurial policies, pricing policies and so on;
(*ii*) Consolidate the existing settlements in the forest and on its fringe. This would mean providing appropriate incentives like the infrastructure, tenurial and financial security, technology, knowledge and resources;
(*iii*) Integrate forestry into rural development by paying attention to land and tree tenure, sustaining and developing traditional forestry knowledge, integrating forestry and agriculture and encouraging participation in multipurpose forestry/agro-forestry. This implies initiating joint forest management programmes with the people, who depend on the forest for their livelihood;
(*iv*) Set up a clear forest ownership structure with a framework of regulations and incentives;
(*v*) Coordinate the authorities responsible for forest functions, notably, forestry, water, and agriculture to achieve convergent approaches to the management of forests;
(*vi*) Ensure participation of local people in all policy planning that affects forests and in forest management and use;

Sustainable forestry has to be vigorously promoted, which

means not merely in making arrangement for the sustainable yield of timber, but also encouraging the capacity of the forest to supply both products and services sustainably. The measures here will include banning or putting restrictions for logging, preventing export of forest products, sustainable forest management, reducing quantity of wood use to manufacture paper and reducing use of wood as fuel. The long term policy to the fuel problem is to develop alternative sources of energy for cooking based on wind, solar or geo-thermal energy and to develop indigenous sources of renewable energy, whatever they may be.

Biological diversity has assumed great importance because of the destruction of ecosystems and species extinction, all of which cause irreversible losses. A broad range of measures are needed to preserve biological diversity. The policies should be both to promote development and at the same time relieve excessive pressure on natural resources. The following measures are needed:

(*i*) Measures that raise yields in agriculture and thus reduce the need for area expansion;
(*ii*) Policies that increase non-farm employment opportunities such as efficient development policies for trade, agriculture and industry;
(*iii*) Sustainable forestry practices that remove subsidies for logging and other activities that cause de-forestation;
(*iv*) Encouraging programmes designed to capture the nature of biological diversity with its diverse range of food, medicines, and other products critical for the local population, thus promoting a development of options for the sustainable use of resources;
(*v*) Programmes to add value to biological resources (e.g. genetic prospecting);
(*vi*) Development of eco-tourism, which can improve, beautify and manage the landscape of the countryside, ensure an intelligent use of mankind's creative ability without destroying the sensitive balance of the ecosystem or destroying areas of natural beauty.

Sustainable Energy and Industry

Biomass and fossil fuels have continued to be the largest sources of energy in developing countries so far. Hydro-electric power has also been an important source of energy, though it is only next to coal-fired power. With carbon emissions being comparatively lower in the developing countries, pollution abatement technologies are not widely deployed in the developing countries. But the scenario has now changed, with the emissions of pollutants rapidly increasing and the threat of greenhouse warming, compelling the restriction on the use of fossil fuels. Hence the use of alternate sources of energy is now necessary to reduce emissions of CO_2 per unit of output. The options available are renewable energy, like the solar energy, biomass, geo-thermal energy, hydro-power, wind and nuclear energy. While taking policy decisions on alternative sources of energy, governments have, no doubt to take into account energy production costs and energy related pollution. Thus the major considerations for promoting sustainable energy in the developing countries are:

(*i*) Cost effectiveness as well as increasing the efficiency of energy use to reduce its polluting effects; and

(*ii*) Promoting the use of renewable and alternative sources of energies in households and vehicle fuels;

(*iii*) Promoting industrial development in such manner, so that the emissions from their activities are such that they can be readily assimilated by the environment, without causing serious environmental problems;

(*iv*) All available technological innovations—pre-combustion, combustion and post-combustion technologies—must be used to control emissions and increase energy efficiency. These must be accompanied by measures to exercise strict environmental controls through enforcement mechanisms and progress monitoring.

Earth Care policies designed for each country context must keep the above considerations in view and aim at the following measures:

(*i*) Formulate national action programmes to promote and support re-afforestation and forest regeneration to achieve sustained provision of adequate biomass energy to meet the needs of the rural and urban low-income groups. In this context, improved biomass stoves should also be promoted and subsidies provided for the development of such stoves.

(*ii*) In the new century, the wind power is being advocated as the foundation of the new energy economy, which through electrolysis can supply both electricity and hydrogen for fuel. Similarly turning sunlight into electricity through solar cells and tapping the Earth's heat as Geothermal energy provide other sources of alternative renewable energy resources, which are bound to accelerate the transition to a new energy era during the present century. According to futurologists, in this transition, natural gas would overtake as the transition fuel during the first quarter of this century.

(*iii*) In the new eco-economy visualized by Lester Brown, wind farms would replace coal mines, hydrogen-powered fuel cells would replace internal combustion engines and the solar energy with solar cells would play the most important roles, in replacing the old energy economy. One of the characteristics of the new energy economy will be that it will rely much more on decentralized small scale power sources, rather than on a few large centralized systems.

The present Conference has assigned a Special Session to discuss "Renewable Energy Technologies" Organisations like the TERI, the Agency for Non-Conventional Energy and Rural Technology, Indian Renewable Energy Development Agency Ltd., Centre for Energy Studies in IIT. Winrock International and Asia and Pacific Centre for Transfer of Technology are already doing excellent work in this context. Their work will be crucial in formulating suitable Earth Care policies to reconcile the expansion of energy and industrial activities with the goals of reducing pollution to acceptably low levels.

Towards a Circular Model of Materials Economy

Managing the Materials Economy

In our modern lifestyle in this material age, we have tended to generate a huge volume of garbage, wastes, metals, throwaway products and toxic chemicals, which damage the environment. Much of this material could be rendered regenerative, by processes of recycling. Scientists call this as "redesigning a new materials economy"; replacing the current linear "flow-through model" with a "circular model", that emulates nature, *one that closes the 'loop'*. In the mining industries for example, the scrap can be reused through recycling. Similarly water can also be recycled. Redesigning also includes discouraging products that are polluting and non-disposable through products that are easily biodegradable and disposable. The classic example is paper *versus* plastic. In our agenda of Earth Care Policies, the circular model of designing a new materials economy should occupy an important place. Regulating hazardous wastes in line with the 'Polluter Pays principle' is yet another method to control hazardous wastes from industrial sources. An autonomous "Industrial Environment Fund Organisation" could be established to levy waste charges from each industry, to establish and operate 'central treatment and disposal' facilities, as done in Thailand. This is a method of minimizing pollution control costs and encouraging efficiency in industrial production processes. It can go a long way in preserving our natural resources.

Sustainable Rural Development Policies

Our rural landscapes, once ruled by virgin nature and viewed as a "terrestrial paradise", and a natural heritage, as well as a strong and safe retreat for man's recreation and rejuvenation is getting transformed into an 'exhausted mine' owing to a 'pillage economy'.

This pillage economy works on a short term 'profit logic' of intermediate struggle for survival, with disastrous assaults on our ecologic environment. In the area of agriculture, this short term approach is reflected in the term 'agribusiness'. It thrives on a myopic view of a world of limitless natural resources and reliance and faith on substitute technologies for the vanishing natural resource capital. With the introduction of green revolution in the annual cycle of the three food crops of wheat, maize and sorghum, against a decennial need for soil replacement and recuperation, it has led to several unintended results and environmental costs. It is totally in contrast with our secular, long-run traditional agriculture systems, evolved on the basis of traditional ecological knowledge and intuitive experiences of societies.

The contrast between these two techniques of food production has led to environmental problems and raised the question as to how to manage the ecologic environment that give the people their sustenance. Thus a commercial approach rooted in the greed for speculative gain and the inability of the traditional farmer to adjust to a technologically oriented society is the heart of our rural problem. This is not a simple matter, because of the complexities of the interactions that determine the dynamics of the natural environment. This represents one aspect of the optimization and utilization of land and water resources in the framework of a change in land use, which the modern economy tries to bring about in the form of agri-business. Obviously, effective policies of Earth Care, oriented to the degree of tolerance of the natural environment to competing uses and conflicting value systems are the need of our times. The 'How' of it is the tricky issue, demanding a development policy which requires a mutual process of adaptation of natural resources, technology and of man himself. This is not a simple matter because of the complexities of the interactions that determine the dynamics of the natural environment. The old saying "you can't see the wood for the trees" is very apt to the current situation. What is needed in this context is to understand the complexity of nature and the web of interactions that manifest themselves in its dynamics.

How to develop our rural environment rationally, and to manage it efficiently, that is by assuring the non-degradation of its resources are the imperatives that impose themselves all the more forcibly in this new century, as the world situation is characterized by:

(*i*) an ungovernable increase in population;
(*ii*) a vast majority of these people (between 2/3 and ¾) who are poorly or insufficiently nourished to grow into healthy individuals;
(*iii*) an industry, with its quest for profit causing immeasurable deleterious effects on the ecologic environment.

With the increasing disparity between rich and the poor and

the patterns of production, consumption and distribution followed in several developing countries being ecologically unfriendly, economically biased and socially unjust, a new paradigm of development is called for. The situation, obviously is serious and tragic. Only the force of public opinion can avert a catastrophe.

In the above context, some important policies that will ensure 'Caring for the Earth', may be outlined. They will include:

(i) The removal of those government policies that exacerbate environmental problems, such as subsidizing the extraction of scarce resources;
(ii) Clarifying property rights, since insecure property rights over land and other natural resources have led people to misuse them or under-invest in their improvement;
(iii) Encouraging flexible types of environmental regulations that rely on economic incentives to encourage compliance. Simpler methods of environmental regulations, such as imposing charges on polluting in-puts, rather than on the pollution itself or providing deposit refund systems to induce producers and consumers of polluting products to return waste for recycling or treatment and safe disposal.

To improve the capacity to implement the above mentioned changes, governments must shift their strategies from top-down management to one focused on strategic intervention. A decentralized approach instead of a huge regulatory bureaucracy would ensure that environmental impact is considered in all areas of policy making. Central Government should devolve responsibility for environmental management to appropriate local and regional levels, and enter into partnerships with the private sector through non-dgovernmental organizations (NGOs) and local communities. Determining the appropriate level of government for environmental management can be determined by considering at which level can effective measures be undertaken. For integrated river basins or watershed management, for instance, institutional arrangements may have to straddle the jurisdiction of several States.

Civil society needs to be involved more intensively. Environmental Impact Assessments should be done in a way that stakeholders can participate at the project level. Thus In the new model of Earth Care Policies, greater decentralisation and broader participation are visualized as the essential prerequisites to work successfully and to move forward in the direction of sustainable development.

Since one view is that poverty is the greatest polluter, poverty reduction has to be an overarching goal, with its strategic concerns, such as human development, sound environmental management, improvement of women's status and fostering economic growth for increasing employment opportunities.

The three pillars of the new poverty reduction strategy are: fostering sustainable economic growth that benefits the poor, promoting social development and encouraging good governance. These strategies have to be prioritized and brought into comprehensive mutual-specific action plans.

In the poverty reduction and environmental care strategy, increasing the access of the poor to essential services, including electricity, water supply and sanitation and most prominently to basic education and primary health care should be addressed to increase the poor's chance of earning income and providing social safety nets.

In all the above policy changes proposed, governments must obviously play a more active role in providing the critical public goods, such as agricultural research, extension services and rural infrastructure. Some aspects of development like the provision of micro credit to the rural poor, for instance could be promoted as 'self help' measures. The Grameen Bank's business strategy based on the voluntary formation of small groups is an example to mobilize the social capital in closely-knit communities in the developing countries.

For transformational change in rural India and meeting the challenge of increasing growth, a threefold strategy of (a) leveraging information technology for rural transformation, (b) leveraging biotechnology for sustainable growth and, (c) linking farmers to remunerative markets would lead to rural partnerships to enhance competitiveness. The first one for instance, will bring about knowledge-based empowerment of the Indian farmer and will also enable creating infrastructure for agri-supply chain management and rural distribution. The second strategy, that of leveraging biotechnology will support large scale farming and social forestry, together with watershed management to create additional avenues of income to the rural poor. The third strategy of linking farmers to remunerative markets will provide the fillip to the food processing industry and lead to value addition to the farmers, by opening up remunerative opportunities to them.

To move in the above directions, the corporate sector companies should develop a "commitment beyond the market". The Indian Tobacco company's strategy followed on these lines by establishing 'e-choupal' in a number of villages has led to transformational change in rural India. This example is worth emulating.

As the population continues to grow, in the next 50 years, demands for food, fuel and fibre will rise enormously. In order to meet these demands, more intensive and extensive exploitation of many natural resources will be required. The stress will be more on agricultural land, forests, water and fisheries. It is in this context that sensible resource management is called for. Food demand is expected to double by 2050. All these things mean that an increase in expenditure for agricultural research and development is very important. Yet, expenditures for agricultural research are stagnating in many countries.

All the above changes require carefully conceived and prioritized policies in several areas.

Population and Carrying Capacity and Human Settlements Planning

According to UN projections, the World population will grow from 6.1 billion in 2000 to 9.3 billion in 2050. The bulk of this increase is expected to be in the developing countries. The medium level projections of the UN indicate that the population in the developing world will increase from 4.9 billion in 2000 to 8.1. billion in 2050, i.e. more than 2.5 times. This would lead almost to the collapse of our ecosystems in many countries. In the developing countries, the linkages between demographic and natural resource issues are dynamic and complex (see Fig. 18.2). Population growth exacerbates the pressure on the resource base at any given level of technological development. This leads to further deterioration of the earth's environment and in the socio-economic condition of the people, with increasing poverty levels and rapid population growth. This is particularly characteristic of the developing world. Another important trend is that this rapid population growth in the developing world is becoming more and more concentrated in cities, which are already facing the problems of increased influx of rural population, leading to congestion, pollution, growth of slums and squatter settlements.

In recent years, studies have not been lacking to suggest measures for containing the population growth to match the carrying capacity of the earth. But government policies and measures have not been equal to the task and implementation of programmes in this direction has been woefully lacking in practice.

Some policies suggested for the developing countries are: (1) Filling the family planning gap and increasing the access to family planning services, by providing a full complement of such services, including reproductive health. (2) Removing the physical and social barriers that prevent women from using family planning services. (3) Creating social conditions that will overcome inhibitions and lead to fertility decline and smaller families. (4) Promoting female education in a substantial measure, which has the potential of reducing fertility by roughly 10 per cent (Summers, 1993). (5) Reducing the average family size to 2 children or less. (6) Changing people's attitudes about reproductive health, gender equity, family size and environmental protection through informal education methods, e.g. soap operas (serialized dramas) and sitcoms (situation comedies) aired on radio and television. The impacts of such measures have been studied and results seem encouraging. Pancha Polston (2000) has reported that Soap operas in Mexico, which continued over a decade, has led to a fall in birth rate by 34 per cent and in promoting progress in achieving replacement-level fertility. According to Population Reference Bureau (2001), 54 countries have reduced average family size to 2 children or less. Among these, Japan and China in Asia figure prominently. The UN's low assumption projection for 2050 (base year 1950) assumes that the entire world is likely to quickly move below replacement-level fertility to 1.7 children per couple.

In our Earth Care Policies for matching population with carrying capacity, developing countries should accord the highest priority to population issues. Family planning, reproductive care, health, environmental and human development programmes should be brought together and designed as a conjunctive

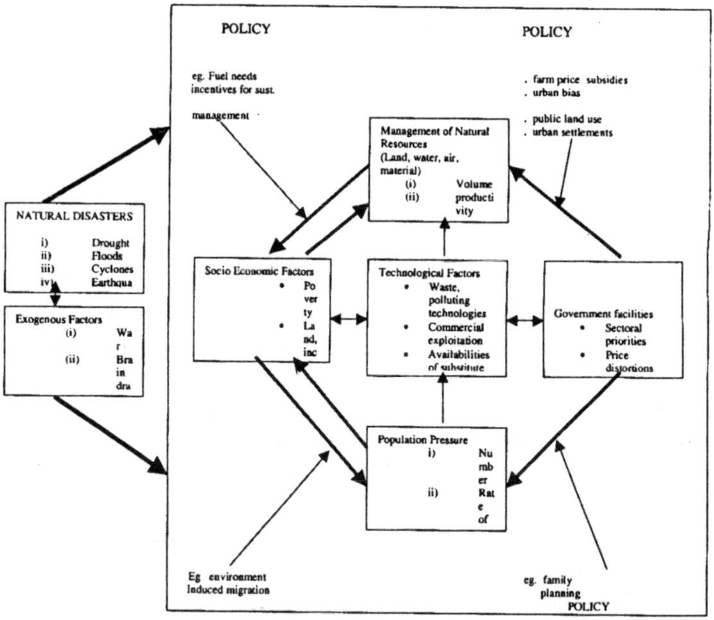

Fig. 18.2: The Linkages Between Demographic and Natural Resource Issues

Source: Adapted from ADB, February, 1990.

programme. Educating girls, enabling women to earn cash incomes and participate fully in decision-making and vigorously pursuing family planning programmes should be conceived as a package of interrelated programmes in rural development. To bring about such close coordination, all those departments, which are now functioning independently or in different ministries should be brought together into one "Population Ministry". This would constitute an important institutional reform in government.

Human Settlement Planning

Human settlement planning, including halting urban sprawl and promoting manageable cities is yet another dimension of Earth Care Policies. The United Nation's projections indicate that by 2050, more than two-thirds of the world's population will be living in cities. Since cities exert a heavy burden on the earth's ecosystems,

Restructuring the Global Economy

Restructuring the Global Economy to make it compatible with the earth's ecosystem, so that economic progress can continue along with ecologically sustainable development is an important aspect of Earth Care Policies. Lester Brown has argued that Economy is part of the Environment, and not the other way. He has stressed the following points:

- Ecological costs of various economic activities should be incorporated into the market price of a product or service in the form of a tax (Environmental tax).
- Other policy instruments that can be used to restructure the economy would include fiscal policy, government regulations, eco-labelling, tax shifting, subsidy shifting and tradable permits.

Thus it is argued that restructuring the tax system is the key to eliminate the crippling economic distortions. According to Brown, "if they use fiscal policy to encourage environmentally constructive activities and to discourage destructive ones, we can steer the economy in a sustainable direction". Tax shifting, i.e. changing the composition of taxes but not their level is another means used by many countries in Europe. It means reducing income taxes for refraining from destructive activities. Lester Brown emphasizes that "if the world is to restructure the economy before environmental destruction leads to economic decline, tax restructuring should be the centre of the effort."

Subsidy shifting is another method to encourage environmentally constructive activities through financing them by shifting funds from environmentally destructive subsidies.

Eco-labelling is now used in many sectors of the economy, including energy-efficient household appliances, forest products from sustainably managed forests, fishery products from sustainably managed fisheries and green electricity from environment-friendly renewable resources.

The whole argument advanced by Lester Brown is based on the fact that the ecological costs must be incorporated into the market price of a product or service in the form of a tax or other economic instruments. While in principle, this will be a good strategy, the worrying aspect is whether in practice, decision makers would be able to understand the ecological consequences of their decisions and give effect to those decisions. Brown himself is aware of the problems and says, "it simply may not be possible".

When all is said and done, one cannot but emphasise the advantage of increasing public awareness on environmental issues and political will to enforce environmental laws and regulations, as the more effective solutions from the perspective of the developing countries. If these could be effectively implemented, the Earth's environment could be preserved for future generations to enjoy.

The Limited Coverage of this Paper

Our discussions in the previous pages show that caring for the Earth is not an easy task and the various problems identified cannot be solved overnight by some new vision. A part of the solution could be by governments acting with strong will and International organizations also strengthening the pressures on Nation States. But this alone are not enough. The civil society on the ground and the attitudes and practices of individuals have also to respond favourably. A concerted effort is needed to inform and educate people about the need for Sustainable Development and Sustainable Lifestyles. Thus moulding the public opinion is an important aspect of the strategy.

In this paper, we have outlined a number of policies for promoting a healthy Earth. Since Earth Care Policies encompass every sector of man's activity, all these could not be covered in a short paper like this. We have touched some important sectors only. An illustrative scheme is outlined in Fig. 18.3, which indicates the principles and commitments needed for effective policies for a healthy Earth, the action strategies necessary as well as some parameters of Earth Care Policies—the Policy orientations, the actions needed for creating a scientific database as a decision-support system (IT strategies) and some broad indications of certain interventions required in the form of fiscal incentives and disincentives, laws and regulations for protection, conservation and abatement of environmental problems, the need for community empowerment on various issues and the Public Sector interventions needed for tackling the critical issues etc.

Towards a New Paradigm of Caring for Mother Earth

The major principles, strategies and actions set out here are those meant to conserve the vitality and diversity of the Earth. They are nothing new and have also been emphasized in many National and International documents. They are meant to be a guide and an agenda for debate, rather than the prescription.

The principal ingredients for a new paradigm for Sustainable Development are as follows:

(*i*) Minimizing the depletion of non-renewable resources. Where possible, their "life" can be extended, for example, by recycling, by substitutes etc.

(*ii*) Keeping the earth's ecosystems within its carrying capacity, so as to bring human numbers and lifestyles into balance with nature's capacity, with the use of benign modern technologies to enhance the capacity by careful management.

(*iii*) Conserving the earth's vitality and diversity by preserving its life-support systems, its bio-diversity and ensuring that uses of renewable resources are sustainable.

(*iv*) Changing the personal attitudes and practices, by re-examining indigenous wisdom, ethics and values of the society and supporting any new practices, only if such policies and actions are absolutely needed for the survival of the planet.

(*v*) Enabling local communities to care for their own environments, by encouraging socially valuable actions through their own institutions and community-based organizations.

(*vi*) Providing a national and regional framework for integrating development and conservation.

- The national framework should deal with issues emanating from globalisation, liberalization and world trade regimes, keeping in view the national interests.
- The regional framework for integrating development and conservation must take into account the interactions with land, air, water, organisms and human activities. They must relate activities and actions to the scale of the region's—micro, meso and macro units.

PRINCIPLES AND COMMITMENTS

Underlying Principles
- ✓ Ecological & Economic Factors
- ✓ Comprehensive and integrated approach
- ✓ Shift from curative to preventive approach
- ✓ POLLUTER PAYS principle
- ✓ Inter- & intra-generational equity

Underlying Commitments
- ✓ Socio-economic justice
- ✓ Right of access to information
- ✓ Preservation of intrinsic worth & diversity
- ✓ Protection of natural heritage
- ✓ Social and environment accountability
- ✓ Establishment of global convention on environmental regimes and duties

↓

Action Strategies
- ✓ Task definition and adoption
- ✓ Participatory cooperation & interaction with stakeholders
- ✓ Establishment of regulatory mechanisms with strict monitoring of implementation
- ✓ Integrated product policy (IPP)
- ✓ Promote sustainable and eco-friendly consumption

↓

Parameters of Earth Care Policies

Policy Orientations
- ✓ Conservation of resources
- ✓ Recycling reclamation & reuse
- ✓ Application of cleaner & greener technologies
- ✓ Eco-labeling
- ✓ IPP
- ✓ Eco-industrial network

Decision-support systems
- ✓ Right to information
- ✓ Awareness & education programmes
- ✓ Data collection/ dissemination
- ✓ Research & Development
- ✓ Knowledge Information centres (e-Choupal)
- ✓ Agri-Clinics

Interventions

FISCAL INCENTIVES & DISINCENTIVES
- ✓ Pricing policy & subsidy
- ✓ Taxes & import duties
- ✓ Public/private partnership
- ✓ Micro-level Planning to channelize development
- ✓ Additional funding sources on soft terms

LAWS & REGULATIONS
- ✓ Protection of health, amenity value & coastal zones
- ✓ Protection of biodiversity
- ✓ Conservation of resources
- ✓ Abatement of desertification
- ✓ Abatement of greenhouse gases

PROGRAMMES FOR SPECIFIC ENVIRONMENTAL THREAT ABATEMENT & COMMUNITY EMPOWERMENT
- ✓ Right to information, communication & environmental reporting
- ✓ Transparency in decision making
- ✓ Facilitation of PILs

PUBLIC SECTOR INTERVENTION
- ✓ Environmental Audit & EIA
- ✓ ICA
- ✓ Designing the materials economy
- ✓ EMS
- ✓ Stabilizing Population & environmental carrying capacity
- ✓ Developing alternate energy resources
- ✓ Food Security
- ✓ Water Security
- ✓ Planning environmentally sound cities for people

Fig. 18.3: Policies for a Healthy Earth.

(*vii*) Providing universal primary education for all children and reducing illiteracy.

- Ensuring the total enrolment and attendance at primary and secondary levels.
- Narrowing the gap in female and male literacy and bringing them on par.

(*viii*) Enhancing security against natural disasters and social strife by evolving pro-active as well as risk-reducing measures in disaster-prone areas like flood plains, coastal zones and areas vulnerable to earthquake and volcano eruptions. This would also include providing early warning signals, shelter and adequate relief facilities, promoting group action by citizen groups, to play a constructive role in emergency.

(*ix*) To conserve the earth's vitality and diversity, taking actions needed to

— Preventing pollution. —
— Restoring and maintaining the integrity of the Earth's ecosystems.
— Conserving biological diversity.
— Ensuring that renewable resources are used sustainably.
— Devising appropriate Earth Care Policies to meet the above objectives in regard to preventing pollution. These will include economic and regulatory measures for reducing emissions of sulphur dioxide, nitrogen oxides, carbon monoxide and hydro carbons.
— Preparing for climate change, induced by the addition of greenhouse gases and international environmental consensus involving principles and rules of collaboration among sovereign states arrived at by common consensus.
— Restoring, increasing and maintaining the integrity of the Earth's natural and modified systems, through an integrated approach to land and water management, using the drainage basin as the unit of management.
— Adopting scientific land use planning in all natural ecosystems—forests, wetlands, scrublands and grasslands as well as any high-quality farm land.

- — Restoring and rehabilitating degraded ecosystems through appropriate scientific measures.
- — Assigning the highest priority to more sustainable agriculture practices in collaboration with the local people, in areas suffering from serious losses of soil erosion, desertification and misuse of land.
- — Halting net-deforestation and protecting large areas of old-growth forest areas and the governments establishing explicit long-term goals in national forest policy.
- — Involving local communities in forest policy formulation as well as in their execution and management to ensure sustainability of yields (Joint Action).
- — Conserving biological diversity by seriously pursuing a combination of measures to safeguard species of genetic stocks, through the establishment and maintenance of protected areas, and adoption of wider strategies that combine economic activities and conservation, with people's participation. For maintaining species and genetic resources, *in situ* and *ex situ* conservation should be practiced.
- — Keeping population within the Earth's carrying capacity is not merely just for survival, but for ensuring sustainable improvement in the quality of life of the people. Earth Care Policies must pay due importance to both these aspects and also to the issues of population growth and sustainable consumption in an integrated way.
- — Distortionary subsidies and prices must be removed.
- — The prices of resources should match with their real costs.
- — To inculcate the sanctity of Mother Earth and as a "Thanks-Giving" method, "Earth-Day" should be celebrated all over the country in Schools, Colleges, Universities, Offices and business establishments. This will motivate "Greener Movements" and ultimately pave the way to "Earth Democracy", with sustainable development and sustainable lifestyles, as its core policies.

Where the voices of the poor and the disadvantaged groups are listened to with justice and freedom;
Where the clear stream of reason has not lost its way into the dreary desert sand of dead habit;
Where the mind is led forward by THEE into ever-widening thought and action towards sustainable development and sustainable lifestyles; Into that heavenly earth, my Father, let our ecosystems awake.

—*K.V. Sundaram*

FOOTNOTES

1. For instance, the average yield per hectare of rice in China is about twice that in India, while in the case of wheat it is 1-1/2 times higher.
2. Ravindra Babu, A., "Combating Land Degradation and Droughts" in *Rio-Johannesburg and Beyond*, LEAD INDIA, Orient Longman Pvt. Ltd. 2002, Hyderabad.
3. Poor and Sayer (1987) *The Management of Tropical Moist Forest Land: Ecological Guidelines*, IUCN Gland, Switzerland.

Appendix-1

(i) A third of the World's cropland is losing topsoil that is undermining its long-term productivity.

(ii) 50% of the World's rangeland is overgrazed and deteriorating into desert.

(iii) The World's forests have shrunk by about half since the dawn of agriculture and are still shrinking.

(iv) Two-thirds of oceanic fisheries are now being fished at or beyond their capacity. Overfishing is now the rule, not the exception.

(v) Overpumping of underground water is common in key food-producing regions.

(vi) Over the last 3 decades, global average temperature has risen from 13.99 degrees Celsius in 1969-71 to 14.43 degrees in 1998-2000, a gain of 0.4°C. If CO_2 concentrations in the atmosphere double pre-industrial levels by the end of this century, reaching 560 ppm, the temperature will rise by 1.4 - 5.8°C. This rise will lead to more extreme climatic events—record heat waves, the melting of ice, rising sea level and more destructive storms.

(vii) In the Arctic Ocean, sea ice is melting. The ice sheet has thinned by 42 per cent and it has shrunk in area by 6 per cent. A recent study by two Norwegian Scientists projects that within 50 years, this ocean would be ice-free during the summer. Sea level would rise leading to the oceans expanding at the expense of continents, with consequences such as inundation of coastal areas, salt water intrusion and beach erosion.

(viii) Water scarcity is increasing, as each year some 80 million additional people are staking their claims to the earth's water resources. One manifestation of emerging water scarcity is dry rivers. Several of the World's major rivers now either run dry part of the year, failing to reach the sea or have little water left, when they get there, e.g. Amu Darya in Central Asia, the yellow river, in China, the Nile in Egypt, the Jordan in Israel, the Ganges in India and the Mekong in Indo-China.

(ix) Falling water tables due to overpumping is another phenomenon being witnessed in many parts of the globe. Northern China is drying out on account of depleting acquifers, leading to the abandonment of wells. In Punjab, the "food basket" of India, the water table is falling by 0.6 metres per year, forcing farmers to drill deeper and deeper. In the Southern Great Plains of USA, practicing irrigated agriculture with water pumped from the Ogallala acquifer with little recharge, the farmers are forced to return to dryland farming.

(x) With excessive demand on fisheries, the world is witnessing the collapse of the fisheries all over—inland, coastal and oceanic fisheries and commercial fishing—is under great threat. Damage to coral reefs, a breeding ground for fish in tropical and sub-tropical waters is also taking a toll.

(xi) The Earth's forested area, estimated at 5 billion hectares at the beginning of the 20th century, has now shrunk to 2.9 billion hectares. This forest loss is concentrated in developing countries. The environmental effects of deforestation are becoming all too visible, with scores of countries suffering from disastrous flooding and alteration in the rainfall cycle, with its effects on the natural vegetation.

(xii) World-wide, almost half of all grasslands are lightly to moderately degraded and 5 per cent are severely degraded. Fodder needs of livestock in nearly all developing countries now exceed the sustainable yield of rangelands and other forage resources. In India, for instance, the demand for fodder in 2000 was estimated at 700 million tons, while the sustainable supply totalled just 540 million tons.

(xiii) With an estimated 36 per cent of the world's cropland now losing topsoil at a rate that is undermining its productivity, our food security will be at risk, if this trend continues. Some examples of stressed relationship, which has affected the biological base are:

- Top Soil loss, declining yields and the abandonment of cropland experienced in Kazakhstan in Central Asia and in Ethiopia, Kenya and Somalia in Africa.

- Shrinking cropland area in China's coastal provinces, with cropland being lost for the construction of factories, roads and expanding cities.
- Increased frequency of dust storms in China.
- Yield losses due to soil erosion in African countries, bringing down the grain harvest by 8 million tons or roughly 8 per cent.
- Desertification of cropland in Algeria.

(xiv) Another major threat is the one concerning the disappearance of species. The archeological record shows five great extinctions, since life began on Earth. We are now in the early stage of the sixth great extinction. Unlike the previous ones, which were caused by natural phenomena, this one will be of human origin. The World Conservation Union—IUCN has pointed to the large increase in the "critically endangered species" in all categories—bird species, mammal species, fish species, amphibians etc.

(xv) Environmental scientists are concerned that some trends of environmental degradation will reinforce each other, i.e. the synergetic effect. Such synergetic trends are described as often irreversible.

Source: Lester R. Brown, *Eco-Economy,* Orient Longman-Hyderabad, 2001.

19

Towards an Innovative Institutional Architecture to Promote the Development and Diffusion of Sustainable Pro-Poor Technologies

SHANTANU MATHUR

Introduction

In the 1980s and up until the mid-1990s the development community supported research and extension structures which relied essentially on formal institutions with a mandate to generate technologies for "transfer" to farming communities through national extension systems. There was little explicit pro-poor emphasis and the lack of proactive poverty focus is evidenced by an approach which focused mostly on scale neutral "technologies" only sometimes with any significant degree of relevance to the rural poor. The emphasis was on crops and commodities produced and consumed by the poorer sections of society.

The lack of in-depth understanding of the capacity and orientation of institutional structures which governed research and extension (R&E) processes, led to less than desired levels of impact on farmer adoption and livelihoods improvements, particularly among the poor. Clearly, new technologies are not in themselves solutions to farmers' problems unless they prove relevant to their needs and are adopted by them. Among the many reasons for low adoption of promising technologies by the poorer farmers was an undue reliance (even if inadvertently) on structures fostering a top-down research process [represented by the more traditional National Agricultural Research and Extension Systems(NARES)].

While such systems did experience success in the rapid transfer of technology-fixes in situations where "one-size fits all" (e.g., scale-neutral technologies or green revolution technologies), in certain circumstances, such processes have tended to undermine the relevance of technologies to those for whom they were intended.

Many evaluations of conventional rural development projects of the 80s and the early 90s show that these initiatives had often sought to promote technology dissemination through top-down credit-induced delivery strategies. Major recommendations from those evaluations suggested adopting pluralistic approaches and involving key stakeholders in developing R&E systems; linking R&E with complementary development activities such as input supply and market support, and provision of rural-finance. Other enabling factors recommended by evaluations include stronger institutional infrastructure, natural resource management and policy environment; developing participatory research capacity among researchers; and addressing recurrent cost and financial constraints.

Evaluations of R&D programmes using participatory approaches showed higher benefits to the rural poor through increasing their adoption of the technologies developed with their involvement—leading to enhanced on-farm production and incomes. In the more recent past, the deployment of more "demand-led" approaches to R&E have demonstrated more positive results.

However, effective, efficient and sustainable mechanisms for farmer community participation in technology development have not yet been rigorously identified, validated and implemented.

Changing Institutional and Policy Environment

A number of participatory research methodologies and organisational approaches have emerged recently. They are based on both: conventional "farming system research" and innovative principles of strategic partnerships. Among the newer concepts emerging in R&E systems is a shift from "transferring technology to a passive recipient", to facilitating R&E farmer linkages in order to enable different stakeholders to interact and develop new ideas and to learn from each other. Accordingly, innovation is seen as an outcome of a social process rather than the sum of a number of individual competencies and experimental outputs.

Conventional R&E approaches, until most recently, were based on pre-packaged information, not necessarily responding to the demands of the diversity of poorer target groups. Alternative approaches involve the use of suitable "institutional arrangements" linking a broad spectrum of change agents (not merely within the research compact) with the ultimate users of technology—the farming communities—to the R&D compact. This is relevant for, both, the development of sustainable agricultural technologies or for developing institutional mechanisms and arrangements (e.g. in a purely development context, the use of input delivery or commercially viable commodity chains/filieres linking productions systems to markets for enhancing development impact.

Innovative approaches to development and diffusion of pro-poor technology are being pioneered in many parts of the developing world and Financial Institutions such as the International Fund for Agricultural Development (IFAD) are beginning to recognize new opportunities for support. However, disparities in scientific capacity in a globalizing inter-regional system of research networks and the paucity of suitable institutional mechanisms to build on the combined strengths of all research partners within the international agricultural research system, remains a challenge. The lack of an appropriate orientation to respond to the needs and aspirations of the communities that stand to benefit from this system also needs to be addressed.

How IFAD and its Partners have Addressed these Challenges

The are two important areas in which IFAD and its partners in the development community are making a significant contribution in enhancing the development and diffusion of pro-poor technology. The first has to do with policy dialogue with those responsible for setting the global agricultural research agenda—through the Global Forum for Agricultural Research (GFAR) and the Consultative Group on International Agricultural Research (CGIAR); and the second, the development of a new and innovative instrument for R&D-farmer partnerships through grant-financed research linkages with Investment Projects.

Policy Dialogue in the Global Partnership Programmes

In 1996, IFAD helped establishing the Global Forum for Agricultural Research (GFAR). This is a programme which facilitates cost-effective partnerships and strategic alliances, which aim to reduce poverty, achieve food security, and conserve and manage biodiversity and natural resources. GFAR brings together all the key stakeholders in global agricultural research from seven key constituencies: developing-country national agricultural research systems, advanced research institutions, universities, non-governmental organizations, farmers' organizations, the private sector, international agricultural research centres, and the donor community. These stakeholders are joining forces to promote cost-effective and strategic alliances which can ensure that the best of science be brought to bear on the problems of poor disadvantaged farming communities. This initiative has implications for changing both international research policy and the institutional arrangements that govern it. The premise is that the systematic creation of science and knowledge with practical significance must involve all actors along the continuum of technology development and diffusion and in so doing, ensuring research results find fruition in farmers' fields.

As the lead agency in GFAR, IFAD is chair of the GFAR Donor Support Group. In this role the Fund has been charged with the responsibility of mobilizing support from the international donor community for the GFAR agenda. IFAD's engagement with the GFAR initiative goes far beyond a resource mobilizing role. The Fund continues to foster a progressive shift of paradigm in agricultural research for development towards a holistic knowledge intensive agriculture accessible to small and poor farmers and indeed built on their own contribution based on their keen understanding of their natural resources base and on their indigenous knowledge systems. Among the elements that IFAD has introduced in GFAR operations are the principles of subsidiarity and complementarity; that research should be demand-driven and implemented through equal partnerships among stakeholders; that priorities for the research agenda should be set with a focus on farmers' perspectives, taking into account the multi-functionality and regional heterogeneity of farming systems; and that research design and technology diffusion should involve the intended users and beneficiaries, particularly farmers. These are consistent with the Fund's own considerations in financing development-led research.

Another global partnership programme to which IFAD participate is the Consultative Group on International Agricultural Research (CGIAR), in which IFAD is co-sponsor with the World Bank, UNDP and FAO. IFAD is on the CGIAR Executive Committee which oversees the definition and formulation of the CGIAR's operational focus, content and governance structure. Through participation in these bodies and through financing pro-poor research programmes, IFAD has brought significant influence to bear on the mandate and research programmes of the CGIAR.

At the heart of the re-organization of the international research system lies a change which needs to be discussed not only in the context of instruments that merely connect, in a mechanistic way, different parts of the global agricultural research system in regional programmes. There is a need to transform relationships among actors, the rules of engagement and the dynamics of consultation. New models of organisation of research and innovative forms of "partnership architecture" have been the subject of discussion at a number of fora which have discussed methodologies, organisation and management of global partnership programmes. These have discussed lessons from experience that can be drawn from initiatives through which a gradual change of roles and attitudes evolved in ways which contribute to greater impact of research outcomes. They have also addressed the dynamics of the circumstances encountered and the strategies used, based on meaningful and productive multi-stakeholder participation to identify pathways for building new partnerships arrangements.

Research Links with Investment Projects—An Innovative Instrument in R&E

IFAD's investment projects are increasingly located in marginal agro-ecologies, in environments for which sustainable agricultural technologies are not easily available. The project areas are often identified in response to prevalent urgency to alleviate rural poverty and represent initiatives which are critical and expedient in the given crisis scenario. IFAD's grant-financed research has supported technology change in resource-poor areas, mainly through financing: the development of appropriate technologies, "tailoring" available prototypes to suit the circumstances of potential IFAD-typical beneficiaries of loan projects; and financing adaptive/action research addressing an identified technology constraint or opportunity directly influencing the livelihoods of IFAD target groups.

IFAD continues to build on the opportunities generated by scientific progress and by the institutional diversification of agricultural research as well as the changing institutional architecture of research organisation. The emphasis on changing the relationships among the rural poor and research institutions and creating a new partnership framework. This is best fostered within a developmental context of a loan project in which researchers are not necessarily the lead players and farmer clients. This re-organization of the research process and the accompanying shift in relations also has to do with issues of decentralisation and empowerment, which are increasingly the vehicle for IFAD's loan projects that attempt to strengthen organisations of the poor and position them to influence policies and R&E institutions. It promotes self-reliance among the poor, providing them the means to increase their own ability to improve productivity and incomes—in the process enhancing the sustainable impact of research linked to development projects.

The Catalytic Role the Development Community can Play

Many scientific achievements are taking place in an environment of globalisation and mutual interdependence of a broad spectrum of actors. They are transforming the institutional context of agricultural research. Advances in genetic sciences are making it possible to 'generate' technologies that promise resilience and adaptability to harsh agricultural environments previously considered unfit for agricultural production. Such developments would potentially change the economics and, indeed, the very structure of agricultural production. It would also dictate the way in which the organization and conduct of agricultural research will need to change, moving increasingly into partnership modes of operation—in response to emerging issues that go beyond the remit of traditional research entities and conventional arrangements.

For instance, the private sector is emerging as an ever-stronger player, with massive investments in state-of-the-art research with potential (spill-over or direct) benefits, for instance, even for smallholder farmers who were not hitherto directly targeted by these private sector initiatives.

There is a growing recognition that local, farmer organizations are often better equipped than their upstream research partners in providing insights into traditional practices and innovations and helping discern the incentive structure of the communities in natural resource utilization and conservation (management) and development. This is because they have access to location-specific, agro-ecological and socio-economic information, and can play a critical role in facilitating the community-level application of basic and strategic research results, emerging from the international agricultural research system, and in translating them into highly adoptable, profitable technologies. Armed with these IFAD's target groups can be positioned to participate effectively and remuneratively in product markets, building on and not eroding their natural—land, water, forest and other resources—and their social capital—their capacity to mobilise themselves and their communities for collective benefit.

There are exceptional opportunities now for new forms of partnerships, due to the emergence of the new technologies. Some of these are in the areas of high-end biotechnology, space and information and communication technologies (ITCs). While many donors such as IFAD may steer clear off the upstream end of these developments which are best supported by other public and private funding, the Fund can continue to play an important leadership role in the downstream application end, e.g. through facilitating trait selection by farmers to drive biotech-based variety improvement or to help diffuse tissue culture propagated elite varieties of relevance to the rural poor who have previously participated in the selection of plant characteristics. Similarly, IFAD's niche in ICTs would lie in promoting knowledge management aspects, including Knowledge Management, empowerment of its target groups through Farmer Field Fora (FFFs) and Telecentres.

These opportunities call for strategic coalitions between public and private sector; among research and development agencies and among these and NGOs, universities, farmer organisations all involved in contributing to rural innovation systems. These relationships are characterised by complementarity; subsidiarity; comparative advantage; institutional synergy, pluralism in funding and increased sensitivity to location-specificity, with better focus on the circumstances of the ultimate beneficiaries.

Through its research grants programme, IFAD will be increasingly supporting multi-stakeholder collaborative research based on mutual strengths and needs of all stakeholders, and in the process strengthening the role of the small farmers in the generation of technologies. A sharpening of focus on socio-economic research and participatory training/coaching which takes into account a broad spectrum of non-bio-physical factors—gender relations, social organisation—contributes to enhancing the self-confidence, dignity and capability of the Fund's main stakeholders—the rural poor.

ANNEXURE

A Brief Outline of IFAD's Strategic Framework

At IFAD we aim to work towards enabling the rural poor to overcome their poverty. Our operational content is driven by three strategic objectives: strengthening the capacity of the rural poor and their organizations; improving equitable access to productive natural resources and technology; and increasing access to financial services and markets. Attention to the differing opportunities and constraints of women and men, and to sources of vulnerability and ways of increasing resilience, are overarching concerns. Central to achieving these strategic objectives is helping the poor to make best use of their limited assets and helping them to develop unrealised opportunities.

I briefly outline these strategic objectives:

Strengthening the Capacity of the Rural Poor and their Organizations

Developing and strengthening organizations of the poor to confront the issues they define - is key to our operations. Increasing the access of the poor to knowledge and building on their own ingenuity so that they can grasp opportunities and overcome obstacles is a part of our Knowledge empowerment strategy. Expanding the influence the poor exert over public policy and institutions; as well as positioning them to deal on better terms with the marketplace - also form important elements of the projects we support.

IFAD works with many different types of poor people's organizations (e.g. traditional village and sub-village work groups, small self-help groups, water users' associations and farmer cooperatives). Building their capacities requires time. However, capacity-building is critical to effective poverty reduction: in its absence, investments in social and economic infrastructure will invariably fail to deliver sustainable benefits.

IFAD also works to strengthen the capacity of local governments and civil society, so they can be more effective in responding to the needs of the rural poor. This will involve developing and promoting processes that increase the accountability and transparency of rural service delivery within decentralized decision-making frameworks.

Improving Equitable Access to Productive Natural Resources and Technology

One of the most important factors leading to entrenched poverty is lack of access to natural resources such as land, water and forests. Where pressure on land and water is great, natural resource degradation has reached alarming levels. This is a major problem for the rural poor, who often live in environmentally fragile zones. Appropriate technologies and research to improve farm productivity by boosting returns to land, water and labour are essential. Also, for IFAD rural poor women throughout the developing world have a primary role in crop production and care of livestock. They engage in multiple economic activities that are critical to the livelihoods of rural poor households. They are responsible for providing for the food, water and fuel needs of their families. Efforts and resources to address gender inequalities by increasing the resilience of rural poor women are central to development objectives.

Increasing Access to Financial Services and Markets

Efforts to increase agricultural productivity can only be effective if they are linked to an appreciation of market potential and can draw on appropriate investment and working capital. Integrated approaches are needed along the full continuum of production, processing and marketing. Diversifying income sources is also necessary, either by producing and marketing non-traditional crops or by exploiting off-farm opportunities more fully. This is in line with the pro-poor job-led growth strategy that Dr. Swaminathan highlighted in a recent IFAD-sponsored event at WSSD Johannesburg. Assistance for rural financial services needs to focus on developing responsive, sustainable rural finance institutions, with an emphasis not just on providing credit but also on encouraging savings. Rural finance is often essential in access to assets and technology adoption.

Part V

Foundation Day Lecture

20

Emerging Knowledge Society and Earth Care Campaign*

K. VENKATASUBRAMANIAN

Hon'ble Prime Minister of India, Shri Atal Behari Vajpayee, has recently unveiled a five point agenda for India's Development as Knowledge Society. The Prime Minister stated "a knowledge-based society will enable us to leap-frog in finding new and innovative ways to meet the challenges of building a just and equitable social order and seek urgent solutions", in his inaugural address to delegates attending the ASSOCHAM Summit, recently held on "India in the knowledge millennium". The five point agenda points to the following:

- Education for developing a learning society
- Global networking
- Vibrant Government-Industry-Academia interaction in policy-making and implementation
- Leveraging of existing competencies in IT, Telecom, Biotechnology, Drug Design, Financial Services, and Enterprise wide Management
- Economic and business strategic alliances built on capabilities and opportunities.

Such an agenda, according to our Hon'ble Prime Minister, will help leveraging of existing competencies in Information technology, Telecom, Bio-technology, Drug design, Financial

---

* Second Foundation Day Lecture, Bhoovigyan Vikas Foundation, New Delhi

Knowledge differs from other resources—each new discovery provides a platform for further discoveries.

There is an urgent need for a time bound project focusing on exploiting knowledge for our future prosperity and well being, and our development as a knowledge society. Rather than projecting into the future with assumptions about how today works, the project should involve constructing a vision of a most desirable future, and then identifying strategies to reach there.

The project should provide a framework for thinking about the sort of future India wants, and define the context for the Government's research, science and technology investments to make India a super power in the new millennium and a super knowledge society. Government of India invests substantially in research, science and technology to generate new innovative, economic, environmental and social capacity. In this way, the Government underpins innovation throughout all sectors. However, it cannot work in isolation, and innovation must be focused on the needs of end-users-whose lives, environment and enterprises will be affected by new knowledge and technological change.

The Government needs confidence that its research, science, and technology investments will be rapidly and effectively exploited to make India a knowledge society. This is more likely where sectors demonstrate their strategic thinking about the future, through bold and dynamic innovation strategies and Government is ready to be a partner in such bold and innovative strategies.

The Union Planning Commission under the Chairmanship of Shri K.C. Pant, has constituted a High Level Task Force for implementing the Prime Minister's Five Point Agenda. The broad areas of relevance cover Information Technology, Telecom, Bio-Technology, Drug Design, Financial Services and Enterprise Wide Management, Global Networking, Education requirements, for developing a learning society, Vibrant partnership between Government, Industry and Institutions, Economic and business strategic alliance built on capabilities and opportunities, and setting up of an Education Development Finance Corporation for meeting the needs of deserving students.

Dr. R.A. Mashelkar, Director General of CSIR, has aptly portrayed the concept of "Knowledge Centered Society", in his presidential address delivered at the 87th Indian Science Congress.

(*d*) *To research* issues related to the knowledge society;
(*e*) *To work* with the creators and developers of knowledge management systems in their efforts to express Indian culture through the information and communications infrastructure;
(*f*) *To encourage* the development of, and link with other groups with related interest;
(*g*) *To do* all such other things which are incidental or conducive to the attainment of the above objects;
(*h*) *Initiate* the production of an annual progress report on India's transformation to knowledge society;
(*i*) *Create* a national forum to engage public debate in discussions pertaining to knowledge society; and
(*j*) *Creation* of an exclusive website on India's knowledge society.

This approach paper mainly gives emphasis on the issues involved in making India a Knowledge Society, which is the need of the hour.

The terms of reference of the taskforce constituted by the Planning Commission for implementing Hon'ble Prime Minister's five point agenda is focused for implementation and the Planning Commission will draw on the talents of everyone concerned with the knowledge platform from eminent Vice-Chancellors, Administrators, Industrialists to ordinary knowledge worker to deal at length issues connected with leveraging of existing competence in select areas; such as global networking; education for development and organizing a learning society; promotion of vibrant government-industry-academia interaction in policy making and implementation; economic and business strategic alliance; setting up of an "Education Development Finance Corporation" for needy and deserving students. This EDFC will be a major input in the growing sphere of Education in the Knowledge Pathway.

India heads the developing world in Knowledge database and, even developed nations like USA is looking towards us for their software requirements. Bill Clinton, Former President of United States of America went on record in India that if he had any urgent software needs, he would first approach India.

We have thus everything to make India a Knowledge Super Power. India was a Knowledge Force in the ancient days. Let us restore again this status to Bharat today.

S.L. Mehta, National Director, National Agricultural Technology Project, ICAR, Krishi Anusandhan Bhawan-II, IARI, New Delhi.

S.S. Menakshisundaram, *I.A.S.*, Secretary to Government of India, Member (Finance), Space Commission & Atomic Energy Commission, Antariksh Bhawan, New BEL Road, Bangalore, India.

S.N. Mishra, Former Director, Institute of Economic Growth, Delhi, and currently Chairman, Society for Economic and Social Research (SESR), Delhi.

M. Moni, Deputy Director General, National Informatics Centre, Ministry of Information & Communication Technology, Government of India and Secretary General, Bhoovigyan Vikas Foundation, New Delhi.

A.M. Michael, Former Director, Indian Agricultural Research institute, New Delhi and former Vice Chancellor, Kerala Agricultural University, Trichur, India.

A. Narayanamoorthy, Reader, Gokhale Institute of Politics and Economics, Pune, India

D.K. Paul, Principal Scientist (IWM), Natural Resources Management Division, Indian Council of Agricultural Research, Krishi Bhawan, New Delhi.

K.V. Raman, Former Member, Agricultural Scientist Recruitment Board, New Delhi & Former Director, National Academy of Agricultural Research Management, Hyderabad.

J.S. Samra, Deputy Director General (NRM), Indian council of Agricultural Research, Government of India, Krishi Bhawan, New Delhi.

K.V. Sundaram, Founder & Chairman, Bhoovigyan Vikas Foundation, New Delhi and Former Chief Technical Adviser, FAO, Rome.

L. Venkatachalam, Assistant Professor, Agricultural Development & Rural Transformation Unit, Institute for Social and Economic Change, Bangalore, India.

K. Venkatasubramanian, Member (Education, Health & Development Policy Research), Planning Commission, Government of India.